Lecture Notes in Computer Science 8484

Commenced Publication in 1973
Founding and Former Series Editors:
Gerhard Goos, Juris Hartmanis, and Jan van Leeuwen

T0213745

Volume Editors

Matthias Jarke
RWTH Aachen University, E-mail: jarke@informatik.rwth-aachen.de

John Mylopoulos
Università di Trento, E-mail: jm@disi.unitn.eu

Christoph Quix
Fraunhofer FIT, St. Augustin, E-mail: christoph.quix@fit.fraunhofer.de

Colette Rolland
Université Paris1, E-mail: colette.rolland@univ-paris1.fr

Yannis Manolopoulos
Aristotle University, Thessaloniki, E-mail: manolopo@csd.auth.gr

Haralambos Mouratidis
University of Brighton, E-mail: h.mouratidis@brighton.ac.uk

Jennifer Horkoff
Università di Trento, E-mail: horkoff@disi.unitn.it

ISSN 0302-9743 e-ISSN 1611-3349
ISBN 978-3-319-07880-9 e-ISBN 978-3-319-07881-6
DOI 10.1007/978-3-319-07881-6
Springer Cham Heidelberg New York Dordrecht London

Library of Congress Control Number: 2014940060

LNCS Sublibrary: SL 3 – Information Systems and Application, incl. Internet/Web and HCI

Typesetting: Camera-ready by author, data conversion by Scientific Publishing Services, Chennai, India

Printed on acid-free paper

Springer is part of Springer Science+Business Media (www.springer.com)

Matthias Jarke   John Mylopoulos
Christoph Quix   Colette Rolland
Yannis Manolopoulos   Haralambos Mouratidis
Jennifer Horkoff (Eds.)

Advanced Information Systems Engineering

26th International Conference, CAiSE 2014
Thessaloniki, Greece, June 16-20, 2014
Proceedings

 Springer

Message from the Chairs

Welcome to the proceedings of the 26th International Conference on Advanced Information Systems Engineering (CAiSE 2014). This year, the conference was held in Thessaloniki, Greece. Thessaloniki is not only the second largest city of Greece, but also a city rich in history, culture, and tourist attractions, both within the city and the nearby peninsula of Chalkidiki. Thessaloniki is located just half an hour north of the archaeological site of Vergina, the ancient capital of Macedonia, where the tomb of Philip (father of Alexander the Great) was discovered. A little farther to the south one can visit mount Olympus, the home of the ancient Gods, as well as Dion, the holy city of ancient Macedonia. From an academic viewpoint, Thessaloniki is home to the largest university of the Balkans – the Aristotle University of Thessaloniki (AUTH) – boasting over 80,000 students and a strong computer science department.

The theme for this year's edition of the conference was "Information Systems Engineering in Times of Crisis." We live in a world where crises of one sort or another – economic, political, social, or geophysical – are becoming the norm. Greece, and much of southern Europe, has been in economic crisis for some time. The weather has been causing emergencies in the past few years of unprecedented scope and scale around the world. And corporations are experiencing unparalleled ups-and-downs, which they somehow have to survive. As scientists and engineers, we have a role to play in addressing these crises and in helping societies and enterprises cope. For this reason, we specifically encouraged contributions that address some of the roles that information systems engineering can play in dealing with crises.

Consistent with the conference theme, we were delighted to have three outstanding keynote speakers whose presentations speak to the point. Eric Dubois (University of Luxembourg) is a prominent member of the CAiSE community and a distinguished researcher in the area of requirements engineering. Eric is director of the "Service Science and Innovation" Department (www.ssi.tudor.lu), an R&D group that is part of the Tudor Centre. His presentation focused on governance models for service systems. Professor Diomidis Spinellis (Athens University of Economics and Business) conducts research on software engineering and related areas. He served as secretary general for information systems (comparable to a CIO position) in the Greek Ministry of Finance right in the middle of arguably one of the deepest and longest national economic crises ever experienced. His keynote described his experiences in this critical position. The third keynote speaker was Professor Bartel Van de Walle (Tilburg University), a founding member and president of the international community on Information Systems for Crisis Response and Management (ISCRAM). His presentation addressed precisely the theme of the conference: risk accelerators in disasters.

As always, research paper sessions showcased ground-breaking research on a rich variety of topics. The papers were selected using the multi-tier review process developed over the past several years. Every submission received three reviews, and those with at least one positive evaluation were the subject of a discussion between their reviewers and an assigned program board member, using Cyberchair's online discussion forum. These discussions resulted in recommendations for acceptance or rejection. Approximately one fourth of the top-ranked submissions were then presented and discussed by the program board during a two-day meeting (February 6–7) in Thessaloniki where final decisions were made. In total, we received 226 submissions for the research track, among which 41 were accepted for an acceptance rate of 18.1%. Accepted papers were presented in 13 sessions: Clouds and Services; Requirements; Product Lines; Requirements Elicitation; Processes; Risk and Security; Process Models; Data Mining and Streaming; Process Mining; Models; Mining Event Logs; Databases; and Software Engineering.

Research papers were submitted either as Formal/Technical, Empirical Evaluation, Experience or Exploratory papers. Formal/Technical papers were expected to present solutions for information systems engineering-related problems, which are novel or significantly improve upon existing solutions. These papers were expected to provide a preliminary validation of the proposed solution, such as a proof-of-concept experiment, or sound arguments that the solution will work and will scale up to real-world sized problems. Empirical evaluation papers evaluated existing problem situations, or validated or refuted proposed solutions through empirical studies, experiments, case studies, simulations, formal analyses, or mathematical proofs, etc. Experience papers applied proposed solutions to real-world problems and drew conclusions about lessons learned. Finally, exploratory papers proposed completely new research directions or approaches. A complete description of each category is available on the CAiSE 2014 website.

As with previous CAiSE conferences, the main conference was preceded by two days of workshops, as well as a doctoral symposium. We are confident that everyone found events of interest in such a rich and diverse program.

The conference would not have been possible without the dedication of dozens of colleagues and students who contributed their time, energy, and expertise to serve on the Organizing Committee, Program Committee, program board, and the actual running of the conference. We extend our heartfelt thanks to each and every one of them. We are particularly grateful to Richard van de Stadt for running CyberChairPRO for us, especially so for being both responsive and helpful. Special thanks also go to the corporations, universities, and research centers who sponsored this event.

Last, but not least, we hope that everyone who attended CAiSE 2014 enjoyed Thessaloniki, and was enriched by the cultural and physical background.

April 2014

Matthias Jarke
John Mylopoulos
Christoph Quix
Colette Rolland
Yannis Manolopoulos
Haris Mouratidis
Jennifer Horkoff

Workshop Chairs

Lazaros Iliadis   Democritus University of Thrace, Greece
Mike Papazoglou   University of Tilburg, The Netherlands
Klaus Pohl   University of Duisburg-Essen, Germany

Forum Chairs

Selmin Nurcan   University of Paris 1, France
Elias Pimenidis   University of East London, UK

Doctoral Symposium Chairs

Óscar Pastor   Universitat Politècnica de València, Spain
Yannis Vassiliou   National Technical University of Athens,
                                 Greece

Organizing Committee Chairs

Anastasios Gounaris   Aristotle University of Thessaloniki, Greece
Apostolos Papadopoulos   Aristotle University of Thessaloniki, Greece

Industrial Chair

Ioannis Kompatsiaris   Institute of Informatics and Telematics, Greece

Publicity Chairs

Christos Kalloniatis   University of the Aegean, Greece
Lin Liu   Tsinghua University, China
Eric Yu   University of Toronto, Canada
Renata Guizzardi   Universidade Federal do Espirito Santo, Brazil
Naoufel Kraiem   Université Manouba, Tunisia

Web and Social Media master

Ioannis Karydis   Ionian University, Greece

Organization

Steering Committee

Barbara Pernici   Politecnico di Milano, Italy
Óscar Pastor   Universitat Politècnica de València, Spain
John Krogstie   Norwegian University of Science and
         Technology, Norway

Advisory Committee

Janis Bubenko Jr.   Royal Institute of Technology, Sweden
Colette Rolland   Université Paris 1 Panthéon Sorbonne, France
Arne Sølvberg   Norwegian University of Science and
         Technology, Norway

General Chairs

Yannis Manolopoulos   Aristotle University of Thessaloniki, Greece
Haralambos Mouratidis   University of Brighton, UK
Colette Rolland   University of Paris 1, France

Program Board Chair

Eric Dubois   Public Research Center H. Tudor, Luxembourg

Program Chairs

Matthias Jarke   RWTH Aachen University, Germany
John Mylopoulos   University of Trento, Italy
Christoph Quix   Fraunhofer FIT, Germany

Tutorial and Panel Chairs

Jaelson Castro   University of Pernambuco, Brazil
Dimitri Karagiannis   University of Vienna, Austria

Program Committee Board

Marko Bajec, Slovenia
Xavier Franch, Spain
Giancarlo Guizzardi, Brazil
Evangelia Kavakli, Greece
Marite Kirikova, Latvia
John Krogstie, Norway
Raimundas Matulevicius, Estonia
Miguel Mira da Silva, Portugal
Ana Moreira, Portugal
Haris Mouratidis, UK

Óscar Pastor Lopez, Spain
Barbara Pernici, Italy
Michael Petit, Belgium
Jolita Ralyté, Switzerland
Stefanie Rinderle-Ma, Austria
Colette Rolland, France
Camille Salinesi, France
Roel J. Wieringa, The Netherlands
Jelena Zdravkovic, Sweden

Program Committee

Wil van der Aalst, The Netherlands
Daniel Amyot, Canada
Yuan An, USA
Paris Avgeriou, The Netherlands
Luciano Baresi, Italy
Carlo Batini, Italy
Boalem Benatallah, Australia
Giuseppe Berio, France
Nacer Boudjlida, France
Sjaak Brinkkemper, The Netherlands
Jordi Cabot, Spain
Albertas Caplinskas, Lithuania
Silvana Castano, Italy
Jaelson Castro, Brazil
Corine Cauvet, France
Isabelle Comyn-Wattiau, France
Panos Constantopoulos, Greece
Fabiano Dalpiaz, The Netherlands
Valeria De Antonellis, Italy
Rebeccca Deneckere, France
Michael Derntl, Germany
Johann Eder, Austria
Neil Ernst, USA
Mariagrazia Fugini, Italy
Avigdor Gal, Israel
Paolo Giorgini, Italy
Stefanos Gritzalis, Greece
Michael Grossniklaus, Germany
Francesco Guerra, Italy

Renata Guizzardi, Brazil
Irit Hadar, Israel
Markus Helfert, Ireland
Brian Henderson-Sellers, Australia
Jennifer Horkoff, Italy
Marta Indulska, Australia
Manfred Jeusfeld, Sweden
Ivan Jureta, Belgium
Haruhiko Kaiya, Japan
Juergen Karla, Germany
Panagiotis Karras, USA
David Kensche, Germany
Christian Kop, Austria
Manolis Koubarakis, Greece
Regine Laleau, France
Alexei Lapouchnian, Canada
Julio Cesar Leite, Brazil
Michel Leonard, Switzerland
Sotirios Liaskos, Canada
Kecheng Liu, USA
Peri Loucopoulos, USA
Kalle Lyytinen, USA
Lech Madeyski, Poland
Alexander Maedche, Germany
Heinrich C. Mayr, Austria
Jan Mendling, Austria
Isabelle Mirbel, France
Selmin Nurcan, France
Andreas L Opdahl, Norway

Michael Pantazoglou, Greece
Anna Perini, Italy
Gilles Perrouin, Belgium
Anne Persson, Sweden
Mario Piattini, Spain
Dimitris Plexousakis, Greece
Geert Poels, Belgium
Klaus Pohl, Germany
Jaroslav Pokorny, Czech Republic
Sudha Ram, USA
Manfred Reichert, Germany
Iris Reinhartz-Berger, Israel
Dominique Rieu, France
Maximilian Roeglinger, Germany
Thomas Rose, Germany
Michael Rosemann, Australia
Gustavo Rossi, Argentina
Matti Rossi, Finland
Antonio Ruiz Cortes, Spain
Motoshi Saeki, Japan
Michael Schrefl, Austria
Víctor E. Silva Souza, Brazil

Guttorm Sindre, Norway
Monique Snoeck, Belgium
Janis Stirna, Sweden
Eleni Stroulia, Canada
Arnon Sturm, Israel
Angelo Susi, Italy
David Taniar, Australia
Ernest Teniente, Spain
Juan-Carlos Trujillo Mondejar, Spain
Irene Vanderfeesten, The Netherlands
Olegas Vasilecas, Lithuania
Panos Vassiliadis, Greece
Yair Wand, Canada
Barbara Weber, Austria
Jan Weglarz, Poland
Hans Weigand, The Netherlands
Mathias Weske, Germany
Carson Woo, Canada
Eric Yu, Canada
Yijun Yu, UK

Additional Referees

Manar H. Alalfi
Konstantinos Angelopoulos
Fatma Başak Aydemir
Ronald Batenburg
Stefan Berger
Pierre Berlioux
Mikael Berndtsson
Martin Berner
Devis Bianchini
Cristina Cabanillas
Carolina Chiao
Jan Claes
Xavier Devroey
Amador Durán Toro
Sergio España
Antonio Ferrandez
Alfio Ferrara
Mariagrazia Fugini
Irini Fundulaki

Luciano Garcia-Banuelos
Lorenzo Genta
Frederic Gervais
Christophe Gnaho
Gregor Grambow
Enrico Graupner
Gerd Groener
Frank Hadasch
Janelle Harms
Marcin Hewelt
Leo Iaquinta
Silvia Ingolfo
Jaap Kabbedijk
Diana Kalibatiene
Christos Kalloniatis
Michael Karlinger
Ravi Khadka
David Knuplesch
Haridimos Kondylakis

Elena Kornyshova
Kyriakos Kritikos
Matthias Kunze
Julius Köpke
Andreas Lanz
Feng-Lin Li
Tong Li
Yuan Ling
Mengwen Liu
Matthias Lohrmann
Amel Mammar
Petros Manousis
Clarissa Cassales Marquezan
Alejandro Mate
Michele Melchiori
Andreas Metzger
Stefano Montanelli
Itzel Morales-Ramirez
Alain Mouttham
Cedric du Mouza
José Antonio Parejo Maestre
Renata Petrevska Nechkoska
Bernd Neumayr
Kestutis Normantas
Karolyne Oliveira
Nicolas Prat
Elda Paja
Ricardo Perez-Castillo

João Pimentel
Pierluigi Plebani
Riccardo Porrini
Alireza Pourshahid
Leo Pruijt
Rüdiger Pryss
Manuel Resinas
Ben Roelens
Andreas Rogge-Solti
David G. Rosado
Tomer Sagi
Mattia Salnitri
Osama Sammodi
Johannes Schobel
Christoph Schütz
Farida Semmak
Vladimir Shekhovtsov
Michael Smit
Monique Soares
Vanessa Stricker
Pablo Trinidad
Justas Trinkunas
Georgia Troullinou
Aggeliki Tsochou
Kevin Vlaanderen
Thorsten Weyer
Apostolos Zarras

Table of Contents

Keynotes

Clouds and Services

Requirements

Product Lines

Requirements Elicitation

Processes

Risk and Security

Process Models

Data Mining and Streaming

Process Mining

Models

Mining Event Logs

Databases

Software Engineering

Information Systems for the Governance of Compliant Service Systems

Eric Dubois

Public Research Centre Henri Tudor, Luxembourg, Luxembourg
eric.dubois@tudor.lu

Abstract. The traditional role of an Information System (IS) is to support operation and management within an organization. In the presentation, we will discuss the specific role that IS can also play to support the management aspects related to the governance of an organization regarding its compliance to norms and regulations. In the new service economy, governance issues are no longer limited to a single organization but should be extended at the level of service value networks, i.e. service systems. In such systems, one of the challenges is for each organization to demonstrate its compliance in a transparent way. In this paper, we discuss how to organize a global governance framework and we illustrate its use in the IT service management. On the basis of some research on TIPA, a process reference model making possible to objectively measure the quality of delivered IT services, we illustrate how IS and Enterprise Architecture can effectively support the deployment of such global governance model.

Keywords: compliance, requirements engineering, goal modelling, enterprise architecture, modelling language, business processes, reference architecture.

1   Introduction

Today, organizations are more and more facing compliance issues coming from international and national regulatory bodies, from standardisation bodies as well as from recognized professional and/or sectorial associations. Demonstrating compliance to all the rules included in the different regulations requires huge and costly efforts. Indeed, the organization has to set-up the appropriate systems (processes, people and IT) 'implementing' the regulations. They also have to establish the necessary evidences to demonstrate their compliance.

In our research, we focus on a specific regulatory context made from non-prescriptive regulations which applies on networked organizations. In contrast with more traditional prescriptive rule-based regulations where the regulatee is just supposed to do exactly the required actions, non-prescriptive regulations such as goal-based, risk-based or principle-based regimes offer more freedom regarding how to implement their requirements and thus open innovation opportunities regarding the implementation within a specific organization. This freedom can be exploited by the organization for differentiating itself from the others in terms of, for example, a better

M. Jarke et al. (Eds.): CAiSE 2014, LNCS 8484, pp. 1–11, 2014.
© Springer International Publishing Switzerland 2014

productivity (optimized processes) or a competitive Quality of Service (QoS) advantage (enhancing its customers' level of trust).

In our context, we consider the application of the regulations to networked organizations, more specifically to IT service value networks called 'service systems'. In [1], they are defined as "a configuration of people, processes, technology and shared information connected through a value proposition with the aim of a dynamic co-creation of value through the participation in the exchanges with customers and external/internal service systems". According to this view, a service system can be itself composed of service systems, cooperating to produce a global business service. In Luxembourg, we have a typical national service system business case where we can find telecommunication companies offering communication services to data centers. Data centers themselves offer services to Archiving companies, which then have their services used by Financial IT Service Providers. Banks finally outsource part of their IT to these IT service providers.

In such value constellation, there are interesting questions regarding the compliance of the whole service system to a set of non-prescriptive regulations and norms. Besides the question of a common interpretation of the requirements by each individual company, there is the question about how the requirements have been implemented by the different companies, the level of interoperability existing between the different implementations and finally the global level of compliance that the global service system can demonstrate. Examples of requirements that apply to this service system are related to security and risk management (like those included in the ISO 27000 or ISO 15408), privacy issues (coming from national laws and EU directives) as well as IT Service Management (like ITIL and ISO 20000). In the rest of the paper, for the purpose of illustration, we will refer to examples associated with ITIL v3. [2]

2   Research Proposition

At the end of the previous section, we have raised a number of problems, which correspond to the following research questions:

1. Is it possible to produce a common reference framework associated with the support for clarifying the interpretation of the regulation and that can be used by an organization for helping it in the implementation?
2. Can we associate objective performance measures to this reference framework so that we can measure the level of assurance in the implemented system?

To answer to these two questions we propose a solution which is summarized in Figure 1 and includes two components:
  • The first component is a Process Reference Framework which is produced through the application of a Goal-oriented Requirements Engineering approach aiming (1) at disambiguating and structuring a consistent set of regulatory requirements and (2) at designing a set of reference processes

together with indicators for measuring their performance level. Regarding (1), we apply a manual process complemented with approaches like those proposed by e.g. [3] for identifying elementary statements. Regarding (2), we use the ISO15504 maturity model [5] for developing references processes. In Section 3, we further detailed this latter element.

- The second component is an Enterprise Architecture Reference Model. This blueprint can be used by an organization for guiding the design of its own implementation according to the level of performance it would like to achieve with respect to their compliance. The proposed approach is based on the production of ArchiMate models [4] derived from the reference processes which also act as frameworks for an information system compliant architecture. This component is further developed in Section 4.

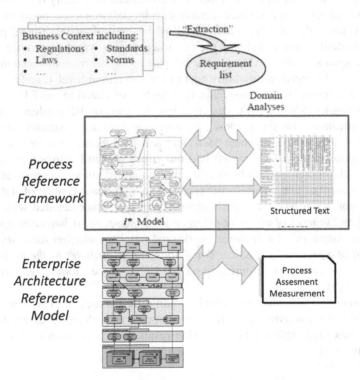

Fig. 1. Presentation of the General Framework

Note that the overall approach supports the (internal and/or external) auditors in their compliance checking process. Each organization has to trace its implementation to the ArchiMate model, this one is itself traceable to the Process Reference Framework which itself is linked to the regulation.

3   The ISO 15504 Process Performance Framework

3.1   Introduction to 15504

For structuring and organizing the requirements inherent to regulations and norms, we have found and experimented a valuable requirements template and associated guidelines that are made available through the 15504 standard [5]. In 15504 standard, a generic requirements' taxonomy together with a predefined requirements' structure define a framework used for eliciting and structuring requirements as well as for assessing and measuring the compliance of deployed Business Processes (BP) against these requirements.15504 (previously known as SPICE) provides an assessment model against which the assurance aspects of an organization in terms of realization of its BP and their contribution to business services objectives can be defined and measured. Built on top of those predecessors, the main originality of 15504 is to standardize the structure of assurance requirements by defining a taxonomy of generic BP assurance goals that are applicable to BP of business domains. Fig. 2 presents the generic guidelines associated with the construction of a process reference and assessment framework (called PAM). On the left part of Fig. 2, from the bottom to the top, one can read the business capability goal of the services at level 1, and then, from 2.1 to 5.2, the different levels of assurance that can be associated to this BP.

According to 15504, a PAM describes requirements on BP implementing QoS assurance attribute with the purpose and outcomes of each assurance attribute. The **purpose** of an assurance attribute *"describes at a high level its overall objectives"* [5]. Each purpose is fully decomposed into **outcomes** and **indicators** (see right part of Fig. 2. Each outcome is an observable achievement of some assurance attribute. An outcome describes that an artefact is produced, a significant change of state occurred, or some constraint has been met. Outcomes can be further detailed with **indicators** focusing on *"sources of objective evidence used to support a judgment about the fulfilment of outcomes"*, for instance: work products (*"an artefact associated with the execution of a process"*), practices (*"activities that contributes to the purpose or outcomes of a process"*), or resources (e.g. *"human resources, tools, methods and infrastructure"*) [5].

Outcomes and indicators are organized into different aspects. The first aspect is related to the main activity while the other aspects are related to different assurance aspects associated with the activity. This result is in a taxonomy of assurance requirements goals.

3.2   Application of the 15504 Framework to ITIL

15504 has been applied by our research team at Tudor centre in several contexts where process needs to be assessed against assurance and performance levels. Produced reference models include Basel II Risk Management in the financial sector, Sarbanes-Oxley, the 27000 series for security management , and COSO. In this paper, we illustrate its application in the the context of service management with the specific ITIL [2] target. The work performed by the Centre in this domain has reached a high level of visibility with the publication of the TIPA (Tudor's ITSM Process Assessment) book [6] and the participation as co-editor of the ISO 20000-4.

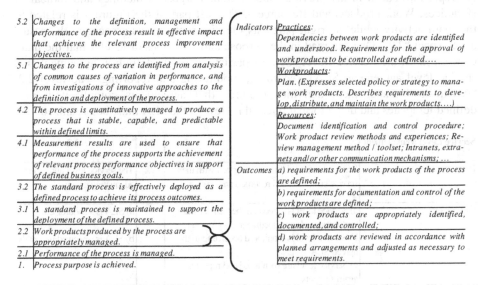

5.2	Changes to the definition, management and performance of the process result in effective impact that achieves the relevant process improvement objectives.
5.1	Changes to the process are identified from analysis of common causes of variation in performance, and from investigations of innovative approaches to the definition and deployment of the process.
4.2	The process is quantitatively managed to produce a process that is stable, capable, and predictable within defined limits.
4.1	Measurement results are used to ensure that performance of the process supports the achievement of relevant process performance objectives in support of defined business goals.
3.2	The standard process is effectively deployed as a defined process to achieve its process outcomes.
3.1	A standard process is maintained to support the deployment of the defined process.
2.2	Work products produced by the process are appropriately managed.
2.1	Performance of the process is managed.
1.	Process purpose is achieved.

Indicators Practices:
Dependencies between work products are identified and understood. Requirements for the approval of work products to be controlled are defined....

Workproducts:
Plan. (Expresses selected policy or strategy to manage work products. Describes requirements to develop, distribute, and maintain the work products....)

Resources:
Document identification and control procedure; Work product review methods and experiences; Review management method / toolset; Intranets, extranets and/or other communication mechanisms; ...

Outcomes a) requirements for the work products of the process are defined;
b) requirements for documentation and control of the work products are defined;
c) work products are appropriately identified, documented, and controlled;
d) work products are reviewed in accordance with planned arrangements and adjusted as necessary to meet requirements.

Fig. 2. Generic guidelines associated with the construction of a PAM

TIPA is an open framework for the assessment of ITSM processes. It describes requirements on 26 processes (see Fig. 3) belonging to 5 groups.

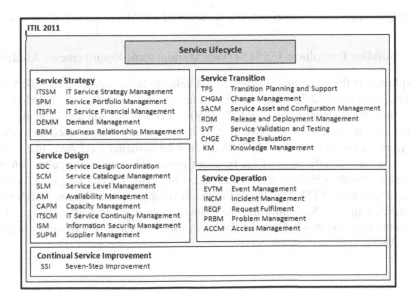

Fig. 3. Primary Life Cycle Process for Service Management

A concrete example is given in Fig.4 with a fragment of the final result associated with Service Level Management. This example illustrates the different ISO 15504 concepts introduced in the previous sub-section: Purpose, Outcomes and Indicators (Practices, Work Products and Resources). The left part of the Figure 4 is related to the main activity while the right part lists the different aspects associated the assurance aspect "2.2". One can read in the purpose and outcomes of level 1 that the main concern is on the Service Level (SL), in particular, on its definition agreement (i.e. service level agreement, SLA), recording, monitoring and reporting. The level 2.2, "day-to-day" management activities requires that agreements comply with predefined templates and that a formal internal review of the SLA must be organized.

Service Level Management	1	2.1	2.2
Purpose	Service Level is defined and agreed with the service customer, and recorded and managed	...	The service level agreement is adequately managed
Outcomes	a) Service level is agreed on the basis of the customer needs and documented b) Service level is monitored according to the agreed SLA c) Service level are monitored and reported against targets		a) SLA is standardised b) SLA is reviewed internally
Indicators	Practices: Agree SL; Monitor SL; Report SL Work Products: SLA; SL Report		Practices: Standardise SLA Work Products: Standardised SLA

Fig. 4. Requirements associated with the Service Level Management QoS attribute

3.3   Building Compliant 15504 Service Management Requirements Models

As explained in the preceding section, 15504 helps to better structure specific types of QoS requirements models with a process reference framework (called PAM). Difficulties arise when creating those PAM: 15504 does not provide any guidance in the incremental elaboration of a PAM. It provides generic concepts used in PAM and rules (meta-requirements, see Fig.2) that must be satisfied by PAM, but gives no guidance to the identification of the business processes, nor the formalization of the knowledge domain which is needed for that. This guidance can be given by GORE techniques, such as *i** [7]. This has led to the development of a rigorous methodology (summarized in Fig. 5) supporting the transformation of natural language flat requirements from the original text of the norm into structured requirements organized in a PAM.

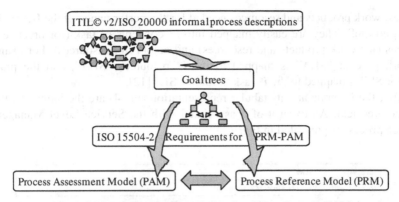

Fig. 5. GORE Techniques applied to the elaboration of a PAM

The proposed methodology relies on a taxonomy of concepts close and compatible to those of 15504. The rules and heuristics that we have discovered regarding the use of *i** in support to the progressive and systematic elaboration of PAM are presented in [8,9]. They are summarized in the next paragraph in the context of the elaboration of the paraphrased result presented in Fig. 6.

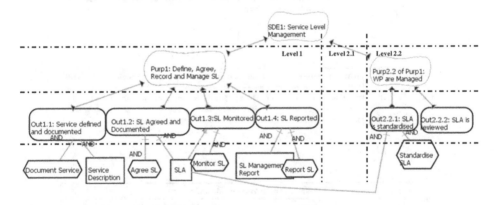

Fig. 6. Requirements Goal Tree Associated with the Service Level Management Attribute

The QoS goals are expressed in terms of *i** soft-goals and goals. The 15504 standard makes an explicit link between the purpose and the set of objectives to be fulfilled when executing BP that implement the service. As indicated in Fig. , purposes are modelled with a soft-goal and this soft-goal can be detailed by refining it into an equivalent collection of other soft-goals and/or goals associated with domain knowledge model. For instance, the soft-goal "Purp1" at the top left of the Fig. 6, corresponds to the first purpose shown in Fig 4.. Since outcomes are objectively observable, they are modelled as goals (which can be further refined) and never with soft-goals. The horizontal lane of outcomes corresponds exactly to the outcomes shown in Fig. 4. Indicators are added and modelled according their types, e.g.

practices, work products and resources needed for the performance of the BP realizing the desired QoS. They are easily mapped into *i** concepts of task (for practices), *i** resources (for work products and resources) and actors (for resources). For example, the work product "SLA" is mapped to the *i** resources "SLA", and the practice "Monitor SL" is mapped to the *i** task "Monitor SL" [12].

Finally, the *i** mode and its tabular representation (Fig.4) are the inputs for the final structured text. An excerpt of it associated with the Service Level Management reference process is presented in Fig. 7.

Process ID	SLM
Process Name	Service Level Management
Process Purpose	The purpose of the Service Level Management process is to ensure that all current and planned IT services are delivered to agreed achievable targets. *[ITIL 2011 - Service Design: p106]* NOTE 1: This is accomplished through a constant cycle of negotiating, agreeing, monitoring, reporting on and reviewing IT service targets and achievements, and through instigation of actions to correct or improve the level of service delivered.
Process Expected Results	As a result of successful implementation of the Service Level Management process: 1. IT and the customers have a common, clear and unambiguous understanding of the levels of service to be delivered;

....⌐

| Base Practices | SLM.BP1: Determine, document and agree on Service Level Requirements (SLRs) Determine, document and agree on service level requirements for services being developed, changed or procured. The SLRs should be an integral part of the overall service design criteria which also include the functional or "utility" specifications. *[ITIL 2011 - Service Design: p112]* [Expected Result 1] |

....

Output Work Products		
ID	Name	Expected results and related BPs
08_02	Service Level Requirements (SLR)	[Expected Result 1] [SLM.BP1]
08_01	Service Level Agreement (SLA)	[Expected Result 1, 3, 6] [SLM.BP2, 7]

Fig. 7. Structured Text associated with a Reference Process

4   IS for Managing Compliant Architectures

In [10], Zachman introduces its framework for managing enterprise architecture. His proposition includes the fundamentals of a conceptual information model that can be used for implementing an information system supporting the management of an enterprise. More recently, ArchiMate [4] appears as an emerging standard associated with a language for describing the different facets of an information system (business, application, infrastructure). Together with its tool support, ArchiMate allows to create a new "second order" information system, the one which is needed for supporting enterprise architects and decision makers in their management of enterprise IS transformations.

We claim that compliance issues require similar "second order" IS supporting organization in the management of their enterprise architecture specifically dedicated to the implementing of the regulations and norms requirements. The existence of such IS also helps in demonstrating the compliance of the organization to the internal and external auditors by explaining how the model is the mirror of the organization.

Our research objective is to support companies in the development of that kind of IS. To this end, we are working on the design of enterprise architecture blueprints associated with the process reference models introduced in the previous section. At this stage, we are using ArchiMate for representing these blueprints in terms of Architecture Reference Models. In Fig. 8, we present an excerpt of such model associated with the Service Level Management reference process. On this model, one can read how we use ArchiMate concepts for representing Purposes in terms of Goals, Expected Results in terms of Requirements, Best Practices in terms of Business Processes and WorkProducts in terms of Business Objects.

Taking this reference architecture as an input, the Enterprise Architect can design its own implementation which if also represented in ArchiMate can easily be traced to the reference model and thereby demonstrate its compliance.

More details regarding the development and use of reference architectures in the telecommunication sector can be found in [11]

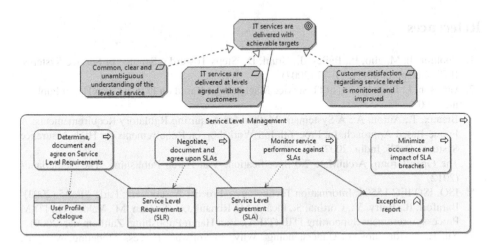

Fig. 8. Excerpt from an ArchiMate Reference Model

5   Conclusion

In this paper, we have introduced the framework that we are developing for support-ing a service system composed from several organizations in their implementation of the requirements coming from different norms, regulations and best practices. We illustrated part of this framework within the context of ITIL best practices.

This framework is produced by Tudor, a Research and Technological Organization whose part of its mission is to support private and public entities in their socio-economic development. Within this context, the proposed framework aims at support-ing these organizations in:

- A reduction of their costs associated with the implementation of non-prescriptive norms and regulations. To this end, reference models reduce the costs associated with the reading and interpreting of requirements included in the texts and also provide some guidance regarding the implementation of the final solution as well as in the demonstration of its compliance to the auditors.
- The development of a differentiating competitive advantage is also supported by the proposed framework. It is based on an objective measurement of the performance of the processes offered through the usage of the ISO 15504 maturity model. QoS assurance elements can be provided to the customers and be part of the Service Level Agreement.

Acknowledgements. The presented results are relying on a team of persons. In the preparation of this paper, specific inputs were provided by: B. Barafort, S. Ghanavati, E. Grandry, N. Mayer, E. Proper, S. Pineau, A. Renault, and A. Rifaut,

References

1. Spohrer, J., Maglio, P., Bailey, J., Gruhl, D.: Steps Toward a Science of Service Systems. IEEE Computer 40(1), 71–77 (2007)
2. van Bon, J.: Foundations of IT Service Management Based on ITIL v3. van Haren Publish-ing (2007)
3. Breaux, T., Anton, A.: A Systematic Method for Acquiring Rgulatory Requiremements: A Frame-Based Approach. In: Proc. 6th Intl Workshop on Requirements for High Assurance Systems, Dehli, India (2007)
4. The Open Group, ArchiMate 2.0 Specification. Van Haren Publishing, The Netherlands (2012)
5. ISO, ISO/IEC 15504: Information Technology – Process Assessment: Part1 - Part5 (2003)
6. Barafort, B., Betry, V., Cortina, S., Picard, M., Renault, A., St-Jean, M., Valdés, O.: ITSM Process Assessment Supporting ITIL (TIPA). Van Haren Publishing, Zaltbommel (2009)
7. Yu, E., Mylopoulos, J.: Understanding "Why" in Software Process Modeling, Analysis, and Design. In: Proceedings of 16th International Conference on Software Engineering, Sorrento, Italy, pp. 159–168 (1994)

8. Rifaut, A., Dubois, E.: Using Goal-Oriented Requirements Engineering for Improving the Quality of ISO/IEC 15504 based Compliance Assessment Frameworks. In: Proc. IEEE Intl. Conf. on Requirements Engineering (RE 2008), Barcelona. IEEE Press (2008)
9. Rifaut, A.: Goal-driven requirements engineering for supporting the ISO 15504 assessment process. In: Richardson, I., Abrahamsson, P., Messnarz, R. (eds.) EuroSPI 2005. LNCS, vol. 3792, pp. 151–162. Springer, Heidelberg (2005)
10. Zachman, J.: A Framework for Information Systems Architecture. IBM Systems Journal 26, 276–293 (1987)
11. Mayer, N., Aubert, J., Cholez, H., Grandry, E.: Sector-Based Improvement of the Information Security Risk Management Process in the Context of Telecommunications Regulation. In: McCaffery, F., O'Connor, R.V., Messnarz, R. (eds.) EuroSPI 2013. CCIS, vol. 364, pp. 13–24. Springer, Heidelberg (2013)
12. Ghanavati, S., Amyot, D., Rifaut, A.: Legal Goal-Oriented Requirement Language (Legal GRL) for Modeling Regulations. In: Proc. 6th International Workshop on Modeling in Software Engineering (MiSE 2014), Hyderabad, India (2014)

Risk Accelerators in Disasters

Insights from the Typhoon Haiyan Response on Humanitarian Information Management and Decision Support

Bartel Van de Walle[1] and Tina Comes[2]

[1] Departement of Management, Tilburg University, The Netherlands
bartel@uvt.nl
[2] Centre for Integrated Emergency Management, University of Agder, Norway
tina.comes@uia.no
www.disasterresiliencelab.org

Abstract. Modern societies are increasingly threatened by disasters that require rapid response through ad-hoc collaboration among a variety of actors and organizations. The complexity within and across today's societal, economic and environmental systems defies accurate predictions and assessments of damages, humanitarian needs, and the impact of aid. Yet, decision-makers need to plan, manage and execute aid response under conditions of high uncertainty while being prepared for further disruptions and failures. This paper argues that these challenges require a paradigm shift: instead of seeking optimality and full efficiency of procedures and plans, strategies should be developed that enable an acceptable level of aid under all foreseeable eventualities. We propose a decision- and goal-oriented approach that uses scenarios to systematically explore future developments that may have a major impact on the outcome of a decision. We discuss to what extent this approach supports robust decision-making, particularly if time is short and the availability of experts is limited. We interlace our theoretical findings with insights from experienced humanitarian decision makers we interviewed during a field research trip to the Philippines in the aftermath of Typhoon Haiyan.

Keywords: Disaster response, humanitarian information management, robust decision support, risk management, preparedness, sensemaking.

1   Introduction

Five weeks after Typhoon Haiyan had made landfall on the Philippines, we lead a small research team to carry out an on-site investigation of the humanitarian response, and in particular of the impact of information on sensemaking and decision making. In the course of our journey, we interviewed 35 decision makers from the United Nations (UN), non-governmental organizations or local government, attended national and local coordination meetings and observed field operations. One compelling finding from this fieldwork was the recognition that humanitarian decision making should be driven by the aim to understand emerging risks and to share information

M. Jarke et al. (Eds.): CAiSE 2014, LNCS 8484, pp. 12–23, 2014.

about them in due time and accessible format. As Jesper Lund, Head of Office for the UN Office for the Coordination of Humanitarian Affairs (OCHA) in the severely affected town of Tacloban stated:

"Managing disasters means to understand what the risks are as they emerge: prevent acceleration of trends that can turn into a disaster."

In this paper we will outline the challenges for humanitarian information management to support such real-time identification and management of emerging risks by focusing on two questions:

1. *How should an information system be designed for sensemaking and decision support in sudden onset disasters?*
2. *How to steer the exploration of a complex system such that the aims of the information system can be achieved while respecting constraints in terms of time and resources available?*

2   Humanitarian Information Management

In the response to Haiyan, the importance of information management has been widely recognized. In most organizations, information management officers (IMOs) work to collect data and convert it into information products, most often a situation report or a map. These information products by their very nature mostly provide a snapshot of the situation; they do not convey analyses or a deeper understanding of the situation and important trends. IMOs try to keep pace with the requests of a plethora of different policy- and decision-makers to satisfy aid organizations, donors, governments, the military, from international to local levels. The multitude of organizations and decisions, the divergence of needs, information sources, temporal and geographical scales, bandwidth constraints and a virtually unlimited variety of information that were openly shared with the whole world, create a frantic pattern of constant requests, surveys, questionnaires, reports and maps pushed from headquarters to the field and back. Marc McCarthy, a member of the UN Disaster Assessment and Coordination (UNDAC) team and deployed in one of the worst hit areas within days after the Typhoon's landfall expressed the resulting confusion and irritation among responders bluntly and succinctly:

"This is the Information Disaster."

Due to the nature of sudden onset disasters and the ad hoc character of the response, no model can be developed to timely explain and predict the behavior of the disrupted socio-economic system or the consequences of decisions on how and where to intervene (DiMario et al. 2009). Therefore, information management in sudden onset disasters should acknowledge that decisions need to be made in near real-time based on uncertain and lacking information about the impact of the disaster. Instead of seeking optimality, this decision-centered approach aims to prevent that essential goals cannot be reached.

2.1   Decision Support in Humanitarian Disaster Response

How humans approach a decision depends on the information and understanding of the systems that affect the results of decisions. Under stress and pressure, we mostly follow intuitive rules (Gigerenzer et al. 2012), which emphasizes the importance of training and professional experience to avoid the most common judgmental biases. To capture expert knowledge, scientists tend to abstract and model parts of the overall problem. Disasters, however, pose complex problems that largely defy such simplifications.

Complexity and uncertainty are certainly not new aspects of decision-making (Rittel & Webber 1973). Yet as organizations and individuals increasingly rely on models for data processing and on Information Systems to share information, decision-makers operate in circumstances that are more difficult than ever before, while they struggle to maintain oversight and control. Turoff, Chumer, Van de Walle and Yao (2004) presented the Dynamic Emergency Response Management Information System (DERMIS) framework for information system design and development that addresses communication, information and decision-making needs of responders to emergencies. As Turoff et al. (2004) stated, the unpredictable nature of a crisis implies that the exact actions and responsibilities of possibly geographically dispersed individuals and teams cannot be pre-determined. Therefore, an information system should be able to support reassigning decision power to where the action takes place, but also the reverse flow of accountability and status information upward and sideways throughout any responding organization.

2.2   Wicked Problems

In policy-making, the term '*wicked problem*' has been coined to refer to problems that are characterized by fundamental uncertainty about the nature, scope and behavior of the involved systems (Van Bueren et al. 2003; Weber & Khademian 2008). Sudden onset disasters confront decision-makers with wicked problems that are further complicated as a disaster entails a catastrophic event generating dramatic impacts that can propagate rapidly through the system (Rasmussen 1997).

The way to understand and analyze a wicked problem depends on the decision-makers' ideas about issues and possible solutions (Rittel & Webber 1973). In literature, wicked problems have hardly been addressed systematically, as there is no standard solution nor algorithm (Coyne 2005). Some approaches aim at adapting knowledge-based models to consider uncertainty and complexity by decomposing the overall system into sub-systems that are modeled separately (Rasmussen 1997). By neglecting interdependencies, important aspects associated to the emergence and interplay of systems are ignored (Pich et al. 2002) leading to inadequate models and flawed expectations regarding both the actual consequences and the manageability of the problem.

Therefore, approaches need to be developed that embrace the lack of situational awareness, resources and time, particularly in the early phases of a disaster. We propose to support decision-makers to structure information for decisions and explore consequences rather than relying on models. Such 'soft' approaches are considered as '*probe, sense and respond*' to test a system's reaction to an intervention instead of a model-based '*analyze and respond*' (Mingers & Rosenhead 2004).

In the response to sudden onset disasters, information management should be targeted at facilitating collaboration between the many organzations and actors involved. The process should systematically identify and reveal information that has the most significant implications for disaster response – on an individual, organizational and regional level. In the words of UN OCHA Head of Office Jesper Lund:

"*I only look at issues, not at numbers.*"

The ultimate challenge in wicked problems is making good decisions on the basis of lacking or inadequate information. The notion of a 'good' decision must be re-interpreted in this context: plans and projects should not be ranked on the basis of their performance at a given (static) point in time. Typically, the dynamics play an important role, as the evolution of the situation, the information available about the problem and the understanding of it continously change. Re-planning 'en cours de route' is often required (Benjaafar et al. 1995). Therefore, good probing should aim at the identification of drivers that considerably change the performance and ranking of alternatives. Information management should enable monitoring the situation, making sense of it and acting upon the (new) understanding (Pich et al. 2002).

2.3 Risk Accelerators as Basis for Information Management

There is a plethora of definitions of 'risk' depending on the context and purpose of use (Frosdick 1997). Although the term is used frequently in day-to-day language and seems to be understood, risks are perceived and judged very differently. Still, most authors agree that risk addresses the (positive or negative) consequences of a situation, an event, a decision or any kind of combination thereof and the probability of the consequences occurring (Fishburn 1984; Haimes et al. 2002).

The notion of risk is most prominent in financial corporations. Financial risk is usually determined by the variance or volatility of expected returns (Rippel & Teply 2011). Further measures focusing on losses comprise different value-at-risk measures that can be used to describe the extent of uncertainty and its related harm. Following this rationale, international engineering standards such as ISO 14971 define the risk associated to an event as the product of the event's probability and harm (Rakitin 2006).

Most approaches to risk management start with an assessment, i.e., the identification of potential risk sources or events, the assessment of those events' likelihood and consequences (Renn 2005). This leads to a focus on 'frequent' or chronic failures that are part of the annual or quarterly reporting. Emerging risks or outliers are typically not considered, and therefore not monitored, controlled and managed.

Organizations that are operating under high-risk circumstances should be very vigilant on avoiding risks resulting in incidents, because their occurrence would have disastrous consequences for the organization itself or the public. "High Reliability Organizations" (HROs) are organizations that operate under these trying conditions and succeed in having less than their fair share of accidents (Weick & Sutcliffe, 2001). Processes in HROs focus on failure rather than success, inertia as well as change, tactics rather than strategy, the present rather than the future, and resilience as well as anticipation (Weick et al., 1999).

The increasing complexity and uncertainty of socio-economic systems have resulted in increasing losses, and an increasing interest in HROs and the way they manage risk (Rothstein et al. 2006). Traditionally, risk management aims at reducing the likelihood of an event or the harm of its consequence. This approach requires that *all* events that may have harmful consequences can be identified and modeled to determine *all* harmful consequences and derive mitigation strategies. To acknowledge the fact that this is not possible in today's complex systems, the events that are not explicitly considered are classified as 'residual' and managed by a contingency or buffer (Renn 2005). In this manner, important risks, particularly those associated with combined or multi-hazards, may be overlooked or neglected. For instance, the 2010 eruption of the Eyjafjallajökull volcano in Iceland was not judged unlikely by geologists (Leadbetter & Hort 2011), yet it was not among the events that airlines considered. This lack of preparedness and vigilance caused supply chain disruptions and losses in the millions of Euros (Jüttner & Maklan 2011). A disaster of an unprecedented type and magnitude was the Fukushima Daiichi disaster in Japan in 2011, a catastrophic failure at the Fukushima I Nuclear Power Plant, resulting in a meltdown of three of the plant's six nuclear reactors. The failure occurred when the plant was hit by the tsunami triggered by the Tōhoku earthquake – an event of a magnitude that was considered extremely unrealistic by experts and government officials.

3   Managing Disaster Risks - Our Approach

We propose a perspective that analyses the multifaceted concept of risk in terms of potential developments of a system. We start the process by identifying unfavorable consequences or paths of development (scenarios) that need to be avoided. Information management, sensemaking and decision support are used to flag these unfavorable paths. Since it is not possible to manage and process information related to *all* possible scenarios, we focus on those that imply the most relevant consequences in terms of plausibility and harm of consequences.

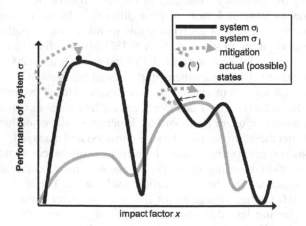

Fig. 1. Risk as a system inherent concept that evolves with changes of the environment

Figure 1 shows the evolution of the performance of a risk system σ as a function of the environment. The performance of the system σ is defined by two characteristics: (i) the potential losses, measured in terms of the performance difference between a satisficing and other potential states; performance can be understood in terms of qualitative and quantitative aims such as economic growth, stability, security, etc.; and (ii) the steepness of decline when the environment changes. As the environment cannot be captured or described in its full complexity, we focus on a set x of *impact factors* x_i that characterize the environment: $x=[x_1,\ldots,x_N]$. The impact factors x_i do not necessarily evolve independently or continuously; shocks such as natural hazards may result in jumps or major disruptions. How x's values actually may or might develop over time needs to be modeled and represented in the scenarios.

We now define *risk drivers* as those components x_i of x whose change leads to a steep decrease of the σ's performance. How steep the decline must be to consider x_i to be a risk driver depends on the perception and preferences of decision makers. Ideally, the set of scenarios should enable them to understand and monitor *all* risk drivers, but this is usually not feasible given restrictions in time and resources; and limitations in knowledge. To identify the most relevant risk drivers, we propose to identify factors that are driving or triggering changes in the σ's performance and impact the evaluation of the decision alternatives.

Good risk management should develop strategies to avoid patterns that may (quickly) lead to undesired consequences. As illustrated in Figure 1, system σ_i (in black) requires a mitigation reaction that corresponds to small changes in the environment to avoid potential large losses initiated by risk driver x. For system σ_j (in grey), the consequences of a small deviation are less severe. Depending on x's development there may be more time to recognize the development and act accordingly. Ultimately, it is the aim to change a system's behavior by exerting controls such that it is less prone to failure and substantial loss.

Due to the dynamics of complex systems, it is crucial to understand the patterns and relations that steer the system's behavior *while* these are emerging. When confronted with lacking information, there is a tendency to assume that relations can be controlled and behave similar to what is known about the system. Uncertainty is then simply added by assuming a limited variance (Draper 1995).

Our concept of risk recognizes that it is impossible to describe all possibly relevant components of x and model their consequences with respect to the system's performance. Ergo, 'risk' is largely a relative concept depending on the current knowledge and organizational or societal preferences and goals. Taking a **relevance- instead of likelihood driven perspective**, we advocate to systematically uncover relevant scenarios by using techniques from information management and decision support, such that systems can be designed that are less prone to substantial losses in any situation.

3.1   Exploration of Complexity through Scenarios

Data interpreted in the context of a disaster will result in assumptions about its possible or likely evolution. Systematically constructing *scenarios* that challenge current mind sets supports probing by helping decision-makers to explore the consequences of their actions against events that may happen and are sufficiently plausible to be envisioned (Wright & Goodwin 2009). Scenarios can be used to plan for possible future humanitarian needs, to steer the assessment to the most critical issues and to create common situation awareness among key stakeholders. By their very nature, scenarios represent diverging paths of the disaster's possible evolution, and can hence also be used as a means to build consensus or compare the impact of different assumptions, forecasts or models on the response planning and strategy. In this sense, they can be used as a tool to embrace different opinions rather than aggregating and averaging them, or choosing just one specific opinion.

Scenarios should address the information needs of decision-makers. Especially at the initial phase of a disaster, the need to act is greatest, yet the least information about what has happened is available. Decisions made in these early stages have consequences for months and years. At a recent UN Workshop on information needs of humanitarian decision makers, the information requirements were categorized into seven categories: context and scope; humanitarian needs; capacity and response planning; operational situation; coordination and institutional structures; internal; and looking forward. Within each of these categories specific questions or kinds of required information were provided (Gralla, Goentzel & Van de Walle 2012). As the resulting extensive list of requirements shows, decision-makers prefer to obtain all relevant observations and information that is available in order to make a decision that reflects the reality of the given situation. Once they know they have all relevant information that is available before they have to make a decision, they can move to sensemaking, which allows them to design response scenarios (Turoff et al 2004).

Scenarios are relevant if they represent a development with significant impact on the current strategy or planning and would – if they were true – require a change. Additionally, scenarios need to be credible and understandable. Credibility can be derived by verifiability and reliability of the source (Schoemaker, 1993). To balance timeliness and potential impact versus credibility, precision and granularity, information management should make trade-offs transparent at run-time by explicitly challenging the adequacy of the information and the constraints on the process (Comes, Wijngaards & Van de Walle, 2014).

Disaster responders operate under pressure and strain, including risks for personal safety and well being of responders on-site. Personal experience and trusted social networks play therefore an important role. As trust often is not transmitted across networks, this leads to a plethora of redundant pieces of information that is collected and processed individually, instead of being shared between different responding communities. It is also often difficult to codify and communicate knowledge that is only applicable to very specific situations. That is why scenarios are appropriate for expressing tacit knowledge (Kim 1998). Not everyone has the same experience with respect to a crisis situation since such events are relatively rare (King 2002), resulting in different reactions of professional responders and population affected. Tacit knowledge can be acquired only through experience such as observation, imitation, and practice (Kim 1998). Again, in the words of Jesper Lund:

"Disaster management is experience. And common sense."

Information is typically perceived as credible when it matches the expectations or experiences of decision-makers (Schoemaker, 1993). In case a scenario flags a risk that is emerging and unexpected, it is essential to annotate the information with the source (reliability by expertise) or the process that was used to derive the information (verifiability). Moreover, the information needs to be represented in an understandable way, making potential cause-effect chains explicit (Comes et al., 2012).

3.2   Providing Information, not Data

As Sebastian Rhodes-Stampa stated for the humanitarian response efforts he was coordinating in Tacloban, information needs could be very different depending who requested the information, and for what purpose. Along with the increasing availability of information management, expectations rose about the availability of detailed data. This lead to the need to manage an ever increasing amount of data, maps and situation reports in various levels of temporal and geographical detail. In his words:

"Granularity is the word of this emergency."

Instead of juxtaposing the same information at different levels of detail, scenarios should be tailored for specific decisions and address decision-makers' needs to avoid information overload, redundancies or the wrong level of granularity. A strategic series of scenarios might for instance include the needs of the population as they are and explore the impact of disaster relief supplies as a basis for the planning of humanitarian logistics. On a more operational level, scenarios can support coordination by presenting information about the current projects and the future presence of aid organizations (building on the so-called Who-What-Where or 3W database), and complementing the efforts with numbers of population and potential migration patterns.

To support sensemaking each scenario should present an understandable development of the situation; i.e., processed information including cause-effect chains rather than raw data. The form and type of information depends on the decision-makers' preferences, their access to technology (such as internet connection, bandwidth or printers) and the time available. Distributed techniques for scenario construction (Comes, Wijngaards & Van de Walle, 2014) enable the integration of experts from various agencies and authorities, bringing together local experts, professional responders, volunteers that work onsite or remotely (such as the Digital Humanitarian Network, a global network of volunteers), and scientists with different backgrounds.

3.3   Addressing the Dynamics

It takes time to collect and process data; to share and communicate information; and to derive an understanding of the problem, construct scenarios and make a decision. This is particularly true if a consensus must be found among different responding actors and organizations. In the very initial phase of humanitarian response, information is typically far from complete, yet the urgency of the response necessitates action nevertheless. As André Pacquet from the International Committee of the Red Cross and responsible for operations in the heavily affected town of Guiuan put it:

"We accept chaos to start operations."

As time passes, the information about the problem and the perception thereof can change. Hence, continuous revisions and corrections are necessary while considering the scarcity of resources available for sensemaking and to support the decision-makers. Therefore, scenario updates need to be conducted in an efficient and responsive manner (Comes, Wijngaards & Schultmann, 2012).

To this end, two aspects need to be respected: relevance and validity. In the context of updating, relevance is assessed in terms of the potential consequences of neglecting the new information. It is therefore necessary to assess if the new information is 'relevant enough' to justify the updating effort. Similarly, already collected information that is still 'sufficiently valid' should be reused. A scenario update can be informational or structural: *information updates* may change the measured or forecasted value of a variable, or its likelihood. A *structural update* requires mechanisms that account for a change in the basis for sensemaking or the evaluation and ranking of alternatives. This is for instance the case, when new impact factors are identified as the understanding about the problem grows, or as expert's previously implicit assumptions become more explicit.

4   Avoid Risk Accelerators: An Agenda for Humanitarian Information Management and Systems

Our approach to manage information and support decision-makers who are facing wicked problems in complex environments can be summarized by answering the two questions posed in the introduction.

Ad 1: Information Systems Design. The behavior of complex systems cannot be predicted and information is imperfect. The difficulty of assessing the consequences of a decision and prioritizing alternatives is compounded by a tendency to simplify the problem and neglect the lack of knowledge (Pathak et al. 2007). To support decision-makers who face complexity, we propose the use of scenarios to systematically explore harmful future developments. This entails continuous sensemaking and seeking to identify risk drivers as they emerge, while evaluating and continuously adapting disaster response strategies. The interpretive information processing mechanisms that are commonly called "intuition" or "experience" need to be supported by appropriate information systems. As Weick (1995) put it, "we need to understand more about Sensemaking Support Systems as well as Decision Support Systems, which means we need to know more about what is being supported". We have referred earlier to the DERMIS design premises as introduced by Turoff et al. (2004) providing a framework for the design of Humanitarian Information Management Systems.

Ad 2: Scenario Construction. Given limitations in time, effort, and resources, scenario construction and design of information products should be guided towards those that most significantly distinguish advantages and drawbacks of promising alternatives or the currently implemented strategies. To understand and detect potential flaws, we use scenarios for probing in a way that is targeted to identify the most critical potential problems while respecting constraints in terms of sufficient plausibility and credibility. To embrace the dynamics of a situation, and potentially swift system changes, information systems need to provide updating procedures to efficiently integrate new information and support sensemaking and decision-making on the basis of the latest understanding of the situation.

Inherent to the complexity of the situation, no method can guarantee to find all critical and loss-prone risks or risk drivers, and to communicate them at the right time to the decision-makers. Yet, in contrast to most modeling and statistical techniques, our method aims at identifying these drivers by referring to professionals, local or remote experts and scientists with different backgrounds to actively challenge current mindsets for critical sensemaking and robust decisions. By referring to different experts per piece of information, we aim at avoiding groupthink and, to some extent, the confirmation bias: experts can creatively think at an individual level about what might go wrong.

To choose and prioritize information products and scenarios, the following questions need to be addressed:

- *Number of information products* to be selected: how can the trade-off be made between a thorough exploration and the constraints on time and resources available?
- *Similarity:* how can the similarity or difference of information products and scenarios be measured in the context of sensemaking and decision support?
- *Reliability:* how can the plausibility and reliability of scenarios, which combine information of different type and quality, be assessed and continuously updated as new information becomes available?
- *Relevance and selection:* how can the most relevant information products be constructed, and how to select a good representative taking into account scenario similarity and reliability?

Each of these questions opens up fields and directions for future research. When designing information systems to answer these questions, it is vital that the decision-makers' needs and the constraints of sudden onset disasters are respected. If the realities of operations are not valued, frustration with the systems may lead to workarounds and the parallel existence of official reporting and information management and direct and direct communications within the respective networks. For instance, Sebastian Rhodes-Stampa expressed his views as follows:

"Provide simple messages, don't overcomplicate stuff. Right now we are victims of our own black magic of sophisticated systems."

The characteristics that need to be taken into account include, among others, the time available before a decision has to be made, and the authority to make it; the requirements of accessibility of information and interoperability of systems; the availability of local experts; the quality of information that local or remote experts, or automated systems can provide; the current workload; and the sensitivity of the experts' assessments to a change in input information. In this manner, future information systems can be designed so that they support decision-makers who are confronted with an increasing number of increasingly complex disasters.

Acknowledgements. The authors thank the Disaster Resilience Lab and its supporters for the inspiring discussions on field research and disaster response. We are grateful to the humanitarian responders who accepted our requests for interviews and discussions, and made this research possible.

References

1. Benjaafar, S., Morin, T., Talavage, J.: The strategic value of flexibility in sequential decision making. European Journal of Operational Research 82(3), 438–457 (1995)
2. Comes, T., Wijngaards, N., Maule, J., et al.: Scenario Reliability Assessment to Support Decision Makers in Situations of Severe Uncertainty. In: IEEE International Multi-Disciplinary Conference on Cognitive Methods in Situation Awareness and Decision Support, pp. 30–37 (2012)
3. Comes, T., Wijngaards, N., Schultmann, F.: Efficient scenario updating in emergency management. In: Proceedings of the 9th International Conference on Information Systems for Crisis Response and Management, Vancouver (2012)
4. Comes, T., Wijngaards, N., Van de Walle, B.: Exploring the Future: Runtime Scenario Selection for Complex and Time-Bound Decisions. Technological Forecasting and Social Change (in press, 2014)
5. Coyne, R.: Wicked problems revisited. Design Studies 26(1), 5–17 (2005)
6. Draper, D.: Assessment and Propagation of Model Uncertainty. Journal of the Royal Statistical Society. Series B (Methodological) 57(1), 45–97 (1995)
7. Dutton, J.: The Processing of Crisis and Non-Crisis Strategic Issues. Journal of Management Studies 23(5), 501–517 (1986)
8. Fishburn, P.C.: Foundations of Risk Measurement. I. Risk As Probable Loss. Management Science 30(4), 396–406 (1984)
9. Frosdick, S.: The techniques of risk analysis are insufficient in themselves. Disaster Prevention and Management: An International Journal 6(3), 165–177 (1997)
10. Gigerenzer, G., Dieckmann, A., Gaissmaier, W.: Efficient Cognition Through Limited Search. In: Todd, P., Gigerenzer, G. (eds.) Ecological Rationality. Intelligence in the World, pp. 241–273. Oxford University Press (2012)
11. Gralla, E., Goentzel, J., Van de Walle, B.: Report from the Workshop on Field-Based Decision Makers' Information Needs in Sudden Onset Disasters, DHN and ACAPS, Geneva (2012), http://digitalhumanitarians.com/content/decision-makers-needs
12. Haimes, Y., Kaplan, S., Lambert, J.H.: Risk Filtering, Ranking, and Management Framework Using Hierarchical Holographic Modeling. Risk Analysis 22(2), 383–398 (2002)
13. Jüttner, U., Maklan, S.: Supply chain resilience in the global financial crisis: an empirical study. Supply Chain Management: An International Journal 16(4), 246–259 (2011)
14. Kim, L.: Crisis construction and organizational learning: Capability building in catching-up at Hyundai Motor. Organization Science 9(4), 506–521 (1998)
15. King, D.: Post Disaster Surveys: experience and methodology. The Australian Journal of Emergency Management 17(3), 39–47 (2002)

16. Leadbetter, S.J., Hort, M.C.: Volcanic ash hazard climatology for an eruption of Hekla Volcano, Iceland. Journal of Volcanology and Geothermal Research 199(3-4), 230–241 (2011)
17. Mingers, J., Rosenhead, J.: Problem structuring methods in action. European Journal of Operational Research 152(3), 530–554 (2004)
18. Pathak, S.D., Day, J.M., Nair, A., Sawaya, W.J., Kristal, M.M.: Complexity and Adaptivity in Supply Networks: Building Supply Network Theory Using a Complex Adaptive Systems Perspective. Decision Sciences 38(4), 547–580 (2007)
19. Pich, M.T., Loch, C.H., de Meyer, A.: On Uncertainty, Ambiguity, and Complexity in Project Management. Management Science 48(8), 1008–1023 (2002)
20. Rakitin, S.R.: Coping with Defective Software in Medical Devices. Computer 39(4), 40–45 (2006)
21. Rasmussen, J.: Risk management in a dynamic society: A modelling problem. Safety Science 27(2-3), 183–213 (1997)
22. Renn, O.: Risk Governance. Towards an integrative approach, Geneva (2005)
23. Rippel, M., Teply, P.: Operational Risk - Scenario Analysis. Prague Economic Papers 1, 23–39 (2011)
24. Rittel, H.W.J., Webber, M.M.: Dilemmas in a general theory of planning. Policy Sciences 4(2), 155–169 (1973)
25. Rothstein, H., Huber, M., Gaskell, G.: A theory of risk colonization: The spiralling regulatory logics of societal and institutional risk. Economy and Society 35(1), 91–112 (2006)
26. Schoemaker, P.J.: Multiple scenario development: its conceptual and behavioral foundation. Strategic Management Journal 14(3), 193–213 (1993)
27. Turoff, M., Chumer, M., Van de Walle, B., Yao, X.: The design of a dynamic emergency response management information system (DERMIS). JITTA 5(4), 1–35 (2004)
28. Weber, E.P., Khademian, A.M.: Wicked Problems, Knowledge Challenges, and Collaborative Capacity Builders in Network Settings. Public Administration Review 68(2), 334–349 (2008)
29. Weick, K.E., Sutcliffe, K.M., Obstfeld, D.: Organizing for high reliability: Processes of collective mindfulness. . Research in Organizational Behaviour 21(1), 81–123 (2008)
30. Van Bueren, E.M., Klijn, E.-H., Koppenjan, J.F.M.: Dealing with Wicked Problems in Networks: Analyzing an Environmental Debate from a Network Perspective. Journal of Public Administration Research and Theory 13(2), 193–212 (2003)
31. Weick, K.E., Sutcliffe, K.M.: Managing the unexpected. Jossey-Bass, San Francisco (2001)
32. Wright, G., Goodwin, P.: Decision making and planning under low levels of predictability: Enhancing the scenario method. International Journal of Forecasting 25(4), 813–825 (2009)

Against the Odds:
Managing the Unmanagable in a Time of Crisis

Diomidis Spinellis

Athens University of Economics and Business
Department of Management Science and Technology
Patision 76, GR-104 34 Athens, Greece
dds@aueb.gr

Abstract. Information technology systems at the Greek Ministry of Finance could be the ideal tools for fighting widespread tax evasion, bureaucratic inefficiency, waste, and corruption. Yet making this happen requires battling against protracted procurement processes and implementation schedules, ineffective operations, and rigid management structures. This experience report details some unconventional measures, tools, and techniques that were adopted to sidestep the barriers in a time of crisis. The measures involved meritocracy, IT utilization, and management by objectives. Sadly, this report is also a story (still being written) on the limits of such approaches. On balance, it demonstrates that in any large organization there are ample opportunities to bring about change, even against considerable odds.

It seemed like a good idea at the time. In 2009, Greece's new government, instead of staffing the ministries' Secretary General positions through the, commonly, opaque political appointments [18, p. 79][19, p. 157], it provided a form to submit online applications. As a professor of software engineering interested in public service, I decided to apply for the position of the Secretary General for Information Systems at the Ministry of Finance, a position that was in effect the Ministry's CIO post. I reasoned that by serving in this position I could apply in practice what I taught to my students; in this case how to provide high quality eGovernment services in an efficient manner. After a couple of interviews and a few weeks of waiting time I started serving, for what was to be a two year term, at the General Secretariat for Information Systems (GSIS).

GSIS develops, runs, and supports the information systems used at the Greek Ministry of Finance. The most important of these at the end of 2009 were TAXIS, the software used in all of 300 Greece's tax offices, TAXISnet, a web application that taxpayers use for electronic filing, and, ICISnet, which supports the customs agencies. Another significant body of work at the time involved the keying-in of tax filing forms, the calculation of tax returns, and the printing of tax assessment forms and payment notices (about 15 million documents per year). In addition GSIS supported diverse tax compliance actions, mainly by running electronic tax compliance checks. Finally, GSIS, contributed input for fiscal policy making in the form of statistical data and ad-hoc calculations.

M. Jarke et al. (Eds.): CAiSE 2014, LNCS 8484, pp. 24–41, 2014.
© Springer International Publishing Switzerland 2014

GSIS reported to the Minister of Finance and was supported by the administrative services of the Ministry of Finance. This meant that staff dealing with GSIS's personnel and procurement were not reporting to me, but to the Ministry's General Secretary. Oddly, GSIS consisted of a single General Directorate. This comprised of three directorates dealing respectively with software, hardware, and data entry. Unlike many other Greek civil service departments, GSIS was lucky to be housed in a modern secure building. In 2009 it employed about 1200 permanent and temporary staff, a number which declined to less than 950 during my tenure. Approximately 135 employees had a university degree, 120 had a technical education degree, while the remaining 620 had a secondary education degree. External contractors handled most of the work associated with the development and maintenance of GSIS's information systems.

Soon I realized that GSIS was in a crisis. The implementation of key IT projects was years behind schedule, some services provided to taxpayers were based on fickle outdated technologies, a large proportion of the staff were not sufficiently qualified or trained, the employees' union demanded a say on the service's operational matters, morale was low, and some managers were unable to deliver the required results. Even worse, I soon discovered that, I did not have at my disposal basic tools of management, namely the formal authority or practical means to hire and fire, promote and demote, reward and discipline, outsource and develop in-house, or reorganize hierarchies. In short, I was in a position of power without authority.

As if those problems were not enough, soon Greece's government debt crisis broke loose [11,17], bringing the Ministry in the eye of the storm. A few months later, it was obvious that GSIS would have to deliver dramatically more and better results with fewer personnel, on lower salaries, with a reduced budget. As the Secretariat's head I had to deliver those results while battling with entrenched bureaucratic inefficiency, inter-departmental intransigence, clientilism, political patronage, drawn-out procurement processes, and an ineffective legal system.

To overcome these problems I targeted the obvious: better utilization of the organization's human capital, exploitation of information technology, management by objectives and results, and improvement of the organization's processes. Unfortunately, the existing Napoleonic state institutional framework — the formalistic, legalistic, and bureaucratic way in which the Greek public administration works [19, pp. 153, 164] — did not provide me with the necessary tools to implement the necessary changes. Consequently, I had to resort to the unconventional techniques detailed in this experience report.

1   Meritocracy

When I started serving at GSIS an experienced colleague told me that 95% of my performance would depend on the people I would select to work with. As time went by I realized he was 100% right. Unfortunately, the Greek public administration lacks well established practices and procedures that guarantee meritocracy. Therefore, meritocracy always depends on the personal choices of all those who serve in management positions — from the Prime Minister to the directors to the section heads.

1.1 Office Staff

Breaking a tradition where department heads would appoint as their advisors former colleagues, acquaintances, friends, or even nephews, I decided to staff the five advisor positions, which were available for my post, through the "OpenGov" web application process I had previously used to apply for my own post. There I published the criteria for the positions and a web form in which applicants had to complete extensive details regarding their knowledge and skills. With the luxury of being able to choose among 750 submitted resumes, I was able to form a team of very capable, hardworking professionals, with valuable work experience in key positions in Greece and abroad. Because applications were submitted electronically through a form with keyed fields, it was easy to evaluate the applications with a small Perl script I wrote for this purpose, and determine those we[1] could call for an interview.

I interviewed the first batch of the short-listed candidates on my own. Then, following an unconventional practice followed by some tech-startups, I had the new members of my team participating in the process by interviewing the following candidates. After each interview round our budding team held a meeting to discuss its results and select the new members. These meetings helped gel our team together, and bring on board staff that was compatible with its technocratic orientation. There were times when team members disagreed with my view. Through our discussions I witnessed in practice how in some contexts a group's performance can surpass that of each group's member [12].

The choice of one of our team's members was particularly interesting. The application came from an existing GSIS employee. I looked for her, and found her sitting in front of an empty desk. I asked her why she applied to work in the department she was already placed, and what I learned was eye-opening. She had returned from secondment to another organization two weeks earlier, and no one had bothered to assign her some work to do. So she applied to join our team in a bid to become productive. She quickly joined us, and as a top graduate of the National School of Public Administration with plenty of experience in managing EU-funded projects, she proved to be a valuable team asset. She became the contact point of our office with the rest of the public administration, handling responsibly and professionally the tens of requests that arrived at my office each day. When I saw her diligently working at 10:00 p.m. on folders overflowing with arcane documents, I couldn't help but wonder how less productive our team would be if we had not published that open call for its staffing.

A few volunteers who, having completed a successful career, were willing to work pro-bono to help get Greece out of the crisis, complemented our team. I was

---

[1] I use the plural to refer to the team work performed by the staff in my office and permanent GSIS staff. Without this team effort, none of the things I am describing could have been achieved.

surprised to find out that it was not formally possible to have these persons join me as advisors without paying them a salary. In a country in a crisis and in a world where volunteer organizations, activists, and NGOs often address problems more effectively than governments, the Greek state was putting barriers in the path of volunteers who wanted to help their country. For reasons of form and substance I was unwilling to have people work in my office without corresponding institutional coverage. Eventually, we solved this issue, by creating an advisory working group which comprised permanent staff members, my advisors, which were hired under a fixed-term contract, and these volunteers.

1.2 Staffing through Open Calls

Having created a culture of meritocracy in my office, we looked how we could extend it throughout the Department. Initially the picture looked bleak. The department's management positions were staffed through a formalistic, bureaucratic, inflexible, and ultimately ineffective system, which used as its main criterion seniority rather than job qualifications, evaluations, and experience [19, pp. 162–166]. To overcome these restrictions we utilized the concept of working groups. A working group and its chair could be setup in a day through a simple formal decision by the Department's General Secretary. Indeed, at GSIS there was already an established tradition of such groups, who were often also receiving extra pay for their services. Sadly, they were often staffed through opaque procedures, sometimes taking into account political party alliances.

Based on the institutional framework of working groups we issued a number of open calls to staff the ones required to complete specific tasks. To stress that the selection was based on merit, we ensured that each call, the skills required for participating in the group, and the decision for the group's composition, were published on the Department's intranet. In the beginning we faced pervasive distrust; some advocated in water-cooler discussions that this process was merely a smokescreen to continue the party games of the past. However, the cynicism subsided, when people saw that some of the appointed working group chairs, could not have been selected based on their party alliance, and that therefore the appointment process was truly meritocratic. (Sadly this started a reverse grumble from people who believed that some positions should be preferentially staffed by people with strong political party credentials.) In total within two years we published and completed 38 open calls for working groups and their chairs.

The meritocratic staffing process I described kick-started a virtuous cycle involving the substantial increase in the engagement of young, highly qualified executives in the working groups, especially in the demanding positions of project coordinators. What drove this cycle? I realized that in the past professional, worthy staff members would avoid their involvement in committees and working groups, because they did not want to be associated with whichever political party was in power at the time. When those people realized that staffing was decided on merit, not only did they participate, but they also urged other colleagues to come forward, declare their interest, and work.

The pride of people who were selected on merit to chair working groups or, later, when it became possible, to be appointed in formal management positions, was revealing. A year after I took office, it was a joy to walk around the building late in the evening and find section heads, team coordinators, and managers working hard to meet a deadline or finish without interruptions work they had not found time to complete during the normal working hours. However, I also felt guilty because I lacked the means to financially reward these people who were working overtime to move the Department forward. Wages were set centrally across the board based simply on seniority. The few funds that were available for overtime pay (each year arriving months late) were a drop in the ocean compared to the actual time these people worked. So, again, I resorted to unconventional means: public recognition of those who put the extra effort, invitations of key people to meetings that I set outside the organization's formal structure, walks by the office of people who worked late for an informal chat, and even the allocation of parking places. As for the overtime payments, we stopped dividing them equally across all the Department's employees, which was until then the custom, and insisted on having these nominal amounts payed to those who actually worked a lot harder than others.

1.3   Staff Evaluation

Another unconventional initiative we undertook in the field of human resource management, involved the genuine assessment of staff. Sadly, this did not fare as well as the other initiatives. The existing way in which civil servants were evaluated was hopelessly inadequate. (See [18, p. 78].) All employees received top marks in their mandatory periodic evaluations. This practice demoralized the best employees, and also provided fertile ground for cronyism to flourish. With the help of an external volunteer advisor, who had extensive experience in managing large organizations, we designed and implemented a 360-degree appraisal [2] for staff working in my office. Under this appraisal scheme employees are evaluated by their superiors, their subordinates (if any), as well as their colleagues working at the same level of the administrative hierarchy. The assessment forms we prepared for the evaluators had fields where one had to describe the work and additional responsibilities of the evaluated staff member, comment on his or her work performance, and identify areas where there was room for improvement.

For the supervisors we designed a more detailed form where they could summarize the information from all evaluators, and rate the staff member's work performance factors (administrative skills, written communication, verbal communication, problem analysis, decision making, delegation of work, work quantity, work quality, staff development, compliance with policies and procedures, and technical ability), as well as personal performance factors (initiative, perseverance, ability to work with others, adaptability, persuasiveness, confidence, judgment, leadership, creativity, and reliability). According to our plan, supervisors would then discuss with each evaluated staff member his or her overall performance, areas for improvement, and his or her career plans. Finally, after this debriefing, the two parties would add to their form any additional comments they might have and sign it.

We started the evaluation process for staff working in my office, hoping that some of the high-level managers who would receive the appraisal forms (as associates of my advisors or as my subordinates) would be take the initiative to adopt this procedure in their directorate or section. Sadly, this did not happen. I did not press the issue further, for I believe that strict instructions and procedures are effective only for performing simple standardized tasks, while more ambitious results (such as the adoption of a work culture based on appraisals) can achieved only through education, leadership, and appropriate incentives. Moreover, two years after this initiative an academic colleague who specializes in human resource management explained to me that 360-degree appraisals are only meaningful in exceptionally mature and well managed organizations, so in this case we were probably over-ambitious.

Interestingly, I never got back my own evaluation forms which I gave to my fellow general secretaries and my superiors. This made me reflect on the upward struggle a widespread introduction of performance appraisals would face. My pessimistic view was further strengthened when legislation passed in 2011[2] introducing performance-based pay for civil servants was put on hold until December 31st 2016 with new legislation[3] passed just a year later.

2   IT Utilization

The performance of GSIS in its IT-related tasks was disappointing for an organization that considered itself the crown jewel in Greek public administration IT service provision. Procurement of hardware and software systems typically took years. For example, a new data center project had commenced in 2002 and was still ongoing in 2010. As a result, there was at the time no disaster recover site. If the existing data center got destroyed by a fire or an earthquake, many critical government revenue management functions would be completely disrupted. Furthermore, GSIS lacked a management information system, a human resource management system, as well as systems to perform tax compliance checks and organize tax audits.

These shortcomings were mainly caused by the sluggish bureaucratic procedures that were in place for public procurement and EU-funded projects. To reach a point where a project's procurement contract could be signed, the project had to jump through dozens of hoops and obtain as many signatures — in a theoretically simple case we counted 28 steps. In addition, during the tender process rival contractors typically appealed against any decision made by the public administration through the judicial system, where cases lingered for months. Consequently, vital projects for our work were years away from completion. Soon I

---

[2] Greek law 4024/2011, article 19. Government Gazette Issue A 226/27-10-2011.

[3] Greek law 4093/2012, article 1, paragraph 3.1.2. Government Gazette Issue A 222/12-11-2012.

concluded that from the time the public administration established the need for an information system it would take at least five years to put it into operation.

As if those problems were not enough, the projects' EU funding often resulted in unworkable specifications. Agencies tended to inflate and gold-plate the specifications, because, first, the agency procuring the project had no motive to keep its budget under control, and, second, it did not know and when, if ever, it would obtain again funds for the project's enhancement. These inflated and, due to delays, outdated specifications resulted in overly complex projects that were a pain to implement, difficult to sign-off, and a challenge to use productively. Adding insult to injury, in some extreme cases, an agency would find itself obliged to deploy the useless system it had ordered in order to avoid having to hand back the funding it had obtained for its implementation. The agency would thus find itself worse off compared to the state it was before it had ordered the system.

The unconventional, guerrilla, methods we employed to solve these problems involved adopting *open source software*, utilizing *agile development methods* to develop software in-house, and *empowering the* IT *market* to develop solutions through the specification of open standards.

2.1   Open Source Software

Open source software [1] can be freely downloaded, adapted, redistributed, and used. Although a large percentage of this software is developed by volunteers and academics, its quality is often comparable to that of proprietary offerings developed by large companies. Some well-known open source software systems, like the Linux kernel, the Python and PHP programming languages, and the the PostgreSQL and the MySQL relational databases are powering critical functions of organizations like Google, Wikipedia, and Facebook. In addition, millions of people around the world are using open source products, such as the Android platform for mobile phones, the Firefox web browser, and the Libre Office suite.

For us at GSIS, the main advantage of open source software was not the ability to read and modify the software's source code, but the fact that we could download and install it for free with a click of the mouse [21], without getting entangled into nightmarish public procurement procedures. Another critical factor concerning the adoption of open source software is the availability of the required technology skills and services [7]. Thankfully, GSIS, as an IT organization, had these available in house.

One of the first systems we installed was MediaWiki; the software driving Wikipedia [4]. This implements a wiki [13], a system that allows anyone to create linkable web pages (articles in the case of Wikipedia), and all others to read and change them. At GSIS we configured the wiki to run on the organization's intranet, so that it could be accessed only by staff members. By developing a few templates we implemented, in less than a month, a bare-bones human resource management system and a repository for organizational knowledge.

Specifically, we asked all employees to create their own wiki page which should contain basic data about themselves: their name, office, department, telephone, responsibilities, specialization, and skills. For some of these elements we specified how they should be coded through MediaWiki templates and predefined "categories". For instance, an employee could specify fluent knowledge of English or experience with SQL. Categories grouped pages together according to their attributes in multiple dimensions. This allowed us to to query the wiki for things such as the employees working in a department or directorate, those who could program in a specific computer language, or those who were experienced tax auditors.

At the beginning of my tenure at GSIS I realized that meeting minutes were only kept for committees that were formally set up, and those minutes were only kept to satisfy the letter of the committee's mandate. In almost all informal meetings, the keeping of minutes was considered an inconvenient luxury. To change this situation, we decided to document the agenda and the minutes of all informal meetings on the wiki. In the first meetings I kept the minutes. This gave me the opportunity to design a template page containing the key elements that should be recorded for each meeting: the place and time it was scheduled, the participants (with links to their personal page on the wiki), the agenda, and the action items. Through the wiki's affordances it was easy for the same page to serve both as the meeting's agenda (participants could easily add items to it), and for the keeping the meeting's minutes (we copied the agenda, changing specific elements into action items; again participants could review and correct the minutes with a click of the mouse). Through the templates we adopted each meeting was automatically categorized (e.g. "Production Board", "Security Team", "SG Office"), and all staff members could read the minutes of all meetings. Open access to all minutes on the wiki (172 entries by the end of my tenure) promoted the administration's transparency, reducing power games with the selective dissemination of information, and cutting down misinformation and false rumors concerning decisions that were taken in the past behind closed doors.

Initially, the introduction of the wiki was met with skepticism. Some claimed that the ability to change any of its contents would lead to misrepresentations and vandalism. Soon, however, it became obvious that employees were considerably more mature than what the naysayers thought, for no such cases occurred. If there was a problem, this was that staff members were reluctant to correct each other's pages, rather than that too many inconsiderate changes were made. Certainly, the wiki's technology helped us in this regard, because MediaWiki keeps a full record of each page's changes and the users associated with them.

It was harder to establish incentives for participating in the wiki. I felt that the administrative enforcement of its use would be counterproductive, for it would lead to formal compliance, rather than embracing the spirit of open cooperation I wanted to promote through its adoption. The wiki's technology gave us a simple incentive mechanism. Links to pages that do not exist on the wiki (e.g. the personal pages of a meeting's participants) are shown in red instead of blue, indicating to all that specific staff members had not yet created their wiki page. Next we established as a rule that those wishing to participate in an open staffing call should have a personal wiki page. This requirement was in full harmony with the spirit of transparency: those wishing to enjoy its advantages should abide by its rules. Finally, to help employees who had difficulty in using the wiki technology, we established a group of "Wiki Samaritans": eager and cheerful executives who undertook to assist those who had trouble using it. Through these means within two years of my term the wiki grew to cover over 2,500 pages of information.

Another open source software we installed and used was *Redmine*, a distributed project management tool. *Redmine* allows the specification of a project's tasks and the relevant deadlines. Based on the data entered, it will show schematically each project's progress, either as a percentage or through Gantt charts. Thereby, everyone involved in a project's implementation or depending on it could see its progress. The deciding factor for progressing in our many projects was the hard and methodical work of their coordinators. On top of that Redmine brought transparency, accountability, and discipline in project management, highlighting the progress made by good coordinators as well as action items that needed our attention.

The fact that we could download Redmine at no cost, without going through a public procurement process, allowed us to deploy it across all GSIS within a few days. As a counterexample, another government body decided, after a thorough study, to obtain a (much more sophisticated) commercial project management system. In order to sidestep the procurement delays it utilized a (supposedly) flexible way to fund project preparatory work through so-called 'technical assistance' EU funding. These efforts began in June 2011 with support from government officials at the highest level. My understanding is that five months later the procurement process was still underway.

2.2   Agile Software Development

It is unrealistic to expect that all the software requirements of a large organization can be met through open source software. Bespoke software development is often needed to satisfy specialized requirements. In the case of GSIS a vital system for combating tax evasion and improving compliance and revenue collection was an audit targeting, assignment, monitoring, and optimization system called "ELENXIS". The project was in the works since 2005. By the time I started my term, the system had begun, after many delays, a painful period of limited pilot operation. Another system, crucial for designing tax policy and improving the functioning of the tax administration, was a management information system (MIS). Its development with EU funding was approved in 2007, but the corresponding request for proposals had not been published until 2009.

To solve these problems we turned to agile software development [6,15]. Our aim was to bypass the prevalent heavy, bureaucratic, and formalistic procurement procedures, and see how we could quickly deliver software that would meet the needs of the citizens and the Ministry's staff.

Unfortunately, the principles of agile software development are at odds with the way government IT projects are traditionally implemented in Greece.

I presented the case for agility to the board of the Federation of Hellenic ICT Enterprises, but got a hostile reaction. We were thus saddled with inflexible practices and contracts for large IT systems like TAXIS, ELENXIS, and the MIS. For instance, for a (theoretically) simple change of the VAT rate a contractor asked to be paid for three effort months. We therefore tried to see how we could specify the use of agile development practices in new funded projects, and also how we could develop software with agile methods in-house by utilizing GSIS staff.

We upgraded a small group of GSIS developers, which was developing for years quietly useful and functional software into an "agile development team". Our goal was for this group to implement simple but effective solutions following Pareto's 80-20 principle under which the 80% of a system's functionality can be implemented with 20% of the required effort. We worked in the same way with staff from the Department's Applications unit and also with advisors who were seconded to my office. Thus, until the 25 million euro ELENXIS project was fully functioning, we ran simple tax compliance queries on the existing databases of GSIS. As an example, one such check would verify whether taxpayers had declared in their tax form the income that partnerships indicated they had paid to their partners. (In many cases we found that, a single digit tended to be dropped with surprising frequency: a 101,345.00 payment would be declared as 11,345.00 income.)

Then the agile development group built within a month a simple application that would assign the cases to the corresponding local tax office and track their progress. (More details on this in Section 3.1.) Furthermore, in place of the MIS, which had not yet been ordered, we implemented a simple system where anyone could enter the title, parameters, and SQL statement corresponding to queries that the Ministry's departments often asked us to run on our databases. A web-based front end would show the available queries, allow authorized users to run them, and offer the results as a downloadable spreadsheet for further processing. This simple application reduced the workload associated with running many boilerplate queries, allowing the staff to concentrate on the increasingly more demanding requests we were receiving.

2.3   The Government as a Regulator Rather Than a Customer

Other systems required bespoke development at a scale too large for them to be implemented in-house with GSIS's limited resources. In such cases, to avoid the quagmire of public procurement, we looked for ways to utilize the local IT market, bypassing the deadly embrace of the government with large EU-funded projects. The unconventional approach we developed and implemented involved limiting the government's role to that of a regulator. Under this approach we would specify technology standards and rules on how specific processes were to run, allowing the market to come up with systems that satisfied these requirements.

We found that through this approach IT companies would swiftly deliver cheaper and better solutions than what we could expect by formally procuring IT systems from government contractors. Two interesting examples involved the implementation of the Single Payment Authority and the use of the Ministry's registry data.

The Single Payment Authority, part of an effort to modernize the public administration, aimed to consolidate fragmented employment practices by disbursing centrally the salary payments of state employees [8, p. 48]. Up until 2010 these were paid by hundreds of bodies scattered throughout Greece [18]. These bodies ranged from universities and hospitals to municipalities and ministries. The wide dispersion of bodies that paid state employees made it difficult to centrally monitor these costs, which in 2010 amounted to 27.8bn euro (24% of the General Government's expenditure) [10, p. 137]. In addition it was suspected that the laxity of controls regarding how small entities paid their salaries left space for mismanagement and graft.

The original plan regarding the Authority was to implement a single payroll system covering the entire government. This would involve collecting the paper files of half a million employees in a central location, entering their data into the new payroll system, and then calculating and paying the salaries through that system. A new general directorate was setup with the necessary directorates and departments, and even offices were rented in a posh business district for housing this new body. Unfortunately, the requisite payroll system did not exist, and, by taking into account the procurement time that was typically required for such system, it would take at least five years to put it into place.

Instead of this grandiose plan we proceeded as follows. First we defined and published technical specifications on how each body's paymaster (for instance the one responsible for the Ministry of Agriculture) would send to GSIS each month a file with the payment details for all state employees that were working there. The details included the employee's name, payment amount, tax and social security identification numbers, withheld amounts, bank account number, and other similar fields. The file format was XML-based and the specification was defined through a corresponding schema file. This allowed the body's technicians to easily verify whether the files they had created were formatted in the specified way. If, for example, a record lacked the beneficiary's social security number, the problem would manifest itself before the file was sent to GSIS. This minimized the communication problems with the scheme's stakeholders.

In addition, we developed in-house a small application that would receive files uploaded over the internet, verify their contents, and prepare payment instructions. Finally, we collaborated with the company that runs the interbank payment system and the state's General Accounting Office to arrange the flow for the beneficiaries' payments. In this way in less than a year Central Payment Authority was managing payments for about 3700 bodies and paying 570,000 state employees.

The decentralised manner in which the system was developed allowed those who were actually running things quickly find the best and cheapest way to comply. Each body formatted its data through whatever way it deemed expedient. Some modified their payroll application in-house, others collaborated with the application's vendor, while smaller ones adopted simple ad-hoc solutions, which involved converting existing reports into the required format. Through a web search we even found a small remote company offering an application that would adapt the payroll data into the Single Payment Authority's format for just 120 euros.

This decentralized implementation did not meet all the requirements of the original system regarding of audits that could be made. However, in practice it turned out that just five simple but effective controls that the new system could implement (payments from multiple bodies, exceeding the statutory maximum salary, salary payments from the private sector, tax filing, and payment arrears to the state) exceeded the throughput capacity of the competent[4] audit service. This demonstrated the agile programming YAGNI (Your Aren't Going to Need It) principle [5, p. 18].

The second example where the GSIS collaborated with the local IT market as a regulator concerns the distribution of the Tax Authority business register. The online availability of the registry could greatly simplify transactions, saving time and money. For example, when a business needs to issue an invoice, instead of typing in all the counterparty's details (name, address, phone, occupation), it could simply fetch them from the register using the counterparty's tax identification number as a key. The easy availability of this data could also reduce the plague of fake invoices, because anyone receiving an invoice could easily check the details written on it as well as whether the listed company was still in business.

To aid the registry's distribution GSIS could implement bespoke applications, and provide them to the taxpayers. This had been the case in the past for applications that filed various tax forms. Instead, we offered the registry's data as a simple web service, which was implemented in a few days. At the same time we published the web service's specifications and issued a call for volunteers to develop clients as open source software. Within a couple of weeks we had at hand clients for a diverse set of platforms and operating systems, including apps for cell phones. Companies that developed accounting and ERP software were soon using this functionality, as were web pages that were setup for this purpose. Sadly, this service ceased being offered without a warning in mid-2013, proving the ambivalent relationship of the State's bureaucracy with public data.

3   Management by Objectives

With increased agility and effectiveness in the areas of people and IT management, we tried leveraging our improved capacity to achieve higher level, fiscal, objectives. This was an audacious move, for we were venturing at the limits of our legally prescribed competences, into areas tainted by chronic ineffectiveness and, possibly, graft. As we shall see in the examples outlined in the following sections, not all ventures had a happy ending.

---

[4] In this work the term "competency" refers to the concept deriving from the principle of legality. A competency prescribes in great detail the legal ability provided to an administrative body to enact legally binding rules, to contribute to their enactment, and to undertake physical operations [23,18]

3.1   Handling Tax Compliance Checks by Regional Tax Offices

In Greece widespread tax evasion [3] and a large shadow economy harm the state's fiscal management, horizontal and vertical equity, and economic efficiency [16]. Although the competent bodies for tax compliance at the Ministry of Finance were the General Secretariat for Tax and Customs Affairs and the Economic Crime Unit, from the beginning of my tenure I felt that GSIS could help significantly in this area through the use of IT. Perhaps naively, I believed that reducing tax evasion would be relatively straightforward, because we could swiftly locate thousands of suspect cases through electronic tax compliance checks, and send them off to the regional tax offices for further processing We therefore activated a previously legislated[5] high-level committee to plan electronic tax compliance checks, and started executing them. We regularly met as a committee to discuss and plan ideas for tax compliance checks. However after a few meetings I began to worry. What had happened with the cases we sent for processing? I was asking the departments who should be overseeing this processing, but I was not getting any concrete answers. I was told that the processing was proceeding "without problems", and bringing in the "expected revenue". However, nobody could tell me the number of cases that had been processed and the amount that was collected.

To obtain a more accurate picture of this process our agile development team developed a small web-based application that would assign the thousands of suspect cases to specific regional tax offices and ask them to process them. For every case that was closed (e.g. by calling in the taxpayer to file an amended declaration and pay a fine), the tax officers had to fill into a form the additional revenue received from taxes and fines. Through this application we could centrally monitor with objective measures the progress on the case workload and also the efficiency of each compliance check. We could also verify that the cases were being processed at a rate that would not result in a backlog buildup. The data we obtained from the application was eye-opening: apparently many regional tax offices were not processing any cases for long periods of time. After a few months the system was operating the (theoretical) workload processing period had climbed to 175 working days against a mutually agreed target of 60 days.

With concrete figures at hand I was able to do three things. First I could present the situation to the Minister of Finance, so that he could mobilize the respective tax office. However, I quickly realized that he was facing at the level of the Ministry the same problems I was facing at GSIS: he did not have at his disposal the necessary management tools, must crucially control of the heads of the regional tax offices. Therefore, the second step involved using publicity to pressure the tax office heads to handle the cases they were assigned. We created a process that would automatically publish on the web each tax office's progress in the handling of the cases. Thus citizens could see how many cases were assigned to their local tax office, (e.g. 1457 cases to an office in a leafy Athens suburb), how many the office had closed in the previous day (zero for this tax office

---

[5] Greek law 3763/2009, article 12. Government Gazette Issue A 80/27-5-2009.

on 2001-04-05), and how much revenue it had collected (for instance, 24,808 euros for a sea-side suburb tax office on the same day). Similar figures showed the cumulative results during the period the system was operating.[6] Finally, as the third step I wrote a small script, which at the end of each business day sent a personal email on behalf of the Secretary General for Tax and Customs Affairs to each tax office head with details of the office's progress on that day. The email was copied to the Minister, the competent Deputy Minister, and the corresponding General Directors. This pressure seems to have paid off, because, according to the data we collected through this system, during 18 months of its operation 690 million euros were collected by closing 260 thousand cases.

3.2   Performance of Regional Tax Offices

With the audacity that arises from naïvité, I thought that management by objectives, which could be centrally monitored from the GSIS databases, could be used for improving the overall performance of the tax administration. For this purpose we studied the effectiveness of the regional tax offices based on a small set of metrics. We found what many suspected: things were not working as they should be. According to the study only 1% of the fines imposed by the Financial Crime Unit were eventually collected by the tax authority, 30% of government pensioners did not declare their entire pension in their tax returns, while no one was monitoring the effectiveness of tax compliance checks. The study also found that just 24 out of a total of 300 local tax offices were responsible for collecting 71% of revenue (another manifestation of the 80-20 rule). Furthermore, the study recommended to measure and monitor a few key performance indicators for each major regional tax office:

- the revenue collection cost,
- the efficiency in closing suspect cases regarding tax compliance,
- the revenue collected from closed cases,
- the gap between collected revenue and the corresponding target,
- the number of temporary audits performed per employee,
- the progress of temporary audits,
- the percentage of the fined amount that was actually collected,
- the ratio of foreclosures to taxpayers in arrears, and
- the level of tax compliance evidenced through the number of suspect cases.

Interestingly, regional tax offices were traditionally monitored only based on the revenue they collected, as if they were a small corner-shop.

Using the infrastructure of the TAXIS information system, which supported most functions of the regional tax offices [22], we implemented a process to derive each month the necessary data, and compute the key performance indicators. Because tax administration was not keen on adopting such sophisticated

---

[6] Sadly, the corresponding web pages are no longer active. However, a representative subset has been archived at http://www.webcitation.org/6HfWwq87N.

indicators, preferring to keep on monitoring performance based solely on collected revenue, we adopted again the approach of publishing the figures on the web, hoping to pressure under-performing tax office heads to improve their operations.[7] The reaction was immediate: tax officers, union leaders, and tabloid press blasted that the information was incorrect, fragmentary, and did not reflect reality. A key argument was that it was unfair to point out that major offices had not conducted any audits within a month, because there were no auditors in their staff. Those shooting the messenger failed to grasp that the KPIs were useful exactly for highlighting and resolving such problems.

The moral of this exercise was that, while there is a lot that can be achieved by publishing metrics as open data and by targeting concrete objectives, not all problems can be addressed through unconventional means. A couple of years later, partly in response to the outlined problems and a corresponding proposal [20], an independent but accountable tax administration body was set up [9, p. 100]. The aims of the new structure were to consolidate tax administration by closing 200 underutilized tax offices and setting operational targets for the remaining ones, assessing managers based on their performance, and obtaining legal powers to direct how local tax office resources should be used. The new structure was to be headed by a non-political appointee with control over core business activities and human resource management.

3.3 Grassroots Pressure

A case where the availability of open data helped an action's implementation concerned the deployment of the Single Payment Authority. During its deployment we tracked on a daily basis the number of government bodies and paymasters that were enrolled and certified. We had set specific goals for each ministry, with a plan of enrolling into the system 100% of employees through a succession of steps, which started with registration, and ended with successfully performing an actual monthly payment. However, many ministries failed to respond to letters and circulars concerning the deployment deadlines. A colleague thought that, given the indifferent response our circulars were receiving, we should try a different approach, namely applying grassroots pressure. Consequently, we developed a website where employees could enter their tax identification number, and see immediately whether their institution was integrated into the Single Payment Authority. Unsurprisingly, many employees, concerned about the fate of their payroll, began pressuring their superiors to join the Single Payment Authority. This increased significantly the rate at which various bodies joined the Authority.

We also saw that the administration failed to follow the project's aggressive time plan. For example, circulars concerning integration into the Single Payment Authority marked "Extremely Urgent" were flowing up and down the administrative hierarchy taking weeks after their dispatch to reach some schools.

---

[7] Sadly, the corresponding web pages are also no longer available. However, a representative subset has been archived at http://www.webcitation.org/6HfXKqfzI.

To avoid these delays, we used *Google Groups* to create a forum serving the government's paymasters. The forum was used extensively for asking questions and receiving informal help from other colleagues. A particular exchange was revealing: the question was asked on 23:16 of a Sunday night, and a reply came just an hour later, at 00:35. The exchange exhibited conscientiousness, industriousness, and diligence that were at complete odds with the indifferent and slothful model of a civil servant portrayed by some popular media.

4   Concluding Remarks

During the two years I served at the Greek Ministry of Finance as Secretary General for Information Systems we restarted dormant projects, deployed many new electronic services, and supported the Ministry's and the Government's work in a number of crucial areas. I am often asked what was the decisive factor behind GSIS's exceptional performance. I was certainly lucky to head a department that had actual implementation capabilities, a culture of project-based management, a technological nous, and many meritocratically selected, well-educated employees.

If I were to select one factor that made a difference, this was the constant struggle to balance short-term with long-term goals. Thus we devoted only half of our team's efforts to the organization's day-to-day running, which too often included fire-fighting (literally in one case). The other half of our efforts went into longer term improvements in the organization's capacity: encouraging good people to head projects and teams, adopting best practices, training, adjusting management structures, leading by example, i.e. demonstrating our expectations to the service's permanent staff. Before we realized how time had passed, we were witnessing that the tiny seeds we had sown had grown to the point of bearing fruit. Thus, in less than a year, through the heroic efforts of its employees, GSIS overcame the crisis it faced, transforming itself into a showcase of solid IT service delivery.

A broader balancing challenge is between the actions required for managing a crisis and those needed to implement sustainable changes. Unconventional techniques, like those described in this experience report, appear to be necessary in times of crisis, in order to cut the Gordian knot of inefficiency and inertia. They can often deliver significant results, and they can even be a potent source of organizational innovation. However, these unconventional techniques are also associated with considerable risks of negative externalities: lack of continuity, stakeholder alienation, and loss of direction. Sustainable changes can be implemented by institutionalizing successful unconventional measures or by adopting reforms in a top-down fashion [18]. The implementation task will require cultivating the ground for change, communicating effectively with all stakeholders, forming alliances [14], as well as acquiring and spending political capital. This will be Greece's challenge in the coming years.

Acknowledgements. I am immensely grateful to the countless permanent GSIS employees as well as the advisors and the seconded members of our team who worked during my term with zeal and diligence to achieve GSIS's goals. I also want to thank Michael G. Jacobides, Nancy Pouloudi, Angeliki Poulymenakou, and Niki Tsouma who contributed valuable comments on earlier versions of this work.

References

1. Androutsellis-Theotokis, S., Spinellis, D., Kechagia, M., Gousios, G.: Open source software: A survey from 10,000 feet. Foundations and Trends in Technology. Information and Operations Management 4(3-4), 187–347 (2011)
2. Antonioni, D.: Designing an effective 360-degree appraisal feedback process. Organizational Dynamics 25(2), 24–38 (1996)
3. Artavanis, N., Morse, A., Tsoutsoura, M.: Tax evasion across industries: Soft credit evidence from Greece. Research paper 12-25, Chicago University, Booth School of Business (June 2012), http://ssrn.com/abstract=2109500
4. Barrett, D.J.: MediaWiki. O'Reilly Media, Inc. (2008)
5. Boehm, B., Turner, R.: Balancing Agility and Discipline: A Guide for the Perplexed. Addison-Wesley, Pearson Education (2003)
6. Cockburn, A.: Agile Software Development. Addison-Wesley, Boston (2001)
7. Dedrick, J., West, J.: An exploratory study into open source platform adoption. In: Proceedings of the 37th Annual Hawaii International Conference on System Sciences, pp. 1–10. IEEE (2004)
8. Directorate-General for Economic and Financial Affairs (ed.): The Economic Adjustment Programme for Greece, Occasional Papers, vol. 61. European Commission, Brussels, Belgium (May 2010)
9. Directorate-General for Economic and Financial Affairs (ed.): The Second Economic Adjustment Programme for Greece, Occasional Papers, vol. 94. European Commission, Brussels, Belgium (March 2012)
10. Directorate-General for Economic and Financial Affairs (ed.): The Second Economic Adjustment Programme for Greece: First Review — December 2012, Occasional Papers, vol. 123. European Commission, Brussels, Belgium (December 2012)
11. Katsimi, M., Moutos, T.: EMU and the Greek crisis: The political-economy perspective. European Journal of Political Economy 26(4), 568–576 (2010)
12. Kerr, N.L., Tindale, R.S.: Group performance and decision making. Annual Reviews of Psychology 55, 623–655 (2004)
13. Leuf, B., Cunningham, W.: The Wiki Way: Quick Collaboration on the Web. Addison-Wesley Professional (2001)
14. Loukis, E., Tsouma, N.: Critical issues of information systems management in the Greek public sector. Information Polity 7(1), 65–83 (2002)
15. Martin, R.C.: Agile Software Development: Principles, Patterns, and Practices. Prentice Hall, Upper Saddle River (2003)
16. Matsaganis, M., Flevotomou, M.: Distributional implications of tax evasion in Greece. Working Paper GreeSE Paper No. 31, The Hellenic Observatory, LSE, London, UK (February 2010), http://eprints.lse.ac.uk/26074/
17. Mitsopoulos, M., Pelagidis, T.: Understanding the Crisis in Greece: From Boom to Bust. Palgrave Macmillan (2012)

18. OECD (ed.): Greece: Review of the Central Administration. OECD Public Governance Reviews, OECD (2011)
19. Spanou, C.: State reform in Greece: Responding to old and new challenges. International Journal of Public Sector Management 21(2), 150–173 (2008)
20. Spinellis, D.: Fair end efficient management of public revenue: Problems and proposals. Hellenic Foundation for European and Foreign Policy. Public debate: Tax evasion and Social Justice (December 2012) (in Greek), http://www.eliamep.gr/wp-content/uploads/2011/12/2011-12-13-tax-system-2.pdf (Current March 2014)
21. Spinellis, D., Giannikas, V.: Organizational adoption of open source software. Journal of Systems and Software 85(3), 666–682 (2012)
22. Stamoulis, D.S., Gouscos, D., Georgiadis, P., Martakos, D.: Re orienting information systems for customer centric service: The case of the Greek Ministry of Finance. In: Smithson, S., Gricar, J., Podlogar, M., Avgerinou, S. (eds.) ECIS 2001: Proceedings of the 9th European Conference on Information Systems, Global Cooperation in the New Millennium, Bled, Slovenia, June 27-29, pp. 977–986 (2001)
23. Yannakopoulos, C.: L'apport de la notion de fait administratif institutionnel à la théorie du droit administratif. Revue interdisciplinaire d'études juridiques 38 (1997)

Queue Mining – Predicting Delays in Service Processes

Arik Senderovich[1], Matthias Weidlich[2], Avigdor Gal[1], and Avishai Mandelbaum[1]

[1] Technion – Israel Institute of Technology
sariks@tx.technion.ac.il, avigal@ie.technion.ac.il,
avim@ie.technion.ac.il
[2] Imperial College London
m.weidlich@imperial.ac.uk

Abstract. Information systems have been widely adopted to support service processes in various domains, *e.g.*, in the telecommunication, finance, and health sectors. Recently, work on process mining showed how management of these processes, and engineering of supporting systems, can be guided by models extracted from the event logs that are recorded during process operation. In this work, we establish a queueing perspective in operational process mining. We propose to consider queues as first-class citizens and use queueing theory as a basis for queue mining techniques. To demonstrate the value of queue mining, we revisit the specific operational problem of *online delay prediction*: using event data, we show that queue mining yields accurate online predictions of case delay.

1 Introduction

The conduct of service processes, *e.g.*, in the telecommunication and health sectors, is heavily supported by information systems. To manage such processes and improve the operation of supporting systems, event logs recorded during process operation constitute a valuable source of information. Recently, this opportunity was widely exploited in the rapidly growing research field of process mining. It started with mining techniques that focused mainly on the control-flow perspective, namely extracting control-flow models from event logs [1] for qualitative analyses, such as model-based verification [2].

In recent years, research in process mining has shifted the spotlight from qualitative analysis to (quantitative) *online* operational support ([3], Ch. 9). To provide operational support, the control-flow perspective alone does not suffice and, therefore, new perspectives are mined. For example, the time perspective exploits event timestamps and frequencies to locate bottlenecks and predict execution times.

To date, operational process mining is largely limited to black-box analysis. That is, observations obtained for single instances (cases) of a process are aggregated to derive predictors for the behaviour of cases in the future. This approach can be seen as a regression analysis over individual cases, assuming that they are executed largely independently of each other. In many processes, however, cases do not run in isolation but *multiple cases* compete over scarce resources. Only some cases get served at a certain point in time (complete execution of an activity and progress in process execution) while others must wait for resources to become available. Cases that did not get served are enqueued and consequently delayed.

M. Jarke et al. (Eds.): CAiSE 2014, LNCS 8484, pp. 42–57, 2014.

In this work, we establish a queueing perspective in process mining. We propose to consider queues as first-class citizens and refer to the various tasks of process mining that involve the queueing perspective as *queue mining*. Further, we present techniques for queue mining following two different strategies. First, following the traditional approach of operational process mining, we enhance an existing technique for time prediction [4] to consider queues and system load. Second, we argue for the application of queueing theory [5,6] as a basis to model, analyse, and improve service processes. Specifically, we mine delay predictors that are based on well-established queueing models and results.

To demonstrate the value of queue mining, we address the specific operational problem of *online delay prediction*, which refers to the time that the execution of an activity for a particular case is delayed due to queueing effects. In addition to the definition of mining techniques for different types of predictors, we also present a comprehensive experimental evaluation using real-world logs. It shows that the proposed techniques improves prediction and that predictors grounded in queueing theory have, in most cases, superior prediction accuracy over regression-based time prediction.

The contributions of our paper can be summarized as follows:

- The queueing perspective is introduced as a novel agenda in process mining, and queue mining is positioned as a new class of mining tasks.
- For the online delay prediction problem, we present techniques for the derivation of predictors of two types; those that enhance existing regression-based techniques for process mining and those that are grounded in queueing theory.
- The value of queue mining techniques is demonstrated empirically by their accuracy in delay prediction. Also, this paper contributes to queueing theory by validating, against real data, delay predictors that have been so far tested only on synthetic simulation runs.

The remainder of this paper is organized as follows. The next section provides motivation for the queueing perspective and background on queueing models. Section 3 defines the queue log as a basis to our queue mining methods and Section 4 states the delay prediction problem. Section 5 introduces delay predictors and brings in mining methods for these predictors. Section 6 presents our experiments and discusses their results. We review related work in Section 7 and conclude in Section 8.

2   Background

We illustrate the need for a queueing perspective, in operational models for services processes, with the example of a bank's call centre. Figure 1(a) depicts a BPMN [7] model of such a process, which focuses on the control-flow of a case, that is, a single customer. The customer dials in and is then connected to a voice response unit (VRU). The customer either completes service within the VRU or chooses to opt-out, continuing to an agent. Once customers have been served by an agent, they either hang-up or, in rare cases, choose to continue for another service (VRU or forwarding to an agent).

Although this model provides a reasonable abstraction of the process from the perspective of a single customer, it fails short of capturing important operational details.

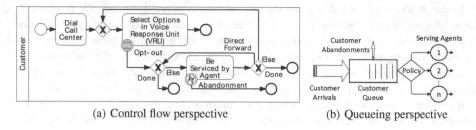

(a) Control flow perspective   (b) Queueing perspective

Fig. 1. Example process in a call centre

Customers that seek a service are served by one of the available agents or wait in a queue. Hence, activity 'Be Serviced by Agent' comprises a waiting phase and an actual service phase. Customers that wait for service may also abandon from the queue due to impatience. To provide operational analysis for this service process and predict delay of processing, such queues and abandonments must be taken into account explicitly.

For the above example, only activity 'Be Serviced by Agent' involves significant queueing since the other activities do not rely on scarce resources of the service provider. Adopting a queueing perspective for this activity, Fig. 1(b) outlines how the activity is conducted under multiple cases arriving at the system and, thus, emphasizes that execution time of one case depend on cases that are already in the system.

The model shown in Fig. 1(b) can be viewed as a single-station queueing system, where one station is served by n homogeneous agents. Such a queueing system is described by a series of characteristics, denoted using Kendall's notation as $\mathcal{A}/\mathcal{B}/\mathcal{C}/\mathcal{Y}/\mathcal{Z}$ [8]. The arrival process ($\mathcal{A}$) is defined by the joint distribution of the inter-arrival times. Whenever no assumption regarding the arrival process is made, $\mathcal{A}$ is replaced by G for general distribution. The processing duration of a single case ($\mathcal{B}$) is described by the distribution of service time. The total number of agents at the queueing station is denoted by $\mathcal{C}$, which stands for capacity. When a case arrives and all agents are busy, the new arrival is queued. The maximum size of the system, $\mathcal{Y}$, can be finite, so that new customers are blocked if the number of running cases is larger than $\mathcal{Y}$. In call centres, which provides our present motivation, $\mathcal{Y}$ is practically infinite and can be omitted. Once an agent becomes available and the queue is not empty, a customer is selected according to a routing policy $\mathcal{Z}$. The most common policy is the FCFS (First Come First Served) policy and in such cases $\mathcal{Z}$ is also omitted.

Queueing models may include information on the distribution of customer (im)patience ($\mathcal{G}$), added following a '+' sign at the end of Kendall's notation. For mathematical tractability and sometimes backed up by practice, it is often assumed that sequences of inter-arrival times, service times and customer (im)patience are independent of each other, and each consists of independent elements that are exponentially distributed. Then, $\mathcal{A}$, $\mathcal{B}$ and $\mathcal{G}$ are replaced by Ms, which stands for Markovian. For example, a $G/M/n + M$ model assumes that arrivals come from a general distribution, service times are exponential, agent capacity is of size n, queue size is infinite, routing policy is FCFS and (im)patience is exponentially distributed.

3   The Queue Log

To mine the queueing perspective of a service process, events that have been recorded during operation must be available. Most existing techniques for process mining assume that these events are process related, indicating start and end of activity execution, cf. [3]. For the queueing perspective we need to record events that relate to queueing transactions, including queue entrance, abandonment, and service start and end. Below, we define a Q-Log for a single queueing station representing a single activity of the service process, but note that the definition can be easily extended to more general queueing models (*e.g.*, multi-class customers and queueing networks).

Definition 1 (Single-Station Q-Log). *A single-station queue log Q is a finite sequence $Q : \mathbb{N}^+ \to \mathcal{Q}$ over queue events $(t, c, p, a) \in \mathcal{Q}$, where*
  - *$t \in \mathbb{N}^+$ is a timestamp,*
  - *$c \in \mathbb{N}^+$ is a unique case (customer) identifier,*
  - *$p \in \mathcal{P} = \{qEntry, qAbandon, sStart, sEnd\}$ is a state change for the case,*
  - *$a \in \mathbb{N}^+$ is a unique agent identifier, set only when $p \in \{sStart, sEnd\}$.*

Below, we write (t_i, c_i, p_i, a_i) for the i-th queue event $Q(i)$ and $|Q|$ for the length of the log. Also, to keep the notation concise, we assume that a Q-Log is ordered by the timestamp, i.e., $t_i \leq t_j$ for all $1 \leq i < j \leq |Q|$.

We refer to *queue mining* as a class of techniques that take a Q-Log as input and derive a model for the operational analysis of the queue and service.

4   The Delay Prediction Problem

In this section, we elaborate on the problem of *online delay prediction*, which will be solved using queue mining in this work. The phenomena of delay has been a popular research subject in queueing theory, see [9]. The interest in delay prediction is motivated by psychological insights on the negative effect of waiting on customer satisfaction [10]. Field studies have found that seeing the line ahead moving and getting initial information on the expected delay, both have a positive effect on the waiting experience [11,12]. Thus, announcing the expected delay in an online fashion improves customer satisfaction.

We refer to the customer, whose delay time we wish to predict as the *target-customer*. The target-customer is assumed to have infinite patience, i.e. the target customer will wait patiently for service, without abandoning, otherwise our prediction becomes useless. However, the influence of abandonments of other customers on the delay time of the target-customer is taken into account. In some service processes (e.g., the one introduced in Section 2), customers may return to a queue after they have been served. In the remainder, we focus on predicting the first delay. Many real-world applications treat returning customers as a negligible phenomenon. For instance, returning customers are only 3% of the cases in the real-life process that we consider in Section 6. We formalize the delay prediction problem as follows.

Problem 1 (Online delay prediction). *Let W be a random variable that measures the first delay time of a target-customer. Denote by* $\widehat{W}$ *the predictor for W. Then, the* online delay prediction *problem aims at identifying an accurate and precise predictor* $\widehat{W}$.

Accuracy and precision are common measures for prediction (see, for example, the use of precision and recall in information retrieval [13]). In our experiments (Section 6), we use, as concrete measures, absolute bias for accuracy and root mean squared error (RMSE) for precision.

5   Delay Predictors: Queue Mining in Action

In order to solve the delay prediction problem, we propose mining techniques for three classes of delay predictors that implement two different strategies. First, we follow the traditional regression-based analysis of operational process mining and enhance a technique presented by van der Aalst et al. for time prediction [4]. We do so by considering a queue to be yet another activity and including a notion of system load in the mining. Our second and third class of predictors, in turn, follow a completely different strategy and are grounded in queueing theory. Here, we present mining techniques for delay predictors that arise directly from a queueing model. These yield delay predictors that are based on queueing theory and a congestion law (*the snapshot principle*).

5.1   State Transition System Predictors

Idea. Our first predictor follows the idea of integrating queueing information into techniques for operational process mining by considering queues as separate activities of the process. Following this line, we rely on a state-of-the-art approach for time prediction based on transition systems that has been presented by van der Aalst et al. [4]. In essence, this approach mines a transition system from a log of recorded activity executions. To this end, different abstractions may be applied to states and state transitions as they are recorded in the log. For instance, a state in the transition system may be defined by the sequence of all activities executed in a case so far, the set of these activities, or only the last executed activity. This abstraction of the process behaviour is then annotated with timing information, *e.g.*, the time needed to finish the process from a particular state averaged over all respective cases.

To use this approach for delay prediction, the queueing phase and the service phase of an activity in a service process are treated as two separate steps and a state is defined as the sequence of executed activities. Then, when a customer is enqueued, we enter an initial state ⟨queue⟩ in the transition system. When a customer enters service, we move to a state ⟨queue, service⟩ and, after service completion, to a state ⟨queue, service, end⟩. If a customer abandons the queue, we transition to a state ⟨queue, end⟩ instead.

The transition system constructed with this approach is based on an evaluation of all cases in isolation and, thus, neglects the influence of other cases. To account for this aspect, we extend the state abstraction to include system load as a context-factor in the spirit of [25]; we represent system load by the number of customers in queue $L(t)$. In practice, $L(t)$ may vary greatly over time, so that including its absolute values leads to a

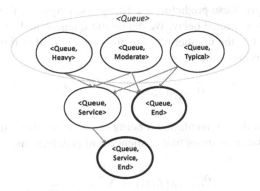

Fig. 2. Transition system extended for three load-classes - High, Moderate, and Typical

'state explosion'. Therefore, we partition $L(t)$ into k clusters, and consider the $\langle$queue$\rangle$ state combined only with these k clusters. For $k = 3$, i.e., assuming that the system can be in one of three load states, namely 'high', 'moderate', and 'typical', the resulting transition system is illustrated in Fig. 2.

Queue Mining. Given a Q-Log, construction of the first version of the transition system is straight-forward. For the resulting system, state $\langle$queue$\rangle$ is annotated with past delay times for customers who waited and eventually got served. Then, the average over these values yields a predictor $\widehat{W}_{PTS}$, referred to as plain transition system predictor.

For the second predictor, we first derive the load clusters using k-means clustering [14]. Based on the partition of $L(t)$ into k load types, we derive the respective transition system. Lastly, we annotate each of the states that represent waiting in a queue under a certain system load with previous delay times. For each state, we receive a different delay predictor, winding up with k predictors $\widehat{W}_{KTS}$, referred to as k-loads transition system predictors. From a statistical viewpoint, the k-loads transition system method may be considered as a regression model that uses system load to predict delays.

5.2 Queueing Model Predictors

Idea. Our second class of predictors does not follow a regression analysis, but is grounded in queueing theory. These predictors relate to the $G/M/n + M$ model, so that upon the arrival of a target-customer, there are n homogeneous working agents at the station. We denote the mean service time by m and assume that service duration is exponentially distributed. Therefore, the service rate of an individual agent is $\mu = 1/m$. Impatient customers may leave the queue and customer individual patience is exponentially distributed with mean $1/\theta$, i.e., the individual abandonment rate is θ. Whenever customers do not abandon the system ($\theta = 0$), the model reduces to $G/M/n$.

We define two delay predictors based on the $G/M/n$ and the $G/M/n+M$ models, respectively. We refer to the first predictor as queue-length (based) predictor (QLP) and to the second as queue-length (based) Markovian (abandonments) Predictor (QLMP) [15].

As their names imply, these predictors use the queue length (in front of the target customer) to predict its expected delay. We define the queue-length, $L(t)$, to be a random
variable that quantifies the number of cases that are delayed at time t. The QLP for a
target customer arriving at time t is:

$$\widehat{W}_{QLP}(L(t)) = \frac{(L(t) + 1)}{n\mu} \tag{1}$$

with n being the number of agents and μ being the service rate of an individual agent.
    The QLMP predictor assumes finite patience and is defined as:

$$\widehat{W}_{QLMP}(L(t)) = \sum_{i=0}^{L(t)} \frac{1}{n\mu + i\theta}. \tag{2}$$

Intuitively, when a target-customer arrives, it may progress in queue only if customers
that are ahead of him enter service (when an agent becomes available, at rate $n\mu$) or
abandon (at rate $i\theta$ with i being the number of customers in queue). For the QLP, $\theta = 0$
and thus the QLMP predictor (Eq. 2) reduces to the QLP predictor (1).

Queue Mining. Given a Q-Log Q that is up-to-date at time t, we extract the current
number of customers in queue and the current number of working agents n as follows
(note that $Q(i) = (t_i, c_i, p_i, a_i)$ denotes the i-th queue event in Q):

- $L(t) = |\{(t_i, c_i, p_i, a_i) \mid p_i = qEntry \wedge \forall (t_j, c_j, p_j, a_j), i \le j : c_j \ne c_i\}|$,
- $n = |\{(t_i, c_i, p_i, a_i) \mid p_i = sStart \wedge \forall (t_j, c_j, p_j, a_j), i \le j : a_j \ne a_i\}|$.

To obtain QLP and QLMP, we only need to estimate two parameters, namely the service
rate (μ) and the abandonment rate (θ). To estimate μ, we go over all pairs of queue
events $(t_i, c_i, p_i, a_i), (t_j, c_j, p_j, a_j)$ for which $c_i = c_j$, $p_i = sStart$ and $p_j = sEnd$,
and average over $t_j - t_i$, which is the service time for case c_i. The result is an unbiased
estimator $\hat{m}$ for the mean service time. We can then deduce a naive moment estimator
for $\hat{\mu}$, $\hat{\mu} = 1/\hat{m}$ [16].
    Estimation of θ is based on a statistical result that relates it to the total number
of abandonments and the total delay time for both served and abandoned customers,
cf., [17]. Practically, we obtain the number of abandonments by counting the respective
queue events. The total delay time is derived by summarizing delay durations for all
customers that experienced queueing. Then, the abandonment rate is estimated as:

$$\hat{\theta} = \frac{|\{(t_i, c_i, p_i, a_i) \mid p_i = qAbandon\}|}{\sum_{(t_i, c_i, p_i, a_i), (t_j, c_j, p_j, a_j), c_i = c_j, p_i = qEntry, p_j \in \{qAbandon, sStart\}} (t_j - t_i)}. \tag{3}$$

5.3 Snapshot Predictors

Idea. An important result in queueing theory is the *(heavy-traffic) snapshot principle*
(see [18], p. 187). A heavy-traffic approximation refers to the behaviour of a queue
model under limits of its parameters, as the workload converges to capacity. In the context of Problem 1, the snapshot principle implies that under the heavy-traffic approximation, delay times (of other customers) tend to change negligibly during the waiting

time of a single customer [15]. We define two snapshot predictors: Last-customer-to-Enter-Service (LES or $\widehat{W}_{LES}$) and Head-Of-Line (HOL or $\widehat{W}_{HOL}$). The LES predictor is the delay of the most recent service entrant, while the HOL is the delay of the first customer in line.

In real-life settings, the heavy-traffic approximation is not always plausible and thus the applicability of the snapshot principle predictors should be tested ad-hoc, when working with real data sets. Results of synthetic simulation runs, conducted in [15], show that the LES and HOL are indeed appropriate for predicting delays.

Queue Mining. Given a Q-Log Q that is up-to-date at time t, we mine these predictors as follows. For the LES, the case c_i that last entered service is the one that satisfies the following condition: there is a queue event (t_i, c_i, p_i, a_i) with $p_i = sStart$ and for all $(t_j, c_j, p_j, a_j), i \leq j$ it holds $p_j \neq sStart$. Then, with $(t_q, c_q, p_q, a_q), c_q = c_i, p_q = qEntry$ as the event indicating queue entrance of the respective customer, the predictor is derived as $\widehat{W}_{LES} = t_i - t_q$.

For the HOL, we observe the case c_i that is still in queue, but would be the next to enter service, i.e., there is a queue event (t_i, c_i, p_i, a_i) with $p_i = qEntry$ and for all $(t_j, c_j, p_j, a_j), j \leq i$ with $p_j = qEntry$ there exists another queue event $(t_k, c_k, p_k, a_k), j \leq k$ with $c_j = c_k$ and $p_k \in \{qAbandon, sStart\}$. Then, the predictor is derived as $\widehat{W}_{HOL} = t - t_i$. Note that this technique for mining the HOL holds only if the FCFS policy is assumed, otherwise the order of $qEntry$ timestamps does not impose the same order on $sStart$.

6   Evaluation

To test the various delay predictors we ran a set of experiments on a real-life queue log. Our experiments show that the snapshot predictors outperform other predictors, in virtually every experimental setting considered. For the predictors based on transition systems we observe that the plain predictor performed poorly, whereas the one integrating the system load leads to significant improvements. Both queueing model-based predictors, in turn, performed worse than the snapshot predictors, since the queueing model assumptions are often violated in real-life processes.

Below, we first describe the real-life queue log used for our experiments (Section 6.1). Then, we define the evaluation's performance measures (Section 6.2), describe our experimental setup (Section 6.3) and report on the main results (Section 6.4). We conclude with a discussion (Section 6.5).

6.1   Data Description

The experiments were conducted on a real-life queue log of a call center of an Israeli bank. The data comes from the Technion laboratory for Service Enterprise Engineering (SEELab)[1]. The dataset contains a detailed description of all operational transactions

---
[1] http://ie.technion.ac.il/Labs/Serveng

that occurred within the call center, between January 24th, 2010 and March 31st, 2011. The log contains, for an average weekday, data on approximately 7000 calls.

For our delay prediction experiments, we selected three months of data: January 2011-March 2011 (a queue log of 879591 records). This amount of data enables us to gain useful insights into the prediction problem, while easing the computational complexity (as opposed to analysing the entire data set). The three months were selected since they are free of Israeli holidays. In our experiments, we focused only on cases that demanded 'general banking' services, which is the majority of calls arriving into the call center (89%). This case selection is appropriate, since our queueing models assume that customers are homogeneous.

We divided the experimental queue log into two subsets: a training log and a test log. This is common practice when performing statistical model assessment [14]. The training log comprises all calls that arrived between January 1st, 2011 and February 28th, 2011; a total of 250488 delays and 247281 completed services. The test log consisted of delays that occurred during March 2011; a total of 117709 delays. We addressed each delayed customer in the test log as the target-customer for whom we aim at solving Problem 1.

6.2 Performance Measures

To evaluate the quality of the delay predictors, we introduce two performance measures: *absolute bias*, for accuracy, and *root mean squared error* (RMSE), for precision. The absolute bias is defined as:

$$|Bias(\widehat{W})| = |E[\widehat{W}] - W|, \tag{4}$$

with W being the delay and $\widehat{W}$ being the delay predictor. We define a point estimate for the absolute bias as:

$$|\widehat{Bias}| = |\frac{1}{k} \sum_{i=1}^{k}(d_i - p_i)|, \tag{5}$$

with $i = 1, ..., k$ being the i-th test-log delay out of k delays, d_i the real duration of the i-th delay and p_i the corresponding predicted delay; $|Bias(\widehat{W})| > 0$ indicates a systematic error in our predictor, thus low accuracy.

For precision define RMSE as:

$$RMSE(\widehat{W}) = \sqrt{E[(W - \widehat{W})^2]}. \tag{6}$$

We consider a point estimate for the RMSE to be the *root average squared error* (RASE), namely,

$$RASE = \sqrt{\frac{1}{k} \sum_{i=1}^{k}(d_i - p_i)^2}, \tag{7}$$

with d_i and p_i defined as before. Low RMSE indicates that the corresponding predictor is precise.

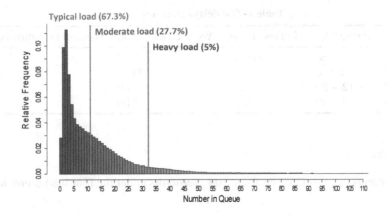

Fig. 3. Relative frequency histogram for number of customers in queue, from training log

We consider the RMSE (and precision) to be more significant, penalizing for any type of deviation from the real delay. In contrast, the absolute bias may result in 0 (high accuracy), but deviate strongly from the delay predictor (*e.g.*, deviating strongly both above and below the real delay). We thus use accuracy as a 'compass' to detect systematic errors in model assumptions, but consider precision to be the indicator for quality of prediction.

6.3 Experimental Setup

The controlled variable in our experiments is the *prediction method* (or the delay predictor). Six various methods are used according to the predictors defined in Section 5, namely the QLP, QLMP, LES, HOL, PTS and KTS predictors. The uncontrolled variables are the two performance measures $|\widehat{Bias}|$ and RASE.

As a preliminary step, we mined the K-loads transition system (applied the KTS) from the training log with $K = 3$. The result was a clustering of the queue-length ($L(t)$) into 3 classes: 'heavy load', 'moderate load,' and 'typical load'. Figure 3 shows the relative frequency histogram of $L(t)$. The vertical lines depict the partition that resulted from running the 3-means algorithm on the training log. For example, 'typical load' is the region where $0 \leq L(t) \leq 12$. Given the partition to $K = 3$ classes of load, we tested our predictors on four different experimental scenarios. Scenario I considered the entire test log and thus we refer to it as the 'all loads' scenario, while Scenarios II-IV relate to the three load-clusters and to delays that are associated with these clusters.

Table 1 summarizes the statistics for the four scenarios. Range $L(t)$ corresponds to the vertical lines in Figure 3, *e.g.*, for typical load the Range $L(t)$ is between 0 and 12. Due to the increase in standard deviation of the delay times as the load increases, we expect that the error (in seconds) will be smaller for the typical load and increasingly larger for the two other load types.

Table 1. Test delays statistics

Load	Range $L(t)$	% of test delays	Average Delay (sec)	Standard Deviation (sec)
Scenario I	0-∞	100.0%	71.5	84
Scenario II	32-∞	5.0%	252.0	125
Scenario III	$12-32$	27.7%	129.0	74
Scenario IV	$0-12$	67.3%	34.0	44

6.4   Results

Figure 4 presents the absolute bias for all six predictors under the four load scenarios.

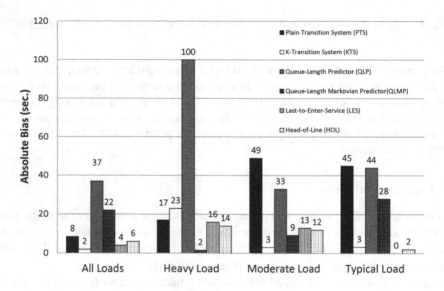

Fig. 4. Sampled bias - Test set delays

The PTS predictor presents a near-zero bias in Scenario I, but when observing its bias across scenarios we note a much larger bias. This originates in the insensitivity of the PTS predictor to system load. The KTS has a negligible bias in all scenarios, except for the one representing heavy load. This result hints at the existence of a finer partitioning of the heavy load scenario.

For the queue-length based predictors (QLP and QLMP), we observe that both predictors appear to be biased. This may point towards violations in the queueing model assumptions. The bias of the snapshot predictors (LES and HOL) is small across scenarios, indicating an absence of a systematic error in these predictors. This observation supports the applicability of the snapshot predictors to service processes in call centers.

Figure 5 presents the RASE in seconds. Snapshot predictors are superior across all scenarios, improving over the PTS by 34%-46%. Note that both snapshot predictors

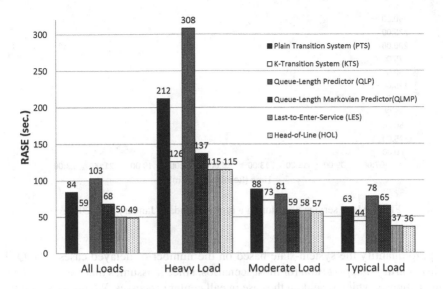

Fig. 5. Root-average squared error in seconds

perform identically in terms of RASE. This empirical proximity between the LES and the HOL, under certain assumptions, has theoretical background in [15] (Theorem 4.4).

The QLP performed worse than PTS across scenarios, except the moderate load scenario, while the QLMP outperformed the PTS in all scenarios except the typical load scenario. In the moderate load scenario, the QLMP performs almost as well as the snapshot predictors. The KTS outperforms both the PTS and queueing model predictors, in all scenarios, except the moderate load scenario.

6.5 Discussion

In the remainder of this section, we divide our discussion according to the three predictor classes.

Transition System Methods: There is no (single) Steady-State
In both transition system methods we consider past delays of customers with similar path-history, when predicting the delay of the target-customer. The problem with the PTS is that, when applied to our real-life process, it considers all past delays. Considering all past delays is appropriate in steady-state analysis, *i.e.*, when the relation between demand and capacity does not vary greatly over time. The KTS (with $K = 3$) performs significantly better, since it captures three different steady-states (three system loads). The performance of this method is second best, in most scenarios, only to snapshot predictors, which may in turn imply that the existence of three steady-states is indeed a plausible hypothesis.

Queue-Length Predictors: Model Assumptions Matter
The queueing model predictors consider the time-varying behaviour of the system and

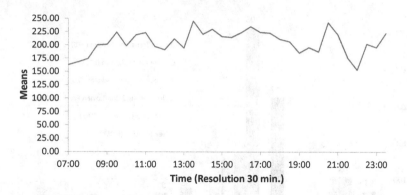

Fig. 6. Mean service time during a typical Sunday (January 2nd, 2011)

attempt to quantify the system-state based on the number of delayed cases. The QLP fails in *accuracy and precision* for most scenarios, since it assumes that customers have infinite patience, which is seldom the case in call center processes. We presume that the QLP would perform better for processes with negligible abandonment rates.

On the other hand, the QLMP outperforms the PTS for most scenarios both in *accuracy and precision*. Therefore, accounting for customer (im)patience is indeed relevant in the context of call centers, and other processes in which abandonments occur [20]. In contrast, the QLMP is inferior when compared to snapshot predictors or the KTS predictor. This phenomena can be explained by deviations between model assumptions and reality. We demonstrate one possible deviation by conducting a short (descriptive) statistical analysis that is relevant for both the QLP and the QLMP. Figure 6 presents the mean service time over a single day (January 2nd, 2011, which is a typical Sunday in our training log).

The horizontal axis presents the time-of-day in a 30 minutes resolution and the vertical axis presents the mean service time in seconds, during each of the 30 minutes. We see that the mean service time is mostly stable, but nonetheless violations do occur during several time points. This fluctuation over the day may cause deterioration in overall performance of both QLP and QLMP, since these predictors assume constant mean service time. We have shown similar violations for both the constant (im)patience time and the exponential service times assumptions, but we do not present them in this paper, due to space considerations.

Snapshot Principle Predictors: Recent History Dominates in Time-Varying Systems
Throughout our experiments, snapshot predictors have shown the largest improvement over the PTS method and outperformed the rest in terms of precision. Thus, we conclude that for the considered queueing process (of a call center), an adequate delay prediction for a newly enqueued customer would be the delay of either the current head-of-the-line (HOL) or the delay of the last-customer-to-enter-service (LES). Our main insight is that in time-varying systems, such as call center, one must consider only recent delay history when inferring on newly arriving cases.

The snapshot principle was shown to work well with multiple service stations as well [18,19]. Therefore, investigating the use of this principle to a queueing network with a complex underlying process may provide competent prediction.

7 Related Work

Our work is related to two streams of research, namely operational process mining and delay prediction in queueing theory.

Lately, process mining has seen a remarkable uptake, providing tools for the creation of process models from event data, over the assessment of the conformance of models and events, to extensions of models for operational support, see [3] for a recent overview. Despite the wide-spread focus on the control flow perspective, process mining techniques would benefit from additional information, such as time and resource utilization. In particular, several approaches addressed the problem of predicting process completion times for running cases. Van der Aalst et al. [21] highlight the importance of capturing resource utilization appropriately and provide techniques for mining a simulation model. The approach creates a Coloured Petri net that comprises resource and timing information and serves as the basis for time prediction. Rogge-Solti and Weske [22] follow a similar approach, but ground the analysis in a probabilistic model, formalised as a stochastic Petri net. Then, Monte-Carlo simulation allows for predicting completion time. A generic framework for time prediction based on state transition systems constructed from process logs was developed in [4]. Our work complements these techniques by focusing on the delay of a case when executing a certain activity instead of estimating the overall completion time. To this end, we add the queueing perspective to process mining and introduce techniques for queue mining. These techniques yield prediction models that take the notion of a queue into account explicitly. We relied on queue models and also enhanced the method based on transition systems of [4] to take queueing effects into account. However, our evaluation illustrated that the predictors that are derived by queue mining and grounded in queue models show superior performance.

Predicting queueing delays has been a popular research subject in queueing theory; see [9] for an overview. Statistical techniques for estimating delays were applied mainly for systems in steady-state [23,17]. Real-time delay predictors that do not assume steady-state, in analogy to Problem 1 addressed in this work, were proposed in [24,15]. We use these predictors as a basis to our queue mining techniques and address the derivation of these predictors from event data.

8 Conclusion

In this paper, we showed how to consider a queueing perspective in operational process mining for service processes. In particular, we state the problem of *online delay prediction* and provide different techniques, jointly referred to as *queue mining*, that take recorded event data as input and derive predictors for the delay of a case cause by queueing. First, we consider mining of regression-based predictors that are based on state transition systems, for which queueing information has been integrated. We further argued for predictors that are grounded in queueing theory and presented mining techniques for predictors that emerge from a queueing model, either based on queueing theory or the snapshot principle. For all predictors, we tested accuracy using a real-life queue log. Our experiments show that predictors grounded in queueing models, in most cases, provide superior performance, improving accuracy by 30%-40% on average compared to the plain regression-based method.

In future work, we intend to expand queue mining to Q-Logs that stem from complex service processes with several stations, *i.e.*, activities that involve queueing. The natural models, when considering such processes, are *queueing networks*. These models are often mathematically intractable and thus the analysis of queueing networks resorts to simulation or approximation methods in the spirit of the *snapshot principle*.

References

1. van der Aalst, W.M.P., Weijters, T., Maruster, L.: Workflow mining: Discovering process models from event logs. IEEE Trans. Knowl. Data Eng. 16(9), 1128–1142 (2004)
2. van der Aalst, W.M.P.: Workflow verification: Finding control-flow errors using petri-net-based techniques. In: van der Aalst, W.M.P., Desel, J., Oberweis, A. (eds.) Business Process Management. LNCS, vol. 1806, pp. 161–183. Springer, Heidelberg (2000)
3. van der Aalst, W.: Process Mining: Discovery, Conformance and Enhancement of Business Processes. Springer (2011)
4. van der Aalst, W.M., Schonenberg, M., Song, M.: Time prediction based on process mining. Information Systems 36(2), 450–475 (2011)
5. Hall, R.W.: Queueing Methods: For Services and Manufacturing. Prentice-Hall, Englewood Cliffs (1991)
6. Bolch, G., Greiner, S., de Meer, H., Trivedi, K.S.: Queueing networks and Markov chains - modeling and performance evaluation with computer science applications. Wiley (2006)
7. Object Management Group (OMG): Business Process Model and Notation, BPMN (2011)
8. Kendall, D.G.: Stochastic processes occurring in the theory of queues and their analysis by the method of the imbedded markov chain. The Annals of Mathematical Statistics 24(3), 338–354 (1953)
9. Nakibly, E.: Predicting waiting times in telephone service systems. Master's thesis, Technion–Israel Institute of Technology (2002)
10. Houston, M.B., Bettencourt, L.A., Wenger, S.: The relationship between waiting in a service queue and evaluations of service quality: A field theory perspective. Psychology and Marketing 15(8), 735–753 (1998)
11. Carmon, Z., Kahneman, D.: The experienced utility of queuing: real time affect and retrospective evaluations of simulated queues. Technical report, Duke University (1996)
12. Larson, R.C.: Perspectives on queues: Social justice and the psychology of queueing. Operations Research 35(6), 895–905 (1987)
13. Manning, C.D., Raghavan, P., Schütze, H.: Introduction to Information Retrieval. Cambridge University Press (2008)
14. Hastie, T., Tibshirani, R., Friedman, J.: The Elements of Statistical Learning. Springer Series in Statistics. Springer New York Inc., New York (2001)
15. Ibrahim, R., Whitt, W.: Real-time delay estimation based on delay history. Manufacturing and Service Operations Management 11(3), 397–415 (2009)
16. Schruben, L., Kulkarni, R.: Some consequences of estimating parameters for the m/m/1 queue. Operations Research Letters 1(2), 75–78 (1982)

17. Brown, L., Gans, N., Mandelbaum, A., Sakov, A., Shen, H., Zeltyn, S., Zhao, L.: Statistical analysis of a telephone call center. Journal of the American Statistical Association 100(469), 36–50 (2005)
18. Whitt, W.: Stochastic-process limits: an introduction to stochastic-process limits and their application to queues. Springer (2002)
19. Nguyen, V.: The trouble with diversity: Fork-join networks with heterogeneous customer population. The Annals of Applied Probability, 1–25 (1994)
20. Gans, N., Koole, G., Mandelbaum, A.: Telephone call centers: Tutorial, review, and research prospects. Manufacturing & Service Operations Management 5(2), 79–141 (2003)
21. van der Aalst, W., Nakatumba, J., Rozinat, A., Russell, N.: Business process simulation: How to get it right. BPM Center Report BPM-08-07 (2008), BPMcenter.org
22. Rogge-Solti, A., Weske, M.: Prediction of remaining service execution time using stochastic petri nets with arbitrary firing delays. In: Basu, S., Pautasso, C., Zhang, L., Fu, X. (eds.) ICSOC 2013. LNCS, vol. 8274, pp. 389–403. Springer, Heidelberg (2013)
23. Woodside, C.M., Stanford, D.A., Pagurek, B.: Optimal prediction of queue lengths and delays in gi/m/m multiserver queues. Operations Research 32(4), 809–817 (1984)
24. Whitt, W.: Predicting queueing delays. Management Science 45(6), 870–888 (1999)
25. Folino, F., Guarascio, M., Pontieri, L.: Discovering Context-Aware Models for Predicting Business Process Performances. In: Meersman, R., et al. (eds.) OTM 2012, Part I. LNCS, vol. 7565, pp. 287–304. Springer, Heidelberg (2012)

PO-SAAC: A Purpose-Oriented Situation-Aware Access Control Framework for Software Services

A.S.M. Kayes, Jun Han, and Alan Colman

Swinburne University of Technology, Victoria 3122, Australia
{akayes,jhan,acolman}@swin.edu.au

Abstract. Situation-aware applications need to capture relevant *context information* and *user intention or purpose*, to provide situation-specific access to software services. As such, a situation-aware access control approach coupled with purpose-oriented information is of critical importance. Existing approaches are highly domain-specific and they control access to services depending on the specific types of context information without considering the *purpose*. To achieve *situation-aware access control*, in this paper we consider *purpose-oriented situations* rather than conventional situations (e.g., user's state). We take *situation* to mean the states of the entities and the states of the relationships between entities that are relevant to the purpose of a resource access request. We propose a generic framework, *Purpose-Oriented Situation-Aware Access Control*, that supports access control to software services based on the relevant situations. We develop a software prototype to demonstrate the practical applicability of the framework. In addition, we demonstrate the effectiveness of our framework through a healthcare case study. Experimental results demonstrate the satisfactory performance of our framework.

Keywords: Situation-aware access control, Context information, Purpose, Situation reasoning, Access control policy.

1 Introduction

In open and dynamic environments, Situation-Aware Access Control (SAAC) applications need to capture and manipulate context information [1] to identify relevant situations and need to adapt their behaviors as the situation changes. In such environments, users demand access to appropriate software services in an anytime and anywhere fashion, as described by Weiser [2], with more flexibility and richer resources, and yet not to compromise the relevant privacy and security requirements of the stakeholders. A security policy (situation-aware access control policy) normally states that the particular services can be invoked based on (i) *the states of the relevant entities* and (ii) *the specific purpose*; which describes the reason for which organizational resources are used [3]. For example, an emergency doctor's request to invoke a healthcare service (access to the emergency patient's records when the patient is in a critical health condition) may be possible from the inside of the hospital but may not from the public bus.

M. Jarke et al. (Eds.): CAiSE 2014, LNCS 8484, pp. 58–74, 2014.

Also, such service access request can be granted for the emergency treatment purpose. In the medical domain the American Health Information Management Association (AHIMA) identifies 18 health care scenarios across 11 purposes (treatment, payment, research, etc.) for health information exchange [4]. Therefore, in order to specify *situations* for SAAC applications, on the one hand, it is required to capture the states of the relevant situation-specific context entities (e.g., user, resource, resource owner) and the states of the relevant relationships between different entities (e.g., the interpersonal relationships between the user and the resource owner). On the other hand, it is required to identify the purpose or user's intention in accessing the software services.

The basic components to achieve situation-awareness have already been defined by Endsley [5], *"the perception of the elements in the environment within a volume of time and space, the comprehension of their meaning, and the projection of their status in the near future"*. Some other research describe situation as the states of the specific kind of entities (e.g., [6],[7],[8]). However, other than the entity states, the states of the relevant relationships between entities are not considered in this situation-awareness research.

Some situation-aware access control approaches have been proposed in the access control literature (e.g., [9], [10]), each of them having different origins, pursuing different goals and often, by nature, being highly domain-specific. They consider the specific types of context information (e.g., the user's state) as policy constraints to control access to software services or resources. However, other than the relevant states, the purpose or user's intention in accessing the services is not considered in these works. In this paper, we consider the basic elements of the situation-aware access control are: the combination of the relevant *entity states* and the *relationship states*, and the *purpose or user's intention*.

The Contributions. In order to address the above-identified research issues and challenges, we present a novel framework PO-SAAC (*Purpose-Oriented Situation-Aware Access Control*, to provide situation-specific access to software services. The novel features of this framework are as follows:

(C1) *Purpose-Oriented Situation Model.* Our framework uses the *purpose-oriented situation* information to provide situation-specific access to software services (authorization), where we present a *situation model* to represent and reason about the different types of situations. The *purpose-oriented situation* can be composed of the *relevant states of the entity and states of the relationships between entities* and the *user's intention or purpose*.

(C2) *Situation-Aware Access Control Policy Model.* Our framework presents a *SAAC policy model* to specify situation-aware access control policies. The policy model supports access control to the appropriate software services based on the relevant situations.

(C3) *Ontology-Based Framework Implementation.* Based on the situation and policy models, we introduce an ontology-based platform for modeling and identifying purpose-oriented situations, and enforcing situation-aware access control policies that take into account the relevant situations. Our ontology-based framework represents the basic elements using the ontology language OWL, extended with SWRL for identifying and reasoning about relevant situations and the corresponding access control policies.

(C4) *Prototype Implementation and Evaluation.* In order to demonstrate the practical applicability of our approach, we have presented a *software prototype* for the development of the situation-aware access control applications. We have carried out a healthcare case study, in order to demonstrate the effectiveness of our framework. To demonstrate the feasibility of our framework, we have conducted a number of experiments on a simulated healthcare environment. We have quantified the *performance overhead* of our framework for measuring the response time. Experimental results have demonstrated the satisfactory performance of our proposed framework.

Paper Outline. The rest of the paper is organized as follows. Section 2 presents a healthcare application scenario to motivate our work. In Section 3, we present the design of our PO-SAAC framework, a situation model to specify different situations and a policy model for specifying situation-specific access control policies. Section 4 presents an ontology-based development platform for our framework. Section 5 describes the prototype implementation along with the viability of the framework. Section 6 discusses related work. Finally, Section 7 concludes the paper and outlines future work.

2   Research Motivation and General Requirements

As an example of the type of situations that a situation-specific access control framework has to consider, in this section we outline a motivating scenario that illustrates the need for the incorporation of purpose-oriented situation information in access control policies. We then distil the general requirements for managing the access to software services in a situation-aware manner.

Motivating Scenario. To exemplify the complexity of achieving situation-awareness in access control systems, we reflect on the area of patient medical records management in the healthcare domain as a motivating scenario.

Scene #1: The scenario begins with patient Bob who is in the emergency room due to a heart attack. While not being Bob's usual treating doctor, Jane, a general practitioner at the hospital, is required to treat Bob and needs to access Bob's emergency medical records from the emergency room of the hospital. Concerning this scene, one of the relevant situation-aware access control policy is shown in Table 1 (see *Policy #1*).

Scene #2: After getting emergency treatment, Bob is shifted from the emergency department to the general ward of the hospital and has been assigned a registered nurse Mary, who has regular follow-up visits to monitor his health condition. Mary needs to access Bob's daily medical records from the general ward with certain conditions (see the corresponding Policy #2 in Table 1).

Concerning the above scenario and their related policies, we can see that a set of constraints include: the user role (e.g., emergency doctor, registered nurse), the

Table 1. Example Access Control Policies

No	Policy
Policy #1	A general practitioner who is a treating doctor of a patient, is allowed to read/write the patient's emergency medical records in the hospital for emergency treatment purpose. However, in an emergency situation (like Scene #1), all general practitioners should be able to access the patient's emergency medical records in the hospital (by playing the emergency doctor role).
Policy #2	A registered nurse within a hospital is granted the right to read/write a patient's daily medical records during her ward duty time and from the location where the patient is located for daily operational purpose.

relevant environmental information (e.g., the emergency room, the interpersonal relationship between doctor and patient), the service (e.g., emergency medical records, daily medical records), and the purpose/user's intention in accessing the services (e.g., emergency treatment, daily operation); and these policies refer to need to be evaluated in conjunction with these relevant information.

General Requirements. To support the situation-aware access control in a computer application like the patients' medical record management system, we need to consider the 3Ws: ***who*** (the appropriate users by playing the appropriate roles) wants to access ***what*** (the appropriate services), and ***when*** (the relevant states and the purpose or user's intention in accessing the services). In particular, a general purpose-oriented situation-aware access control framework is required to manage the access to services in such applications by taking into account the different types of relevant situations. As different types of elementary information are integrated into the access control processes, some important issues arise. These issues and their related requirements are as follows:

(R1) *Representation of purpose-oriented situations:* What access control-specific elementary information should be identified as part of building a purpose-oriented situation model specific to SAAC? Furthermore, how to represent and reason about the different types of situations?

(R2) *Specification of situation-aware access control policies:* How to define the access control policies based on the relevant situations to realize a flexible and dynamic access control scheme?

(R3) *Implementation framework:* How to realize the relevant situations and the corresponding situation-specific access control policies in an effective way, in oder to access/manage software services?

3   Purpose-Oriented Situation-Aware Access Control

In this section, we present our Purpose-Oriented Situation-Aware Access Control (PO-SAAC) framework for software services.

3.1   Purpose-Oriented Situation Model

A situation consists of the set of *elementary information* (the combination of the relevant states and the user's intention or purpose-oriented information). In our purpose-oriented situation model, we define the simple situation (*atomic situation*) and the complex situation (*composite situation*) that are used in specifying situation-specific access control policies.

3.1.1 Representation of Situation

Different atomic situations can be defined based on the data/information from the organization (domain-specific).

Definition 1 (Atomic Situation, S_a). A *Situation* used in an access control decision is defined as the states of the relevant entities and the states of the relevant relationships between different relevant entities at a particular time that are relevant to a certain goal or purpose of a resource access request. A *Purpose* is the user's intention in accessing software services. The *Situation* and *Purpose* are domain-dependent concepts, and their values can be obtained based on the access request (i.e., from the sensed contexts, inferred contexts, etc.).

An atomic situation 'S_a' is the logical conjunction of 'P' and 'St'.

$$S_a = P \wedge St \tag{1}$$

where 'P' denotes the purpose or user's intention in accessing the service, e.g., considering our application scenario (*Scene #1*), *purpose* = "*EmergencyTreatment*"; and 'St' denotes the state of the relevant entity, e.g., *location(Jane)* = "*Hospital*", or the state of the relevant relationships between entities, e.g., *interpersonalRelationship(Jane, Bob)* = "*NonTreatingDoctor*".

A purpose 'P' can be identified based on the currently available contexts (i.e., the *states* of the relevant entity and the relationships between entities).

Example 1. Consider *Policy #1* related to our application scenario: a user, who is a general practitioner, by playing an emergency doctor (ED) role can access a patient's emergency medical records (EMR) in the hospital for emergency treatment (ET) purpose, when the patient is in a critical condition. The following rule (2) is used to identify that the purpose is 'ET' (i.e., a user by playing the 'ED' role can access a patient's medical records for 'ET' purpose, when the patient's health condition is critical),

$$Purpose(p) \wedge User(u) \wedge Role(r) \wedge Owner(o) \wedge Resource(res)$$
$$\wedge\ isPlayedBy(r, u) \wedge\ equal(r, \text{``}ED\text{''}) \wedge\ isOwnedBy(res, o) \tag{2}$$
$$\wedge\ healthStatus(o, \text{``}Critical\text{''}) \rightarrow equal(p, \text{``}ET\text{''}).$$

Example 2. Consider the policy mentioned in *Example 1*, in which the relevant elementary information is represented as an atomic situation ($s_{a1} \in S_a$),

$$s_{a1} = User(u) \wedge Purpose(p) \wedge intendedPurpose(u, p) \wedge equal(p, \text{``}ET\text{''})$$
$$\wedge\ Location(l) \wedge\ hasLocation(u, l) \wedge equal(l, \text{``}Hospital\text{''}). \tag{3}$$

3.1.2   Reasoning about Situation

The process of inferring a new composite situation (complex situation) from the one or more already defined/existing atomic situations is refereed to *reasoning about situation.* One of the main advantages of our framework to situation-awareness is its reasoning capability; that is, once facts about the world is stated, other facts can be inferred using an inference engine through the reasoning rules.

Definition 2 (Composite Situation, S_c). Given a collection of atomic situations, the composite situations can be defined by performing logical composition (AND, OR or NOT) on the same purpose-oriented atomic situations.

Example 3. Consider *Policy #2* related to our application scenario. The daily operation (DO) purpose can be identified using the following rule (4).

$$Purpose(p) \land User(u) \land Role(r) \land Owner(o) \land Resource(res)$$
$$\land isPlayedBy(r, u) \land equal(r, ``RN") \land isOwnedBy(res, o) \qquad (4)$$
$$\land healthStatus(o, ``Normal") \rightarrow equal(p, ``DO").$$

Two atomic situations regarding the mentioned policy are represented as,

$$s_{a2} = User(u) \land Purpose(p) \land intendedPurpose(u, p) \land equal(p, ``DO")$$
$$\land Location(l) \land hasLocation(u, l) \land equal(l, ``GW"). \qquad (5)$$

$$s_{a3} = User(u) \land Purpose(p) \land intendedPurpose(u, p) \land equal(p, ``DO")$$
$$\land Time(t) \land hasRequestTime(u, t) \land equal(t, ``DT"). \qquad (6)$$

A policy associated with the situation 's_{a2}' can be read as, a user by playing a registered nurse (RN) role, who is located with a patient in the general ward (GW) of the hospital, can access the patient's daily medical records (DMR) for daily operation (DO) purpose, when the patient's health condition is normal.

An example policy associated with the situation 's_{a3}' can be read as, a user by playing the 'RN' role can access the patient's 'DMR' during her ward duty time (DT) for 'DO' purpose, when the patient's health condition is normal.

A composite situation 's_{c1}' ($s_{c1} \in S_c$) with these two atomic situations (s_{a2} and s_{a3}) can be identified using the following logical conjunction, $s_{c1} = s_{a2} \land s_{a3}$.

3.2   Software Services

A service is a self-contained software entity and may be composed of other services (service composition). We consider the resource (e.g., patient medical record) in a service oriented manner, in order to provide fine-grained access control and grant the right access to the appropriate parts of a resource by the appropriate users. A *service* can be seen as a *pair* <*res, op*> with '*res*' being a requested resource and '*op*' being the action/operation on the resource. For example, the write operation on the emergency medical records is defined as <*EMR, write*> or *writeEMR()*. In this way, the fine-grained access control to resources can be realized by managing the access to the service operations.

3.3   The SAAC Policy Model for Software Service

Based on the formalization of the RBAC model in [11], we present a formal definition of our policy model. Our policy model for SAAC applications that extends RBAC with relevant situations, which is defined in the previous section. Our goal in this research is to provide a way in which the role-permission assignment policies can be specified by incorporating dynamic attributes (i.e., relevant situations) as policy constraints.

Definition 3 (SAAC Policy Model). Our policy model for access control can be formally described as a tuple, where R, S, Ser, and $SAACPolicy$ represents Roles, Situations, Services, and Policies, respectively (Formula (7)):

$$M_{SAAC} = (R, S, Ser, SAACPolicy) \qquad (7)$$

1. **Roles (R):** A set of roles $R = \{r_1, ..., r_m\}$. A role reflects user's job function or job title within the organization. A user is a human-being (who is a service requester) whose service access request is being controlled.
2. **Situation (S):** A set of situations $S = \{s_1, ..., s_n\} = S_a \cup S_c$ specified by using the situation model. S is used to express the relevant situations (atomic, S_a or composite, S_c) in order to describe the SAAC policies.
3. **Services (Ser):** A set of services $Ser = \{ser_1, ..., ser_o\} = \{(res, op) | res \in Res, op \in OP\}$, where Res is a set of component parts of resources, $Res = \{res_1, ..., res_p\}$ and OP is a set of operations on the resources, $OP = \{op_1, ..., op_q\}$. In our policy model, a service is a well-defined and self-contained software entity with an invocable interface to provide certain capability to perform certain operations on resources.
4. **Policies (SAACPolicy):** A set of policies $SAACPolicy = \{sp_1, ..., sp_r\} \subseteq R \times S \times Ser$. Our model has situation-aware role-service assignment policies to provide situation specific access to software services.

Our policy model extends the concept of common *role-permission assignments* (*RPA*) in RBAC (*RPA* $\subseteq R \times P$) [11], by introducing the concept of purpose-oriented situation, called *situation-aware role-service assignments*.

Example 4: Based on our policy model (*Role(r)* $\wedge$ *Situation(s)* $\wedge$ *Service(ser)* $\rightarrow$ *(r, s, ser)* $\in$ *SAACPolicy*), the following rule (shown in Table 2) expresses the policy mentioned in Example 1, i.e., a User '*u*' by playing the Role '*r*' (emergency doctor (ED) role) can invoke the Service '*ser*' (*writeEMR()* service), if a Situation '*s*' (*s* denotes s_{a1} mentioned in Example 2) is satisfied.

Table 2. An Example Situation-Aware Access Control Policy

If
$SAACPolicy(sp_1) \wedge Role(r) \wedge equal(r, ``ED") \wedge hasRole(sp_1, r) \wedge$
$Service(ser) \wedge equal(ser, ``writeEMR()") \wedge hasService(sp_1, ser) \wedge$
$Situation(s) \wedge equal(s, ``s_{a1}") \wedge hasSituation(sp_1, s)$
Then
$canInvoke(u, ser)$

The identification of the relevant information to represent the *purpose-oriented situations* and specify the corresponding *SAAC policies* satisfies requirements R(1)

and R(2), which is discussed earlier. To meet requirement R(3), we in the next section propose an *ontology-based development platform*.

4 Ontology-Based PO-SAAC Framework

We have introduced an ontology-based PO-SAAC framework to model relevant purpose-oriented situations and situation-specific access control policies. The principal goal of our framework is to formalize the situation-aware access control concepts using a logic-based language. To achieve this goal, we have already identified relevant concepts in the previous section.

In the literature, there are many languages that have been developed for specifying computer-processable semantics. In the present age, ontology-based modeling technique has been proven as a suitable logical language for modeling dynamic contexts/situations (e.g., [12], [13]). The ontology-based modeling approach to achieve situation-awareness (e.g., [7], [8]) is not only beneficial from the representational viewpoint but also beneficial from the reasoning viewpoint; that is, once facts about the world is stated in terms of the ontology, other facts can be inferred using the inference engine through the inference rules.

To model the PO-SAAC ontology, in this paper, we adopt the OWL language as an ontology language to represent the situations, which has been the most practical choice for most ontological applications because of its considered trade-off between computational complexity of reasoning and expressiveness [13].

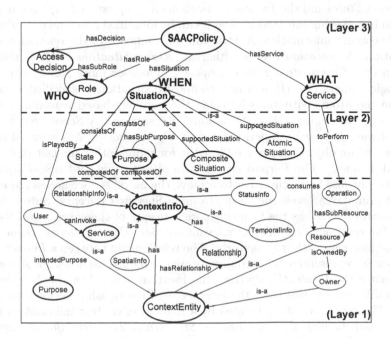

Fig. 1. The PO-SAAC Core Ontology

In order to support the process of inferring *new composite situations*, we need to define a set of reasoning rules that are associated with the existing or already defined situations. In addition, several of the reasoning rules require mathematical computation, which is not supported by the OWL language. Towards this end, the expressivity of OWL can be extended by adding SWRL rules to an ontology. We express the user-defined reasoning rules using the SWRL which provide the ability to identify the purposes and to reason about new composite situations.

Core Concepts. A graphical representation of the PO-SAAC ontology is shown in Figure 1. We model our ontology based on the 3Ws: *who* (user/role) wants to access *what* (service) and *when* (relevant states and purpose). The ontology facilitates software engineers to analyze and specify purpose-oriented situation information of service invocation for access control in a situation-aware manner. The ontology is divided into three layers. The top layer (*Layer 3*) shows the core concepts/elements for specifying the SAAC policies. The middle layer (*Layer 2*) shows the situation modeling concepts. The bottom layer (*Layer 1*) shows the basic concepts for defining the context information and services (resources). The ontology models the following core concepts.

The top layer has the following core concepts, which are organized into *SAACPolicy* hierarchy, namely *Role*, *Situation*, *Service*, and *AccessDecision* classes. A policy captures the *who/what/when* dimensions which can be read as follows: a *SAACPolicy* specifies that a user (who is playing a *Role*) has *AccessDecision* ("Granted" or "Denied") to *Service* if a *Situation* is satisfied.

The middle layer has the situation modeling concepts. A *Situation* consists of the relevant *States* and the *Purpose* of user's access request. A *Purpose* is a user's intention in accessing the services; and it can be identified based on the currently available context information. A *State* can be composed of the relevant context information. A *Situation* can be either an *AtomicSituation* binding a simple situation or a *CompositeSituation* composed by one or more atomic situations using logical operators. (How a new composite situation is specified/reasoned based on the atomic situations by using the ontology-based reasoning rule, is discussed in "Reasoning About Situations" Subsection.) A *Service* consumes a set of software *Resources* to perform certain *Operations*. A *Role* is linked to the *User* class by an object property *isPlayedBy* for representing the fact that a role is played by a user. The *Purpose* class has an object property *hasSubPurpose* to model the purpose hierarchy, so as to achieve the users' service access request at different granularity levels (detail in "Domain-Specific Concepts" Subsection).

The bottom layer has the following core concepts of the context entities and context information. The different relevant entities (*User*, *Resource*, *Owner*) are organized into *ContextEntity* hierarchy. The relationship between a *Resource* and its *Owner* is represented by an object property named *isOwnedBy*. A context characterizes the *ContextEntity* (e.g., the location of user) or the *Relationship* between different entities (e.g., the interpersonal relationship between user and owner). The contexts are represented by a number of context information types (*ContextInfo*), namely *RelationshipInfo*, *StatusInfo*, *TemporalInfo*, and *Spatial-Info*. To specify the different relationships between different entities, an object property *hasRelationship* is used which links *ContextEntity* and *Relationship* classes. A general and extensible context model specific to access control is proposed in our earlier paper [14].

Domain-Specific Concepts. The PO-SAAC core ontology (shown in Figure 1) serves as an entry-point for the domain ontologies. The domain-specific concepts extend the core ontology's corresponding base concepts. It is important for the application developers, providing a way to include domain-specific concepts into the core ontology. Figure 2 shows an excerpt of the representation of the *Purpose* ontology for the healthcare domain (e.g. treatment purpose, research purpose) to exchange patients' medical records. A purpose is identified based on the currently available context information. To identify the purpose, we specify a set of user-defined SWRL rules. An example rule shown in Table 3 identifies the *Purpose* is *DailyOperation(DO)*, based on the current contexts.

Table 3. An Example Rule that Captures the *Purpose* is *DO*

Purpose(?purpose) ∧ Role(?role) ∧ roleID(?role, "RegisteredNurse") ∧ User(?user) ∧ is-PlayedBy(?role, ?user) ∧ Resource(?resource) ∧ Owner(?owner) ∧ isOwnedBy(?resource, ?owner) ∧ healthStatus(?owner, "Normal") → **intendedPurpose**(?user, "DO")

The different purposes at various granularity levels of a user's service access request are individually identifiable, so as to achieve fine-grained control over access to services. As such, the *Purpose* class contains an important data type property (*xsd:int* type) named *granLevel*, which indicates the granularity level. By doing so, we can provide different levels of purpose granularity. For example, an

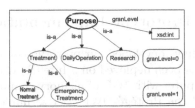

Fig. 2. An Excerpt of Purpose Ontology

Emergency Doctor can access a patient's emergency medical records for the *Treatment* purpose, at *granLevel* 0 (highest level), which means she also can access for all the other sub-purposes (at the lower granularity levels). A General Practitioner can access a patient's some medical records (e.g., daily medical records) for the *NormalTreatment* purpose. However, she can not access a patient's emergency medical records for *EmergencyTreatment* purpose.

We also consider the granularity levels of the healthcare *Role* and *Resource* (patient's medical records) hierarchies, in order to facilitate different fine-grained control for different types (roles) of users, so as to achieve fine-grained control over access to resource components at various granularity levels [14].

Reasoning about Situations. Various types of ontology-based inferences can be performed for the situation identification and reasoning, service composition and policy evaluation, including implicit knowledge reasoning as well as consistency checking. A set of reasoning rules are specified for implicit knowledge reasoning, which reasons about the implicit knowledge conveyed by the specification. For example, the rule specified in *Example 3* is written in OWL/XML that is used to reason about a new composite situation ($s_{c1} = s_{a2} \cap s_{a3}$, $s_{c1} \subseteq S_c$). The specification of these two atomic situations (s_{a2} and s_{a3}) are discussed in *Example 3*. An example policy associated with this composite situation s_{c1} specifies a registered nurse (RN) can access a patient's daily medical records from the general ward (GW) during her ward duty time (DT) for daily operation (DO) purpose. The specification of this composite situation is shown in Table 4.

Table 4. An Example Composite Situation *RNFromGWAtDTForDO*

```
<CompositeSituation rdf:ID="sc1_RNFromGWAtDTForDO">
     <supportedSituation rdf:resource="#sa2_RNFromGWForDO"/>
     <supportedSituation rdf:resource="#sa3_RNAtDTForDO"/>
</CompositeSituation>
<Situation>
     <owl:intersectionOf rdf:parseType="Collection">
          <Situation rdf:about="#sa2_RNFromGWForDO"/>
          <Situation rdf:about="#sa3_RNAtDTForDO"/>
     </owl:intersectionOf>
     <rdfs:subClassOf>
          <Situation rdf:about="#CompositeSituation"/>
     </rdfs:subClassOf>
</Situation>
```

5   Prototype Implementation and Evaluation

We have developed our prototype in Java2 SE using widely supported tools and it has been deployed on a Intel(R) Core(TM) Duo T2450 @ 2.00 GHz processor computer with 1GB of memory running Windows XP Professional OS. We have used the Protégé-OWL API to implement the core and healthcare ontologies. During the SAAC policy evaluation phase, an access query is used to process the user's service access request. We have used the SWRL rules to evaluate the policies. We have used the Jess Rule Engine for executing the SWRL rules. In particular, the query language SQWRL, which is based on OWL and SWRL, is adopted to process service access requests.

5.1   Prototype Architecture

A high-level architecture of our prototype framework is shown in Figure 3. We have implemented a set of *Software Components*, which can support the software engineers to develop Situation-Aware Access Control (SAAC) applications using this framework.

Currently a simple Java class *SAACDecisionEngine* is used to check the user's request to access the services and makes situation-specific access control decisions. We have implemented *PolicyEnforcementPoint* as part of the *SAACDecisionEngine*. Once the *SAACDecisionEngine* receives the request in accessing software services, it queries the *PolicyManager* class for the relevant policies. The *PolicyDecisionPoint*, and *PolicyAdministrationPoint* are implemented as parts of the class *PolicyManager* that are used to allow the

Table 5. An Example SAAC Policy (simplified)

```
<SAACPolicy rdf:ID="sp1">
        <hasDecision rdf:resource="#AccessDecision_Granted"/>
        <hasRole rdf:resource="#EmergencyDoctor_ED"/>
        <hasService rdf:resource="#Service_EMR_Write"/>
        <hasSituation rdf:resource="#s_{a1}_EDFromHospitalForET"/>
</SAACPolicy>
```

engineers to add, edit, and delete access control policies. We have developed a number of *ContextProviders* (which capture low-level context information) and the *ContextReasoner* (which infers high-level information) as parts of the *SituationManager*. The *SituationManager* is used to identify relevant purposes and situations. The ontology knowledge bases are stored in the form of the OWL concepts, SWRL rules and SQWRL queries (PO-SAAC Ontology).

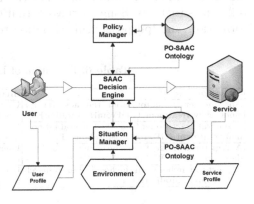

Fig. 3. Our Prototype Architecture

5.2 Developing a SAAC Application for Healthcare

A situation-aware application in the healthcare domain is built to illustrate the operation of our situation-aware access control. The environment of our application is the patients' medical records management (PMRM). The main goal that we aim with this application is to access different medical records of patients based on the relevant situations. We simulate the Java programs and the relational databases as different context sources. For example, our prototype application has context sources: SystemTime (which provides current_time), Location (which provides location_address), User_Pass relational table (containing usr_id and password), User_Role table (containing usr_id and usr_role_id), Patient_Pofile table (containing patient_id, patient_name and connected_people_id), patient Health_Profile (which provides patient_id, heart_rate and body_temperature), etc.

Policy Specification. Table 5 shows the *Policy #1* written in OWL that is related to our application scenario. In this policy, the access decision (*"Granted"* decision) is based on the following policy constraints: *who* the user is (user's *role*, e.g., "*ED*"), *what* service being requested (*service*, e.g., "*writeEMR()*"), and *when* the user sends the request (*purpose-oriented situation*). The '*purpose*' and '*situation*' regarding this policy are specified in Examples 1 and 2.

Case Study. To demonstrate the effectiveness of our framework, we present a case study. Consider our application scenario (*Scene #1*), where Jane, by playing an emergency doctor role, wants to access the requested service *writeEMR()* (i.e., the write access to the emergency medical records of patient Bob). The bottom layer of our PO-SAAC ontology captures the relevant context information (interpersonal relationship, location, health status, etc.). The middle layer of the ontology captures the relevant situation based on the captured information and situation specification rules. For the PMRM application we have specified different situations. Some of these 'situations' and their associated 'context information' and 'purpose' using situation reasoning rules are shown in Table 6.

Table 6. Definition of Different Situations

Situation	Situation Definition (high-level description)
An emergency doctor from the hospital for emergency treatment (EDFromHospitalForET)	User_Role(ED) ∧ Location_ED(Hospital)∧ Purpose(ET)
A general practitioner from the hospital for normal treatment (GPFromHospitalForNT)	User_Role(GP) ∧ Location_GP(Hospital)∧ Purpose(NT)
A registered nurse from the general ward for daily operation (RNFromGWForDO)	User_Role(RN) ∧ Location_RN(GeneralWard) ∧ Purpose(DO)
A guest researcher from the hospital for research (GRFromHospitalForR)	User_Role(GR) ∧ Location_GR(Hospital)∧ Purpose(R)

Our ontology (top layer) also captures the relevant SAAC policy. Based on this information, the ontology returns the SAAC decision, i.e., Jane's service access request is *Granted* (see an access query in Table 7 and result in Table 8), because the ontology captures relevant situation, and satisfies a SAAC policy which is stored in the policy base (ontology knowledge base).

Table 7. An Example Access Query (Simplified)

SAACPolicy(?policy) ∧ User(?**user**) ∧ Role(?**role**) ∧ Situation(?**situation**) ∧ Service(?**service**) ∧ AccessDecision(?**decision**) → **sqwrl:select**(?user, ?role, ?situation, ?service, ?decision)

Table 8. Access Query Result (Shown Only One Entry)

?user	?role	?situation	?service	?decision
Jane	ED	EDFromHospitalForET	EMR_Write	Granted

5.3   Performance Evaluation

We evaluate the runtime system performance using our prototype system, where we adopt our PO-SAAC approach to identify and reason about the relevant purpose-oriented situation.

Experimental Setting. With the goal of evaluating the runtime performance of the various stages of our prototype framework, we have conducted two sets of experiments on a Windows XP Professional operating system running on Intel(R) Core(TM) Duo T2450 @ 2.00 GHz processor with 1GB of memory.

Measurement. The main purpose of this experimental investigation is to quantify the performance overhead of our approach. Our main measures included *situation identification time* and *policy evaluation time.* The first measure indicates how long it took to identify/infer a relevant situation (by capturing the currently available context information and identifying the purpose using this information). The second measure indicates how long it took to determine a user's access permission on a requested service (by incorporating the identified situation into the access control process and making situation-aware access control decision). We calculate the average *end-to-end response time* (T_{RT}), time from the arrival of the user's service access request (query) to the end of its execution, which equals to the time for identifying relevant situation and time for evaluating relevant policy.

Results and Analysis. We have examined the performance of PO-SAAC. The main finding was that the time for *making situation-aware access control decision* (based on the *situation identification time* and *policy evaluation time*) is acceptable, as they impose just a small, acceptable overhead.

The *first test* focuses on measuring the response time of our prototype in the light of increasing number of policies. First, we have selected 20 policy rules in which 5 situation types (ST) act as the policy constraints (e.g., the situation-aware policy rule for emergency doctor for emergency treatment purpose is shown in Table 5). We have varied the number of policies up to 100 with 15 different types of situation variations. Each of these variations is executed 10 times for each of following cases: 5 ST (situation types), 10 ST, and 15 ST. For each setting, the average value of the 10 execution runs is used for the analysis (see test results in Figure 4(a)). The test results show that the average response time increases when the number of situation types and policies increases. For example, it varies *between 4.1 and 5.2 seconds* for 15 types of situation information and for the variation of 20 to 100 policy rules. We can see that the average response time seems to be linear. Overall, the performance is acceptable.

In the *second test*, we have again evaluated the total response time (situation identification and policy evaluation time) over various size of the knowledge base. We have varied the number of policies up to 500 with respect to 138 different types of health professionals [15] (i.e., 138 roles). To build the ontology KB of increasing sizes, we have specified 2000 policies. In order to measure the response time, we have run each experiment 10 times and the average value of the 10 execution runs is used for the analysis (see test results in Figure 4(b)). As the size

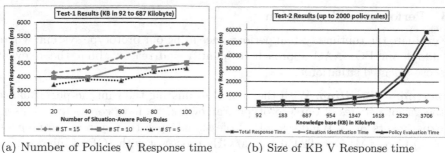

(a) Number of Policies V Response time   (b) Size of KB V Response time

Fig. 4. Average Response Time Over Different Number/Size of Policies/KB

of the ontology KB increases beyond 1618 kilobyte, the computational overhead increases dramatically. This is due to the large number of policy rules (larger KB size), fully utilizing the memory capacity of the computer. At the point of the KB being 1618 kilobyte (500 policy rules for the 138 health professional roles), it takes *approximately 10 seconds* to process the request. We can see that changes to the number of access control policies do not have much impact on the response time, when the ontology knowledge base (KB) size is small. Overall, the runtime performance is acceptable for a reasonable sized KB.

6   Related Work and Discussion

In [9], Kim and Lim propose the Situation-Aware Role-Based Access Control (SA-RBAC) model, which extends the basic RBAC model [11] and dynamically grants roles (or permissions) to users based on the situation information of the user. The SA-RBAC model is used to deal with the situation information by considering the combination of the required credentials of users, and the context information such as location, time, and system resources relevant to the user's access request. In [16], Yau and others have defined the situation as a set of context attributes of users, systems and environments over a period of time affecting future system behavior. Later, Yau and Liu have presented a Situation-Aware Access Control (SA-AC) based privacy-preserving service matchmaking approach [10]. SA-AC model incorporates situation-aware constraints into RBAC model, such that the states of service providers, requesters and environments, which can affect the access control decisions. These approaches only consider the states of the relevant entities as the policy constraints. In open and dynamic environments, however, the states of the relevant relationships between different entities are also important consideration in access control decision making. In our PO-SAAC approach, a situation not only involves the states of the specific types of context entities but also the states of the relevant relationships between different relevant entities. Moreover, in our approach, the purpose or user's intention in accessing the services is also considered for modeling situation.

Previous works on ontology-based context/situation-awareness also provide valuable insights for modeling a fine-grained ontology-based SAAC framework.

The CONtext ONtology (CONON) [6], situation theory ontology (STO) [7] and situation-awareness (SAW) ontology [8] research describe 'situation' as the states of the specific kind of entities (e.g., attributes of users or other relevant entities). However, this research are highly domain-specific and they do not consider several important concepts which are important consideration for situation modeling in today's dynamic environments: the states of the relevant relationships between entities, and the purpose or user's intention in accessing the services.

Byun and Li [3] have proposed a privacy preserving access control model for relational databases where purpose information associated with a given data element specifies the intended use of the data element. Their access control policy normally states that the particular resources can be accessed only for the specific purpose; and a purpose describes the reason for data access and data collection. In [17], the authors presented a purpose-based access control model (usage access control and purpose extension) for medical information system, where 'usage' means usage of rights on digital objects, and 'purpose' dictates how access to data items should be controlled. A major difference of our approach with respect to these purpose-based access control approaches is that, we not only consider the purpose information but also consider the different granularity levels of purpose information. In addition, different from these approaches, our approach can dynamically identify the appropriate purpose or user's intention in accessing the requested services based on the currently available context information.

7   Conclusion and Future Work

In this paper, we have presented a new Purpose-Oriented Situation-Aware Access Control framework for software services. One of the main contributions of this paper is the *PO-SAAC model* for specifying the purpose-oriented situations and the corresponding situation-specific access control policies. Another contribution of this paper is an *ontology-based development platform*, in order to formalize PO-SAAC model using OWL and SWRL. The practical applicability of our framework is demonstrated through the implementation of a software prototype. In addition, we have developed a SAAC application in the healthcare domain and presented a case study. The case study shows that our framework captures relevant situations at runtime and invokes software services in a situation-aware manner. The experimental results have shown that our framework has satisfactory performance. Future work focus on the scalability of our framework in the mobile platform will be an important issue to be addressed.

Acknowledgment. Jun Han is partly supported by the Qatar National Research Fund (QNRF) under Grant No. NPRP 09-069-1-009. The statements made herein are solely the responsibility of the authors.

References

1. Dey, A.K.: Understanding and using context. Personal Ubiquitous Computing 5(1), 4–7 (2001)
2. Weiser, M.: Some computer science issues in ubiquitous computing. Commun. ACM 36(7), 75–84 (1993)
3. Byun, J.-W., Li, N.: Purpose based access control for privacy protection in relational database systems. The VLDB Journal 17(4), 603–619 (2008)
4. Dimitropoulos, L.L.: Privacy and security solutions for interoperable health information exchange: nationwide summary. AHRQ Publication (2007)
5. Endsley, M.R.: Design and evaluation for situation awareness enhancement. In: Proceedings of the Human Factors Society 32nd Annual Meeting, Santa Monica, CA, USA, pp. 97–101 (1988)
6. Wang, X.H., Zhang, D.Q., Gu, T., Pung, H.K.: Ontology based context modeling and reasoning using owl. In: Proceedings of the Second PerCom Workshops, pp. 18–22 (2004)
7. Kokar, M.M., Endsley, M.R.: Situation awareness and cognitive modeling. IEEE Intelligent Systems 27(3), 91–96 (2012)
8. Yau, S.S., Huang, D.: Development of situation-aware applications in services and cloud computing environments. International Journal of Software and Informatics 7(1), 21–39 (2013)
9. Kim, Y.G., Lim, J.: Dynamic activation of role on rbac for ubiquitous applications. In: Proceedings of the 2007 International Conference on Convergence Information Technology, pp. 1148–1153 (2007)
10. Yau, S.S., Liu, J.: A situation-aware access control based privacy-preserving service matchmaking approach for service-oriented architecture. In: ICWS, pp. 1056–1063 (2007)
11. Sandhu, R.S., Coyne, E.J., Feinstein, H.L., Youman, C.E.: Role-based access control models. IEEE Computer 29, 38–47 (1996)
12. Bettini, C., Brdiczka, O., Henricksen, K., Indulska, J., Nicklas, D., Ranganathan, A., Riboni, D.: A survey of context modelling and reasoning techniques. Pervasive and Mobile Computing 6, 161–180 (2010)
13. Riboni, D., Bettini, C.: Owl 2 modeling and reasoning with complex human activities. Pervasive and Mobile Computing 7, 379–395 (2011)
14. Kayes, A.S.M., Han, J., Colman, A.: An ontology-based approach to context-aware access control for software services. In: Lin, X., Manolopoulos, Y., Srivastava, D., Huang, G. (eds.) WISE 2013, Part I. LNCS, vol. 8180, pp. 410–420. Springer, Heidelberg (2013)
15. ASCO: Health professionals (Jul 2013), http://www.abs.gov.au/
16. Yau, S.S., Karim, F., Wang, Y., Wang, B., Gupta, S.K.S.: Reconfigurable context-sensitive middleware for pervasive computing. IEEE Pervasive Computing 1(3), 33–40 (2002)
17. Sun, L., Wang, H., Soar, J., Rong, C.: Purpose based access control for privacy protection in e-healthcare services. JSW 7(11), 2443–2449 (2012)

Optimal Distribution of Applications in the Cloud

Vasilios Andrikopoulos, Santiago Gómez Sáez,
Frank Leymann, and Johannes Wettinger

IAAS, University of Stuttgart
Universitätsstr. 38, 70569 Stuttgart, Germany
{andrikopoulos,gomez-saez,leymann,wettinger}@iaas.uni-stuttgart.de

Abstract. The emergence of the cloud computing paradigm introduces
a number of challenges and opportunities to application and system developers. The multiplication and proliferation of available offerings by
cloud service providers, for example, makes the selection of an appropriate solution complex and inefficient. On the other hand, this availability
of offerings creates additional possibilities in the way that applications
can be engineered or re-engineered to take advantage of e.g. the elastic
nature, or the pay per use model of cloud computing. This work proposes
a formal framework which allows to explore the possibility space of optimally distributing application components across cloud offerings in an
efficient and flexible manner. The proposed approach introduces a set of
innovative in their use concepts and demonstrates how this framework
can be used in practice by means of a running scenario.

Keywords: application topology, distribution optimization, cloud
computing, operational expenses.

1   Introduction

The cloud computing paradigm offers a well documented set of benefits to
enterprises and individuals with respect to transferring capital to operational
expenses, potentially unlimited access to computational resources, and utility-
based charging for the use of these resources [4]. In this respect, cloud computing
offers a platform for innovative information systems that are partially or completely implemented using cloud offerings. In order however to reap the full
benefits of cloud computing, application design and development must move
beyond the mere re-packaging of applications in virtual machines (VMs) and
offering them as part of Infrastructure as a Service (IaaS) solutions [1]. For example, novel services like Database as a Service (DBaaS) offerings can be used
in designing and realizing new applications, or while migrating and accordingly
adapting existing applications for the cloud. Furthermore, when considering the
variation of pricing models across cloud providers [22], it becomes possible to
select from different cloud offerings, e.g. different configurations of the AWS

M. Jarke et al. (Eds.): CAiSE 2014, LNCS 8484, pp. 75–90, 2014.

EC2 service[1], in order to identify an optimal in terms of operational expenses distribution of the application.

Toward this goal, a number of approaches provide decision support for migrating existing applications to the cloud, see for example [2,10,16]. However, these approaches do not consider as part of their process the *application topology*, i.e. the combination of *application-specific components*, *middleware solutions* like the application server used, and the underlying *infrastructure* (VMs on either a local server, or on cloud offerings) hosting both of them and allowing the application to operate. Using the taxonomy proposed in [1], such approaches usually provide support for migration type III, meaning that the whole *application stack* (components, middleware and OS) is bundled in a VM image and moved to a cloud provider for hosting. In this respect, these approaches are limited in their capabilities when considering the distribution of the application across cloud offerings and/or local, in-house servers.

On the other hand, initiatives like the TOSCA standard [6], Cloud Blueprints [20] or CloudML [7] allow for a portable and interoperable topological description of the application stack that can be used for the distributed deployment of the application across cloud providers. Using these initiatives, it becomes possible for the application developer to explore the application design space and model which cloud offering to use to host which parts of the application stack. However, what these approaches lack is decision support capabilities towards *optimally* selecting the best of the identified application topologies in a given situation. This is a deficiency that this work aims to address by bringing together cloud migration decision support with these cloud-aware topology description approaches. The proposed approach does not make any assumptions with respect to the technologies used and as such it is suitable for use in both generic and domain-specific information systems.

The main contribution of this work can therefore be summarized as a technology-agnostic formal framework that provides the means to:

- Model, verify and automatically generate alternative scenarios for the distribution of an application stack across cloud offerings. Applications in this context may entail a complete information system, or only part of it.
- Evaluate each one of these distribution scenarios with respect to various dimensions using different criteria, and allow the selection of an optimal scenario given the application needs.

The remaining of this paper is structured as follows: the following section (Section 2) discusses a motivating scenario that illustrates the challenges that this work is addressing. Section 3 builds on existing models and languages to provide a formalization of the notion of application topology and affiliated concepts. Section 4 uses this formalization to develop a method for the optimal selection between alternative (acceptable) application topologies, which is demonstrated in practice in Section 5. Related approaches are discussed in Section 6, and the paper concludes in Section 7 by providing also the outline for future work.

---

[1] Amazon Web Services (AWS) EC2: http://aws.amazon.com/ec2/

2   Motivating Scenario

For purposes of further motivating this work we adapt the Web Shop application topology discussed in [6]. We abstract away from the TOSCA notation used in [6] and represent the topology of the application as the nodes and edges with solid lines in the graph of Fig. 1. The application itself consists of three tiers: front end, back end and persistence as a database. The WebShop_Frontend component is developed as a set of PHP files deployed in a PHP container. The container is in turn configured and deployed as an Apache Web server module, with the server running inside a Windows 2003 Server OS installed on top of an IBM zSeries server. The WebShop_Backend component is a Web application packaged in a WAR (Web application ARchive) file running inside an Apache Tomcat servlet container (requiring also the installation of the Oracle Java Virtual Machine (JVM) in the same OS), while the MySQL RDBMS is used as a database server for the ProductDB database. The latter two tiers are deployed in a Windows 7 image provided by the Amazon Web Services (AWS) EC2 service as part of their Reserved Instances offerings[2].

The application topology in Fig. 1 is already deployed in a distributed manner, in the sense that the components from the different tiers are deployed and operated in different infrastructure solutions, with the front end in a physical server on premises, and the back end and persistence in an IaaS offering. However, the application topology shown in Fig. 1 is only one of the possibilities for distributing the application. As also shown in Fig. 1, and marked with dashed lines in the figure, it is also possible to separate the back end from the persistence tier and deploy them in different EC2 offerings (denoted by the 'alt_hosted_on' relationship), one or both of which could be an Ubuntu Linux OS image. Furthermore, the ProductDB database could also be migrated to the Amazon RDS[3] DBaaS solution, which is compatible with the MySQL RDBMS.

Each one of these topologies has a different impact on essential characteristics of the application such as operational expenses, deployment time, scalability opportunities, performance, etc. Different pricing models are used, for example, for IaaS and DBaaS offerings, taking into account different parameters, e.g. number of CPUs per VM in the former case and size of egress traffic per month in the latter. Furthermore, migrating the ProductDB to AWS RDS can be better suited for profiting from some characteristics offered out of the box by DBaaS offerings, e.g. multi-instance management, high availability, automated scaling, etc., as re-engineering the application to deal with data consistency issues across database replicas is not required.

There are therefore two major challenges that this work is addressing: first, *how to infer the existence of possible topologies* for a given application, and second, *how to optimally select amongst these alternative topologies* for a given set of characteristics like operational costs. In the following section we introduce a formal framework that provides us with the fundamentals necessary towards dealing with these challenges.

---

[2] AWS EC2 Instance Types: http://aws.amazon.com/ec2/instance-types/
[3] AWS Relational Database Service: http://aws.amazon.com/rds/

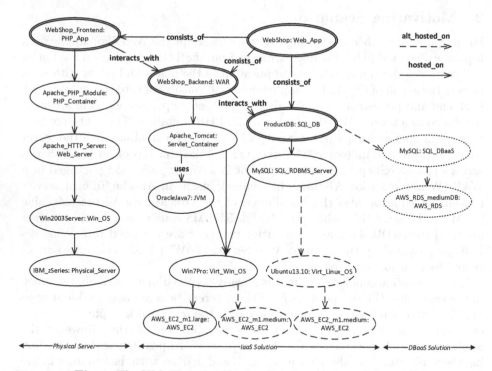

Fig. 1. The Web Shop Application Topology (adapted from [6])

3 Application Topology Fundamentals

So far we have been using the term 'application topology' in a rather informal manner to denote the model for the deployment of the application components in middleware solutions (e.g. the Apache Tomcat container in Fig. 1), and the consequent deployment of the resulting software stack in an appropriate infrastructure solution (e.g. the zSeries server, or the EC2 VM offering). Before proceeding further we first formalize this notion:

Definition 1 (Application Topology). *An application topology is a labeled graph* $G = (N^L, E^L, s, t)$ *where* N *is a set of nodes,* E *is a set of edges,* L *a set of labels, and* s, t *the source and target functions* $s, t : E^L \to N^L$. *The topology graph is called* typed, *if the label set* L *contains only elements* <name:type> *(for nodes) and* <type> *(for edges), in which case the graph is denoted by* T.

Most existing works for cloud-oriented topology description like the TOSCA specification [6], the Cloud Blueprinting approach [20], and the CloudML language [7], or involving such a description as in, e.g. the MOCCA [13] framework, use this typed topology graph model, in order to provide a concrete description of the application and middleware components and cloud offerings involved under a unified model. Similar approaches are also used by cloud service providers like

Amazon with CloudFormation[4], as well as the OpenNebula initiative[5] or Open-Stack Heat[6], with a clear orientation towards facilitating and/or automating the deployment, provisioning and management of applications on cloud solutions. For this purpose they need a complete and a priori defined description of the application topology that can be distributed across multiple cloud offerings.

However, as discussed in the previous section, this is a limited view of the possibilities available in distributing the application across cloud solutions. Looking at the case of the Web Shop application, it can be observed that there is a conceptual distinction between the application components on one hand (denoted with double lines in Fig. 1), and the middleware components like the Apache Web server and the cloud offerings like the AWS EC2 service on the other. More specifically, while the former part is unique and specific for the Web Shop application, the latter can actually be reused and even shared across multiple applications similar to the Web Shop. In this respect, the typed topology model used by approaches like TOSCA should therefore only be interpreted as *one possible instantiation* of the application topology. In order to be able to model and explore this possibility space, the notion of a *type graph with inheritance* as formally defined in [5] and [12] can be used:

Definition 2 (Type Graph with Inheritance, following [5]). *A type graph with inheritance TG_I is a triple (TG, I, A) consisting of a type graph $TG = (N, E, s, t)$ (with a set of nodes N, a set of edges E and a target function $s, t : E \to N$), an inheritance graph I sharing the same set of nodes N, and a set $N^A \subseteq N$, called abstract nodes. For each node $n \in I$ the* inheritance clan *relation is defined by $clan(n)_I = \{n' \in N \mid \exists \, \text{path} \; n' \xrightarrow{*} n \in I\}$ where $n \in clan(n)_I$ (i.e. the* path *of length 0 is included).*

TG_I is therefore a graph where the nodes and edges are types, and where edges denoting the inheritance/subtype relation type, as in UML class diagrams, is allowed between nodes. Bardohl et al. use the concept of *abstract* nodes in [5] for types that have only inheritance relations with other nodes, meant to denote generic classes of nodes like e.g. Web Server. Using the clan morphism relation $clan(n)_I$ allows for navigating the inheritance-type edges in TG_I graphs, which is instrumental in producing typed graphs. In this respect, thinking of the application topological description as a graph morphism over TG_I produces potentially multiple typed topology graphs depending on the availability of sibling nodes in inheritance relations with abstract nodes (e.g. 'Apache HTTP Server' and 'IBM WebSphere' for the 'Web Server' node). The concept of *viable topology* builds on this capability:

Definition 3 (Viable Topology). *A typed topology T is viable w.r.t. a type graph with inheritance TG_I, iff all elements of T are labeled (typed) over the elements of TG_I, i.e. there exists a graph morphism $m : TG_I \to T$ which uses the inheritance clan relation.*

---

[4] AWS CloudFormation: http://aws.amazon.com/cloudformation/

[5] OpenNebula.org: http://opennebula.org/

[6] OpenStack Heat: https://wiki.openstack.org/wiki/Heat

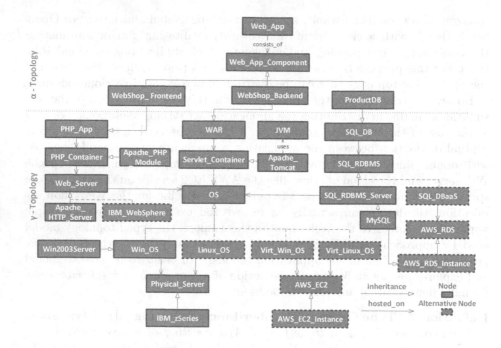

Fig. 2. The (Extended) μ-topology of the Web Shop Application

Based on this definition, the topology of the Web Shop application of Fig. 1 can therefore be classified as viable under the TG_I graph of Fig. 2. In addition to including the same types as the typed topology of Fig. 1 connected through edge types inheritance, 'consists_of' and 'hosted_on', the TG_I also incorporates types like 'Linux_OS' as a subtype of the 'OS' node that were not included in Fig. 1 (marked with dashed lines in Fig. 2). There are two ways to look at the morphism m that translates TG_I to T: *top-down*, with T being generated or validated against TG_I, and *bottom-up*, with TG_I being abstracted from one particular typed topology T and potentially being reused across different viable topologies. In order to facilitate the discussion, the following terms are being introduced:

Definition 4 (μ, α and γ-topology). *The type graph with inheritance TG_I for a viable application topology T is called its μ-topology. We denote by α-topology the application-specific sub-graph of a μ-topology, and by γ-topology the non application-specific (and therefore reusable) sub-graph of a μ-topology.*

In the μ-topology of Fig. 2, for example, the upper nodes (above the dotted line) belong to the α-topology of the Web Shop application, while the lower nodes (below the line) belong to its γ-topology. The distinction between α- and γ-topology is purely functional in nature, and the border between them can be moved dynamically per application to accommodate the application needs. For example, if the Web Shop front-end component requires exclusively a Windows 2003 Server OS due to the way that it was implemented, then the whole subgraph under it can be moved to the α-topology of the application to reflect this fact. Alternatively, all the necessary components for the front end (PHP container, Web server and OS) can be bundled together with the Web Shop front end component, in which case the 'WebShop_Frontend' node in the graph of Fig. 2 can be replaced by an equivalent 'WebShop_FrontendBundle' (in the α-topology) that is connected directly with the 'Physical_Server' node with a 'hosted_on' relation. In this manner, resource requirements as explicit constraints on the possible topologies, as discussed in both [6] and [20], can be specified.

Finally, a set of viable topologies $\mathcal{V}$ for an application can be generated given the α-topology of the application and a generic γ-topology that can even be standardized in a domain or enterprise by merging the two graphs using the inheritance relationship. Using the resulting μ-topology, a set of viable topologies can then be inferred from the μ-topology by applying different morphisms $m^{(i)} : TG_I \rightarrow T^{(i)}, i \geq 1$ to it, resulting in different topologies $T^{(i)} \in \mathcal{V}$. We assume without loss of generality that there always exists a viable topology for an application, i.e. $|\mathcal{V}| \geq 1$. In the following sections we only consider viable topologies in the discussion, unless explicitly stated otherwise.

4 μ-Topologies and Distribution Optimization

The introduction of μ-topologies provides us the tools to deal with the first of the challenges identified in Section 2, i.e. inferring the existence of possible (viable) topologies for an application. The richer in terms of available types the γ-topology used is, the bigger the size of the viable topologies set $\mathcal{V}$ for the application. In the following we build on the introduced formalisms in order to address the second identified challenge, i.e. optimal w.r.t. a given set of dimensions selection among these possible topologies for a given set of parameters, in a formal manner.

For this purpose, we first introduce (a set of) utility functions as the means to quantitatively evaluate a topology along one or more dimensions, and then we formulate the optimal topology selection problem in order to identify the steps involved in solving it.

4.1   Optimization Utility Function

Let's assume a set of functions $\mathbb{F}$ on the domain of real numbers $\mathbb{R}$ of the form $\mathbb{F} = \{f(a_1, \ldots, a_n) \,|\, n \geq 1, f : \mathbb{R}^* \rightarrow \mathbb{R}\}$, and a mapping function f_{map} from each topology in the set of *all* viable topologies for all applications $\mathbb{V}$ to this set $f_{map} : \mathbb{V} \rightarrow \mathbb{F}$. We then denote by $u^{(i)} \in \mathbb{F}$ the function $u^{(i)}(a_1, \ldots, a_n) = f_{map}(T^{(i)})$ and by $A^{(i)}$ the set of arguments $\{a_1, \ldots, a_n\}$ of $u^{(i)}$; as a shorthand for $u^{(i)}(a_1, \ldots, a_n)$ we equivalently use $u(T^{(i)})$ in the rest of this document. Providing concrete values $P^{(i)} = (p_1, \ldots, p_n)$ for the arguments $A^{(i)}$ allows for the *evaluation* of the function, i.e. $eval(u(T^{(i)}), (p_1, \ldots, p_n)) = u^{(i)}(p_1, \ldots, p_n)$.

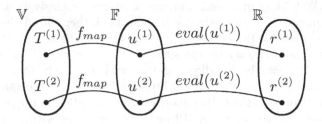

Fig. 3. Schematic Representation of the Sets $\mathbb{V}, \mathbb{F}, \mathbb{R}$ and the Mappings Between Them

Function $u^{(i)}$ is essentially the *utility function* for the topology $T^{(i)}$, in the sense that it evaluates the dimension on which the optimization takes place by providing a mapping from the set $\mathbb{V}$ to $\mathbb{R}$ as shown in Fig. 3, where $r^{(i)} = eval(f_{map}(T^{(i)}), (p_1, \ldots, p_n)) = eval(u^{(i)}(a_1, \ldots, a_n), (p_1, \ldots, p_n)), r^{(i)} \in \mathbb{R}$. For purposes of simplifying the discussion we assume that functions $u^{(i)}$ are by definition monotonic.

Different utility functions can be defined for the same topology depending on which dimension is taken under consideration. Furthermore, the concrete definition of each utility function depends on the types of the nodes in the μ-topology of the application. For example, for the initial topology $T^{(1)}$ of the Web Shop application in Fig. 1 the operational expenses of the application are decomposed into the expenses $opex_{zSeries}$ of operating the IBM zSeries server hosting the Web Shop front end for a time period of τ months, and into the cost $opex_{EC2\_m1.large}$ of using the AWS 'EC2 m1.large' offering for the same time period. For the former, $opex_{zSeries}$ can be calculated using a method like the one discussed by Walker in [23] as the product of the electricity cost, power consumption for operation and cooling, server utilization and number of hours of operation. Assuming that utilization z is stable over time we can simplify the formula as:

$$opex_{zSeries}(h_\tau, z) = k_e \times h_\tau \times z \tag{1}$$

where k_e is the cost of electricity per hour of operation and h_τ the total hours of operation in τ. For the latter, as discussed in [2], the cost calculation function can be inferred by the (publicly available) pricing policies in each cloud provider's Web site. In particular for the 'EC2 m1.large' Reserved Instances offering in the European Region using Linux, operational expenses (in US dollars) can be written analytically as $opex_{EC2\_m1.large}(h_\tau) = k_{initial} + h_\tau \times k_{perHour}$, or in prices of December 2013 [7]:

$$opex_{EC2\_m1.large}(h_\tau) = \begin{cases} 243 + h_\tau \times 0.17 & \text{with 1-year contract} \\ 384 + h_\tau \times 0.134 & \text{with 3-year contract} \end{cases} \tag{2}$$

where h_τ, as in the case of $opex_{zSeries}$, is the total amount of hours that the offering has been used in period τ, and $k_{initial}, k_{perHour}$ the initial cost for the reservation of instances and the cost of the offering per hour of use, respectively.

---

[7] As defined in http://aws.amazon.com/ec2/pricing/#reserved

Assuming that the application owner has a fixed budget k_{max} that is allowed to spend on operational expenses, it follows from Equations 1 and 2 that

$$u(T^{(1)}) = u^{(1)}(k_{max}, h_\tau, z) = k_{max} - (opex_{zSeries}(h_\tau, z) + opex_{EC2\_m1.large}(h_\tau))$$

and $A^{(1)} = \{k_{max}, h_\tau, z\}$.

The utility function $u^{(i)}$ and arguments set $A^{(i)}$ for each topology in $\mathcal{V}$ can be defined in a similar fashion. In principle, if utility (and therefore optimization of the distribution) considers more than one dimensions, e.g. cost and deployment time, then it can be written as a weighted and normalized sum of functions. However for the purposes of this work, we restrict the discussion to single-dimension optimization and leave the multiple dimension problem for future work.

4.2   Optimal Topology Selection

Following from the above, optimizing the distribution of an application for a given set of parameters (values) $\mathcal{P}$, which constitutes the *application profile*, can therefore be viewed as the (partial) ordering of the set $\mathcal{V}$ of the viable topologies for the application based on the evaluation of their utility functions for (potentially a subset of) $\mathcal{P}$.

More specifically, starting from the partial ordering

$$eval(u(T^{(1)}), \mathcal{P}) \gtrsim eval(u(T^{(2)}), \mathcal{P}) \gtrsim \ldots \gtrsim eval(u(T^{(m)}), \mathcal{P}), m = |\mathcal{V}|$$

and given the assumption that the utility functions $u^{(i)}$ are monotonic in nature, then ordering the evaluation of these functions allows for the ordering of the viable topologies, e.g. and without loss of generality:

$$eval(u(T^{(1)}), \mathcal{P}) \leq \ldots \leq eval(u(T^{(m)}), \mathcal{P}) \Rightarrow T^{(1)} \leq \ldots \leq T^{(m)}. \qquad (3)$$

Given therefore an application profile $\mathcal{P}$ and by identifying the appropriate utility functions in the set $\mathcal{U} \subset \mathbb{F}$ for the set of viable topologies $\mathcal{V}$, the optimal distribution of the application can be selected by Equation 3. $\mathcal{V}$ can be first trimmed down to a smaller size (which would allow for better performance given the number of evaluations and comparisons required) by applying a set of *filter* functions $\sigma^{(1)} \circ \cdots \circ \sigma^{(k)}(T^{(i)})$ where

$$\sigma^{(j)}(T^{(i)}) = \begin{cases} T^{(i)} & \text{if condition}(j)=\text{true,} \\ \emptyset & \text{otherwise.} \end{cases}$$

with condition(j),$1 \leq j \leq k$ written as logical formulas e.g. $Apache\_Tomcat \in T^{(i)}$ to denote whether an Apache Tomcat typed node appears in $T^{(i)}$.

In terms of automating this process, optimally distributing an application across cloud offerings with respect to one or more dimensions (e.g. operational expenses) and for a set of predefined constraints $\mathcal{C}$ (e.g. the data layer of the

application must remain on premises) can be decomposed into the following
steps:

1. If no μ-topology is available, then construct and merge the α-topology of the
   application with an available γ-topology.
2. Generate the set of viable topologies $\mathcal{V}$ from the μ-topology by traversing
   the typed graph with inheritance.
3. Prune down $\mathcal{V}$ by iteratively applying the filter functions $sigma^{(j)}$ for each
   $j \in \mathcal{C}$.
4. For each viable topology $T^{(i)}$ remaining in $\mathcal{V}$, identify the utility function
   $u^{(i)}$ that is relevant for the optimization dimension.
5. Construct the set of parameter values $\mathcal{P} = \bigcup_i^{|\mathcal{V}|} P^{(i)}$, $\forall u^{(i)} \in \mathcal{U}$.
6. Calculate $r^{(i)} = eval(u(T^{(i)}), \mathcal{P})$, $\forall T^{(i)} \in \mathcal{V}$ (or equivalently $\forall u^{(i)} \in \mathcal{U}$).
7. Select the topology corresponding to the value $max\{r^{(i)} \mid 1 \leq i \leq |\mathcal{V}|\}$.

In the following section we demonstrate how these steps can be applied in
practice for the Web Shop application presented in Section 2 in order to optimize
the distribution of the application in terms of operational expenses and with a
set of architectural constraints.

5   Evaluation

The evaluation of our methodology presented in this work is based on the Web
Shop application described in Section 2. More specifically, as discussed in the
previous sections, Fig. 2 outlines some of the alternative viable topologies for
the application, such as hosting the database on AWS RDS instead of a virtual
machine, and so on. In the following we show how the proposed method can be
used to optimize the distribution of the application w.r.t. operational expenses.
For evaluation purposes we came up with a synthetic application profile $\mathcal{P}$ for
the Web Shop application to be used in the fifth step of the optimization process
discussed in the previous section. This profile, shown in Table 1, ensures that
alternative viable topologies hosted on different Cloud providers are comparable.
Furthermore, for reasons of completeness we also considered similar offerings to

Table 1. Web Shop Application Profile Parameters

Parameter		Value
h_τ	Hours of Usage	5,040
τ	Months of Usage	15
$n_{I/O}$	Number of I/O Ops	5,000
$d_{storage}$	Storage in GB	5,000
d_{egress}	Outgoing Traffic in GB	50,000
loc	Infrastructure Location	Europe

AWS EC2 and RDS provided by Windows Azure and Rackspace that we do not show explicitly in Fig. 2 but nevertheless include in the following discussion.

In terms of the proposed method, Fig. 2 already illustrates a μ-topology for the application containing offerings from only one cloud provider (AWS). Traversing the graph in the figure and generating viable topologies follows from the use of inheritance clan relation in the choice of e.g. Linux instead of Windows for the back end of the application. In order to limit the search space we define the constraint set $\mathcal{C} = \{c_{front}, c_{provider}\}$ where $c_{front} = IBM\_zSeries \in T^{(i)} \wedge \exists \text{path} \in T^{(i)} : WebShop\_FrontEnd \xrightarrow{*} IBM\_zSeries$, i.e. the application front end must be deployed on an IBM zSeries server, and $c_{provider} = (AWS\_EC2 \in T^{(i)} \vee AWS\_RDS \in T^{(i)}) \oplus (Azure\_VM \in T^{(i)} \vee Azure\_SQL \in T^{(i)}) \oplus \ldots$, i.e. cloud offerings only from one provider at a time are allowed to avoid latency between providers. The remaining viable topologies in $\mathcal{V}$ after applying the filter functions $\sigma^{front} \circ \sigma^{provider}$ for the offerings of the three cloud providers (AWS, Azure and Rackspace) are depicted in Table 2. For example, $T^{(1)}$ is the initial topology, $T^{(2)}$ is its variation that uses two smaller Amazon EC2 m1.medium instances, both with a different operating system, for a separate deployment of the Web Shop's back end and persistence tiers, etc.

The equivalent provider offerings that can be used, and the monetary cost projected for each $T^{(i)}$ for the application profile $\mathcal{P}$ is calculated by utilizing the Nefolog system [24]. For a given application usage profile and time interval, Nefolog provides cloud offerings matching and cost estimation capabilities as RESTful services. For the given application profile and viable topologies, we first used the *Offerings Matcher* service to identify a set of offerings from the two additional to AWS providers (Windows Azure and Rackspace) that are equivalent to the AWS offerings used in Fig. 1. We then invoked the *Cost Calculator* service for each of the identified offerings, and the results of the service invocation was stored in an $N \times M$ matrix, where N is the Cost Calculator operation query parameters (using the application profile in Table 1) and M the projected cost of each Cloud offering for each $T^{(i)}$ topology. The total cost of operational expenses $opex^{(i)}$ for each $T^{(i)}$ with application profile parameters from Table 1 is shown in Table 2.

By denoting with $opex_{max}$ the maximum calculated cost (\$154,134 for a Windows server and database solution in Rackspace for 15 months of use), choosing for utility function

$$u^{(i)}(h_\tau, \tau, n_{I/O}, d_{storage}, d_{egress}, loc) = opex_{max} - opex^{(i)}(h_\tau, \tau, \ldots)$$

(so that the utility function is monotonically decreasing with the cost) and by using the application profile in Table 1 it can be seen that:

$$r^{(9)} < r^{(8)} < r^{(7)} < r^{(6)} < r^{(3)} < r^{(5)} < r^{(1)} < r^{(2)} < r^{(4)} \Rightarrow$$
$$T^{(9)} < T^{(8)} < T^{(7)} < T^{(6)} < T^{(3)} < T^{(5)} < T^{(1)} < T^{(2)} < T^{(4)}$$

From this it can therefore be concluded that for the given application profile, the *optimal w.r.t. operational expenses distribution of the Web Shop application*

Table 2. Cost Analysis for a Subset of the Viable Topologies of the Web Shop Application

Topology	Provider	Cloud Offerings Used	Total Cost
$T^{(1)}$	AWS	Backend: *EC2 m1.large* (Windows) ProductDB: *in the same VM*	$77,037
$T^{(2)}$	AWS	Backend: *EC2 m1.medium* (Windows) ProductDB: *EC2 m1.medium* (Linux)	$75,942
$T^{(3)}$	AWS	Backend: *EC2 m1.medium* (Windows) ProductDB: *RDS db.m1.medium* (MySQL)	$84,904
$T^{(4)}$	Azure	Backend: *VM Large A3* (Windows) ProductDB: *in the same VM*	$75,504
$T^{(5)}$	Azure	Backend: *VM Medium A2* (Windows) ProductDB: *VM Medium A2* (Linux)	$84,504
$T^{(6)}$	Azure	Backend: *VM Medium A2* (Windows) ProductDB: *SQL ProductDB* (Microsoft SQL)	$86,139
$T^{(7)}$	Rackspace	Backend: *Cloud Server 8GB* (Windows) ProductDB: *in the same VM*	$96,351
$T^{(8)}$	Rackspace	Backend:*Cloud Server 4GB* (Linux) ProductDB: *Cloud Server 4GB* (Linux)	$105,432
$T^{(9)}$	Rackspace	Backend: *Cloud Server 4GB* (Windows) ProductDB: *Cloud Database 4GB* (MySQL)	$154,134

is represented by the viable topology $T^{(4)}$, i.e. using a single Windows Azure VM to host both the back end and persistence tier of the application. Looking only at topologies that are deployed on AWS offerings, it can also be seen that it is cheaper to distribute the application back end and persistence tier across two smaller VMs instead of a larger one. It is obvious from the above that elasticity is not considered in these results. Adding to the application profile the use of multiple VMs to cope with variation in demand would potentially result in a different ordering of the topologies. However, adding this capability to the presented framework is at this point in time future work.

6   Related Work

As discussed in the introductory section, decision support-oriented approaches like Kingfisher [21], CloudGenius [16], CloudAdoption [10] and MDSS [2] focus on assisting application designers in migrating their applications to the cloud. The main focus of these works is on optimal cloud offering selection for a given application that is essentially treated as a monolithic artifact. These approaches are therefore limited in their usefulness in light of multiple potential application topologies considering the distribution of the application across offerings.

The Cloud Blueprinting approach [19,20] defines a blueprint as an abstract description of cloud service offerings that facilitates the selection, customization and composition of cloud services into service-based applications. Blueprint templates allow the application developers to define the requirements of the application in terms of functional capabilities, QoS characteristics, and deployment and provisioning resources as target blueprints. In this respect, target blueprints are equivalent to α-topologies. However, the blueprinting approach is geared towards matching requirements with available solutions in a repository, having no equivalent concept to γ-topology, and lacking therefore the ability to generate viable topologies for an application.

The proposed approach shares a similarity with other existing works, in the sense that they use application topologies to optimize for a set of dimensions usually involving operational expenses. For example, the work in [18] presents DADL, a language to describe the architecture, behavior and needs of a distributed application to be deployed on the cloud, as well as describing available cloud offerings for matching purposes. Similarly, in [3], the authors propose an approach that matches and dynamically adapts the allocation of infrastructure resources to an application topology in order to ensure SLAs. CloudMig [8] is another approach that builds on an initial topology of the application that is adapted through model transformation in order to optimize the distribution of the application across cloud offerings. The optimization in this case also focuses on SLA compliance in a trade-off relation to operational expenses. The approach in [17] uses a Palladio-based application topology model in order to distribute an application across different cloud providers aiming at optimizing for availability and operational expenses.

Nevertheless, all of the above approaches assume that the application topology is already known (and fixed), and are restricted to VM-based IaaS solutions. Our approach takes into account also non-VM cloud offerings like DBaaS offerings, and allows for the dynamic generation of acceptable application topologies, which may also include alternative application stacks based on the richness of the γ-topology of the application. This observation also applies to the most relevant for our proposal work, the MOCCA framework [13] which also discusses the optimization of the application to cloud offerings based on introducing variability points in the application topology.

In terms of non-cloud scenarios, optimization of the application distribution has been discussed as part of various approaches like [11,14] and [15]. These approaches focus on performance engineering that is not discussed in the scope of this work, and in this sense they can be useful in extending the current work. However, it is necessary to evaluate first to which extend their underlying application topology models can be leveraged for cloud applications.

7 Conclusions

The previous sections motivated the need for moving away from the practice of thinking of applications as monolithic stacks to be deployed in one VM, either in the cloud or in in-house servers. Multi-tiered applications in particular can be seen as an aggregation of application-specific components, middleware solutions supporting these components, and of the underlying infrastructure in which they are being deployed and provisioned. The availability of cloud offerings beyond the VM-oriented IaaS solutions, and the proliferation of cloud services competing for market share create both opportunities and challenges for application engineers. Optimizing the distribution of an application across potentially multiple cloud offerings is therefore an important requirement for reaping the benefits of the cloud computing paradigm.

Toward this goal, in this work we proposed a theoretical framework that supports decision making in identifying the optimal application distribution. For this purpose we approached application topology models as typed graphs and leveraged existing work on introducing inheritance relationships between nodes in them. Using the concept of type graph with inheritance we introduced the concept of μ-topologies as an abstraction over two distincts parts of an application topology: α-topology, the application specific aspect of the model, and γ-topology, being reusable across different applications. We then showed how μ-topologies can be used to generate viable topologies as alternative deployment scenarios for the application, taking into account different types of cloud offerings. Based on this foundation we then proposed a generic definition of the optimization distribution problem as a mapping from the application topology domain to the set of real numbers, which allows for the (partial) ordering of alternative solutions and therefore simplifies the optimization.

One clear deficiency of the proposed approach is the ability to scale with the number of nodes in the μ-topology. Rich γ-topologies are of course necessary in order to be able to generate as many alternative solutions as possible, but the richer the γ-topology used is, the larger the space that needs to be searched through. Realizing the topology generation and selection algorithm discussed in Section 4.2, evaluating its complexity for real-world examples and dealing with potential scalability problems is in our immediate future plans.

For purposes of illustrative examples and evaluation throughout this work the focus was on operational expenses, and showing how the most cost-efficient application topology can be identified. Beyond offering the opportunity for concrete examples and easily verifiable results with publicly available information, this choice was also based on what is perceived to have driven the growth of cloud computing, i.e. cost reduction due to economies of scale on the provider side. However, the presented framework is not limited to optimization for operational expenses. As discussed in the previous section, there are a number of available performance engineering approaches that can be used to extend this work, e.g. [11,14,15]. To this goal, investigating the role of the workload of the application as reflected in its distribution across (topological) nodes is of interest for future work, as well as the effect of network latency between cloud offerings of the same and different providers (see also the discussion in [1] building on [9]). Finally, evaluating the impact of different scalability strategies, expanding on works like [21,22], is as mentioned in Section 5 an example of an additional optimization dimension to be introduced in future work.

Acknowledgment. This work is partially funded by the FP7 EU-FET project 600792 ALLOW Ensembles.

References

1. Andrikopoulos, V., Binz, T., Leymann, F., Strauch, S.: How to Adapt Applications for the Cloud Environment. Computing 95(6), 493–535 (2013)
2. Andrikopoulos, V., Song, Z., Leymann, F.: Supporting the migration of applications to the cloud through a decision support system. In: Proceedings of the 6th IEEE International Conference on Cloud Computing (CLOUD 2013), pp. 565–572. IEEE Computer Society (2013)
3. Antonescu, A.F., Robinson, P., Braun, T.: Dynamic topology orchestration for distributed cloud-based applications. In: Second Symposium on Network Cloud Computing and Applications (NCCA), pp. 116–123 (2012)
4. Armbrust, M., et al.: Above the Clouds: A Berkeley View of Cloud Computing. Tech. Rep. UCB/EECS-2009-28, EECS Department, University of California, Berkeley (2009)
5. Bardohl, R., Ehrig, H., De Lara, J., Runge, O., Taentzer, G., Weinhold, I.: Node type inheritance concept for typed graph transformation. Tech. Rep. 2003-19, TU Berlin (2003), http://citeseerx.ist.psu.edu/viewdoc/download?doi=10.1.1.4.9257&rep=rep1&type=pdf
6. Binz, T., Breitenbücher, U., Kopp, O., Leymann, F.: TOSCA: Portable Automated Deployment and Management of Cloud Applications. In: Advanced Web Services, pp. 527–549. Springer (2014)
7. Brandtzæg, E., Mohagheghi, P., Mosser, S.: Towards a domain-specific language to deploy applications in the clouds. In: The Third International Conference on Cloud Computing, GRIDs, and Virtualization, Cloud Computing 2012, pp. 213–218. IARIA (2012)
8. Frey, S., Hasselbring, W.: The cloudmig approach: Model-based migration of software systems to cloud-optimized applications. International Journal on Advances in Software 4(3 and 4), 342–353 (2011)
9. Gray, J.: Distributed Computing Economics. Queue 6(3), 63–68 (2008)
10. Khajeh-Hosseini, A., Greenwood, D., Smith, J.W., Sommerville, I.: The cloud adoption toolkit: supporting cloud adoption decisions in the enterprise. Software: Practice and Experience 42(4), 447–465 (2012)
11. Koziolek, A., Koziolek, H., Reussner, R.: Peropteryx: automated application of tactics in multi-objective software architecture optimization. In: Proceedings of the joint ACM SIGSOFT QoSA and ISARCS, pp. 33–42. ACM (2011)
12. de Lara, J., Bardohl, R., Ehrig, H., Ehrig, K., Prange, U., Taentzer, G.: Attributed graph transformation with node type inheritance. Theoretical Computer Science 376(3), 139–163 (2007)
13. Leymann, F., Fehling, C., Mietzner, R., Nowak, A., Dustdar, S.: Moving applications to the cloud: An approach based on application model enrichment. International Journal of Cooperative Information Systems 20(03), 307–356 (2011)
14. Malek, S., Medvidovic, N., Mikic-Rakic, M.: An extensible framework for improving a distributed software system's deployment architecture. IEEE Transactions on Software Engineering 38(1), 73–100 (2012)

15. Martens, A., Koziolek, H., Becker, S., Reussner, R.: Automatically improve software architecture models for performance, reliability, and cost using evolutionary algorithms. In: Proceedings of the First Joint WOSP/SIPEW International Conference on Performance Engineering, pp. 105–116. ACM (2010)

16. Menzel, M., Ranjan, R.: Cloudgenius: decision support for web server cloud migration. In: Proceedings of the 21st International Conference on World Wide Web, WWW 2012, pp. 979–988. ACM, New York (2012)

17. Miglierina, M., Gibilisco, G., Ardagna, D., Di Nitto, E.: Model based control for multi-cloud applications. In: 5th International Workshop on Modeling in Software Engineering (MiSE), pp. 37–43 (2013)

18. Mirkovic, J., Faber, T., Hsieh, P., Malaiyandisamy, G., Malaviya, R.: DADL: Distributed Application Description Language. Tech. Rep. ISI-TR-664, USC/ISI (2010), ftp://www.isi.edu/isi-pubs/tr-664.pdf

19. Nguyen, D.K., Lelli, F., Papazoglou, M.P., Van Den Heuvel, W.J.: Blueprinting approach in support of cloud computing. Future Internet 4(1), 322–346 (2012)

20. Papazoglou, M.P., van den Heuvel, W.: Blueprinting the cloud. Internet Computing 15(6), 74–79 (2011)

21. Sharma, U., Shenoy, P., Sahu, S., Shaikh, A.: Kingfisher: Cost-aware elasticity in the cloud. In: Proceedings of INFOCOM 2011, pp. 206–210. IEEE (2011)

22. Suleiman, B., Sakr, S., Jeffery, R., Liu, A.: On understanding the economics and elasticity challenges of deploying business applications on public cloud infrastructure. Journal of Internet Services and Applications, 1–21 (2011)

23. Walker, E.: The real cost of a cpu hour. Computer 42(4), 35–41 (2009)

24. Xiu, M., Andrikopoulos, V.: The Nefolog & MiDSuS Systems for Cloud Migration Support. Technical Report 2013/08, Universität Stuttgart, Fakultät Informatik, Elektrotechnik und Informationstechnik, Germany (November 2013), http://www2.informatik.uni-stuttgart.de/cgi-bin/ NCSTRL/NCSTRL_view.pl?id=TR-2013-08&engl=0

Identifying Modularity Improvement Opportunities in Goal-Oriented Requirements Models

Catarina Gralha, Miguel Goulão, and João Araújo

CITI, Departamento de Informática
Faculdade de Ciências e Tecnologia, Universidade Nova de Lisboa
Lisbon, Portugal
acg.almeida@campus.fct.unl.pt, {mgoul,joao.araujo}@fct.unl.pt

Abstract. Goal-oriented Requirements Engineering approaches have become popular in the Requirements Engineering community as they provide expressive model elements for requirements elicitation and analysis. However, as a common challenge, they are still struggling when it comes to managing the accidental complexity of their models. In this paper, we provide a set of metrics, which are formally specified and have tool support, to measure and analyze the complexity of goal models, in particular *i** models. The aim is to identify refactoring opportunities to improve the modularity of those models, and consequently reduce their complexity. We evaluate these metrics by applying them to a set of well-known case studies from industry and academia. Our results allow the identification of refactoring opportunities in the evaluated models.

Keywords: Goal-Oriented Requirements Models, *i**, software metrics, model assessment.

1 Introduction

Goal-oriented Requirements Engineering (GORE) has a great impact and importance in the Requirements Engineering community, helping in identifying, organizing, and structuring requirements, as well as in exploring and evaluating alternative solutions to a problem [1]. There are several GORE approaches, such as *i** [2], KAOS [3], and GRL [4]. When modelling real-world systems with a GORE approach, the models can quickly become very complex. A common challenge for the GORE approaches is to manage the complexity of their models. While real-world problems have an unavoidable essential complexity, we need to minimize, as much as possible, the accidental complexity introduced by the way we model those problems [5].

A possible way of minimizing the accidental complexity of a model is to improve its modularity. In particular, this can be achieved by identifying model refactoring opportunities. In this paper, we focus on the *i** framework, and how we can manage the accidental complexity of *i** models. In order to identify refactoring opportunities for these models, we define a metrics suite for assessing their complexity and the complexity of the elements defined in them. By collecting such metrics on several different models, we are able to establish a typical usage profile of the modelling mechanisms.

M. Jarke et al. (Eds.): CAiSE 2014, LNCS 8484, pp. 91–104, 2014.

In practice, this profile is built using descriptive statistics analysis on the metrics collected from different model elements. For example, the number of goals and tasks for a system agent may indicate whether this agent holds too many responsibilities in the system. This can hint the modeler for a refactoring opportunity where this agent should in fact be decomposed into several sub-agents.

The objective of this paper is to provide a metrics suite, along with the corresponding tool support, targeted to the measurement and analysis of the complexity of $i*$ models, with the goal of identifying refactoring opportunities to improve the modularity of those models. The identification of such opportunities can be useful during the development of the system, where a better modularization can lead to a sounder distribution of responsibilities among the system components. If performed in a timely fashion, this is likely to contribute to relevant costs savings through the reduction of the model's accidental complexity. Refactoring opportunities identification is also an asset in the context of preventive maintenance, as a facilitator for future requirements changes.

Our metrics suite is integrated in an eclipse-based $i*$ editor, so that metrics can be computed during the requirements modelling process, whenever the requirements engineer requests them. The metrics are defined using the Object Constraint Language (OCL) [6] upon the $i*$ metamodel. This makes our metrics set easily extensible, as improving the metrics set can be done by adding new OCL metrics definitions to the ones presented in this paper.

In [7], we proposed and validated a metrics suite for evaluating the completeness and complexity of KAOS goal models, formally specified (using OCL) and incorporated in a KAOS modelling tool. The metrics suite was evaluated with several real-world case studies. The work described in this paper shares a common approach to metrics definition and tool implementation. However, the goals and structure of the KAOS approach are significantly different from those of the $i*$ framework. In particular, $i*$ has a modularity mechanism – the actor's boundaries – which is not present in KAOS, that paves the way for a significantly different approach to modularity, by encapsulating model elements within the actors boundaries. This is reflected in the choice of relevant complexity metrics. Actor's boundaries are a key mechanism in the metrics suite proposed in this paper. Our goal is to use these metrics to leverage the modularity of $i*$ models.

This paper is organized as follows. Section 2 describes background information on the $i*$ framework. Section 3 describes the metrics set, defined using the Goal-Question-Metrics approach, and a concrete example of its application to a real-world model. Section 4 reports the evaluation process, including a presentation of the case studies used, the results obtained by applying the metrics on those case studies, and a discussion on the results. Section 5 discusses the related work. Section 6 draws some conclusions and points out directions for future work. While the paper is self-contained, additional information such as the complete $i*$ metamodel, the detailed specification of auxiliary metrics, and the fully detailed statistical analysis of the case studies presented in this paper can be found in this paper's companion site[1].

---

[1] http://ctp.di.fct.unl.pt/~mgoul/CAiSE2014Companion/

2   The *i** Approach

i* [2] was developed for modelling and reasoning about organizational environments and their information systems. It focuses on the concept of *intentional actor*. Actors in their organizational environment are viewed as having intentional properties such as *goals*, *beliefs*, *abilities* and *commitments*. *i** has two main modelling components: the *Strategic Dependency* (SD) model and the *Strategic Rationale* (SR) model. The SD model describes the dependency relationships among the actors in an organizational context. In this model, an actor (called *depender*) depends on another actor (called *dependee*) to achieve *goals* and *softgoals*, to perform *tasks* and to obtain *resources*. The SR model provides a more detailed level of modelling than the SD model, since it focuses on the modelling of intentional elements and relationships internal to actors. Intentional elements (*goals*, *softgoals*, *tasks* and *resources*) are related by *means-end* or *decomposition* links. *Means-end links* are used to link *goals* (ends) to *tasks* (means) in order to specify alternative ways to achieve goals. *Decomposition links* are used to decompose tasks. A task can be decomposed into four types of elements: a *subgoal*, a *subtask*, a *resource*, and/or a *softgoal*. Apart from these two links, there are the *contribution links*, which can be *positive* or *negative*.

In this work we are particularly interested in assessing the complexity of *i** models. To support this, we needed a flexible platform upon which we could define our metrics set. To the best of our knowledge, none of the existing *i** tools provides adequate support for a flexible definition of such metrics (detailed comparison of the existing *i** tool support can be found in [8, 9]). One of the important requirements of the tool was that it should be extensible, so that new metrics (which can potentially target different quality attributes) can be easily added. To fill this gap, we implemented an Eclipse-based *i** editor using Epsilon [10], EMF/GMF [11, 12] and Ecore Tools [13].

Figure 1 presents a fragment of the *i** metamodel implemented in our tool, showing only the concepts which will be used in the metrics definitions proposed in this paper. This metamodel is the basis for the tool support for the specification of *i** models, and their evaluation with model metrics. The root of the metamodel is the

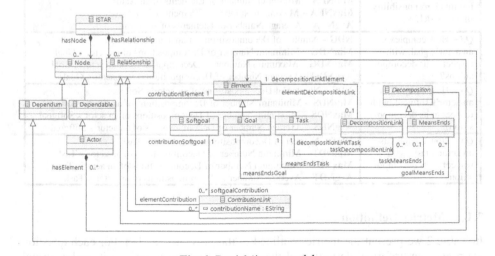

Fig. 1. Partial *i** metamodel

metaclass *ISTAR*, which contains all the nodes and relationships of an *i** model. This top-level metaclass serves as a basis for model analysis. The remaining metaclasses can be easily mapped into some of the concepts described earlier in this section.

3   A Metrics Set for *i** Complexity Evaluation

The purpose of this study is to evaluate the complexity of *i** models. We propose a metrics-based analysis framework for *i** models, using the Goal-Question-Metric (GQM) approach [14]. Table 1 summarizes the GQM-based proposal for a set of metrics that will allow satisfying the goal of *complexity evaluation*. The first column presents *questions* that will allow evaluating whether the overall goal is being achieved. The second column shows a set of *metrics* that provide quantitative information to answer the corresponding question. *Q1* concerns complexity, as perceived when regarding the model as a whole. In particular, we are interested in the number of actors, elements, and their ratio, within a model. The remaining questions are targeted to assessing the complexity of model elements, namely the amount of responsibilities supported by an actor (*Q2*), and the number of decompositions of actor's goals (*Q3*), softgoals (*Q4*) and tasks (*Q5*). For each of these elements-centered questions, we define a basic metric (e.g. *NEA*, for *Q2*) and three additional distribution metrics presenting the *minimum*, *maximum* and *average* values for the basic metric.

Table 1. Goal-Question Metric for *i** models evaluation

Goal: Complexity evaluation	
Question	**Metric**
Q1 – How complex is the model, concerning the number of actors and elements?	NAct – Number of Actors NElem – Number of Elements
Q2 – Does an actor have too much responsibility in the model?	NEA – Number of Elements of an Actor MinNEA – Minimum Number of Elements of an Actor MaxNEA – Maximum Number of Elements of an Actor AvgNEA – Average Number of Elements of an Actor
Q3 – How complex is an actor's goal, with respect to its decompositions?	NDG – Number of Decompositions of an actor's Goal MinNDG – Minimum Number of Decompositions of an actor's Goal MaxNDG – Maximum Number of Decompositions of an actor's Goal AvgNDG – Average Number of Decompositions of an actor's Goal
Q4 – How complex is an actor's softgoal, with respect to its decomposition?	NDS – Number of Decompositions of an actor's Softgoal MinNDS – Minimum Number of Decompositions of an actor's Softgoal MaxNDS – Maximum Number of Decompositions of an actor's Softgoal AvgNDS – Average Number of Decompositions of an actor's Softgoal
Q5 – How complex is an actor's task, with respect to its decompositions?	NDT – Number of Decompositions of an actor's Task MinNDT – Minimum Number of Decompositions of an actor's Task MaxNDT – Maximum Number of Decompositions of an actor's Task AvgNDT – Average Number of Decompositions of an actor's Task

3.1   Metrics Definition

In Table 2 we present the metrics outlined in the previous section. For each question we present an informal definition of the metrics specified to answer it, and a formal definition using OCL upon the metamodel fragment presented in figure 1. When required, we include pre-conditions in the formal definition. For example, when defining metrics to compute the average decomposition of *goals*, *softgoals*, or *tasks*, a typical pre-condition is to ensure that there are *goals*, *sofgoals*, or *tasks*, to be decomposed. Elements without decompositions may have been modeled in order to be final elements. It would not make sense analyzing the extent to which they are decomposed. For the sake of brevity, we omit trivial auxiliary metrics definitions with basic counts in the paper. The full metrics suite definition in OCL, including all auxiliary metrics, can be found in the paper's companion site.

Regarding question *Q1*, the values of *NAct* (number of actors) and *NElem* (number of elements) are measures for the SD/SR model size. Size can be used as a surrogate for overall model complexity, and used to compare the complexity among different models. For example, different candidate models for the same system can be compared, using these metrics, with respect to their overall complexity.

Concerning question *Q2*, a high value for *NEA* (number of elements of an actor) can be an indicator that a particular actor has too much responsibility. The *minimum*, *maximum* and *average* values help the requirements engineer recognizing cases where the responsibility is higher than expected. Complexity can also be used for supporting project estimation efforts.

Questions *Q3*, *Q4* and *Q5*, provide different perspectives on the complexity associated with a particular actor. The value of *NDG* (number of decompositions of an actor's goal), presented in *Q3*, measures the complexity of the *goal* decompositions associated with an *actor*. The value of *NDS* (number of decompositions of an actor's softgoal), presented in *Q4*, measures the complexity of the *softgoal* decompositions associated with an *actor*. Finally, the value of *NDT* (number of decompositions of an actor's task), presented in *Q5*, measures the complexity of the *task* decompositions associated with an *actor*. The *minimum*, *maximum* and *average* values for *NDG*, *NDS* and *NDT* help the requirements engineer identifying out of the ordinary *goal*, *softgoal*, or *task* decomposition complexities, respectively. Note that the minimum value is computed only for goals, softgoals, or tasks, which are decomposed. As such, it excludes leaf elements in its computation.

Table 2. Metrics to satisfy the complexity goal

Q1 – Is there a suitable number of actors and elements in the model?	
Name	**NAct** – Number of Actors
Informal definition	Number of actors in the SD/SR model
Formal definition	context ISTAR def:NAct():Integer = self.hasNode -> select (n : Node | n.oclIsKindOf(Actor)) -> size()
Name	**NElem** – Number of **Elements**
Informal definition	Number of elements in the SD/SR model
Formal definition	context ISTAR def:NElem():Integer = self.NEOAB() + self.NEIAB()
Requires	**NEOAB** – Number of Elements Outside Actors' Boundaries (see companion site) **NEIAB** – Number of Elements Inside Actors' Boundaries (see companion site)

Table 2. (*Continued.*)

Q2 – Does an actor have too much responsibility in the model?	
Name	**NEA** - Number of Elements of an Actor
Informal definition	Number of elements inside an actor's boundary in the SR model
Formal definition	context Actor def:NEA():Integer = self.hasElement -> select(e : Element I e.oclIsKindOf(Element)) -> size()
Name	**MinNEA – Min**imum Number of Elements of an Actor
Informal definition	Minimum number of elements inside an actor's boundary in the SR model

Formal definition	context ISTAR
	def:MinNEA():Integer = self.hasNode -> select(n : Node I n.oclIsKindOf(Actor)) ->
	    iterate(n : Node; min : Integer = -1 I let aux : Integer n.oclAsType(Actor).NEA() in
	        if min = -1 then aux else min.min(aux) endif)

Name	**MaxNEA – Max**imum Number of Elements of an Actor
Informal definition	Maximum number of elements inside an actor's boundary in the SR model

Formal definition	context ISTAR
	def:MaxNEA():Integer = self.hasNode -> select(n : Node I n.oclIsKindOf(Actor)) ->
	    iterate(n : Node; max : Integer = -1 I let aux : Integer = n.oclAsType(Actor).NEA() in
	        if max = -1 then aux else max.max(aux) endif)

Name	**AvgNEA – A**verage Number of Elements of an Actor
Informal definition	Average number of elements inside an actor's boundary in the SR model
Formal definition	context ISTAR pre:self.NAct() > 0 context ISTAR def:AvgNEA():Real = self.NEA() / self.NAct()
Requires	**NEA – Number of Elements of an Actor** **NAct – Number of Act**ors

Q3 – How complex is a goal, with respect to its decompositions?	
Name	**NDG – N**umber of **D**ecompositions of an actor's **G**oal
Informal definition	Number of decompositions associated with a goal in the SR model
Formal definition	context Goal def:NDG():Integer = self.goalMeansEnds -> select(me : MeansEnds I me.oclIsKindOf(MeansEnds)) -> size()
Name	**MinNDG – Min**imum **N**umber of **D**ecompositions of an actor's **G**oal
Informal definition	Minimum number of decompositions associated with a goal that is inside an actor's boundary in the SR model

Formal definition	context Actor
	def:MinNDG():Integer = self.hasElement ->
	    select(e : Element I e.oclIsKindOf(Goal) and e.oclAsType(Goal).NDG() > 0) ->
	        iterate(e : Element; min : Integer = -1 I let aux : Integer = e.oclAsType(Goal).NDG()
	    in
	            if min = -1 then aux else min.min(aux) endif)

Name	**MaxNDG – Max**imum **N**umber of **D**ecompositions of an actor's **G**oal
Informal definition	Maximum number of decompositions associated with a goal that is inside an actor's boundary in the SR model

Table 2. (*Continued.*)

Formal definition	context Actor
	def:MaxNDG():Integer = self.hasElement ->
	  select(e : Element | e.oclIsKindOf(Goal) and e.oclAsType(Goal).NDG() > 0) ->
	    iterate(e : Element; max : Integer = -1 | let aux : Integer = e.oclAsType(Goal).NDG()
	in
	      if max = -1 then aux else max.max(aux) endif)

Name	**AvgNDG – A**verage **N**umber of **D**ecompositions of an actor's **G**oal
Informal definition	Average number of decompositions associated with a goal that is inside an actor's boundary in the SR model
Formal definition	context Actor pre:self.NGWDI() > 0 context Actor def:AvgNDG():Real = self.NDG() / self.NGWDI()
Requires	**NDG – N**umber of **D**ecompositions of an actor's **G**oal **NGWDI – N**umber of **G**oals **W**ith **D**ecompositions **I**nside (see companion site)

Q4 – How complex is a softgoal, with respect to its decomposition?	
Name	**NDS – N**umber of **D**ecompositions of an actor's **S**oftgoal
Informal definition	Number of decompositions associated with a softgoal in the SR model
Formal definition	context Softgoal def:NDS():Integer = self.softgoalContribution -> select(cl : ContributionLink | cl.oclIsKindOf(ContributionLink)) -> size()
Name	**MinNDS – Min**imum **N**umber of **D**ecompositions of an actor's **S**oftgoal
Informal definition	Minimum number of decompositions associated with a softgoal that is inside an actor's boundary in the SR model

Formal definition	context Actor
	def:MinNDS():Integer = self.hasElement ->
	  select(e : Element | e.oclIsKindOf(Softgoal) and e.oclAsType(Softgoal).NDS() > 0) ->
	    iterate(e : Element; min : Integer = -1 | let aux : Integer =
	      e.oclAsType(Softgoal).NDS() in if min = -1 then aux else min.min(aux) endif)

Name	**MaxNDS – Max**imum **N**umber of **D**ecompositions of an actor's **S**oftgoal
Informal definition	Maximum number of decompositions associated with a softgoal that is inside an actor's boundary in the SR model

Formal definition	context Actor
	def:MaxNDS():Integer = self.hasElement ->
	  select(e : Element | e.oclIsKindOf(Softgoal) and e.oclAsType(Softgoal).NDS() > 0) ->
	    iterate(e : Element; max : Integer = -1 | let aux : Integer =
	      e.oclAsType(Softgoal).NDS() in if max = -1 then aux else max.max(aux) endif)

Name	**AvgNDS – A**verage **N**umber of **D**ecompositions of an actor's **S**oftgoal
Informal definition	Average number of decompositions associated with a softgoal that is inside an actor's boundary in the SR model
Formal definition	context Actor pre:self.NSWDI() > 0 context Actor def:AvgNDS():Real = self.NDS() / self.NSWDI()
Requires	**NDS – N**umber of **D**ecompositions of an actor's **S**oftgoal **NSWDI – N**umber of **S**oftgoals **W**ith **D**ecompositions **I**nside (see companion site)

Table 2. (*Continued.*)

Q5 – How complex is a task, with respect to its decompositions?	
Name	**NDT** – Number of Decompositions of an actor's Task
Informal definition	Number of decompositions associated with a task in the SR model
Formal definition	context Task def:NDT():Integer = self.taskDecompositionLink -> select(dl : DecompositionLink | dl.oclIsKindOf(DecompositionLink)) -> size()
Name	**MinNDT** – Minimum Number of Decompositions of an actor's Task
Informal definition	Minimum number of decompositions associated with a task that is inside an actor's boundary in the model

Formal definition	context Actor
	def:MinNDT():Integer = self.hasElement ->
	    select(e : Element | e.oclIsKindOf(Task) and e.oclAsType(Task).NDT() > 0) ->
	        iterate(e : Element; min : Integer = -1 | let aux : Integer = e.oclAsType(Task).NDT()
	in
	        if min = -1 then aux else min.min(aux) endif)

Name	**MaxNDT** – Maximum Number of Decompositions of an actor's Task
Informal definition	Maximum number of decompositions associated with a task that is inside an actor's boundary in the SR model

Formal definition	context Actor
	Def:MaxNDT():Integer = self.hasElement ->
	    select(e : Element | e.oclIsKindOf(Task) and e.oclAsType(Task).NDT() > 0) ->
	        iterate(e : Element; max : Integer = -1 | let aux : Integer = e.oclAsType(Task).NDT()
	in
	        if max = -1 then aux else max.max(aux) endif)

Name	**AvgNDT** – Average Number of Decompositions of an actor's Task
Informal definition	Average number of decompositions associated with a task that is inside an actor's boundary in the SR model
Formal definition	context Actor pre:self.NTWDI() > 0 context Actor def:AvgNDTI():Real = self.NDT() / self.NTWDI()
Requires	**NDT** – Number of Decompositions of an actor's Task **NTWDI** – Number of Tasks With Decompositions Inside (see companion site)

3.2   Example

Figure 2 shows a fragment of the Media Shop (MS) case study, whose main objective is to allow an online customer to examine the items in the Medi@ internet catalogue (books, newspapers, magazines, audio CD, videotapes, and the like) and place orders. The figure, taken from our tool, shows the actor Media Shop and some of its elements, as well as the model metrics.

The tool allows to create *i** models using a visual language and provides metrics values for the model. These values can be updated at any time of the construction process. As such, they can be valuable to detect potential problems early in the process, such as a high accidental complexity caused by a modelling option.

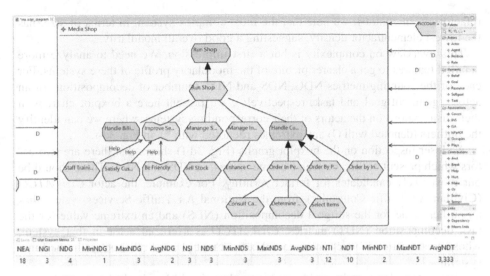

NEA	NGI	NDG	MinNDG	MaxNDG	AvgNDG	NSI	NDS	MinNDS	MaxNDS	AvgNDS	NTI	NDT	MinNDT	MaxNDT	AvgNDT
18	3	4	1	3	2	3	3	3	3	3	12	10	2	5	3,333

Fig. 2. Application of the tool and the metrics to the Media Shop case study

4   Evaluation

4.1   Case Studies

To evaluate the presented metrics, we modelled *i** case studies, namely Media Shop (MS) [15], Newspaper Office (NO) [16], Health Care (HC) [2], Health Protection Agency (HPA) [17] and National Air Traffic Services (NATS) [17] with our tool, and then collected the corresponding metrics. The case studies MS, NO, and HC have been extensively used in the literature, while HPA and NATS are real-world case studies, also available in the literature. They target different domains and have different essential complexities. A common characteristic of these models is that they are available with full details, making them good candidates for evaluation.

4.2   Results and Discussion

In this section we present the main findings from our statistics analysis of the collected metrics. The statistics data files and scripts for performing the statistics analysis outlined here can be found in the paper's companion site.

Concerning model size (*Q1,* Fig. 3a and Fig. 3b), the NATS (National Air Traffic Services) system has, approximately, twice the size of the second largest system (HPA, Health Protection Agency). The HC (Health Care) system has less actors, but more elements than the MS (Media Shop) and NO (Newspaper Office) systems, which have a very similar size. In fact, if we compute the elements to actors ratio (Fig. 3c), we note that HC has a higher ratio than all the other systems, which have very similar ratios. This may suggest that HC could be an interesting candidate for refactoring. In contrast, we note that the most complex system, in terms of size, has the lowest element/actor density, suggesting a good overall modularity.

This overview on complexity is but a first impression. We need to analyze more detailed features to get a clearer picture of the modularity profile of these systems. For each of the counting metrics NDG, NDS and NDT (number of decompositions of an actor's goal, softgoal and task, respectively), we present here a boxplot chart with their distributions on the actors of their corresponding systems, where we can identify the outliers (denoted with O) and extremes (denoted with *), in Fig. 3d-f.

A closer inspection on the boxplot graphs (Fig. 3d-f) shows that there are two actors which present outlier, or even extreme values, in NDS and NDT. These should be our most likely candidates for further scrutiny. For example, the actor *Civil ATCO* (Civilian Air Traffic Controller), from the National Air Traffic Services system, has an outlier value for the softgoal decomposition (NDS) and an extreme value for the task decomposition (NDT) metrics. *Civil ATCO* is a crucial actor in that system, whose specification is much more complex than that of most other actors in the same system.

There are at least two possible problems that should be checked, concerning the *Civil ATCO* actor's decomposition. A first potential problem is that this actor may have too many responsibilities. A typical refactoring would be to decompose the actor into *sub-actors*, using the *is-part-of* relationship, where each *sub-actor* would be responsible for a *sub-system*. This anti-pattern and its proposed refactoring are similar to god classes [18] and their refactoring, in object-oriented design. Note that, sometimes, the extra complexity is not of an accidental nature, but rather of an essential one. In such case, this analysis is still useful, in the sense that it highlights an actor in the system which has an extremely high essential complexity associated with it. This may hint project managers to assign more resources to quality assurance activities (e.g. inspections and testing) to artifacts related to the implementation of the requirements associated with this actor.

It may also be the case that the requirements engineer may over-decompose these goals, softgoals, or tasks, by following a functional decomposition strategy, leading to poor modularity. This is similar to the *functional decomposition* anti-pattern [18], where the encapsulation principle is neglected. Another consequence is that the abstraction level of the model lowers: including too many (design) details may obfuscate the requirements model, making it harder to understand and evolve. Abstracting away the unnecessary detailed decompositions can improve the overall modularity of the requirements model.

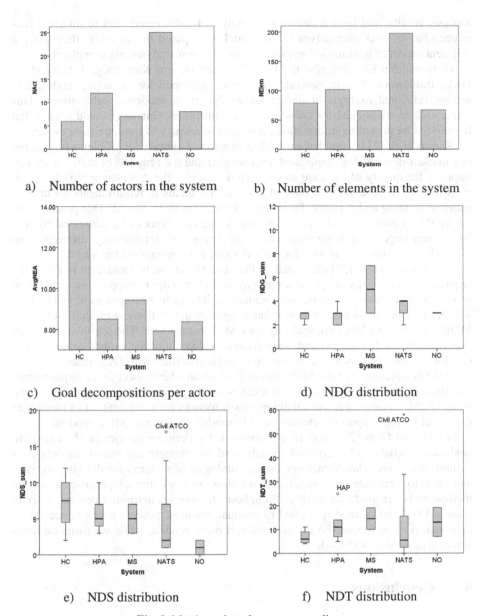

a) Number of actors in the system   b) Number of elements in the system

c) Goal decompositions per actor   d) NDG distribution

e) NDS distribution   f) NDT distribution

Fig. 3. Metrics values for our case studies

5   Related Work

Horkoff and Yu [19] evaluate seven goal satisfaction analysis procedures using available tools that implement those procedures. They evaluate three sample goal models. The results help to understand the ways in which procedural design choices affect analysis results, and how differences in analysis results could lead to different recommendations over alternatives in the model. Compared to our work, they study a different aspect of goal modelling, i.e. goal satisfaction analysis, not complexity.

Hilts and Yu [20] describe the Goal-Oriented Design Knowledge Library (GO-DKL) framework. This framework provides an approach for extracting, coding and storing relational excerpts of design knowledge from academic publications. This framework was designed for knowledge reuse purposes. Our work could extend that framework by providing information about the complexity of those existing models.

Ramos et al. [21] claim that early identification of syntactical problems (e.g., large and unclear descriptions, duplicated information) and the removal of their causes can improve the quality of use case models. They describe the AIRDoc approach, which aims to facilitate the identification of potential problems in requirements documents using refactoring and patterns. To evaluate use case models, the AIRDoc process uses the GQM approach to elaborate goals and define questions to be addressed by metrics. Their target quality attributes are reusability and maintainability, different from ours. Their metrics were neither formally defined nor implemented in a tool.

Vasconcelos et al. [22] claim that GORE and MDD can be integrated to fulfill the requirements of a software process maturity model in order to support the application of GORE methodologies in industry scenarios. The proposed approach, called GO-MDD, describes a six-stage process that integrates the i^* framework into a concrete MDD process (OO-Method), applying the CMMi perspective. The fourth stage of this process concerns the verification, analysis and evaluation of the models defined in the previous stages; and uses a set of measurements, specified with OCL rules, that evaluate the completeness of the MDD model generation with respect to the requirements specified in the i^* model. The set of metrics used in this stage is presented in [21], using GQM. Compared to ours, their approach focuses on a different set of metrics as their goal was to support the evaluation of i^* models to generate MDD models.

Franch and Grau [23] propose a framework for defining metrics in i^* models, to analyze the quality of individual models, and to compare alternative models over certain properties. This framework uses a catalogue of patterns for defining metrics, and OCL to formulate these metrics. In a follow up work, Franch proposes a generic method to better guide the analyst throughout the metrics definition process, over i^* models [24]. The method is applied to evaluate business process performance. Their approach is more focused on the process, and more generic, while we focus on modularity assessment of i^* models.

6   Conclusions

In this paper, we proposed a metrics suite for evaluating the complexity of i^* goal models, formally specified (using OCL), implemented and incorporated in an eclipse based modelling tool. The metrics were proposed using the GQM approach. The selected questions allow evaluating the complexity of the model as a whole concerning its size, and the complexity of an actor and its model elements (i.e. goals, softgoals and tasks). The set of metrics provide quantitative information to answer the corresponding questions. The contribution of this paper is that evaluating complexity at early stages to identify modularity problems of the models allows avoiding eventual extra costs in during the later stages of software development and also during software maintenance and evolution. The realization that the modularity of a requirements model can be improved can trigger requirements refactoring opportunities, like decomposing a system's actor using an is-part-of relationship between sub-actors, or abstracting over-decomposed goals, softgoals, or tasks. These metrics were validated by applying them to well-known industrial and academic case studies. The results of these metrics also reveal a pattern of usage in goal modelling concerning modularity of those models.

For future work, we intend to replicate this evaluation with other i^* models and extend the metrics set to cover other model quality attributes, such as correctness. The final aim is to provide a metrics-based modelling support in GORE tools. In particular, with an increased number of evaluated models, we will be able to, for example, identify thresholds for suggesting merging and/or decomposing model elements to reduce complexity of an i^* model. As a cross-validation for those thresholds, we plan to conduct an experiment with requirements engineers to assess the extent to which those thresholds are correlated with an increased difficulty in i^* model comprehension. We also plan to define and apply refactoring patterns for GORE models.

Acknowledgments. The authors would like to thank FCT/UNL and CITI – PEst-OE/EEI/UI0527/2011, for the financial support for this work.

References

1. Van Lamsweerde, A.: Goal-oriented requirements engineering: a guided tour. In: Proceedings Fifth IEEE International Symposium on Requirements Engineering, pp. 249–262. IEEE Comput. Soc. (2001)
2. Yu, E.: Modelling Strategic Relationships for Process Reengineering, PhD dissertation, University of Toronto, Canada (1995)
3. van Lamsweerde, A.: Requirements Engineering: From System Goals to UML Models to Software Specifications. Wiley (2009)
4. ITU-T: Recommendation Z.151 (10/12): User Requirements Notation (URN)–Language definition. , Geneva, Switzerland (2012)
5. Brooks, F.P.: The Mythical Man-Month: Essays on Software Engineering. Addison-Wesley Publishing Company, Reading (1995)
6. ISO/IEC JTC1, O.M.G.: Information technology - Object Management Group Object Constraint Language (OCL), ISO/IEC 19507 (2012)
7. Espada, P., Goulão, M., Araújo, J.: A Framework to Evaluate Complexity and Completeness of KAOS Goal Models. In: Salinesi, C., Norrie, M.C., Pastor, Ó. (eds.) CAiSE 2013. LNCS, vol. 7908, pp. 562–577. Springer, Heidelberg (2013)
8. Almeida, C., Goulão, M., Araújo, J.: A Systematic Comparison of i * Modelling Tools Based on Syntactic and Well-formedness Rules. In: Castro, J., Horkoff, J., Maiden, N., Yu, E. (eds.) 6th International i* Workshop (iStar 2013). CEUR, vol. 978, pp. 43–48. CEUR Workshop Proceedings (2013)
9. i* wiki, http://istarwiki.org/ (last access: March 2014)
10. Kolovos, D., Rose, L., García-Domínguez, A., Paige, R.: The Epsilon Book. Eclipse Foundation (2013)

11. Steinberg, D., Budinsky, F., Paternostro, M., Merks, E.: EMF: Eclipse Modeling Framework. Addison-Wesley Professional (2009)
12. Eclipse: GMF, http://www.eclipse.org/modeling/gmp/?project=gmf-tooling (last access: March 2014)
13. Eclipse: Ecore tools, http://wiki.eclipse.org/index.php/Ecore_Tools (last access: March 2014)
14. Basili, V.R., Caldiera, G., Rombach, H.D.: The goal question metric approach. Encyclopedia of Software Engineering 2, 528–532 (1994)
15. Castro, J., Kolp, M., Mylopoulos, J.: A Requirements-Driven Development Methodology. In: Dittrich, K.R., Geppert, A., Norrie, M. (eds.) CAiSE 2001. LNCS, vol. 2068, pp. 108–123. Springer, Heidelberg (2001)
16. Silva, C., Castro, J., Tedesco, P., Silva, I.: Describing Agent-Oriented Design Patterns in Tropos. In: Brazilian Symposium on Software Engineering (SBES 2005), pp. 10–25 (2005)
17. Lockerbie, J., Maiden, N.A.M., Engmann, J., Randall, D., Jones, S., Bush, D.: Exploring the impact of software requirements on system-wide goals: a method using satisfaction arguments and i* goal modelling. Requir. Eng. 17, 227–254 (2011)
18. Brown, W.J., Malveau, R.C., McCormick, H.W., Mowbray, T.J.: AntiPatterns: Refactoring Software, Architectures, and Projects in Crisis. Wiley (1998)
19. Horkoff, J., Yu, E.: Comparison and evaluation of goal-oriented satisfaction analysis techniques. Requir. Eng. 18, 199–222 (2012)
20. Hilts, A., Yu, E.: Design and evaluation of the goal-oriented design knowledge library framework. In: Proc. 2012 iConference (iConference 2012), pp. 384–391 (2012)
21. Ramos, R., Castro, J., Araújo, J., Moreira, A., Alencar, F., Santos, E., Penteado, R., Carlos, S., Paulo, S.: AIRDoc – An Approach to Improve Requirements Documents. In: Brazilian Symposium on Software Engineering, SBES 2008 (2008)
22. De Vasconcelos, A.M.L., de la Vara, J.L., Sanchez, J., Pastor, O.: Towards CMMI-compliant Business Process-Driven Requirements Engineering. In: Eighth Int. Conf. Qual. Inf. Commun. Technol (QUATIC 2012), pp.193–198 (2012)
23. Franch, X., Grau, G.: Towards a Catalogue of Patterns for Defining Metrics over i* Models. In: Bellahsène, Z., Léonard, M. (eds.) CAiSE 2008. LNCS, vol. 5074, pp. 197–212. Springer, Heidelberg (2008)
24. Franch, X.: A Method for the Definition of Metrics over i* Models. In: van Eck, P., Gordijn, J., Wieringa, R. (eds.) CAiSE 2009. LNCS, vol. 5565, pp. 201–215. Springer, Heidelberg (2009)

Understandability of Goal-Oriented Requirements Engineering Concepts for Enterprise Architects

Wilco Engelsman[1,2] and Roel Wieringa[2]

[1] BiZZdesign
w.engelsman@bizzdesign.nl
[2] University of Twente
r.j.wieringa@utwente.nl

Abstract. ArchiMate is a graphical language for modelling business goals and enterprise architecture. In previous work we identified possible understandability issues with the goal-oriented notations in ArchiMate. [**Problem**] We investigated how understandable the goal-oriented concepts really were in two quasi-experiments with practitioners. [**Principal ideas/results**] Only three concepts were understood by most or all subjects; the stakeholder concept, the goal concept and the requirement concept. The other concepts were misunderstood by most of our subjects. We offer explanations for these (mis)understandings. [**Contribution**] This paper provides new insights into the understandability and hence usability of goal-oriented concepts by practicing enterprise architects.

Keywords: GORE, ArchiMate, Evaluation.

1 Introduction

In large companies the gap between business and IT is usually bridged by designing and maintaining an enterprise architecture (EA). An enterprise architecture is a high-level representation of the enterprise, used for managing the relation between business and IT.

Large organizations must model their enterprise architectures in order to coordinate IT projects and the management of IT costs. In addition, in recent years EA is used to increase the flexibility of the organization and to justify the contribution of IT to business goals. This means that EAs need to be used not only to coordinate IT projects, but also for the following kinds of analysis:

- to determine the impact of changes in the business environment on the organizational goals and the EA,
- to determine the value of a certain architectural element and
- to assess which projects that implement the architecture have the most business value.

This requires an extension of EA modelling languages with concepts such as business goal and business value, and support for tracing business goals to EA

M. Jarke et al. (Eds.): CAiSE 2014, LNCS 8484, pp. 105–119, 2014.

components. In this paper, we empirically investigate such an extension on understandability.

The context of our work is the ArchiMate language for enterprise architecture modelling [27]. In previous work [9,23] we defined a set of goal-oriented concepts based on the concepts found in goal-oriented requirements engineering (GORE) and extended ArchiMate with these concepts. These goal-oriented extensions have been adopted in the Open Group standard for enterprise architecture modelling [27]. In subsequent work we provided initial empirical validation of the usability of this extension [10]. This validation showed that some users of the language experienced difficulty in understanding the extension to ArchiMate, and we proposed a simplification of the goal-oriented extension. In this paper, we present and analyze further data about understandability of goal-oriented concepts by enterprise architects, and we present explanations of the understandability issues. We present tentative generalizations about goal-oriented concepts in the context of enterprise architecture. We believe that the population of enterprise achitects have no difficulty in using the stakeholder, goal and requirement concept. Regarding the relations, the influence relation is the best understood relation. These findings should also be true for the languages we based the motivation extension of ArchiMate on, namely i*, Tropos, KAOS and GBRAM.

We start with listing the research questions in the next section. Next we describe our research methodology in section 3. We detail our conceptual framework in section 4. Section 5 presents our data and analyzes the implications of these data for goal-oriented requirements concepts. In section 6 we provide answers to our research questions. Section 7 discusses related work and in section 8 we discuss some implications for practice and for further research.

2   Research Problem

We want to know how understandable the goal-oriented requirements extension to an enterprise architecture language is for practicing enterprise architects. So our population of interest is the population of enterprise architects, and in our research we investigate a small sample of them, and we investigate the understandability of the goal-oriented extension of the ArchiMate language. At the end of the paper we discuss the generalizability of our results to the larger population of interest. Here we state our research questions:

Q1: How understandable is the motivation extension of ArchiMate by enterprise architects?
Q2: Which concepts are understood correctly? Why?
Q3: Which concepts are not understood? Why?
Q4: What kind of mistakes are made? Why?

We will define the concept of understandability, used in Q1, as the percentage of language users who understand the concept correctly. Q2 and Q3 ask which concepts are understood by all users or misunderstood by at least some users, respectively. For the concepts that are misunderstood, Q4 asks what kinds of mistakes are made.

In all cases, we want to know not only an answer to the journalistic question what is the case, but also the research question why it is the case.

3   Research Methodology

In terms of design research methodology, our empirical study is an evaluation of a technology implemented in practice, namely ArchiMate [29]. However, Archi-Mate (version 2.0) has only recently been implemented and although it is used, it has not been used long enough on a large scale to make an evaluation by survey possible. Moreover, although surveys may reveal large-scale trends, they are inadequate at providing the detailed data about understandability that we need.

Our data comes from two groups of practitioners who followed a course on ArchiMate. Their homework provided the material we needed to assess understandability of goal-oriented concepts to enterprise architects, and to answer our research question above. The first group had 7 participants, and the second group had 12 participants. Their homework was an excercise based on an actual problem within the organization. These were real requirements engineering or EA design problems and therefore a fair representation of the difficulty level.

The participants of the two groups self-selected into the course, and so they may be more motivated or more talented than the "average" enterprise architect. They were also highly motivated to pass the course, since they were sent by their employer. They had to pass their homework exercises in order to get a certificate. Not passing the exam would have relfected badly on the subject and weakened their position in the organization.This would make understandability problems all the more telling.

All participants had at least 5 years of experience as an enterprise architect (or a similar role) and all had at least a bachelors degree (not necessarily in computer science or software engineering). The median experience is based on the linkedin profiles of the subjects. They have had some modelling experience, since this is common in their role of architect or business analyst. Since we did not do random sampling, and the groups are too small for statistical inference anyway, we cannot draw any statistical inferences from our results. We can only give descriptive statistics of our sample, but not draw statistical conclusions about the population of enterprise architects.

A controlled experiment would have given us more flexibility, but this is beyond our budget to do such an experiment with practitioners (i.e. we would have to pay them commercial fees).

However, because we have detailed data from the homework done by the participants, we will analyze possible causes for (mis)understanding goal-oriented concepts in ArchiMate, and then consider whether these explanations provide a reason for expecting (mis)understanding of goal-oriented concepts to occur outside our sample in a similar way that it happened in our sample. We will also compare our results with those in the published literature to see if results similar to ours have been found in other studies too, which would strengthen the plausibility of generalizations.

The first author (Engelsman) has been a teacher in the first but not in the second course. On both courses, he did the correcting of student assignments. The assignments were relatively small compared to real-world enterprise architecture concepts. That reduces the generalizability of our results, but in a useful direction: We expect that in larger, real-world projects, understandability problems would increase, not decrease compared to what we have observed in our courses. This is useful because our findings provide suggestions for improvement of teaching and using goal-oriented concepts in enterprise architecture in practice.

The first author was involved in the definition of GORE concepts in Archi-Mate. Correction was done twice, and we assume that few mistakes in correcting the assignments have been made. A sample of the corrections of the student exercises have been discussed between the two authors of this paper, and no mistakes were found. However, later we will see that even if we would increase or decrease the percentages (in)correct in the gradings with as much as 10 points, this would not change our explanations and qualitative generalizations.

4   Defining Understandability

Many authors operationalize understandability in terms of the time needed to understand a model [8,12] or the number of mistakes made in answers to questions about a model [16,21,22,25]. Houy et al. [14] surveyed these definitions of model understandability and classified them in five types:

- Recalling model content. Subjects are given a model, and are given time to study the model. Afterwards they have to recall how the model looked like.
- Correctly answering question about model content. Subjects are given a model and are given time to study the model. Afterwards they are presented with a questionnaire and have to answer questions about the information in the model (e.g. the constructs used in a model).
- Problem solving based on the model content. Subjects are given a model to analyze, and are asked to solve problems (answer questions) based on this model. For example, if the model were a route for a bus, they were asked questions about the route of the bus.
- Verification of model content. Subjects are given a model and a textual description. They have to answer questions regarding the correctness of the model content based on the problem description.
- Time needed to understand the model. Subjects are given a model to study. The time needed to answer questions about the model is measured.

Another interesting approach to measuring understandability, not mentioned by Houy et al., is that of Caire et al. [5], who measured the ability of subjects to guess the definition of an i* construct by looking at the icons.

All of these measures indicate a passive form of understanding because they concern the understanding of a given model. We are however interested in a more active kind of understanding of a modeling language, this is needed when an analyst uses the language to build models. Such an active concept of understanding is used by, for example, Carvallo & Franch [6] and by Matulevičius

& Heymans [17], who measured the number of mistakes made in constructing i* models, and by Abrahao et al., who measured the time needed to build a model [1].

We define the understandability of a concept for a set of language users in this paper as the percentage of language users who, whenever they use the concept when building a model, use it correctly. Understandability is thus relative to a set of language users. In this paper we measure the understandability of goal-oriented concepts in ArchiMate 2.0 in a sample of 19 language users. From our observations, we draw conclusions about understandability of ArchiMate in general, and of goal-oriented concepts in general, for enterprise architects.

5 Data Analysis

Table 1 summarizes the scores that the 19 enterprise architects received on their homework. The numbers are the percentage of correctly used concepts by each subject. When a subject did not use a concept at all, the corresponding cell contains "na". Subject 1-7 are the subjects from 2011 and subject 8 - 19 are the subjects from 2012. The avg column shows the percentage of users that always uses the concept correctly. Looking at this column we see that only four concepts were used correctly by at least half of the subjects: the concepts of stakeholder, goal, requirement and influence. We now discuss our findings in detail.

Table 1. Understandability of goal-oriented concepts in ArchiMate by a sample of 19 practitioners. Row i column j shows the percentage of times that practitioner i used concept j correctly.

Practitioner	1	2	3	4	5	6	7	8	9	10	11	12	13	14	15	16	17	18	19	avg
Stakeholder	100	100	100	100	100	100	100	100	100	100	100	100	100	100	100	100	100	100	100	100
Driver	66,6	100	100	100	77	na	69	50	38	100	55	100	100	100	69	33	100	85	100	47
Assessment	25	8,3	100	44	100	na	13	50	100	100	100	71	100	100	83	90	100	97	100	47
Goal	94	82	100	95	100	92	98	100	100	50	100	100	100	100	100	100	100	100	100	68
Requirement	100	100	100	75	100	na	100	100	0	80	100	91	62	100	100	100	100	95	85	57
Decomposition	0	na	na	100	100	83	24	na	62	na	100	100	100	50	na	na	79	57	15	26
Influence	100	50	na	100	100	100	100	na	100	na	100	100	100	100	100	100	100	100	100	79
Realization	100	100	100	100	100	100	100	100	100	100	100	100	100	100	100	100	100	100	100	100

5.1 Description of Model Complexity

In total the 19 subjects constructed 246 diagrams and on average the models contained 9 concepts. However, complexity of the models varied. Some diagrams contained as little as 2 concepts, and others contained 35 concepts. Not every diagram contained every concept. This is because ArchiMate uses views to reduce model complexity. There are roughly three kind of views. The first is a stakeholder view, showing the stakeholders, drivers, assessment and initial goals. The second is a goal refinement view showing the modeling of goals, goal influence, goal decomposition and goal realization through requirements. The third view shows the realization of requirements by architecture components. Figure 1

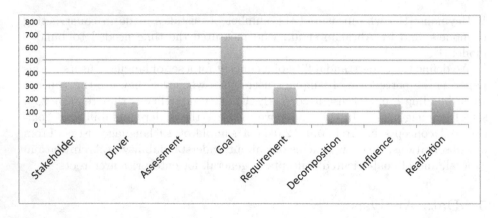

Fig. 1. Frequency of use of goal-oriented concepts in 246 EA models

shows the frequency with which different concepts were used. The most frequently used concepts are those of goal, stakeholder and assessment. We have included an median sized model in the appendix A. This is an actual (translated) model constructed by one of the subjects. It contains more than nine concepts, but that is just an average. The example illustrates the size of the models.

5.2   Analysis of GORE Concepts and Relations in ArchiMate

Stakeholder. The first concept under analysis is the stakeholder concept. This concept is based on definitions from TOGAF, i* and Tropos. TOGAF defines a *stakeholder* as an individual, team, or organization (or classes thereof) with interests in, or concerns relative to, the outcome of the architecture [26]. This seems more general than the definition of actor in i* and Tropos as entities with intentional properties such as goals, beliefs, abilities, and commitments [30]. The motivation extension of ArchiMate adopted the more general definition of TOGAF [9,27].

In our experiments the stakeholder concept was perfectly understood by every student. There was not a single mistake made in all instances of use. This can be explained by the fact that the TOGAF stakeholder concept is a well known concept by the subjects. Its definition is very clear, and it is substantially different than the other concepts used in the motivation extension, so that it is not easy to confuse the stakeholder concept with any other concept. For these reasons we think this finding will generalize to other ArchiMate users too. To the extent that the concept of actor in i* and Tropos coincides with that of TOGAF stakeholder, we expect that users of i* and Tropos will find the actor concept unproblematic too, and to be able to use it without mistakes.

Driver. The driver concept is not found in the GORE literature, but used in the EA literature. TOGAF defines driver as the key interests that are crucially important to the stakeholders in the system, and determines the acceptability of the system [26]. The motivation extension of ArchiMate adopted this definition [9, 27]. In our experiments only nine subjects (47%) understood the driver concept correctly. The most common mistake made with driver was that it was used as a goal. For example, subjects modeled the goal 'to improve Financial Information' as a driver. But the driver corresponding to this goal is the key interest 'Financial Information'. Apparently the definition of driver is not very clear, and it is so close to the concept of a goal that it generates more confusion than clarity. We see no reason why this would not confuse other practicing enterprise architects, so we think that this finding will generalize to other ArchiMate 2.0 users as well.

Assessment. The concept of an assessment too is based on definitions found in the EA literature. The Business Motivation Model (BMM) defines an assessment as a judgment about some influencer that affects the organization's ability to employ its means or achieve its end [4]. The motivation extension of ArchiMate attempted to make this more concrete by defining an assessment as the *outcome of the analysis of some stakeholder concern* [9, 27]. In our experiments nine subjects used the concept perfectly. The most common mistake was that the assessment concept was used as a goal. For example, correct use of an assessment would be 'the financial information is incorrect'. This is a possible outcome of an analysis of the key stakeholder interest 'financial information'. However the subjects used the concept often to denote a goal like 'improve financial information', just as we saw with the driver concept above. The distinctions between a key interest, an analysis of a key interest, the outcome of the analysis, and the goal motivated by this outcome, were lost on most of our subjects. Moreover, the outcome of an analysis of a key interest can indeed be to 'improve something'. For these reasons we think this confusion will be present in other enterprise architects who use ArchiMate, as well as in users of the assessment concept in BMM.

Goal. The ArchiMate definition of goal is based on a combination of the EA literature and the GORE literature. KAOS defines goals as desired system properties that have been expressed by some stakeholder(s) [28]. This seems more technical and solution oriented than the i* and Tropos concepts of a goal as the intentions of a stakeholder i* [30]. BMM defines goal as a state or condition of the enterprise to be brought about or sustained through appropriate means BMM [4]. ArchiMate defines goal as *some end that a stakeholder wants to achieve* [9, 27]. In our experiments 13 subjects understood the goal concept perfectly. The most common mistakes made were that a goal was either used as a driver or as a requirement. For example, the subjects would write down 'financial information' as a goal, but it should actually be something like 'improve financial information'. When it was used as a requirement, it was written down as 'the system should have 100% availability'. We can reuse our explanation that the distinction between driver, goal and requirement were lost by the subject in that instance. The concept of goal can therefore be understood and used by practicing enterprise architects, but mistakes are made too. Since the

ArchiMate concept of a goal is similar to that in KAOS, i* Tropos and the BMM we expect that this will happen in users of those languages too. This calls for clearer guidelines in the application of the goal concept.

Requirement. We based our definition of the requirements concept on the GORE literature. In KAOS a requirement is a goal assigned to an agent of the software being studied [28]. In GBRAM a requirement specifies how a goal should be accomplished by a proposed system [2]. The ArchiMate motivation extension defines requirement as *some end that must be realized by a single component of the architecture* [9, 27]. In our experiments in total 11 subjects (57%) perfectly understood the concept. In general the requirement concept was reasonably well understood. This can be explained by the fact that it is a well known concept already known in practice by the subjects.

However, there were quite a large number of mistakes. Many subjects specified requirements that were goals not yet allocated to a system. For example, instead of the 'the system should have a financial reports function', they specified the goal 'improve financial reports'. We see again that semantically close concepts are confused by practitioners, even though the definitions of the concepts are clear. We expect this confusion to be present in other users of ArchiMate as well.

The decomposition relation. ArchiMate 2.0 based this relation on a combination of concepts from the EA and GORE literature. i* defines a decomposition as an element that is linked to its component nodes. [30]. BMM uses a similar definition, but it is more aimed at goals. BMM defines decomposition as an end that includes an other end BMM [4]. In Tropos, a parent goal is satisficed if all of its chlidren goals are satisficed [3]. In KAOS the conjunction of all the subgoals must be a sufficient condition entailing the goal KAOS [28].

The motivation extension of ArchiMate defines decomposition as a *some intention that is divided into multiple intention.* [9, 27]. This was understood correctly by only five subjects (26%). When the decomposition relation was used incorrectly, it was used as a influence relation, which in ArchiMate is defined as a contribution relation. For example, correct decomposition of the goal 'improve correctness financial information' should be 'improve correctness financial information regarding outstanding debt AND improve correctness financial information sales'. This decomposes a goal into more detailed goals. However, many subjects decomposed the goal 'improve correctness financial information' into the component goal 'acquire a financial reports system that records sales information'. But this is an influencer, i.e. a new goal that contributes to the original goal. The confusion is probably caused by the fact that satisfaction of an influencer increases the satisfaction of the influenced goal, just as satisfaction of the components increases the satisfaction of the composite goal. Based on this analysis we expect other users of ArchiMate to have similar problems.

The influence relation. In i* a contribution is a link of elements to a soft goal to analyze its contribution [30]. Tropos defines contribution analysis as goals that can contribute positively or negatively in the fulfillment of the goal to be analyzed [3]. ArchiMate defines this as a goal G1 contributes to another goal G2 if satisfaction of G1 influences the satisfaction of G2 positively or negatively [9, 27]. The influence relation was understood correctly by 15 subjects (79%). In the cases were the relation was not used correctly, the subjects linked requirements with goals on a 1 on 1 basis, which amounted to stated the same goal twice. Others used a standard ArchiMate association relation where they should have used an influence relation. To further reduce the misunderstandings of the influence relation, better guidelines must be found.

The realization relation. This relation is based on relations found in the GORE literature. i* defines a means-end relation, which is a relation between an end and a means [30]. KAOS defines a relation for linking requirements to operations [28]. The ArchiMate motivation extension defines the realization relation as a relation that some end that is realized by some means [9, 27]. All subjects used the realization relation correctly. This can be easily explained by the fact that the support tool only allows connecting a requirement to a goal and an architecture element to a requirement so that the relation cannot be used incorrectly. 100% correct use therefore has no implication for (mis)understanding of the concept by tool users.

6   Answers to Research Questions

Q1: How understandable is the motivation extension of ArchiMate by enterprise architects? As shown by the last column of table 1, not all of the motivation extension is understood very clearly.

Q2: Which concepts are understood correctly? Why? Only the stakeholder, goal, requirement concepts and the influence relation were understood by the majority (scoring more than 55%). However the requirement concept was a borderline case where a lot of mistakes were made. Our explanation of this level of understanding is that they are well known concepts already used in practice, and that they have a semantic distance that prevents confusion. However, the distance between requirement and goal is smaller than the other concepts and immediately we saw an a drop in understandability.

Q3: Which concepts are not understood? Why? The concepts of driver, assessment and decomposition were not very well understood. They were often confused with other concepts, such as that of a goal. Our explanation is that drivers, assessments and goals are very closely related and may even overlap, and that the definition of the decomposition relation overlaps with the definition of the influence relation.

Q4: What kind of mistakes are made? Why? The subjects made two types of mistakes. Drivers and assessments were modelled as goals. A driver is related to a stakeholder and an interest area of the stakeholder. A goal is a statement of desire about this interest area. This makes goals and drivers conceptually very close and created confusion in our subjects.

The same is true for the assessment concept. An assessment is the outcome of some analysis. It is not defined what this outcome should be. It can very well be a goal or something else, which is confusing again. The use of the requirement concept to model a goal is similar. Because both concepts are closely related, the difference between desired functionality from the viewpoint of a stakeholder is very much similar to the stated functional need of a system. The only difference is the perspective.

The second type of mistake is that an influence relation was expressed by means of a decomposition relation. Again, the definitions turn out to be too close to each other for many of our subjects.

7 Related Work

The Business Rules Group has published a model that relates business goals and elements found in EA, called the business motivation model [4], which is now an OMG standard. The difference with ArchiMate is that the BMM provides no concrete modelling notations. It provides plans and guidelines for developing and managening business plans in an organized manner, all related to enterprise architecture.

Clements & Bass extend software architecture modelling with GORE, but remove all notational conventions of GORE techniques and return to a classic bulleted list of possible goals and stakeholders [7]. This makes goal-oriented modelling usable for requirements and architecture engineering workshops with practitioners, but does not help to support the kinds of analysis that we mentioned earlier in the introduction.

Stirna et al. describe an approach to enterprise modelling that includes linking goals to enterprise models [24]. However they do not describe concrete modelling notations that are needed to extend existing EA modelling techniques. Jureta and Faulkner [15] sketch a goal-oriented language that links goals and a number of other intentional structures to actors, but not to EA models. Horkhoff and Yu present a method to evaluate the achievement of goals by enterprise models, all represented in i* [13].

An important obstacle to applying GORE to real-world problems is the complexity of the notation. Moody et al. [20] identified improvements for i* and validated the constructs of i* in practice , based on Moody's theory of nottions [18].

Caire et al. [5] also investigated the understandability of i*. They focussed on the ease of understanding of a concept by infering its definition by its visual representation. They had novices design a new icon set for i* and validated these icons in a new case study. This contrasts with our work because they focus on notations and we focus on concepts.

Carvallo & Franch [6] provided an experience report about the use of i* in architecting hybrid systems. They concluded that i* could be used for this purpose for stakeholders and modellers, provided that i* was simplied. Our work extends on these findings. We also found out that related concepts are hard to distinguish (i.e the distinction between driver,assessment,goal, the distinction between requirement and goal and the distinction between decomposition and influence).

Matulevičius & Heymans [17] compared i* and KAOS to determine which language was more understandable. The relevant conclusions for this work were that the GORE languages had ill defined constructs and were there hard to use, GORE languages also lacked methodological guidelines to assist users in using the languages. These conclusions were also found in our work.

Another contrast is that most of the empirical studies of the usability of GORE languages have been done with students, while we do our empirical studies with practitioners.

8   Discussion

8.1   Generalizability

To which extent are our results generalizable beyond our sample of practitioners? In our experiments every subject had at least five years experience, the minimal of a bachelors degree. Enterprise architects usually have the same educational background as our subjects. Our subjects were responsible for translating business strategy and business goals into requirements models and they had to design an enterprise architecture based on these requirements. This is similar to the tasks enterprise architects have to perform in general.

Moreover, the results from this study match with our previous research. In our previous work [10] we reported about a real-world project in which practicing enterprise architects used ArchiMate to redefine an enterprise architecture and link it to changed business objectives. They used the stakeholder and goal concepts as intended. They had some trouble understanding the requirement concept and often formulated requirements as if they were business goals. We also saw that the subjects had a difficult time to see the difference between goals and drivers. The driver concept was too general to use for the subjects. The same was true for the distinction between driver, goal and assessment. Those finding and their explanations agree with the ones reported about in this paper.

All of this justifies the claim that other enterprise architects may understand and misunderstand goal-oriented ArchiMate concepts in the same way as our subjects did. This is a weak generalization, as it says "this can happen more often" without giving any quantification how often it could happen [11]. But such a quantification is not needed to draw some implications for practice, as we do below.

Because the goal-oriented concepts that we used have been taken from other existing goal-oriented languages, we hypothesize that our conclusions may be generalized to those languages too. Again, we cannot quantify this beyond the weak claim that this may happen in those languages too. But we do claim that our findings are sufficiently generalizable to motivate similar research for those languages.

8.2   Validity

Construct validity is the extent to which theoretical constructs are applied and measured correctly in our study. The only theoretical construct that we use is that of understandability, and we defined it in section 4. Our definition agrees with that used by other authors [6, 17] but with that of all other authors. Our definition refers to the number of mistakes made when building models, and not the the amount of time (indicator of effort) required to build the models. Other definitions refer to the number of mistakes or the amount of time needed to answer questions about the models. Comparison of our results with that of studies that use another definition of understandability should be done with caution.

Internal validity is the support for our causal explanations of the phenomena. Could subjects have misunderstood some concepts for other reasons than the ones we hypothesize? For example because they lack competence or because they were explained badly in the training? We cannot exclude these other explanations, but find them less plausible because all subjects had similar background and experience, and because the teachers similarly have several years of experience teaching these concepts. And even if these explanations were true for some subjects, this would not invalidate our explanation in terms of semantic closeness of concepts.

External validity is the support for generalization from our quasi-experiment. Because our explanations do not refer to particular properties of our sample but are stated in terms of the language itself, and because other practitioners are relevantly similar in background and experience to those in our sample, we think our conclusions are generalizable. But we do not claim that they are generalizable to the entire population of practicing enterprise architects, nor to all other goal-oriented languages.

8.3   Implications for Practice

ArchiMate 2.0 is now an Open Group standard, and the concepts we investigated in this paper will remain present in the language. However, one practical implication of this paper is that in future training programs we will not teach all concepts anymore. We will make a distinction between the recommended minimal concepts and less important concepts. We will recommend that future users of the language at least should use the stakeholder concept, the goal concept and the requirement concepts.

A second implication is that we need more practically usable guidelines for the use of the concepts that we do recommend, because other than the goal and realization concepts, we expect that many practitioners will misunderstand and incorrectly apply the basic concepts of goal and requirement and the relations of influence and decomposition. This is a topic for future research.

8.4   Future Research

In addition to work on the guidelines mentioned above, we intend to combine our work with the results of usability and understandability of notations done by Moody [18,19], Caire [5] and Heymans [17]. The focus of Moody and Caire was on the understandability of the notation. Heymans focussed more on the conceptual use of GORE concepts. If we combine their work with ours we will improve understandability the conceptual and notational level. This could lead to more clearly defined and usable GORE languages.

We also intend to investigate the utility of goal-oriented concepts in ArchiMate as well. They have been added in order to facilitate traceability between business goals and enterprise architecture. Are they actually used this way in practice? We plan to do additional surveys and experiments with practicing enterprise architects to investigate this.

References

1. Abrahão, S., Insfran, E., Carsí, J.A., Genero, M.: Evaluating requirements modeling methods based on user perceptions: A family of experiments. Information Sciences 181(16), 3356–3378 (2011)
2. Anton, A.I.: Goal-based requirements analysis. In: Proceedings of the Second International Conference on Requirements Engineering, pp. 136–144. IEEE (1996)
3. Bresciani, P., Perini, A., Giorgini, P., Giunchiglia, F., Mylopoulos, J.: Tropos: An agent-oriented software development methodology. Autonomous Agents and Multi-Agent Systems 8(3), 203–236 (2004)
4. Business Motivation Model: Business motivation model version 1.0. Standard document (2007), http://www.omg.org/spec/BMM/1.0/PDF (September 22, 2009)
5. Caire, P., Genon, N., Moody, D., et al.: Visual notation design 2.0: Towards user-comprehensible re notations. In: Proceedings of the 21st IEEE International Requirements Engineering Conference (2013)
6. Carvallo, J.P., Franch, X.: On the use of i^* for architecting hybrid systems: A method and an evaluation report. In: Persson, A., Stirna, J. (eds.) PoEM 2009. LNBIP, vol. 39, pp. 38–53. Springer, Heidelberg (2009)
7. Clements, P., Bass, L.: Using Business Goals to Inform a Software Architecture. In: 18th IEEE International Requirements Engineering Conference, pp. 69–78. IEEE Computer Society Press (2010)
8. Cruz-Lemus, J.A., Genero, M., Manso, M.E., Morasca, S., Piattini, M.: Assessing the understandability of UML statechart diagrams with composite states: A family of empirical studies. Empirical Software Engineering 14(6), 685–719 (2009)
9. Engelsman, W., Quartel, D.A.C., Jonkers, H., van Sinderen, M.J.: Extending enterprise architecture modelling with business goals and requirements. Enterprise Information Systems 5(1), 9–36 (2011)
10. Engelsman, W., Wieringa, R.: Goal-oriented requirements engineering and enterprise architecture: Two case studies and some lessons learned. In: Regnell, B., Damian, D. (eds.) REFSQ 2011. LNCS, vol. 7195, pp. 306–320. Springer, Heidelberg (2012)
11. Ghaisas, S., Rose, P., Daneva, M., Sikkel, K.: Generalizing by similarity: Lessons learnt from industrial case studies. In: 1st International Workshop on Conducting Empirical Studies in Industry (CESI), pp. 37–42. IEEE Computer Society Press (2013)

12. Hadar, I., Reinhartz-Berger, I., Kuflik, T., Perini, A., Ricca, F., Susi, A.: Comparing the comprehensibility of requirement models expressed in use case and Tropos: Results from a family of experiments. Information and Software Technology (2013)
13. Horkoff, J., Yu, E.: Evaluating goal achievement in enterprise modeling – an interactive procedure and experiences. In: Persson, A., Stirna, J. (eds.) PoEM 2009. LNBIP, vol. 39, pp. 145–160. Springer, Heidelberg (2009)
14. Houy, C., Fettke, P., Loos, P.: Understanding understandability of conceptual models - what are we actually talking about? - supplement. Tech. rep., UniversitÃts- und Landesbibliothek, Postfach 151141, 66041 SaarbrÃcken (2013), http://scidok.sulb.uni-saarland.de/volltexte/2013/5441
15. Jureta, I.J., Faulkner, S.: An agent-oriented meta-model for enterprise modelling. In: Akoka, J., Liddle, S.W., Song, I.-Y., Bertolotto, M., Comyn-Wattiau, I., van den Heuvel, W.-J., Kolp, M., Trujillo, J., Kop, C., Mayr, H.C. (eds.) ER Workshops 2005. LNCS, vol. 3770, pp. 151–161. Springer, Heidelberg (2005)
16. Kamsties, E., von Knethen, A., Reussner, R.: A controlled experiment to evaluate how styles affect the understandability of requirements specifications. Information and Software Technology 45(14), 955–965 (2003)
17. Matulevičius, R., Heymans, P.: Comparing goal modelling languages: An experiment. In: Sawyer, P., Heymans, P. (eds.) REFSQ 2007. LNCS, vol. 4542, pp. 18–32. Springer, Heidelberg (2007)
18. Moody, D.: The "physics" of notations: Toward a scientific basis for constructing visual notations in software engineering. IEEE Transactions on Software Engineering 35(6), 756–779 (2009)
19. Moody, D., van Hillegersberg, J.: Evaluating the visual syntax of UML: An analysis of the cognitive effectiveness of the UML family of diagrams. In: Gašević, D., Lämmel, R., Van Wyk, E. (eds.) SLE 2008. LNCS, vol. 5452, pp. 16–34. Springer, Heidelberg (2009)
20. Moody, D.L., Heymans, P., Matulevičius, R.: Visual syntax does matter: improving the cognitive effectiveness of the i* visual notation. Requirements Engineering 15(2), 141–175 (2010)
21. Nugroho, A.: Level of detail in UML models and its impact on model comprehension: A controlled experiment. Information and Software Technology 51(12), 1670–1685 (2009)
22. Purchase, H.C., Welland, R., McGill, M., Colpoys, L.: Comprehension of diagram syntax: an empirical study of entity relationship notations. International Journal of Human-Computer Studies 61(2), 187–203 (2004), http://www.sciencedirect.com/science/article/pii/S1071581904000072
23. Quartel, D.A.C., Engelsman, W., Jonkers, H., van Sinderen, M.J.: A goal-oriented requirements modelling language for enterprise architecture. In: Proceedings of the Thirteenth IEEE International EDOC Enterprise Computing Conference, EDOC 2009, pp. 3–13. IEEE Computer Society Press, Los Alamitos (2009)
24. Stirna, J., Persson, A., Sandkuhl, K.: Participative enterprise modeling: Experiences and recommendations. In: Krogstie, J., Opdahl, A.L., Sindre, G. (eds.) CAiSE 2007 and WES 2007. LNCS, vol. 4495, pp. 546–560. Springer, Heidelberg (2007)
25. Storrle, H.: On the impact of layout quality to understanding UML diagrams. In: 2011 IEEE Symposium on Visual Languages and Human-Centric Computing (VL/HCC), pp. 135–142. IEEE (2011)
26. The Open Group: TOGAF Version 9. Van Haren Publishing (2009)
27. The Open Group: ArchiMate 2.0 Specification. Van Haren Publishing (2012)

28. van Lamsweerde, A.: From system goals to software architecture. In: Bernardo, M., Inverardi, P. (eds.) SFM 2003. LNCS, vol. 2804, pp. 25–43. Springer, Heidelberg (2003)
29. Wieringa, R.J.: Design science as nested problem solving. In: Proceedings of the 4th International Conference on Design Science Research in Information Systems and Technology, Philadelphia, pp. 1–12. ACM, New York (2009)
30. Yu, E.: Towards modelling and reasoning support for early-phase requirements engineering. In: Proceedings of the Third IEEE International Symposium on Requirements Engineering, pp. 226–235. IEEE Computer Society Press (2002)

A   Example Model

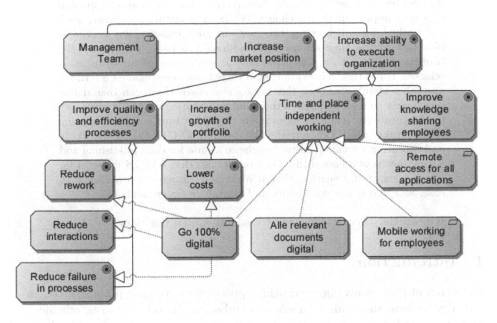

Fig. 2. Example model

FACTS: A Framework for Anonymity towards Comparability, Transparency, and Sharing

Exploratory Paper

Clemens Heidinger, Klemens Böhm, Erik Buchmann, and Kai Richter

Karlsruhe Institute of Technology (KIT), Germany

Abstract. In past years, many anonymization schemes, anonymity notions, and anonymity measures have been proposed. When designing information systems that feature anonymity, choosing a good approach is a very important design choice. While experiments comparing such approaches are enlightening, carrying out such experiments is a complex task and is labor-intensive. To address this issue, we propose the framework FACTS for the experimental evaluation of anonymization schemes. It lets researchers implement their approaches against interfaces and other standardizations that we have devised. Users can then define benchmark suites that refer to those implementations. FACTS gives way to comparability, and it includes many useful features, e.g., easy sharing and reproduction of experiments. We evaluate FACTS (a) by specifying and executing a comprehensive benchmark suite for data publishing and (b) by means of a user study. Core results are that FACTS is useful for a broad range of scenarios, that it allows to compare approaches with ease, and that it lets users share and reproduce experiments.

Keywords: Privacy, Anonymity, Evaluation, Benchmarking.

1 Introduction

In the recent past, many anonymization approaches have been proposed, i.e., anonymity notions, anonymization schemes (subsequently referred to as 'schemes'), and measures for their evaluation. It is difficult to compare them and to decide when to use which scheme. It is hard to answer important questions, e.g.:

- Given a data set, a scheme, and an attack, how much information can the attack disclose?
- Given a data set and a set of queries, which scheme maximizes query accuracy while offering, say, Differential Privacy?

We see three dimensions that must be considered when comparing approaches, namely attacks, measures and benchmarks:

Attacks. Schemes have to make assumptions on the data set to be anonymized, and on the capabilities required to break anonymization. This allows to state if and to which degree the schemes give protection. Example 1 introduces our running example. In order to ease presentation, we use well-known approaches with well-researched vulnerabilities.

M. Jarke et al. (Eds.): CAiSE 2014, LNCS 8484, pp. 120–135, 2014.

Example 1: Each row in Table 1a describes one individual. The data set contains attributes (quasi-identifiers) which might allow to identify a person ("Zip", "Age" and "Sex"). It further has a sensitive attribute ("Disease"). Table 1b shows how a k-Anonymization scheme has transformed this data. This transformation cannot shield from attacks that disclose the sensitive attribute value for an individual. This is because, for all tuples with the same values of identifying attributes, the value of the sensitive attribute is the same. However, k-Anonymization implicitly assumes that there is no correlation between quasi-identifying and sensitive attributes. The so-called homogeneity attack can exploit this to break the anonymization of Table 1b. Another scheme is required; see for instance Table 1c for an anonymization outcome with l-Diversity.   ●

Table 1. Examples for Anonymization

(a) Original data set

Zip	Age	Sex	Disease
13053	28	F	Lupus
13053	29	F	Lupus
13068	21	M	AIDS
13053	23	F	AIDS

(b) Outcome with k-Anonymity ($k = 2$)

Zip	Age	Sex	Disease
130*	[28, 29]	F	Lupus
130*	[28, 29]	F	Lupus
130*	[21, 23]	*	AIDS
130*	[21, 23]	*	AIDS

(c) Outcome with l-Diversity ($k = l = 2$)

Zip	Age	Sex	Disease
130*	[21, 28]	*	Lupus
130*	[23, 29]	F	Lupus
130*	[21, 28]	*	AIDS
130*	[23, 29]	F	AIDS

[10] has shown that any scheme that preserves some utility has to rely on assumptions. Attacks in turn exploit such assumptions. This may result in new schemes to shield against them, i.e., we observe a stream of new attacks and countermeasures, for many scenarios. We say that *approaches belong to the same scenario* if they share certain basic requirements. For example, in scenario data publishing of microdata (S_{PUB}) one releases modified data sets without any means to undo these modifications. With scenario database-as-a-service (S_{DAAS}) in turn, a requirement is to have de-anonymization mechanisms for authorized individuals. Besides S_{PUB} and S_{DAAS} there are many more scenarios, e.g., statistical databases (S_{STATS}) and data mining (S_{MINING}). Differential Privacy [7] for example assumes independent database records – [11] then describes an attack exploiting dependencies between records, together with a respective new scheme. To find out if a scheme can be used in a certain real-world context, it is important to test the anonymized data against such attacks.

Measures. Besides formal proofs of anonymity and complexity analyses, quantitative measures are needed to assess the applicability of a scheme for real-world applications. An example is the probability that the anonymity of a data set can be broken if it has been anonymized with a certain scheme. Regarding performance, it is interesting to know if there is an optimal scheme that can anonymize a certain data set in reasonable time, or if a heuristic scheme is needed. Further measures consider data quality and query accuracy – we address them later in this article. However, the sheer number of schemes, attacks, and application requirements makes it hard to identify the best scheme for a given setting.

Making the right choice is important to account for high-level privacy requirements, cf. [3].

Benchmarks. Schemes may be related in that they aim at the same kind of protection, e.g., against linking values of sensitive attributes to individuals. However, related schemes typically have been evaluated with different experiments. For example, [12] uses the UCI Adult data set, while the related scheme [17] uses an IPUMS census data set: One cannot compare their measurements of data quality or of query accuracy.

Example 2:   Queries on non-anonymized data sets may need to be modified to be executed on the anonymization output. Query-processing techniques then must be tailored to schemes. With our running example, the query SELECT * FROM Table 1a WHERE Age BETWEEN 22 AND 28 needs to be modified so that values of "Age" map to the generalized intervals in Table 1b. Different measures for the loss of accuracy exist. To have experiments that are comparable, not only the data must be identical, but also those modifications of the queries and the accuracy measures.   ●

The three dimensions of evaluation problems described above call for a framework that supports a detailed comparison of schemes based on the requirements of real-world applications. Such requirements exist in various categories that are orthogonal to each other. At first, technical requirements must be considered, e.g., the memory footprint or the scalability of an anonymization scheme regarding the number of input tuples. Secondly, the anonymization scheme must consider the eventual use of the anonymized data. For example, if a scheme removes all data values that deviate from the average, but the use case needs to perform outlier detection, this scheme is inappropriate. The third category considers privacy preferences, attacker models and how sensitive information is represented in the data. For example, sensitive information could be materialized as set-valued data, e.g., from a shopping cart analysis, and an adversary might know typical shopping carts. Thus, FACTS must be flexible enough to implement a wide range of different schemes, attacks, and measures.

Designing such a framework is challenging, given the wide variety of possible attacks, measures and benchmarks. Although in this paper we limit examples and discussions to S_{PUB} and S_{DAAS}, we strive for a framework that also works for other scenarios, e.g., S_{STATS} and S_{MINING}. In this context, the heterogeneity of scenarios is challenging. For instance, data quality is not important for S_{DAAS}, but for S_{PUB}, it is.

In this paper, we propose FACTS, a **F**ramework for **A**nonymity towards **C**omparability, **T**ransparency, and **S**haring. It allows to compile benchmarks together with the implementations of schemes and of attacks, data sets, query-processing techniques etc. When designing FACTS, we have devised standards for the anonymization application, namely for interfaces that researchers proposing new approaches must implement and for data they must provide. Users can then define, share, update, and execute benchmarks for anonymization that refer to the standards. FACTS addresses comparability, as Example 3 illustrates.

Example 3: An author of a query must implement two methods whose interfaces are given by FACTS: one for the query on anonymized data sets, another one for the query on the original data. In $\mathbf{S}_{\text{PUB}}$, this allows to measure the loss of query accuracy (cf. Example 2). In $\mathbf{S}_{\text{DAAS}}$, it allows to quantify the performance costs of decrypting query results and to verify that results are the same as without encryption.   ●

Our evaluation is twofold. On the one hand, we have developed various benchmarks, including one $\mathbf{S}_{\text{PUB}}$ and one for $\mathbf{S}_{\text{DAAS}}$, described in a complementary technical report [9]. Here, we report on a user study with 19 participants that has continued for three months. The evaluation shows that FACTS addresses its objectives well, e.g., FACTS standards allow to compare approaches fairly by enforcing compliance with benchmarks. We have implemented the framework and the benchmarks in full and make everything available under a free license on our website [1]. The vision is that over time it will become common among anonymization researchers to refer to suitable benchmarks.

2 Background: Terminology and Examples

We now introduce our terminology and discuss how schemes have been evaluated.

Anonymization. Our understanding of the term anonymity is broad and includes approaches such as encryption, see below. Any *scheme* takes an *original data set* as input, with *original values* in its cells. With $\mathbf{S}_{\text{STATS}}$, a set of functions that operate on the data is input as well. Schemes generate an *anonymization output*. With $\mathbf{S}_{\text{PUB}}$ and $\mathbf{S}_{\text{DAAS}}$, this output is the entire anonymized data set, with $\mathbf{S}_{\text{STATS}}$ it is anonymized query results. Any scheme seeks to protect against a certain kind of disclosure of sensitive information. The *protection model* states which information to protect. *Anonymity notions* state characteristics the output of or the information processed by schemes must have. An anonymity notion may refer to a certain protection model, i.e., any scheme compliant with the notion protects the information specified by the protection model. Adversaries execute *attacks* that try to break the protection. *Adversary models* describe the adversary, i.e., her capabilities and her background knowledge. An anonymity notion may include a reference to an adversary model: A scheme complies with the anonymity notion iff the adversary of the referenced adversary model cannot get to the information it aims to protect. Finally, *anonymity* is given if a scheme protects the information specified by the protection model against adversaries as defined by the adversary model. Thus, schemes such as pseudonymization or partitioning [2] can offer "anonymity" according to this definition.

Example 4: With $\mathbf{S}_{\text{PUB}}$, the original data sets contain quasi-identifying and sensitive attributes. An assumption is that each tuple belongs to one individual. A protection model is that any sensitive attribute value must not be linked to the respective individual. The anonymity notion k-Anonymity [15] specifies the following rule for anonymization output: For any tuple, there are at least $k-1$ other tuples with the same values for the quasi-identifying attributes. $\mathcal{S}_{\text{k-Anonymity}}$, a scheme for k-Anonymity, with k set to 2, computes the output in Table 1b. It generalizes original values, to build so-called *QI blocks*. This anonymization however cannot protect from adversary Alice who wants to disclose the disease Bob has. The adversary model is that Alice has knowledge about individuals, as follows. Alice knows that Bob is in the database, lives in a zip-code area beginning with 130, and is 21 years old. She concludes that Bob has AIDS. That is, she executes the so-called homogeneity attack [13]. We refer to it as $\mathcal{A}_{\text{HG}}$. l-Diversity [13] protects against $\mathcal{A}_{\text{HG}}$, see Table 1c.   •

Experiments. 'Approach' is our generic term for any new concept an anonymization researcher might propose. Approaches include schemes, attacks, query processing, and measures. Next to anonymity, schemes may have further goals: With $\mathbf{S}_{\text{PUB}}$, a goal is to maximize data quality for subsequent analyses. For $\mathbf{S}_{\text{STATS}}$, the data set is hidden, and the user can enter a given set of statistical queries – a goal is to maximize the accuracy of their results. For $\mathbf{S}_{\text{DAAS}}$, a goal is to maximize performance of query processing. In general, researchers strive to find schemes that are good regarding a combination of goals, as quantified by *measures*. Measures used in the literature are *anonymity*, *data quality*, *query accuracy*, and *performance*. For instance, anonymity measures quantify to which degree an adversary can break the anonymization, i.e., disclose the information specified in the protection model, and data-quality measures quantify how much the anonymized data set differs from the original one. An *experiment* to evaluate an approach has *experiment parameters*, at least an original data set and a measure. With our terminology, a *benchmark* is a set of experiments. A *benchmark suite* bundles benchmarks with schemes that use them, and contains their parameters and runs such bundles. It yields *measure values*, i.e., values from the respective experiments as output. One benchmark may be used in several suites. We differentiate between benchmark specification and benchmark execution with suites. This is because one might have an interesting benchmark, e.g., containing a new data set, but might not have a scheme using it. In general, we see two user roles: *researchers* and *users*. Researchers are inventors/implementer of an approach. Users deploy approaches. They do not necessarily know the inner structure of the approach they use. A researcher can also be a user.

Example 5:   Continuing Example 4, we illustrate how the measure of [12] (we refer to it as $\mathcal{M}_{\text{Anon-Dist}}$) quantifies the threat posed by $\mathcal{A}_{\text{HG}}$. $\mathcal{M}_{\text{Anon-Dist}}$ is the maximum distance between (a) any distribution of values of the sensitive attribute of a *QI* block in the anonymized data set and (b) the distribution of values of the sensitive attribute of the original data set. $\mathcal{A}_{\text{HG}}$ can conclude that an individual has a sensitive attribute value if the distance is large, as we now explain. Experiment e quantifies anonymity with $\mathcal{M}_{\text{Anon-Dist}}$:

```
e = { original data set: Table 1a, anonymity measure: 𝓜Anon-Dist }
```

Benchmark B contains e as the only experiment, i.e., $B = \{e\}$. Benchmark suite $\mathcal{B}$ runs B for two schemes.

```
𝓑 = { ( experiment: e ∈ B, scheme: 𝓢k-Anonymity, parameters: {k = 2} ),
       ( experiment: e ∈ B, scheme: 𝓢1-Diversity, parameters: {k = 2, l = 2} ) }
```

$\mathcal{B}$ executes and generates Tables 1b and Table 1c as the anonymization output. For Table 1b, the distributions (a) are {Lupus, Lupus} and {AIDS, AIDS}. For Table 1c, the distributions (a) are {Lupus, AIDS}, both times. Distribution (b) is {Lupus, Lupus, AIDS, AIDS}. The distributions (a) for Table 1b have a greater distance to distribution (b) than the distributions (a) for Table 1c. $\mathcal{M}_{\text{Anon-Dist}}$ thus calculates a higher degree of disclosure for Table 1b.   ●

3   FACTS

We now present FACTS, our framework for easy comparability for anonymization research. In this section we give an overview, describe the key concepts, and say how to implement benchmarks.

3.1   Overview

FACTS is a framework for easy comparison of anonymization approaches. A core issue when designing FACTS has been to come up with class models of approaches. Class models are our standardizations of behavior and of processes in the context of anonymization. In FACTS, researchers provide implementations of class models, by implementing them against interfaces we, the designers of FACTS, have specified. Researchers further have to comply with the standards class models specify for data generation. Users configure benchmarks and benchmark suites within FACTS that refer to these implementations. Benchmark suites bundle all data, i.e., data sets, the implementations of class models, and experiment results. FACTS stores everything in a central repository. Users can execute benchmark suites to compare the state of the art with ease. The idea is that users who are experts of an anonymization sub-domain create benchmark suites for approaches where a comparison is interesting.

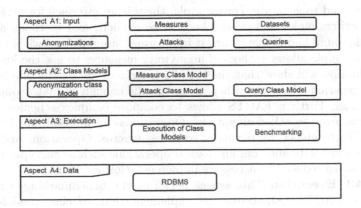

Fig. 1. FACTS – Overview

3.2 Aspects

FACTS covers four aspects. First, users define benchmark suites, i.e., the specification which approaches to compare based on which data, parameter settings etc. Benchmark suites refer to implementations of class models. We have defined class models as the second aspect, and there are class models of schemes, attacks, and queries. The third aspect is that FACTS executes these class models and performs the benchmarking. FACTS stores all results and protocols of executing benchmark suites in a repository, this is the fourth aspect. See Figure 1.

3.3 Benchmarks

We now describe how to realize benchmarks by means of the four aspects. For specifics of our implementation in Java, we refer to the documentation on the FACTS website [1].

Aspect A1: Input In this aspect, a user configures benchmark suites. Standardized interfaces and data representations ensure that all input plays well together, e.g., the scheme knows how to access the input data set. Benchmark suites refer to one or more experiments. An experiment has the following parameters:

1. An original data set D.
2. A scheme *anon*, possibly with parameters, referred to as *params(anon)*.
3. An attack *attack*. It may have parameters, referred to as *params(attack)*.
4. A set of queries Q where each $q \in Q$ may have parameters *params(q)*.
5. A measure $\mathcal{M}$.

Users may omit (3) or (4) if the experiment does not make use of attacks or queries, e.g., experiments on the performance of schemes.

Aspect A2: Class Models Class models let researchers model approaches with a set of interfaces they need to implement and standardized formats of the data they need to generate. For example, there is an interface for attacks that lets researchers make background knowledge explicit, and methods accessing such background knowledge return it in a format standardized within FACTS. This for example allows authors of anonymity measures to use the knowledge. Our evaluation will show that the FACTS interfaces are on the one hand sufficiently generic and, on the other hand, specific enough to make comparisons indeed easier. Further, FACTS allows to compose complex schemes, attacks, and queries from so-called operations. Operations can be used individually, or they can be combined by means of so-called macros. Operations and macros allow to encapsulate and combine logical operations such as encryption or randomization, to reduce the necessary implementation work.

Aspect A3: Execution This aspect performs the benchmarking, with measurements. FACTS instantiates the implementations of class models of Aspect **A2** with the data of Aspect **A1**. That is, FACTS runs the schemes, attacks, and queries. Experiments are logged, including time, date of execution, and the input data set.

Aspect A4: Data This aspect stores all data, i.e., benchmark suites (**A1**), the class models and their implementations (**A2**), and the measurement results and execution logs (**A3**). FACTS stores all data sets and implementations of approaches for later runs of the same suite. This is transparent to the users; FACTS takes care of the data storage. For instance, users and researchers do not need to know the schema of the database or other internals of the framework. They do not need to concern themselves with logging or with the storage of implementations. They only have to comply with a few standardizations for data generation. One example of such a standardization is that a user has to provide a name for a benchmark suite.

3.4 Illustration

We now exemplarily describe how to implement an anonymity benchmark in FACTS. Our benchmark lets an adversary attack a copy of the data that has been anonymized with some scheme one wants to test. The benchmark specifies a fragment of the original data as background knowledge of the adversary, and it allows to quantify the effect of various parameters of interest. In the following, we discuss the implementation of the four aspects of FACTS.

Aspect A1: Input Listing 3 shows how to configure the input of the anonymity benchmark suite by invoking the respective methods implemented in FACTS. First, we import the input data from a file (Lines 1-3) and set up up a new experiment (Line 4-5). We further specify a scheme *anon* (Line 6) and an attack *attack* (Line 8), and link them to the experiment and the benchmark suite (Lines 7 and 9). Note that *anon* and *attack* must have been modeled in Aspect 2. Finally, we tell FACTS to use the anonymity measure *AnonDist* (Line 10). *AnonDist* implements the distance measure $\mathcal{M}_{\text{Anon-Dist}}$, as introduced in Example 5.

```
1   CSV csv = new CSV(new File(inputData));
2   Dataset input = csv.importDataset();
3   Datasets original = new Datasets().add(input);
4   Measurement m = benchmarkSuite.createMeasurement();
5   m.setInputDatasets(original);
6   AnonymityClassModel anon = new anon();
7   m.setAnonymityClassModelImplementation(anon);
8   AttackClassModel attack = new attack();
9   m.setAttackClassModelImplementation(attack);
10  m.setMeasure(new AnonDist());
```

Listing 3. Configuration of anonymity benchmarks

Aspect A2: Class Models With this aspect, we provide implementations of *anon* and *attack*, which inherit from the FACTS classes *AnonymityClassModel* and *AttackClassModel*. Listing 4 illustrates the implementation of background knowledge, which is part of *attack*. In our example, we consider the distribution of the attribute "Disease" of the original data. Thus, `backgroundKnowledge` (Line 1) has the original data set as one parameter. We use methods implemented in

FACTS to count each value of the attribute named "Disease" (Lines 3-6). Another FACTS method adds the background knowledge to the framework (Line 7).

```
1  public void backgroundKnowledge(Dataset original, Dataset anonymized,
       Dataset preconditions, Parameters p, OperationAssembler
       knowledgeLogic)
2  {
3      Attribute a = original.getAttribute("Disease");
4      a.setAggregate(AggregateType.COUNT);
5      a.setGroupByAttribute(true);
6      Dataset knowledge = original.aggregateSelect(a);
7      knowledgeLogic.addOperation(new NullOperation(), knowledge);
8  }
```

Listing 4. Statistics of original data set as background knowledge

Aspect A3: Execution The third aspect is about running our anonymity benchmark (Listing 5). Line 1 runs the scheme *anon*, which produces the anonymized data set *anon(D)*. Next, Line 2 executes *attack*. Finally, Line 3 executes the anonymity measure. It accesses the values guessed by *attack* and compares them to the original values specified during anonymization *anon*.

```
1  m.runAnonymization();
2  m.runAttack();
3  m.runMeasure();
```

Listing 5. Execution of anonymity benchmarks

Aspect A4: Data The final aspect is storing and logging of all classes, models and test data in a relational database. Since FACTS handles this internally, no additional code is required.

4   Features and Use Cases

In this section, we describe important features of our framework, namely comparability, reproducibility, workability, collaboration, and understandability, together with respective use cases. These use cases will form the basis of our evaluation in the next section.

Feature 1 (**Comparability**). Comparability means quantifying anonymity, data quality, query accuracy, and performance of approaches. This is to decide which approach is best for a given real-world problem.

FACTS gives way to comparability by means of benchmarks.

Use Case (**U**BENCHMARK). FACTS lets users define, update, and access benchmarks for anonymization. For anonymization approaches that are related, e.g., approaches that aim for the same protection model, a user creates a benchmark suite that compares them, together with attacks and queries, under a set of measures. When a researcher proposes a new attack, users can update benchmark suites to include it, or create new ones.

Feature 2 (**Reproducibility**). Reproducibility lets unbiased third parties repeat and verify experiments.

Experts in their respective scientific fields have stressed the importance of reproducibility. For example, [4] states that more research is necessary to get to good experiment tools. FACTS supports reproducibility use cases such as the following one:

Use Case ($\mathbf{U}_{\text{COMMITTEE}}$). Authors of a new scheme, attack, or query-processing technique add an implementation of their approach to the FACTS repository and to a benchmark suite. They use this benchmark suite to evaluate their technique. A respective conference committee can later retrieve the benchmark suite. The committee can rerun measurements without difficulty and award a reproducibility label.

Feature 3 (**Workability**). Workability lets one explore effects of modifications of evaluation parameters.

Workability allows to evaluate if an approach achieves good results solely because experiment parameters were chosen to its advantage. Parameter values however may be hidden in an implementation. It can be hard to identify and to vary them subsequently. FACTS addresses this:

Use Case ($\mathbf{U}_{\text{WORKABILITY}}$). Alice is developing a new approach. FACTS requires Alice to specify the parameters with interfaces she has to implement, be it for anonymization, attacks, or queries. Bob now wants to evaluate this new approach. He retrieves and changes parameters of any benchmark with the approach. To this end, he can use FACTS methods that we have already implemented. He does not need to search for parameters in the code. This lets Bob observe how parameters affect benchmark results with ease.

Feature 4 (**Collaboration**). Collaboration within the community allows for faster development of new approaches.

In publications, details such as the concrete data set, initialization or termination procedures and the values of parameters are not always given [16]. This makes it hard for researchers to build upon existing work, i.e., when implementing a new approach by reusing some of the implementation of an existing one.

Use Case ($\mathbf{U}_{\text{SHARING}}$). FACTS gives way to sharing of operations. Suppose that researchers have developed a new scheme for $\mathbf{S}_{\text{DAAS}}$ that protects against adversaries trying to find out the order of tuples. The authors search the FACTS repository and find an operation which randomizes a data set. It might have been developed for schemes of $\mathbf{S}_{\text{PUB}}$ originally.

Another use case of collaboration is to let the community assist in solving a task:

Use Case ($\mathbf{U}_{\text{ASSISTANCE}}$). A user wants to find out if her data set can be anonymized such that her quality criteria are met. The community helps her to find suitable schemes. For example, suppose that Alice wants to outsource her data to a $\mathbf{S}_{\text{DAAS}}$ provider. She wants to know if there exists an anonymization that allows executing certain queries in under one second on her data set. Alice creates a benchmark suite with her data set and queries. Other users can retrieve it and add schemes and query-processing techniques.

Feature 5 (**Understandability**). Understandability lets the user perceive the impact of all input parameters of an experiment on the experimental results.

Given an experimental result such as a diagram, it can be hard to understand how exactly it has been computed, e.g., why one value is larger than another one: For example, there may be several (parametrized) schemes and attacks, operating on different background knowledge. FACTS supports understandability by allowing the user to execute series of anonymization experiments with varying parameters, by providing logs of intermediate results that one can analyzes with data-analyitcs tools, and by providing convenience methods to generate diagrams. A use case for understandability, but also for reproducibility and collaboration, is as follows:

Use Case ($\mathbf{U}_{\mathrm{DIAGRAM}}$). Researcher Carl is developing a new scheme. He uses FACTS to implement it and creates a new benchmark suite with performance experiments. Carl wants to graph anonymization performance, to find settings where the scheme is slow. His workflow is to implement the scheme, generate the graph, and to refine the implementation. Our final use case is to simplify benchmarks for understandability:

Use Case ($\mathbf{U}_{\mathrm{SIMPLIFY}}$). Tony has a large data set with activities of his waste-management business. He wants his business associate Silvio to access the data, but conceal it from the authorities. This is a $\mathbf{S}_{\mathrm{DAAS}}$ scenario and requires anonymization. However, Silvio complains that certain queries are slow. Tony lets Christopher evaluate which data the problem occurs with. To this end, Christopher gradually reduces the data set size and measures query-execution times. With FACTS, he can use methods already implemented to retrieve an evaluation data set, to reduce its size, and to start measurements. Christopher observes that processing is slow if a certain client is in the data set. Tony is now able to eliminate the problem, once and for all.

Discussion Our evaluation will show that FACTS is general enough to be applicable to the very different scenarios $\mathbf{S}_{\mathrm{PUB}}$ and $\mathbf{S}_{\mathrm{DAAS}}$. Furthermore, FACTS is directly applicable to many other scenarios where input and output data can be represented as relations, e.g., association-rule mining of shopping carts, search histories, location-based services, social networks, or statistical databases. Anonymization scenarios for continuously changing data, e.g., data streams or incrementally updated databases, would require to adapt our interfaces and their implementations of Aspects A1 and A4. However, generic benchmark functionality, e.g., performance measurements, should work as is.

5 Evaluation

We evaluate FACTS by means of an exploratory study. We declare success if FACTS allows to model state-of-the-art schemes, attacks, and measures, and if FACTS allows to execute and to compare them by means of benchmark suites. Further, we seek confirmation that the framework indeed has the features we have identified earlier.

We have conducted a user study to evaluate how well FACTS realizes reproducibility and collaboration. We reenact the use cases $\mathbf{U}_{\mathrm{ASSISTANCE}}$ and $\mathbf{U}_{\mathrm{COMMITTEE}}$

with this study. It is based on an instance of $U_{\text{BENCHMARK}}$ and a benchmark suite, $\mathcal{B}_{\text{DaaS}}$, for scenario S_{DAAS}. We stress however that our main contribution is not one specific benchmark suite but the idea of a *framework* to build and share such suites. Additionally, our technical report [9] includes a benchmark suite $\mathcal{B}_{\text{pub}}$, the use case U_{DIAGRAM} and an alternative instance of $U_{\text{BENCHMARK}}$. Supplementary evaluation material is available on the project website [1].

We now describe the user study that was realized as an instance of use case $U_{\text{ASSISTANCE}}$ and has led to the development of benchmark suite $\mathcal{B}_{\text{DaaS}}$. We have specified three tasks with $U_{\text{ASSISTANCE}}$: (1) Anonymize specific data sets in a S_{DAAS} scenario and produce anonymization output, (2) develop query-processing techniques for each anonymization (cf. Example 2), and (3) attack the anonymization output of other study participants. In a user experiment, we have let participants solve these tasks. After the solutions were handed in, we have verified their reproducibility ($U_{\text{COMMITTEE}}$). We have further compared the different solutions with performance and anonymity measures ($U_{\text{BENCHMARK}}$).

Evaluation Setup. Our experiment consists of three phases where users solve different tasks with FACTS. After the three phases were completed, we handed out a user survey regarding FACTS. It is available on our website [1]. We designed the survey with care so as to not enforce positive results with the way of asking questions. Likert-scale questions did not follow patterns, i.e., positive answers have been sometimes to the left, sometimes to the right. Further, our participants answered the survey anonymously, and they knew that we could not trace negative answers back to them. We now describe the tasks, followed by a description of the participants, and incentives. Our three tasks are:

Task 1. Folksonomies [14] let users annotate digital objects with free-text labels. For example, with Last.fm, users annotate music, with Flickr photos. Folksonomies contain data that is sensitive regarding privacy. A user study [5] confirms that users see a significant benefit in being able to control who is allowed to see which data. Schemes let users only access data when the data creators have given the respective authorization. Thus, the first task is to develop schemes for CiteULike folksonomies of varying size.

Task 2. Users issue queries against folksonomies for various reasons, e.g., personal organization or communication with other users. We have identified seven types of common folksonomy queries [8]. For example, one type of query is "retrieve all tags applied to a specific object". $\mathcal{B}_{\text{DaaS}}$ includes parameters suitable for each of these seven query types for each CiteULike folksonomy data set. To continue the example, $\mathcal{B}_{\text{DaaS}}$ computes the most frequent object as one of the query parameters for each data set. This is because the most frequent object results in a large query result and thus a long query-processing time. This is an interesting extreme case that should be included in a meaningful benchmark. Thus, the second task is to develop fast processing techniques for each query type given and its parameters.

Task 3. The frequency of attribute values in folksonomies follows a power-law distribution. With improper anonymization, this leaves room for statistical attacks [6]. $\mathcal{B}_{\text{DaaS}}$ specifies as the adversary model someone with statistical background knowledge. $\mathcal{B}_{\text{DaaS}}$ computes this knowledge from the original data sets and makes the frequency of values of each attribute of the original data set available to an adversary. Thus, the third task of $\mathcal{B}_{\text{DaaS}}$ is develop attacks against the schemes developed in Task 1, given this adversary model.

Participants. We have let 19 students of computer science solve the tasks. We divided the students into four groups where three groups had five members and one group had four members. We instructed them in the fundamentals of (i) database anonymization, (ii) query processing on anonymized data, and (iii) statistical attacks. To test their understanding regarding (i) to (iii), we issued assignments to them. Two of originally 21 students did not pass them, and we did not let them participate in the subsequent evaluation.

Incentives. The participants joined the experiment as part of a practical course. Their main incentive for participation was to pass the course. To do so, participants had to earn points. Completion of the three tasks (i)-(iii) had earned them points. We had issued bonus points if participants committed their implementations of FACTS class models to the repository, or if they had developed and shared FACTS operations.

Results

Comparability with $\mathcal{B}_{DaaS}$ One outcome of the study has been the FACTS benchmark suite $\mathcal{B}_{\text{DaaS}}$. We have imported the data set, queries, and adversary model (along with the data representing statistical background knowledge) from a previous research project of ours [8] into FACTS. $\mathcal{B}_{\text{DaaS}}$ thus allows us to compare the approaches of students in an evaluation setup actually used in research. We have observed that FACTS allows us, the conductors of the study, to compare approaches with ease. We justify this claim in different ways. (1) The final result of queries on the anonymization output does always equal that of the queries on the respective original data set, for all approaches by different participants. (2) The same set of queries executes for each approach. In the past years, we had lectured this practical course without FACTS. There have been many comparison tasks that were cumbersome without the standardizations. Participants had submitted query-processing techniques that returned fewer result tuples, and they had used other query parameters than what we had specified. With FACTS, (1) its benchmarking checks correctness of results, and (2) always runs the same queries.

Reproducibility with $\mathcal{B}_{DaaS}$ We evaluate reproducibility by letting participants upload solutions and then letting them rerun them.

Our first indicator for reproducibility is if participants are able to execute approaches without errors. We say that schemes are without error if they produce an anonymization output. We say that query-execution techniques are without error if they terminate, and if they compute the correct result for all queries. We say that attacks are without error if they write their guesses for original values for each anonymized cell in the proper place for FACTS, and anonymity measures compute. A scheme writing only zeros to all cells would thus be error-free, but query execution based on it would fail. To evaluate if participants were able to reproduce the results of approaches by other participants, we have asked respective questions in the survey about the total number of schemes, queries, and attacks that participants had executed, and for how many of them participants have observed no errors. By means of answers to these questions, we have calculated the share of error-free executions, cf. Table 2. Our apriori expectations have been that the values are close to our measurements. The numbers reflect that one group has had errors with queries and attacks with our benchmark runs. The values calculated with the survey are lower, but relatively close to ours. We conclude from these observations that FACTS allows users to run approaches from the FACTS repository without difficulty and that FACTS standardizations allow to observe implementation errors that would be in the way of (fair) comparisons and reproducibility otherwise.

Table 2. Reproducibility: Error-Free Executions

Approach	Study Answers	Our Measurements
Schemes	85 %	100 %
Query-Processing Techniques	68 %	75 %
Attacks	61 %	75 %

Our second indicator for reproducibility is if measurement values from several experiment runs on varying platforms lead to similar results. To do this comparison, we could rely on our execution of $\mathcal{B}_{DaaS}$ and the executions of $\mathcal{B}_{DaaS}$ by each group. We did observe similar results. For example, all performance measurements have had Group 4 as the fastest before Group 1 and Group 3 and have reported errors for Group 2. Results are not identical however because execution times depend on the computational power of clients.

We state that there is reproducibility with three of four groups ($\mathbf{U}_{COMMITTEE}$) because we were able to execute all of their approaches without error, and our measurement results were similar to theirs. We thus see strong indications that FACTS does allow for reproducibility.

Collaboration with $\mathcal{B}_{DaaS}$. To evaluate the collaboration feature, we have asked respective questions in the survey. In a nutshell, users deem that the concept to collaborate with anonymization operations through the FACTS repository is useful. Our complementary technical report provides more details, also on other aspects of our evaluation.

6   Conclusions

Nowadays, a broad variety of anonymization approaches exists. We observe that requirements, goals, adversary models, implementations, or evaluation parameters are publicly available only for a few of them. It is very difficult to answer which approach is best regarding anonymity, data quality, query accuracy, and performance. To deal with this situation, we have proposed a framework, FACTS, that allows to compare anonymization approaches with ease. Researchers can implement their approaches within FACTS against so-called class models. We have systematically devised interfaces of class models that ease comparing and benchmarking approaches. Besides comparability, FACTS has other useful features, e.g., to support researchers in the documentation and presentation of experiment results. Our evaluation shows that FACTS allows to define comprehensive benchmark suites for anonymization scenarios, and that it addresses user needs well. Our vision is that FACTS will give way to a higher degree of comparability within the research area.

References

1. http://facts.ipd.kit.edu/
2. Abramov, J., Sturm, A., Shoval, P.: A Pattern Based Approach for Secure Database Design. In: Salinesi, C., Pastor, O. (eds.) CAiSE Workshops 2011. LNBIP, vol. 83, pp. 637–651. Springer, Heidelberg (2011)
3. Barhamgi, M., Benslimane, D., Oulmakhzoune, S., Cuppens-Boulahia, N., Cuppens, F., Mrissa, M., Taktak, H.: Secure and Privacy-Preserving Execution Model for Data Services. In: Salinesi, C., Norrie, M.C., Pastor, Ó. (eds.) CAiSE 2013. LNCS, vol. 7908, pp. 35–50. Springer, Heidelberg (2013)
4. Bonnet, P., et al.: Repeatability and workability evaluation of SIGMOD 2011. ACM SIGMOD Record 40(2) (2011)
5. Burghardt, T., Buchmann, E., Müller, J., Böhm, K.: Understanding User Preferences and Awareness: Privacy Mechanisms in Location-Based Services. In: Meersman, R., Dillon, T., Herrero, P. (eds.) OTM 2009, Part I. LNCS, vol. 5870, pp. 304–321. Springer, Heidelberg (2009)
6. Ceselli, A., et al.: Modeling and Assessing Inference Exposure in Encrypted Databases. TISSEC 8(1) (2005)
7. Dwork, C.: Differential privacy. In: Bugliesi, M., Preneel, B., Sassone, V., Wegener, I. (eds.) ICALP 2006. LNCS, vol. 4052, pp. 1–12. Springer, Heidelberg (2006)
8. Heidinger, C., et al.: Efficient and secure exact-match queries in outsourced databases. World Wide Web (2013)
9. Heidinger, C., et al.: FACTS: A Framework for Anonymity towards Comparability, Transparency, and Sharing (Extended Version). Technical report, Karlsruhe Institute of Technology, KIT (2013), http://digbib.ubka.uni-karlsruhe.de/volltexte/1000037502
10. Kifer, D., Machanavajjhala, A.: No Free Lunch in Data Privacy. In: SIGMOD (2011)
11. Kifer, D., Machanavajjhala, A.: A Rigorous and Customizable Framework for Privacy. In: PODS (2012)

12. Li, T., Li, N.: On the Tradeoff Between Privacy and Utility in Data Publishing. In: KDD (2009)
13. Machanavajjhala, A., et al.: l-Diversity: Privacy Beyond k-Anonymity. In: ICDE (2006)
14. Peters, I.: Folksonomies: Indexing and Retrieval in the Web 2.0. Walter de Gruyter (2009)
15. Samarati, P.: Protecting Respondents' Identities in Microdata Release. TKDE 13(6) (2001)
16. Vandewalle, P., et al.: Reproducible research in signal processing. SPM 26(3) (2009)
17. Wang, H., Liu, R.: Privacy-preserving publishing microdata with full functional dependencies. DKE 70(3) (2011)

Trust-Aware Decision-Making Methodology for Cloud Sourcing*

Francisco Moyano[1], Kristian Beckers[2], and Carmen Fernandez-Gago[1]

[1] Department of Computer Science
University of Malaga, 29071 Malaga, Spain
{moyano,mcgago}@lcc.uma.es
[2] paluno - The Ruhr Institute for Software Technology -
University of Duisburg-Essen, Germany
firstname.lastname@paluno.uni-due.de

Abstract. Cloud sourcing consists of outsourcing data, services and infrastructure to cloud providers. Even when this outsourcing model brings advantages to cloud customers, new threats also arise as sensitive data and critical IT services are beyond customers' control. When an organization considers moving to the cloud, IT decision makers must select a cloud provider and must decide which parts of the organization will be outsourced and to which extent. This paper proposes a methodology that allows decision makers to evaluate their trust in cloud providers. The methodology provides a systematic way to elicit knowledge about cloud providers, quantify their trust factors and aggregate them into trust values that can assist the decision-making process. The trust model that we propose is based on trust intervals, which allow capturing uncertainty during the evaluation, and we define an operator for aggregating these trust intervals. The methodology is applied to an eHealth scenario.

Keywords: trust, cloud computing, decision making, security, domain knowledge elicitation.

1 Introduction

There is an increasing trend to outsource IT services and infrastructures to the cloud [1]. This model, also called cloud sourcing[1], is replacing traditional outsourcing engagements due to its advantages [2]. These include the provision of elastic IT resources and cost savings as a result of reduced operational costs for complex IT processes [3].

---

* This research was partially supported by the EU project Network of Excellence on Engineering Secure Future Internet Software Services and Systems (NESSoS, ICT-2009.1.4 Trustworthy ICT, Grant No. 256980), and by the Spanish Ministry of Science and Innovation through the research project ARES (CSD2007-00004). The first author is funded by the Ministry of Education through the national F.P.U. program.

[1] Techopedia: http://www.techopedia.com/definition/26551/cloudsourcing

M. Jarke et al. (Eds.): CAiSE 2014, LNCS 8484, pp. 136–149, 2014.

Security and trust are significant barriers for the adoption of clouds in companies [4]. Lack of trust in cloud providers lies within the nature of clouds: storage and management of critical data, and execution of sensitive IT processes are performed beyond the customers control. As a consequence, new security threats arise[2,3], and IT decision makers must balance the advantages and these threats before making decisions. These decisions range from selecting a cloud provider to determining how much data or which part of the infrastructure moving to the cloud.

Trust includes the expectation that we hold on another party regarding the outcome of an interaction with that party. Even when there is not any agreed definition for trust, it is generally accepted that it can help in decision-making processes in the absence of complete information [5,6]. Given that information about cloud providers, due to internal policy or strategic reasons, may be uncertain and incomplete, trust can enhance the cloud sourcing decision-making process.

We present a methodology that evaluates trust in cloud providers and that can help IT decision makers to make more informed decisions during the outsourcing process. The methodology provides a systematic way to gather knowledge about cloud providers and to exploit this knowledge in order to yield trust values that can be used as inputs to the decision-making process. The methodology pinpoints which aspects of the providers should be analysed, indicators that decision makers can use to quantify these aspects, and how these quantifications can be aggregated into trust values. We use trust intervals in order to quantify trust and we define a summation operator to aggregate trust intervals. The methodology constitutes a guide that decision makers can follow to evaluate their trust in cloud providers under several dimensions or viewpoints.

The paper is structured as follows. Related work is discussed in Section 2. We explain the methodology in Section 3, whereas in Section 4 we present its application to an eHealth scenario. We discuss some aspects of the methodology in Section 5 and we conclude the paper in Section 6, where we also outline some directions for future research.

We present an extended version of this paper in a technical report, which is available for the interested reader[4].

2 Related Work

Cloud provider evaluation is a necessary step for cloud sourcing decision-making, but clouds can be evaluated under different angles, including performance [7], scalability [8], accountability [9] and transparency [10].

The impact of trust for cloud adoption and some trust-related factors that influence users when selecting cloud providers have been identified in previous

---

[2] http://www.infoworld.com/d/security-central/
gartner-seven-cloud-computing-security-risks-853
[3] Top Threats to Cloud Computing V1.0,
https://cloudsecurityalliance.org/topthreats/csathreats.v1.0.pdf
[4] Technical report: http://www.uml4pf.org/publications/trust.pdf

works [11][12]. In this direction, Sarwar et al. [13] review several works that elicit relevant trust aspects in the cloud. Ahmad et al. [14] argue that trust in the cloud must be built upon a deep knowledge about the cloud computing paradigm and the provider.

In many works, trust depends on the verification of Service Level Agreements (SLAs) [15] or the measurement of Quality of Service (QoS) attributes [16]. However, these works are usually focused on cloud services evaluation and selection rather than on the cloud providers themselves.

Pavlidis et al. [17] propose a process for trustworthy selection of cloud providers. This selection is based on how well the cloud provider fulfils the customer's security and privacy requirements. It also aims to reduce uncertainty by justifying trust relationships and by making trust assumptions explicit. Compared to our approach, we consider other aspects of the cloud providers and we use trust intervals instead of probabilities and weights.

Supriya et al. [18] propose a fuzzy trust model to evaluate cloud service providers that uses the attributes defined by the Service Measurement index (SMI) [19]. Examples of these attributes are assurance, performance and security. Even though uncertainty is embedded in the fuzzy engine, the authors do not provide guidelines on quantifying the attributes or on eliciting cloud knowledge. Qu et al. [20] introduce customers' feedback in the evaluation, although this evaluation is focused on cloud service selection, rather than on cloud provider selection.

As a conclusion from our literature review, trust has already been incorporated in the evaluation of clouds. However, in most cases, the purpose of this evaluation is service selection, rather than cloud provider selection. Most contributions are also focused on the metrics rather than on a concrete methodology to gather and quantify all the information. Uncertainty or subjectivity, which are intrinsic to the notion of trust, are usually laid aside. This paper aims to fill these gaps. The existing literature provides valuable information about the aspects of cloud providers that are usually considered by cloud customers before moving to the cloud, and our approach builds upon this knowledge.

3   Trust-Aware Methodology for Decision Making

In this section, we present a methodology to evaluate trust in cloud providers. A high-level overview of the methodology is depicted in Figure 1. The first step consists of gathering knowledge about the cloud provider. Next, we elicit and quantify a set of trust factors about the provider's stakeholders and about the cloud provider as a whole. In parallel, we specify trust thresholds that are based on the scenario requirements. These thresholds are minimum trust values that we expect for a given scenario. In the following step, the factors are aggregated into three dimensions or viewpoints: a stakeholder dimension, a threat dimension, and a general dimension. In order to perform the aggregation, we define a summation operator. Finally, the information is graphically visualized.

Next sections discuss each step in detail.

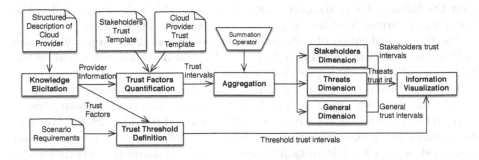

Fig. 1. Overview of the Methodology

3.1 Domain Knowledge Elicitation

The goal of this step is to gather knowledge about the cloud provider and the cloud domain. We propose context-pattern for a structured domain knowledge elicitation [21]. These patterns contain a graphical pattern and templates with elements that require consideration for a specific context. In addition, our context-pattern contains a method for eliciting domain knowledge using the graphical pattern and templates. For this work we use a specific context pattern, the so-called *cloud system analysis pattern* [22,23]. It describes stakeholders and other systems that interact with the *Cloud*, i.e. they are connected to the cloud by associations. For example, the *cloud provider* offers its resources to *cloud customers* as *Services*, i.e., *IaaS*, *PaaS*, or *SaaS*. However, it is also possible to use other methods for structured domain knowledge elicitation during this step of our method such as the one proposed in [24]. Once we have gathered general knowledge about the provider, we focus on the trust factors in the next step.

3.2 Trust Factors Quantification

The goal of this step is to quantify the factors that are used to evaluate trust. Factors are aspects and non-functional requirements that may influence a trust decision.

The Stakeholder Trust Template (STT) in Table 1 is a modification over the original stakeholder template [21], and identifies the trust factors that we consider for each stakeholder. In Table 2 we present an excerpt of the Cloud Provider Trust Template (CPTT)[5], which identifies the trust factors that we consider for the cloud provider. In each table, the first two columns show the name of the factor and its meaning respectively, whereas the last column provides hints for quantifying the factors.

Quantification in our methodology entails providing two values for each factor: the factor value itself and a confidence value. The latter refers to the confidence

---

[5] The complete table is in the Technical Report:
http://www.uml4pf.org/publications/trust.pdf

that the factor value is accurate. The role of this value is to make explicit the uncertainty derived from having partial and subjective information.

For the quantification of each factor and confidence value, we decide to use only integer numbers from 0 to 3. More justification on this decision and on the trust engine[6] in general is provided in Section 5.

In our methodology, threats are sub-factors of two trust factors: *direct interaction* and *3rd party referrals*. The former refers to information about threats derived from previous direct experience with the cloud provider, whereas the latter requires asking external organizations for this information. We use the threats identified by the Cloud Security Alliance[7], which summarize the experience of a large industrial consortium in the field of cloud computing.

Once we have a factor value and its corresponding confidence value, we calculate a *trust interval* for each factor, as explained in the next definition.

Definition 1 (Trust Interval). *Let v and c be a factor value and its corresponding confidence value, respectively. These values are integer numbers between 0 and 3. We form the trust interval as:* $TI = [\dfrac{vc}{3}, \dfrac{vc}{3} + (3 - c)]$.

This interval is in the domain of the real numbers. 0 and 3 are lower and upper bounds of the interval, respectively. For the rationale of this definition we refer the reader to the contribution by Shakeri et al. [25]. Given that we use integer values, there is a finite set of possible intervals during quantification. For example, when the factor value is 2 and the confidence value is 1, the resulting trust interval is $[\dfrac{2}{3}, \dfrac{8}{3}]$. Note that when $c = 0$, we have the maximum uncertainty, that is, the interval is $[0, 3]$ and has the maximum width. When $c = 3$, uncertainty is minimum, that is, the interval width is zero because we know the trust value.

Table 1. Stakeholder Trust Template

Direct Interaction	Evaluation of previous direct interaction with the stakeholder.	Analyse the number of incidents and overall satisfaction with the stakeholder in the past.
3rd Parties referrals	Referrals from 3rd parties regarding interactions with the stakeholder.	Ask other organisations about their general satisfaction with the stakeholder.
Knowledge	Stakeholder knowledge on its task.	Check number of years of experience and whether the stakeholder has any certification.
Willingness	Willingness of the stakeholder to perform the task.	Take into account the aforementioned factors; research on the motivations of the stakeholder (e.g. bonuses); check how long it takes him to finish his task.

Before proceeding to the aggregation of the trust intervals, decision makers define trust thresholds as explained in the next section.

---

[6] A trust engine is a set of rules or mathematical functions that yield trust values.
[7] Threats are listed in the Technical Report:
http://www.uml4pf.org/publications/trust.pdf

Table 2. Excerpt of the Cloud Provider Trust Template

SLA and Contracts	Quality of SLAs and signed contracts that express the conditions and liabilities regarding the service offered by the cloud provider.	Check if there was some abuse of the contract or SLAs.
Security	Provider's concern and actions on security.	Check whether the cloud provider participates in cloud standards bodies such as CloudAudit, Open Cloud Computing Interface, CSA and ENISA. Does the cloud provider perform security assessment?
Transparency	Transparency of the provider.	How difficult is to retrieve data from the cloud provider? Does it publish its privacy and security policies?
Direct interaction	Own experience in the interaction with the cloud provider.	Evaluate direct experience against threats.
3rd parties referrals	Referrals from 3rd parties regarding interactions with the cloud provider.	Evaluate 3rd parties referrals against threats.

3.3 Trust Thresholds Definition

This step, which is performed in parallel with the quantification step, defines trust thresholds according to the scenario requirements. These thresholds represents the minimum trust that decision makers expect for each trust factor. The goal is to have a yardstick that can be used to check whether cloud providers meet our trust expectations.

For each trust factor, the decision maker assigns an expected factor value and a confidence value. In this case, the confidence value expresses how sure the decision maker is about the need to expect the corresponding factor value. As in the quantification step, for each factor, a trust interval is derived from these values by using Definition 1.

3.4 Trust Aggregation

During the previous steps we have calculated trust intervals for different factors of stakeholders and cloud providers. This step reduces the number of trust intervals by aggregating them.

Before defining the operator that performs the aggregations, we need another definition.

Definition 2 (Interval Accuracy). *Given a trust interval $[a, b]$, we define the interval accuracy as $IA = 3 - w$, where $w = b - a$ is the width of the interval.*

The maximum possible width of a trust interval is 3 (see Definition 1). When the width is maximum, the interval accuracy is 0 because uncertainty is maximum. On the other hand, when the width of a trust interval is 0, the interval accuracy is 3 because uncertainty is minimum.

Next we define a summation operator that aggregates trust intervals.

Definition 3 (Summation Operator). *Given two trust intervals* $[a, b]$ *and* $[c, d]$, *where* $a \neq c$ *or* $b \neq d$, *we define the summation operator* $\oplus$ *as* $[a, b] \oplus [c, d] = [e, f]$ *where* $[e, f]$ *is a new trust interval that can be obtained as:* $e = \dfrac{IA_1 a + IA_2 c}{IA_1 + IA_2}$ *and* $f = \dfrac{IA_1 b + IA_2 d}{IA_1 + IA_2}$. IA_1 *and* IA_2 *are the interval accuracy of* $[a, b]$ *and* $[c, d]$, *respectively. If* $a = c$ *and* $b = d$, *then* $[a, b] \oplus [c, d] = [a, b] = [c, d]$.

The resulting interval after a summation is somewhere in between the two source intervals. The uncertainty, represented by the interval accuracy, determines how close e is to a or c, and how close f is to b or d. This is why we weight a, b, c and d by the interval accuracy. The higher the interval accuracy, the more the values of the corresponding interval contributes. Note that the operator has an identity element: $[0, 3]$. This makes sense as this interval expresses the maximum uncertainty and does not add any knowledge to the trust value.

In order to present meaningful trust information, we suggest performing three aggregations that correspond to three dimensions or viewpoints: the stakeholders dimension, the threats dimension and the general dimension. Next subsections explain each of them.

Stakeholders Dimension. This dimension illustrates the level of trust in the cloud provider according to the stakeholders working in it. This aggregation is performed by summing all the intervals of all the factors for each stakeholder, and then summing the resulting intervals for all the stakeholders.

Threats Dimension. This dimension shows the amount of trust in the cloud provider according to the threats defined by the Cloud Security Alliance (CSA)[3]. For each threat, we aggregate the trust intervals of the *direct interaction* and *3rd party referrals* factors.

We believe that having independent trust intervals for each threat is convenient, instead of aggregating all the different threats together, because decision makers can make more fine-grained decisions. For example, if the trust interval is low for the threat *Data Loss & Leakage*, the decision maker can decide not to move the customers data of the organisation to the cloud provider. However, if trust intervals of the other threats for the same cloud provider are high, some services or infrastructures could be outsourced to that cloud provider. If we aggregated all the threats into a unique trust interval, we would lose this valuable information.

General Dimension. This dimension depicts trust in the cloud provider with regards to the rest of trust factors that are not threats, including *Security*, *Transparency* and *Accountability*.

After the trust aggregation step, there are ten trust intervals for a cloud provider: one for the stakeholders dimension, eight for the threats dimension (i.e. one for each threat) and one in the general dimension.

3.5   Trust Information Visualization

The last step consists of plotting the trust intervals for each dimension for comparison purposes and decision making.

In the Y-axis, we represent possible trust values, whereas in the X-axis we represent the three dimensions. For each dimension, we draw a line from the lower bound to the upper bound of its trust intervals. This arrangement allows fast comparison between providers in each dimension. Likewise, it allows comparing the trust intervals with the trust thresholds.

This is better illustrated in the next section, where we apply the methodology to an eHealth scenario.

4   Evaluation in an eHealth Case Study

In this section we present an application of our methodology to a case study provided by the EU project NESSoS[8]. The scenario concerns managing *Electronic Health Records* (EHRs) in clouds. EHRs contain any information created by health care professionals in the context of the care of a patient. Examples are laboratory reports, X-ray images, and data from monitoring equipment.

Security concerns in this scenario include the confidentiality and integrity of EHRs during communication and storage; data separation of EHRs and other data of the eHealth applications; availability of EHRs; availability of network connection; and data origin authentication. Some of these concerns, like confidentiality and integrity, require authentication mechanisms.

Given these security concerns, the CSA threats that become more relevant are the following: *Insecure Interfaces and APIs (Threat 2)*, because these are essential for security functionalities like authentication; *Malicious Insiders (Threat 3)*, because they could steal EHRs and use them for blackmailing or similar criminal activities. *Shared Technology (Threat 4)* and, specially, *Data Loss & Leakage (Threat 5)*, can lead to a loss of confidentiality of EHRs or data separation. *Account or Service Hijacking (Threat 6)* leads to bypass authentication controls, including those for data origin authentication; *Unknown Risk Profile (Threat 7)* and *Unknown Causes (Threat 8)*[9] can also have a negative effect on all the security concerns.

For this scenario, we consider the following cloud vendors: Amazon, Apple, Microsoft and Google. For space limitations, we lay stakeholders evaluation aside and we focus on evaluating trust in the threat and general dimensions. Next subsections include each step in our methodology.

---

[8] The NESSoS project: http://www.nessos-project.eu

[9] Note that the original CSA Top Threats are just 7, but the CSA documented cloud security incident referenced numerous incidents that cannot be categorized because of a lack of information. This lead us to adding an additional threat.

Trust Factor Quantification and Thresholds Definition Threats quantification is based on a data set from CSA, which mapped 11 491 cloud security incidents to these threats[10].

As explained before, for each trust factor (including the threats), we assign a factor value and a confidence value. For example, in the case of *Threat 1* for Amazon, we assigned factor value 0 and confidence value 2. The rationale, which must also be included as part of the analysis, is that we found three incidents on record and one that had a significant amount of user accounts affected. As another example, for *Security* trust factor in Microsoft, we assigned factor value 3 and confidence value 2. The rationale is that Microsoft considers some certifications (e.g. ISO 27001) and complies with the CSA control matrix and FedRAMP. Applying Definition 1, we obtain the trust interval [0, 1] for the first example, and [2, 3] for the second example[11].

In parallel and based on the security requirements of the scenario, we define minimum trust values for each trust factor. These thresholds, already aggregated in the threat and general dimensions, are presented in Table 4.

Trust Aggregation We aggregate the trust intervals of every factor for a given cloud provider. As an example, consider the following: Apple has trust interval [0, 2] for *Security* and [0.33, 2.33] for transparency. We use the operator in Definition 3 to aggregate these intervals. The resulting interval is [0.17, 2.17]. We would now aggregate this trust interval with the one corresponding to *Accountability and Auditing*, and so forth, until we reach a final trust interval in the general dimension. The resulting trust interval in the general dimension for each cloud provider is shown in Table 3.

Table 3. Trust Intervals for Cloud Providers

	Threat 1	Threat 2	Threat 3	Threat 4	Threat 5	Threat 6	Threat 7	Threat 8	General
Amazon	[0,1]	[0.67,1.67]	[0,3]	[0.33,2.33]	[1.33,2.33]	[0,3]	[0.33,2.33]	[0,1]	[0.34,1.86]
Apple	[0.67,1.67]	[0,1]	[0,0]	[0.33,2.33]	[1.33,2.33]	[0.33,2.33]	[0.67,1.67]	[0.67,2.67]	[0.02, 2.02]
Microsoft	[2,3]	[0.33,2.33]	[1.33,2.33]	[0.67,2.67]	[0.67,1.67]	[0.67,1.67]	[1.33,2.33]	[0,1]	[0.8, 2.25]
Google	[1.33,2.33]	[0,1]	[0.33,2.33]	[1.33,2.33]	[0,1]	[0.33,2.33]	[0.33,2.33]	[0,1]	[0.53, 2.39]

---

[10] Documented Cloud Security Incidents: https://cloudsecurityalliance.org/download/cloud-computing-vulnerability-incidents-a-statistical-overview/
[11] The Technical Report shows the whole quantification for one of the considered cloud providers: http://www.uml4pf.org/publications/trust.pdf

Table 4. Trust Thresholds

Threat 1	Threat 2	Threat 3	Threat 4	Threat 5	Threat 6	Threat 7	Threat 8	General
[1.0,1.0]	[0.67,2.67]	[0.33,2.33]	[2.0,2.0]	[2.0,2.0]	[0.67,2.67]	[0.33,2.33]	[0.33,2.33]	[0.67,2.67]

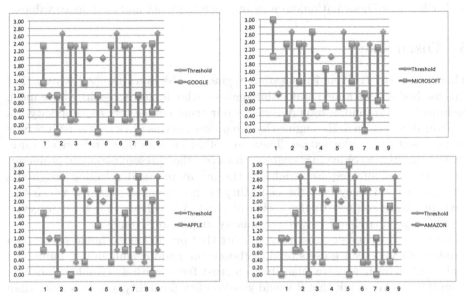

Note that the x-Axsis legend abbreviates Threat 1 to Threat 8 with just the values from 1 to 8. General dimension is value 9

Fig. 2. Contrasting Trust Thresholds and Trust Intervals

We assume that we have no direct previous experience with the providers. Therefore, there is no need to aggregate trust intervals in the threat dimension, which this time only considers information from *3rd party referrals*, in this case, from CSA. Trust intervals for each threat and cloud provider are presented in Table 3. Note that due to space limitations, we laid the stakeholder dimension aside.

Trust Visualization. Figure 2 allows comparing the trust intervals with the trust thresholds[12].

As a conclusion, we see in Figure 2 that no cloud provider upholds all trust thresholds. However, at this point, we can say that Amazon violated "only" the trust thresholds for threats 2 and 8. Google violates the trusts thresholds for threat 5 significantly and threats 2, 4, and 6 just slightly. Microsoft has significant trust threshold violations for threats 4 and 5, while threats 2, 4 and 5 are just violated. Apple has significant misses for threats 2 and 3, while threats 6, 7 and 8 have just minor violations of the threshold. The cloud provider that

---

[12] Other interesting figures, including a comparison of cloud providers, are depicted in the Technical Report: http://www.uml4pf.org/publications/trust.pdf.

best meets the trust expectations in the general dimension is Microsoft, followed by Google. To sum up, our analysis would lead us to either not pursue any cloud provider for our scenario at this time and repeat the analysis later, or to confront the cloud providers with the results and ask for a detailed justifications for their security mechanisms, especially regarding threats 2 and 8. Once the decision maker has more information, he may improve the trust and confidence values.

5   Discussion

There are many trust and reputation engines in the literature [26]. Given that this methodology is aimed at decision makers, who do not necessarily have much technical background, a requirement for our trust engine was its simplicity. As explained in Section 3, the engine that we present in this work uses trust intervals to represent trust information. There are other engines that are easier to use, such as summation or average engines. However, they present two main problems. First, they usually require weighting the attributes, and selecting weights is difficult. Second, they lack the capability to represent uncertainty, which is a concept highly coupled to the notion of trust. We believe that trust intervals present a good trade-off between simplicity and expressiveness.

Best practices in risk assessment indicate that practitioners should set an even number of choices since users tend to choose the middle value in odd numbered scales [27]. This is why we quantify each trust factor with 4 possible values (i.e. from 0 to 3). We think that 2 would give too few flexibility, whereas more than 4 would be confusing.

A disadvantage of our methodology is that it relies on data that in many cases may not be accessible or available. Cloud providers may be reluctant to provide certain information and it might not be straightforward to gather knowledge about the stakeholders of a cloud provider.

Another source of imprecision is subjectivity. By definition, trust is subjective and therefore some of the information that the methodology requires may have a subjectivity bias. The results of the trust evaluation may not be completely accurate, but we advocate that even minimal or partially subjective information is better than blind decision-making. In order to avoid strong subjectivity bias, it is important to state the rationale for each factor quantification.

Subjectivity draws a line between trust and trustworthiness. Having a trustworthiness value would help in determining trust. Whereas trust usually depends on subjective information and may change among trustors, trustworthiness is an objective measure of many different qualities. The ideal situation occurs when trust in a trustee matches the trustworthiness of that trustee [28]. This is the reason why we claim that we are evaluating trust and not trustworthiness.

6   Conclusion and Future Work

We have proposed a methodology that allows IT decision makers to evaluate their trust in cloud providers. We have applied this methodology to an eHealth scenario, where an organization (e.g. a hospital) is planning to outsource the management and storage of EHRs to the Cloud.

In order to perform the evaluation, we have chosen four real cloud providers: Amazon, Apple, Microsoft and Google. We have retrieved information from two main sources: the Cloud Security Alliance and the providers' web pages. The former is a valuable source of information about security incidents, which is indispensable for evaluating trust in the threat dimension. The latter allowed us to determine more general information about the providers, such as their compliance to security or privacy standards. However, we noticed that in general it is hard to find information about cloud providers. Often we had to browse through several sub-sites in order to find meaningful information. Due to these issues, our analysis is most likely done on incomplete information. It is also important to point out that some factors are susceptible to subjective evaluation and that we have not considered the stakeholders dimension or direct experience information.

As future work, we plan to study how to evaluate a cloud provider's reputation, which can provide a valuable input for trust evaluation. We also intend to retrieve information about cloud stakeholders in order to perform a comprehensive empirical study. We would like to study the impact of small changes to different trust factors in the final results. Finally, we plan to provide tool support for the proposed methodology.

References

1. Neovise Research Report: Use of Public, Private and Hybrid Cloud Computing (2013)
2. Martorelli, W., Andrews, C., Mauro, S.P.: Cloud Computing's Impact on Outsourcing Contracts (January 2012)
3. Mell, P., Grance, T.: The NIST Definition of Cloud Computing. Working Paper of the National Institute of Standards and Technology (NIST) (2009)
4. Ponemon Institute Research Report: Security of Cloud Computing Users Study. Technical report, Ponemon Institute, sponsored by CA Technologies (March 2013)
5. Yan, Z., Holtmanns, S.: Trust Modeling and Management: from Social Trust to Digital Trust. Computer Security, Privacy and Politics: Current Issues, Challenges and Solutions (January 2008)
6. Griffiths, N.: A Fuzzy Approach to Reasoning with Trust, Distrust and Insufficient Trust. In: Klusch, M., Rovatsos, M., Payne, T.R. (eds.) CIA 2006. LNCS (LNAI), vol. 4149, pp. 360–374. Springer, Heidelberg (2006)
7. Bubak, M., Kasztelnik, M., Malawski, M., Meizner, J., Nowakowski, P., Varma, S.: Evaluation of Cloud Providers for VPH Applications. In: CCGrid2013 - 13th IEEE/ACM International Symposium on Cluster, Cloud and Grid Computing (May 2013)
8. Gao, J., Pattabhiraman, P., Bai, X., Tsai, W.T.: SaaS performance and scalability evaluation in clouds. In: 2013 IEEE Seventh International Symposium on Service-Oriented System Engineering, pp. 61–71 (2011)

9. Nuñez, D., Fernandez-Gago, C., Pearson, S., Felici, M.: A metamodel for measuring accountability attributes in the cloud. In: 2013 IEEE International Conference on Cloud Computing Technology and Science (CloudCom 2013), Bristol, UK. IEEE (2013) (in press)

10. Pauley, W.: Cloud provider transparency: An empirical evaluation. IEEE Security & Privacy 8(6), 32–39 (2010)

11. Rashidi, A., Movahhedinia, N.: A Model for User Trust in Cloud Computing. International Journal on Cloud Computing: Services and Architecture (IJCCSA) 2(2) (2012)

12. Ko, R., Jagadpramana, P., Mowbray, M., Pearson, S., Kirchberg, M., Liang, Q., Lee, B.S.: TrustCloud: A Framework for Accountability and Trust in Cloud Computing. In: 2011 IEEE World Congress on Services (SERVICES), pp. 584–588 (July 2011)

13. Sarwar, A., Khan, M.: A Review of Trust Aspects in Cloud Computing Security. International Journal of Cloud Computing and Services Science (IJ-CLOSER) 2(2), 116–122 (2013)

14. Ahmad, S., Bashir Ahmad, S.M.S., Khattak, R.M.: Trust Model: Cloud's Provider and Cloud's User. International Journal of Advanced Science and Technology 44 (2012)

15. Chakraborty, S., Roy, K.: An SLA-based Framework for Estimating Trustworthiness of a Cloud. In: International Joint Conference of IEEE TrustCom/IEEE ICESS/FCST, pp. 937–942 (2012)

16. Manuel, P.: A trust model of cloud computing based on Quality of Service. Annals of Operations Research, 1–12 (2013)

17. Pavlidis, M., Mouratidis, H., Kalloniatis, C., Islam, S., Gritzalis, S.: Trustworthy selection of cloud providers based on security and privacy requirements: Justifying trust assumptions. In: Furnell, S., Lambrinoudakis, C., Lopez, J. (eds.) TrustBus 2013. LNCS, vol. 8058, pp. 185–198. Springer, Heidelberg (2013)

18. M, S., L.j, V., Sangeeta, K., Patra, G.K.: Estimating Trust Value for Cloud Service Providers using Fuzzy Logic. International Journal of Computer Applications 48(19), 28–34 (2012)

19. Garg, S.K., Versteeg, S., Buyya, R.: SMICloud: A Framework for Comparing and Ranking Cloud Services. In: Proceedings of the, Fourth IEEE International Conference on Utility and Cloud Computing, UCC 2011, pp. 210–218. IEEE Computer Society, Washington, DC (2011)

20. Qu, L., Wang, Y., Orgun, M.A.: Cloud Service Selection Based on the Aggregation of User Feedback and Quantitative Performance Assessment. In: Proceedings of the IEEE International Conference on Services Computing, SCC 2013, pp. 152–159. IEEE Computer Society, Washington, DC (2013)

21. Beckers, K., Faßbender, S., Heisel, M.: A meta-model approach to the fundamentals for a pattern language for context elicitation. In: Proceedings of the 18th European Conference on Pattern Languages of Programs (Europlop). ACM (2013) (accepted for publication)

22. Beckers, K., Küster, J.-C., Faßbender, S., Schmidt, H.: Pattern-based support for context establishment and asset identification of the ISO 27000 in the field of cloud computing. In: Proceedings of the International Conference on Availability, Reliability and Security (ARES), pp. 327–333. IEEE Computer Society (2011)

23. Beckers, K., Côté, I., Faßbender, S., Heisel, M., Hofbauer, S.: A pattern-based method for establishing a cloud-specific information security management system. Requirements Engineering, 1–53 (2013)
24. Greenspan, S.J., Mylopoulos, J., Borgida, A.: Capturing more world knowledge in the requirements specification. In: Proceedings of the 6th International Conference on Software Engineering, ICSE 1982, pp. 225–234. IEEE Computer Society Press, Los Alamitos (1982)
25. Shakeri, H., Bafghi, G., A, S, Yazdi, H.: Computing Trust Resultant using Intervals. In: IEEE (ed.): 8th International ISC Conference on Information Security and Cryptology (ISCISC) 15–20 (2011)
26. Jøsang, A., Ismail, R., Boyd, C.: A survey of trust and reputation systems for online service provision. Decision Support Systems 43(2), 618–644 (2007)
27. Ontario: Standards of Sound Business and Financial Practices. Enterprise Risk Management: Application Guide. Technical report, Deposit Insurance Corporation of Ontario (2011)
28. Pavlidis, M.: Designing for trust. In: Proceedings of the CAiSE Doctoral Consortium 2011. CEUR-WS, vol. 731 (June 2011)

Analyzing Variability of Software Product Lines Using Semantic and Ontological Considerations

Iris Reinhartz-Berger[1], Nili Itzik[1], and Yair Wand[2]

[1] Department of Information Systems, University of Haifa, Israel
iris@is.haifa.ac.il, nitzik@campus.haifa.ac.il,
[2] Sauder School of Business, University of British Columbia, Canada
yair.wand@ubc.ca

Abstract. Software Product Line Engineering (SPLE) is an approach to systematically reuse software-related artifacts among different, yet similar, software products. Previewing requirements as drivers of different development methods and activities, several studies have suggested using requirements specifications to identify and analyze commonality and variability of software products. These studies mainly employ semantic text similarity techniques. As a result, they might be limited in their ability to analyze the variability of the *expected behaviors* of software systems as perceived from an external point of view. Such a view is important when reaching different reuse decisions. In this paper we propose to introduce considerations which reflect the behavior of software products as manifested in requirement statements. To model these behavioral aspects of software requirements we use terms adapted from Bunge's ontological model. The suggested approach automatically extracts the initial state, external events, and final state of software behavior. Then, variability is analyzed based on that view.

Keywords: Software Product Line Engineering, Variability analysis, Requirements Specifications, Ontology.

1 Introduction

Software Product Line Engineering (SPLE) is an approach to systematically reuse software-related artifacts among different, yet similar, software products [6], [19]. Reuse of artifacts, such as requirements specifications, design documents and code, often results in the creation of a myriad of variants. Managing such a variety of artifacts' variants is a significant challenge. Thus, SPLE promotes the definition and management of software product lines (SPLs), which are families of similar software systems, termed software products. An important aspect of SPLE is managing the *variability* that exists between the members of the same SPL. In this context, variability is defined as "the ability of an asset to be efficiently extended, changed, customized, or configured for use in a particular context" [10].

In SPLE, different artifacts need to be managed. Of those, requirements management is of special interest due to several reasons. First, requirements represent the expectations of different stakeholders from the requested system. These stakeholders

M. Jarke et al. (Eds.): CAiSE 2014, LNCS 8484, pp. 150–164, 2014.

include users and customers and not just developers. Second, requirements are the drivers of other development activities, including analysis, design, implementation, and testing. Finally, requirements are relevant to many development methods, including agile ones (through concepts such as user stories).

Several studies have suggested using requirements specifications in order to identify and analyze commonality and variability of software products. In these studies, requirements are operationalized or realized by features, and variability is usually represented as feature diagrams, the main aid for representing and managing variability in SPLE [5], [11]. The current studies commonly apply only semantic similarity metrics, that is, seek similarities of terminology, in order to identify common features, create feature diagrams, and analyze the variability of the resultant feature diagrams. As we will show via examples, using only semantic considerations might limit the ability to analyze the variability of the *expected behaviors* of software systems as perceived from an external point of view of a user or a customer. Such a view is important for reaching different reuse decisions, e.g., when conducting feasibility studies, estimating software development efforts, or adopting SPLE. In addition, current variability analysis methods take into account intermediate outcomes of the behavior that may not matter to external stakeholders, such as users and customers. For example, a system may intermediately keep information in case a transaction fails, but this would be of no interest when the behavior ends successfully. Hence, when analyzing variability of software products, we aim at minimizing the impact of intermediate outcomes which cannot be used for (and might confound) comparing the products from an external point of view.

In this work we propose to overcome the shortcomings of pure semantic-based variability analysis by combining semantic similarity with similarity of software behavior as manifested in requirement statements. To compare software behavior we apply an ontological view of dynamic aspects of systems which we proposed in earlier work [20], [21]. For a given requirement, we consider the behavior it represents in the application ("business") domain. Taking an external point of view, behavior is described in terms of the initial state of the system before the behavior occurs, the external events that trigger the behavior, and the final state of the system after the behavior occurs. We use semantic metrics to evaluate the similarity of related behavioral elements and use this similarity to analyze variability.

The rest of this paper is structured as follows. Section 2 reviews related work, exemplifying limitations of current approaches. Section 3 briefly provides the ontological background and our framework for classifying software variability. Section 4 introduces the ontological approach to variability analysis and demonstrates its applicability. Section 5 presents preliminary results and discusses advantages and limitations. Finally, Section 6 summaries the work and presents future research directions.

2   Related Work

As mentioned above, the main approach to variability analysis in SPLE is semantic – based on text similarity measures. Semantic text similarity measures are commonly classified as knowledge-based or corpus-based [9], [16].

Corpus-based measures identify the degree of similarity based on information derived from large corpora (e.g., [4], [12], and [22]). Latent Semantic Analysis (LSA) [12], for example, is a well-known method that analyzes the statistical relationships among words in a large corpus of text. Sentence similarity is computed as the cosine of the angle between the vectors representing the sentences' words.

Knowledge-based measures use information drawn from semantic networks. Many of these methods use WordNet [26] for measuring word (or concept) similarity. This can be done in different ways, including measuring path length between terms on the semantic net or using information content, namely, the probability to find the concept in a given net. Several measures have been suggested to extend word similarity to sentence similarity. These measures consider sentences as vectors, sets, or lists of words and suggest ways to calculate sentence similarity using word similarities (e.g., [13], [14], and [16]). The MCS method [16], for example, calculates sentence similarity by finding the maximum word similarity score for each word in a sentence with words in the same part of speech class in another sentence. The derived word similarity scores are weighted with the inverse document frequency scores that belong to the corresponding word.

In the context of analyzing software products variability, different studies have suggested ways to use textual requirements to generate variability models in general and feature diagrams in particular. Examples of such studies are [7], [17], and [25]. In [25], for instance, the semantic similarity of the requirements is measured using LSA. Then, similar requirements are grouped using a hierarchical agglomerative clustering algorithm. Finally, a Requirements Description Language enables the specification and composition of variant features.

All the above methods employ only semantic considerations. Furthermore, the similarity calculation takes into consideration the full text of a requirement statement. As mentioned before, such statements might include aspects (e.g., intermediate outcomes) that are less or not relevant for analyzing variability from an external perspective. We illustrate the limitations of the current methods and motivate our approach, using a series of examples.

The first example refers to the following requirements:

(1) "The system should be able to report on any user update activities";
(2) "Any user should be able to report system activities".

Applying the well-known and commonly used semantic similarity method LSA[1], the similarity of these sentences is 1. This would imply that their semantic meanings are identical, and hence no variability between these requirements exists. It is clear, however, that these requirements are quite different: the first represents behavior that is internal and likely aims at detecting suspicious user update activities. The second requirement represents a behavior triggered by an external user who intends to report his/her system activities.

As a second example, consider the following two requirements:

(3) "The system will allow different functions based on predefined user profiles";
(4) "Different operations should be allowed for different user profiles".

---

[1]   We used LSA implementation that can be accessed via http://lsa.colorado.edu/.

In this case, LSA results with a low similarity value of 0.38, failing to reflect the situation accurately: the two requirements represent very similar domain behaviors.

Finally, the following two requirements can be considered similar from an external point of view, although they differ in their levels of details of intermediate actions.

(5) "When the client activates an activity she is allowed to perform, the system displays the outputs of the activity."

(6) "If the user is authorized to perform an action, the system initializes the parameters needed by the action. The user performs the action and the system responds that the action was performed. Finally, the user requests to display the outputs, and the system presents the action's outcomes."

However, the LSA-based value of the similarity of these two requirements is relatively low (0.57), failing to reflect their similarity from an external point of view.

To overcome the above limitations, we propose to combine a semantic approach and considerations which reflect system behavior as manifested in requirements statements and modeled ontologically.

3   Bung's Ontology and Software Variability Classification

We use concepts from Bunge's ontological model [2, 3] and its adaptations to software and information systems [23, 24] in order to define behaviors and use them for variability analysis. We have chosen this ontology because it formalizes concepts that are important for representing functionality and behaviors. Specifically, these concepts include things, states, events, and transformations. Furthermore, Bunge's ontological model has already served us to define software variability classes [20, 21].

Bunge's ontological model [2], [3] describes the world as made of *things* that possess *properties*. Properties are known via *attributes*, which are characteristics assigned to things by humans. A *state variable* is a function which assigns a value to an attribute of a thing at a given time. The *state* of a thing is the vector of state variables' values at a particular point in time. For a state s, s.x denotes the value of the state variable x in s. An *event* is a change of a state of a thing. An event can be external or internal. An *external event* is a change in the state of a thing as a result of an action of another thing. An *internal event* is a change which arises due to an internal transformation in the thing. Finally, a state can be stable or unstable: a *stable state* can be changed only by an external event. An *unstable state* will be changed by an internal event.

We exemplify the above concepts using a library management domain. In this domain, *book status* can be considered a state variable, defining whether a book is borrowed, on the shelf, or in repair; *ready to lend* can be considered a stable state, when it can accept the external event – *borrow book* (generated by a reader); and *book becomes past-due* can be considered an internal event, which is initiated when a certain period has passed from borrowing and the book is not yet returned.

Using these concepts, we defined in [20] *a behavior* as a triplet (s_1, E, s^*). s_1 is termed the *initial state* of the behavior and s^* – the *final state* of the behavior. We assume that the system can respond to external events when in s_1 (i.e., s_1 is an input sensitive state, see [20], [21]). s^* is the first stable state the thing (the real domain or a system) reaches when it starts in state s_1 and the external events sequence $E=<e_1,...,$

e_n> occurs. The full behavior includes intermediate states the thing traverses due to its own transformations in response to the external events. However, only (s_1, E, s*) are "visible" from an external (user) point of view.

In our example, *borrowing* can be considered a behavior, which starts in the state *ready to lend* (i.e., when the book status is "on the shelf" and the librarian is "available"), is triggered by the external event *borrow book,* and ends in the state *book is borrowed* (i.e., the book status is "borrowed" and the librarian is "available" again).

We further made two assumptions regarding the things whose behavior we model [21]: *no interruption* (external events can affect a thing only when it or at least one of its components is in a stable state) and *stability assumption* (all things we deal with in practice will eventually reach stable states).

Finally, we defined similarity of behaviors in terms of similarity of their external events and states [20]:

Event similarity: Two external events are considered similar if they appear to be the same in the application domain.

State similarity: Two states s and t are considered similar with respect to a set of state variables X, iff $\forall x \in X$ s.x = t.x. X is termed the *view of interest*.

Based on these definitions we identified eight classes of external variability, namely, variability that refers to software *functionality* as visible to users (see Table 1).

Table 1. External variability classes based on systems' behaviors

#	s_1	E	s*	Class Name
1.	similar	similar	similar	Completely similar behaviors
2.	similar	not similar	similar	Similar cases and responses, different interactions
3.	similar	similar	not similar	Similar triggers, different responses
4.	similar	not similar	not similar	Similar cases, different behaviors
5.	not similar	similar	similar	Different cases, similar behaviors
6.	not similar	not similar	similar	Different triggers, similar responses
7.	not similar	similar	not similar	Different cases and responses, similar interactions
8.	not similar	not similar	not similar	Completely different behaviors

In the current work, we use textual software requirements as the basis for automatic identification of domain behaviors and their elements (namely, the initial and final states and the external events). We use semantic measurements in order to refine event and state similarity definitions.

4   Deriving Domain Behaviors from Software Requirements

Perceiving a software system as a set of intended changes in a given domain, we focus on systems' behaviors as specified by or represented in functional requirements. Functional requirements commonly refer to *actions* (what should be performed?) and *objects* (on what objects, also termed *patients*, should the action be performed?). They can further refer to the *agents* (who performs the action?), the *instruments* (how the action is performed?), and the *temporal constraints* (when is the action preformed? in what conditions is it performed?).

There are different ways to write and phrase functional requirements. For our purpose, we assume that they are specified as *user stories* or *descriptions of use cases*.

We further assume that each use case or user story represents a *single behavior* of the requested system[2]. For example, consider the following requirement which describes a typical use case in a library management system:

> When the home page is displayed, a borrower borrows a book copy by herself. She enters the copy identification number after she provides the borrower number. If the copy identification number and the borrower number are valid, the system updates the number of available copies of that title.

Our approach consists of four steps: (1) *pre-processing* which checks the quality of the individual requirements and identifies the need for corrections or improvements; (2) *extraction of the main behavioral elements* from a requirement, e.g., the requirement's agents (who?), actions (what?), and patients (on what objects?); (3) *Classification* of the extracted main behavioral elements according to the ontological definition of behavior (in terms of states and events); and (4) *measuring requirements variability* based on the framework presented in [20], [21].

Pre-processing is out of the scope of this paper. It may use existing quality models, such as that presented in [1]. In the following sub-sections we elaborate on steps 2-4.

4.1   Extraction of the Main Behavioral Elements

In order to extract the main behavioral elements of software requirements we use semantic role labeling (SRL) [8]. This approach labels constituents of a phrase with their semantic roles in the phrase. Currently, we refer to five semantic roles which are of special importance to functional requirements. These roles, their labels, and the aspects they fulfill in functional requirements are listed in Table 2.

Table 2. The semantic roles we use in our work

Label	Role	Assigned to	Aspects fulfilled in requirements
A0	Agent	Agents, causers, or experiencers	Who?
A1	Patient	Undergoing state change or being affected by the action	On what?
A2	Instrument	Instruments, benefactives, attributes	How?
AM-TMP	Temporal modifier	Time indicators specifying when an action took place	When?
AM-ADV	Adverbial modifier	Temporally related (modifiers of events), intentional (modifiers of propositions), focus-sensitive (e.g., only and even), or sentential (evaluative, attitudinal, viewpoint, performative)	In what conditions?

Using SRL[3], we specify for each requirement R a list of behavioral vectors $BV_R = \{bv_i\}_{i=1..n}$. Two types of behavioral vectors are identified: action and non-action vectors. The following definitions formally specify the behavioral vectors for these two types. Examples are provided immediately afterwards.

---

[2]   If this is not the case, a pre-processing done by a requirements engineer is needed to split the requirements statements to separate expected behaviors.

[3]   We specifically use the system at `http://barbar.cs.1th.se:8081/` or `http://en.sempar.ims.uni¬stuttgart.de/`.

Definition 1. An *action vector* represents an activity (identified by a verb) in the behavior: $bv_i ::= (Agent_i, Action_i, Patient_i, Instrument_i, Source_i)$, where:

-   $Agent_i$, $Patient_i$ and $Instrument_i$ are as explained in Table 2.
-   $Action_i$ is the verb predicate of the phrase.
-   $Source_i \in \{$AM-TMP, AM-ADV, None$\}$ indicates whether the vector originates from a modifier (temporal or adverbial) or a non-modifier phrase, respectively.

An action vector is derived from a non-modifier phrase or a compound modifier phrase that is further parsed to reveal its constituting components (e.g., agents and actions).

Definition 2. A *non-action vector* represents the temporal or adverbial pre-condition of the behavior (or part of it): $bv_i ::= (Modifier_i, Source_i)$, where:

-   $Modifier_i$ includes the atomic modifier phrase
-   $Source_i \in \{$AM-TMP, AM-ADV$\}$ indicates whether the vector originates from a temporal or adverbial modifier, respectively.

A non-action vector is derived from an atomic modifier phrase which includes no verb (and thus is not further parsed by SRL).

Table 3 lists the derived behavioral vectors for our previous requirement of the library management example. Vector #5 is a non-action vector. All other vectors represent actions. We further replace pronouns with their anaphors (i.e., the nouns to which they refer) using the algorithm in [18] (e.g. the agent "she" becomes "a borrower").

Table 3. Examples of behavioral vectors

#	Agent	Action	Patient	Instrument	Modifier	Source
1	[4]	is displayed	the home page			AM-TMP
2	a borrower	Borrows	a book copy	by herself		None
3	[5]~~She~~ [a borrower]	Enters	the copy identification number			None
4	[5]~~She~~ [a borrower]	Provides	the borrower number			AM-TMP
5	[4]				the copy identification number and the borrower number are valid	AM-ADV
6	The system	Updates	the number of available copies of that title			None

The next step in the analysis is to arrange the behavioral vectors of each requirement in a temporal order. We do this by constructing temporal graphs:

Definition 3. Given a requirement R and its derived list of behavioral vectors BV_R, the *temporal graph* is defined as $TG_R = (BV_R, E)$, where $e = (bv_1, bv_2) \in E$ implies that $bv_1, bv_2 \in BV_R$ and bv_1 temporally precedes bv_2 (notation: $bv_1 \dashrightarrow bv_2$).

The construction of edges in this graph is done in two steps. First, we use *syntactic ordering*, based on the order of the argument vectors in the requirement's phrasing.

---

[4] Note that since we are interested in automated analysis, we cannot incorporate here assumptions about what causes these actions (e.g., the system or an external user).

[5] Replacement of a pronoun by the relevant noun is indicated with ~~pronoun~~ [noun].

Second, we apply *semantic ordering*, using the machine learning algorithm suggested in [15], to update the syntactic edges based on six types of temporal relations derived from the text. These relations are listed in Table 4. Whenever a semantic relationship contradicts a syntactic one, we use the semantic relationship as shown in the table.

Table 4. The temporal relations for overriding syntactic edges with semantic ones; W, X, Y, and Z are temporal phrases or events, ⤳ indicates their order

The graph after phase 1	Detected semantic temporal relation	The graph after phase 2
W ⤳ X ⤳ Y ⤳ Z	Y before X Y ibefore X	W ⤳ Y ⤳ X ⤳ Z
W ⤳ X ⤳ Y ⤳ Z	X begins Y^6 X ends Y^6 X includes Y^6 X simultaneous Y^6	(graph: W with arrows to X above and X below, converging to Z)

Fig. 1 exhibits the temporal graph for our example (Table 3). The changes the semantic ordering causes to the syntactic order (the gray arrows) are depicted with the black arrows[7].

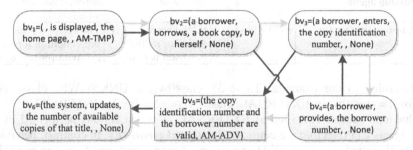

Fig. 1. The temporal graph generated for our example; Ellipses represent action vectors and rectangles – non-action vectors

4.2   Classification of the Behavioral Vectors

We now turn to the classification of the dynamic aspects of the requirements to initial states, external events, and final states. To this end, we first classify each behavioral vector into external, internal, or unknown (with respect to the requested system). In particular, we examine the Agent and Action components of action vectors: the agent can be *internal*, *external*, or *missing* (as in passive phrases)[8]; independently, the action

---

[6] In all these cases X and Y are executed in parallel (at least partially).

[7] We assume that the requirements are well-written (i.e., include no ambiguities and contradictions) after the pre-processing step. Thus, the temporal graph is a directed acyclic graph.

[8] We maintain a list of terms representing internal agents, including: "the system", "the application", and the explicit name and abbreviation of the requested system. The requirements analyst may update this default list to include the main components of the requested system.

can have an *active* or a *passive* meaning[9]. All non-action vectors are considered internal, as they do not represent an actual action, but a pre-condition for the behavior (or part of it). Accordingly, we identify six generic cases (see Table 5).

Table 5. Classifying behavioral vectors into internal, external, and unknown

Case	Classification class(bv)	Example	Comments
1. An **action vector** with an **external agent** and an **active meaning**	EXTERNAL	"a borrower borrows a book"	The action is performed by an external agent
2. An **action vector** with an **external agent** and a **passive meaning**	INTERNAL	"a borrower receives an email message"	The system acted on an external agent
3. An **action vector** with an **internal agent** and an **active meaning**	INTERNAL	"the system updates the number of available copies"	The action is performed by the system
4. An **action vector** with an **internal agent** and a **passive meaning**	EXTERNAL	"the system receives the number of available copies"	The system is acted on
5. An **action vector** with a **missing agent**	UNKNOWN	"a book is borrowed"	The vector cannot be deterministically classified
6. A **non-action vector**	INTERNAL	if "the book copy is valid" or if "the borrower is new"	The vector represents a pre-condition for the behavior (or part of it)

Returning to our example (Table 3): class(bv_1) = UNKNOWN; class(bv_2) = class(bv_3) = class(bv_4) = EXTERNAL; class(bv_5) = class(bv_6) = INTERNAL.

Behavioral vectors classified as EXTERNAL represent actions performed by external agents and therefore are considered ***external events (E)***. In contrast, behavioral vectors classified as INTERNAL represent actions performed or pre-conditions checked by the system. They are considered to reflect states: initial, final, or intermediate. As an initial state describes the state *before* the behavior occurs, only internal behavioral vectors that *precede* (in the temporal graph) the sequence of external behavioral vectors will be taken into consideration for defining the initial state of the behavior. Of those, only vectors whose sources are modifiers (and thus represent pre-conditions) are considered the ***initial state of the behavior (s_1)***. Following similar arguments, only internal behavioral vectors which *follow* the sequence of external behavioral vectors will be taken into consideration for defining the final state of the behavior. Of those, only action vectors whose sources are not modifiers (and thus represent actual internal actions) are considered the ***final state of the behavior (s*)***. All other internal behavioral vectors, i.e., those interleaved with the external behavioral vectors, are considered to be manifested by intermediate states. Such actions (and related states) are not currently taken into consideration in our analysis, which is based on an external view of behaviors.

---

[9] Note that passive actions can use an active form of the verb (e.g., "receive" and "get"). Thus, we maintain a list of such verbs.

Behavioral vectors for which the agent is unknown are classified at this stage into multiple behavioral elements (e.g., both initial state and external events). The decision whether these vectors represent internal or external actions is taken in a later stage, when calculating for each vector the most similar counterparts.

We next formally define the behavior associated with a requirement and exemplify this definition on our requirement:

Definition 4. Given a requirement R, its derived list of behavioral vectors BV_R, and its temporal graph TG_R, the *behavior associated with* R is defined as a triplet $B_R=(s_1, E, s^*)$, where:

- The *initial state (s_1)* includes all internal or unknown vectors originated from modifiers (i.e., may represent pre-conditions) and *precede* all external vectors in the temporal graph representing the behavior. Formally expressed,
  s_1 = {bv∈ BV_R | class(bv) ∈ {INTERNAL, UNKNOWN} and bv.Source ∈ {AM-TMP, AM-ADV} and ¬∃path p∈ TG_R such that bv'⇢ bv∈p and class(bv') = EXTERNAL}
- The *external events (E)* include all potentially external behavioral vectors (namely, external vectors and action vectors with unknown agents). Formally expressed,
  E = {bv ∈ BV_R | class(bv) ∈ {EXTERNAL, UNKNOWN}}
- The *final state (s^*)* includes all internal or unknown vectors that do not originate from modifiers (i.e., may represent actual actions) and *follow* all external vectors in the temporal graph representing the behavior. Formally expressed,
  s^* = {bv ∈ BV_R | class(bv) ∈ {INTERNAL, UNKNOWN} and bv.Source = None and ¬∃path p∈ TG_R such that bv⇢ bv'∈p and class(bv') = EXTERNAL}

In our previous example, we obtain the classification of behavioral vectors as shown in Table 6. Note that bv_1 appears twice as its agent is unknown and hence it can be considered either an external event or an initial state. bv_5 = (the copy identification number and the borrower number are valid, AM-ADV) does not appear at all as it represents a pre-condition originated from an adverbial modifier and appearing after external events. Thus, bv_5 cannot be considered an initial neither final state (but rather an intermediate state).

Table 6. An example of the outcome of the behavioral vectors classification phase

S_1 (initial state)	E (external event to which the system responds)	S* (final state the system is expected to have)
bv_1=(, is displayed, the home page, , AM-TMP)	bv_1=(, is displayed, the home page, , AM-TMP) bv_2=(a borrower, borrows, a book copy, by herself , None) bv_4=(a borrower, provides, the borrower number, , None) bv_3=(a borrower, enters, the copy identification number, , None)	bv_6=(the system, updates, the number of available copies of that title, , None)

4.3   Measuring Requirements Variability

Having two requirements, their behavioral vectors, and the classification of the vectors to initial states, external events, and final states, we now define *behavioral similarity*. The definitions are followed by an example.

Definition 5 (Behavioral Vectors Similarity). Given two behavioral vectors, the vectors similarity is calculated as follows:

1. If the two vectors are *action vectors*, the vectors similarity is the weighted average of their component semantic similarities. Formally expressed,

$$VS\ (v_1,\ v_2)\ =\ \frac{\sum_{comp \in \{Agent,Action,Patient,Instrument\}} \delta_{comp}*w_{comp}*sim(v_1.comp,v_2.comp)}{\sum_{comp \in \{Agent,Action,Patient,Instrument\}} \delta_{comp}*w_{comp}},$$

   where:
   - w_{comp} is the weight given to a specific vector component (agent, action, patient, or instrument), $\sum_{comp \in \{Agent,Action,Patient,Instrument\}} w_{comp}=1$.
   - δ_{comp} is 1 if the component comp exists (i.e., it is not empty in both v_1 and v_2) and 0 otherwise.
   - $sim(v_1.comp, v_2.comp)$ is the semantic similarity of the two vectors' components.

2. If the two vectors are *non-action* vectors, the vectors similarity is the semantic similarity of their modifier components. Formally expressed,
   $VS\ (v_1, v_2) = sim(v_1.Modifier, v_2.Modifier)$, where
   - $sim(v_1.Modifier, v_2.Modifier)$ is the semantic similarity of the modifier components of the two vectors.

3. If one vector is an *action vector* (say v_1) and the other is a *non-action vector*, the vectors similarity is the semantic similarity between the corresponding phrases. Formally expressed, $VS\ (v_1, v_2) = sim(v_1, v_2.Modifier)$, where:
   - $sim(v_1, v_2.\ Modifier)$ is the semantic similarity between the concatenation of the agent, action, patient, and instrument components of the first vector and the modifier component of the second vector.

Definition 6 (Behavioral Element Similarity). Given two requirements, R_1 and R_2, and their behavioral vectors that are classified as the same element bh (initial state, external events, or final state), the behavioral element similarity is calculated as the average of the maximal pair-wise similarities. Formally expressed:

$$BS\ (R_1, R_2 \mid bh) = \begin{cases} 0 & R_1.bh \neq \emptyset\ and\ R_2.bh = \emptyset \\ \frac{\sum_{i=1}^{n} \max_{j=1..m} VS(v_i,v\prime_j)}{n} & R_1.bh = \{v_1, ..., v_n\}\ and\ R_2.bh = \{v\prime_1, ..., v\prime_m\}, \\ 1 & R_1.bh = \emptyset \end{cases}$$

where:
- $R_1.bh$, $R_2.bh$ are the behavioral vectors classified as the element bh in requirements R_1 and R_2, respectively; $R_i.bh=\emptyset$ means that no behavioral vectors were classified as bh.
- $VS\ (v_i, v\prime_j)$ is the behavioral vector similarity of v_i and $v\prime_j$.

As an example consider the following requirements:

1.	"When a borrower borrows a book copy by herself, she enters the copy identification number and the borrower number. The system updates the number of available copies of that title."
2.	"When a librarian lends a book copy to a borrower, she enters the copy identification number and the borrower number. The system updates the number of available copies of that title and stores the lending details (when, by whom, to whom)."

For calculating component semantic similarities we used an MCS version that handles phrases rather than complete sentences. We set the component weights to 0.3,

0.4, 0.2, and 0.1 for agents, actions, patients, and instruments, respectively, perceiving agents and actions as the dominant components in behavioral vectors similarities. We obtain initial state similarity for the given requirements of 1 (no special pre-conditions in both requirements), external events similarity of 0.78 (due to differences in the agents that initiate the events), and final state similarity of 1 (as the final state of the first requirement is included in the final state of the second requirement). Note that we chose an asymmetric metric for defining behavioral element similarity, meaning that BS $(R_1, R_2 \mid bh) \neq$ BS $(R_2, R_1 \mid bh)$, as we perceive similarity as the ability to reuse behavior R_2 when behavior R_1 is required. The asymmetry in this measure reflects the possibility that it might be acceptable to substitute one behavior for another, but not the second for the first, as exemplified by the two requirements above.

Based on the behavioral element similarity, we classify the outcome of comparing each pair of requirements to one of the eight variability classes in Table 1. To this end, we define *event similarity threshold* (th_e) and *state similarity threshold* (th_s):

1. Initial states are considered similar if and only if BS $(R_1, R_2 \mid s_1) > th_s$.
2. External events are considered similar if and only if BS $(R_1, R_2 \mid E) > th_e$.
3. Final states are considered similar if and only if BS $(R_1, R_2 \mid s^*) > th_s$.

Assuming an event similarity threshold greater than 0.5 (e.g., 0.8), the variability class to which requirement 1 belongs with respect to requirement 2 is # 2 (see Table 1: similar cases and responses, different interactions). This class accurately describes the requirements variability.

5   Preliminary Results

To evaluate the proposed approach, we compared its outcomes to evaluations by experts. We provided five experts, each having 10 to 25 years of experience in requirements engineering and software development, with 10 requirements. For each requirement, four alternative systems to be considered were presented to the experts. Each alternative was describes as a requirement. The full set of requirements and alternatives is discussed in [20][10]. We asked the experts to rank the four alternatives for each requirement based on the similarity to the given requirement in terms of the amount of changes needed to adapt the alternatives to the requirement. Since experts' ranking requires some subjective considerations, there was no full agreement between the experts regarding the ranking of the alternatives. Therefore, we defined for each pair of alternatives, Si and Sj (i, j=1…4, i>j), relation "Si is not better than Sj" (Si≤Sj). For each requirement there were four possible alternatives yielding six such relations. This provided a total of 60 relations for the 10 requirements. There were 55 relations on which most experts (at least four out of the five experts, 80%) agreed.

We conducted the analysis described in this work for the same set of requirements. We used the behavioral element similarities to calculate overall similarity, which can serve as a basis for ranking alternatives. The weight of initial state similarity was set to 0.2, the weight of external events – 0.3, and the weight of final state similarity – 0.5. This reflected an assumption that the final state of behaviors (usually specifying

---

[10] It can be accessed at http://mis.hevra.haifa.ac.il/~iris/research/OA/ QuestionnaireEng.pdf.

system output) is the dominant element in defining behavior similarity. We followed a similar procedure using the well-known semantic similarity method LSA, which as noted is based only on semantic considerations. Table 7 summarizes the results of the ontological approach and LSA with respect to experts[11].

Table 7. Comparing the results of the ontological approach and LSA with experts

	Ontological approach	LSA
Number of experts' relations found by the method (out of 55)	51 relations (93%)	45 relations (82%)

As can be seen, our approach performed better than LSA in comparison to rankings by experts. We believe that our approach has an additional advantage to better performance – it is self-explanatory. Users of the approach, who are expected to be requirements analysts, can see not only the overall calculated similarity, but also more details: initial state, external events, and final state similarities. This can help make their reuse decisions more evidence-based and feasibility studies more systematic.

Analyzing the relations missed by the ontological approach, we observed the following. First, some of the requirements included phrases that explain reasons, e.g., "so the librarian can make inter-library loans". These phrases were interpreted by the approach as an integral part of the behavior (part of the external events in this case). Second, in a few cases, where the requirements statements included very complicated sentences, SRL failed to correctly identify the agents, actions, patients and/or instruments of the different phrases. Finally, we observed that in some cases our approach resulted with the conclusion that two alternatives are very similar to the given requirement and the experts subjectively preferred one alternative over the other.

6   Summary and Future Work

We proposed a method to analyze variability and similarity of software requirements based on combining semantic and behavioral aspects of requirement statements. To formalize the external (user-oriented) aspects of software behavior we used an ontological model where a specific functional requirement is modeled as a triplet: initial state, external events, and the final state of the system. We have shown how such a representation can be obtained automatically by: (1) applying semantic analysis to requirements statements to identify behavioral vectors; (2) describing the vectors in common terms; (3) ordering the vectors temporally based on modifiers identified in the semantic analysis; and (4) extracting the initial state, external events, and final state for each functional requirement. We then suggested a way to measure the similarity of two requirements based on each element of their behavioral triplets and classified pairs of requirements to one of eight variability classes. In a preliminary evaluation, the approach yielded results more similar to experts' evaluations than those of a well-known semantic similarity measure – LSA.

---

[11] Elaborations can be found at
http://mis.hevra.haifa.ac.il/~iris/research/SOVA/.

In the future, we intend to extend the approach in several ways. First, we intend to consider additional semantic roles, e.g., location modifiers. Second, we plan to refine the similarity measures to include a choice of specific state variables rather than complete behavioral vectors, thus having a way to reflect user views more faithfully. This will enable us to analyze variability of software requirements from different points of view that may reflect different purposes or stakeholders. Users may consider two software behaviors similar while developers may consider them different, or vice versa. Similarly, such differences might exist among users. The choice of state variables to represent different points of view can be included in the behavioral analysis and hence in the similarity calculation. Third, we also intend to take into account in the variability analysis different ordering of the occurrence of external events.

References

1. Berry, D.M., Bucchiarone, A., Gnesi, S., Lami, G.,Trentanni, G.: A new quality model for natural language requirements specifications. In: The International Workshop on Requirements Engineering: Foundation of Software Quality, REFSQ (2006)
2. Bunge, M.: Treatise on Basic Philosophy. Ontology I: The Furniture of the World, vol. 3. Reidel, Boston (1977)
3. Bunge, M.: Treatise on Basic Philosophy. Ontology II: A World of Systems, vol. 4. Reidel, Boston (1979)
4. Burgess, C., Livesay, K., Lund, K.: Explorations in context space: Words, sentences, discourse. Discourse Processes 25(2-3), 211–257 (1998)
5. Chen, L., Babar, M.A.: A systematic review of evaluation of variability management approaches in software product lines. Information and Software Technology 53(4), 344–362 (2011)
6. Clements, P., Northrop, L.: Software Product Lines: Practices and Patterns. Addison-Wesley (2001)
7. Dumitru, H., Gibiec, M., Hariri, N., Cleland-Huang, J., Mobasher, B., Castro-Herrera, C., Mirakhorli, M.: On-demand feature recommendations derived from mining public product descriptions. In: 33rd IEEE International Conference on Software Engineering (ICSE 2011), pp. 181–190 (2011)
8. Gildea, D., Jurafsky, D.: Automatic Labeling of Semantic Roles. Computational Linguistics 28(3), 245–288 (2002)
9. Gomaa, W.H., Fahmy, A.A.: A Survey of Text Similarity Approaches. International Journal of Computer Applications 68(13), 13–18 (2013)
10. Jaring, M.: Variability engineering as an Integral Part of the Software Product Family Development Process, Ph.D. thesis, The Netherlands (2005)
11. Kang, K.C., Cohen, S.G., Hess, J.A., Novak, W.E., Peterson, A.S.: Feature-oriented domain analysis (FODA) – feasibility study. Technical report no. CMU/SEI-90-TR-21). Carngie-Mellon University, Pittsburgh (1990)
12. Landauer, T.K., Foltz, P.W., Laham, D.: Introduction to Latent Semantic Analysis. Discourse Processes 25, 259–284 (1998)
13. Li, Y., McLean, D., Bandar, Z.A., O'Shea, J.D., Crockett, K.: Sentence Similarity Basedon Semantic Nets and Corpus Statistics. IEEE Transactions on Knowledge and Data Engineering 18(8), 1138–1150 (2006)

14. Malik, R., Subramaniam, V., Kaushik, S.: Automatically Selecting Answer Templates toRespond to Customer Emails. In: The International Joint Conference on Artificial Intelligence (IJCAI 2007), pp. 1659–1664 (2007)
15. Mani, I., Verhagen, M., Wellner, B., Lee, C.M., Pustejovsky, J.: Machine learning of temporal relations. In: The 21st International Conference on Computational Linguistics and the 44th Annual Meeting of the Association for Computational Linguistics, pp. 753–760 (2006)
16. Mihalcea, R., Corley, C., Strapparava, C.: Corpus-based and knowledge-based measures of text semantic similarity. In: The 21st National Conference on Artificial Intelligence (AAAI 2006), vol. 1, pp. 775–780 (2006)
17. Niu, N., Easterbrook, S.: Extracting and modeling product line functional requirements. In: The 16th IEEE International Requirements Engineering Conference (RE 2008), pp. 155–164 (2008)
18. Raghunathan, K., Lee, H., Rangarajan, S., Chambers, N., Surdeanu, M., Jurafsky, D., Manning, C.: A Multi-Pass Sieve for Coreference Resolution. In: The conference on Empirical Methods in Natural Language Processing (EMNLP 2010), pp. 492–501 (2010)
19. Pohl, K., Böckle, G., van der Linden, F.: Software Product-line Engineering: Foundations, Principles, and Techniques. Springer (2005)
20. Reinhartz-Berger, I., Sturm, A., Wand, Y.: Comparing Functionality of Software Systems: An Ontological Approach. Data & Knowledge Engineering 87, 320–338 (2013)
21. Reinhartz-Berger, I., Sturm, A., Wand, Y.: External Variability of Software: Classification and Ontological Foundations. In: Jeusfeld, M., Delcambre, L., Ling, T.-W. (eds.) ER 2011. LNCS, vol. 6998, pp. 275–289. Springer, Heidelberg (2011)
22. Turney, P.D.: Mining the web for synonyms: PMI-IR versus LSA on TOEFL. In: Flach, P.A., De Raedt, L. (eds.) ECML 2001. LNCS (LNAI), vol. 2167, pp. 491–502. Springer, Heidelberg (2001)
23. Wand, Y., Weber, R.: On the ontological expressiveness of information systems analysis and design grammars. Information Systems Journal 3(4), 217–237 (1993)
24. Wand, Y., Weber, R.: An Ontological Model of an Information System. IEEE Transactions on Software Engineering 16(11), 1282–1292 (1990)
25. Weston, N., Chitchyan, R., Rashid, A.: A framework for constructing semantically composable feature models from natural language requirements. In: The 13th International Software Product Line Conference (SPLC 2009), pp. 211–220 (2009)
26. WordNet, http://wordnet.princeton.edu/

Similarity Analysis within Product Line Scoping: An Evaluation of a Semi-automatic Approach

Markus Nöbauer[1], Norbert Seyff[2], and Iris Groher[3]

[1] InsideAx GmbH, 4031 Linz, Austria
markus.noebauer@insideax.at
[2] University of Zurich, 8050 Zurich, Switzerland
seyff@ifi.uzh.ch
[3] Johannes Kepler University (JKU), 4020 Linz, Austria
iris.groher@jku.at

Abstract. Introducing a product line approach in an organization requires a systematic scoping phase to decide what products and features should be included. Product line scoping is a non-trivial activity and traditionally consumes a lot of time and resources. This issue highlights the need to complement traditional scoping activities with semi-automatic approaches that allow to initially estimate the potential for reuse with small efforts. In this paper we present an evaluation of a tool-supported approach that enables the semi-automatic analysis of existing products in order to calculate their similarity. This approach is tailored to be used within the configuration-based systems domain, where we have used it to identify similarity within two types of industrial standard software products. The results of this evaluation highlight that our approach provides accurate results and leads to time savings compared to manual similarity analysis.

1 Introduction

Adopting a product line (PL) approach supports companies to foster systematic reuse [1],[2]. However, the transition from single-system development to a PL approach is often non-trivial and costly [3]. PL scoping is an important activity in existing PL engineering processes [2]. Within PL scoping, companies investigate which existing products are potential candidates for a PL. Therefore, they have to identify the commonality that potential members of the PL share and their variations [4],[5]. Most existing scoping approaches require large upfront investments [6],[7]. Scoping highly depends on the development practices within the organizations, the architecture of the system, and the business domain. In [8] about 16 different scoping approaches and industrial applications have been identified. However, only 6 industrial case studies for these approaches exist. Those approaches aim to deliver a full PL scope while our goal is to deliver a first estimation if further scoping investments are justified.

According to our experience, small and medium sized companies (SME) would require more lightweight, automated and therefore time and cost-effective approaches for initially estimating the reuse potential within their existing products. This is also highlighted by current research in the agile software engineering domain [7],[9],[10]

M. Jarke et al. (Eds.): CAiSE 2014, LNCS 8484, pp. 165–179, 2014.
© Springer International Publishing Switzerland 2014

that emphasis the need for more lightweight approaches. However, agile approaches such as the scoping game [7] require the participation of various stakeholders which could also limit its applicability. Within our research we aim at addressing the bespoke issue by investigating semi-automatic similarity analysis to support PL scoping for configuration-based standard software products.

In this context we presented a first solution [11], which allows to semi-automatically identify key information on the reuse potential of existing standard software product configurations. Such configurations represent large software products such as Enterprise Resource Planning (ERP) systems. These kind of products aim to support a wide range of possible business activities in different industry domains. Therefore, standard software products are by their nature highly flexible and configurable software systems. However, the configuration of standard software products is a time consuming non-trivial task, similar to coding in traditional software development. The goal of our work is to provide a semi-automatic approach to estimate the variability within product configurations. We are aware of the fact that traditional scoping approaches [4],[12] include important activities such as domain assessment and risk analysis and consider product plans or organizational issues. Our automated approach is not meant to replace traditional scoping but to complement it with an initial similarity calculation that could trigger additional scoping measures.

We have conducted two industrial case studies in order to validate our approach. Within the first case study we have applied our approach to ERP system customizations for 5 different customers from different industry branches. The second case study has included more than 50 different business intelligence systems. Both case studies aimed at investigating whether the similarity calculation provides correct results and indicates the start of a product line for the products under comparison. In the first case study we have compared the calculated similarity values to a manual estimation performed by domain experts. Furthermore, we have evaluated the efficiency of our approach in terms of time savings by comparing the manual estimation to the tool-supported calculation. The second case study focused on the scalability of our approach on large sets of products and the extensibility to handle less standardized configurations. We also have evaluated the integration of domain knowledge by using synonym definitions to identify semantically equivalent settings.

The results of the case studies suggest that our approach is capable of semi-automatically calculating the similarity between existing standard software product configurations and thus supports a key scoping activity which is the analysis of existing systems. Domain experts clearly indicated that they would benefit from our tool-supported approach compared to manual methods to investigate the reuse potential within a software product portfolio. Apart from time-savings, our approach provides objective results on the similarity between the different products. This helps to prevent misjudgments and discussions between engineers, which are not based on facts but potentially false opinions.

This paper is structured as follows: In Section 2 we present our tool-supported approach that allows semi-automatic product line scoping. Section 3 and 4 present the conducted case studies and the identified results. Section 5 discusses related work and Section 6 concludes the paper with lessons learned and an outlook on future work.

2   Lightweight Product Line Scoping

2.1   Conceptual Solution

Our approach is focused on standard software products (i.e. customer specific software configurations). These kinds of products are developed and maintained by large software vendors such as Microsoft or SAP and typically contain a rich set of features. Smaller partner companies sell these products to their customers and configure or extend the product to meet the customers' needs. This is mainly done by setting values in available configuration options. In [11] we presented an initial solution to perform tool-supported product line scoping for configuration-based standard software products in order to support these small partner companies. We foresee a semi-automatic approach where customer-specific product configurations are compared in order to identify commonalities and variations. The variability in our case lies in the differences between the configuration settings of the products under comparison. This means each product contains a set of features that are configured according to the needs of a customer. The comparison is based on whether a feature is part of a product and if yes how it is configured. An analyst can provide additional domain knowledge as input to our approach to calculate similarity. Our approach is based on the following steps in order to perform a similarity analysis for configuration-based products:

Step 1: The domain expert selects a set of products for analysis. The selected products are instances of a particular standard product (e.g. ERP system without customizations) that defines the schema of the available configuration settings. The result of this step is a list of products for further analysis.

Step 2: In this step the domain expert defines the scope of the analysis. Therefore the relevant configuration settings that should be compared are selected. Many software products contain settings that do not influence the behavior of the product and are thus not relevant for scoping (e.g. audit settings). Such settings can be excluded from analysis. Moreover, settings can also be grouped if they belong to a logically related feature (e.g. credit card and limit settings). During similarity calculation (cf. step 4) grouped settings are only considered similar if all individual setting values are similar. The output of step 2 is a new configuration schema which only includes relevant configuration settings and newly defined groups of settings.

Step 3: The domain expert can define how the similarity between the selected configuration settings is calculated. Checking on exact equality of settings might often be too strict. Therefore we support an approach that also allows a more fuzzy comparison. The domain expert can define so called *dictionaries* to deal with different naming conventions. A dictionary contains lists of synonyms to identify semantically equal configuration settings (e.g. "revenue", "rev." and "turnover"). The domain expert can also provide upper- and lower boundaries for numerical values of settings (e.g. credit card limits between 2900€ – 3100€ shall be considered similar). These *similarity ranges* are defined using mathematical formulas (e.g. a range of 10% around a default value). We not only support defining similarity ranges for specific configuration settings (e.g. credit card limit) but also for global data types (e.g. Floating Point). For example an analyst can decide to round all floating point numbers. The combination of 1.2, 1.4, 0.9 and 1.7 would be transformed to 1,1,1,2. The output of step 3 is a domain specific definition of similarity for the configuration settings selected in step 2.

Step 4: In this step the similarity analysis is performed by comparing the configuration setting values for the selected products. We compare the configuration values for each of the selected settings of all products to calculate a similarity percentage value per setting. We take the most frequent setting value among the selected products as basis and compare it with all other values. Values are identified as similar if they are identical or if they are within a similarity range defined in step 3. If there is a domain specific similarity defined for a specific setting (e.g. credit card limit between 2900€ – 3100€) and the data type of this setting also has a similarity definition in place (e.g. round floating points), the tool uses the more specific definition from the setting to calculate the similarity value. As an example let us consider the comparison of 4 products with the values *true, true, false, true* for the setting *credit card payment allowed*. We take the most frequent value (in this case the value *true*) as basis and compare all values with it. In our example 75% of the values (3 out of 4) are equal to the base value *true*. In addition we calculate an overall similarity value as the percentage of similar settings within all the products under analysis. For example, if a set of products is compared and out of the 100 settings defined in the schema, 20 are regarded as similar in all product configurations, the overall similarity value is 20%. The results of step 4 are a calculated similarity value for each setting or group of settings and a total similarity value for all products under analysis.

Step 5: Finally the domain expert can draw conclusions based on the calculated results. The analysis results guide the decision whether to invest in a product line.

2.2 Tool Support

We have developed an internally available tool prototype to perform a similarity analysis based on configuration settings. The tool supports importing product configurations from multiple source systems, defining similarity evaluation rules, and comparing the different product configurations. In contrast to the initial prototype described in [11], we have extended the tool's capability to process different types of configuration settings from XML files and SQL data sources.

Setup. The setup of the tool consists of three steps. First the binaries are installed on a Microsoft Windows-based computer. This step requires almost no additional human input. The second step is to configure the connections to the products under analysis. In case where the products use an SQL database only a connection client is required (ODBC). Furthermore we provide add-ons for non-SQL products to export the configurations to XML, for example QlikView (see case study in section 4). In a final step the product configurations are loaded, either from an SQL data source or XML files. The effort to make the tool ready for analysis was on average half an hour for each case study. However, if the products under analysis cannot be accessed either by using SQL connections or one of our plugins for XML export, the tool cannot be used out of the box and additional development effort is required.

Data Management. Meta data is required to handle product configurations. XML schema definitions are used to describe how product configurations are structured. These schemas are either delivered with the standard software product itself, or deduced from the actual configurations. Moreover, domain knowledge about the customer's context is essential in order to tailor the analysis. For example, it can be advised to compare all products for a specific industry branch. Therefore our tool contains master data about customers and the products in use. Every customer has at least one legal entity. Each legal entity belongs to one or more industry branches (e.g. retail, construction). A legal entity uses one or more products. Each product is built for one or more business areas (e.g. sales, procurement) and there can be multiple products built for one business area. Each product has at least one configuration. This product configuration is an instance of a schema definition. This structure is used to tailor the analysis scope (e.g. compare all product built for sales in retail industry).

2.3   Limitations

A main issue regarding our approach is that in its current form it can only be used for identifying the reuse potential within configuration-based systems (e.g. ERP systems). This means it cannot be applied without modifications in other software domains where the system behavior is not configured. Furthermore, the system behavior may also be influenced by its application data (e.g. the chart of ledger accounts in an ERP system) which is not considered by our approach. We only analyze existing product configurations. This does not reflect all possible product configurations and therefore cannot reveal the complete variability. Each feature has equal influence on the calculated similarity. Currently we do not support weighting of features (e.g. based on their granularity). Focusing on existing product configurations means that we currently do not support other typical product line scoping activities such as planning future products as members of the product line. The tool compares the values of each configuration setting and calculates the similarity. Therefore the effort increases with each additional product under analysis. However, we have conducted a case study on 54 products (see section 4) which can be seen as typical repository size for an SME and the tool was able to finish the calculations within seconds.

3   Industrial Evaluation I – Microsoft Dynamics AX

3.1   Case Study Setting

In order to get insights on our approach we conducted a case study at InsideAx, a small company that is a partner for Microsoft Dynamics AX. Dynamics AX is a business software solution from Microsoft for medium to large enterprises. Partners, such as InsideAx, configure, customize and sell the ERP product to customers.

Standard software, such as Dynamics AX has high reuse potential and would therefore suggest the application of software product lines. However, as partner companies do not own the software product, their influence on the evolution of the system is limited. In fact they have to cope with massive changes within short time periods. This volatile environment and the limited resources of a small company have so far prevented InsideAx to invest in PL engineering.

At InsideAx employees are basically aware of the benefits of PLs and some even believe that the introduction of PL engineering would be beneficial for their company. However, no detailed analysis of existing product configurations was conducted, which leaves the company in uncertainty about the reuse potential of their software.

Furthermore, initial informal discussions among domain experts at InsideAx have indicated that experts might have different opinions on the similarity and thus the reuse potential of particular software products.

In order to eliminate this uncertainty we analyzed their product configurations with the help of our tool. The results could then be used to support decisions on further steps regarding the introduction of PL engineering at the company.

3.2   Evaluation Method

The goal of this study was to provide first evidence that our approach provides correct similarity calculations. Within a small company we used our approach to calculate the similarity between different product configurations to deliver a first estimation if further scoping investments are justified. Particularly we were interested in providing initial answers to the following questions:

Q1: Will the calculated results indicate the need for introducing a PL approach?
Q2: Will the calculated results differ from domain expert estimates?
Q3: Will domain experts benefit from knowing the calculated results?

Steps 1 to 4 were conducted as described in Section 2.1 by one of the authors of this paper, who is also an employee of InsideAx. He first selected five customized products (step 1) which are all derived from the same base product but operating in different industry branches (construction, retail, and manufacturing). He selected the business areas *Purchase*, *Sales*, and *Inventory Management* (i.e. their configuration settings) for comparison as they reflect key business areas (step 2). Next, the domain expert provided similarity ranges (step 3) and the tool calculated a pairwise similarity between the products and the overall similarity value for all three business areas (step 4).

In parallel three domain experts at InsideAx were asked to estimate the similarity of the mentioned products and business areas. They used a scale from 0% to 100% (0% meaning that there is no overlap and 100% meaning that two products are identical). To support the estimation process, they had full access to the configured products, their documentations and requirements. The first expert was an ERP consultant with 3 years experience, the second expert was a data analysis consultant with 4 years experience and the third expert had 2 years experience in developing and customizing ERP products. We then compared the tool-calculated similarity with the domain experts' estimates. Finally, we discussed these results in a workshop with the domain experts.

3.3   Results

The author calculated the similarity for the selected products (P1 to P5) with the help of the tool and spent about 15 minutes in total to perform steps 1 to 4. Table 1 shows the pairwise calculated similarity values for the business activities Sales, Inventory and Purchase.

Table 1. Calculated Similarity for Products (P1-P5)

	Purchase				Inventory				Sales			
	P1	P2	P3	P4	P1	P2	P3	P4	P1	P2	P3	P4
P2	60 %				48 %				58 %			
P3	60 %	40 %			52 %	48 %			54 %	46 %		
P4	53 %	68 %	53 %		52 %	45 %	52 %		42 %	56 %	35 %	
P5	47 %	60 %	47 %	93 %	48 %	48 %	48 %	59 %	39 %	50 %	31 %	65 %

For *Purchase* the pairwise similarity calculations resulted in a similarity range from 40% to 93% (58% on average). In addition to the pairwise comparison the tool also calculated the overall similarity value. Within *Purchase* 33% of all features are similar. The pairwise similarity comparison for *Inventory* provided a range from 48% to 59% (50% on average). In total 41% of all features are similar. For *Sales* the pairwise similarity comparison resulted in a range from 31% to 65%, while the average similarity for *Sales* is 47%. Within *Sales* the total similarity rate is 31%.

Furthermore, we received the estimates of the domain experts. However, one expert was not familiar with all products under analysis and therefore just provided a comparison for those he knew. Table 2 highlights the pairwise similarity estimates. We present the minimum and maximum estimates and the individual estimates for the three domain experts in brackets.

A comparison between the calculated values and the estimates revealed that the expert's opinion and tool calculations differ significantly with hardly any exact matches. To still enable a meaningful comparison, we defined a 20-percentage point interval around each automatically calculated similarity value as a more relaxed comparison criterion. For example, if the tool has calculated a 70% similarity, we defined an interval from 60% to 80%. We then counted the number of expert estimates that were within the defined ranges.

For the business area *Purchase*, eight out of ten estimates do not differ more than 20 percentage points on the scale form 0% to 100%. However, the two remaining estimates on purchase vary between 30 (P3-P5) and 70 (P4-P5) percentage points. For *Inventory* only 4 estimates are within the 20-percentage point limit. This leaves 6 estimates which differ significantly (40 percentage points at most). Also for *Sales* only 4 out of 10 estimates are within the 20-percentage point limit.

The first domain expert who only provided estimates for 18 out of 30 requested comparisons provided 3 estimates, which were within the corresponding intervals. All of them could be linked to the business area *Purchase*. Eight estimates were actually lower, leaving seven estimates to be higher than the calculations. The second domain expert performed best. 5 out of 10 estimates were within the corresponding intervals. All of them were within the business area *Purchase*. 7 out of 10 estimates were within the intervals for the business area *Inventory* and still 3 out of 10 for *Sales* were within the given range. 14 estimates were higher than the tool-calculated results. The third domain expert was able to provide three estimates within the given range. Only one estimate for each business area was within the interval. Again, most estimates were too optimistic (17 out of 23).

Table 2. Similarity Estimates by Domain Experts

	Purchase				Inventory				Sales			
	P1	P2	P3	P4	P1	P2	P3	P4	P1	P2	P3	P4
P2	85 85,85,85				80-95 95,80,95				65-95 65,85,95			
P3	55-75 -,75,55	55-75 -,75,55			70-75 -,70,75	70-75 -,70,75			70-75 -,70,75	70-75 -,70,75		
P4	55-65 55,65,55	55-65 55,65,55	45-55 -,55,45		25-65 25,50,65	25-65 25,50,65	50-75 -,50,75		15-65 15,65,65	15-65 15,65,65	70-85 -,70,85	
P5	35-55 55,55,35	35-55 55,55,35	25-55 -,55,25	25-95 95,75,25	25-65 25,45,65	25-65 25,45,65	55-75 -,55,75	60-85 85,60,65	15-55 15,55,55	15-55 15,55,55	60-75 -,60,75	55-85 85,60,55

3.4   Findings

Will the calculated results indicate the need for introducing a PL approach? The case study was conducted for customized ERP products. While ERP software is commonly known as Standard-Software, we expected a high reuse potential. Reviewing the calculated similarity results, this assumption seems to be somewhat correct. In total, 31% to 41% of the features were similar in all the customized products, regardless of industry branch or business area. A pairwise comparison indicated even higher values. Although we have not defined a clear schema in order to decide which result indicates to introduce a PL, we expected a significantly higher overall similarity value than 50% for each business area. This assumption was based on the published scoping threshold in [6] where 50% is understood as break-even point. However, as we couldn't identify a similarity value higher than 41% we conclude that the results do not clearly indicate the need for introducing a PL approach.

Will the calculated results differ from domain expert estimates? The results highlight that tool calculations and expert estimates vary strongly. Therefore, we performed a more detailed manual analysis of the product configuration settings together with the domain experts. The tool's calculations were validated and for selected settings the corresponding product configurations were analyzed. Although no overall similarity was calculated manually, the experts agreed that the tool's calculations were correct and can be seen as the ground truth for this comparison. Comparing calculated and estimated similarity shows that 33% of the estimates were within a 20 % points interval around the calculated results. In general the domain experts estimated a higher similarity than tool calculations revealed. The discussion with the domain experts in the debriefing session revealed the reasons. In many cases new projects are based on existing customized products from past projects. The domain experts know this and somehow assume that these products show high similarity. However, in reality, these products undergo major changes in most cases and diverge. Table 2 indicates this effect comparing product P1 and product P2, which was initially built based on P1. Although the product has undergone major changes, domain experts still assumed high similarity between the products. In general the domain experts make their estimates based on their experience. None of the domain experts performed a detailed comparison of all product configuration settings, which would not have been possible in a reasonable amount of time.

Will domain experts benefit from knowing the calculated results? Having a different view on the overall situation might lead to conflicts between domain experts. In the debriefing workshop we told domain experts about the tool results and compared them to their estimates. Most experts did not expect that the products were tailored to individual customer needs to that extent. They liked the fact that they could compare their estimates with the calculated values. They argued that the calculated values provide guidance and support in resolving conflicts between domain experts.

3.5   Threats to Validity

Conducting one single case study does not allow computing any statistical significance regarding the correctness of the calculated similarity values, which is a threat to *conclusion validity*. Discussions with domain experts and a conducted manual analysis revealed the appropriateness of the calculated similarity in this case.

One of the authors used our tool to calculate the similarity values within this study, which can be seen as a threat to *internal validity*. However, the debriefing meeting with the consultants revealed the correctness of the input and the configuration.

Our similarity calculation mechanism was developed for the domain of configurable software products. However, our study only focuses on Dynamics AX. This can be seen as a threat to *construct validity*. Also, we did not utilize the dictionary concept in the first case study.

The size and the number of products used in our study were limited, which is a threat to *external validity*. We focus on configuration-based systems and do not provide support for a broader system range. Input from a skilled domain expert, who is familiar with the tool is needed. Not yet investigating the tool's usability in more detail can be seen as threat.

4   Industrial Evaluation II – QlikView

4.1   Case Study Setting

The second case study at InsideAx was focused on a product for data analysis and business intelligence. Domain experts at InsideAx use a product named QlikView to build data analysis applications for their customers. The process of building these applications contains three key steps. In a first step QlikView extracts, transforms, and loads data from multiple source systems such as ERP systems. A domain expert defines so-called measures in a second step. A measure in QlikViev is a formula to calculate a business relevant value (e.g. contribution margin). In a last step the measures are visualized and set in relation to other measures (e.g. revenue in contrast to contribution margin). These analysis results are used to lead a company and optimize a departments' work.

Business intelligence applications such as QlikView are built in tight collaboration with the customers' decision makers, and therefore are more individual than a standard software product. Still, domain experts at InsideAx believe there is a common set of recurring QlikView measures on most business areas and industry branches. However, no in depth analysis has been conducted so far.

Within this study we analyzed a set of customer specific products in order to identify similar QlikView measures. The products are characterized by business area and the customers' industry branch.

4.2   Evaluation Method

The goal of this study was to show that our similarity calculation approach works with a larger example (scalability of the approach). Furthermore, the dictionary concept was applied for the first time. In contrast to the first case study, the size of the system under analysis does not allow comprehensive manual calculations or estimates in a reasonable amount of time. This is why we did not include domain experts in this case study. We have framed our evaluation goal in three research questions (RQs):

Q1: Will the calculated results indicate the need for introducing a PL approach?
Q2: Will the dictionary concept influence the calculated results?
Q3: Will the approach be scalable to the given problem size?

In step 1 we selected 54 different products from 12 customers in 6 different industry branches. All of these 54 products use the data analysis capabilities of QlikView. In contrast to the first case study these products are not derived from a common base product. Each of these 54 products can be seen as individually developed product. QlikView only defines how measures are created but does not include a predefined list of measures (such as a configuration schema in an ERP system). Therefore we defined an initial dictionary containing synonym lists of measures to allow a domain specific comparison. For example, the measures *Profit Margin* and *Contribution Margin* are identical and should therefore be identified as similar during the similarity calculation. The dictionary containing the synonym lists was created by one of the authors of this paper who has 6 years experience in developing business applications.

In step 2 we grouped the products by business area (e.g. Sales, Finance, and Project).

In step 3 we incrementally refined the dictionary while importing product configurations into our tool. We assigned newly imported measures to existing synonym lists if they were semantically similar. For example, the imported measure *Profit Contribution* was added to the synonym list that already contains the measures *Profit Margin* and *Contribution Margin*.

In a next step we performed a similarity analysis on the groups of products built for a specific business area (step 4). The tool identified the number of measures occurring in all products within this group and calculated a similarity value.

4.3   Results

In total, we analyzed 54 different products from 12 customers in 6 different industry branches. These products were grouped into 7 business areas. In total all products together contained 930 measures. We defined a dictionary containing 27 synonym lists to group semantically equal measures. 109 measures were highly individual and could not be grouped with others.

The author spent about 40 minutes to create the initial dictionary (step 1) and 5 minutes to group the products into business areas (step 2). Step 3, the refinement of the synonym lists, took again about 45 minutes. The calculation itself has been performed within seconds (step 4).

Table 3 shows the results from the analysis based on the product's business area. The second column shows the number of products per business area. The number of products varies between two for *Project* up to 17 for *Sales*. The third column contains the number of customers running a product for this business area. For example there are two customers running a product to analyze *Project* but 10 customers analyzing *Sales*. The next column shows the total number of identified measures within the products per business area. For the business area *Project*, 29 measures were identified while for the business area *Sales* we found 460 measures. The fifth column shows the number of synonym lists used to group the measures. This means that the comparison of measures can be reduced from the number of measures to the number of synonym lists. For example, for the business area *Sales* the tool had to compare 64 measures instead of 460 measures because they were identified as semantically equal in the dictionary. The last column shows the calculated similarity of all products in the given business area. For the business area *Project*, the two compared products are 63% similar. This means 63% of identified measures are used in both products. In the business area *Sales*, only 8% of the identified measures (or their synonyms) are present in all 17 products. In general, the calculated similarity decreases with the number of compared products.

Table 3. Calculated similarity for products grouped by business area

Business Area	# Products	# Customers	# Measures	# Synonym lists	Similarity
Project	2	2	29	15	63%
Production	3	2	46	18	50%
CRM	6	3	55	19	25%
Procurement	6	4	71	27	23%
Finance	9	7	118	26	16%
Warehouse	11	7	151	34	14%
Sales	17	10	460	64	8 %

4.4   Findings

Will the calculated results indicate the need for introducing a PL approach? Providing a clear answer to this question is difficult in this case. Comparing the calculated similarity to a threshold of 50% like published in [6], the results suggest that no PL approach is needed and a single-system development approach can also be perused in the future. In case where the calculated results reach the threshold value (see business areas *Project* and *Production* in Table 3) only two products were compared. In all other cases the calculated similarity was significantly lower than the desired threshold. However, our study also indicates that the different granularity of the products under investigation had a significant impact on the results. For example we found five very specialized *Sales* applications built for one customer. A way to address this issue could be to merge these specialized applications and compare more general applications in a next evaluation. In order to at least partly assure the validity of the calculated similarity values, we performed a manual similarity analysis for 6 products with 71 measures from the business area *Procurement,* which is about 10% of total products under analysis. This manual analysis revealed the correctness of the calculations.

Will the dictionary concept influence the calculated results? Solutions developed with QlikView are in general harder to compare as less standardization is available. Therefore, we introduced the dictionary concept. We observed that synonym lists within the dictionary have a significant impact on the calculated results. We initially provided a predefined set of synonym lists. Therefore many terms were mapped to these synonyms and the reported similarity value was high. With ongoing analysis we refined the set of synonym lists by splitting existing synonym lists into smaller more precise lists. As a result the calculated similarity decreased. This also means that the calculated similarity strongly depends on the analyst's domain knowledge and ability to define adequate synonym lists for domain specific terms.

Will the approach be scalable to the given problem size? The study has shown that our approach can be used with a larger number of products. In contrast to the first case study where 5 products were compared in 3 business areas we managed to analyze 54 products in 7 business areas. We could not identify any performance problems within this case study as the tool calculated the similarity within seconds. However, the manual definition of the dictionary (step 1) and the iterative refinement (step 3) consumed a significant amount of time (about 1,5 hours in total).

4.5   Threats to Validity

Although the example is larger than the one in the previous case study and we can draw first conclusions regarding the scalability of our approach, we still cannot compute any statistical significance regarding the correctness of the calculated results. This can be seen as a threat to *conclusion validity.* More case studies would be needed to further evaluate the correctness of the similarity calculation in different settings. The number of products in some of the business areas (such as *Production* and *Project*) was very limited. Manual analysis revealed the correctness of the calculations for a limited set of products in the business area *Procurement.*

As one of the authors of this paper was also the developer of the tool similar threats to internal validity as described for the first case study (cf. Section 3.5) apply. Particularly, the dictionary had a significant influence on the similarity calculation in this case study. Although the dictionary was built iteratively, which allows for validation and correction, it was created and validated by one person only.

Similar to the first case study, we focused on a specific product (QlikView), which is a threat to *construct validity.* Although we applied the dictionary concept, we did not use similarity range definitions.

As discussed in the first case study, or approach focuses on configuration-based systems. This could mean that it underrepresents *external validity.* A domain expert who is familiar with the tool is needed. Although in this study we successfully used our approach in a larger setting, we did not investigate the tool's performance in detail. However, we expect the problem size of the second study to be typical for SMEs.

5   Related Work

Schmid and Schank [6], PuLSE-BEAT is introduced, a tool for supporting the product line scoping approach called PuLSE-Eco presented in [13]. To identify the optimal scope, a product map is used which is a matrix with the product characteristics (features) on one axis and the products on the other axis. The product characteristics are elicited from stakeholders, existing systems, and the product plan. In our approach, product characteristics (we call them feature definitions) are derived from existing systems. In PuLSE-Eco the benefit analysis step decides what to develop for reuse and what not. Benefit functions describe the benefit of having a certain characteristic inside the scope. In our approach we analyze the similarity of the different products and calculate a similarity value to decide what should be inside the scope.

John [8] describes the CAVE approach. It utilizes existing documentation in order to identify communalities and variability. CAVE foresees the steps; Preparation, Analysis and Validation. In the first step a domain expert selects user documentation for analysis. In the second step a domain expert browses the selected documents and tags elements based on extraction patterns. The results of the second step are product line artifacts that are validated by a group of domain experts.

Scoping based on source code is presented in de Medeiros et al. [14]. The authors present a tool-based approach containing three modules. The feature identification module receives legacy systems source code and outputs the features composing the legacy system. The similarity comparison module identifies copied source code from legacy systems and calculates the similarity of feature implementations. The third module visualizes the results for domain experts. Duszynski et al. [15] present an approach that analyzes the source code of multiple variants for commonalities to support migration towards a product line. The reuse potential of system parts is assessed using occurrence matrices. Instead of a pair-wise comparison of existing variants, the authors propose to describe the similarity between a set of variants in a matrix. The matrix contains the different elements of the variants that are compared, the variants and the occurrence of the elements in the variants. The similarity rate is categorized as core (element occurs in all variants), shared (element occurs in some variants), and unique (element occurs in only one variant). In contrast to [14] and [15] we focus on configuration settings of standard software products rather than on source code. In the second case study we calculate similarity of products based on measures defined in these products. We compare formula definitions in this case but do not analyze the source code for similarity. Although many measures realize the same business concept (e.g. calculate the contribution margin) the implementation itself greatly differs because the information sources for this measure are different for most of the systems (e.g. different tables from different ERP systems are used to retrieve the input data for the calculation). Code scoping techniques would thus reveal that the implementations of these products are highly different.

6   Conclusion and Lessons Learned

We presented a tool-supported approach that enables companies to semi-automatically perform a similarity analysis of existing product configurations. We consider it as a lightweight approach which complements existing approaches and supports companies to initially answer the question if a product line approach would suit their needs. The presented solution enables SMEs to estimate the similarity in standard software products. The case studies have shown that our approach can be applied to different types of products (ERP, data analysis) and also scales to a larger number of products. The similarity calculation is automated and reveals quick insight on the existing product portfolio. It can be repeated and refined without major changes on the tool.

In order to evaluate our approach we have conducted two industrial case studies in the field of business software. Starting a product line from existing solutions is recognized as an option to improve productivity and quality. In the initial case study we have shown that the tool can be used by domain experts and reveals valuable results. Furthermore the evaluation shows that domain experts give different estimates on the reuse potential that not only differ from the calculated value, but also from one another. If a company is planning to introduce software product lines they should not rely only on their domain experts estimates, but take (semi-)automatic scoping into consideration. Although the calculated results did not clearly indicate the need for introducing a product line approach, it provoked an intense discussion in the company.

In the second case study we started with a large set of existing products, built for different customers and purpose. In contrast to the first case study these products were less standardized. Therefore we intensively used the dictionary concept and defined many synonym lists to identify semantically equivalent configuration settings. This case study revealed the importance of domain knowledge when performing a scoping analysis. The dictionary concept was proven to be a valuable way to make domain knowledge explicit and reusable for automatic processing. Moreover, the second case study has shown that our approach scales also to a large number of less standardized products. Also, the more products under analysis are domain specific the more domain knowledge is required. We have learned that less standardized software products like QlikView in case study two, are harder to compare than strictly standardized software products like the ERP systems in case study one.

Future work will include extending the tools functionality to implement a more sophisticated similarity calculation method in order to identify clusters of similar parts. Moreover, we will work on the dictionary concept. The second evaluation has shown that we need to address the different granularity of dictionaries and synonym definitions in order to handle products of different granularity for analysis.

References

1. van der Linden, F., Schmid, K., Rommes, E.: Software Product Lines in Action: The Best Industrial Practice in Product Line Engineering. Springer (2007)
2. Clements, P., Northrop, L.M.: Software Product Lines:Practices and Patterns. Addison-Wesley (2007)
3. Krueger, C.: Easing the transition to software mass customization. In: 4th Int. Workshop on Software Product-Family Engineering (PFE), pp. 282–293 (2002)
4. Schmid, K.: A comprehensive product line scoping approach and its validation. In: 22nd Int. Conf. on Software Engineering (ICSE), pp. 593–603 (2002)

5. Schmid, K.: Scoping Software Product Lines: An Analysis of an Emerging Technology. In: 1st Conference on Software Product Lines (SPLC), USA, (2000)
6. Schmid, K., Schank, M.: PuLSE-BEAT – A Decision Support Tool for Scoping Product Lines. In: van der Linden, F.J. (ed.) IW-SAPF 2000. LNCS, vol. 1951, pp. 65–75. Springer, Heidelberg (2000)
7. Dalgarno, M.: The Scoping Game at miniSPA2007, http://blog.software-acumen.com/2007/07/19/the-scoping-game-at-minispa2007/ (September 2, 2013)
8. John, I.: Using Documentation for Product Line Scoping. IEEE Software 27(3), 42–47 (2010)
9. da Silva, I.F.: An Agile Approach for Software Product Lines Scoping. In: Proceedings of the 16th Int. Software Product Line Conference, Brazil (2012)
10. Leitner, A., Kreiner, C.: Software product lines – an agile success factor? In: O'Connor, R.V., Pries-Heje, J., Messnarz, R. (eds.) EuroSPI 2011. CCIS, vol. 172, pp. 203–214. Springer, Heidelberg (2011)
11. Noebauer, M., Seyff, N., Groher, I., Dhungana, D.: A Lightweight Approach for Product Line Scoping. In: 38th EuromicroConference on Software Engineering and Advanced Applications (SEAA), Turkey, pp. 105–108 (2012)
12. John, I., Knodel, J., Lehner, T., Muthig, D.: A Practical Guide to Product Line Scoping. In: 10th Int. SPL Conference (SPLC), USA, pp. 3–12 (2006)
13. DeBaud, J.M., Schmid, K.: A systematic approach to derive the scope of software product lines. In: 21st Int. Conf. on Software Eng., USA, pp. 34–43 (1999)
14. de Medeiros, T.F.L., LemosMeira, S.R., Almeida, E.S.: CodeScoping: A Source Code Based Tool to Software Product Lines Scoping. In: 38th Euromicro Conf. on Software Eng. and Advanced Applications, Turkey, pp. 101–104 (2012)
15. Duszynski, S., Knodel, J., Becker, M.: Analyzing the Source Code of Multiple Software Variants for Reuse Potential. In: 18th Working Conference on Reverse Engineering (WCRE), Ireland, pp. 303–307 (2011)

An Exploratory Study of Topic Importance
in Requirements Elicitation Interviews

Corentin Burnay[1,2,3], Ivan J. Jureta[1,2,3], and Stéphane Faulkner[2,3]

[1] Fonds de la Recherche Scientifique – FNRS, Brussels
[2] Department of Business Administration, University of Namur
[3] PReCISE Research Center, University of Namur
{corentin.burnay,ivan.jureta,stephane.faulkner}@unamur.be

Abstract. Interviewing stakeholders is a common way to elicit information about requirements of the system-to-be and the conditions in its operating environment. One difficulty in preparing and doing interviews is how to avoid missing the information that may be important to understand the requirements and environment conditions. Some information may remain implicit throughout the interview, if the interviewed stakeholder does not consider it important, and the business analyst fails to mention it, or a topic it relates to. We propose the so-called Elicitation Topic Map (ETM), which is intended to help business analysts prepare elicitation interviews. ETM is a diagram that shows topics that can be discussed during requirements elicitation interviews, and shows how likely it is that stakeholders tend to discuss each of the topics spontaneously (as opposed to being explicitly asked questions on that topic by the business analyst). ETM was produced through a combination of theoretical and empirical research.

Keywords: Elicitation, Interviews, Context, RE Topics, Exploratory study.

1 Introduction

Research Context - Requirements Elicitation via Interviews: Requirements Engineering (RE) focuses on the elicitation, modelling, and analysis of requirements and environment of a system-to-be, in order to produce its specification. Requirements elicitation [1–4], only *elicitation* hereafter, refers to activities done in RE, in order to obtain information from stakeholders of the system-to-be; the aim is to use this information to understand conditions in the system's operating environment, and the stakeholders' requirements from the system [5].

Elicitation is important, because misunderstanding stakeholders, or in some other way missing important information, can result in the specification of the wrong system - one that fails to satisfy requirements, and/or is inconsistent with the conditions in its operating environment (e.g., it does not comply with applicable legislation). *Elicitation often involves communication with stakeholders,* through, for example, structured, semi-structured, or unstructured interviews, workshops, and so on [2, 3]. Hereafter, we write *interviews* to refer to any form of direct communication with stakeholders, which

M. Jarke et al. (Eds.): CAiSE 2014, LNCS 8484, pp. 180–195, 2014.
© Springer International Publishing Switzerland 2014

is done in order to elicit information. Interviews provide invaluable information through verbal and nonverbal communication.

General Issue - How to Uncover Important Context Defaults during Interviews?
A difficulty when doing interviews, is that the business analyst and stakeholders have different backgrounds, experiences of existing systems, and expectations from the future system. They will come into interviews with different assumptions about the environment, requirements, and system-to-be. In itself, it is not a problem that different stakeholders hold different assumptions. It becomes a problem if some of their key assumptions remain implicit in interviews. If, instead of remaining hidden, some of these assumptions were known, then this could have helped with, for example, requirements inconsistencies, stakeholder negotiations, or the identification of other requirements.

A more technical way to see this, is to look at it through the notion of non-monotonic reasoning in artificial intelligence [6–9]: when the business analyst is doing elicitation interviews, she is asking the stakeholder questions; the stakeholder's thinking before answering could be - roughly speaking - seen as an inference that the stakeholder makes on the basis of her defaults (statements that can be rejected when there is new information) and her certain knowledge (statements which remain relevant despite of any new information) [8]; the stakeholder's answer are the conclusion of her reasoning process. If we see things this way, then it can be useful for the requirements engineering to try to reveal at least some of the stakeholder's defaults, in order to understand the requirements better, discuss other requirements, or otherwise.

This is, for RE research, the issue of how to make sure that elicitation interviews reveal as much as feasible of the defaults that may be important for RE. It is not a new research issue. Any contribution on how to prepare elicitation interviews, is also inevitably interested in how to use these interviews to elicit as much as feasible of the important information for RE [4, 10–13]. An approach to this issue that has not received attention, consists of trying to understand what domain-independent categories of information the stakeholders tend to talk spontaneously about during interviews, and which others tend to remain implicit. The latter group are the defaults mentioned above.

Contributions - Map of Elicitation Interview Topics, and their Relative Importance: The contributions of this paper are the so-called *Elicitation Topic Map (ETM)*, a list of topics to discuss in elicitation interviews, and indications of the relative importance of these topics. Topic importance reflects our measure of the stakeholders' tendency to share spontaneously the information on these topics: a topic is more important if we observed, in our sample of stakeholders, that they were more willing to share information about it spontaneously. This does not mean that less important topics in the ETM are less important for the analysts: it simply means that fewer stakeholders would spontaneously share information on them; if the analyst needs information on lower importance topics, she will have to be proactive in finding that information (for example, the analyst would need to stimulate stakeholders to discuss those topics).

Overview of Research Methodology: The ETM was produced through three phases of research. It is easier to understand the rationale for them, by starting from the third and last phase. The goal of the third phase was to evaluate topic importance. This was done by selecting professionals, all of whom had acted as stakeholders in RE projects, and sending each of them the same set of 30 topics. We asked each individual to evaluate, for each topic, if she would share information on it spontaneously, or only if asked.

In order to have the 30 topics to evaluate, the second phase of research focused on identifying the topics. They were identified through interviews with business analysts, coming from five RE and systems engineering projects done in Belgian small and medium size businesses; projects differed in terms of number of participants (from 15 to 150) and in terms of the system domain (pharmacology, finance, etc.). To prepare interviews done in the second phase, our first phase consisted of adapting our past research on a generic model of context [14, 15]. Our model of context suggested groups of topics, without suggesting specific ones.

Organization: This paper is organized as follows. Section 2 introduces basic terminology and relates it to standard RE terminology. Sections 3–5 present the three phases of research. Section 6 presents the raw data and the analysis technique we applied to it to produce ETM. Section 7 presents hypotheses for future research in RE, that ETM suggests. Section 8 overviews related work, and Section 9 summarizes our conclusions.

2   Baseline

We start from the observation that there is explicit and implicit information when doing an elicitation interview. *Explicit information* is that which the stakeholder shared with the business analyst who did the interview. *Implicit information* is that which the stakeholder did not share by the end of the interview. The fact that some information is explicit or implicit does not matter for its relevance for understanding the requirements and the environment of the system-to-be. The stakeholder decides what information to share, and thereby which information will be explicit or implicit.

Stakeholder's decisions to share undoubtedly depends on many factors, such as the business analyst's questions, the stakeholder's assumptions about the system-to-be and its environment, her understanding of her role in the systems engineering process, and so on. The goal of the ETM is to influence primarily the set of questions that the business analyst asks, rather than the other factors. We see the elicitation interview as an exchange of information and questions between stakeholders and business analysts.

Although the number of stakeholders and analysts in an interview will have an influence on the content and procedure of the interview in practice, they do not influence the contributions in this paper - the ETM is not designed with a specific interview duration and number of participants in mind. This exchange can be more or less controlled; more, for example, if the analyst wishes to proceed in the exact same way with every stakeholder and in every interview, perhaps through the same list of questions. We see any interview as a conversation about a set of topics, regardless of how controlled that conversation is, or the analyst may want it to be.

In this paper, the term **Topic** designates an entity that different pieces of information refer to. A topic can be, for example, a time period (talking about the events in March 2013), a physical object (the company's product packaging), event (merger with another company), position (CEO), etc. Another key term in this paper is **Topic Set**, which refers to a set of Topics that are somehow related. For example, if there is a Topic for past events, another for current events, and a third for future events, then there can be a Topic Set about time, which includes all the three Topics. It is important to keep in mind that Topic is not a subclass of Topic Set, and that same Topic can be in more than one Topic Set. We have also found no universal set of Topic Sets, or of Topics per Topic Set; we are reporting in this paper those Topics and Topic Sets that proved useful with regards to the issue we are interested in, namely, providing an ETM and an evaluation of Topic importance in it.

It is important to understand how the notion of Topic in this paper relates to common concepts in requirements modelling languages, such as RML [16], ERAE [17, 18], Telos [19], KAOS [20] or i* [21]. A requirements modelling language suggests concepts and relations to use, to represent information about requirements, environment, and the system-to-be. If an elicitation interview results in explicit information about key actors in the environment, and how they depend on the system-to-be to achieve some specific goals, then, for example, an i* model can be used to capture these as instances of its agent, role, and goal concepts, and its dependency relation. In a way, the concepts and relations of the language can be seen as suggesting Topics to discuss. If the language is i*, then Topics would be the agents and roles in the environment, the goals of the agents, and the dependencies between them for achieving these goals. The difference between Topics, and concepts and relations in requirements modelling languages, is that a Topic may correspond one to one to a concept or relation, or to more concepts and relations among those in the language. Our aim in defining the Topics was not to suggest an ontology for requirements modelling languages. Some languages may be able to capture the information associated to some Topics more easily than others, but that discussion is beyond the scope of this paper, and influences in no way the contributions here.

3   The First Phase: Defining Topic Sets

The purpose of the first phase of our research was to define Topic Sets. To do so, we started from the idea that all elicitation interviews can be said to be context-specific. This means that an interview is specific to a time, place, project, analyst doing the interview, stakeholder being interviewed, and so on. In other words, to say that elicitation is context-specific, is simply to say that no two elicitation interviews are alike.

The useful conclusion to draw here, from the observation that elicitation is context-specific, is that context influences the answers that stakeholders give. Therefore, if we keep the same analyst who interviews, the same stakeholder who is being interviewed, and the same questions, and change something else in the context (such as interview location, time, and so on), then we may get different explicit information from the interview. Notice that we are careful to say that we actually do not know if a change to context would in fact change the information that the stakeholder chooses to share.

Consequently, phase one involved two tasks: (i) identify Context Dimensions, that is, groups of variables which characterize the context, so that if they change, then we say that context changed from an old context to a new context; (ii) determine, through experiment, which of the Context Dimensions influence people's decision-making: namely, given some Context Dimensions, we want to identify those that have the following property: The same individual, when facing the problem in the old context would solve it in one way, and when in the new context, would solve it in another way. We reported elsewhere our work on the two tasks above [14, 15].

To identify Context Dimensions, we drew on conceptualizations of context in philosophy [22, 23], artificial intelligence [24] and computer science. In computer science, for instance, fields like ubiquitous computing and context-awareness are particularly interested in the notion of context, and, so to speak, what context is made of (see [25, 26] for surveys). This interest has lead to some operational definitions of context (e.g., [27]). These definitions decompose context into a series of dimensions. We identified six of these Context Dimensions in our past work, and use them in this paper as Topic Sets, with each Context Dimension being a Topic Set. They are the following:

- **Items** deal with salient entities inside the context, e.g., a person, an object, etc.
- **Rules** deal with constraints in the context, e.g., laws, targets, habits, etc.
- **Localizations** deal with the position of the context in space and time;
- **Activities** deal with the set of objectives of Items, e.g., intentions, desire, etc.
- **Relationships** deal with the connections / links between Items and/or Rules.
- **Granularities** deal with the nature, quantity and level of any additional piece of information that is provided about things occurring in the context.

4   The Second Phase: Identifying Topics for Topic Sets

The output of phase one are a list of six Topic Sets. While interesting on their own, the Topic Sets are not very useful for elicitation, as they are too general. Asking questions about items, rules, localization, and so on, still are much too generic recommendations on what to discuss during interviews.

To identify Topics for Topic Sets, we selected business analysts, and did interviews with them. The aim in the interviews, was to discuss the Topic Sets, their perception of the relevance of Topic Sets, and to identify Topics that they would have, or actually had discussed with stakeholders. The resulting Topics are given in Table 2. The rest of this section describes how we found these Topics.

Participants: We had access to five systems engineering or reengineering projects, which involved professional business analysts. Projects took place at small and medium sized companies (up to 250 employees) located in Belgium and Luxembourg. When we did our study, all projects had ended in the 12 months that preceded our study. We interviewed the business analysts involved in these projects. The interviews took place at the respective companies that employed these individuals. In addition, we had access to requirements documentation produced for the projects. We chose projects so as to cover different domains and project sizes. Names of systems engineering buyers and providers remain anonymous in this paper. This was a condition to satisfy in order to gain access to project documentation and the people involved. Table 1 gives an overview of project characteristics.

Procedure: The research in this stage was interpretative. As suggested in [28], it was mostly based on interviews and project documentation. The interviews were semi-structured, in that the goal in each interview was to discuss all Topic Sets identified

Table 1. Summary of project characteristics

Name	# Stakeholder	Industry	Description
PP	60	Pharmacology	Reporting system for customers' feedback
FD	15	Finance	Implementation of a CRM system
ML	20	Accounting	Automation of accounting dashboards
AP	90	Communication	Design of a BI system
BD	100	ICT	Scheduling tool for human resources

in phase one. At any time during an interview, subjects were free to mention any aspect outside the scope of the Topic Sets, or challenge the Topic Sets. The process was iterative: we analyzed documents generated during the project, and asked questions to analysts, when some aspects emphasized during the interviews did not correspond to observations in the documentation. Such iterations happened up to three times (three interviews and documentation analyses, for each analyst). An interview typically involved three parts, each dealing with particular types of questions:

- Overall discussion with direct references to Topic Sets, e.g., "Do you think it is relevant to discuss Rules during an interview with a stakeholder?";
- Specific discussion about what Topics might be in each Topic Set, e.g., "What aspects related to Rules would you want to elicit?" or "Do you consider culture of the company is a relevant aspect to be discussed with stakeholders when you want to collect information about Rules";
- Concluding discussion with broader questions such as, e.g., "Do you see other aspects that we did not mention during this interview?".

Results: The result of phase two is a list of 30 Topics, organized by Topic Set. They are shown in Table 2. The limit of 30 Topics was decided taking into account the largest set of Topics on which we could work and for which methodological concerns (in terms of validity, data collection and treatment) remained manageable. Hereafter, we refer to these Topics by mentioning the identifier they have in Table 2. For example, if we write I2, we are referring to the Topic of Objects that could be related to the system, as shown in Table 2. Some of the Topics identified during interviews have been removed from the final list, e.g., "Important financial ratios" has been identified as a Topic in the ML project (see table 1), but was rejected because it dealt with aspects that are only relevant in the scope of an accounting reporting system. Similarly, "Assignments from management team about ergonomics" has been rejected because too precise, and partially redundant with R4.

5   Third Phase: Evaluating Topic importance

The goal of phase three was to evaluate if system stakeholders would share spontaneously or not the information about the Topics identified in phase two.

Our premise is that if our data suggests that stakeholders tend to spontaneously share information about a Topic, then that topic is likely to produce explicit information in elicitation interviews. If data suggests that stakeholders do not tend to spontaneously share information about a Topic, then this information will remain implicit in elicitation interviews, unless the business analyst asks the stakeholders about it. The rest of this

Table 2. A list of Topics, by Topic Sets

Item	I1. Actors who are going to use the system I2. Objects that could be wired to the IS I3. Other systems that are in use in the firm I4. Inputs and outputs expected of the system I5. Units/structure that compose the firm	Localization	L1. Place where the system will be used L2. Repetitive trends in the firm L3. Frequency of recurring events in the firm L4. Recurring events in the firm L5. History and evolution of the firm
Activity	A1. Core business of the firm A2. Reason why the company needs the IS A3. Purpose of the IS, what it is going to do A4. Goals assigned to you and the colleagues A5. Vision and strategy of the firm	Connection	C1. Type of relations between colleagues C2. Power of agents who are going to use the IS C3. IS criticality for people of the firm C4. Strength of relationships between colleagues C5. Connection between Requester and Provider
Rule	R1. Laws or regulations applying to the firm R2. Norms/guidelines/standards in the firm R3. Habits, traditions or culture of the firm R4. Recommendations from the management R5. Best practices that apply to the firm	Granularity	G1. Atmosphere in the company G2. Legal or financial status of the firm G3. Relevant monitoring metrics of the firm G4. Synergies inside the firm G5. Special facts about the firm

section describes how we collected the data. Section 6 discusses the conclusions that can be drawn from that data, and presents the ETM.

Participants: Participants in phase three are 40 people. Data were initially collected from 51 people, but we rejected answers from those with no experience as stakeholders of IT project. The target group for the survey was defined by randomly selecting people from the alumni's network of the University of Namur. Stakeholders from companies described in Table 1 were also invited to take part in the survey.

Procedure: Data collection took the form of an online survey. Subjects were asked to recall the last project in which they were involved as stakeholders who had been interviewed by business analyses. More precisely, subjects were asked to remember the beginning of the project, when they first got interviewed by a business analyst or equivalent (hereafter BA). Two series of questions were then submitted to subjects. A first series was interested in the Topics themselves. Questions took the following form: "During an interview with the business analyst, would you mention X" where X is to be replaced by one Topic, e.g., the first question of the series takes X= "actors that are going to use the system-to-be (e.g., employees, customers, suppliers, other companies, ...)". Subjects were asked, for each possible X in Topics listed in Table 2, whether they would discuss it with the BA. For each question, the subject had the choice between:

– "A: I would discuss this aspect even if not asked by the BA"
– "B: I would discuss this aspect only if I was asked to do so by the BA"

We interpret A as suggesting that the subject would spontaneously share information on the Topic. We interpret B as suggesting that the information on the Topic would remain implicit, unless the BA asks questions about it. We acknowledge that there could have been more alternatives, e.g., "C: I would be reluctant to discuss this aspect even if asked by the BA". Yet, given the exploratory orientation of this study, we decided to stick to a binary scale. This enables to stay consistent with our initial explicit/implicit distinction [14] and keep simple and easily interpretable results. We refer to the resulting set of answers as Topic evaluation.

In the second part of the questionnaire, subjects were asked to evaluate how frequently, in their own experience, the Topic Sets are discussed with BAs during interviews. In this second section, no Topics are mentioned, and subjects are asked to answer,

Table 3. Result of our Quantitative Study

(a) Topics Evaluations

	I1	I2	I3	I4	I5	R1	R2	R3	R4	R5	L1	L2	L3	L4	L5
A	36	23	24	32	19	12	21	15	21	23	26	9	18	19	5
B	4	17	16	8	21	28	19	25	19	17	14	31	22	21	35

	A1	A2	A3	A4	A5	C1	C2	C3	C4	C5	G1	G2	G3	G4	G5
A	36	38	35	19	13	7	25	25	8	6	6	5	16	17	4
B	4	2	5	21	27	33	15	15	32	34	34	35	24	23	36

(b) Topic Sets Evaluations

	I	R	L	A	C	G
Never	0	1	2	1	1	9
Very Rarely	2	3	3	0	3	7
Rarely	1	8	5	5	7	8
Occasionally	9	20	16	13	20	12
Very Frequently	26	7	13	18	8	3
Always	2	1	1	3	1	1

considering the Topic Groups from a general point of view. Given our objective to measure frequency, a six-level Likert scale of frequency was proposed to subjects: "Never", "Very Rarely", "Rarely", "Occasionally", "Very Frequently" or "Always". We choose a scale with more than two levels (unlike Topic evaluations) because Topic Sets are more generic and thereby less concrete to the stakeholders. We refer to the resulting set of answers as Topic Sets evaluation.

Results: The collected data are summarized in Table 3a for *Topics evaluations*, and Table 3b for *Topic Sets evaluations*. Results are presented under the form of contingency tables, given that all the variables that we used in our survey are categorical. Numbers reported in the tables are occurrences, e.g., from Table 3a, we learn that I1 has been evaluated as being explicit by 36 of our stakeholders (Answer A), while 4 of them evaluated that same Topic as being implicit (answer B). Heads of the columns are the identifiers from Table 2. We use hereafter the notation $CT=X * Y$ to define a contingency table formed by the crossing of the dimension X by the dimension Y. For instance, the contingency table presented in Table 3a would be noted $CT= Topic\ evaluations*Topics$, while the one in Table 3b would be described by $CT= Set\ evaluations*Sets$.

6   Data Analysis and the Elicitation Topic Map

We applied Correspondence Analysis (CA) to the data collected in phase three. CA is conceptually similar to Principal Component Analysis: it aims to summarize within two or three dimensions most of the variance of a data set. CA is particularly useful in the scope of our study because it provides a graphical representation for the contingency tables we built from collected answers. Such displays are convenient for identifying patterns in data. CAs were performed with the R package FactoMineR [29]. This section describes the CAs we performed to analyze our data. Next section presents some hypotheses we draw from these analyses in combination with previous qualitative study.

6.1   Analysis of Topics: The Elicitation Topic Map

The most significant output from our quantitative study is the ETM. ETM is obtained from a CA performed on the data presented in Table 3a, i.e. with $CT= Topic\ evaluations*Topics$. Result of the CA is presented in Figure 1. The graph shows the distances between Topics, and distances between Topics and some Points of Interest (bold text). Points of Interest (PIs) can be seen as the representation, on the diagram, of stakeholders' behaviour regarding the sharing of information: one point represents spontaneous

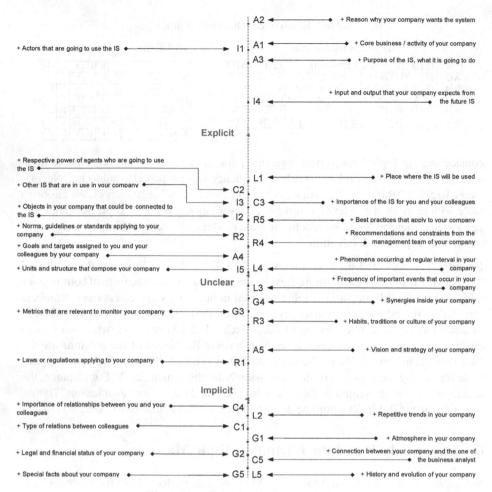

Fig. 1. The Elicitation Topic Map (ETM)

sharing (the label Explicit in Figure 1), another one (Implicit in Figure 1) the tendency not to spontaneously share the information on the topic.

Read the graph as follows: the closer a Topic is to a PI, the more it is associated by our stakeholders to the related sharing behaviour. For instance, L1 can be considered to be an explicit Topic, because it is relatively close to the Explicit PI. Yet, it is less explicit than A1 or A2, because the latter are at a larger distance from Implicit PI.

ETM is helpful during elicitation in that it provides indications about the risk of omissions of certain Topics. For example, observe that A5, and A4 to a lesser extent, are closer to the Implicit PI, i.e. they are associated to implicit sharing behaviour. This does not mean that they are not relevant to RE, e.g., understanding the strategy and vision of the company may be critical to make appropriate specification design decisions. However, it means that stakeholders are likely not to mention these Topics spontaneously during interviews. Consequently, the BA might decide to prepare her interview with questions that focus specifically on understanding the vision, strategy, and targets of the business. It also suggests that it may be useful to the BA to prepare for these interviews by researching the vision, strategy, and targets that the business had already publicly announced in press releases, annual reports, and such.

6.2 Analysis of Topic Sets

Rather than working on Topic evaluations, we now look at the data on Topic Sets evaluations; that data is Table 3b. The mechanisms for presenting and reading the CAs stay the same as for the preceding section: axes are abstract dimensions built to represent the variance within our data set, and are interpreted in the next paragraph.

Figure 2a presents the CA on Table 3b, with *CT= Set evaluations*Sets*. We observe that Activities and Items topics are very close to the *Always* and *Very frequently* PIs. This is interpreted as the fact that our stakeholders tend to spontaneously share information on Topics in these Topic Sets. In sharp contrast, Granularity is close to *Very Rarely* and *Never* answers, thereby suggesting implicit behaviour. Connections, Localization, and to a lesser extent Rules are associated with Occasionally and Rarely answers. Figure 2 can be used in the same way as the ETM. It provides BAs with indications about the expected sharing behaviour of stakeholders toward the Topic Sets, e.g., Figure 2a suggests that it may require more effort to elicit Localizations than Items.

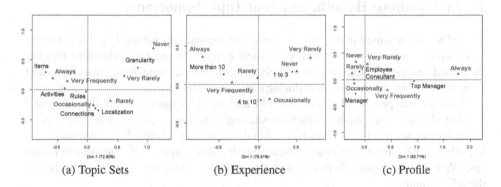

| (a) Topic Sets | (b) Experience | (c) Profile |

Fig. 2. Correspondance Analysis on Topic Sets Evaluations

6.3 Analysis of Experience and Profile

We now focus on the analysis of Experience (i.e. the number of projects in which the stakeholder has been involved) and Profile (i.e. the position that the stakeholder was holding in most of these projects). These two characteristics are studied because they are easily identifiable by BAs at the beginning of an interview. Again, the mechanisms for presenting and reading the CAs stay the same as for the ETM section. Our aim here is not to provide a detailed discussion of such characteristics, but rather to illustrate their potential impact. Further research could however go on the investigation of other stakeholders' characteristics that influence sharing of Topics and Topic Sets.

Experience: A CA for the experience of the stakeholder is presented in Figure 2b, and is computed from *CT=Experience*Sets Evaluations*. In our survey, we use three different levels: people who participated from 1 to 3 projects, from 4 to 10 projects, and finally those with more than 10 projects. The analysis suggests that experienced stakeholders are associated with *Very Frequently* to *Always* answers. This suggests an explicit sharing behaviour about Topics. Stakeholders with smaller experience selected more *Very Rarely* and *Never* answers, while stakeholders which took part to 4 to 10 projects favour the *Occasionally* answer.

Profile: A CA for the profile of the stakeholder is presented in Figure 2c. It is computed from *CT=Profile*Sets Evaluations*. We use four groups of profiles: employees (i.e. working for the buyer with negligible responsibilities in the project), consultants (i.e. people from outside the company helping on the project), managers (i.e. people with some responsibilities in the project) and top managers (i.e. CEO/direction of the buying company). The impact of profile on sharing behaviour is less evident, as the distances between our data points (i.e. our profiles) are smaller than in previous figures. It is still possible to observe that stakeholder with more responsibilities - managers and top managers - are more often associated with *Always*, *Very Frequently* and *Occasionally* PIs. On the contrary, stakeholders with less responsibilities - employees and consultants - are more often associated with *Rarely*, *Very Rarely* and *Never* PIs.

7   Implications: Hypotheses about Topic Importance

The ETM we presented in this paper is based on the samples we used, and it is hard to claim much generality to it. In terms of practice, it can be used as a checklist that has the added benefit of suggesting how likely information on some Topics will be shared spontaneously by the stakeholders during elicitation interviews.

From the perspective of research, ETM and the data from our samples suggest a number of hypotheses about information sharing behavior of stakeholders during elicitation interviews. We believe that it is worth doing further empirical research into these hypotheses. We have not yet completed the empirical research to validate these hypotheses. We therefore present them as interesting research issues that may be of interest to the RE community.

The approach here is exploratory: we observe patterns of answers, and then suggest hypotheses that could explain these patterns. The hypotheses are always about sharing behaviour of stakeholders during an interview with a BA, in the scope of an IT project. They should not be considered outside these particular settings. They are to be read as potential explanations why stakeholders behave differently toward different Topics.

7.1   Some Overall Hypotheses about Topic Importance

We are interested here in hypotheses that can be formulated regardless of the Set to which a Topic belongs. Such hypotheses are called overall hypotheses, and are usually dealing with some general characteristics of Topics. In other words, we expect these hypotheses to hold for any new Topic that is added to the ETM, whatever the Topic Sets to which it may belong. Some overall hypotheses are:

- Information on Topics dealing with information systems (e.g., A3, L1, I3) are spontaneously discussed;
- Information on Topics that pertain to information that stakeholders encounter on a daily basis (e.g., A1, G3, R5) are spontaneously discussed;
- Information on Topics dealing with concrete concepts (e.g., I4, R2, L4) (as opposed to abstract concepts, e.g., C1, G1, A5) are spontaneously discussed.

These three hypotheses (and their opposites), if validated, could be used by interviewers as guidelines for understanding where to seek information that is not represented in the ETM. For instance, an BA may be interested in "The strengths/weaknesses of the firm (SWOT)", which is not represented in the ETM. Using previous hypotheses, she could estimate the Topic is likely to remain implicit during an interview with a BA, because it does not refer to any information system, and deals with abstract concepts. Hence, the BA could decide to include questions in her interview that focus on collecting sufficient information about that supposedly implicit Topic.

7.2 Some Specific Hypotheses about Topic Importance

Some hypotheses can also be suggested, that only apply within a particular Topic Set. The interest of such specific hypotheses for BAs is basically the same as for overall hypotheses. The main difference is that their usage are restricted to Topics existing within the related Topic Set. Some examples of specific hypotheses are listed below. It is important to note that the latter does not list all the possible hypotheses that can be suggested from our results: it simply lists some of the most evident ones.

- Rules that are dictated by the business (e.g., R2, R4, R5) are made explicit;
- Activities about how a business runs (e.g., A4, A5) are kept implicit;
- Localizations that suggest some distance (e.g., L2, L5) are kept implicit;
- Items capable of accomplishing some tasks (e.g., I1, I4) are made explicit;
- Connections involving human relationships (e.g., C1, C4) are kept implicit;
- Granularities with coarse grain (e.g., G5, G1, G2) are kept implicit.

8 Related Work

Importance of context (i.e. environment, domain) is hardly new to RE. Contextualism - which claims that peculiarities of context must be understood before the requirements can be derived - is often presented as an alternative design philosophy to systems design [30]. Papers like [31] - in which it is argued that the machine is to be considered within its environment and cannot be dissociated from it - or [32] - presenting ethnographic analysis as valuable to RE - are further evidence of the importance of context to RE.

As already discussed in this paper, domain modelling languages also emphasize the importance of context in RE [16, 18–21]. This importance has also been highlighted in the NATURE research project, e.g., [33] stresses the importance of a representation dimension in RE, which copes with the tools (formal or not) that can be used to express knowledge about the system, while [34] propose a conceptual model to support the documentation of domain theories. More recently, authors have emphasized the importance of relating requirements to context. Some emphasize the importance of context and empirical validation of RE models as a direction for future research to accelerate the transfer of research results into RE practice [35]. Others even identify context study as an important research area on which RE should re-focus [36]. Modelling the domain requires information to be collected, and hence elicited. This has also been the center of attention in RE. Efforts have been devoted to the definition of elicitation methods that provide ways for acquiring contextual information. From Contextual Inquiry [37] to Inquiry Cycle [38] , context is put at the center of the acquisition effort. Other approaches indirectly account for the context of use of a system during elicitation. CREWS [39] for instance suggests that elicitation can be guided by the use of scenarios and use-cases. SCRAM [40] also positions scenarios as an important tool for RE. Alternatively, several viewpoints can be adopted to cover different concerns related to a system and therefore support completeness of elicitation (e.g., [41, 42]).

The question of how stakeholders behave during elicitation when being interviewed about context has been the center of less attention in RE. Some research has been devoted to the risks related to stakeholders' behaviour during interviews, e.g., personal, social or cognitive factors, and suggest ways to handle those risks [43]. A framework for the communication issues during elicitation has even been proposed [44]. None of these studies handles the distinction between implicit and explicit information. Still, the existence of implicit information is recognized in RE - through for instance concepts such as Tacit knowledge [45, 46] or Implicit Requirements [47, 48] - and should be accounted for during elicitation.

9   Conclusions and Limitations

In this paper, we discussed the importance of distinguishing between the information stakeholders have that is made explicit during interviews, and the information that they keep implicit. Such distinction brought us to the question of how to discover the implicit information that stakeholders may have. As an answer, we introduced the ETM, a list of RE relevant Topics that are mapped by order of importance. In this paper, importance is understood from the point of view of stakeholders, and express the likelihood of a topic to be discussed explicitly. To build the ETM, we used a combination of a qualitative study (to identify Topics) and quantitative study (to determine the importance of Topics). The ETM enabled us to formulate a set of 9 hypotheses about the sharing behaviour of stakeholders during interviews. Ways for further research are clear: new Topics should be added to the list, and larger-scale validations/replications of already proposed Topics are required, so as to make the ETM more representative. Moreover, hypotheses suggested in this paper, if validated, can make synergies for achieving more complete interviews, and hence, perhaps, systems that fit their requirements better.

Limitations in our study should be kept in mind when using our results. Threats to validity exist, e.g., non-response error, small sampling and selection bias, among others are potential threats to the validity of our study. Also, answers are based on what people say that they do rather than on a direct observation. These threats might introduce bias to our results, but do not hold us back from drawing relevant preliminary results.

References

1. Christel, M.G., Kang, K.C.: Issues in requirements elicitation. Technical Report CMU/SEI-92-TR-12 ESC-TR-92-012 (1992)
2. Goguen, J.A., Linde, C.: Techniques for requirements elicitation. In: Proc. IEEE International Symposium on Requirements Engineering, pp. 152–164 (1993)
3. Zowghi, D., Coulin, C.: Requirements Elicitation: A Survey of Techniques, Approaches, and Tools. In: Engineering and Managing Software Requirements, pp. 19–46. Springer, Heidelberg (2005)
4. Davis, A.M., Dieste, O., Hickey, A.M., Juristo, N., Moreno, A.: Effectiveness of Requirements Elicitation Techniques: Empirical Results Derived from a Systematic Review. In: 14th International Requirements Engineering Conference, pp. 179–188. IEEE (September 2006)
5. Zave, P.: Classification of research efforts in requirements engineering. ACM Computing Surveys (CSUR) 29(4), 315–321 (1997)
6. McDermott, D., Doyle, J.: Non-monotonic logic I. Artificial intelligence 13(1), 41–72 (1980)
7. McCarthy, J.: Circumscription - a form of non-monotonic reasoning. Artificial Intelligence 13(1), 27–39 (1980)
8. Reiter, R.: A logic for default reasoning. Artificial Intelligence 13(1-2), 81–132 (1980)
9. Moore, R.: Semantical considerations on nonmonotonic logic. Artificial Intelligence 25(1), 75–94 (1985)
10. Sampaio do Prado Leite, J.C., Gilvaz, A.P.: Requirements Elicitation Driven by Interviews : The Use of Viewpoints. In: IWSSD. (1996) 85–94
11. Lecoeuche, R., Mellish, C., Robertson, D.: A framework for requirements elicitation through mixed-initiative dialogue. In: Proc. 3rd IEEE International Conference on Requirements Engineering, pp. 190–196 (1998)
12. Davey, B., Cope, C.: Requirements Elicitation - What' s Missing? Information Science and Information Technology 5 (2008)
13. Yamanka, T., Komiya, S.: A Method to Navigate Interview-driven Software Requirements Elicitation Work. WSEAS Transactions on Information Science and Applications 7(6), 784–798 (2010)
14. Burnay, C., Jureta, I.J., Faulkner, S.: Context Factors: What they are and why they matter for Requirements Problems. In: Proc. 25th International Conference on Software Engineering and Knowledge Engineering, pp. 30–35 (2013)
15. Burnay, C., Jureta, I.J., Faulkner, S.: Context-Driven Elicitation of Default Requirements: an Empirical Validation. CoRR abs/1211.2 (November 2013)
16. Greenspan, S., Mylopoulos, J., Borgida, A.: Capturing more world knowledge in the requirements specification. In: Proc. 6th International Conference on Software Engineering, pp. 225–234 (1982)
17. Dubois, E., Hagelstein, J., Lahou, E., Ponsaert, F., Rifaut, A.: A knowledge representation language for requirements engineering. Proceedings of the IEEE 74(10), 1431–1444 (1986)
18. Hagelstein, J.: Declarative approach to information systems requirements. Knowledge-Based Systems 1(4), 211–220 (1988)
19. Mylopoulos, J., Borgida, A.: Telos: Representing knowledge about information systems. ACM Transactions on Information Systems 8(4), 325–362 (1990)
20. Dardenne, A., Van Lamsweerde, A., Fickas, S.: Goal-directed requirements acquisition. Science of Computer Programming 20, 3–50 (1993)

21. Yu, E.S.: Towards modelling and reasoning support for early-phase requirements engineering. In: Proc. 3rd International Symposium on Requirements Engineering, pp. 226–235 (1997)
22. Gauker, C.: Zero tolerance for pragmatics. Synthese 165(3), 359–371 (2008)
23. Stalnaker, R.: On the Representation of Context. Journal of Logic, Language and Information 7(1), 3–19 (1998)
24. McCarthy, J., Buvac, S.: Formalizing context (expanded notes) (1997)
25. Dourish, P.: What we talk about when we talk about context. Personal and Ubiquitous Computing 8(1), 19–30 (2004)
26. Baldauf, M.: A survey on context-aware systems. International Journal of Ad Hoc and Ubiquitous Computing 2(4), 263–277 (2007)
27. Lenat, D.: The Dimensions of Context-Space. Technical Report 512 (1998)
28. Walsham, G.: Doing interpretive research. European Journal of Information Systems 15, 320–330 (2006)
29. Lê, S., Josse, J., Husson, F.: FactoMineR: An R Package for Multivariate Analysis. Journal of Statistical Software 25(1), 1–18 (2008)
30. Potts, C., Hsi, I.: Abstraction and context in requirements engineering: toward a synthesis. Annals of Software Engineering 3(1), 23–61 (1997)
31. Jackson, M.: The meaning of requirements. Annals of Software Engineering 3(1), 5–21 (1997)
32. Viller, S., Sommerville, I.: Social analysis in the requirements engineering process: from ethnography to method. In: Proc. IEEE International Symposium on Requirements Engineering, vol. 6, pp. 6–13 (1999)
33. Pohl, K.: The three dimensions of requirements engineering. In: Advanced Information Systems Engineering (1993)
34. Jarke, M., Pohl, K., Jacobs, S., Bubenko, J., Assenova, P., Holm, P., Wangler, B., Rolland, C., Plihon, V., Schmitt, J.R., Sutcliffe, A., Jones, S., Maiden, N., Till, D., Vassiliou, Y., Constantopoulos, P., Spanoudakis, G.: Requirements engineering: an integrated view of representation, process, and domain (1993)
35. Cheng, B.H., Atlee, J.M.: Research directions in requirements engineering. In: Future of Software Engineering (FUSE), pp. 285–303. IEEE Computer Society (2007)
36. Jarke, M., Loucopoulos, P., Lyytinen, K., Mylopoulos, J., Robinson, W.: The brave new world of design requirements. Information Systems 36(7), 992–1008 (2011)
37. Holtzblatt, K., Jones, S.: Contextual inquiry: A participatory technique for system design. In: Participatory design: Principles and Practice, pp. 180–193 (1993)
38. Potts, C., Takahashi, K., Anton, A.: Inquiry-based requirements analysis. IEEE Software 11(2), 21–32 (1994)
39. Maiden, N.: CREWS-SAVRE: Scenarios for acquiring and validating requirements. Automated Software Engineering 5(4), 419–446 (1998)
40. Sutcliffe, A., Ryan, M.: Experience with SCRAM, a scenario requirements analysis method. In: Proc. 3rd IEEE International Conference on Requirements Engineering (1998)
41. Mullery, G.P.: CORE - A method for controlled requirement specification. In: Proc. 4th International Conference on Software Engineering, pp. 126–135 (1979)
42. Easterbrook, S.: Domain Modelling with Hierarchies of Alternative Viewpoints. In: First IEEE International Symposium on Requirements Engineering (January 1993)
43. Cohene, T., Easterbrook, S.: Contextual risk analysis for interview design. In: Proc. 13th International Conference on Requirements Engineering, pp. 95–104 (2005)

44. Coughlan, J., Lycett, M., Macredie, R.D.: Communication issues in requirements elicitation: a content analysis of stakeholder experiences. Information and Software Technology 45(8), 525–537 (2003)
45. Goguen, J.A.: Formality and Informality in Requirements Engineering. In: Proc. 4th International Conference on Requirements Engineering, pp. 102–108 (1996)
46. Stone, A., Sawyer, P.: Identifying tacit knowledge-based requirements. IEEE Proceedings-Software 153(6), 211–218 (2006)
47. Singer, L., Brill, O.: Utilizing Rule Deviations in IT Ecosystems for Implicit Requirements Elicitation. In: Managing Requirements Knowledge (MARK), pp. 22–26 (2009)
48. Daramola, O., Moser, T., Sindre, G., Biffl, S.: Managing Requirements Using Semantic Case-Based Reasoning Research Preview. In: Requirements Engineering: Foundation for Software Quality, pp. 172–178 (2012)

Expert Finding Using Markov Networks
in Open Source Communities

Matthieu Vergne[1,2], Angelo Susi[1]

[1] Center for Information and Communication Technology, FBK-ICT
Via Sommarive, 18 I-38123 Povo, Trento, Italy
{vergne,susi}@fbk.eu
[2] Doctoral School in Information and Communication Technology
Via Sommarive, 5 I-38123 Povo, Trento, Italy
matthieu.vergne@unitn.it

Abstract. Expert finding aims at identifying knowledgeable people to help in decision processes, such as eliciting or analysing requirements in Requirements Engineering. Complementary approaches exist to tackle specific contexts like in forum-based communities, exploiting personal contributions, or in structured organisations like companies, where the social relationships between employees help to identify experts. In this paper, we propose an approach to tackle a hybrid context like an Open Source Software (OSS) community, which involves forums open to contributors, as well as companies providing OSS-related services. By representing and relating stakeholders, their roles, the topics discussed and the terms used, and by applying inference algorithms based on Markov networks, we are able to rank stakeholders by their inferred level of expertise in one topic or more. Two preliminary experiments are presented to illustrate the approach and to show its potential benefit.

Keywords: Expert Finding, Open Source Software, Requirements Engineering, Markov network.

1 Introduction

A requirement for a system defines what this system should achieve to meet the expectations of the stakeholders who depend on it. In Requirements Engineering (RE), researchers deal with requirement-related issues such as eliciting, modelling and analysing, documenting and checking that the requirements are fulfilled [2,9]. Specific difficulties in this area are, for example, the huge amount of stakeholders to deal with, the stakeholders' heterogeneity and distribution, the difficulty to express needs and solve their conflicts [16]. Although methodologies exist to support the analyst in dealing with the full RE process, a broad mastering is generally infeasible for a single person [4,8] and makes RE processes human- and knowledge-intensive [1,12]. These difficulties show the need to support the management of the information about the requirements in an efficient and customised way. One such way is to rely on available stakeholders considered as *experts* to provide reliable information or to analyse the information provided by others.

M. Jarke et al. (Eds.): CAiSE 2014, LNCS 8484, pp. 196–210, 2014.

Aiming at recommending stakeholders, two main approaches have been considered in requirements elicitation: forum-based approaches, which rely on the contribution of stakeholders in forums to evaluate their knowledge [1], and social network-based approaches, which exploit relationships between stakeholders to evaluate them relatively to the others [11]. However, while these two approaches show interesting results in their specific contexts, they are not designed to exploit the information provided by a hybrid context like an Open Source Software (OSS) project. In such a context, a large community of anonymous stakeholders provide few relations between each others and OSS-related companies can participate through some representatives only.

In this paper, we propose a novel approach exploiting concepts borrowed from both forum- and social network-based works to fill this gap. In particular, we show how they relate to two complementary perspectives to evaluate expertises, that we call *content-based* and *social-based* perspectives, which justifies their use in a unified way. While this approach could be considered in a broader scope than RE, we mainly inspire from works and build on concepts used in the RE field, justifying the scope of this paper. In our approach, we basically reuse the concept of *role* provided in social networks, the concepts of *topic* and *term* provided in forum-based works, and the concept of *stakeholder* common in both (and more broadly in RE). By relating instances of these concepts depending on evidences extracted from available data sources, we build a new model where specific stakeholders are related to instances of the other concepts, allowing us to evaluate their expertise. We translate this model into a Markov network, which allows us to produce inferences based on the modelled expertise, in order to rank a stakeholder based on selected topics or roles for instance.

In the following, Section 2 provides an overview of the state of the art in expert finding and stakeholders recommendation in RE, focusing particularly on the two approaches mentioned previously. Then, we highlight the main limitations we want to tackle in Section 3 and describe how we do so in Section 4. We present in Section 5 two preliminary experiments, one with a small, illustrative example where our approach has been successfully applied, and another on an existing OSS project. Finally, we highlight the limits of our results and discuss how our approach can be improved in Section 6 before to conclude.

2   State of the Art

2.1   Expert and Expertise

By looking at different dictionary definitions of *expert*, we can identify a broad agreement on the concept among dictionaries like the Collins[1], Oxford[2], Cambridge[3] and Merriam-Webster[4] dictionaries. Considering the last one, more precise, you can be identified as an expert by "having or showing special skill or knowledge because of what you have been taught or what you have experienced". This definition shows two perspectives: when one *has* special skills or knowledge, whether people assess them or not,

---

[1] http://www.collinsdictionary.com/
[2] http://www.oxforddictionaries.com/
[3] http://dictionary.cambridge.org/
[4] http://www.merriam-webster.com/

and when one *shows* special skills or knowledge, whether he actually has them or not. Ericsson [5] investigates more deeply three criteria (p. 14): a *lengthy domain-related experience*, based on evidences that one has extended knowledge ; a *reproducibly superior performance*, based on evidences that one has extended skills ; a *social* criteria, where a community agree on the status of expert that one could have. We retrieve the two former criteria in the *expertise* notion provided by Sonnentag et al. [5] (p. 375) with the *long experience* and the *high performance*. These two criteria are specialisations of the "*has*" definition, that we will call *content-based* perspective, while the social criteria represents the "*shows*" definition, that we will call *social-based* perspective.

Several works already provide approaches to model expertises and retrieve experts. Pavel and Djoerd [17] exploit documents produced by people to build a language model for each person and infer to which extent this person has contributed to the document, which helps to evaluate the expertise of this person in the topics related to the document. Similarly, Mockus and Herbsleb [14] tackle the expert finding problem in collaborative software engineering, where the amount of code written in a piece of a software appears as a good evidence of his or her expertise in this piece. Taking a more social point of view, Zhang et al. [20] compare several algorithms used to retrieve experts using social networks built from forums of online communities, identifying askers and repliers and exploiting evaluations of the replies provided by participants. Finally, Karimzadehgan et al. [7] exploit at the same time the organisational relationships between employees of a company and the content of e-mails they have sent in mailing lists. This makes it an hybrid solution to expert finding and the closest work to our approach, to the best of our knowledge. All these works can be classified as taking a content-based perspective [14,17], a social-based perspective [20] or both [7].

2.2   Stakeholder Recommendation in RE

A recommendation system (RS) is a software application which provides items estimated to be valuable for a given user task in a given context. RSs have been widely used in e-commerce to provide users with personalised product, content or service recommendations (e.g. Amazon product recommendation, MovieLens movie recommendation) [12]. While a few works consider the expert finding problem in RE [18], by generalising to stakeholder recommendations one can find works and literature reviews comparing them [15]. Relying on these reviews, we can identify two main approaches that we can relate to the content-based and social-based perspectives identified so far.

A first approach comes from Castro-Herrera et al. [1], where the participation of the stakeholders in a forum is exploited to evaluate their knowledge on different topics. Since several threads can be related to the same topic or one thread can mix several topics, they cluster the messages by *topic* depending on their common *terms* (resulting in abstract topics represented as vectors of terms). Then, looking at the authors of the messages, the stakeholders are related to the topics in which they participate. The result is that other stakeholders can be recommended to participate in a new topic by identifying its similarity with already existing ones. From the expert finding point of view, we can see this approach as a way to exploit the knowledge provided by the stakeholders through their contributions to identify their topics of expertise, illustrating the *content-based* perspective.

In a second approach, Lim et al. have worked on StakeNet [11] for the aim to prioritise the requirements to implement depending on how the stakeholders rate them. For this aim, starting from a reduced set of well-identified stakeholders, each of them suggests people that he or she assumes to have some influence on the project. A *role*, like student, security guard or director, and a level of *salience*, a value on a scale between 1 and 5, are provided to describe how the suggested stakeholder influences the project. Based on these suggestions, a *social network* is built and classical measures are applied to evaluate the global influence of each stakeholder. From the expert finding point of view, we can see this approach as a way to evaluate the expertise of a stakeholder by aggregating the suggestions of other stakeholders, illustrating the *social-based* perspective.

3   Motivation and Problem

In the RE literature, we can find two approaches illustrating well the content-based and social-based perspective separately. However, due to the complementarity of these perspectives, a hybrid context needs to consider both of them. For instance, in the context of OSS projects, it is usual to use forums where the community can exchange ideas and discuss about issues or answer questions from newcomers [10], supporting the forum-based approach and its content-based perspective. However, companies providing OSS-related services (e.g. integration, adaptation and training) can be involved in these communities, with only a few members (e.g. representatives) actually participating in the forum, leading to have a whole set of stakeholders ignored. On the other way, companies can exploit the roles of their employees and the feedback from their co-workers to identify who are the relevant people to contact for specific issues [11,19], supporting the social-based perspective. But when considering the participants of a forum or a mailing list, where several thousands of anonymous people can join and leave at any time, personal suggestions of other stakeholders is unable to cover the whole picture. Especially when indirect evaluations, such as message evaluation, is not available, like in mailing lists.

Consequently, we aim at improving expert finding in RE by designing a more comprehensive approach, also integrating the content-based and social-based perspectives already developed in the current state of the art. To do so, we provide a new model which reuses the concepts exploited in the existing approaches, namely *stakeholders*, *roles*, *topics* and *terms*, and relate them based on evidences extracted from available sources of data. Then, we use *Markov networks* (MN), a technique computing probabilities based on graphical models (probabilistic models based on graphs), to infer the probability for each stakeholder to have some expertise and build corresponding rankings. Karimzadehgan et al. [7] also provides an hybrid solution which considers topics and terms in a probabilistic way, but we additionally consider *roles* in our model, while they consider social relationships only as a way to post-process the probabilities. Another main difference is that, using MNs, we can adapt the query to the needs of the user, such as considering several topics or integrate specific terms and roles, while the inference technique in their approach is based on a single topic.

4 Approach

4.1 Concepts and Relations

As we aim to recommend experts, we have to consider the people who will be recommended. In RE, the people involved in a project are usually called *stakeholders* and, because we consider that any person involved in a project is a potential expert to work with, we will use the same term in our approach. Each stakeholder can have one or several *roles*, such as being a developer or a manager in a company, but also being a contributor in the forum of an OSS (more specific ones can be considered). Each stakeholder can also know about some *topics*, such as security, community management, interface or specific features of the OSS. Going further, we can see that each stakeholder uses *terms*, whether it is in his contributions in the forum or in official documents he redacts as employee of a company involved in an OSS.

At this point, we have stakeholders who are related to roles, topics and terms. In our approach, we go further by exploiting the fact that knowing about a topic, like *interface*, implies generally to know some terms related to this topic, like *interface* (the name of the topic itself), *button*, *screen* and so on. In the same way, having a specific role, like *developer*, implies generally to know about some specific topics, like *interface* and *programming*, and to use specific terms. We exploit all these relations in our model to describe the expertises of each stakeholder.

Once all the concepts we consider and their relations have been presented, we have to consider the outcomes we build from them. First of all, we define an *expert* using a relative point of view: being more expert than another person means having more expertise compared to this person. This definition takes the side of *relative* experts rather than of *absolute* ones, as described by Chi [5] (chapter 2), with the latter considering people *above a threshold* to be experts even if nobody reaches this threshold in the considered community. For the notion of *expertise*, we use the definition provided by the Oxford Dictionaries by considering the expert knowledge or skill in a particular field, thus the topics she knows, the terms she uses, but also the roles she has, which supports the presence of both knowledge and skills. Consequently, someone having more expertise than someone else in a particular field is considered as more expert in this specific field, and similarly someone ranked as more expert in a field is assumed to have more expertise.

All the concepts introduced here are described in Figure 1. The relations are directed to clarify their interpretation, but we consider the relations in both directions (e.g. a term is related to a topic as well as the topic is related to the term).

4.2 Model

In order to model the experts and their expertises, we use a *weighted graph* representing the instances of the concepts and relations previously defined. We have a set of stakeholders S, a set of roles R, a set of topics T and a set of terms C which correspond to the nodes of the graph, and a weighted edge for each relation between these nodes. Basically, each stakeholder in S is related to all elements in R, T and C, each role in R is related to all elements in S, T and C and equivalently for each topic in T and each

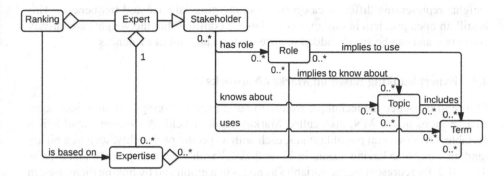

Fig. 1. UML model of the concepts and relations of our approach

term in C, forming a complete 4-partite graph, as shown in Figure 2. The weight of an edge represents the amount of evidences supporting the corresponding relation. For instance if we have no evidence that a stakeholder $s \in S$ knows about a topic $t \in T$, these nodes are related by an edge with a zero weight written as a tuple $\langle s, t, 0 \rangle$. Having the tuples $\langle s_1, t, 5 \rangle$ and $\langle s_2, t, 10 \rangle$ describes two relations showing that we have twice the amount of evidence that s_2 knows about the topic t compared to s_1.

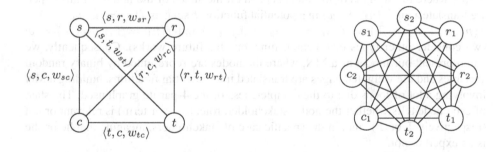

Fig. 2. Examples of models with 1 node (left) or 2 nodes (right) for each S, R, T and C, showing the different relations and the 4-partite structure (only nodes of the same type are not related)

The actual value of the weight depends on the interpretation of *evidence*. Lim et al. [11], in their social network, use the salience elicited from the stakeholders to weight their edges, while Castro-Herrera et al. [1] exploit the frequencies of appearance of terms and normalise them in vectors. Both these approaches as well as others can be exploited, with the main challenge being to have consistent weights depending on the sources used to retrieve them. Considering the technique we use, described in Subsection 4.3, the inference is independent on the scale, so having the weights 5 and 10, or respectively 1 and 2, have no influence on the results. Consequently, any arbitrary scale can be chosen for a given category of weight, and the remaining challenge is to merge weights representing different categories, like merging salience and frequencies. This is still an open problem in our approach, thus we consider that the weights are already consistent and can be simply added to have the total amount of evidences.

4.3 Expert Ranking Based on Markov Networks

Before to introduce the technique we use to build expert rankings, we introduce some basic notions of the MN, also called Markov random field. A *random variable* is a variable having several possible states, each with a specific probability, such as a binary random variable x having a state in $V_x = \{\top, \bot\}$ with $P(x = \top) = 0.8$ and $P(x = \bot) = 0.2$. By representing the variables as nodes in a graph and by linking them, we can identify for each complete sub-graph contained in this graph a set of fully-connected variables called a *clique*. On each clique $g = \{x_1, ..., x_n\}$, where x_i can take any state in V_i, we can define a *potential function* $f_g : V_1 \times ... \times V_n \to \mathbb{R}^+$ which returns a value based on the state of the variables in the clique. Finally, a MN $N = (X, F)$ is defined via a set of random variables, $X = \{x_1, ..., x_n\}$, and a set of potential functions over cliques in X, $F = \{f_1, ..., f_m\}$.

Notice that we do not explicit the links between the nodes in the definitions of the network, as they are already defined through the cliques (each clique implies that we have all the possible links between the variables concerned). In the specific case where all the potential functions are defined on pairs of nodes, the MN represents a weighted graph, where the weights of the links depend on the states of the nodes. In this paper, we translate a tuple $\langle n_1, n_2, w \rangle$ in a potential function f such as $f(n_1 = \bot, n_2 = \bot) = f(n_1 = \bot, n_2 = \top) = f(n_1 = \top, n_2 = \bot) = 0$ and $f(n_1 = \top, n_2 = \top) = w$ (we consider other types of potential functions for future works). Consequently, we can represent our model as a MN, where the nodes are represented by binary random variables and the weighted edges are translated into potential functions, building a MN involving a lot of loops due to the completeness of the 4-partite graph used. The state of each node tells whether the node (stakeholder, role, topic or term) is relevant or not (respectively $\top$ or $\bot$), and, in the specific case of stakeholders, meaning that he or she is an expert or not.

The aim of MNs is to compute probabilities based on these random variables and potential functions. Considering the nodes $X = \{x_1, ..., x_n\}$, where x_i is assigned a state $v_i \in V_i$, and each clique g_i assigned to a potential function f_i, the probability to be in a specific state $\chi = \{v_1, ..., v_n\}$ is computed as $P(\chi) = \frac{\prod_{i=1}^m f_i(g_i)}{Z}$ where $Z = \sum_\chi \prod_{i=1}^m f_i(g_i)$ is the normalisation factor which allows to build a probability ($\sum_\chi P(\chi) = 1$). If we are interested in a subset of variables, it is possible to compute a partial probability by summing all the cases for the remaining variables, for instance $x = \{x_1, x_2\}, P(x_1 = \top) = P(x_1 = \top, x_2 = \top) + P(x_1 = \top, x_2 = \bot)$. Finally, assuming that some variables have a given state, we can compute a conditional probability, where the computation is done only with the configurations where the given states hold (including the normalisation factor). For instance, with the combinations having $x_2 = \top$:

$$P(x_1 = \top | x_2 = \top) = \frac{\prod_{i=1}^m f_i(g_i)|_{x_1=\top, x_2=\top}}{(\prod_{i=1}^m f_i(g_i)|_{x_1=\bot, x_2=\top}) + (\prod_{i=1}^m f_i(g_i)|_{x_1=\top, x_2=\top})}$$

An interesting property is its *scale independence*: if we apply a scaling factor α on the potential functions $f'_i = \alpha.f_i$ and compute the probability P' based on these functions, we can see that we get the same results:

$$P'(\chi) = \frac{\prod_{i=1}^{m} f'_i(g_i)}{Z'} = \frac{\prod_{i=1}^{m} \alpha.f_i(g_i)}{Z'} = \frac{\alpha^m \prod_{i=1}^{m} f_i(g_i)}{Z'}$$

$$Z' = \sum_{\chi} \prod_{i=1}^{m} f'_i(g_i) = \sum_{\chi} \prod_{i=1}^{m} \alpha.f_i(g_i) = \alpha^m \sum_{\chi} \prod_{i=1}^{m} f_i(g_i) = \alpha^m Z$$

$$P'(\chi) = \frac{\alpha^m \prod_{i=1}^{m} f_i(g_i)}{\alpha^m Z} = \frac{\prod_{i=1}^{m} f_i(g_i)}{Z} = P(\chi)$$

This property is of particular importance because it reduces the problem of data merging by allowing us to choose any arbitrary scale as a reference and to re-scale data extracted with different scales to this reference. The remaining problem is to consider the trust or reliability of the data, which is still an open problem in our approach.

Using this technique on our model, we build a *query* based on which kind of expert is searched, for instance someone knowing about the topics $t_{security}$ and $t_{cryptography}$. These topics provide the condition we want to match, thus the probability for a stakeholder s to be an expert is $P(s = \top | t_{security} = \top, t_{cryptography} = \top)$. By computing these probabilities for all the stakeholders, we are able to rank them from the most to the least probable expert on the corresponding topics. It is possible to combine as much topics as wanted for the query, as well as other elements like roles and terms.

4.4 Recommendation Process

In order to recommend stakeholders as experts, we need to build our model based on *sources of data*, from which we should be able to retrieve all the elements used as nodes in our graph-based models (stakeholders, roles, topics and terms) and their weighted relations. These sources can be document-based, like forums, e-mails or reports, or other models, like goal-models or social networks built from social recommendations. Based on these sources, the necessary extractors have to be designed: a *node extractor*, which retrieves the nodes, and a *relation extractor*, which retrieves the weighted relations between these nodes (e.g. algorithms 1 and 2 in Section 5). With these extractors and the sources as inputs, we first extract all the nodes using the node extractors on each source of data, before to extract all the relations using the relation extractors. We split the extraction process because we do not make any assumption on which source will provide the relevant nodes and relations and in which order they will be parsed: by extracting the nodes first, we ensure that the relation extraction step will consider all the relevant nodes. After each extraction step we aggregate the elements extracted from the different sources: a simple union for the nodes and a merging of the similar relations by summing their weights, merging from instance $\langle s, t, 2 \rangle$ and $\langle s, t, 3 \rangle$ into $\langle s, t, 5 \rangle$.

After the nodes and relations are extracted, we can build the MN, as described in Subsection 4.3, and query it. To build the query, the properties searched for the experts to recommend (having some roles, knowing about some topics or using some terms) should be present in the network nodes. For instance, if the network contains a topic *security*, it is possible to query for an expert in this topic, possibly combining it with other topics, but also with roles and terms. If the element is not present, it cannot be queried and an equivalent need to be found, e.g. *cryptography*, which is in the network. In our approach, when we look for an expert in a topic which is not in the network, we replace this topic by the corresponding term if it exists, otherwise we ignore it. Notice that querying for an expert with a given role does not mean that only people having this role will be considered (it is not a filtering function), but that people being more related to this role (directly or indirectly, as described in the model) will be considered as more experts.

Once the MN and the query $Q = \{x_1, ...x_q\}$ are built, the probability of each stakeholder $s \in S$ to be an expert is computed as a conditional probability based on the query $P(s = \top | x_1 = \top, ..., x_q = \top)$. The stakeholders are then ranked by decreasing order of probability to infer the ranking of recommendation. The recommendation can be enriched with the probabilities to provide an evaluation of the recommendations, so that a ranking like $((s_1, 0.98), (s_3, 0.95), (s_2, 0.43), (s_4, 0.22))$ allows to select only the first two as potential experts because of their high probability. An important remark is that, as we consider relative expertise, the main information provided by our rankings is not which rank is assigned to which stakeholder, but which stakeholder is ranked higher or lower than another. In particular, the rankings (A, B, C, D) and (D, A, B, C) fully agree on (A, B, C) and disagree on the ordering of D compared to the others. By considering rank comparisons, these two rankings are completely disagreeing, which is not our interpretation here. Moreover, having a partial ordering (several stakeholders at the same rank) leads to have less informative rankings, because no order is provided between some stakeholders and the interpretation of lack of information to rank them is more natural than a strictly equal expertise.

The complete process is illustrated in Figure 3.

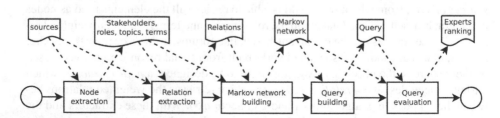

Fig. 3. Recommendation process, from left to right, with the artefacts on the top and the tasks on the bottom. The directed arrows shows the inputs and outputs of each task.

4.5   Supporting Tool

The approach has been implemented in Java and external libraries have been used to extract the data from the sources and compute the MN. We retrieve nouns to identify terms and topics using the software GATE [3], a free and open source Java software to manage text processing with natural languages. It was chosen because it appears as a reference regarding natural language processing, aggregating well known tools like

Lucene and WordNet and providing a complete extraction process. The MN is built and the queries are evaluated using libDAI [6], a free and open source C++ library made to compute graphical models. It was chosen because, among all the tools or libraries able to compute graphical models like Bayesian networks and MNs, it was one of the few able to compute MNs in particular and the only one explicitly supporting loops, which is a major constraint considering our loop-intensive models described in Subsection 4.3. The global architecture of our tool is presented in Figure 4.

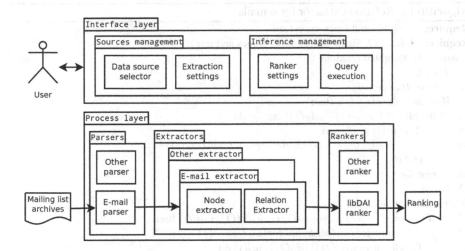

Fig. 4. Architecture of the implemented tool

5   Preliminary Experiments

5.1   Illustrative Example

In order to stress our approach in a controlled situation, we have lead an experiment with 3 participants Alice, Bob and Carla, discussing via e-mail about 2 cooking-related threads : Asian food and European dessert (the names and topics have been renamed to preserve anonymity). The experiment has started just after its presentation to the participants and has lasted 2 days during which 30 messages were exchanged, with 8 contributions from Alice (4 for Asian food, 4 for European dessert), 9 from Bob (4 for Asian food, 5 for European dessert) and 13 from Carla (6 for Asian food, 7 for European dessert). To build a gold standard, the participants were asked to fill a form for each discussion after the experiment, asking for their level of knowledge in the discussion (newbie, advanced, expert) and the most knowledgeable participant from their point of view. Bob and Alice were identified as experts in European dessert while Carla was the expert in Asian food.

In order to build our model, we have designed a *node extractor* and a *relation extractor* which fit to our source of data: the set of e-mails exchanged. The node extractor uses Algorithm 1 to consider an authors as a *stakeholder*, the nouns in the subject of the

---

Algorithm 1. Node extractor for e-mails.

Require: $mail$: Natural language e-mail
Ensure: S, R, T, C: Extracted stakeholders, roles, topics and terms
 1: $S \leftarrow \{stakeholder(authorOf(mail))\}$
 2: $R \leftarrow \emptyset$
 3: $T \leftarrow \{topic(x)|x \in nounsOf(subjectOf(mail))\}$
 4: $C \leftarrow \{term(x)|x \in nounsOf(bodyOf(mail))\}$

Algorithm 2. Relation extractor for e-mails.

Require: $mail$: Natural language e-mail
Require: S, R, T, C: Stakeholders, roles, topics and terms
Ensure: L: Weighted relations
 1: $L \leftarrow \emptyset$
 2: $a \leftarrow author(mail)$
 3: **if** $stakeholder(a) \in S$ **then**
 4:     **for all** $t \in termsOf(bodyOf(mail))$ **do**
 5:         **if** $term(t) \in C$ **then**
 6:             $L \leftarrow merge(L, \{\langle stakeholder(a), term(t), 1\rangle\})$
 7:         **end if**
 8:     **end for**
 9: **end if**
10: **for all** $topic \in T$ **do**
11:     **if** $nounOf(topic) \in nounsOf(subjectOf(mail))$ **then**
12:         $L \leftarrow merge(L, \{\langle stakeholder(a), topic, 1\rangle\})$
13:         **for all** $t \in nounsOf(bodyOf(mail))$ **do**
14:             **if** $term(t) \in C$ **then**
15:                 $L \leftarrow merge(L, \{\langle topic, term(t), 1\rangle\})$
16:             **end if**
17:         **end for**
18:     **end if**
19: **end for**

---

e-mails as *topics*, and the nouns in the body as *terms*. We did not consider *roles* in this experiment, but the MN does not differentiate the types of nodes: using roles in place of topics for instance, assuming the weights are the same, leads to the exactly same result. Thus, while they should be considered for a proper validation, we claim that it is not critical for our preliminary experiments. The relation extractor uses Algorithm 2 to relate the terms in the body and the topics in the subject to the author, as well as the terms and topics together.

The extraction process has identified 3 stakeholders, 4 topics, 293 terms and 2063 relations, building a MN of 300 nodes and 2063 functions. The 4 topics include the 2 more than the expected ones because the participants were asked to launch the discussions by themselves, letting them formulate the discussion subjects. The results, displayed in Table 1, consider an empty query aiming to ask for expert without specifying any constraint (all the nodes in the MN can have any state), while the query with "European dessert" or "Asian food" implies to ask for experts in the corresponding topics

Table 1. Results of the experiment. The rank can be compared to the gold standard (GS) to check the fitness.

Stakeholder	$Q = \emptyset$	Rank	GS	Q =European dessert	Rank	GS	Q =Asian food	Rank	GS
Carla	0.50088	1	-	0.49941	3	2	0.49978	1	1
Bob	0.49959	2	-	0.49969	2	1	0.49946	3	2
Alice	0.49908	3	-	0.50106	1	1	0.49975	2	2

(restricting these topic nodes to the state $\top$). Alice and Bob appear as more expert than Carla on European dessert, while it is the opposite on Asian food, as shown by our gold standard.

5.2 OSS-Based Experiment: XWiki

While the previous experiment allows to have a better control on the data, another experiment has been run on an OSS project to fit better to the contexts targeted by this approach. Our tool has been applied on the mailing list of the XWiki[5] OSS community, which involves also a company selling support and training on this OSS. We have used the mailing list archives[6] from January to May 2013, retrieving 805 e-mails in 255 threads. We did not use *roles* in this preliminary experiment, but we plan to do so in future works by exploiting some data available from the XWiki community, as discussed in Section 6.

In order to build our model, we have used the Algorithm 1 and Algorithm 2 to extract the nodes and relations from the e-mails. An additional effort has been made to clean the data, especially to identify unique authors by aggregating different e-mail addresses for similar names of author, and to remove noise in the body of the e-mails like quotations. However, this process still need to be improved because some noise, like huge source code excerpts, is removed manually by forbidding special terms which appear in this noise. In order to make the computation tractable, we systematically remove the nodes having the smallest total weight (i.e. summing all the weights of its relations) and their relations. We do so in an iterative way until we reach a targeted configuration (e.g. 10 stakeholders, 10 topics and 100 terms).

The extraction process has identified 120 stakeholders, 216 topics, 4854 terms and 75470 relations, and different reduction policies and potential functions have been applied to build the MN. Some preliminary experiments have shown that we are able to build a ranking from this dataset and we were able to assess the coherency of some results by having obvious experts like main contributors generally highly ranked, and participants of specific discussions highly ranked for the topics of their discussions. We did not build a proper gold standard, but we plan as future work to build one based on the rankings provided by some requirement analysts. For instance, by reducing the network to 5 stakeholders, 10 topics and 100 terms, we come with two committers, *committer 1* (a main committer) and *committer 2*, and three other forum participants,

---

[5] http://dev.xwiki.org
[6] http://lists.xwiki.org/pipermail/users/

participant 1, *participant 2* and *participant 3*. During the time span considered, *committer 1*, *committer 2* and *participant 1* have discussed about data migration issues during an XWiki upgrade on the forum. By querying the MN on "Data migration", which are topics available after the reduction process, these 3 stakeholders are generally ranked as the top 3. More investigation is needed to improve and assess the validity of our approach in this context, but these preliminary experiments provide a good support.

6 Discussion

The illustrative example and the OSS-based experiment suffer a lot of limitations due to, respectively, their restricted context and preliminary state. However, the aim of this paper is to present our approach and to illustrate it and show potential benefits by exploiting the results we were able to get from these experiments, saving the proper validation for future work. In particular, the OSS-based experiment provides a relevant context for our purpose but, due to the amount of noise (e.g. systematic quotations, huge source code excerpts) and the difficulty to remove it systematically, we need to use more advanced techniques to improve our results. Moreover, while the presented experiments do not use any role, the OSS-based experiment provide some sources of data that we can use to retrieve and relate them, such as a Hall of Fame which describes specific types of committers and contributors, and organisational models which describe the different types of actors involved.

Looking at the approach, several points can be discussed. First of all, a MN computation is not scalable due to the computation of the full graph. We can see it particularly well in the OSS experiment where the reduction of the network was mandatory to use the libDAI library. Another way to compute our model could be to compute part of the MN in a smarter way, using optimisation techniques, or to use other techniques which are more local like social network measures (e.g. PageRank, degree centrality) or search based techniques (e.g. hill climbing, genetic algorithms). Another point is the lack of relation between two nodes of the same type in our model: we could consider for instance that topics are co-related, such as "security" and "cryptography", or two stakeholders working in the same office or on the same OSS module are related. We can also discuss the querying process, where asking for an expert in a specific role does not mean that only people having this role will be ranked due to the probabilistic property of our approach. Such filtering behaviour could be considered to improve its adaptivity, for instance weighting the elements of the query to give them some importance. Finally, we can discuss the interpretation of the probabilities used to infer the ranking, especially their proximity leading to a probable lack of robustness, or the inability to identify a clear threshold to differentiate actual experts from novices. We are currently looking at other potential functions and information to exploit in our data to tackle this problem.

We can also consider related works to improve or extend our approach. For instance, Massa and Avesani [13] describe trust metrics for recommendations based on collaborative filtering, which could inspire us for the merging of the weights coming from different sources. In particular, the frequency of the term in a forum, which can be above thousand, compared to roles provided by official documents, which can be one or two evidences, implies to use some normalisation methods and trust metrics. Yarosh et al [19] provide a taxonomy which includes roles and topics, but also other concepts and classifies them as selection criteria or tasks to achieve, which could be interesting to extend the expressiveness of our approach. Finally, we consider that the scope of this approach can also be discussed because, although we focus on RE works to inspire us, we could imagine to use it in other domains or to use more restrictive assumptions which holds in RE to improve the performance of our approach.

7 Conclusion

This paper focuses on expert finding to improve the support of RE processes in large and dynamic contexts like OSS projects. We show how current approaches in RE, based on forums and social networks, relate to two complementary perspectives to evaluate expertises, namely content-based and social-based perspectives. We provide a novel approach by combining and enriching concepts from these works to build a model that we translate into a Markov network to infer the probability that stakeholders have some searched expertises. We show in an illustrative example how this approach can be successfully applied and present a preliminary experiment in a real OSS case, before to discuss the results and limitations of our approach.

As future work, we plan to improve our approach by considering normalisation and trust metrics to manage heterogeneous sources of information as well as to optimise the MN computation or to use more local techniques to improve the scalability. The query expressiveness should be also improved to allow a better control of the inference process and adapt the results to the needs of the user of our approach. Other potential functions are investigated in order to improve the confidence and robustness of our rankings. Finally, we plan to further exploit the data provided by the OSS case to exploit roles and to design a complete case study.

Acknowledgements. The authors are grateful to Itzel Morales-Ramirez for her help in exploiting the tool GATE for the nouns extraction. This work is a result of the RISCOSS project, funded by the EC 7th Framework Programme FP7/2007-2013, agreement number 318249.

References

1. Castro-Herrera, C., Cleland-Huang, J.: Utilizing recommender systems to support software requirements elicitation. In: Proc. of the 2nd International Workshop on RSSE, pp. 6–10. ACM, New York (2010)
2. Cheng, B.H.C., Atlee, J.M.: Current and future research directions in requirements engineering. In: Lyytinen, K., Loucopoulos, P., Mylopoulos, J., Robinson, B. (eds.) Design Requirements Engineering. LNBIP, vol. 14, pp. 11–43. Springer, Heidelberg (2009)
3. Cunningham, H., Bončeva, K., Maynard, D.: Text Processing with GATE. University of Sheffield, Dept. of Computer Science, Sheffield (2011)
4. Damian, D., Izquierdo, L., Singer, J., Kwan, I.: Awareness in the wild: Why communication breakdowns occur. In: Second IEEE ICGSE, pp. 81–90 (August. 2007)
5. Anders Ericsson, K.: The Cambridge Handbook of Expertise and Expert Performance. Cambridge University Press (June 2006)

6. Mooij, J.M.: libDAI: a free and open source C++ library for discrete approximate inference in graphical models. JMLR 11, 2169–2173 (2010)

7. Karimzadehgan, M., White, R.W., Richardson, M.: Enhancing expert finding using organizational hierarchies. In: Boughanem, M., Berrut, C., Mothe, J., Soule-Dupuy, C. (eds.) ECIR 2009. LNCS, vol. 5478, pp. 177–188. Springer, Heidelberg (2009)

8. Kwan, I., Damian, D.: The hidden experts in software-engineering communication (NIER track). In: Proc. of the 33rd ICSE, pp. 800–803. ACM, New York (2011)

9. van Lamsweerde, A.: Requirements engineering: from system goals to UML models and software specifications. Wiley, John Wiley, Hoboken, Chichester (2007)

10. Laurent, P., Cleland-Huang, J.: Lessons Learned from Open Source Projects for Facilitating Online Requirements Processes. In: Glinz, M., Heymans, P. (eds.) REFSQ 2009 Amsterdam. LNCS, vol. 5512, pp. 240–255. Springer, Heidelberg (2009)

11. Lim, S.L., Quercia, D., Finkelstein, A.: StakeNet: using social networks to analyse the stakeholders of large-scale software projects. In: Proc. of the 32nd ACM/IEEE ICSE, vol. 1, pp. 295–304. ACM, New York (2010)

12. Maalej, W., Thurimella, A.K.: Towards a research agenda for recommendation systems in requirements engineering. In: 2nd International Workshop on MARK, pp. 32–39 (September 2009)

13. Massa, P., Avesani, P.: Trust metrics in recommender systems. In: Computing with Social Trust. HCI Series, pp. 259–285. Springer, London (2009)

14. Mockus, A., Herbsleb, J.D.: Expertise browser: a quantitative approach to identifying expertise. In: Proc. of the 24th ICSE, pp. 503–512. ACM, New York (2002)

15. Mohebzada, J.G., Ruhe, G., Eberlein, A.: Systematic mapping of recommendation systems for requirements engineering. In: ICSSP, pp. 200–209 (June 2012)

16. Nuseibeh, B., Easterbrook, S.: Requirements engineering: a roadmap. In: Proc. of the Conference on The Future of SE, ICSE 2000, pp. 35–46. ACM, New York (2000)

17. Serdyukov, P., Hiemstra, D.: Modeling documents as mixtures of persons for expert finding. In: Macdonald, C., Ounis, I., Plachouras, V., Ruthven, I., White, R.W. (eds.) ECIR 2008. LNCS, vol. 4956, pp. 309–320. Springer, Heidelberg (2008)

18. Vergne, M., Morales-Ramirez, I., Morandini, M., Susi, A., Perini, A.: Analysing user feedback and finding experts: Can goal-orientation help. In: iStar 2013 Workshop (2013)

19. Yarosh, S., Matthews, T., Zhou, M., Ehrlich, K.: I need someone to help!: a taxonomy of helper-finding activities in the enterprise. In: Proc. of the Conference on CSCW, pp. 1375–1386. ACM, New York (2013)

20. Zhang, J., Ackerman, M.S., Adamic, L.: Expertise networks in online communities: structure and algorithms. In: Proc. of the 16th International Conference on WWW, pp. 221–230. ACM, New York (2007)

Unifying and Extending User Story Models

Yves Wautelet[1], Samedi Heng[2], Manuel Kolp[2], and Isabelle Mirbel[3]

[1] KU Leuven, Belgium
yves.wautelet@kuleuven.be
[2] Université catholique de Louvain, Belgium
{samedi.heng,manuel.kolp}@uclouvain.be
[3] University of Nice Sophia Antipolis, France
isabelle.mirbel@unice.fr

Abstract. Within Agile methods, *User Stories* (*US*) are mostly used as primary requirements artifacts and units of functionality of the project. The idea is to express requirements on a low abstraction basis using natural language. Most of them are exclusively centered on the final user as only stakeholder. Over the years, some templates (in the form of concepts relating the WHO, WHAT and WHY dimensions into a phrase) have been proposed by agile methods practitioners or academics to guide requirements gathering. Using these templates can be problematic. Indeed, none of them define any semantic related to a particular syntax precisely or formally leading to various possible interpretations of the concepts. Consequently, these templates are used in an ad–hoc manner, each modeler having idiosyncratic preferences. This can nevertheless lead to an underuse of representation mechanisms, misunderstanding of a concept use and poor communication between stakeholders. This paper studies templates found in literature in order to reach unification in the concepts' syntax, an agreement in their semantics as well as methodological elements increasing inherent scalability of US-based projects.

Keywords: User Story Template, Agile Requirements Modeling, eXtreme Programming, Scrum.

1 Introduction

User Stories (*US*) constitute the main key artifact serving for requirements engineering in agile methods; this is particularly the case in *eXtreme Programming* (*XP*) [6]. US are very operational documents describing user functionalities on a low-level basis. Basically, a US is made to be written in natural language even if initially a few templates have been proposed. With the years, practitioners developed more templates which they used at their best convenience (e.g. [15,13] for formal sources and [10,4,14,16] for informal ones). The US template is structured in the following way: *As [the WHO], I want/want to/need/can/would like [the WHAT], so that [the WHY]*. In other words, US allow inherently to address the three following fundamental elements (called the *dimensions* in this research) of requirement engineering: *WHO wants the functionality, WHAT*

M. Jarke et al. (Eds.): CAiSE 2014, LNCS 8484, pp. 211–225, 2014.

functionality end-users or stakeholders want the system to provide and *the reason WHY the end-users or stakeholders need the system for*. These dimensions are materialized by a *syntax* in a US template, like the elements between angle brackets in: *As a <role>, I want <goal> so that <benefit>*.

With practically no definition (called *semantics* in the rest of the paper) associated with the elements constituting the US templates, the interpretation is often hazardous. This leads to a need of accuracy, precision and unification. We consequently propose to build a unified model defining a set of US templates. We therefore started from frameworks issued of *Goal-Oriented Requirements Engineering (GORE)*. The use of GORE frameworks, inherently high-level, is a deliberate choice of the authors. Indeed, to the best of their knowledge, they include the richest sets of modeling constructs for system analysis. Alternative choices could have been made and the priority among GORE frameworks within the research could have been different leading to build a different model. The aim is, however, not to evaluate each possible unified model but to build one that could allow to associate a single (one option only) syntax/semantic to every (no lack) dimension of a US template. For this purpose, the unified model is evaluated empirically onto sets of US issued of real life projects.

Finally, we argue that a unified syntax coupled with precise semantics would allow to enhance the potential of these requirements artifacts. Indeed, the use of a well-defined set of non-redundant terms would:

- reduce communication issues between the agile project stakeholders;
- reduce scalability issues of US-based agile methods (see [19]). Indeed, by furnishing constructs that can be better structured, hierarchized and grouped on the basis of their nature, the (iterative) planning of the software development could be based on elements with a higher abstraction level (i.e. broader scope). It will allow to divide the software problem into pieces better manageable for huge software developments;
- ease the querying and reasoning onto US.

2   Research Method

Figure 1 illustrates the research process. First, the dataset has been built; on that basis we have defined a candidate model which has finally been validated on two real life case studies. These steps are depicted into this section.

2.1   Building the Dataset

Initially, the way of writing US was rather fuzzy; it mostly consisted of a small text of maximum 2 lines to describe some functional expectation or scenario involving the final user. Even if [9] proposed an initial way of writing US, many users of agile methods have been suffering from the lack of guidance in how to write an effective US [19]. Some of them thus proposed their own solutions and plenty of templates used in an ad-hoc manner appeared. In line with this, the research sources that have been taken into account are of two types:

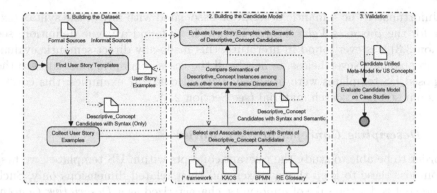

Fig. 1. Followed Research Process

- academic: which consisted in overviewing the US templates found in "formal" or semi-formal sources (published scientific articles or books);
- practice: which consisted in overviewing the US templates found in "informal" sources (mostly websites and blogs).

The aim was to list and basically classify the US templates that are used in practice. No higher importance was given to formal sources, even if Table 1 explicitly shows the number of syntaxes issued of both types of sources.

Basic references for agile development as well as sources found using scientific publications search engines where primarily taken into account. Then, a web search on google[1] allowed us to fill the set of US templates with others issued of the daily use of agile methods practitioners. The search included informal sources like websites, blogs, etc. (i.e. html pages); only sources considered relevant (i.e. referring to a practical use) were taken into account. The search included: (1) "User Story Template"; (2) "User Story" ∧ "XP"; (3) "User Story" ∧ "eXtreme programming"; (4) "User Story" ∧ "Agile"; (5) "Agile Requirement" ∧ "User Story". The first ten pages (i.e. 100 links since 10 pages multiplied must be multiplied by 10 sources by page) provided were taken into account. All pages were carefully scrutinized; relevant US templates were included. We finally included 20 US templates issued of formal sources and 65 of informal ones[2]; this constitutes our first research material.

---

[1] The data was collected by a junior researcher (PhD candidate) onto the Belgian French google version. Another local version or its consultation at another moment of time can lead to the collection of other templates. However, since we have collected a significant number of them, it would have impacted redundancy or brought genuine occurrences in a non-significant amount with no impact on the model.

[2] The addition of the figures in Table 1 within one dimension surpasses the number of collected templates. Indeed, into one template we can find several syntaxes for a dimension; e.g. the US template *As a [type of user], I want [capability or feature] so that [business value or benefit]* generates 2 occurrences for the WHAT and the WHY.

Unfortunately, no semantic description associated with any of the syntax (except for the *Business Value* syntax for which we found a vague definition, see section 3.3) was ever found in literature, this made any direct semantic evaluation impossible. Nevertheless, in nearly all the cases, examples associated to the proposed US templates were provided. We collected 237 examples; this constitutes our second research material (see Section 2.3).

2.2 *Descriptive_Concepts* in User Stories

In order to be able to study the relevant concepts within US templates, we first decompose these to keep the syntaxes and their related dimensions only. Such an element is, for the sake of uniformity, characterized as a *Descriptive_Concept* (*D_C*) in the present study. Figure 2 shows the *D_C* in the form of a class. When building the dataset, each element that we find in a US template and that relates to one of the 3 dimensions will be an instance of that class. As an example, for the template *As a <role>, I want <goal> so that <benefit>*, we will have 3 instances of the *D_C* class, one for *role*, one for *goal* and one for *benefit*. The attribute *dimension* thus compulsorily takes one of the values *WHO* (e.g. for *role*), *WHAT* (e.g. for *goal*) or *WHY* (e.g. for *benefit*) and the attribute *syntax* takes the syntax found within the dimension. Finally, the attribute *semantic* will eventually be instantiated later through the use of GORE frameworks.

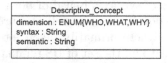

Fig. 2. The Descriptive_Concept class

2.3 Building the Candidate Model

Three sets of *D_C* instances can be distinguished: one for the WHO, one for the WHAT and one for the WHY dimension. For each dimension, a table was built including each of the *D_C* instances found and their number of occurrences.

Then, the syntax of each instance of the *D_C* class was associated to a semantic issued of GORE, business modeling or general requirements engineering literature. More precisely, we used the following sources:

- the i* modeling framework [26], an agent and goal-oriented framework which has been applied in many fields including requirement engineering, software process development, business redesign, business organization, security, etc. [25]. The framework was taken "at large" since it includes the contributions of the whole Tropos [8] methodology[3]. [26] was used as a main source since it encompasses significant work done around the framework;

---

[3] Tropos is the software development methodology using i* in the requirements stages.

- the KAOS framework [23], a requirements engineering framework based on goal modeling. [23] was used as a main source since it encompasses significant work done around the framework;
- the Business Process Model Notation framework [18], a well-known and industry adopted framework for representing business processes;
- A glossary of requirements engineering terminology [12], which collects, defines and translates most of the concepts used in software engineering.

In order to build the model, each instance of the *D_C* class leads to consult these sources in a sequential order. Indeed, the syntax of each instance was compared to the different syntaxes proposed in the frameworks. When a match was found between the syntax issued of a US template and one issued of the consulted framework, we proceeded to a preliminary adoption[4]. This means that the semantic issued of the framework was associated to the *D_C* so that we dispose of a couple syntax/semantic that can be further evaluated later. We can take the example of the *D_C* associated with the syntax <role>: the i* framework was firstly taken into account. Within this framework, the syntax *role* was present. A match was thus directly found and the semantic associated to the *role* in the i* framework was adopted for the *D_C* attribute *semantic*. If it was not the case, we would have done the same process for the second framework (KAOS), and so on. If finally no match could be established in any of the evoked frameworks, it was left out of the study. This stage is referred to as *Syntax Included and Semantic Association* in Section 3.

After the process depicted in the previous paragraph was performed for each *D_C* instance of a particular dimension, each semantic was firstly compared to the other ones of the same dimension in order to evaluate possible redundancy/overlap/mismatch. When issues were identified, some of these instances were left out for the semantic evaluation onto US examples. This stage is referred to as *Comparison of Associated Semantic* in Section 3.

Each remaining *D_C* was then compared to each of the set of US examples (known as *second research material*). The goal was to find how many examples could be related to the semantics of each *D_C* to evaluate its relative importance. This stage is referred to as *Semantic Evaluation on Examples* in Section 3.

The model was built by a senior researcher (PhD graduate). After, it was evaluated by a junior and two other senior researchers. Elements that lead to discussions were carefully evaluated and discussed until a consensus was found.

2.4 Validation

Once the final model has been built, it has been evaluated onto two sets of US issued of two real-life projects. This has been done by a junior researcher then cross checked by a senior one. We started from the US sets and evaluated to what class of the unified model it belongs in order to determine coverage and completeness. Results are discussed in Section 5.

---

[4] We always respected the defined framework hierarchy to ensure higher internal consistency of the produced model.

3   Selected Semantic Associated to the D_C Class Instances

Table 1 summarizes the different syntaxes that we have found for the WHO, WHAT and WHY dimensions. The reader can find between brackets next to each syntax, the respective number of occurrences found in US templates (*number of occurrences found in formal sources + number of occurrences found in informal sources*). The syntaxes in bold are the ones that were associated with a semantic; the other ones were left out of the process of building the candidate model before a semantic was associated. Full rationale for each of these dimensions is given in the rest of this section.

Table 1. Instances for Descriptive_Concept and Related Syntax

WHO	WHAT	WHY
Role (13 + 31)	**Goal (4 + 18)**	Business Value (7 + 18)
Type of User (8 + 15)	Something (3 + 10)	Benefit (7 + 18)
User (0 + 10)	Action (4 + 7)	Reason (4 + 14)
Actor (0 + 6)	**Feature (4 + 7)**	**Goal (3 + 6)**
System Role (0 + 1)	Function (1 + 7)	Achievement (0 + 4)
Persona (0 + 1)	Desire (0 + 6)	Rationale (0 + 2)
"x" (0 + 1)	**Functionality (1 + 4)**	Desire (0 + 2)
	Capability (3 + 1)	Outcome (0 + 1)
	Task (1 + 2)	Result (0 + 1)
	Activity (1 + 2)	"z" (0 + 1)
	Outcome (0 + 2)	
	Behaviour (0 + 1)	
	Description (0 + 1)	
	What (0 + 1)	
	"y" (0 + 1)	

3.1   The WHO Dimension

Syntax Included and Semantic Association. As shown in Table 1, we found six different syntaxes into the WHO dimension. We decided to group *User* and *Type of User* into a single instance of the D_C class since a *User* inherently refers to a *Type of User* through its instantiation. In the same way, we have preliminarily left out the syntaxes *System Roles, Persona* and "*x*" because the number of their instances found was not significant and only supported by informal sources.

Using the method depicted in Section 2.3, the semantics associated to the remaining syntaxes were:

- Role: *A role is an abstract characterization of the behavior of a social actor within some specialized context or domain of endeavor* [26];

- User: *A user is a person who uses the functionality provided by a system* [12];
- Actor: *An actor is an active entity that carries out actions to achieve goals by exercising its know-how* [26].

Comparison of Associated Semantic. As explained in the research method, the semantics we have associated to the syntax of *Role*, *User* and *Actor* have been compared to each other. We first emphasize that the semantics associated to *Role* and *Actor* are issued of the i* framework and, as such, can thus be evaluated complementarily. Concretely, i* includes both concepts because the framework distinguishes *Actors* at a high-level of abstraction and, as mentioned in their definition, *Roles* are used into a specific context. Concretely, this high-level of abstraction is not present in the WHO entities into the US examples that we have studied and each of them always refer to a specific context. Consequently, none instances would be qualified as an *Actor* but rather as a *Role* with respect to the semantic issued of i*. The *D_C* with syntax *Actor* is thus judged non-relevant and eliminated from the candidates to be integrated in the unified model.

Semantic Evaluation on Examples. The semantics associated to *Role* and *User* were further compared to the list of examples built-up as a research dataset. In every of the studied US examples, we found either the word *User* used as example (so not instance of *D_C*) within the WHO dimension, or a specific role played by a user of the system. At this stage, *User* can thus be the syntax of an instance of the *D_C* class or the syntax of a US example. This is misleading so that we suggest to only keep the instance of the *D_C* class associated to the syntax *Role*; the syntax *User* can be used in a US but only as an instance of *Role*. Figure 3 thus only owns one class related to the WHO dimension; the *Role*.

3.2 The WHAT Dimension

Syntax Included and Semantic Association. *Something* was directly left out of the study. Indeed, even if the number of occurrences is high (3 + 10), no semantic could be found in the source frameworks and it is inherently too vague/imprecise/broad to be taken into account. No semantic could be associated to *Action* and *Function*. The only semantic we found for *Action* (*... an auxiliary operation associated with a state transition* [23]) is in the context of UML [17] state chart diagrams, which are design diagrams documenting the states of the object so non relevant for the present purpose. Similarly, we also only found a semantic related to *Function* in the context of object-oriented design which was stated as non relevant for the present context. They were thus left out before evaluation. No direct semantic for *Desire* was found into the envisaged frameworks, we nevertheless can point to the *Belief-Desire-Intention* (*BDI*) model [11] for a semantic related to *Desire*. The BDI paradigm nevertheless refers to the design stage of an agent paradigm and, when integrated with i* elements, the desire explicitly refers to an actor goal. So the concept is redundant with the goal concept and located specifically into a design context; we have thus decided to leave it out of the evaluation. Finally, we have preliminarily left out the syntaxes *Outcome*, *Behavior*, *What* and *"y"* because the number of their occurrences was not significant (1 or 2 informal sources only).Using the method depicted in section 2.3, the semantics associated to the remaining syntaxes were:

- Goal: we decided to include semantics of hard- and soft-goals to evaluate the opportunity of including both notions into our unified model for US. More particularly we associated the following semantics:
  - hard-goal: *A hard-goal is a condition or state of affairs in the world that the stakeholders would like to achieve* [26];
  - soft-goal: *A soft-goal is a condition or state of affairs in the world that the actor would like to achieve. But unlike a hard-goal, there are no clear-cut criteria for whether the condition is achieved, and it is up to the developer to judge whether a particular state of affairs in fact achieves sufficiently the stated soft-goal* [26].
- Feature: *A feature is a delimitable characteristic of a system that provides value for stakeholders* [12];
- Functionality: *Functionalities are the capabilities of a system as stated by its functional requirements* [12];
- Capability: *A capability represents the ability of an actor to define, choose, and execute a plan for the fulfilment of a goal, given certain world conditions and in the presence of a specific event* [26];
- Task: *A task specifies a particular way of attaining a goal* [26];
- Activity: *An activity represents work that a company or organization performs using business processes. An activity can be atomic or non-atomic (compound). The types of activities that are a part of a Process Model are: Process, Sub-Process, and Task* [20].

Comparison of Associated Semantic. The *Feature* and *Functionality* could be compared since they both refer to properties (characteristic or capability of a system). This similarity could be problematic. We first of all decided to look for enhancements in the semantics of *Feature* to gain confidence with interpretation/identification onto the set of examples. We notably consulted literature about Feature-Oriented Development. [5] defines a feature as *a unit of functionality of a software system that satisfies a requirement, represents a design decision, and provides a potential configuration option*. The *Feature* thus is unique when compared to the other semantics because it refers to part of the system that satisfies a functional or non-functional requirement [7] and thus inherently shapes part of the structure of the system-to-be. Due to the perceived similarity in semantic between the concepts of *Feature* and *Functionality*, we decided to only keep one. We have thus chosen to integrate the *Feature* as a candidate *D_C* because of the higher presence of the term in the US templates and in the context of agile development in general and the most precise semantics we have.

Then we can legitimately be willing to compare the *Capability* and *Task* since both semantics are issued from the i*/Tropos framework and both point, in the chosen semantic, to the achievement of a goal. When comparing them, one can notice that they differ in the way they relate to a subject. While the *Task* is a particular way of attaining the *Goal* not related to any subject, the *Capability* explicitly refers to an ability (*define, choose and execute a plan*) of a particular actor to fulfill a *Goal*. Inherently, [26] defines the *Capability* on a design level rather than on an analysis one. We will nevertheless keep it into the evaluation in order to consider its relevance in the use of US where elements are often expressed at the frontier between analysis and design.

Finally, the *Task* and *Activity* must be semantically compared too because the application of these semantics can be conflicting. Within the definition of an *Activity*, we find an explicit reference to the *Task* syntax. In BPMN, the *Task* refers to some atomic behavior which is not compulsorily the case with i*. Both the *Task* and the *Activity* refer to behavior in order to achieve a higher level element known as business process for BPMN and *Goal* for the i* framework. We believe that these elements can thus be seen as overlapping but do not use the same terminology since they belong to different modeling paradigms. Since we give higher priority to i*, we decide to eliminate the *Activity* from the candidate *D_C* instances and only keep the *Task* as candidate.

Semantic Evaluation on Examples. Empirically, we were able to find occurrences of each of the *D_C* instances selected within the studied examples.

Following the used semantics, there is nevertheless an over representation of the Capability (88% of the cases). Indeed, in a lot of cases, the US is expressed in its WHAT dimension as a capability of a role instance.

We distinguish the *Task* from the *Capability* through the way they are expressed; the *Task* is expressed like a general intention constraining the system while the *Capability* is expressed as a direct system offering. The *Task* should thus be kept in order to be able to specify a way of acting to achieve a *Goal*; it can, in a sense, be seen as a way of constraining the system-to-be for achieving a goal during the requirements stage. For example, the US *As ..., I am required to log into the system so that ...* represents a *Task* for the WHAT dimension because it is expressed in the form of a constraint on the system, while *As a ..., I can start a new game* represents a *Capability* for the same dimension because it is expressed in a more direct manner.

Instances of the *Hard-goal* are also present, for example *As a borrower, I want to pay off my loan*. It nevertheless always concerns an "Epic" US i.e. US that need to be refined. Similarly, occurrences of the *Soft-goal* in the WHAT dimension are also present but are even more rare; we for example find *As a player, I want nice looking background art that integrates with the game boards*. This shows that elements issued of GORE frameworks are envisaged in the context of US and we can make further use of it in the context of agile development.

We finally discuss the *Feature* element. Examples such as *Search for ...*, *Undo/redo move*, ... are sometimes considered as instances of *Feature* in the studied US but we do not believe this is in line with the semantic that we have associated to the *Feature*. It is rather aligned with the one that we have associated to *Capability*. A *Feature* is indeed, according to our semantics, a broader aspect of the system requiring to fulfill the 3 conditions set up in [5]. The US *As a salesman I want car to be equipped with GPS so that I can easily set my direction* could be considered as clearly integrating a Feature into the WHAT dimension. We nevertheless point to the interpretation as a *Goal* and leave the *Feature* concept not as a *D_C* instance but rather an element that can be used at higher level to group US around a central theme. This way of doing is in line with the use of the *Feature* element in the Scrum method.

3.3   The WHY Dimension

Syntax Included and Semantic Association. Some information was found into informal literature about agile development related to the syntax *Business Value*. [1] indeed points out that *business value is a concept that describes the relative worth of any development effort to the business. Business value is often unquantifiable, but often relates to money ... The relative business value of stories can generally be determined by asking questions to get to the root value proposition of each.* We do not really consider this as semantic for evaluation since it is more about the characteristics of *Business Value* than the description of how *Business Value* could be expressed in itself. It inherently refers to an umbrella term of a goal or objective to be attained. No *Business Value* syntax relating to semantics was found in the input frameworks. As we will see in the rest of this section, we do have a set of semantics directly referring to objectives to be attained that are defined in a much more precise manner. Even if the representation of the syntax is very high into the studied templates, we believe that leaving it out of the model to favor precise semantics is the best option.

No semantic associated to the syntax *Benefit* and *Reason* was found in the envisaged frameworks. For the same reason *Business Value* was left out, we decided not to consider them. We have also preliminarily left out the syntaxes *Achievement, Rational, Desire, Outcome, Result* and *"z"* because the number of their instances found was not significant.

Using the method depicted in section 2.3, the semantics associated to the remaining syntax, the goal which includes both the *Hard-goal* and the *Soft-goal*, are the same as in the WHAT dimension.

Comparison of Associated Semantic. The analysis of the WHY dimension will thus firstly be limited to the evaluation of examples with respect to i* hard-goal and soft-goal definitions.

Semantic Evaluation on Examples. On the evaluation, most of the examples could not be considered as goals because, even if they are expressed as objectives, they are onto a too low level to be considered as (abstract) i* goals. We indeed could only find alignment with the *Hard-goal* and *Soft-goal* semantics on 53% of the cases, leaving the rest without association.

We thus need the inclusion of other *D_C* instances to cover the WHY dimension. Nevertheless, as evoked earlier in this Section, no satisfying instance was found among the collected syntaxes; we thus suggest relaxing the dimension characteristic of the *Task* element so that it can be used into the WHY dimension. Indeed, we intuitively believe that the semantics associated to the *Task* element would fit most of the examples found into the WHY dimension because they are expressed as a requisite on a lower level basis. If we take the following example ... *so that I know my recent deposit went through*. We assume that it cannot be considered as a *Hard-goal* because it is expressed on a too low level basis, a corresponding *Hard-goal* could be for example *Make deposits* while *knowing that the recent deposit went through* is only a way of attaining the higher-level *Hard-goal* (could be to attain a soft-goal too). By including the *Task* element into the WHY dimension we were able to cover all of the examples.

4   A Unified Model for User Stories

Figure 3 represents the instances of the *D_C* class that have been selected on the basis of the previous study to be part of the unified model.

Each instance has become a class itself meant to be instantiated within the requirements gathering stage. The links between the classes represent the possible links between the elements into a US template issued of the model.

The link between the classes conceptually represents the link from one dimension to the other. Concretely, the unidirectional association from the *Role* to one of the class *Capability*, *Task* or *Goal* implies that the target class instantiates an element of the WHAT dimension (always tagged as *wants/wants to/needs/can/would like* in the model). Then, the unidirectional association from one of these classes instantiating the WHAT dimension to one of the classes instantiating the WHY dimension (always tagged as *so that* into the model) implies that the target class eventually (0 as minimal cardinality) instantiates an element of the WHY dimension. An US template we can derive from the model is: *As a <Role>, I want/want to/need/can/would like <Task> so that to <Goal>*.

Let us finally note that the *Goal* class is represented as an interface because it cannot be instantiated as such; it is either a *Hard_Goal*, either a *Soft_Goal*. As shown within the research, the instance of *Hard_Goal* and *Soft_Goal* can be related to the WHAT or WHY dimensions. Also, if a *Hard_Goal* is related to the WHAT dimension, it can be linked to a *Soft_Goal* in the WHY dimension, not if the WHAT dimension is a *Soft_Goal*. This because it has never been found in any of the examples so we believe it is impossible to have a *Soft_Goal* as desired state to fulfill a *Hard_Goal*.

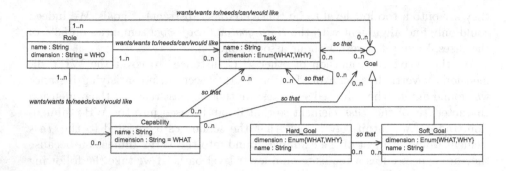

Fig. 3. Unified Model for User Story Descriptive Concepts

5 Validation

The unified US model has been applied to two different case studies in order to evaluate the coverage – i.e. *Is each of the elements required?* – and completeness – i.e. *Are more elements required?* – of the model.

The first case study is the development of an application to ease carpooling. Carpooling is the sharing of car journeys so that more than one person travels into the car; it takes increasing importance to save gas, reduce traffic, save driving time and control pollution. *ClubCar* is a multi-channel application available as an Android application, SMS service and IVR system. Users of ClubCar are riders and/or drivers, they can register by SMS, voice or through the Android app. Roughly speaking the software allows drivers to propose rides and submit their details with *dates, times, sources* and *destinations* while riders can search for available rides [21]. The project included a total of 28 US.

The second case study is called CalCentral has been developed by the University of Berkeley. CalCentral ... *is an online system that delivers a unified and personalized experience to students, faculty and staff, facilitating the navigation of campus resources, delivering personal notifications from key campus systems, and supporting learning and the academic experience* [3]. US are used as requirement artefacts in the project; the list of 95 US that is available at [2].

Figure 4 summarizes results of the application of the conceptual model on the two case studies. It notably shows that each of the concepts included into the model has been required to characterize each of the US of the cases (even if the *Task* concept has not been required in the WHY dimension of the carpooling case). If we consider the two case studies, we thus have full coverage. In other words, each of the elements included in the unified model are necessary for concrete representation of the US found in these two real life projects. This means that, as far as these two projects are concerned, no element is superfluous. Similarly, all of the US of the case studies taken into account could be covered by using the set of elements considered in our model. We thus also have full completeness. This concretely means that we are able to interpret each US of these projects with the set of US templates that we can derive from our unified model. As such, the US is thus associated with a well defined structure.

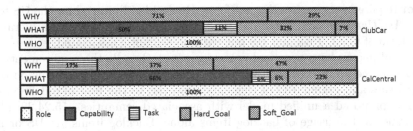

Fig. 4. Elements Coverage in the Carpooling and CalCentral Case Studies

Finally, the reader should note that the WHY dimension was not present in each of the US; it was thus only evaluated when it was present in the US.

6 Threats to Validity

One may argue that the choice made in the semantics was arbitrary. The choice has been made to start from GORE frameworks because these are the ones proposing the most advanced concepts for requirements representation and have a significant supporting community. Similarly, one may argue that each couple syntax/semantic of each of the frameworks used as source do form a whole and that we can hardly take a concept from one method and another from another. That is the reason why we proceeded sequentially and gave priority to the best ranked source. We nevertheless admit that the choices of the used framework and their respective priority could have been different leading to some differences in the proposed model and associated semantic.

The number of collected examples for each US template was unequal which could have biased the relative importance of each of the concepts found. We have always been aware of this reality but we do not consider it as an issue since we were studying the whole coverage of the model. Moreover, the validation is aimed to partially solve this issue by showing such a relative importance of the D_C instances onto real life case studies.

One may question about the level of abstraction of the US expressed in agile projects and question whether i* hard- and soft-goals semantics could be suitable to characterize elements in US by nature operationally oriented. The results that have been presented show that high-level elements are in a few occasions present notably in the form of Epic US.

7 Related Work

[19] highlights the difficulties of Agile practitioners to deal with a project involving a huge number of US for implementing the information system of an hospital. Indeed, when dealing with about 800 US, the hierarchy was rather difficult to determine and the big picture of the system while performing the planning game. Scalability is thus definitely an issue in agile projects with US

as poor requirements engineering artifacts. He decided to introduce the US template "*As [User], I want[Task], so that [Goal]*" in order to define a hierarchy in the form of Goal, Task and US but with no semantic associated.

Series of papers have proposed enhancements to handle the requirements engineering process into agile software development, most of them focus on scalability issues and granularity of elements; however, to the best of our knowledge none has proposed a unified model with associated semantics. [15,24,22] identified issues in the usage of backlog items alone. Backlog items are US or non US-based but still a text based requirements sets. It does indeed not allow to represent the business strategy (or the long-term business goals). They highlight the project should thus include not only the backlog items, but also Epics, Themes, Visions. The backlog items are the lowest requirement items and respectively Epic, Themes and Vision are elements representing the software problem through higher level entities. They however did not provide any explanation on how to map the blacklog items to the upper levels.

8 Conclusion and Future Work

Various syntaxes with no associated semantics have made the use of US ad-hoc and mostly operational only. This has lead to several problems in the use of agile methods notably in large development projects. This paper has provided a set of concepts with syntax and associated semantic for a more precise use of US. The objective is to be able to address larger projects with the same requirements artifacts and to include the overall benefits of GORE into agile methods use. The use of the framework could indeed help – through hierarchization and stepwise refinement – to enhance scalability possibilities of agile methods. Refinement of *Goals* using *Tasks* and *Capabilities* and grouping around *Features*, the project can be divided easier into loosely coupled parts that can be developed rather independently within balanced iterations.

Future work includes the identification of representational gaps overcome by practitioners in US modeling and overviewing how our framework and GORE in general could address these issues. In parallel, the evaluation of the ability of practitioners to use the proposed framework instead of their usual templates will also be evaluated. A Computer Aided Software Engineering (CASE)-tool is currently under development and will be used to support experiments.

References

1. Agile Skills Project Wiki, Agile skills inventory, business value, http://www.agileskillsproject.org/agile-skills-inventory/business-value
2. Calcentral Team, Calcentral user stories (2013), https://confluence.media.berkeley.edu/confluence/display/MYB/CalCentral+User+Stories
3. Calcentral Team, Calcentral's mission statement (2013), https://confluence.media.berkeley.edu/confluence/display/MYB/Mission+Statement

4. Ambler, S.W.: Introduction to user stories (2012),
   http://www.agilemodeling.com/artifacts/userStory.htm
5. Apel, S., Kästner, C.: An overview of feature-oriented software development. Journal of Object Technology 8(5), 49–84 (2009)
6. Beck, K., Andres, C.: Extreme Programming Explained: Embrace Change, 2nd edn. Addison-Wesley Professional (2004)
7. Bosch, J.: Design and use of software architectures: adopting and evolving a product-line approach. Addison-Wesley, Harlow (2000)
8. Castro, J., Kolp, M., Mylopoulos, J.: Towards requirements-driven information systems engineering: the tropos project. Inf. Syst. 27(6), 365–389 (2002)
9. Cohn, M.: User Stories Applied: For Agile Software Development. Addison Wesley Longman Publishing Co., Inc., Redwood City (2004)
10. Cohn, M.: Advantages of the "as a user, i want" user story template (2008),
    http://www.mountaingoatsoftware.com/blog/
    advantages-of-the-as-a-user-i-want-user-story-template
11. Dennis, L.A., Farwer, B., Bordini, R.H., Fisher, M., Wooldridge, M.: A common semantic basis for bdi languages. In: Dastani, M., El Fallah Seghrouchni, A., Ricci, A., Winikoff, M. (eds.) ProMAS 2007. LNCS (LNAI), vol. 4908, pp. 124–139. Springer, Heidelberg (2008)
12. Glinz, M.: A glossary of requirements engineering terminology, version 1.4 (2012)
13. Keith, C.: Agile Game Development with Scrum. Addison-Wesley (2010)
14. Klugh, D.: User story authorship: Defining the user role (2011),
    http://agilerepublic.com/?p=29
15. Leffingwell, D.: Agile software requirements: lean requirements practices for teams, programs, and the enterprise. Addison-Wesley Professional (2010)
16. North, D.: Whats in a story (2012), http://dannorth.net/whats-in-a-story/
17. OMG: Omg unified modeling language (omg uml). version 2.4.1. Tech. rep., Object Management Group (2011)
18. OMG: Business process model and notation (bpmn). version 2.0.1. Tech. rep., Object Management Group (2013)
19. Patton, J.: Finding the forest in the trees. In: Johnson, R.E., Gabriel, R.P. (eds.) OOPSLA Companion, pp. 266–274. ACM (2005)
20. Shapiro, R., White, S.A., Bock, C.: BPMN 2.0 Handbook Second Edition: Methods, Concepts, Case Studies and Standards in Business Process Management Notation. Future Strategies Incorporated (2011)
21. Shergill, M.P.K., Scharff, C.: Developing multi-channel mobile solutions for a global audience: The case of a smarter energy solution. SARNOFF 2012, New Jersey (2012)
22. Vähäniitty, J., Rautiainen, K.T.: Towards a conceptual framework and tool support for linking long-term product and business planning with agile software development. In: Int'l Conference on Software Engineering, pp. 25–28. ACM (2008)
23. Van Lamsweerde, A.: Requirements engineering: From System Goals to UML Models to Software Specifications. Wiley (2009)
24. Vlaanderen, K., Jansen, S., Brinkkemper, S., Jaspers, E.: The agile requirements refinery: Applying scrum principles to software product management. Information and Software Technology 53(1), 58–70 (2011)
25. Yu, E., Amyot, D., Mussbacher, G., Franch, X., Castro, J.: Practical applications of i* in industry: The state of the art. In: Proc. RE, pp. 366–367. IEEE (2013)
26. Yu, E., Giorgini, P., Maiden, N., Mylopoulos, J.: Social Modeling for Requirements Engineering. MIT Press (2011)

How does Quality of Formalized Software Processes Affect Adoption?

María Cecilia Bastarrica[1], Gerardo Matturro[2], Romain Robbes[1],
Luis Silvestre[1], and René Vidal[3]

[1] Computer Science Department, Universidad de Chile
[2] Departamento de Ingeniería de Software, Universidad ORT Uruguay
[3] Amisoft, Soluciones y Servicios TI

Abstract. Defining software processes allows companies to evaluate and improve them enhancing development productivity and product quality, as well as allowing certification or evaluation. Formalizing processes also helps eliminating ambiguity, and enables tool support for evolution and automatic analysis. But these benefits cannot be fully achieved if practitioners do not adopt the process. Some challenges related to adoption have already been identified. In this paper we analyze the influence of the quality of the specified process on its adoption. Adoption is measured in terms of work products built during projects: work products that were not built, those that were built but late during the project, and those that were built in time. We illustrate this analysis by evaluating the adoption of a formalized process in a small Chilean company along five projects. We conclude that certain kinds of errors in process specification may threaten its adoption and thus its potential benefits.

1 Introduction

Defining software processes is perceived as beneficial as it allows to count on a pre-stablished way of working enabling planning, evaluation and improvement. Defined processes also enable companies to obtain an ISO certification or a CMMI evaluation that may provide commercial benefits. Formalizing the defined process also brings the advantages of formal methods: eliminating ambiguity, and being able to automatically analyze the process being able to find errors otherwise hidden [10]. However, if the formalized process is not adopted, all these benefits may not be attained. Process adoption has been identified as a challenge by several authors [12][16], but to the best of our knowledge, it is still not clear how the quality of the software process specification influences adoption.

For the last five years we have been working with small companies in Chile aiding them defining and formalizing their software processes with varying levels of success [19]. We use SPEM 2.0 [1] for the formalization and EPF Composer[2] as

---

[1] SPEM 2.0 - http://www.omg.org/spec/SPEM/
[2] Eclipse Process Framework Composer - http://www.eclipse.org/epf/

M. Jarke et al. (Eds.): CAiSE 2014, LNCS 8484, pp. 226–240, 2014.
© Springer International Publishing Switzerland 2014

the supporting tool, following the current trend [11]. Some of these companies admit they are not rigorous in following their defined process but they are not aware of the causes. Others say that the resulting process is too detailed and that it is difficult for practitioners to understand and follow. These factors are similar to those reported in the literature [16][17]. However, we have found that companies where all the reported factors affecting adoption were addressed still have trouble in applying the process.

In this paper we focus on the influence that the quality of the software process specification has over its adoption. To this end we have recorded the actual use of the software process in Amisoft, a small Chilean company. This process has been formalized and applied for two years at the moment this research took place. They have achieved an ISO certification and recently a CMMI level 2 evaluation. We registered information about two development and three maintenance projects [18]. For each project, the manager manually tailors the organizational process defining a subset of all the work products that are required. A Gantt chart is built for each project indicating the expected date of construction and modification of each work product. During project execution, expected work products' state is recorder weekly. The process adoption is evaluated in terms of expected work products that are actually built in time, those that are late, and those that never get to be built during the project.

We have built AVISPA (Analysis and VIsualization for Software Process Assessment) [10], a tool that builds blueprints and highlights error patterns for a given process model. Error patterns are identified with process elements that are graphically abnormally different from the remaining elements [13]. Counting on this tool, the process engineer only needs to analyze highlighted elements, demanding little experience and also little previous knowledge for effective process model analysis, adding usability as well. Some of these errors are the existence of overloaded roles, too demanded work products and waste work products, among others. These situations indicate possible errors in the process design or specification. We use some of these patterns and create new ones in order to try to identify characteristics of the process specification that may affect its adoption. Among our hypotheses about the possible factors related to the specified process quality that may threaten process adoption we find:

1. no role is responsible for the work product,
2. two or more roles are responsible for the work product,
3. too many roles are assigned to the work product,
4. the responsible role is overloaded,
5. no templates are available for the work product,
6. the work product is potentially waste, i.e., nobody needs it.

The rest of the paper is structured as follows. Section 2 presents background concepts about software process adoption and several factors affecting it. The hypotheses about the issues in process quality that may affect adoption and their application to the company's process are discussed in Sect. 3. The empirical study conducted in the company is described in Sect. 4. Section 5 reports the data analysis and the validation of the hypotheses. A survey conducted to check our hypotheses with the company's employees is described in Sect. 6, the threats to the validity are descibed in Sect. 7 and some conclusion are stated in Sect. 8.

2   Software Process Adoption

Several factors can influence the successful deployment and adoption of new process models. At the individual level, Chroust considers that process models and their support in the form of a software engineering environment, have a high pervasiveness and impact on the software development process and the people working with it [2]. To this author, an individual's views, perceptions and motivations to accept and enact software process models outweigh all other factors with respect to quality, cost, and time, and are key factors for success. Among the human or "soft" factors, he mentions the need for learning the new process and the additional qualifications required, the fear of added complexity, the loss of flexibility and creativity, and the amount of new documentation that must be created and kept up to date, in detriment to "productive work". Even though we have witnessed the influence of these factors on adoption, we focus on the influence that process specification quality has on its adoption. We address some of these issues in the employees' interviews in Sect. 6. At the organizational level, Rifkin considers that the difference between success and failure in the adoption of software process innovations is related to upper-management commitment and sponsorship, the ability or persuasiveness of change agents, the divisibility of the innovation, how disruptive the innovation is, and whether the change is planned and managed [17]. This issue is actually completely necessary in practice to enable any kind of success in adopting formalized software processes. The company that illustrates this research has a highly qualified manager that encourages people involved in development to strictly follow the defined process.

Other factors that influence process adoption in small companies, had also been identified in [20]: notation expressiveness and understandability, supporting tools usability and availability, and the level of interoperability of these tools with others used by the company. On the other hand, O'Connor and Coleman have studied the barriers to the adoption of software process models that are based on industry "best practices", such as CMM/CMMI and ISO 9000. The main factors they have found are Documentation (overhead which can delay development activity and whose merits are difficult to convey to engineers), Bureaucracy (time and resources which the managers believe are required to manage and apply the software process), and the perception of limiting Creativity and Flexibility [14].

As stated by Persee [15], the trick to the success will not come from merely building a good process; it will come from using it: using it over time, refining it, making it better and better, and allowing it to become a permanent part of the organization's business approach. We try to isolate in this paper some of the factors that may promote the adoption of a good process. The introduction of a new process into an organization can be seen as a particular case of an innovation in the way software development activities have to be done in the future. Hammed, Counsell and Swift define innovation as an idea, a product, a process or a technology that is new to the adopting unit, and also define adoption of an innovation as the process that results in the introduction and use of a product, process, or practice that is new to the adopting organization [8]. When the innovation in question involves a change to software development practices, there are particular difficulties in encouraging individual developers to adopt and sustain the use of disciplined, repeatable processes [7]. In particular, if a methodology is not regarded as useful by developers, its prospects for successful deployment may be severely undermined. In other words, to the extent a methodology is not useful, that is, it does not enable developers to be more productive and achieve higher levels of performance in their job, they are not likely to use it in a sustained manner, even if it is mandated [16]. We establish some hypotheses about the causes that make motivated developers not to use the process and we check them against historical data of five projects in the same company.

One theoretical model widely used for addressing the technology adoption process is the technology acceptance model (TAM) [3], which is based on the relationships among perceived attributes of a technology, attitudes toward a technology, and actual usage. This model employs the constructs perceived usefulness of a technology and perceived ease-of-use of it as main determinants for explaining adoption. We use some of these concepts for building the survey questions described in Sect. 6. In [4], they analyze the factors that affect software developers' acceptance and utilization of electronic process guides. The results show that perceived usefulness is a strong and highly significant determinant of current system usage and future use intentions. If a process is represented in electronic or paper-based form, it is not regarded as useful and it will not be fully adopted by developers. As stated by Heijstek and van Vliet, most of the times new processes are adopted to some extent, but not to the extent needed to achieve any real benefit [9]. Partial adoption can come in the form of just performing some of the activities prescribed by the model, not performing the activities in the way they are defined, and/or when not all of the defined work products are elaborated and used during process execution.

This leads to define adoption of a software process as the fact that the process model is followed to the extent that ensures process compliance, that is, when performing the process, developers actually comply with process requirements in order to ensure process success and delivery of desired outcomes. In defining a process model one can take two different but complementary approaches. One is the "activity approach" that focuses on tasks or activities that relate to work to be done, and the other one is the "work product approach", that focuses on work products that relate to artifacts to be built. According to Gonzalez-Perez and Henderson-Sellers, a methodology that focuses on expressing its work products rather than its process is arguably more people-oriented, being better at dynamically reorganizing the work to be done and opportunistically exploiting unforeseen circumstances [5]. As noted by Goodman, this last perspective can support work product "states" for work product promotion/demotion, and assumes that work product production and activity execution are synonymous [6]. From this second perspective, process adoption can be reflected on the work products actually elaborated and used during process execution. This is precisely the approach taken in this study, in order to analyze process adoption in the target company.

3   Process Model Quality Analysis

We say that a software process is not fully adopted if there are work products that, being necessary for a project, have either not been developed, or have been late during the project execution. We state a series of hypotheses that may explain why a software process could have adoption difficulties, and analyze the APF process from the point of view of these hypotheses. The hypotheses are derived from our hands-on experience with the software companies collaborating with the ADAPTE project[3], documented in our previous work [1,10], where we analyzed the software processes of Amisoft, BBR Engineering, and DTS (hypotheses 1, 4, and 6). Additional hypotheses where formulated and refined based on the additional analysis that we carried on for this paper (hypotheses 2, 3, and 5).

(1) No role is responsible for the work product. EPF Composer allows to assign a role responsible for each work product. This role should be in charge of assurig that the work product is appropriately built and modified. If there is nobody in charge of the timely construction of the work product, it is likely that nobody would take responsibility for it, so not assigning a responsible role for a work product may cause it not to be built in time. AVISPA allows identifying work products with no responsible role assigned. Analyzing APF with this pattern we found that only three work products had no responsible role.

(2) Two or more roles are responsible for the work product. On the other hand, there may be two or more roles responsible for a certain work product. In this case, although the process specification makes sure at least one role will take care of the work product, this situation of shared responsiblility may prevent all of them to assume it. For computing this situation we extend AVISPA so that it colors those elements with two or more responsible roles. We found five work product with two or more responsible roles in APF.

(3) Too many roles are assigned to a work product. There are certain work products that are used and/or modified by more than one role. This is not necessarily a problem in itself, but if there are too many roles that interact with a work product coordination may become an issue for finishing appropriately and in time. We assumed that up to three roles would be fine, but having four or more roles modifying a work product could be a source of problems. We extended AVISPA so that those work products with four or more roles modifying it are colored, and we found several of these elements.

(4) Overloaded role is responsible for the work product. Oveloaded roles are those assigned to too many work products, either as responsibile or modifying them.

---

[3] http://www.adapte.cl/?page_id=36

If an overloaded role is in charge of a work product, he/she may have other pri-oritary tasks to do. AVISPA provides an error pattern for identifying overloaded roles. The Project Manager is by far the role involved in more work products in APF, so his work products are candidates to be delayed.

(5) No template is available for the work product. EPF Composer allows to associate a template to each work product. Counting on a predesigned template makes it easier to build the work product in time so we expect that those elements with no template are more likely to be delayed. We extended AVISPA creating a new error pattern that colors those work products with no template associated. We found only a few work products in APF with no template.

(6) Potentially waste work product. If a work product needs to be used as an input for certain task but the specified process does not state it, this task may not be correctly executed. This situation is not always easily detected. However, if a work product is neither marked as deliverable nor it is specified as input of a task, it is potentially waste. Waste work products are those that are neither needed for any task in the process nor deliverables. The AVISPA tool is able to identify potentially waste work products. APF presents several work products that are potential waste, at least in the formalized process; some of them may be underspecifications (i.e., input for some task or deliverables), or actually waste work products.

4 Empirical Study

4.1 Case Study

Our case study was conducted at Amisoft, a software services company based in Santiago, Chile, that builds and maintains custom-order software. Amisoft employs 43 people, and has on average 2 development contracts a year and 7 permanent maintenance contracts. In the last years, Amisoft transitioned from an informal software development process, to a formally specified process –APF– based on the Rational Unified Process (RUP). Further, in order to know if the process is a net benefit for the company and if employees actually follow it, Amisoft keeps track of the artifacts that are produced during projects. A full-time metric analyst is in charge of tracking the adoption to the process.

We study 2 development and 3 maintenance projects developed at Amisoft. Table 1 contains summary statistics of the projects. SITMIX, SITLA, SITCO and SITCORTE are systems specifically developed for the Chilean Judiciary. They allow to automate manual processes and to eliminate paperwork. The main functionality of these systems is a configurable workflow integrated with a doc-ument management system. Currently Amisoft is in charge of the maintenance of these systems for its customers; that is why only SITMIX is a development project for our case study. AMILEX is a product developed by Amisoft that en-capsulates the knowledge acquired in paperless management workflow systems. Since the process is tailored for every project, the work products created during each project vary. In particular, there are (unsurprisingly) significant differences

Table 1. Description of Projects Analyzed in the Empirical Study

Project	Type	Team	Months	Description
SITMIX	Dev.	1 project manager + 5 developers	12	Mixed courts information system
AMILEX	Dev.	1 project manager + 3 developers + 0.5 architect	7	Parameterizable workflow and digital folder
SITLA	Maint.	0.5 project manager + 3 developers	6	Labor Courts information system support
SITCO	Maint.	0.5 project manager + 3 developers	6	Collection, Labor and Social Courts information system
SITCORTE	Maint.	0.5 project manager + 5 developers	6	Courts of Appeal information system

between the processes followed by development and maintenance projects; in addition, individual processes vary, particularly among development projects.

4.2 Methodology

In this study, we perform a two-step investigation: we first analyze the process adoption spreadsheet of each project to confirm our hypotheses, and then we perform a follow-up employee questionnaire of the hypotheses.

Process adoption spreadsheet. The process adoption spreadsheet is maintained by the metrics analyst, and it tracks each work product weekly. Each work product that is expected to be delivered before that date is checked in order to know if it is present. The work product is then marked, for that week, as either delivered or late. At the end of the project, the weekly information is consolidated in order to define 3 possible statuses for a given work product:

- **Delivered on time (OT).** The work product was present in the project, and each time its delivery was expected, it was indeed present.
- **Delayed (D).** At least once during the project, the work product suffered a delay of at least one week.
- **Not delivered (ND).** At the end of the project, the work product was still not delivered.

Based on the data that we have for each work product of each project, we look for evidence towards the validation or invalidation of each of our hypotheses.

Employee survey. In order to follow up on the first analysis, we also conducted a survey of the project managers of Amisoft, specifically designed to provide further evidence for or against our hypotheses. Project managers are all Computer Science Engineers with more than three years experience. They are in charge of scheduling activities, controlling that milestones are met, and making sure that team members apply the company's software process. They are also in charge of requirements analysis for their projects.

Table 2. General work product statistics

Project Id	Work products	OT	D	ND
SITMIX	30	18	10	2
AMILEX	37	22	13	2
SITLA	19	7	12	0
SITCO	34	27	3	1
SITCORTE	34	28	3	0

5 Process Adoption Spreadsheet

Table 2 presents the general results of our study. Each row presents a project, and for each project: (1) the total number of work products in the tailored process; (2) the number of work products that were delivered in time; (3) the number of work products that were delayed; and (4) the number of work products that were not delivered. From this table, we can see that a minority of work products are not delivered (which is reassuring for Amisoft). For development projects, a third of the work products experience delays or are not delivered. For maintenance projects, there are fewer delays, with more than 80% of the work products being delivered in time, which is within Amisoft's goals. Table 3 presents a summary of the work products, whether they comply with our hypotheses, and, for each project, whether they were delivered on time, or experienced issues.

(1) No role is responsible for the work product. We found weak evidence for this claim. Only three work products fit the pattern (MUS, ICF, DDD). Of those, DDD is only present in the process of project AMILEX; ICF has been delivered in time each time, and MUS has not been delivered for project SITCO. In all cases, MUS, ICF, and DDD are subsumed by the hypothesis that they may be waste as well; as such, the evidence is overall inconclusive.

(2) Two or more roles are responsible for the work product. We again find that a low number of work products suffer from this issue. There are 5 overall: TEC, CGP, SRQ, ARR, and PMD. Of those, PMD was the only one that did not encounter delays of any kind. On the other hand, TEC and CGP were late in both development projects, while SRQ was not performed in SITMIX, and ARR was delayed in AMILEX. Of note, TEC was late in both SITMIX and AMILEX, but it was performed in time for all three maintenance projects; these 3 projects did not include CGP, ARR, or SRQ in there processes. Overall, it seems that there is reasonable initial support for the hypothesis, even though the number of work products concerned is small, and 3 out of 5 of these work products were not present in maintenance projects.

(3) Too many roles are assigned to the work product. We consider the threshold of too many roles to be 4. Using that threshold, we find that 11 work products have too many roles involved for their proper implementation (LAA, CGP, CGI, ARR, MRR, PCC, PPP, PVP, PRP, PMD, and ACE). Of those, 9 feature a delay on at least one project, which yields strong evidence towards this factor

Table 3. Work product behavior for each hypothesis: H1 - no responsible role, H2 - two or more responsible roles, H3 - too many interacting roles, H4 - assigned to an overloaded role, H5 - no template available, H6 - defined as waste. For the projects the meaning is: ✗ - not delivered, ! - delayed, ✓ - in time, – - not in process

Work product	Hypotheses						Statuses				
	H1	H2	H3	H4	H5	H6	SITMIX	AMILEX	SITLA	SITCO	SITCORTE
LNE	N	N	N	Y	N	Y	✗	✗	–	–	–
TEC	N	Y	N	Y	N	N	!	!	✓	✓	✓
LAA	N	N	Y	Y	N	Y	!	!	✓	✓	✓
PEE	N	N	N	Y	N	N	!	!	!	✓	✓
CGP	N	Y	Y	Y	N	N	!	!	–	–	–
CGI	N	N	Y	Y	N	N	!	!	✓	✓	✓
SRQ	N	Y	N	Y	N	N	✗	✓	–	–	–
ARR	N	Y	Y	Y	N	N	✗	✓	–	✓	✓
MRR	N	N	Y	Y	N	N	!	✓	!	✓	✓
PAC	N	N	N	N	N	N	!	✓	✓	✓	✓
PRH	N	N	N	Y	N	N	!	✓	✓	✓	✓
PRV	N	N	N	Y	N	N	!	✓	✓	✓	✓
ESC	N	N	N	Y	N	Y	✓	✗	✓	✓	✓
PEA	N	N	N	Y	N	Y	✓	!	✓	✓	✓
PCC	N	N	Y	Y	N	Y	✓	!	–	–	–
PPR	N	N	N	Y	N	Y	✓	!	!	!	!
PPP	N	N	Y	Y	N	N	✓	!	✓	✓	✓
LRR	N	N	N	Y	N	N	✓	!	✓	✓	✓
PVP	N	N	Y	Y	N	N	✓	!	!	!	!
CPU	N	N	N	Y	N	N	–	✓	✓	✓	✓
PRP	N	N	Y	Y	N	Y	–	!	!	!	!
VPP	N	N	N	Y	N	N	✓	✓	–	–	–
PLP	N	N	N	Y	N	N	✓	✓	–	–	–
PMD	N	Y	Y	Y	Y	N	–	✓	✓	✓	✓
PAP	N	N	N	N	N	N	✓	✓	✓	✓	✓
MCU	N	N	N	Y	N	N	–	✓	–	–	–
MDD	N	N	N	N	N	N	✓	✓	✓	✓	✓
MUS	Y	N	N	N	Y	Y	✓	✓	✓	✗	✓
ICF	Y	N	N	N	Y	Y	✓	✓	✓	✓	✓
PIR	N	N	N	N	N	N	–	✓	✓	✓	✓
GLS	N	N	N	Y	N	Y	✓	✓	✓	✓	✓
ESS	N	N	N	N	N	N	✓	✓	✓	✓	✓
ERS	N	N	N	Y	N	N	✓	–	✓	✓	✓
DDD	Y	N	N	N	Y	Y	–	✓	–	–	✓
DDR	N	N	N	N	Y	Y	–	✓	✓	✓	✓
SAD	N	N	N	N	Y	N	✓	✓	–	–	–
ACE	N	N	Y	Y	N	Y	–	✓	✓	✓	✓
Total	3	5	11	15	5	13	–	–	–	–	–

being a possible cause for delays. As said above, the higher the number of roles, the more probable these coordination issues arise. We also note that development projects are more concerned with this issue (9 work products) than maintenance projects (only 3 work products are affected).

(4) Overloaded role is responsible for the work product. The most overloaded role by far is the project manager; therefore, we only investigate this particular role. Our analysis brings strong evidence that if a role is overloaded, it is a factor in work products that are delayed or not delivered: of the 17 work products the project manager is involved in, 15 experienced delays. Clearly, the project manager has many things on his plate, and a lot of them can pass through. We note that of these 15, only 2 concern maintenance projects (15 concern development projects), highlighting again the asymmetry between both kinds of

projects. It seems that if changes to the process could delegate some of these tasks to other roles, this would significantly help process adoption all around.

(5) No templates are available for the work product. We do not find support for this hypothesis. The presence/absence of a template seems uncorrelated with the adoption of the process. If anything, it appears to be negatively correlated: of the six work products that do not have a template (PMD, MUS, ICF, DDD, DDR, SAD), only one, MUS, encountered issues, in only one project.

(6) Potentially waste work product. Waste is defined as a work product that is generated, but that is neither delivable nor used in any other task. This hypothesis seems to be a good factor for explanation of adoption as well, although the reasoning is not obvious at first glance. There are 13 work products marked as "waste". Of those, only 8 suffer any kind of delay, which does not provide a very strong support for waste being an issue. However, examining the work products marked as waste, we find that several of them were victim of underspecification. More precisely, several work products marked as "waste" were actually deliverables to the client, and as such employees are very aware of their importance. The waste work products that are actually client deliverable are: ACE, DDR, GLS, MUS, and ICF. Of these, only MUS was not delivered; all other work products were delivered, on time. Removing these 5 work products from the "waste" category yields a different pictures: of the 8 work products that remain, only DDD does not suffer any delay, which makes "real waste" work products a strong predictor of adoption to the process. In short, perceived utility seems like an important factor. Of note, taking into account the fact that deliverables to the clients are seen as important further weakens the evidence towards the no-responsible role hypothesis, as two of the three work products without a responsible role are deliverables to the client.

6   Survey Results

Since we have several competing hypotheses, we attempted to shed more light by getting feedback from the project managers of Amisoft. Specifically, we sent a questionnaire via email to all the project managers, asking them whether they recalled having experienced delays in delivering work products according to our hypotheses. The questionnaire contained one question per hypothesis, plus a last question asking for other causes for the delays. All responses were free-form text, that we analyzed and summarize here. Five project managers replied to our questionnaire, although the fact that it was done by email, and that the managers are busy, had the consequence that some responses were quite succinct and as such not always easy to interpret. Of note, 4 of the 5 managers that responded were from projects we investigated in the first step, while the last one was not.

No role responsible for the work product. The project managers were unanimous on this hypothesis: they do not recall any instance of this fact being the cause of delays, going so far as saying that all work products have assigned roles. Given that a small minority of work products were found to have no responsible role, this confirms that our first hypothesis has very weak support in practice: even if there is (in rare instances) a work product that is not assigned to any role formally in the process, someone in practice is responsible for it.

Two or more roles responsible for the work product. We find limited additional support for this hypothesis. In particular three of the managers mentioned that the responsibilities for some work products are sometimes unclear, especially for the testing plan (PPR), resource allocation (ARR), and the requirement specification (ERS). However the additional evidence is limited since both PPR and ERS do not have two responsible roles—only several involved roles—in the process definition, although in practice the distinction between responsible and involved role might not be as clear-cut as it is in the process specification.

Too many roles assigned to a work product. One product manager replied saying that due to the size of his team, having too many people involved was not a problem. Given that that team was SITMIX, the largest one in the projects we analyzed, we can extrapolate that other teams did not run into that problem either. As such, it seems that this may be a valid hypothesis, but not in the particular circumstances at Amisoft, where teams are small. On the other hand, another manager mentions that the work product ERS has too many roles, and that it is a problematic situation. Another manager mentions a work product that involves an architect, a developer, and the project manager, but does not precise which. Overall, managers have conflicting opinions about this hypothesis, preventing us from reaching a clear conclusion.

Overloaded roles are responsible for the work product. The evidence is much clearer for this hypothesis. All managers agree that the project manager is over-loaded. Two managers mention that this is an explicit risk to the project, that is taken into account in order to mitigate it (by dividing up tasks, and delegating them to other people). One manager is also aware of this strategy to reduce his load, but mentions he is unable to delegate tasks, since his team is too small. Finally, another manager mentions the quality assurance (QA) roles as also being affected by overloading, although he is the only one.

No templates are available for the work product. For this hypothesis, all managers find that the templates are present, and are adequate, except for specific work products, where they could be improved (with TEC being explicitly mentioned once). As such, the evidence gathered by the questionnaire leads us to reject this hypothesis, at least for the case of projects at Amisoft.

Potentially waste work product. We find convincing evidence that there is perceived waste in the process, coming from three of the project managers. For some work products, it is unclear who will use them once they are produced, or why they are important. A few work products are mentioned by name. These include PRV, ERS, PLP, and PCC, and (less precisely) activities related to verification and validation, and activities related to process monitoring (i.e., metric collection regarding the process itself). From this, we can conclude that waste, as perceived by the managers, is an issue that is present in the process.

Other reasons. Finally, there are several other reasons for delays that are mentioned in the free entry space that we let for the project managers to fill. There are two main reasons:

- Dependencies between tasks is a problem referenced by four of the five interviewed managers. By dependencies between tasks, we mean the situation that arises when a task is delayed because of waiting upon the completion of another task. In particular, three managers mention the Quality Assurance area as being a bottleneck in that regard.

- External factors, such as changes in personnel, and changes to requirements made by clients are mentioned as source of delays, that propagate to other tasks. However these factors cannot be attributed to the process itself.

7 Discussion

7.1 Aggregating the Evidence

Combining the evidence we gathered in the two steps of our investigation, we can order our hypothesis from the least likely to the most likely to incurr delays in delivering work products.

Unlikely hypotheses

- *No role responsible for the work product:* we found very few work products which did not have a responsible role specified, and a low correlation with delays or work products undelivered. Further, all project managers stated that all work products are in the responsibility of someone.

- *No templates are available for the work product:* we found a similar situation as with the previous hypothesis. There are few work products matching the hypothesis, a low correlation, and projects managers concurr.

Moderately likely hypotheses

- *Two or more roles responsibles for the work product:* We found that there are few work products matching with the hypothesis, but that they have a high correlation with problematic work products. On the other hand, other hypotheses seem to have more explaining power, and project managers gave little additional support in the questionnaire.

- *Too many roles assigned to a work product:* This hypothesis has a good correlation with problematic work products. However, project managers have conflicting opinions about it, with at least one manager saying that Amisoft's teams are too small for it to be an issue.

Likely hypotheses

- *Potentially waste work product:* at first, we found a moderate correlation between potential waste and problematic work products. However, a detailed inspection reveals that some of the "waste" is not really waste, as it concerns work products directly relevant to the client (deliverables), hence which are very likely to be done anyways. With this new knowledge in hand, we find that waste is a much better explanation. This is further confirmed by the managers, of whom most agree that there is waste in the process, conforting this hypothesis.

• *Overloaded roles are responsible for the work product:* finally, this hypothesis has the strongest support. It has a strong correlation with problematic work products, and managers strongly echo this in their comments.

7.2 Difference between Development and Maintenance Projects

We observe that maintenance projects have less problematic work products than development ones. A follow-up with the company's CEO gave us some possible reasons, for whom the most important is the type of contract for each type of project, and the impact this has on the process. Maintenance projects usually have a monthly contract, while development projects have contracts based on functionality milestones. As such, there is more pressure in development projects to produce deliverable work products and functionality fast, leading to a lower priority towards other artifacts in the process, which are either for internal use, or that are perceived to have a lower added value (such as verification and validation activities).

7.3 Additional Hypotheses

Beyond the hypoteses checked, there are others not investigated yet.

• *Synchronization issues.* Managers reported that some tasks were delayed because they were waiting on other tasks to be finished, that behave as bottlenecks (e.g., QA activities). Since managers are keenly aware of this issue, it seems to be a salient one.

• *Early vs late tasks.* Related to synchronization issues, the fact that a task is late in the project or in an iteration could lead to it being more likely to be delayed, as the delays tend to accumulate with time.

• *Verification and validation.* Managers and the company's CEO mentioned on several occasions that tasks from the Verification and Validation software engineering discipline frequently were the most problematic. A quick glance at the problematic work products reveals that the most problematic ones (the ones delayed in 4 out of 5 projects), belong to the verification and validation area: PPR, PVP, and PRP. As such, exploring this in more details would be worthwhile.

• *Internal vs external tasks.* Managers often put more emphasis on work products that are more relevant to the client, as progress is more easily seen that way. We have seen hints of this being a factor when we investigated waste, but this phenomenon deserves a fuller investigation.

7.4 Threats to Validity

As with any empirical study, this work is subject to several threats to validity, that we sumarize in Table 4.

Table 4. Threats to validity of the study

Threat	Description
Single case study.	We only analyzed 5 projects from a single company. Different companies will have different characteristics, in terms of size of the company and of the teams working there, different market niches, different cultures, and different software engineering practices. Further, each project has a host of speficities that make it unique, such as the client, the composition of the team, etc. Our study needs to be replicated in a variety of distinct contexts to see whether the findings hold in general, or are specific to this case.
No qualitative analysis of the work products	So far, the process monitoring at Amisoft considers that a work product is delivered only by its presence or absence in the system. There is no inspection of the quality of the work product itself. Some of the work products may be present in the system, but in an incorrect or incomplete state. A manual analysis of the work products would be necessary in order to know if this is the case.
Effect of process tailoring	At Amisoft, each project has a specific process, tailored from the generic process. As such, the set of artifacts to be delivered for each project may vary. The fact that some artifacts were not delivered because they were not in the process to start with makes it harder to compare projects with one another.
Project manager questionnaires	Our questionnaires also have several potential issues. We only sent the questionnaire to project managers, as it would have been prohibitive to send it to all employees at Amisoft, in terms of the effort involved both at Amisoft to fill it (for that reason we also refrained from asking for subsequent clarifications), and on our side to aggregate the information. We chose to send the questionnaire to project managers since they have a good view of their team members, but this choice also inccurs bias in the responses.

8   Conclusion

In this paper we analized the impact that the quality of formalized software processes has on their adoption. We stated six hypotheses about the reasons that may cause work products to be delayed or never built during project execution. The process itself was analyzed using AVISPA, a graphical tool that highlights potentially problematic elements in the process.

The formalized sofware process adoption was analyzed in two different dimensions. First an empirical study about actual use of the process in practice was conducted in two development and three maintenance projects in the same company. In this study each work product that was either late or not developed in each project was recorded. And then a questionnaire was applied to all five project managers about their personal perception about the stated hypotheses.

We could realize that the process was well specified for defining one and only one responsible for each work product, and there is also a template defined for each work product in the process model. So these issues were not supposed to be the causes for not following the process as expected, at least in this company. Both, the empirical study and the questionnaire corroborated these facts. We found some evidence that work products where four or more roles interact or those where there are more than one role responsible for them are somewhat likely to be delayed. Finally, we found strong evidence that work products that are specified as waste and those that are responsible of an overloaded role are almost always late. In general, all six hypotheses seamed reasonable, but empirical analysis resulted that they were not true in all cases.

References

1. Bastarrica, M.C., Hurtado, J.A., Bergel, A.: Toward Lean Development in Formally Specified Software Processes. In: 18th EuroSPI 2011, Denmark (June 2011)
2. Chroust, G.: Soft Factors impeding the Adoption of Process Models. In: Proceedings of the 28th EUROMICRO 2002, Dortmund, pp. 388–394 (September 2002)
3. Davis, F.D., Bagozzi, R.P., Warshaw, P.R.: User acceptance of computer technology: A comparison of two theoretical models. Management Science 35(8), 982–1003 (1989)
4. Dyba, T., Moe, N.B., Mikkelsen, E.M.: An Empirical Investigation on Factors Affecting Software Developer Acceptance and Utilization of Electronic Process Guides. In: METRICS 2004, Chicago (September 2004)
5. Gonzalez-Perez, C., Henderson-Sellers, B.: A work product pool approach to methodology specification and enactment. Journal of Systems and Software 81(8), 1288–1305 (2008)
6. Goodman, F.A.: Defining and deploying software processes. Auerbach Publications, Boca Raton (2005)
7. Green, G.C., Collins, R.W., Hevner, A.R.: Perceived control and the discussion of software process innovations. Journal of High Technology Management Research 15(1), 123–144 (2004)
8. Hameed, M.A., Counsell, S., Swift, S.: A conceptual model for the process of IT innovation adoption in organizations. Journal of Engineering and Technology Management 29, 358–390 (2012)
9. Heijstek, A., van Vliet, H.: Less is More in Software Process Improvement. In: M. Biro and R. Messnarz (eds.) EuroSPI 2005, pp. 6.1–6.12 (2005)
10. Hurtado, J.A., Bastarrica, M.C., Bergel, A.: AVISPA: A Tool for Analyzing Software Process Models. Journal of Software Evolution and Process (2013), http://onlinelibrary.wiley.com/doi/10.1002/smr.1578/abstract
11. Kuhrmann, M., Fern_andez, D.M., Steenweg, R.: Systematic software process development: where do we stand today? In: ICSSP 2013, pp. 166–170 (May 2013)
12. Münch, J., Armbrust, O., Kowalczyk, M., Soto, M.: Software Process Definition and Management. Springer (2012)
13. Nierstrasz, O., Ducasse, S., Demeyer, S.: Object-Oriented Reengineering Patterns. Square Bracket Associates (2009)
14. O'Connor, R., Coleman, G.: An investigation of barriers to the adoption of software process best practices models. In: Proceedings of the 18th Australasian Conference on Information Systems, Toowoomba, Australia (December 2007)
15. Persee, J.: Process Improvement Essentials. O'Reilly, Sebastopol (2006)
16. Riemenschneider, C.K., Hardgrave, B.C., Davis, F.D.: Explaining Software Developer Acceptance of Methodologies: A Comparison of Five Theoretical Models. IEEE Transactions on Software Engineering 28(12), 1135–1145 (2002)
17. Rifkin, S.: Why software process innovations are not adopted. IEEE Software 18(4), 110–112 (2001)
18. Robbes, R., Vidal, R., Bastarrica, M.C.: Are Software Analytics Efforts Worthwhile for Small Companies? The Case of Amisoft. IEEE Software 30(5), 46–53 (2013)
19. Ruiz, P., Quispe, A., Bastarrica, M.C., Hurtado, J.A.: Formalizing the Software Process in Small Companies. In: 8CCC, Colombia (August 2013)
20. Simmonds, J., Bastarrica, M.C., Silvestre, L., Quispe, A.: Variability in Software Process Models: Requirements for Adoption in Industrial Settings. In: PLEASE 2013, San Francisco, USA (May 2013)

Context-Aware Staged Configuration of Process Variants@Runtime

Aitor Murguzur[1], Xabier De Carlos[1], Salvador Trujillo[1], and Goiuria Sagardui[2]

[1] Software Production Area, IK4-Ikerlan Research Center, Spain
{amurguzur,xdecarlos,strujillo}@ikerlan.es
[2] Embedded Systems Group, Mondragon University, Spain
gsagardui@mondragon.edu

Abstract. Process-based context-aware applications are increasingly becoming more complex and dynamic. Besides the large sets of process variants to be managed in such dynamic systems, process variants need to be context sensitive in order to accommodate new user requirements and intrinsic complexity. This paradigm shift forces us to defer decisions to runtime where process variants must be customized and executed based on a recognized context. However, there exists a lack of deferral of the entire process variant configuration and execution to perform an automated decision of subsequent variation points at runtime. In this paper, we present a holistic methodology to automatically resolve process variability at runtime. The proposed solution performs a staged configuration considering static and dynamic context data to accomplish effective decision making. We demonstrate our approach by exemplifying a storage operation process in a smart logistics scenario. Our evaluation demonstrates the performance and scalability results of our methodology.

Keywords: Runtime Variability, Late Selection, Context-awareness, Dynamic Software Product Lines, Smart Logistics.

1 Introduction

In recent years, emerging technologies, such as Machine-to-Machine (M2M) communications, Cloud Computing, Service-oriented Computing (SOC), Business Process Management (BPM) and Big Data analytics, have been leveraged to support businesses achieving their goals under changed marked conditions, e.g., reducing the time to market and costs. From the marriage of the latter technologies, smart services are commonly deployed and extended into a variety of smart devices and elastic cloud platforms, to improve decision making, rapid provisioning and deployment, and to provide greater flexibility. Atop of such service-based platforms, process-intensive and event-based applications offer a large number of processes as a catalyst for collaboration, integration and control, e.g., enabling the Business Process as a Service (BPaaS) concept [1].

Variability management for such processes is indeed becoming challenging, e.g., in smart logistics [2]. In this light, new techniques and tools are being developed to address the shortcomings of standard solutions to deal with large

M. Jarke et al. (Eds.): CAiSE 2014, LNCS 8484, pp. 241–255, 2014.

sets of process variants and adequate process variants to meet new requirements, context changes and intrinsic complexity. Process variability approaches
[3,4] handle different process variants, which are entirely or partially common to
several domain stakeholders and assets to which processes are applied. Process
variants share a common part of a core process whereas concrete parts fluctuate
from variant to variant. In dynamic conditions, such variants need to be context sensitive with the aim of adequately providing multiple stakeholders/assets
configurations and reasoning [5], and thus, drive customization based on context
information [6]. Therefore, context-awareness demands innovative solutions that
allow process-based applications to change during runtime.

This paradigm shift has imposed the emergence of Dynamic Software Product
Lines (DSPLs) [7], which support late variability, i.e., defers product configuration to runtime, exploiting traditional Software Product Line (SPL) concepts.
Regarding to the BPM field, a configurable process model is capable of dynamically (re-)binding variation points at runtime, considering context information.
Once context data is detected from external sensors or new user requirements,
the system decides which alternatives of the configurable process must be activated or deactivated and executes the decision via runtime binding. At a glance,
the key properties of DSPLs are: (i) support runtime variability, (ii) are able to
handle unexpected and environmental changes, (iii) may change variation points
at runtime, (iv) may support context-awareness and self-adaptive properties, and
(v) may include an automated decision making.

Some of the above-mentioned properties are partially supported by existing
work in the literature, such as the Worklets approach [8] which enables user-
driven selection of self-contained sub-processes aligned to each activity depending on the particular context at runtime, or the DyBPEL engine [9] which has
the ability to adapt running and compliance Business Process Execution Language (BPEL) instances when the corresponding process variant schema evolves.
However, there is a lack of deferral of the entire process variant customization
and execution to perform an automated decision making at runtime. This would
reduce the time to change from one process variant to another, as well as scaling-
up and modifying process variant alternatives during operation.

In this paper, we aim to solve such problem by focusing on process models
variability at runtime. The main contributions provided by this paper can be
summarized as follows: **c1** - we propose a novel methodology and a prototype
toolkit called `LateVa` to automatically resolve process variability at runtime; and
c2 - we demonstrate through an experimental smart logistics case study that our
methodology is scalable and can be used in dynamic settings.

The paper is organized as follows: In Section 2, we present a detailed overview
of the case study at the ACME Corp. and the problems associated with the
complexity of its operational processes. In Section 3, we present a methodology
based on an automated customization of process variants using the late selection
of fragments at runtime to address the issues raised by the case study. The results
of our evaluation are detailed in Section 4. Section 5 discusses related work, while
we conclude the paper with a summary and future next steps in Section 6.

2   Case Study: Smart Logistics

ACME Corp. is a leading innovative company that provides goods handling systems with a multiplicity of solutions for automated warehouses and storage, baggage handling, sorting systems and picking facilities. ACME Corp. designs and develops Warehouse Management Systems (WMS) for each customer (i.e. offering an ad-hoc solution for each customer to satisfy their business needs) in four areas, namely healthcare, retail, industrial components and food.

In essence, a WMS is a key part of the supply chain which primarily aims to control the movement and storage of goods (also referred to as articles) within a warehouse. Each WMS is complex and comprises a large number of operational processes [2], such as storage, retrieval and picking.

- *Storage*: The goods storage process allows goods to be stored based on different location search strategies (e.g. manual location, fixed location, next empty location, storage unit type, etc.) detailed in a WMS.
- *Retrieval*: The retrieval process enables the complete removal of goods from a warehouse, following disparate extraction strategies (e.g. FIFO, LIFO, least quantity, expiration date, etc.). Such extracted goods are typically moved to an intermediate area for custom shipping configurations.
- *Picking*: The picking process merges both retrieval and storage processes. It consists of taking and collecting goods in a specified quantity before shipment to satisfy customer orders. After each picking operation, the transport unit (e.g. pallet, box) with its remaining articles is routed back to a specific warehouse location based on pre-established storage strategies.

Inside an automated warehouse, the aforementioned operational processes can be modeled and executed by a BPM platform in order to track and control all warehouse flows, and enable multi-agent interaction, such as physical devices (e.g. conveyor systems, transelevators, pick to light systems, RFID, presence sensors, etc.) and warehouse operators (e.g. maintenance manager, workstation agents, picking operator, etc.) [10]. Hence, logistics process automation provides a smart visualization of existing operational processes for each WMS solution and complex event triggering from dozens of sensors; however, adopting a standard BPM platform in a smart logistics scenario presents four major issues:

Large set of process variants. Processes may have common parts and details that can vary for each WMS solution, influenced in various ways by warehouse types, storage areas, location types and conformance checking. As a result, designing ad-hoc processes for each WMS becomes time, resource and cost consuming, as well as an error prone task.

Constantly changing context data. In each automated warehouse, installed sensors are able to provide near real-time data, for instance, about warehouse locations, conveyor systems and the status of goods in transit. It is therefore essential that such events are picked up just-in-time for appropriate decision making. Further, although processes may include different wait states for event catching, inadequate event processing could have a negative impact on the execution of subsequent activities, often requiring manual intervention.

Scalability. An initial warehouse layout can be enlarged to accommodate large amount of orders and/or improve its productivity rates. Previously deployed processes have to be re-designed tackling new requirements. This often involves designing, testing and deploying updated operating processes.

High-availability. WMS execution may not be interrupted and 24/7 service availability is most required. However, any unexpected process execution error would completely stop the system. This would result in expensive system downtime until a system engineer could take corrective action.

3   Process Variants@Runtime

In this section, we present a *fragment-based re-use* methodology used to manage the variability of process models at runtime, that covers the modeling and execution phases of the process life-cycle. In Section 3.1, we present a brief summary of our foundations [11]. Due to space constraints, the formal definitions of LateVa foundations are provided as supplement[1]. We detail the different steps of our methodology in Section 3.2. In Section 3.3, we describe the implementation of the methodology in our LateVa toolkit.

3.1   Foundations

We follow the Base-Variation-Resolution (BVR) modeling approach [12] from the Software Product Line Engineering (SPLE), which states the separation of model commonality, variability and possible configurations into separate models.

Base Model. The first input of our methodology is a *base model*. It represents the commonality shared by a process family in a particular domain and place-holder activities (variation points) that are subject to vary. This configurable process model may be seen as the intersection or Greatest Common Denominator (GCD) of all related process variants. Variation points identify specific parts in a base model where variant binding occurs. In light of this binding time, we distinguish three types of variation points, as illustrated in Fig. 1: *a) static variation point* - resolved at configuration-time (design-time); *b) partial variation point* - partially resolved at configuration-time, simplifying the spectrum of runtime fragment choices within a variation model; and *c) dynamic variation point* - fully determined at runtime. The latter type of variation point may have two different behaviors: *with-flag* which indicates just-in-time resolution and with *no-flag* in which the resolution is performed at base model instance initialization. In this paper, as will be shown later, we only focus on those two.

Process Fragment. A process *fragment*, or simply fragment, describes a single variant realization option for each variation point within a particular base model. Likewise in a base model specification, it may include different kind of variation points for upholding nested variation points and control flow elements.

---

[1] http://tinyurl.com/lateva-formaldef

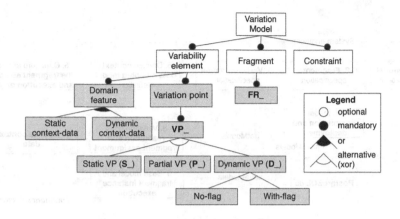

Fig. 1. Variations of the variation model

Variation Model. The third input of our methodology is a *variation model* which details all the particularities of a process variant that must be satisfied for valid process variant configuration. It offers abstraction for the base model and its variation points when enhancing a customization, in addition to decision support. Fig. 1 contains a feature diagram for the variation model subtypes that are differentiated in our approach, using the notation proposed by Batory [13]: *a) Variability elements* - stand for a family of process variants, their corresponding domain features and variation points. A feature captures a property of the domain that is relevant for a user. It is related to its parent as mandatory, optional, alternative (xor) and or relations [14]; *b) Fragments* - characterize variation points' realization options; and *c) Constraints* - represent constraints to valid process variant resolutions (complex feature-feature, feature-variable and variable-variable cross-tree relationships).

3.2   Methodology

We describe the methodology in two phases where each phase subsumes several sub-steps. An illustrative overview of the methodology is given in Fig. 2 (a).

Process Variability Specification and Deployment (LateVa Modeler). This is achieved via steps numbered 1-5 in Fig.2 (a). Following process family identification, a system engineer provides three inputs as described in Section 3.1: *a)* a base model representing the commonality and variability of a process family (will be exposed as a business service) by employing the OMG standard Business Process Model And Notation (BPMN) version 2.0; *b)* process fragments in BPMN2; and *c)* a variation model for decision support exposed as a feature model given their common industrial adoption [15]. Variation points are modeled using custom BPMN2 activity constructs (e.g. for each type of variation point) supported in our Activiti plugin (see Fig. 3).

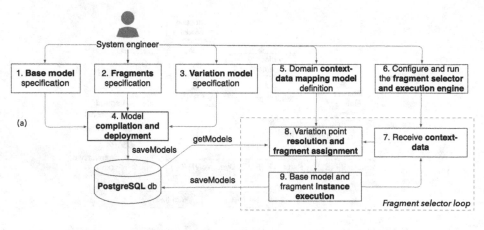

(a)

(b)

contextVariableName	featureName	contextValue	defaultValue	parseType
operationalFlow	OperationalFlow	HighRates	HighRates	Static
scanner	VP_Scanner	Barcode	Barcode	Static
checkpoint	VP_Checkpoint	P2	P2	Static
boxWidth	boxWidth	280	287	Dynamic
boxLength	boxLength	490	491	Dynamic
boxHeight	boxHeight	501	530	Dynamic
boxWeight	boxWeight	5	6	Dynamic
boxInCorridor	boxInCorridor	2	3	Dynamic

Fig. 2. (a) Methodology (b) Context-data/feature mapping example

In Step 3, the variations for portraying a single variation model (shown in grey in Fig. 1) are: concrete domain feature names and variation points representing domain variability, features with the VP_ extension mapped to variation points in a base model, for fragments we use features with FR_ extension and cross-tree constraints between variability elements and fragments. We distinguish between two context data types, which can be directly mapped to domain features: *static context data* variable/value pairs for static preferences which rarely change over time and are known at base model initialization, and *dynamic context data* variable/value pairs which change and alter over time as they become unpredictable in practice. Therefore, our model could contain features capturing domain abstraction and features associated with domain data.

After all models (base models, fragments and variation models) are defined, they are compiled and deployed to the *models repository*. In this step, we make use of a variation model compiler (the `Clafer` compiler [16]) to check that predefined features and constraints are well-defined prior to deployment. Since features related to variation points and fragments use direct naming compounds for corresponding process model IDs (see patterns below for creating variation point and fragment features), the compiler does not check if the inserted base model and fragment references already exist in the models repository. Still, such functionality is supported by the fragment engine which directly retrieves mapping names and threats exceptions in case of mismatch.

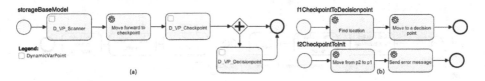

Fig. 3. (a) Storage base model and D_VP activities (b) f1 and f2 fragment samples

Pattern for representing variation point features

{S_,P_,D_} + VP_ + {baseModelVPName} + {parentFeatureName}

Pattern for representing fragment features

FR_ + {fragmentId} + {parentFeatureName}

The resolution of process variants is context sensitive. Such resolution could differ from context to context depending on domain context data values and variation model constraints. Those relationships between features, variables, and context data variable/value pairs are represented by *context model mapping* in Step 5 (see Fig. 2 (b) mapping example for the smart logistics case study). Each context data row must define its *contextVariableName* - a concrete variable name in a domain context model, *featureName* - represents a feature or a variable in a variation model, *contextValue* - context information of a context variable, *defaultValue* - a valid value which can be assigned for a context variable, and *parseType* - represents the aforementioned static and dynamic data types.

Staged Process Variants Configuration and Execution (LateVa Engine). Base models generated in the previous steps need to be resolved prior to execution. After Step 6, the engine takes system properties for granted. We can configure the engine to work in two different running modes:

- *allin* mode (initialization/startup runtime resolution strategy): runs a two-staged resolution prior to base model instance initialization. Useful when context data values are not altered rapidly over time, so the engine does not necessarily postpone decision making, i.e., variation point resolution and fragment assignment.
- *staged* mode (n-staged online/pure-runtime resolution strategy): performs n-staged online resolution until all variation points are self-determined. Required when a variation point's execution is dependant on fluctuating data (just-in-time dynamic data), and thus faces a critical decision. Critical dynamic variation points are indicated with-flag while non-critical (with noflag) are resolved at base model instance initialization.

Both running modes start by handling messages, as represented in Step 7 of Fig. 2. When a JavaScript Object Notation (JSON) message is received an internal context object is created based on context model mapping. In addition to static and dynamic variable-value pairs, a JSON message includes three common values, namely *mappingId* - refers to a valid context model mapping identifier,

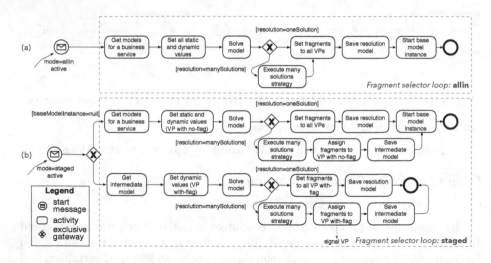

Fig. 4. (a) *allIn* and (b) *staged* running modes of the fragment selector engine

service - describes a business service (base model) that should be executed, and *instance* - identifies a running base model instance. It could also contain extra data that will be ignored by the engine, but recognized by others (e.g. data visualization). If context model mapping and business service description are encountered, the engine follows a pre-established run strategy.

Example of a JSON message for the smart logistics case study

```
{message:{"date":"2013-10-25", "time":"09:40:13", "mappingId"
    :"Geneva", "service":"StorageOP", "instance":"4401", "
    domain":"SmartLogistics", "operationalFlow":"HighRates",
    "scanner":"Barcode", "checkpoint":"P2", "boxWidth":"280",
    "boxLenght":"480", "boxHeight":"520", "boxWeight":"5", "
    boxInCorridor":"0"}}
```

Bearing in mind the two running strategies, steps 8-9 in Fig. 2 are executed differently for each configuration (see Fig. 4). In *allin* mode, the fragment selector loop starts by retrieving base model and variation model definitions for a given business service. Here, we automatically transform a variation model to a constraint satisfaction problem (CSP). Proposals using constraint solving to reason on feature modes have been studied over the past two decades [17]. In our case, every optional feature becomes a boolean variable of the CSP with domain {false,true} or {0,1}, whereas every mandatory domain feature becomes a {true} or {1} variable.

The second activity in Fig. 4 (a) determines context data values in two-stages. Firstly, static context data is parsed for putting features into one:

Example of static feature constraint

```
vSpecModel.addConstraint(one(concreteFeature));
```

Additionally, dynamic values are specified by setting `Integer` constraints:

Example of dynamic feature constraint

```
concreteFeature . addConstraint ( equal ( joinRef ( $this ( ) ) ,
    constant ( ( int ) constraintValue ) ) ) ;
```

After parsing all context values and setting up constraints to the variation model, the solver starts running propagation and search to derive possible valid configurations. We handle three situations:

- *No solution* after allin: Apart from the functionality provided in Fig. 4 (a), the fragment selector engine must deal with unexpected situations, such as no solution found after model solving. Pro tem, the engine rollbacks all operations for an unexpected message.
- *One solution* after allin: The engine assigns fragments to applicable variation points from the resulting solution, saves this model (resolution model) in the models repository and enhances a base model instance. When the execution reaches a variation point, it starts a valid fragment execution.
- *Many solutions* after allin: When the solver returns more than one valid solution for the current context, we may select between four different strategies: (i) *get-first* to get the first feasible fragment, (ii) *get-default* to select the fragment marked as default, (iii) *recommender* system to decide which is the suitable solution for the given context, and (iv) *manual-selection* to enable system-user decision making. In this paper, the engine automatically runs a *get-first* strategy, i.e., it returns the first correct resolution from all possible configurations and establishes this as an input for the "one solution" flow.

The second run mode, namely the *staged* mode, may activate two different branches depending on whether the received context data is for a running instance or not. This is indicated by the *instance* variable.

In a first stage (the upper workflow in Fig. 4 (b)), both static and dynamic constraints for dynamic variation points with no-flag are set (with-flag indicates that a variation point is critical and thus needs just-in-time data for its proper resolution). In the event of many solutions, the get-first strategy is performed to assign fragments for dynamic variation points with no-flag and an intermediate model is saved. Otherwise, one solution flow performs assignations for all dynamic variation points in order to ensure a valid customization.

The n-staged flow (the lower workflow in Fig. 4 (b)) is activated to handle "just-in-time" context messages. For each dynamic variation point in a wait state (with staged flag = true), the engine establishes constraints for an intermediate model which is restored from the models repository by the specified instance ID. The solver uses this altered model as an input, and concludes if a sound configuration exists. If just one exists, all with-flag dynamic variation points are determined by a suitable fragment. Many solutions after n-staged, however, implies the activation of a many-solution strategy (e.g. get-first) to assign a fragment for pending dynamic variation points with-flag. These are then re-activated by signal-catching to initiate a concrete fragment instance.

3.3   Implementation in LateVa Toolkit

We implement our methodology in the `LateVa` toolkit to manage the variability of process models at runtime. The implementation is standalone and employs open source frameworks such as Activiti[2] for base model and process fragment modeling and execution, Clafer[3] for variability representation with its alternative backend using Choco[4] constraint solver, ActiveMQ[5] as the engine broker and Camel[6] for integration. A prototype implementation of the toolkit encompasses two modules: the `LateVa-modeler` for representing models (as an Activiti extension) and the `LateVa-engine` for executing late variability.

4   Evaluation

In this section, we perform an experiment to synthesize a storage process for the ACME Corp. case study and discuss the experimental results and threats to validity of the proposed methodology.

4.1   Experimental Setup

We developed a case scenario to automatically configure and enhance a storage process to test an automated warehouse operation in the Geneva apparel industry. The warehouse layout consists of a single material entry point in which goods are packed in carton boxes (288x492x531mm), two corridors each containing 2000 locations, 2 picking workstations and a single material retrieval point. Due to space limitations, the full description of the storage process example is given online at: `http://aitormurguzur.com/projects/lateva/caise2014`

4.2   Results of Discussion

We generated 1 base model with 3 dynamic variation points (1 with no-flag: D_VP_Scanner, and 2 with-flag: D_VP_Checkpoint and D_VP_Decisionpoint, as depicted by Fig. 3), 5 fragments and 1 variation model with 22 features and 8 constraints, covering 3x2x2 = 12 process variant customizations for the Geneva layout. These models were used to generate **a test case for 157 storage operations**. We ran the experiment as a standalone application on a 13inch MacBook Air with 8GB 1600 MHz DDR3 RAM, and Core i7 running @2 GHz.

In this paper, we focus on understanding the performance of our approach in relation to the smart logistics case study. We use the non-intrusive `perf4j` library to perform measurements. Dynamic variation point execution performance is measured by total processing time. Fig. 5 shows the minimum, maximum and

---

[2] `http://activiti.org`
[3] `http://clafer.org`
[4] `http://www.emn.fr/z-info/choco-solver`
[5] `http://activemq.apache.org`
[6] `http://camel.apache.org`

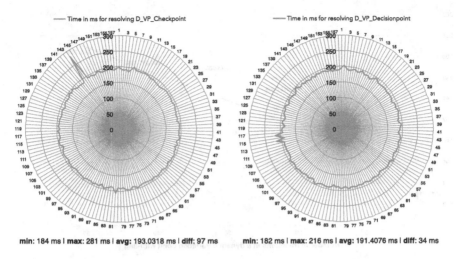

Fig. 5. TTR of dynamic variation points with-flag

average time taken by each with-flag dynamic variation point before fragment execution. Consequently, the average time-to-resolution (TTR) that a base model instance has to wait for using this kind of variation points is **192.2197 ms**. The delay can be omitted by including events and exclusive gateways in the modeling phase, however, `LateVa` solves several issues raised at the beginning of the paper:

Large set of process variants. This is achieved by separating operational process variability in disjointed models. The key model (the variation model) captures variability at the domain level in which different processes have been assembled. This allows users to focus on domain concepts rather than on each BPMN2 elements.

Constantly changing context data. The variation model may contain two types of domain features: features for domain abstraction and features/variables mapped to context data. Dynamic context data can be controlled by establishing constraints and automatically customizing process variants.

Scalability. Our approach supports *variability by extension* [18], i.e., it allows variable segments of operational processes to be captured in fragments and weaved into a base model. Consequently, the base model is minimal in that it only contains elements common to all processes. Specific variation points elements (i.e. fragments) are added and/or updated when needed. This also applies to new context data types.

High-availability. Unexpected situations are dealt effectively and appropriate fragments are updated when necessary. Fragment replacement only affects new configurations while running base model instances will assure their correct execution path.

Looking beyond the particulars of the case study, we lend to generalization by checking how our approach operates with increasing `LateVa` fragments, i.e., approach scalability. We added 50 extra fragments to `D_VP_Checkpoint`, so that

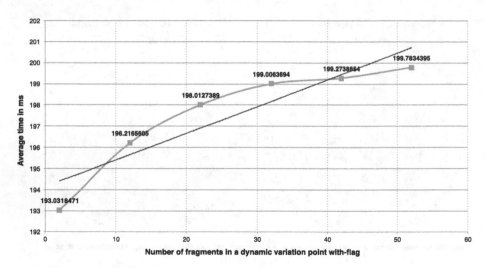

Fig. 6. TTR of `D_VP_Checkpoint` by increasing fragments in the variation model

the number of possible variant configurations increases to 312 (3x52x2). First results are encouraging which indicate that the engine suffers a minimal delay of **1.3503 ms** when the number of applicable fragments grow for a particular dynamic variation point with-flag, as illustrated in Fig. 6. All datasets are available at: `http://git.io/3sUrCA`

4.3   Threats to Validity

Our experiments did not consider a certain number of factors that may affect our proposed methodology and generalized outcomes on scalability.

- *Correctness*: Our approach guarantees the syntactical correctness (correct structure of process variants), but not behavioral (soundness [19], e.g., by avoiding deadlocks and livelocks) correctness of the resulting process variants. For the former, we avoided disconnected nodes by representing process fragments with initial and final states and enabling "call activity" behavior from BPMN2 elements within new activity constructs (variation points). However, it may become impossible to guarantee behavioral correctness of the customized models adopting the variability by extension strategy [18]. In our case, this is due to the large number of possible combinations of solver options, considering both static and dynamic context variable/value pairs at runtime, as well as evolutionary variation models, i.e., the process engineer may also add or modify fragments in the variation model.
- *Dynamic context data*: In this paper, we only employed `Integer` values for constraint solving, but the variation model should consider other data types, such as, strings and reals in future releases.
- *Base model, fragment and variation model scalability*: Although initial tests on model scalability show promising results, we plan to consider more scalability and performance tests, and also evaluate the presented methodology

against different industrial case studies. In addition, only dynamic variation points were considered in the presented case study; however, static and
partial variation points need to be incorporated in future tests.

5   Related Work

The work presented is related to other fields of research, such as process variability, context-aware configuration of process variants, process flexibility and
DSPLs. In this section, we briefly introduce related research in these areas and
explain the novelty of our proposed approach.

Previous work on *process variability* [18,20] can be divided into two main
groups: approaches adopting a single configurable process model [3,4,21] and
fragment-based re-use approaches [6,9,8]. C-EPC [3] is an extension of the Event-
driven Process Chain (EPC) to support multiple process families of EPC process
variants by means of configurable nodes and configurable alternatives. Orthog-
onally, the PESOA project [4] was proposed to provide mechanisms to capture
variability of UML activity diagrams and BPMN, enriching them with stereotype annotations using feature models in an abstract way (they do not transform
variation points to selected variants). C-YAWL [21] is an extension of the Yet Another Workflow Language (YAWL) which applies hiding/blocking operations to
customize a configurable process model. They all provide useful methods to deal
with process variability; however, they are merely focused on design-time process
variability, rather than customizing process variants at runtime. Furthermore,
they are based on conceptual modeling rather than executable process models.

Context-aware process modeling and variability has been also studied in the
past. A context-aware framework for the explicit modeling of context is provided
in [22], which includes system stakeholders' reasoning about business processes
in appropriate manner. The importance of context sensitive process modeling
has been also discussed in other studies [5], in order to deal with changing user
requirements and the complex and dynamic nature of environments. In a similar
vein, context-awareness has been translated to the process variability field. For
instance, the Provop approach [6] provides five steps to customize base models
based on context information. Although the latter allows for context-aware process variants customizations employing a base model, such customizations are
user-supported rather than automated and they are not executable in practice.

Process variability and *flexibility* concepts are closely connected. Process flexibility is concerned not only with variability but also with runtime aspects of
process models, as described by Reichert and Weber [23]. Hence, runtime variability may be seen as a flexibility type (also referred to as late selection or late
binding) which defers placeholder activity resolution to runtime. The work that
is closer to our proposal is the Worklets approach [8], which enables a dynamic
runtime selection of self-contained sub-processes aligned to each activity depending on the context of the particular instance. When activities become enabled
appropriate fragment selection is achieved by using Ripple Down Rules (RDR),
which include hierarchically organized selection rules. With respect to the mentioned work, the main novelties of our approach are two-fold: we provide a staged

configuration and execution of process variability at runtime, which can perform customizations in different ways (allin, staged). Secondly, all customizations are performed automatically while in Worklets the selection is realized interactively by end-users (user interaction).

Context-awareness and intrinsic complexity of environments has caused *DSPLs* to support late variability in systems in order to cater for changes at runtime. Baresi et al. [9] propose a methodology based on Common Variability Language (CVL) and DyBPEL for managing process reconfiguration at runtime using DSPLs. This proposal has been focused on handling process variants at design-time and supporting adaptation at runtime; however, our approach merely binds variation points at runtime. Despite the fact that DSPLs have been applied to other research areas such as, model-driven engineering [24] or service-oriented systems [25], to the best of our knowledge this is the first work tackling the issue of DSPLs in process variability.

6 Conclusion

In this paper, we have addressed the problem of a smart logistics scenario and presented a novel fragment-based re-use approach for an automated management of process models variability at runtime. We introduced a methodology implemented in the LateVa toolkit, to manage large sets of variants that utilize context data and constraint solving for process variant customization. In the experiment, we developed a base model, 5 fragments and a variation model for a warehouse storage operation. The evaluation generated 157 tests and concluded that the approach provides an average TTR of **192.2197 ms** for dynamic variation point with-flag. The initial scalability tests for our approach have provided positive results for its adoption as an alternative in scenarios where: large set of process variants, dynamic context data, scalability and/or high-availability are the norm, not the exception. Our future work will involve a large-scale empirical evaluation using different real case studies while carefully collecting scalability/performance metrics and dealing with models complexity and maintainability. We also plan to concentrate on three parts: testing of other many-solution strategies when the solver gets many solutions, abstractions for enabling user-defined dynamic process configuration [26], and how to deal with data variability for the automated generation of context model mappings.

References

1. Böhmer, M., Daniluk, D., Schmidt, M., Gsell, H.: Business object model for realization of individual business processes in the logistics domain. In: Efficiency and Logistics, pp. 237–244 (2013)
2. Derguech, W., Gao, F., Bhiri, S.: Configurable process models for logistics case study for customs clearance processes. In: Daniel, F., Barkaoui, K., Dustdar, S. (eds.) BPM Workshops 2011, Part II. LNBIP, vol. 100, pp. 119–130. Springer, Heidelberg (2012)
3. Rosemann, M., van der Aalst, W.: A configurable reference modelling language. Information Systems 32(1), 1–23 (2007)

4. Puhlmann, F., Schnieders, A., Weiland, J., Weske, M.: Variability Mechanisms for Process Models. Technical report (2005)
5. Saidani, O., Nurcan, S.: Context-awareness for adequate business process modelling. In: RCIS, pp. 177–186 (2009)
6. Hallerbach, A., Bauer, T., Reichert, M.: Capturing variability in business process models: The provop approach. Journal of Software Maintenance and Evolution: Research and Practice 22(6-7), 519–546 (2010)
7. Bencomo, N., Hallsteinsen, S., de Almeida, E.S.: A view of the dynamic software product line landscape. Computer 45(10), 36–41 (2012)
8. Adams, M., ter Hofstede, A.H.M., Edmond, D., van der Aalst, W.M.P.: Worklets: A service-oriented implementation of dynamic flexibility in workflows. In: Meersman, R., Tari, Z. (eds.) OTM 2006. LNCS, vol. 4275, pp. 291–308. Springer, Heidelberg (2006)
9. Baresi, L., Guinea, S., Pasquale, L.: Service-oriented dynamic software product lines. Computer 45(10), 42–48 (2012)
10. Ao, Y., He, W., Xiao, X., Lee, E.: A business process management approach for rfid enabled supply chain management. In: ETFA, pp. 1–7 (2010)
11. Murguzur, A., Sagardui, G., Intxausti, K., Trujillo, S.: Process variability through automated late selection of fragments. In: Franch, X., Soffer, P. (eds.) CAiSE Workshops 2013. LNBIP, vol. 148, pp. 371–385. Springer, Heidelberg (2013)
12. Bayer, J., Gerard, S., Haugen, Y., Mansell, J., Müller-Pedersen, B., Oldevik, J., Tessier, P., Thibault, J.P., Widen, T.: Consolidated product line variability modeling. In: SPLC, pp. 195–241 (2006)
13. Batory, D.: Feature models, grammars, and propositional formulas. In: Obbink, H., Pohl, K. (eds.) SPLC 2005. LNCS, vol. 3714, pp. 7–20. Springer, Heidelberg (2005)
14. Kang, K., Cohen, S., Hess, J., Nowak, W., Peterson, S.: Feature-Oriented Domain Analysis (FODA) Feasibility Study. Technical report (1990)
15. Berger, T., Rublack, R., Nair, D., Atlee, J.M., Becker, M., Czarnecki, K., Wasowski, A.: A survey of variability modeling in industrial practice. In: VaMoS (2013)
16. Antkiewicz, M., Bąk, K., Murashkin, A., Olaechea, R., Liang, J., Czarnecki, K.: Clafer tools for product line engineering. In: SPLC, Tokyo, Japan (2013)
17. Benavides, D., Segura, S., Ruiz-Cortés, A.: Automated analysis of feature models 20 years later: A literature review. Information Systems 35(6), 615–636 (2010)
18. Rosa, M.L., van der Aalst, W.M., Dumas, M., Milani, F.P.: Business process variability modeling: A survey. ACM Computing Surveys (2013)
19. van der Aalst, W.M.P., van Hee, K.M., ter Hofstede, A.H.M., Sidorova, N., Verbeek, H.M.W., Voorhoeve, M., Wynn, M.T.: Soundness of workflow nets: Classification, decidability, and analysis. Form. Asp. Comput. 23(3), 333–363 (2011)
20. Valença, G., Alves, C., Alves, V., Niu, N.: A Systematic Mapping Study on Business Process Variability. IJCSIT 5(1) (2013)
21. Gottschalk, F., van der Aalst, W.M., Jansen-Vullers, M.H., Rosa, M.L.: Configurable workflow models. IJCIS 17(2) (2008)
22. Balabko, P., Wegmann, A.: Context based reasoning in business process models. In: IRI, pp. 120–128 (2003)
23. Reichert, M., Weber, B.: Enabling Flexibility in Process-Aware Information Systems: Challenges, Methods, Technologies. Springer (2012)
24. Morin, B., Barais, O., Jezequel, J., Fleurey, F., Solberg, A.: Models@ run.time to support dynamic adaptation. Computer 42(10), 44–51 (2009)
25. Parra, C., Blanc, X., Duchien, L.: Context Awareness for Dynamic Service-Oriented Product Lines. In: SPLC, pp. 131–140 (2009)
26. Lapouchnian, A., Yu, Y., Mylopoulos, J.: Requirements-driven design and configuration management of business processes. In: Alonso, G., Dadam, P., Rosemann, M. (eds.) BPM 2007. LNCS, vol. 4714, pp. 246–261. Springer, Heidelberg (2007)

Prioritizing Business Processes Improvement Initiatives: The Seco Tools Case

Jens Ohlsson[1], Shengnan Han[1,2], Paul Johannesson[1], Fredrik Carpenhall[3], and Lazar Rusu[1]

[1] Department of Computer and Systems Sciences,
Stockholm University Kista, Sweden
[2] IAMSR, Åbo Akademi University, Turku, Finland
{jeoh,shengnan,pajo,lrusu}@dsv.su.se
[3] Fagersta, Sweden
{fredrik.carpenhall}@secotools.com

Abstract. Chief Information Officers (CIOs) face great challenges in prioritizing business process improvement initiatives due to limited resources and politics in decision making. We developed a prioritization and categorization method (PCM) for supporting CIOs' decision-making process. The method is designed in a collaborative research process engaging CIOs, process experts and researchers. In this experience paper, we firstly present the PCM, and then we describe the lessons learned when demonstrating the PCM prototype at a big international company, Seco Tools. The results show that the PCM can produce a holistic analysis of processes by eliciting the "collective intelligence" from process stakeholders and managers. The PCM activities create a top-down social process of process management. By using the PCM the company managed to prioritize business process improvement initiatives in a novel way. This paper contributes to theories/know how on business process management, as well as propose a novel method that can be used by CIOs of large corporations in prioritizing process initiatives.

Keywords: business process improvement, process prioritization, process categorization, demonstration, strategic decision making, industry experience.

1 Introduction

Chief Information Officers (CIOs) are usually responsible for the improvement of business processes [1]. The evidence shows that 60% of business process improvement initiatives, e.g., Six Sigma and Lean IT failed in reality [2]. What can CIOs do to tackle this failure? The answer relies probably on how they make strategic decisions on *what* and *how* to prioritize improvement initiatives through a transparent process. More importantly, CIOs need to establish a supportive culture for implementations of prioritized processes in order to ensure the sustainability and long-term value delivery of these processes [3]. In the business process management (BPM) practice, the available guidelines and methods for process prioritization are *"either of very high level and*

M. Jarke et al. (Eds.): CAiSE 2014, LNCS 8484, pp. 256–270, 2014.

hence not of much assistance when attempting to implement BPM initiatives, or, on the contrary, are so detailed that it can take a significant effort to simply identify the critical processes" ([4] , p. 178). Moreover, these methods focus on activity- level analysis, managers may stuck in *"the complexities of the techniques and tools, and lose sight of the requirement to deliver corporate value"* [5]. Finally, project prioritization by CIOs is mostly politically driven, which means that executives of business units, that are more influential, get funding for projects regardless of their contributions to business strategy and values [6]. Therefore, a new more neutral method for prioritizing process improvement initiatives is needed. The method should 1) *identify* the processes to be improved; 2) *indicate* how to improve; and 3) *avoid* politics. As a result a novel method of prioritization decisions is created. The design requirement of the method is that it should be useful, efficient and reliable. *"Useful"* means the method can solve prioritization problems and support managers' decision making in prioritization. *"Efficient"* means the method is easy to use and produces results by using limited resources and within a short time. *"Reliable"* means the method can produce good quality results that managers can rely on in decision making.

We adopt design science research methodology [7, 8] to develop and evaluate the new method, which we refer to as the prioritization and categorization method (PCM). Orlikowski [9] asserts the importance of engaging practice in research. Van de ven [10] also promotes the "engaged scholarship" approach in order to gain collective achievement and "co-product" knowledge "that can both advance the scientific enterprise and enlighten a community of practitioners" ([10], p.27). Since January 2011, the first author and a group of CIOs and BPM experts formed a think-tank, Duqtor (www.duqtor.com). The purpose of the think-tank is to facilitate dialogue and collaboration between practitioners and researchers. One initiative, that is core in this paper, is to engage CIOs and experts in collaboration for designing a method in prioritizing business processes improvement initiatives. The managers engaged in the design endeavour came from big organizations in Scandinavia, e.g., Atlas Copco, Postnord, Vattenfall, Västerås Stad, Bombardier Nordic, SSAB, Scania, Siemens Industrial Machinery, Seco Tools, Statkraft (Norway), Sandvik, and a Swedish consulting company Knowit. In February 2012, the PCM, a prototype built on Excel, was introduced for demonstration and testing in companies, e.g. Seco Tools.

In this paper, we mainly focus on the practical experience we obtained from the demonstration of the PCM at Seco Tools. During the demonstration we collected data on the perceptions and viewpoints of decision makers with regard to the use of the PCM in real decision making context. The experience is documented, analysed, and interpreted. The results are served as the foundation for improving the PCM to better fulfilling its design requirements and goals. This paper contributes to theories/know how on business process management, as well as propose a novel method that can be used by CIOs of large corporations.

This paper is organized as follows. In section 2, we briefly review the related research. We then give an overview of the PCM in section 3. In section 4, we describe how PCM was introduced at Seco Tools and the results from the demonstration. In section 5, we discuss the lessons learned. The paper concludes with a discussion of PCM contributions to research and to practice.

2   Related Research

Dumas et al. ([11], p.5) define a business process as " a collection of inter-related events, activities and decision points that involve a number of actors and objects, and that collectively lead to an outcome that is of value to at least one customer". Business process management (BPM) has rapidly evolved as a management philosophy and discipline with a specific focus on business processes [3]. It considers the continuous improvement and the fundamental innovation of business process to ensure that strategic goals and objectives of the organization can be achieved [12]. Harrington [13] presents the five stages of business process improvement, i.e. organising for improvement, understanding the process, streamlining, measurements and control, and continuous improvement. One of the key activities in the stages is to select the critical processes for improvement. The selection criteria are proposed by previous research; for examples, effectiveness, efficiency and adaptability [13]; strategic importance, process scope, needs to improve, and difficulty of improvement [14]; competition outperforming, many conflicts/high frequency/excessive non-structured communication, and continuous incremental improvement [15]; and importance, dysfunction, and feasibility [11]. The literature also presents the dimensions in order to clearly understand business process characteristics; for examples, flow, effectiveness, efficiency, cycle time and cost [13]; and time, cost, quality, and flexibility [11].

A number of BPM maturity models (e.g. [16, 17]) are developed and introduced to organizations for process improvement and innovation in order to achieve a successful process management. The analysis of maturity level of process and BPM is the indicator for improvement. However, the models lack applicability to practitioners [18]. Previous research has introduced a very few methods specifically for prioritizing processes improvement initiatives, for example, the business value scoring method [4], the process performance scoring method [19], and the value matrix of process and strategy alignment [12]. However, these methods only describe the process performance, and indicate where to prioritize, the information on how to improve is mostly missing. Six Sigma and Lean are the two methods that are widely used in the business for continuous process improvement, but they cannot easily be justified for the purpose of process prioritization. Bandara et al. conclude that prioritization "remains as a 'mystery phase' in most available guidelines" ([4], p. 178).

Although there is no standardized methodology yet for selecting and prioritizing processes for improvement, the literature recommends that the selection criteria should focus on: i) the strategic importance of the process; ii) the performance of the process; 3) flexibility for the process improvement, e.g. resource allocation, people's readiness for change, and organization supportive culture. Previous research shares certain agreements with regards to analysing and understanding process. Quantitative and formal methods are recommended. However, these methods focus on process activity level. Managers may get lost in the complexity of these methods and tools [5]. Moreover, the results bring little values for understanding BPM as an enterprise-wide capability [5]. We are called upon to develop creative thinking in analysing processes which serves as the foundation for process selection and prioritization [11].

BPM is fundamentally a CIO and senior management responsibility [1]. Process governance is crucial for the success of business process as well for sustaining and optimizing process improvement performance [3]. Hence, a new method is required for supporting managers' decision making in prioritizing process improvement initiatives.

3   Prioritization and Categorization Method – PCM

The PCM consists of two models, the process assessment heat map (PAHM) and the process categorization map (CM). The CIOs and practitioners have formulated the perspectives of the heat map and the dimensions of categorization map in the design process. Both concepts are recognizable to business people and help to understand and adapt the processes for prioritizing improvement initiatives [20].

3.1   Process Assessment Heat Map – PAHM

The heat map helps to analyse processes from five distinct perspectives (see Table 1). The **Positioning** perspective is aimed at assessing the alignment of the process with the business strategy, objectives and values. Strategic positioning is the approach that Porter [21] has recommended for analysing process activities in business. With a proper positioning, companies would be able to identify to which degree the process is aligned with business strategy, objectives and values [5], [14]. We argue that positioning processes with the help of PAHM support companies to open employees' minds for generating critical thinking about process prioritization and to create common understanding of business processes and possible improvements. The **Relating** perspective is designed for investigating the attitudes, roles, risks and rewards of stakeholders exposed to the process. Literature has recognized the importance of people and culture-related activities in the context of BPM. A focus on these issues results in longer and stronger process improvements and improved management [3]. The **Preparing** perspective is directed at analysing availability and quality of key capabilities necessary for process improvements. The **Implementing** perspective is focussed on analysing the performance of the process that is subject to analysis. The **Proving** perspective is focussed on the degree to which processes are appropriately monitored and measured. Therefore it is necessary to define the proper metrics and to define the right KPIs levels.

Table 1 shows the working definitions of the five perspectives, and the sample questions, which were adapted from [3], [22]. Because each organization has its own strategy and business processes, the model allows managers to define and refine crucial aspects and questions in each perspective as relevant to the heat map (PAHM). The motivation for this design choice is twofold. First, the questions used, should motivate and engage managers and stakeholders to provide tactical knowledge and sample experiences. Therefore, the questions should be directly related to their work life, experience and context. Second, the information included in the heat map should be focused on each relevant process and on each relevant perspective, so that prioritization and decision making fits a specific organization. Relevant information to fill out the heat map is collected based on interviews with managers and stakeholders.

Table 1. PAHM Perspectives and Sample Questions

PAHM perspectives	Sample questions
Positioning assesses the alignment of the process with the business strategy, objectives and values.	How clear has management positioned the process role, mandate and importance in relation to the business strategy and operational model? Is the process well described in the management system?
Relating assesses the attitudes, roles, risks and rewards of stakeholders exposed to the process.	Do stakeholders share risks and rewards among the units/departments? Do stakeholders have clear understanding of the process? Are all key stakeholders in agreement with the process interfaces and improvement roadmap?
Preparing assesses the availability and quality of key capabilities for improving the process.	Do people have the right skills and competence? Are necessary resources secured? Do we depend on a key person? Do people commit to the process?
Implementing assesses the performance of the process that is subject to analysis.	What are customers' (internal, external) perceptions about the performance? How well do interfaces work around supporting processes? How effective is the process?
Proving assesses the degree to which the process is appropriately monitored and measured.	How well is business impact measured? What is the right level of process evaluation/measuring? What are the relevant KPIs? What is the relevant feedback loop?

We adopt Hammer's colour regimes and quantitative measurements [22] in the heat map. If a process according to the perspective chosen is considered by CIOs or stakeholders to be eligible for improvement, the colour red is used to indicate the improvement potential to be more than 50%. If it is considered to have an improvement potential between 20% and 50%, the colour amber is used. If the process is considered to have less than 20% improvement potential, the colour is green. The heat map offers the opportunities to provide comments and motivations for the assessment based on current performance and expected improvements. The colour and comments are documented as shown in Fig. 1 (G=Green, A=Amber, R=Red).

PROCESS	POSITIONING	RELATING	PREPARING	IMPLEMENTING	PROVING	ADVICE
Create Forecast	G: visible activities	G:	A: Process flow interfaces red (very manual), resources red, skillset green	R: frontend information from the different markets. Should be relevant (by product and realistic growth ambitions)	A: We are at same service level as competition.	Closer to the markets, get outside Sweden (developing markets in particular) , get closer to product level (selected)

Fig. 1. The PAHM represented after one interview/one stakeholder

All assessments based on interviews are then consolidated in one table (See also Fig. 4). This table also presents an aggregated view of all individual assessments. If an interviewee assesses one of the processes from one perspective as red, then the aggregated view for this person will be red. For example, in Fig. 1, if the interviewee assigned red to a process from the implementation perspective, the aggregated view of this process from this interviewee is also red. The process with the highest number of red assessments will be then getting the highest priority.

3.2   Process Categorization Map – CM

The PCM offers the possibility to position processes in a space that is defined by three dimensions, i.e., differentiating, formality and governance in the value network. The result is presented in what is labelled as the categorization map (CM) (Fig. 2). The map is aimed to obtain indicative information on how the prioritized processes resulted from the heat map can be improved, e.g. which type of process support system should be used, and what degree of change in the process is desired, i.e. incremental improvement or reengineering.

Fig. 2. CM map

The dimensions for selection are based on three criteria. First, the fundamental criterion for prioritizing a process is the degree to which it contributes to the business strategy [14]. It is important that the process must make it possible for the company to differentiate itself from competitors by creating added value. Hence, we define differentiation as the degree to which a process is superior to analogous processes of competitors, and supports the value proposition of the organization. A continuous scale is used with differentiating processes and common processes as the extremes.

Second, BPM systems have become the inseparable mirror of process management. Information technology capabilities have to support process management capabilities [3]. If a process is fully aligned and supported by information technology, then it can become formalized and contribute to cost-effective execution [23]. As a contrast, if a process is unpredictable and knowledge intensive, operational cost in an organization will increase considerably [24]. Hence an assessment of the degree of formality is crucial for the analysis. **Formality** means the degree to which a process is strictly managed, repeatable, predictable, automatable, and involves applications rather than people. Formality is scored on a continuous scale with formal and informal as the extremes.

Third, it is the phenomena that companies in the different value networks collaborate to co-create values for consumers and create network value, i.e. revenues for individual network partners [5]. The positioning of a specific process in a value creation network helps companies to allocate limited resources to support value creation and relation building with network partners. This leads to serious (re)considerations of establishing process governance structure and mechanism, e.g. process ownership, accountability, responsibility, or decision rights [25]. So network governance is identified as the third dimension. **Value network governance**, thereby, is defined as the degree to which a process interacts with front-end or back-end network partners/customers in the value network, which determines process governance.

So back-end and front-end are opposites. The detailed operationalization for the three dimensions is offered in table 2.

Figure two shows an example how a process can be positioned. In the map you see a business process. Letter A that illustrate the current *as-is* positioning, and T that indicates the *to-be* positioning of the same process. The map is constructed as a six-cell grid in two dimensions rather than a cube in three dimensions. The reasons for this design choice are that: 1) the visualization of results in two dimensions is easy to understand, and 2) a process that has the characteristics of being common and informal, independent from the question if it is a back or front process *ideally* should not exist. However, we realize that such a process may remain in reality and A* is then used to indicate this instance. The CM is engaged in the assessments from level 1 to level 3, which is the core corporate processes (level 1), process areas (level 2), and main processes (level 3) [26]. The reasons for this design are because we aim to avoid the complexity in the assessment; as well top management is not interested in syntactic details of the lower business processes.

Table 2. CM Dimensions and Sample Questions

CM dimensions	Sample questions
Differentiation assesses the degree to which a process is superior to analogous processes of competitors, thereby differentiating the value proposition of the organization (scale: differentiating to common).	Does the process in scope differentiate your company versus your competitors? Does the process in scope perform poorer than your competitors?
Formality assesses the degree to which a process is strictly managed, repeatable, predictable, automatable, and involves applications rather than people (scale: formal to informal).	Does the process in scope reside on tacit knowledge? How strict is the process in scope managed? How much of the process in scope is done in an unstructured way? How much of the process is done with manual work?
Value network governance assesses the degree to which a process interacts with front-end or back-end network partners/customers in the value network, which determines process governance (scale: back to front).	Does the process interact with suppliers, consumers or others actors in the value network? Where is the ownership of the process in scope? Who is accountable and responsible for the process?

4   The Seco Tools Project

Seco Tools is a global company with 5,600 employees in 42 countries, and annual sales of 7,000 MSEK (~1 BUSD). The company has an established reputation as a world leading manufacturer and supplier of carbide cutting tools and related equipment. "Passion for customer" is the core driver for their business. Seco Tools actively contribute to improving customers' productivity and competitiveness by providing powerful machinery solutions to leading companies in the automotive, aerospace, oil and gas, energy and medical industries, among many others around the world.

4.1   The CIO's Motivation

Seco Tools launched "one Seco program" to improve their business processes in 2011. However, the senior management team did not share the same view on BPM and did not agree on how to establish a process-oriented organization. The CIO and senior vice president (VP) of process and IT was responsible for implementing the "one SECO program". The aim of this program was to create a common understanding and culture with regard to BPM, and to decide on the budget for process improvement projects. The manager faced the following challenges:

1) Seco Tools stems from the traditional "manufacturing" industry. The company has a rather conservative and strong organization culture.

2) Business and IT do not share a common understanding of the business. They have a clear vision on process ownership, and quite a different understanding of each other's work. As the CIO/VP said: *"I have the feeling that there were two parties sitting on respective sides of the fence and no common understanding."*

3) All businesses ask for improvements in their business areas. But the CIO/VP has limited budgets/resources for executing all projects. He said *"The demand is three times larger than what we could do with existing budgets and resources."*

4) The CIO/VP needed clear evidence as well as consensus in prioritizing process improvement projects, to be able to say "no" to other projects. Without transparency and trustworthiness in the decision-making process, the CIO would endanger his position and support in the company.

The CIO/VP decided to use the PCM in prioritizing process improvement initiatives. He articulated the motivation that

"Because of our strong manufacturing culture in the company, we will never accept management consultants, who bring a model, perfectly with a three or four letter acronym. This is deemed to fail from the start. The BPM maturity models, which are a kind of off-the-shelf survey that is conducted by doing impractical assessments in numbers, would not be our way forward. By engaging myself in the PCM design process with other CIOs and academic researchers, I learned to appreciate the value and relevance of the method in solving our problem. We jointly discover the common problems in prioritizing process improvement initiatives. With this background, I strongly believe the worth of testing the PCM in my company."

The aims of the project for Seco Tools were to: 1) prioritize the process that has high improvement potential, for example, to achieve "operational excellence" in operational process, "product & services innovation" at the back-end, and "passion for customer" at the front end; 2) to find out which processes have improvement potential and can be handled in the future. The project was done between January and April 2012;[1] 3) for research purposes, we aimed to demonstrate the method and use it to solve the prioritization problems. Moreover, we gathered feedback to improve the PCM in future research.

---

[1] The CIO/VP shared the experience and his reflections with the public in March 2013. The video is available at *http://bambuser.com/v/3434182* *(in Swedish)*. The quotations we cited in this paper are translated by the first author from Swedish to English.

4.2   The PCM Demonstration Procedure

The demonstration was completed by following the **four steps.**

1. The CIO firstly selected 40 processes that were intended for improvement. He then contacted the former CEO, who has worked for 30 years for the company; then he selected the VP in the Asian region, and the global process manager. They together identified 12 out of 40 processes for assessment, including a few simple lower-level processes. The pre-selection was guided by using the PCM.
2. The CIO and the three managers reviewed and agreed on the core questions in the assessment. Then the three managers further recommended other stakeholders based on their informal network to perform the assessments and interviews. Altogether they selected 20 key stakeholders (both owner and customers of the processes) from different business functions, different countries and from different levels in the organization, i.e., strategic, functional as well as operational. These managers were the CIO/Senior Vice President, Global Distribution Manager, Country Managing Director, Global Process Manager, Director Operations and Human Resources, Quality Manager, Process Owners and Process Improvers.
3. Interviews with each manager were conducted by involved researchers. In the first part of the interviews the heat map (PAHM) was used. This took about one and half hours. In the second part of the interview the CM assessment was central. This part took about 30 minutes. The researchers didn't impose personal opinions and kept neutral in the interviews.

    First the 12 selected processes for the assessment were introduced. Next the five perspectives in combination with the key questions for generating a PAHM were discussed. The managers were asked to decide on a colour, green, amber or red, based on their knowledge and experiences of the process and on discussion of the key questions with involved researchers. The managers were asked to give concrete reasons and to motivate why they chose a specific colour. They were also asked to give their advice on how to improve the process. All these comments were documented in the heat map.

    Next, the interviews were focused on process categorization. The CM, the three dimensions and the key questions, and the *as-is* and *to-be* analysis were introduced by the researchers. The managers did the *as-is* analysis of the process by answering and reflecting on the three dimensions and the questions for the current situations first. As a follow up, they went through the same questions again but with a future oriented thinking, i.e. two to three years, of where they would like to see the process *to-be* to move to. The discussions during the completion of the task related to the heat map helped the managers to get familiar with the assessment. Their learning and reflections served as the basis for generating the CM. The intensive interaction during the interviews had generated active learning and reflection for both involved managers and researchers.
4. Finally, the results from the individual interviews were consolidated, calibrated and coordinated at the end. The evaluation results were presented and discussed at a Business Process Council meeting where 18 top managers of Seco Tools participated in March 2012.

4.3   Results

We only present one of the examples of the results. We focus on the process to Create Forecasts. The process received the highest numbers of red in the assessment.

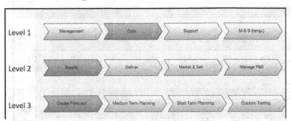

Fig. 3. Create forecast process at Seco Tools

The forecast process is presented and analysed here to illustrate the kind of results that can be derived from using the PCM. The process under discussion is a level 3 process that is part of the "supply" domain and a core processes at the corporate level (see Fig. 3).

Figure four shows the heat map of the process. Each cell presents the results from an assessment by an individual manager (R1 -interviewee 1 - to R20- interviewee 20). The results show that the process has high potential for future improvement in the overall assessment. A majority of the managers (17) assessed the process as having more than 50% improvement potential (illustrated by the colour red). The other three managers consider it to be an amber process. The results from the five perspectives indicated that the improvement should be focused on Implementation (14 red, 4 amber) and Proving (10 in red, and 7 in amber). The company should also pay attention to the Preparing perspective, as the 18 managers perceived its potential for improvement (4 in red and in amber). It seemed that most of the managers (12, 60%) were satisfied with the process performance from the perspectives of Positioning and Relating.

The CM of the "create forecast process" is shown in Fig. 5. Most of the managers (13) described the as-is state (marked as A) of the process as having the characteristics of being formal, common and back (closer to supplier). Four managers believed that the process was common, informal and back (mark as A*). A majority of them (13) prescribed the to-be state of the process as informal, differentiating and near the vertical line between the front and back dimension. Although the other seven managers had different perceptions of the to-be state of the process, they also believed that the process should possess the characteristics of being near the vertical line between the front and back dimension. The relative distance between the as-is dots and the to-be dots was clearly shown in the map, which indicated that the process should be reengineered [27]. The to-be process required the seamlessly collaboration of the supporting processes at the back (with suppliers) and front (with customers) dimension. This suggested the need for change in the process management and resource allocation for establishing and ensuring this inter-organizational process collaboration.

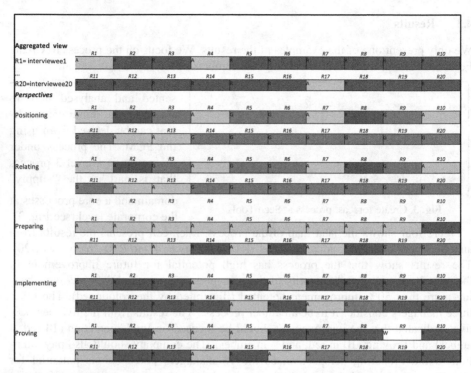

Fig. 4. PAHM: Create forecast process (manipulated picture)

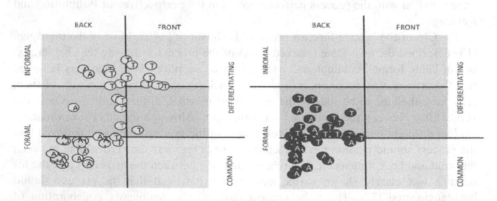

Fig. 5. PCM – Process Create Forecast (left) in comparison with another process at Seco Tools

Figure five also showed the CM of another process that we evaluated at Seco Tools. Comparing these two processes, we can easily find out that the managers had different views of the two processes' characteristics. The create forecast process as we discussed needs big changes and should be reengineered. In comparison, another process needs a small improvement, as the as-is and to-be dots are mostly located in the "formal, common and back" area. The company only needs to improve the process to be "differentiating" to a small degree. The CM results indicate how to improve the process in scope.

4.4   Top Management Decision in Prioritizing Process Improvement Initiatives

The top management team discussed the overall results of the 12 processes from the PCM analysis, particularly which processes to prioritize to generate a better value from the process prioritization projects for the business. The managers also tried to identify if the organizational capabilities were aligned for a successful implementation for the prioritized processes. The team reflected the shared view of the purposes and challenges for implementing the process driven operations in the organization. The two most important problems were raised at the end of the discussions: 1) the process performance varied a lot among different processes; 2) and the process performance measurement was missing in almost all the processes, therefore the proving perspective of PAHM should be improved. Because the consensus is achieved in the PCM demonstration based on the assessments from managers at different levels, the team was comfortable to make the decisions [21]. Accordingly, they made the following decisions: 1) five processes were prioritized for improvement, including create forecast process; 2) at least two KPIs per process should be published on a regular basis in order to improve process transparency and performance, in order to enhance the "proving" perspective; and 3) the organizational capabilities, e.g., people, culture and IT priorities (reliability, cost, agility, quality) should be in focus for supporting a successful implementation of the prioritized processes.

5   Lessons Learned

Five lessons from this demonstration stand out.

First, the PCM is a *useful, efficient and reliable* method in supporting prioritization decisions. The PCM can produce a holistic analysis of processes with good quality within a short time by interviewing 20 people. It assists the managers in gaining a common understanding of the processes' performance, and to reach consensus about where to prioritize and where to invest the resources. Therefore, the PCM can solve the problems in prioritizing process improvement initiatives. The CIO/VP stated:

"The method is a tremendous help to me, in that it creates, together with the management board, a common picture regarding our as-is state and to-be state. It was a foundation, where we could agree which process works well and which does worse. This consensus was not present at all before we did this demonstration. We know where to assign our resources to the prioritized process. The processes that work fine can wait. " He continued that: *"The method helped us to decide what, where in the processes the improvements should take place, but then, the how, is the next question the method can indicate. Should we go for a large change project or implementing an existing process with everyday business operation through small adjustment?"*

Based on analysis of the process characteristics, the categorization map (CM) can give an indication for the "how" question. For instance, if the *to be state* of a process should be formal and common, then the company can automate the process; if the *to be state* of a process should be informal and differentiating, then the company should focus on business process reengineering for big changes. The *"to be"* state also implies that companies should allocate limited resources, and capabilities for ensuring a successful implementation of the prioritized processes [3].

Second, top management should initiate and participate in the assessment. The CIO/VP recognized the power of "collective intelligence" in the demonstration process. He identified the key stakeholders based on his formal and informal network in the company, and then those key stakeholders recommended other influential persons from their own social network. In doing so, a top- down social process in decision making was created. This ensures the right people are included in the interviews. Therefore, politics in decision making is avoided. Involving right people also increases the data quality of the assessment. Consequently, it improves the quality and reliability of the results which are used for strategic decision making. The CIO/VP reflected that:

"It is very important to do a good preparation work and to choose the right interviewees. They are not only from the management group, but also from a more heterogonous group of key stakeholders, informal leaders in the organization, such as individuals who have not formal leadership but have a strong position and great knowledge of the business. The number should be manageable, given the size of the business and decent coverage of the business areas. You have to adopt the method to your own business." He further explained that: *"By using the method in the decision-making process, I took help from the ones that have spent their entire carrier in the business; those who know how things really work. ...I get a sense of what is important at present, and what I should do next."*

Third, the interviews guided by the PCM, were conducted with the right people, which creates openness, transparency and trust in the decision-making process. The interviewees' names were known by the whole organization. The selection of the right people was a deliberate choice. People who were not involved would "buy in" to the decision because they saw their peers who they trusted participated in the decision making. This effect was very much appreciated by the CIO/VP: *"I was a little bit worried, how the people who were not interviewed would interpret this. It turned out, because of our openness regarding who was interviewed and that we had made a consensus decision, it was quite well accepted."*

Fourth and lastly, the interviewer(s)/facilitators should preferably remain neutral in the assessment. This helped in avoiding personal influences and creating trust during the interview sessions enabled the interviewees to open up their thinking and transferred more intangible knowledge during the interviews. Involving two interviewers proved to give a better result than only one considering the limited time for interviews, since taking both notes and facilitating the interviews was too challenging.

The general learning outcomes of this demonstration are that, 1) the PCM can identify the processes to be improved and indicate how to improve. The PCM produces a holistic analysis of processes from the five perspectives of PAHM and the three dimensions of CM. The PCM can solve the prioritization problem in organizations, and it is useful in a real decision-making context. 2) The CIO and process stakeholders have deepened their understanding of how process prioritization and categorization can be facilitated, operated and analysed by the PCM in the organization. 3) The CIO/VP at Seco Tools recommended that it is crucial to choose the right people in the interviews for ensuring the full benefits of using the PCM, especially, avoiding politics in decision making. In other words, people in both the formal network and informal network in the organization should be identified and included in the assessments [28]. Moreover, the top-down social process created in adapting the PCM in decision making, has improved the communication between business and IT, enhanced the information/knowledge sharing among managers at different levels, and established a supportive culture for an effective process management.

6   Conclusion

This paper presents the PCM and depicts the experience from Seco Tools in prioritizing process improvement initiatives by demonstrating the method. The evidences support that the PCM is a novel method in prioritizing process improvement initiatives. It clarifies the prior theoretical "mystery" in prioritization by providing a holistic analysis of processes from the five perspectives of PAHM and three dimensions of CM. The PCM can identify processes to be improved and indicate how to improve.

A significant benefit of using the PCM is that practitioners can gain a better and common understanding of processes, improvement potentials and how to improve processes. This builds up a solid foundation for decision making in prioritizing process improvement initiatives. Furthermore, the company creates a novel way of making decisions by using the PCM. The prioritization process was transparent, open, and trustworthy. This supported top management in making the right decisions, and created a good "buy in" of the decisions made. Additionally, the top-down social process in using the PCM has been beneficial for the company in eliciting the "intelligence" from the right people and creating a culture for process management. Therefore, the PCM can avoid politics in decision making for prioritizing process initiatives.

Building upon the experience from the Seco Tools project, we further developed a web-based application of the PCM. The PCM has now been tested and evaluated by a number of Swedish companies and public organizations. We will evaluate the PCM in different contexts and improve the method in future research.

References

1. Zairi, M.: Business Process Management: A Boundaryless Approach to Modern Competitiveness. Business Process Management J. 3, 64–80 (1997)
2. Chakravorty, S.S.: Where Process-Improvement Projects Go Wrong. World Street Journal (January 2010)
3. Rosemann, M., vom Brocke, J.: The Six Core Elements of Business Process Management. In: vom brocke, J., Rosemann, M. (eds.) Handbook on Business Process Management 1, pp. 107–122. Springer, Heidelberg (2010)
4. Bandara, W., Guillemain, A., Coogans, P.: Prioritizing Process Improvement: an Example from the Australian Financial Services Sector. In: vom Brocke, J., Rosemann, M. (eds.) Handbook on Business Process Management 2, pp. 177–195. Springer, Heidelberg (2010)
5. Franz, P.H., Kirchmer, M., Rosemann, M.: Value-driven Business Process Management: Impact and Benefits. Accenture (2012)
6. Alter, A.: How can CIOs Keep Prioritization Politics in Check? CIO Insight (July 2004)

7. Hevner, A.R., March, S.T., Park, J., Ram, S.: Design Science in Information Systems Research. MIS Q. 28, 75–105 (2004)
8. Peffers, K., Tuunanen, T., Rothenberger, M.A., Chatterjee, S.: A Design Science Research Methodology for Information Systems Research. J. Manage. Inf. Syst. 24, 45–77 (2007)
9. Orlikowski, W.J.: Practice in Research: Phenomenon, Perspective and Philosophy. In: Orlikowski, W.J., Golsorkhi, D., Rouleau, L., Seidl, D., Vaara, E. (eds.) Cambridge Handbook of Strategy as Practice, pp. 23–33. Cambridge University Press (2010)
10. Van de Ven, A.H.: Engaged Scholarship: A Guide for Organizational and Social Research. Oxford University Press (2007)
11. Dumas, M., La Rosa, M., Mendling, J., Reijers, H.A.: Fundamentals of Business Process Management. Springer, Heidelberg (2013)
12. Burlton, R.: Delivering Business Strategy through Process Management. In: Vom Brocke, J., Rosemann, M. (eds.) Handbook on Business Process Management 2, pp. 5–37. Springer, Heidelberg (2010)
13. Harrington, H.J.: Business Process Improvement: The Breakthrough Strategy for Total Quality, Productivity, and Competitiveness. McGraw-Hill (1991)
14. Davenport, T.H.: Process Innovation: Reengineering Work through Information Technology. Harvard Business Press (1993)
15. Hammer, M., Champy, J.: Reengineering the Corporation: A Manifesto for Business Revolution. Harper Business (1993)
16. Rosemann, M., de Bruin, T.: Towards a Business Process Management Maturity Model. In: Proceedings of the 13th European Conference on Information Systems (ECIS), pp. 521–532 (2005)
17. Weber, C.V., Curtis, B., Gardiner, T.: Business process maturity model (BPMM), version 1.0 (2004), http://www.omg.org/spec/BPMM/1.0
18. Röglinger, M., Pöppelbuß, J., Becker, J.: Maturity Models in Business Process Management. Business Process Management J. 18, 328–346 (2012)
19. Huxley, C.: An Improved Method to Identify Critical Processes. Queensland University of Technology, Australian (2003)
20. Silva, A.R., Rosemann, M.: Processpedia: an Ecological Environment for BPM Stake-holders' Collaboration. Business Process Management J. 18, 20–42 (2012)
21. PorterM. E.: What is Strategy?Harv. Bus. Rev.74, 61-80 (1996)
22. Hammer, M.: The Process Audit. Harv. Bus. Rev. 85, 1–11 (2007)
23. van der Aalst, W.M.P.: Business Process Management: A Comprehensive Survey.ISRN Software Engineering, 1–37 (2013)
24. Swenson, K.D. (ed.): Mastering the Unpredictable: How Adaptive Case Management Will Revolutionize the Way that Knowledge Workers Get Things Do. Meghan-Kiffer Press, Tampa (2010)
25. Markus, M.L., Jacobson, D.D.: Business Process Governance. In: vom Brocke, J., Rosemann, M. (eds.) Handbook on Business Process Management 2, pp. 201–222. Springer, Heidelberg (2010)
26. Davis, R., Brabänder, E.: ARIS Design Platform: Getting Started with BPM. Springer, London (2007)
27. Hammer, M.: What is Business Process Management? In: vom Brocke, J., Rosemann, M. (eds.) Handbook on Business Process Management 1, pp. 3–16. Springer, Heidelberg (2010)
28. Krackhardt, D., Hanson, J.R.: Informal networks. Harv. Bus. Rev. 71, 104–111 (1993)

Cloud Forensics: Identifying the Major Issues and Challenges

Stavros Simou[1], Christos Kalloniatis[1], Evangelia Kavakli[1], and Stefanos Gritzalis[2]

[1] Cultural Informatics Laboratory, Department of Cultural Technology and Communication,
University of the Aegean, University Hill, GR 81100 Mytilene, Greece
{SSimou,chkallon}@aegean.gr, kavakli@ct.aegean.gr
[2] Information and Communication Systems Security Laboratory,
Department of Information and Communications Systems Engineering,
University of the Aegean, GR 83200, Samos, Greece
sgritz@aegean.gr

Abstract. One of the most important areas in the developing field of cloud computing is the way that investigators conduct researches in order to reveal the ways that a digital crime took place over the cloud. This area is known as cloud forensics. While great research on digital forensics has been carried out, the current digital forensic models and frameworks used to conduct a digital investigation don't meet the requirements and standards demanded in cloud forensics due to the nature and characteristics of cloud computing. In parallel, issues and challenges faced in traditional forensics are different to the ones of cloud forensics. This paper addresses the issues of the cloud forensics challenges identified from review conducted in the respective area and moves to a new model assigning the aforementioned challenges to stages.

Keywords: Cloud Computing, Cloud Forensics, Cloud Forensics Process, Cloud Forensics Challenges, Digital Forensics.

1 Introduction

In the last years, the growing demand of computing power and resources, lead the traditional forms of services to mutate very rapidly. During this period users have been experiencing a huge demand on applications and services on cloud computing, which is definitely one of the most important services offered in this era. According to the 3rd Annual Future of Cloud Computing Survey, cloud adoption continued to rise in 2013, with 75 percent of those surveyed reporting the use of some sort of cloud platform – a 67 percent rise from the previous year. Addressing this growth in the worldwide market for cloud computing it is expected to reach $158.8 billion by 2014, an increase of 126.5 percent from 2011 [1]. Recent International Data Corporation (IDC) cloud research shows that spending on public IT cloud services will reach $47.4 billion in 2013 and is expected to be more than $107 billion in 2017. Over the 2013–2017 forecast period, public IT cloud services will have a compound annual growth rate (CAGR) of 23.5%, as companies build out the infrastructure needed to deliver public cloud services. By 2017, IDC expects public IT cloud services to drive 17% of the IT product spending. [2].

M. Jarke et al. (Eds.): CAiSE 2014, LNCS 8484, pp. 271–284, 2014.

Although, organizations are adopting cloud computing technology there is still a great consideration about security and the continuously increasing number of digital crimes occurring in cloud environments. According to a newly-released report sponsored by McAfee, global cyber activity is costing up to $500 billion each year, which is almost as much as the estimated cost of drug trafficking [3]. Investigators have to conduct digital forensic investigation on cloud computers to identify, preserve, collect and analyze all the evidentiary data in order to proper present them in a court of law. This type of forensic has been named as cloud forensics. The ability of cloud forensic investigators to carry out an investigation depends completely on the tools and methods used, to acquire the appropriate digital evidence from a device. The current digital forensic methods, tools and frameworks used to conduct a digital investigation cannot meet the requirements and the standards for the new technology on cloud environment. This happens due to the fact that computer technology is continuously changing and the forensic technology is unable to follow that pace.

Since cloud forensics is a newly developed research area our main and primary focus was to conduct a thorough analysis of the respective literature in order to present an analytic review of the challenges and issues raised so far in the respective field. For conducting this analysis we begun with the most cited papers presented in respective scientific journals, conferences and industrial reports like "Digital Investigation", "Advances in Digital Forensics", "International Journal of Digital Evidence", "Emerging Digital Forensics Applications for Crime Detection, Prevention, and Security", "Systematic Approaches to Digital Forensic Engineering", "Digital Forensic Research Workshop", "Cyber Security, and Cyber Warfare and Digital Forensic" etc.. After conducting this analysis we have broaden our research to less related academic reports and papers from the field of security in information systems.

The findings of this study constitute an initial but robust set of requirements that analysts and developers need to consider when designing information systems or individual services in the cloud. Also this research introduces future research efforts that need to be conducted and tools that need to be implemented for assisting in the process of cyber-crime investigation in cloud-based environments.

2 Technical Background

2.1 Cloud Computing

Companies and organizations are looking for new services and solutions on the Internet, aiming on the reduction of the cost on their infrastructure and support (human resources) and, in parallel, to increase their systems' scalability. In order to accomplish their objectives, they outsource services and equipment. This solution is a step towards cloud computing. Cloud computing is not owned by companies and the respective IT systems are not usually managed by them. Instead, Cloud Service Providers (CSPs) supply these services after signing contracts with companies. A CSP maintains the computing infrastructure (high availability computer systems in clusters, data centers) required for providing the various services, runs the cloud software and delivers the cloud services to the Cloud Consumers through the Internet.

Cloud computing uses virtualization techniques for providing equipment, software and platform support as remote services. Cloud model is composed of five essential characteristics, i.e., on-demand self-service, broad network access, resource pooling, rapid elasticity and measured service, three service models, i.e., Software as a Service (SaaS), Platform as a Service (PaaS) and Infrastructure as a Service (IaaS), and four deployment models, i.e., private cloud, community cloud, public cloud and hybrid cloud" [4]. Cloud computing provides many advantages to companies and organizations in comparison to traditional private environments.

2.2   Digital and Cloud Forensics

In the digital world were modern users live and interact on a daily basis the number of crimes involving computer devices is growing rapidly. This has an immediate impact to the people who aim to assist law enforcement, using digital evidence to uncover the digital crime. A new battlefield is set and the investigators are trying to cope and bring to justice the people responsible for these kinds of crimes. Digital forensics is the field where the investigators use forensic processes to search for digital evidence in order to use them in a court of law, or to a company's internal investigation. Digital forensics has been defined as the use of scientifically derived and proven methods toward the preservation, collection, validation, identification, analysis, interpretation, documentation and presentation of digital evidence derived from digital sources for the purpose of facilitating or furthering the reconstruction of events found to be criminal, or helping to anticipate unauthorized actions shown to be disruptive to planned operations [5].

Forensic techniques and tools have been created for assisting the investigation process, aiming to acquire, preserve and analyze evidence. Digital forensics deals with the digital evidence found in the area where the crime committed. When we refer to evidence we mean all kind of digital evidence found on any type of digital devices, present or futures. The most important element in the digital forensics is to maintain the integrity and the chain of custody of the digital evidence. Any alteration to the evidence simply means that the case is lost in a court of law.

Identification of evidence in cloud environments is a difficult process due to the different deployment and service models and also the limitation of seizing (physically) the computer device containing the evidence. In the early stages of the new era, investigations on cloud environments were based on methodologies and tools from the digital forensic field. Rapid advances in cloud computing require new methodologies, frameworks and tools for performing digital forensics in cloud environments. Cloud forensic is a subset of digital forensics and it was first introduced by Ruan (2011), to designate the need for digital investigation in cloud environments, based on forensic principles and procedures.

Crime investigators in cloud environments have to deal with a number of different issues compared to network or computer investigation. The most important is that the evidence can reside everywhere in the world in a virtualization environment. The investigators' main concern is to maintain that the evidence has not been compromised by third parties, in order to be presented and being acceptable in the court of law. Third parties are involved in the cloud forensic process due to their collaboration with CSPs. Service providers sign contracts with other companies possibly in different geographically locations, for help and assistance.

Various cloud forensics techniques are developed and used depending on the cloud deployment and service model the respective crime or incident under investigation have taken place. In service models like PaaS and SaaS for example, consumers do not have the control of the hardware and they depend on the CSP for the logs, whereas in IaaS, consumers have the ability to make an image of the instance and acquire the logs. As for the deployment models, in public cloud consumers do not have the physical access and the privacy compared with the ones in private cloud.

3   The Cloud Forensic Process

3.1   Related Work

Since 2001, various methods and frameworks have been introduced regarding the way of conducting proper digital forensic investigation, including different stages and phases. The First Digital Forensic Research Workshop (DFRWS) [5] defined a generic investigative process that could be applied to the majority of investigations involving digital systems and networks. The model establishes a linear process, which includes identification, preservation, collection, examination, analysis, presentation and decision. In this workshop a discussion was conducted about the use of the term collection and preservation, and the possibility of the first being a subcategory or a separate step with the other.

The Abstract Digital Forensic model [6] was based on DFRWS model and consists of nine stages which are identification, preparation, approach strategy, preservation, collection, examination, analysis, presentation and returning evidence. It adds three more stages and describes what each one of them concern.

In 2003, the Integrated Digital Investigation Process [7] model was introduced based on the crime scene theory for physical investigations. It allows technical requirements for each phase to be developed and for the interaction between physical and digital investigations to be identified. This framework consists of 17 phases organized into five groups: readiness, deployment, physical crime scene investigation, digital crime scene investigation and review.

The Enhanced Digital Investigation Process model [8] separates the investigations at primary and secondary crime scenes while depicting the phases as iterative instead of linear. It is based on the IDIP model and expands the deployment phase into physical and digital crime investigations while introducing the primary crime scene phase. The reconstruction is only made after all investigations have taken place.

The hierarchical, objectives based framework [9] for the digital investigations process in 2005, proposes a multi-layer, hierarchical framework which includes objectives-based phases and sub-phases that are applicable to various layers of abstraction, and to which additional layers of detail can easily be added as needed. The framework includes the stages of preparation, incident response, data collection, data analysis, presentation of findings and incident closure.

In 2006, the Forensic Process [10] proposed consisting of four phases: collection, examination, analysis and reporting. In this model, forensic process transforms media into evidence for law enforcement or for organization's internal usage. First collected data is examined, extracted from media and transforms it into a format that can be processed by forensic tools. Then data is transformed into information through analysis and finally the information is transformed into evidence during the reporting phase.

The Digital Forensic Investigation Framework (DFIF) [11] groups and merges the same activities or processes that provide the same output into an appropriate phase. The proposed map simplifies the existing complex framework and it can be used as a general DFIF for investigating all incident cases without tampering the evidence and protect the chain of custody. The framework consists of five phases which are preparation, collection and preservation, examination and analysis, presentation and reporting and disseminating the case.

In 2010, Digital Forensic Evidence Processes [12] defined nine stages, identification, collection, preservation, transportation, storage, analysis - interpretation and attribution, reconstruction, presentation and destruction. All of these should be done in a manner that meets the legal standards of the jurisdiction and the case.

The Harmonized digital forensic investigation process model [13] introduced in 2012, proposed several actions to be performed constantly and in parallel with the phases of the model, in order to achieve efficiency of investigation and ensure the admissibility of digital evidence. The phases defined in terms of scope, functions and order. These are: incident detection, first response, planning, preparation, incident scene documentation, identification, collection, transportation, storage, analysis, presentation and conclusion.

The Forensic Investigations Process [14] in cloud environments was based on the Forensic Process with the four stages. Due to the evolution of cloud computing the stages were changed to apply basic forensic principles and processes. The four distinct steps are: a) determine the purpose of the forensics requirement, b) identify the types of cloud services (SaaS, IaaS, Paas), c) determine the type of background technology used and d) examine the various physical and logical locations, which are client side, server side and developer side.

In 2012, Cloud Forensics Process [15] focused on the competence and admissibility of the evidence along with the human factor. The process consists of four stages which includes a) ascertain the purpose of the cloud forensic, b) ascertain the type of the cloud service, c) ascertain the type of the technology behind the cloud and d) carry out specific investigation on the base of stage c such as ascertain the role of the user, negotiate with the CSP, collect potential evidence, etc.

Finally, in 2012, the Integrated Conceptual Digital Forensic Framework for Cloud Computing [16] proposed, based on McKemmish and NIST. It emphasizes on the differences in the preservation of forensic data and the collection of cloud computing data for forensic purposes. It consists of four stages, identification and preservation, collection, examination and analysis, reporting and presentation.

In the following section we propose a cloud forensics process as it was derived from the aforementioned findings.

3.2   The Process

In order to identify the cloud forensic process an extensive literature review on the fields of both digital and cloud forensics was conducted. Based on the above frameworks it is obvious that some of the existing models follow similar approaches while others are moving in different areas of investigation, but the outcome in most occasions is almost the same. The model used in this paper is similar to DFWR model with three additions! Firstly we propose the inclusion of collection phase in the preservation stage, secondly we include the analysis stage in the examination stage and finally the decision stage is excluded, due to the fact that it cannot be considered "forensic".

This model is convenient for analyzing and associating challenges in cloud forensics and was derived based on the suggestions and drawbacks located from the investigation of similar approaches presented before. The model is consisted of four steps: i) *Identification* which is the first stage and deals with identifying all possible sources of evidence in a cloud environment in order to prove that the incident took place. It is crucial, because the next processes depend upon the evidence identified here. ii) *Preservation – Collection* which deals with the collection of the evidence, from the locations they reside in clouds, the different types of media and the tools used to do so. Also, investigators need to isolate and preserve the evidence by preventing people from using the digital device or by duplicating digital evidence. Integrity and unauthorized alterations of digital evidence must be ensured. The most important issue in this step is to maintain the chain of custody of the evidence and to ensure the validity and the integrity of them in order to be used in a court of law. Preservation could be a different process in a cloud forensic framework running concurrently with all the other processes, iii) *Examination – Analysis* which involves the extraction of data from the previous stage and the inspection of the huge amount of data identified in order to locate the proper evidence for the incident occurred. The data found will be analyzed by different tools and techniques for revealing any useful information in order to prove if someone is guilty or not. In this stage also, data reconstruction will take place, iv) *Presentation* stage which is the final stage and deals with the presentation of the evidence in a court of law. A well-documented report with the findings must be produced using expert testimony on the analysis of the evidence. Evidence must be presented in a way that the jury will understand all the technical details due to the fact that cloud computing is a very complicated environment for ordinary Internet users to understand.

4   Cloud Forensic Challenges

In this section we present the cloud forensics challenges identified from the review conducted in the respective area. Also we move one step further and accomplish a categorization of the respective challenges based on the cloud forensics process stages presented in section 3. It should be mentioned that most of the challenges presented apply basically on public clouds while fewer have applicability on private cloud architectures as well.

4.1   Identification Stage

Access to Evidence in Logs. Logs play a vital role in an investigation. Having access to log files in order to identify an incident is the first priority for the investigators. In cloud environments where data are stored in unknown locations due to systems' distribution locating logs is a hard and painful process. The detection of logs also depends on the service model. In PaaS and SaaS, checking system status and log files is not feasible because the client access is completely limited to the API or the pre-designed interface. It is just partly applicable in IaaS cloud model as it provides the Virtual Machine which behaves almost the same as an Actual Machine [17]. On the other hand many CSPs do not provide services to gather logs and sometimes intentionally hide the details from customers.

Physical Inaccessibility. In a cloud environment, data location is a difficult task due to the geographical distribution of the hardware devices. The established digital forensic procedures and tools assume that physical access to the hardware is a fact [18]. However, in cloud forensics there is no possibility to seize the hardware containing data, because the data are stored in distributed systems usually in different jurisdictions. Thus, this challenge applies to all three service models.

Volatile Data. Data stored in a Virtual Machine instance in an IaaS service model will be lost when the VM is turned off or rebooted. This reflects to the loss of important evidence such as registry entries, processes and temporary internet files. In case an adversary launches an attack on a VM with no persistent storage synchronization, when the attack is completed, the adversary can shut down the Virtual Machine instance leading to a complete loss of volatile data, if no further countermeasures are installed [19]. Respective literature [18, 20, 21, 22] place the specific challenge to preservation and collection stages. Actually this challenge can fit into both stages, because first we have to identify volatile data and then we have to preserve and collect them from any instance.

Distribution - Collaboration. The distribution of computer systems (in all three service models) in the cloud environment makes the investigators to confront problems with different jurisdictions and laws. To access information, they need to wait for a warrant which sometimes can be costly and time consuming. This is why international collaborations between law enforcement and CSPs must be taken into consideration [23]. New guidelines need to be written and adopted by all countries for the aforementioned reasons.

Client Side Identification. Evidence can be found not only in the providers' side but also in the clients' side interface. In most of the scenarios, the user agent (e.g. the web browser) on the client system is the only application that communicates with the service in the cloud. This especially holds for SaaS and IaaS scenarios. Hence, in an exhaustive forensic investigation, the evidence data gathered from the browser environment should not be omitted [19].

Dependence on CSP - Trust. In all respective literature authors point out the CSPs contribution on cloud forensic process. CSPs are responsible for helping and assisting the investigators and the clients with all the information and evidence they can get in their cloud infrastructures. The problem arises when the CSPs are not willing to provide the information reside in their premises. A good reason for not doing so is the fear that these are going to be used against their companies. In all three models, especially in SaaS and PaaS we need to depend on the CSP to identify, preserve and collect all the evidence that could lead us to the incident. Another major issue is the CSPs dependence on third parties. CSPs sign contracts with other CSPs in order to be able to use their services. This means that the investigation has to cover all the parties involved with an immediate impact to the chain of custody. This challenge applies not only to identification stage, but also to preservation and collection stage.

Service Level Agreement (SLA). In many cases important terms regarding forensic investigations are not included in the SLA signed between CSP and customer. This is because there is a lack of customer awareness, a lack of CSP transparencies, trust boundaries and a lack of international regulations. CSPs cannot provide transparency to customers, because they either do not know how to investigate criminal incidents or the methods and techniques they are using are not appropriate in cloud environments [24]. Suppose a customer signed a contract with a CSP regarding the deletion of all data after the contract expires. It is hard for the customer to verify that the CSP has fulfilled the agreement. Service Level Agreements concern the stages of identification, preservation and collection.

4.2 Preservation – Collection Stage

Integrity and Stability. The integrity preservation and the stability of the evidence is essential in cloud investigation for IaaS, PaaS and SaaS. We must preserve data in our effort to acquire evidence in multi-jurisdiction environments, a difficult task to deal with, without violating any law. If the integrity is not preserved (could be compromised by the CSP or the hypervisor [17]), then the evidence will not be admissible to the court of law. Finally, it is difficult to maintain the stability of the data because of the transient nature and dedicated description of the data in a Cloud [15]. According to [16], this challenge applies to analysis stage.

Privacy. The virtualization of the systems in IaaS and multi-jurisdiction affect the privacy of the clients. Investigators must ensure that all regulations and standards are retained in order to collect the evidence without breaching clients' privacy. CSPs also must find a mechanism to ensure clients that their information will not be accessed by any member of the staff even if they have been deleted.

Time Synchronization. In all three service models the time concerning data is also crucial and requires hard work to come with the correct results. This is due to the fact that data are stored in multiple geographical regions with different time zones. Investigators need to gather all the time stamps from the devices and establish an accurate time line of events [20].

Internal Staffing. This issue concerns all three service models and all four stages, from identification to preservation. To conduct an investigation in cloud forensics a number of people must be involved as a team. This team should consist of investigators with technical knowledge, legal advisors and specialized external staff with deep knowledge in new technology and skills [24].

Chain of Custody. The most important thing to present evidence in a court of law is to make sure that the chain of custody of the evidence is maintained throughout the investigation. Any interruption in the chain of custody will be a problem and the evidence will be questionable. Because of the multi-jurisdictional laws and the involvement of the CSPs for maintaining the chain is a huge challenge. Imagine an investigation where the CSP has to submit data to the investigators. The personnel responsible for collecting the data are not trained to preserve evidence according to specific forensic techniques. In this case the chain of custody will not be maintained. For a case to stand in court the investigators have to ensure that the chain of custody should contain information such as, who collected the evidence, how and where the evidence was collected, how the evidence was stored, who accessed the evidence, etc. [16]

Imaging. In IaaS to make an image of the instance to acquire evidence can be accomplished by taking a snap-shot of the VM. In this case client does not need to shut down the VM to clone the instance. The term "Live Investigation" was introduced for the aforementioned method. The method gathers data in rest, in motion and in execution. Using different images of the instance can provide to investigators any change or alteration made. For PaaS and SaaS clients do not have the ability to access the device. This simply means that there is no possibility of making an image, leading to lose potential evidence when a criminal activity takes place.

Bandwidth Limitation. The volume of data is increasing rapidly resulting to an increase of evidence. In the previous paragraph we referred on the VM imaging in IaaS model. In order to collect data, investigators need to download the VM instance's image. The bandwidth must be taken into consideration when they are downloading these large images.

Multi-jurisdiction. To acquire evidence from the three models in cloud from different jurisdictions is another issue for the investigators. Due to cloud characteristics system's data are usually spread in places around the globe. Thus, it is very difficult, almost impossible, to conduct evidence acquisition when investigators are dealt with different legal systems, where the related laws or regulations may vary by countries [15]. Any evidence retrieval must be according to the laws and privacy policies of the specific jurisdiction where forensic investigation took place in order to maintain the chain of custody. Otherwise, the evidence cannot stand in a court of law.

Multi-tenancy. In cloud environments where IaaS and PaaS services are used, customers share the same storage in VMs. This has an immediate effect on the investigation. Evidence retrieval in multi-tenant environments must maintain the confidentiality, preserve the privacy of the tenants and finally ensure that the data to be collected concern specific tenant and no other. Due to the multi-tenancy the data can be contaminated by people who have access into the same storage unit with result of losing important evidence.

4.3   Examination - Analysis Stage

Lack of Forensic Tools. Data analysis in cloud environments requires appropriate forensic tools. Many of the tools used for a cloud investigation, have been designed and introduced for digital forensic investigations. With the systems distributed all over the world and with no physical access to the computer devices, these kinds of tools cannot fully cover the investigations in IaaS, PaaS and SaaS models. New software tools must be developed to assist in the preservation – collection stage acquiring data more efficient and new certified tools must be produced to help the investigators in data examination and analysis.

Volume of Data. The amount of data, stored in the CSPs' data centers is extremely large and it's increasing on a daily basis. This has an immediate impact on the analysis of the information in order to find useful evidence for the investigation. Appropriate capture and display filters have to be developed and set up in order to make the data volume present in Cloud Infrastructures proccessible [21]. It is very difficult to analyze the VMs directly, even if the CSPs cooperate with investigators, because the VMs for SaaS and PaaS may have a huge storage system, and contain many other applications [25].

Encryption. Many cloud customers in all three service models store their data in an encrypted format to protect them from criminal activities. When an investigation is conducted the encrypted data will not be useful once the encryption keys cannot be acquired. The evidence also can be compromised if the owner of the data is the only one who can provide the key, or if the key is destroyed. Furthermore, many CSPs are using encryption methods to store clients' data in the cloud [23].

Reconstruction. During the investigation, crime scene reconstruction might take place. In cloud environments where data are spread across different regions and countries with time differences, to reconstruct the crime scene and place the facts in a logical order might be a difficult work [17]. On the other hand, if a VM instance is forced to shut down, all data and potential evidence will be lost and the reconstruction phase cannot be executed.

Unification of Log Formats. Analyzing data acquired from the service models is a time consuming process, especially if we have to deal with and identify a number of different log formats. Unification of log formats in cloud is a difficult operation when we have to access the huge amount of different resources available. [24].

Identity. In traditional digital forensic associating a user with the data stored in their computer device is comparatively straight forward (assuming that the device belongs to them and found in their house). In cloud investigation is more complicated, because data are stored in multiple remote locations in multi-tenant environments, and are accessed through clients. Hence, to determine that someone is the owner of the data from a large number of cloud users distributed globally is an intricate process [23]. Another prospective is when a user engages a criminal movement through their VM from a veiled IP address and afterwards claims that their credentials have been compromised from another person.

4.4   Presentation Stage

Complexity of Testimony. In a court of law where the jury (often) consists of people with only the basic knowledge in computer systems, the investigators must be ready to deal with this situation. They have to be prepared to give a clear and simple under-standing on the terms of cloud computing, cloud forensics and how they work and explain how the evidence acquired preserved and documented during the investigation. This is an important issue towards the progress of the trial.

Documentation. Another challenge is to persuade the jury that the evidence acquired during the investigation has been documented properly and there had been no changes to the evidence in the previous stages. Investigators must ensure that all parties have been involved in the investigation, followed methods and principles in order to maintain the chain of custody of the evidence that has been collected. Documentation of digital evidence concerns all stages.

4.5   Uncategorised

Compliance Issues. Companies and organizations such as banks, brokers, hospitals, etc. are not transitioning easily to cloud environments, due to trustworthy data retention issues, together with laws and regulations. There are several laws in different countries, which mandate the trustworthy data retention [18]. Cloud environments yet, are not being able to comply with the forensic requirements set by laws and regulations, hence the transition of those organizations to cloud is impractical. The same applies to credit card companies, as achieving compliance with standards set in this field cannot be met [19].

5   Discussion

Based on the review analysis it is obvious that cloud forensics is far more demanding than digital forensics and this is why there is a need for the introduction of new frameworks and methodologies on cloud investigation in order to proper preserve evidence and maintain the chain of custody in all stages of the investigation. Since cloud forensic is a new field, methodologies and frameworks were based on the digital forensics. To the best of our knowledge no author developed and introduced a framework or methodology, concerning cloud forensics that covers every aspect and every phase in a cloud forensic investigation. Most of the work conducted on cloud forensics, refers to challenges, issues and threats, suggestions and solutions on the service models. Challenges, though, apply on different phases and processes in an investigation.

The categorization of stages presented above is based upon models and frameworks introduced and proposed by academics and the industry. To assign challenges to phases, DFRW model was used with a slight differentiation as presented in section 3. Cloud forensic as mentioned earlier is a new technology, hence, there are many different opinions on the categorization of the challenges. After thorough study on the literature on cloud forensics table 1 was designed for assigning challenges according to the respective stage and service model they belong to. The table also captures the

Table 1. Cloud Forensics Overview

Cloud Forensic Challenges / Stage	Applicable to			Related Work
	IaaS	PaaS	SaaS	
Identification				
Access to evidence in logs	partly	√	√	[16], [17], [18], [19], [20], [21], [22], [23], [24], [25], [26], [27]
Physical inaccessibility	√	√	√	[18], [23], [24], [25], [27]
Volatile data	√	X	X	[17], [18], [19], [20], [21], [22], [24], [25]
Distribution – Collaboration	√	√	√	[23], [24], [26]
Client side identification	√	X	√	[17], [19], [22]
Dependence on CSP – Trust	√	√	√	[18], [19], [20], [22], [24], [25], [26]
Service Level Agreement (SLA)	√	√	√	[19], [24], [26]
Preservation – Collection				
Integrity and stability	√	√	√	[15], [16], [17], [18], [26]
Privacy	X	√	√	[16], [17], [20], [21]
Time synchronization	√	√	√	[18], [20], [24]
Internal Staffing	√	√	√	[24], [26]
Chain of custody	√	√	√	[16], [18], [19], [20], [21], [24], [27]
Imaging	X	√	√	[15], [17], [18], [19], [20]
Bandwidth limitation	√	X	X	[18], [22], [25]
Multi-jurisdiction	√	√	√	[15], [23, [24], [26], [27]
Multi-tenancy	√	√	√	[18], [21], [24], [26]
Examination – Analysis				
Lack of forensic tools	√	√	√	[16], [18], [20], [23], [26], [27]
Volume of data	X	√	√	[15], [17], [21], [25]
Encryption	√	√	√	[16], [20], [23], [24]
Reconstruction	√	√	√	[16], [17], [18]
Unification of log formats	√	√	√	[24]
Identity	√	√	√	[19], [23]
Presentation				
Complexity of testimony	√	√	√	[16], [17], [18], [20], [27]
Documentation	√	√	√	[15], [16]
Uncategorised				
Compliance issues	√	√	√	[18], [19]

√ denotes that a challenge is present and X denotes that a challenge is not present according to the referenced authors.

related work produced by authors on every challenge. Some of the challenges' assignments may refer to more than one stage (see Section 4), but for the convenient presentation of the table each challenge is assigned to one stage.

Preservation of digital evidence along with challenges, such as maintaining chain of custody and documentation, should be applied throughout the digital investigation process. They should run concurrently with all other processes/stages in order to ensure that the evidence will be presented as admissible in a court of law. Procedures must be followed and documented from the moment an incident has occurred until the end of the investigation.

In the field of cloud forensics the most important identifiable challenge is the access to evidence in logs, as all respective authors refer to. To win an investigation, evidence must be presented in a court of law, otherwise no case exists. Once logs are the most valuable and powerful evidence all authors focused on the base on how logs can be identified and accessed in a distributed environment as cloud. The problem relies on the CSPs' dependencies, another sensitive issue to which authors referred thoroughly. Due to the physical inaccessibility, identifying, preserving and collecting evidence depend mostly on CSPs. This is why trusted relations with consumers should be built by allowing the transparency and cooperation in the first stages of an investigation. This could also be ensured with clear written and well-presented SLAs between CSP and consumer.

Forensic tools' challenge is another priority for the authors, as most of them identified that the current tools cannot be efficient and productive for collection and analysis of potential digital evidence. Developers should modify existing tools or produce new ones in order to overcome problems, such as encrypted data, acquiring evidence or the enormous amount of data which sometimes has to be analyzed in a short period of time. Again, by developing appropriate tools the chain of custody could be maintained in a better way and the collection of data would not compromise the evidence making them questionable by the jury.

References

1. http://www.mjskok.com/resource/2013-future-cloud-computing-3rd-annual-survey-results (accessed November 2013)
2. IDC, Worldwide and Regional Public IT Cloud Services 2013 –2017 Forecast, http://www.idc.com/getdoc.jsp?containerId=242464 (accessed November 2013)
3. FOXBusinessReport, Matt Egan. Cyber Crime Costs Global Economy Up to $500B a Year (July 22, 2013), http://www.foxbusiness.com/technology/2013/07/22/report-cyber-crime-costs-global-economy-up-to-1-trillion-year/ (accessed November 2013)
4. Peter, M., Grance, T.: The NIST definition of cloud computing (draft)." NIST special publication 800.145: 7 (2011)
5. Palmer Gary, L.: A Road Map for Digital Forensic Research – report from the First Digital Forensic Research Workshop (DFRWS), Utica, New York, USA, August 2001. Technical Report DTR-T001-01, Digital Forensic Research Workshop, Utica, New York, USA (November 2001)
6. Mark, R., Carr, C., Gunsch, G.: An examination of digital forensic models. International Journal of Digital Evidence 1(3), 1–12 (2002)

7. Brian, C., Spafford, E.H.: Getting physical with the digital investigation process. International Journal of Digital Evidence 2(2), 1–20 (2003)

8. Venansius, B., Tushabe, F.: The enhanced digital investigation process model. In: Proceedings of the Fourth Digital Forensic Research Workshop (2004)

9. Lang, B.N., Clark, J.G.: A hierarchical, objectives-based framework for the digital investigations process. Digital Investigation 2(2), 147–167 (2005)

10. Kent, K., Chevalier, S., Grance, T., Dang, H.: Guide to integrating forensic techniques into incident response, pp. 800–886. NIST Special Publication (2006)

11. Rahayu, S.S., Yusof, R., Sahib, S.: Mapping process of digital forensic investigation framework. International Journal of Computer Science and Network Security 8(10), 163–169 (2008)

12. Cohen, F.B.: Fundamentals of digital forensic evidence. In: Handbook of Information and Communication Security, pp. 789–808. Springer, Heidelberg (2010)

13. Aleksandar, V., Venter, H.S.: Harmonized digital forensic investigation process model. In: Information Security for South Africa (ISSA). IEEE (2012)

14. Hong, G., Jin, B., Shang, T.: Forensic investigations in cloud environments. In: 2012 International Conference on Computer Science and Information Processing (CSIP). IEEE (2012)

15. Chen, G., Du, Y., Qin, P., Du, J.: Suggestions to digital forensics in Cloud computing ERA. In: 2012 3rd IEEE International Conference on Network Infrastructure and Digital Content (IC-NIDC). IEEE (2012)

16. Ben, M., Choo, K.-K.R.: An integrated conceptual digital forensic framework for cloud computing. Digital Investigation 9(2), 71–80 (2012)

17. Mohsen, D., Dehghantanha, A., Mahmoud, R., Shamsuddin, S.B.: Forensics investigation challenges in cloud computing environments. In: 2012 International Conference on Cyber Security, Cyber Warfare and Digital Forensic (CyberSec). IEEE (2012)

18. Shams, Z., Hasan, R.: Cloud Forensics: A Meta-Study of Challenges, Approaches, and Open Problems. arXiv preprint arXiv:1302.6312 (2013)

19. Dominik, B., Wegener, C.: Technical issues of forensic investigations in cloud computing environments. In: 2011 IEEE Sixth International Workshop on Systematic Approaches to Digital Forensic Engineering (SADFE). IEEE (2011)

20. George, G., Storer, T., Glisson, W.B.: Calm Before the Storm: The Challenges of Cloud. In: Emerging Digital Forensics Applications for Crime Detection, Prevention, and Security, p. 211 (2013)

21. Poisel, R., Tjoa, S.: Discussion on the challenges and opportunities of cloud forensics. In: Quirchmayr, G., Basl, J., You, I., Xu, L., Weippl, E. (eds.) CD-ARES 2012. LNCS, vol. 7465, pp. 593–608. Springer, Heidelberg (2012)

22. Zimmerman, S., Glavach, D.: Cyber Forensics in the Cloud. IAnewsletter 14.1 (Winter 2011)

23. George, S., Venter, H.S., Fogwill, T.: Digital forensic framework for a cloud environment (2012)

24. Ruan, K., Carthy, J., Kechadi, T., Crosbie, M.: Cloud forensics: An overview. Advances in Digital Forensics 7, 35–49 (2011)

25. Ting, S.: A Log Based Approach to Make Digital Forensics Easier on Cloud Computing. In: 2013 Third International Conference on Intelligent System Design and Engineering Applications (ISDEA). IEEE (2013)

26. Shahrzad, Z., Benford, D.: Cloud Forensics: Concepts, Issues, and Challenges. In: 2012 Third International Conference on Emerging Intelligent Data and Web Technologies (EIDWT). IEEE (2012)

27. Reilly, D., Wren, C., Berry, T.: Cloud computing: Pros and cons for computer forensic investigations. International Journal Multimedia and Image Processing (IJMIP) 1(1), 26–34 (2011)

Dealing with Security Requirements
for Socio-Technical Systems: A Holistic Approach

Tong Li and Jennifer Horkoff

University of Trento, Trento, Italy
{tong.li,horkoff}@disi.unitn.it

Abstract. Security has been a growing concern for most large organizations, especially financial and government institutions, as security
breaches in the socio-technical systems they depend on are costing bil-
lions. A major reason for these breaches is that socio-technical systems are
designed in a piecemeal rather than a holistic fashion that leaves parts of
a system vulnerable. To tackle this problem, we propose a three-layer security analysis framework for socio-technical systems involving business
processes, applications and physical infrastructure. In our proposal, global
security requirements lead to local security requirements that cut across
layers and upper-layer security analysis influences analysis at lower layers. Moreover, we propose a set of analytical methods and a systematic
process that together drive security requirements analysis throughout the
three-layer framework. Our proposal supports analysts who are not security experts by defining transformation rules that guide the corresponding
analysis. We use a smart grid example to illustrate our approach.

Keywords: Security Requirements, Goal Model, Multilayer, Socio-
Technical System, Security Pattern.

1 Introduction

Like all non-functional requirements, security requirements have a global influence over the design of a socio-technical system. Socio-technical systems
(STSs) are organizational systems consisting of people, business processes, software applications, and hardware components. Such systems often include a
rich physical infrastructure consisting of not only computers, but also build-
ings, cable networks and the like. Due to their ever-increasing complexity, STSs
have been experiencing a growing number of security breaches [5], caused by
security flaws and vulnerabilities.

A common theme for many of these breaches is that security solutions are
not designed in a holistic fashion. Rather, they are dealt with in a piecemeal
fashion, by different analysts and at different times, using different analysis
techniques. For example, Mouratidis [13] and Liu [11] analyze security issues at
organizational level; Herrmann [9] analyzes security requirements in business
process level; Lamsweerde investigate security requirements for software [21].
This leads to security gaps and vulnerabilities for parts of a STS, while others

M. Jarke et al. (Eds.): CAiSE 2014, LNCS 8484, pp. 285–300, 2014.

may be costly and over-protected. For example, when designing an encryption function for a smart meter system, a designer may focus only on the software (application layer). In this case, the software can implement encryption by calling functions implemented by an external hardware chip. However, with this design alternative, calling the external functions means that the software first sends unencrypted text to the chip, creating a vulnerability which can be exploited by non-authorized people (business layer) via bus-snooping (physical layer) [1]. By focusing only on the software, vulnerabilities from the physical layer and business layer perspectives are missed.

To tackle this problem, we propose a holistic approach to security engineering where STSs consist of three layers: a business layer, a (software) application layer, and a physical infrastructure layer. Within this framework, each layer focuses on particular concerns and has its own requirements and specifications, which are captured by goal-oriented requirements modeling language. In particular, specifications in one layer dictate requirements in lower layers. In this manner, the security requirements analysis carried out in one layer seamlessly leads to the analysis in the next layer down. Thus, security requirements derived in different layers can cooperate properly to deliver security to systems. Go back to the aforementioned encryption example, if a holistic view is taken, alternative security treatments are identified: 1) apply software-based encryption, which avoid hardware access issues; 2) apply hardware-based encryption, as well as additional protections on corresponding hardware. In this way, security mechanisms applied in different layers are coordinated, and the aforementioned vulnerability can be avoid.

Based on this framework, a systematic process is provided to drive security analysis both within one layer and across layers. To support analysts without much security knowledge, we propose a set of analytical methods and corresponding transformation rules to facilitate the security analysis process. This security analysis framework is particularly designed for existing systems that have a determined functional design. Our approach takes a number of high-level security requirements as input, analyzes their influences over three layers, and produces holistic security treatments that consist of coordinated security mechanisms in different layers.

In the reminder of this paper, we first describe a smart grid example in Section 2, which is used to illustrate our approach throughout the paper. Next, in Section 3 we introduce our research baseline on requirements and specification models, and security requirements analysis. Section 4 presents the three-layer security analysis framework, while Section 5 describes a set of security requirement analysis methods and a systematic analysis process. Section 6 compares our proposal to other work, and finally in Section 7 we conclude the whole paper and discuss future work.

2   Motivating Example

In this section, we introduce a smart grid example, which leverages information and communication technologies to enable two-way communications between customers and energy providers. This example involves a number of scenarios, and we exclusively focus on a *real-time pricing* scenario. In this scenario, the service provider periodically collects customer's energy consumption data, based on which they can create new prices to balance loads on the power grid. A business layer requirement model for this scenario is shown in Fig. 1. We will introduce details of the goal-oriented modeling language in Section 4.

Because this system involves a wide scope of artifacts, which vary from business processes to physical devices, it is difficult to provide a cost-benefit security treatment to protect the whole system from damages. As reported by National Vulnerability Database, on average, 15 new vulnerabilities of the Supervisory Control and Data Acquisition system (a major control system used in power grid systems) are publicly disclosed each day. Not surprisingly, the presence of these vulnerabilities leads to many attacks on smart grid systems [5].

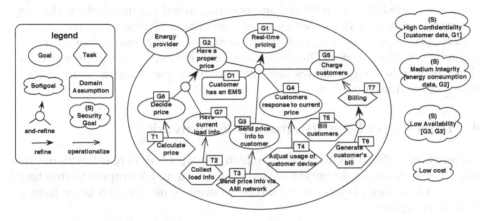

Fig. 1. High-level requirements of real-time pricing scenario

3   Baseline

In this section, we introduce existing work, used as the baseline of our research. We first introduce the requirements problem, which specifies fundamental tasks that need to be addressed during requirements analysis. Then, we describe several requirements modeling language [10,22,6,2], which are intended to capture requirements or tackle the requirements problem.

Requirements Problem. Zave and Jackson [23] define a Requirements Engineering ontology to specify what is the requirements problem. This definition consists of three concepts: a *Requirement* is an optative property that specifies stakeholder's needs on the system-to-be; a *Domain Assumption* is an indicative property that is relevant to the system; a *Specification* is an optative property, which is able to be directly implemented by the system-to-be. Based on these three basic concepts, they define the requirements problem amounts to finding a set of specifications

S, which can satisfy all system requirements R under domain assumptions K. Thus, the requirements problem is represented as $K, S \vdash R$.

Requirements Modeling Language. Jureta et al. [10] propose a goal-oriented requirements modeling language *Techne*, which includes all related concepts for addressing the requirements problem as defined by Zave and Jackson. In addition, it is able to model stakeholder's priority over different requirements, based on which, the best solution can be obtained amongst candidate solutions. Yu [22] proposes the i^* framework for modeling organizational environments and system requirements. Specifically, it captures relationships among social actors via dependency relations. Chung adopts NFR to analyze security requirements [2]. In this work, a security requirement is represented as a *security goal*, which is specified in terms of *sort* and *parameter*. Giorgini et al. [6] model trusts relations between social actors in order to analyze social security issues. In this work, we base our three-layer framework on a combination of above approaches to model both functional and non-functional requirements (including security requirements), as well as social interactions. Particularly, we use the concepts *actor, goal, softgoal, quality constraint, task,* and *domain assumption* and the relations *refine, preferredTo, dependency, contribution,* and *trust*, provided by those approaches. Fig. 3 shows how we combine these concepts and relations in our conceptual model.

4   Three-Layer Security Analysis Framework

Stakeholder's global security needs, which are captured as non-functional requirements, influence designs in all parts of the system. We propose to structure a system into three layers, and analyze security issues in each layer from a holistic viewpoint.

4.1   Three-Layer Structure

In this work, we have focused on three particular layers, which have received much attention from the security community. As shown in Fig. 2, at the most abstract layer, we consider the business layer, which highlights social dependencies, trusts, and business processes. At the next layer of abstraction, we consider software applications and their related IT infrastructures. Finally, we consider the physical infrastructure layer, which focuses on deployments of software applications and placements of devices.

As an essential part of the three-layer structure, we propose to analyze the requirements problem for each layer respectively. Each layer has its own requirements R, which are operationalized into proper specifications S under corresponding domain assumptions K. As shown in the left part of Fig. 2, we apply goal-oriented modeling to each of the three layers with the aim of analyzing their requirements problems respectively.

We base our three-layer security analysis approach on the proposed three-layer structure, which is shown in the right part of Fig. 2. Our approach starts with high-level stakeholder's security requirements; and then analyzes them throughout three layers with regard to layer-specific goal models; and finally generates a set of alternative global security treatments.

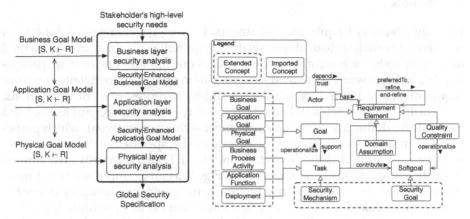

Fig. 2. Framework overview   **Fig. 3.** Conceptual model of the Goal Model within the three-layer framework

4.2 Three-Layer Conceptual Models

In this section, we specify conceptual models that we use for modeling and analyzing the three-layer architecture. Apart from concepts and relations we adopt from existing approaches, mentioned in Section 3, we further extend and make use of new concepts. Fig. 3 shows an overview of conceptual model of the three-layer framework, where the newly introduced concepts are highlighted in the dashed rectangles.

Extended Requirement Concepts and Relations. As we build goal models for different layers capturing different concerns, we specialize *Goal* into layer-specific goals that focus on a particular aspect. *Business Goal* represents stakeholder's high-level requirements for his business. *Application Goal* represents stakeholder's requirements regarding software applications that he uses to perform related business activities. *Physical Goal* represents stakeholder's requirements on physical devices and facilities that support execution of software. Accordingly, we assign *Task* in different layers with operational definitions. In the business layer, a task is a *Business Process Activity*; in the application layer, an *Application Function* is deemed as a task; and in the physical layer, a task is specialized into a *Deployment* action.

Apart from that, a number of relations are also proposed. *Operationalize* is a relation that presents how a goal/softgoal is operationalized into a task/quality constraint. This relation emphasizes the relationship between requirements and specifications, and indicates when a stakeholder's requirements are translated into operational specifications. For example, the business goal *Have current load info* shown in Fig. 1, which is desired by the *Energy Provider*, is operationalized into the task *Collect load info* in the same layer, which can accomplish this goal. *Support* is a cross-layer relation, which specifies a task designed in one layer is supported by requirements in the next layer down. Fig. 9 contains examples of this relation.

Extended Security Requirement Concepts. Chung [2] leverages non-functional requirements analysis to deal with security requirements, which are represented as *security goals*. Each security goal consists of one *sort* and one or more *parameters*. In our framework, we extend *security goals* to express more detailed security requirements, and introduce *security mechanisms* to represent security solutions.

Security Goal represents stakeholder's security needs with regard to asset and interval. We define a security goal as a specialization of softgoal, which particularly focuses on security issues. A security goal is specified in the format: *<importance><security attribute>[<asset>, <interval>]*. Take the security goal *Medium Integrity [energy consumption data, G2]* (in Fig. 1) as an example, its four dimensions together describe a security requirement "protecting integrity of energy consumption data during the execution interval of G2 to a medium degree".

- *Security Attribute* specifies a characteristic of security. Particularly, we adopt security attributes use in [17,4], which is shown in Fig. 5. The security attributes we consider in our work constitute a minimum set, which serves as a starting point and can be extended in the future.
- *Asset* is anything that has value to an organization, such as data, service. Fig. 4 shows an overview of all the types of assets that we have considered in our framework, as well as the interrelationships among them. Normally different assets are concerned in different layers. For example, we only consider *Service* and *Data* as assets in the business layer.
- *Interval* of a security goal indicates within which temporal interval the security goal is concerned. In this work, an interval is specified in terms of the execution period of a goal or task.
- *Importance* of a security goal indicates to which degree stakeholders want the security goal to be satisfied. We consider the value of importance within an enumeration {*very low, low, medium, high, very high*}.

Security Mechanism is a concrete mechanism provided by the "system-to-be" in order to achieve one or more security goals. We define the security mechanism

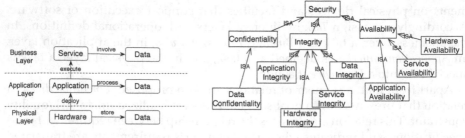

Fig. 4. Overview of assets   **Fig. 5.** Hierarchy of security attributes

as a specialization of task in goal model, which contributes to security goals and satisfies them. Thus, in our framework, security mechanisms are parts of specifications, and also influences requirements in its lower layers.

5   Security Analysis Methods

In this section, we propose a systematic process and a set of security analysis methods to guide security analysis both within one layer and across layers. Fig. 6 shows an overview of the analysis process, which starts from security analysis in the business layer and follows a top-down manner to propagate influences of security analysis in one layer to lower layers. Within one single layer, we refine and simplify security goals to identify concrete and critical ones, which are then operationalized into possible security mechanisms that are left to security analysts to select. After security analysis has been done for all layers, security treatments applied in each layer are synthesized to generate holistic security treatments.

We propose security analysis methods and corresponding transformation rules to guide the aforementioned analysis steps, which have been implemented using Datalog rules. We developed a prototype for a CASE tool, which automates some of the analysis steps as indicated in Fig. 6. Due to space limitation, we only describe and illustrate a small part of the transformation rules. A full list of the 23 transformation rules is available online [1]. In the reminder of this section, we describe details the proposed security analysis methods in subsections, each of which support one or several analysis task shown in Fig. 6.

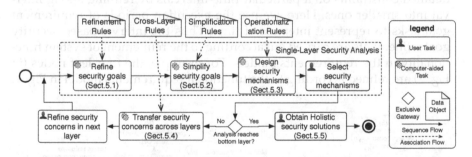

Fig. 6. An overview of the three-layer security requirements analysis process

5.1   Refinement Methods

A coarse-grained security goal is normally more difficult to analyze and operationalize than a fine-grained one, as it may be too abstract to be satisfied by specific security mechanisms. Thus, it is advisable for an analyst to refine a security goal till he obtains satisfiable ones. A security goal can be refined along

---

[1] http://goo.gl/Pd0TGw

any of its dimensions (security attributes, asset, or interval), i.e. there are three refinement methods. Fig. 7 shows an example of security goal refinements for security goal *Medium Integrity [energy consumption data, G2]* (Fig. 1). Note that a refinement process can be flexible in the sense that different refinement methods can be applied in any sequence and to any extent. Given the reference models that are shown in the left part of Fig. 7, the example presents only one possible way to refine the goal.

- **Security attributes-based refinement:** refining security goals via security attributes helps the security analysis to cover all possible aspects of security. According to the hierarchy of security attributes shown in Fig. 5, a security goal that talks about a high-level security attribute can be refined into several sub-security goals that talks about corresponding low-level security attributes. For example, in Fig. 7, the security goal *Medium Integrity [energy consumption data, G2]* is refined into four sub-security goals.
- **Asset-based refinement:** refinement of security goals can also be done by refining assets via *part-of* relations, which propagates a security goal on an asset to all its components. The *part-of* relation is an abstract one, which can be specialized into particular types of *part-of* relation of different conceptual models, such as data schema, software architecture model etc. For example, the security goal *Medium Data Integrity [energy consumption data, G2]* (Fig. 7) is refined according to the *part-of* relations among energy consumption data, water consumption data, and electricity data.
- **Interval-based refinement:** because an interval specifies the temporal period, for which a security goal is concerned, the security analyst can put more detailed constraints on a particular time intervals by refining a long interval into smaller ones. Here, we use the execution periods of requirement goal/tasks to represent intervals of time. Thus the interval-based security goal refinements are carried out according to the refinement of system functionality in the requirements models. For example, the four leaf nodes (in Fig. 7) are refined according to the functional requirements model in Fig. 1.

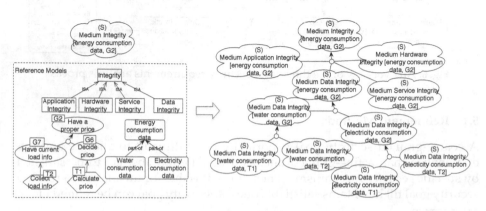

Fig. 7. Security goals refinements

5.2 Simplification Methods

When dealing with a large number of security goals, analysts may not have enough time to go through each of them to determine which is critical and requires further treatments. Especially as the refinement methods, which are intended to cover every potential facet of security goals, easily result in many detailed security goals. To release analysts from scrutinizing all security goals, we introduce simplification methods, which identify critical security goals that need to be treated and exclude others.

In order to determine the criticality of security goal, we consider two particular factors: **applicability** and **risk level**. The applicability specifies whether a security goal is sensible with regard to the content of the four dimensions of a security goal. The risk level identifies to which extent the satisfaction of a security goal is threatened. The criticality of a security goal is determined by considering: 1) If a security goal is applicable and its risk level is either high or very high, then we treat this security goal as a critical one, which is highlighted with a character "C". 2) All other security goals are deemed as non-critical and will be removed from following security analysis. It is worth noting that this criticality analysis can be adjusted depending on analyst time and the domain. For example, if analyst time allows, a security goal, which is at the medium risk level, could be adjusted as critical security goal.

For the analysis of applicability, we consider not only related requirements and simple specifications, but also detailed specifications, i.e. design information. For instance, how business activities are arranged, how application components interact with others, and where physical devices are placed. Based on this information, we propose layer-specific inference rules to determine the applicability of a security goal in one layer. For example, the security goal *Medium Data Integrity [water consumption data, T1]* (Fig. 7) is not suitable, because the asset *water consumption data* would not be changed during the execution of *T1*. Due to space limitation, in each layer we only present one rule as an example, which are shown in Table 1.

For the risk level analysis, we carry out a trust-based approach, which consider the trust between the owner of a security goal and the actor that potentially

Table 1. Rules for determining applicability of security goal

Rule	Rationale
BUS.A.1	If a business process activity takes a data asset as input, the confidentiality of this asset might be impaired within this activity. Thus, corresponding security goals are identified as applicable.
APP.S.1	If an application component is called by another component for a data asset, the integrity and confidentiality of that data asset may be impaired during functioning of that component. Thus, corresponding security goals are identified as applicable.
INF.S.1	If a hardware device stores a data asset, the integrity and confidentiality of that data asset may be impaired during deployment task of that device. Thus, corresponding security goals are identified as applicable.

impairs the security goal. For example, the maintainer of a smart meter may impair the integrity of that meter, if a customer owns a security goal that aims to protect the integrity of the smart meter, then our analysis considers to which extent the customer trusts the maintainer. Table 2 represents how we infer the risk level of security goals with regard to the trust level and the importance of security goals. Note that the letter L, M, H, V stands for low, medium, high, and very high level of risk respectively.

Table 2. Risk level evaluation matrix

Trust \ Importance	very low	low	medium	high	very high
very bad	H	H	V	V	V
bad	M	H	H	V	V
neutral	L	M	H	H	V
good	L	L	M	H	H
very good	L	L	L	M	H

5.3 Operationalization Methods

To bridge the gap between security requirements and security specifications within an individual layer, we propose operationalization methods which generate possible security mechanisms that could satisfy critical security goals. As security mechanism analysis and design requires additional security knowledge, which is normally not easy to obtain in reality, we exploit the power of security patterns to reuse security knowledge that tackles known security problems. Particularly, we survey existing work on security patterns [17,8,19], and extract the parts of them that are suitable for our security analysis framework. Note that the selection of security patterns is not intended to be exhaustive, and may evolve over time.

A security pattern consists of a security attribute and a security mechanism that is supposed to satisfy that security attribute. Each security mechanism can contribute to one or several security attributes, and we use *Make* and *Help* links to represent their contributions. For example, one security pattern shown in Fig. 8 is *Auditing* has a *Make* contribution to *Service Integrity*. According to these security patterns, when operationalizing a critical security goal, we identify security mechanisms that contribute to the security attribute of the security goal. It is worth noting that security patterns, shown in the Fig. 8, may also have either positive or negative influences on other non-functional goals, such as *Time, Cost*, which are documented in the specification of the security patterns.

5.4 Cross-Layer Analysis Methods

After finishing single-layer security analysis in one layer, indicated in Fig. 6, we analyze its influences on lower-layers. In our framework, the influences are

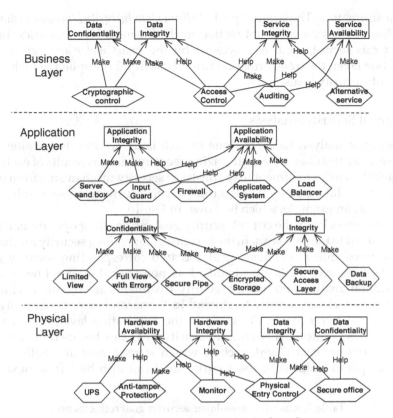

Fig. 8. Applicable security patterns in three layers

reflected in two ways, which require different analysis methods. Accordingly, a number of inference rules are proposed to automate the cross-layer transformations, parts of which are shown in Table 3.

Firstly, each of the security mechanisms should be transformed into at least one goal in the lower-layer goal model. Because security mechanisms are critical for satisfying security goals, additional security goals are derived to ensure correct implementations of the corresponding functional goals. Fig. 9(a) shows an example of this transformation. The security mechanism *Encryption* is transformed into a function goal of *smart meter application*, because that application is supposed to execute the *encryption* activity. Apart from this functional goal, the transformation also introduces two security goals, which concerns *application integrity* and *application availability* of the smart meter application during the execution of *encrypt data*. Note that the importance of these two new security goals is *Medium*, which is the same with the corresponding security goal in the business layer.

Secondly, if a security goal has not been fully satisfied in one layer, this security goal will be refined into security goals in next layer down according to the newly available information in that layer. Fig. 9(b) shows an example of this transformation. The security goal *Medium Data Integrity [energy consumption data, Measure energy data]* is not treated in the business layer. Considering the asset of this security goal is processed by the *smart meter application* in the application layer, the transformation rule *BUStoAPP.2* is applied, which results in two sub-security goals.

5.5 Global Security Analysis

After security analysis has been done in each layer, we can derive alternative global security treatments by synthesizing security analysis results of each layer. Each global security treatment may consist of security mechanisms from one or several layers. Take a snippet of the three-layer security analysis results of the smart grid as an example, which is shown in Fig. 10.

In the business layer, the critical security goal can be either operationalized as *Auditing* or left to the next layer. In the first case, the *Auditing* security mechanism is transformed into a functional goal and two corresponding security goals. As the two security goals are identified as non-critical after refinement and simplification analysis, no further security treatments are required. Thus, we derive the first global security treatment. In the second case, the security goal is refined into two sub-security goals in the application layer, one of which is identified as critical. This critical security goal can be operationalized as either *Firewall* or *Input Guard*, each of which starts a new alternative. Apart from the operationalization, the security goal can also be left to next layer,

Table 3. Rules for cross-layer security goal refinements

Rule	Rationale
BUStoAPP.1	If a security goal concerns a service asset, which is supported by an application component, then the security goal introduces security goals that concern the integrity and availability of that application.
BUStoAPP.2	If an untreated security goal that concerns data confidentiality or data integrity targeting at a business process activity, which is supported by an application in the application layer, then this security goal will be refined to sub-goals that concern corresponding applications.

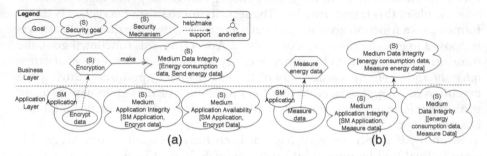

Fig. 9. Examples of security transformation

which further introduces another two alternatives. Finally, we derive 5 global security treatments in this example. Among these alternatives, the *Alt.3* contains a security mechanism from only one layer, i.e. *Input Guard*; while the *Alt.2* contains two security mechanisms from two different layers, i.e. *Firewall, Anti-tamper protection*.

6   Related Work

NFR-Based Requirements Analysis. Chung proposes to treat security requirements as a class of NFRs, and apply a process-oriented approach to analyze security requirements [2]. In a subsequent work, Chung and Supakkul integrate NFRs with FRs in the UML use case model [3], which enable NFRs to be refined through functional requirement models. Another complementary work done by Gross and Yu propose to connect NFRs to designs via patterns [7]. However, all of these NFR-based approaches mainly focus on information system analysis, and lack of supporting requirements analysis in the business layer and the physical layer.

Security Requirement Analysis. A large number of security requirement analysis approaches have been proposed over last two decades. Most of these approaches focus on analyzing security requirements with regard to a particular aspect of information system. There are approaches that focus on the social and

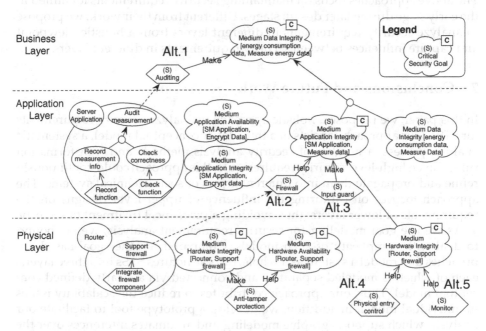

Fig. 10. A snippet of three-layer security analysis result of the smart grid example

organizational aspect. Mouratidis et al. [13] capture security intentions of stake-holders and interdependence among stakeholders; Giorgini et al. [6] investigate social relationships by integrating trust and ownership into security analysis; Liu et al. [11] analyze organizational risks by considering dependencies among social actors. Another branch of work deals with security requirements for business process. Rodríguez et al. [15] propose an extention of UML activity diagram to model security requirements within business process model, as well as a method that guides construction of the secure business process models. Herrmann et al. [9] propose a systematic process to elicit and analyze security requirements from business processes models. Most work is dedicated to analyzing security requirements of software, such as Attack Tree [18], Misuse case [20], and obstacle analysis [21]. All of these approaches are complementary to our approaches, as each of them could fit into one layer of our framework.

From Security Requirements to System Design. A number of approaches have been proposed to transform security requirements captured in the high-abstraction level to the security design in the low-abstraction level in order to maintain security requirements throughout the whole life-cycle of system development. Mouratidis and Jürjen [14] translate security requirements into design by combining Security Tropos with UMLsec. Menzel et al. [12] propose an approach that transfers security requirements, which are captured at the business process layer, to security configuration for service-based systems by using patterns. Similarly, Rodríguez [16] et al. apply the MDA technique to transform secure business process model into analysis class diagram and use case diagram. The above approaches focus on maintaining security requirements identified in the early stage during later design stages. Different from their work, we propose to analyze security requirements in different layers from a holistic viewpoint and capture influences between security requirements in different layers.

7   Conclusions and Future Work

In this paper, we propose a holistic approach to analyze security requirements for STSs. Our approach consists of a three-layer conceptual model, a systematic analysis process, a number of security analysis methods and transformation rules. Given high-level security requirements, this approach could continuously refine and propagate them into different layers of socio-technical systems. The approach focuses on capturing the influence of upper-layer designs on the requirements of lower layers, thus avoiding a piece-meal treatment of security.

As we use goal modeling for security requirement analysis, we are bound to deal with complexity of such models. Compared to other goal-based approaches that model a system as a whole, ours structures STSs into three layers, each of which is modeled separately and connected via a clearly defined conceptual model. Thus, our approach contributes to reduce the scalability issues in individual model. In addition, we develop a prototype tool to facilitate our analysis, which supports graphic modeling and automates inferences over the transformation rules. However, our approach has limitations on its evaluation.

So far, our approach is only applied to a single scenario of the Smart Grid case, which is an illustrative example rather than a practical evaluation.

In the future, we plan to extend our framework by incorporating real security regulations and laws, such as ISO standards, in order to provide more practical and grounded security analysis. Moreover, the security patterns we leveraged during security goal operationalization should be updated in light of recent advances in the field [19] synchronized with the cutting edge of that field. Finally, with the help of the prototype, we intend to apply our approach to a practical case study that has a reasonable scale to evaluate and further improve our work.

Acknowledgements. This work was supported in part by ERC advanced grant 267856, titled "Lucretius: Foundations for Software Evolution".

References

1. Carpenter, M., Goodspeed, T., Singletary, B., Skoudis, E., Wright, J.: Advanced metering infrastructure attack methodology. InGuardians White Paper (2009)
2. Chung, L.: Dealing with security requirements during the development of information systems. In: Rolland, C., Cauvet, C., Bodart, F. (eds.) CAiSE 1993. LNCS, vol. 685, pp. 234–251. Springer, Heidelberg (1993)
3. Chung, L., Supakkul, S.: Representing nfrs and frs: A goal-oriented and use case driven approach. In: Dosch, W., Lee, R.Y., Wu, C. (eds.) SERA 2004. LNCS, vol. 3647, pp. 29–41. Springer, Heidelberg (2006)
4. Firesmith, D.: Specifying reusable security requirements. Journal of Object Technology 3(1), 61–75 (2004)
5. Flick, T., Morehouse, J.: Securing the smart grid: next generation power grid security. Elsevier (2010)
6. Giorgini, P., Massacci, F., Zannone, N.: Security and trust requirements engineering. In: Aldini, A., Gorrieri, R., Martinelli, F. (eds.) FOSAD 2005. LNCS, vol. 3655, pp. 237–272. Springer, Heidelberg (2005)
7. Gross, D., Yu, E.: From non-functional requirements to design through patterns. Requirements Engineering 6(1), 18–36 (2001)
8. Hafiz, M., Adamczyk, P., Johnson, R.E.: Organizing security patterns. IEEE Software 24(4), 52–60 (2007)
9. Herrmann, P., Herrmann, G.: Security requirement analysis of business processes. Electronic Commerce Research 6(3-4), 305–335 (2006)
10. Jureta, I., Borgida, A., Ernst, N., Mylopoulos, J.: Techne: Towards a new generation of requirements modeling languages with goals, preferences, and inconsistency handling. In: Proc. of RE 2010, pp. 115–124 (2010)
11. Liu, L., Yu, E., Mylopoulos, J.: Security and privacy requirements analysis within a social setting. In: Proc. of RE 2003, Monterey, California, pp. 151–161 (2003)
12. Menzel, M., Thomas, I., Meinel, C.: Security requirements specification in service-oriented business process management. In: Proceedings of International Conference on Availability, Reliability and Security, ARES 2009, pp. 41–48. IEEE (2009)
13. Mouratidis, H., Giorgini, P.: A natural extension of tropos methodology for modelling security. In: Proc. of the Agent Oriented Methodologies Workshop (OOPSLA 2002). Citeseer, Seattle (2002)
14. Mouratidis, H., Jurjens, J.: From goal-driven security requirements engineering to secure design. International Journal of Intelligent System 25(8), 813–840 (2010)

15. Rodríguez, A., Fernández-Medina, E., Trujillo, J., Piattini, M.: Secure business process model specification through a uml 2.0 activity diagram profile. Decision Support Systems 51(3), 446–465 (2011)
16. de Rodríguez, G.I.G.R., Fernández-Medina, E., Piattini, M.: Semi-formal transformation of secure business processes into analysis class and use case models: An mda approach. Information and Software Technology 52(9), 945–971 (2010)
17. Scandariato, R., Yskout, K., Heyman, T., Joosen, W.: Architecting software with security patterns. Tech. rep., KU Leuven (2008)
18. Schneier, B.: Attack trees. Dr. Dobb's Journal 24(12), 21–29 (1999)
19. Schumacher, M., Fernandez-Buglioni, E., Hybertson, D., Buschmann, F., Sommerlad, P.: Security Patterns: Integrating security and systems engineering. John Wiley & Sons, (2013)
20. Sindre, G., Opdahl, A.L.: Eliciting security requirements with misuse cases. Requirements Engineering 10(1), 34–44 (2005)
21. Van Lamsweerde, A., Letier, E.: Handling obstacles in goal-oriented requirements engineering. IEEE Transactions on Software Engineering 26(10), 978–1005 (2000)
22. Yu, E.: Towards modelling and reasoning support for early-phase requirements Engineering, pp. 226–235. IEEE Computer Soc. Press (1997)
23. Zave, P., Jackson, M.: Four dark corners of requirements engineering. ACM Trans. Softw. Eng. Methodol. 6(1), 1–30 (1997)

IT Risk Management with Markov Logic Networks

Janno von Stülpnagel[1], Jens Ortmann[1], and Joerg Schoenfisch[2]

[1] Softplant GmbH
Agnes-Pockels-Bogen 1
80992 Munich, Germany
{janno.stuelpnagel,jens.ortmann}@softplant.de
http://www.softplant.de/
[2] Research Group Data and Web Science
University of Mannheim, Germany
joerg@informatik.uni-mannheim.de
http://dws.informatik.uni-mannheim.de

Abstract. We present a solution for modeling the dependencies of an IT infrastructure and determine the availability of components and services therein using Markov logic networks (MLN). MLNs offer a single representation of probability and first-order logic and are well suited to model dependencies and threats. We identify different kinds of dependency and show how they can be translated into an MLN. The MLN infrastructure model allows us to use marginal inference to predict the availability of IT infrastructure components and services. We demonstrate that our solution is well suited for supporting IT Risk management by analyzing the impact of threats and comparing risk mitigation efforts.

Keywords: IT Risk management, IT Infrastructure, Markov logic networks, Availability.

1 Introduction

IT risk management tries to find, analyze and reduce unacceptable risks in the IT infrastructure. Most commonly risk is defined as a set of triplets, each triplet consisting of a scenario, its probability and its potential impact [1]. In the IT environment these scenarios are typically called threats.

If a new threat surfaces, the IT risk management needs to asses its probability and evaluate its potential impact. Today's IT infrastructure has complex dependencies and a threat to a single component can threaten a whole network. Furthermore, single threats often have a very low probability but the combination of many threats can be a major risk to an IT infrastructure. Therefore, it is not enough to look at infrastructure components individually to determine the possible impact of a threat. While each year a huge number of new threats surfaces, old threats do not vanish [2].

A fast response to a new threat is important to minimize the chance of exploitation. However, a manual threat analysis takes time. The complexity of

M. Jarke et al. (Eds.): CAiSE 2014, LNCS 8484, pp. 301–315, 2014.

today's IT infrastructure provides many indirect ways a single threat can affect different IT services and each must be analyzed. At the same time, the number of new threats is increasing, which leaves even less time to evaluate each new threat [3]. A semi-automated approach allows an easier handling of this complexity, but to our knowledge there exists none that incorporates dependencies and combinations of multiple threats. Even the tools to monitor and report risk are still in a premature state and there is a demand for tool supported risk assessment [4]. While the measurement of IT infrastructure availability is already part of IT service management [5], it is only moderately used in IT risk management [4].

Our approach has two major features. First, it employs a reusable top-level model of the infrastructure dependencies. Second, the measured availabilities are added to each infrastructure component. The use of measured availabilities frees us from the need to model each measured threat manually. If a new threat surfaces, it can be added to the model and expected changes to the availabilities can be calculated. In this paper, we focus on impacts that make infrastructure components unavailable.

We start our approach by creating a dependency graph of the central components and services. To predict availabilities of IT components and services we need a way to represent (1) the logic of dependency of IT infrastructure, (2) probabilistic values for availabilities and (3) new threats. The dependencies in IT infrastructure can easily be modeled with first-order logic, but, first-order logic alone has no way to calculate how a threat influences the probability that an infrastructure component is available.

Markov logic networks (MLN)[6] offer a single representation of probability and first-order logic by adding weights to formulas. Together with a set of constants, the MLN specifies a probability distribution over possible worlds. Marginal inference computes the probability for specific values of variables in these possible worlds.

Thereby, we can create a reusable IT infrastructure model that includes infrastructure dependencies and measured availability. The model can be used to calculate a prediction how new threats affect the availability of IT components in an IT infrastructure. This provides a fast and quantitative solution to determine if a new threat is acceptable or needs to be mitigated.

We demonstrate and evaluate our solution in a case study where we implement the MLN for a small part of an IT infrastructure. We show how the change of availabilities through a new threat can be predicted and how to analyze a risk mitigation approach for this threat.

2   Background

2.1   Markov Logic Networks

Markov logic networks generalize first-order logic and probabilistic graphical models by allowing soft and hard first-order formulas [6]. Hard formulas are regular first-order formulas, which have to be fulfilled in every possible world. Soft formulas have weights that support worlds in which they are satisfied,

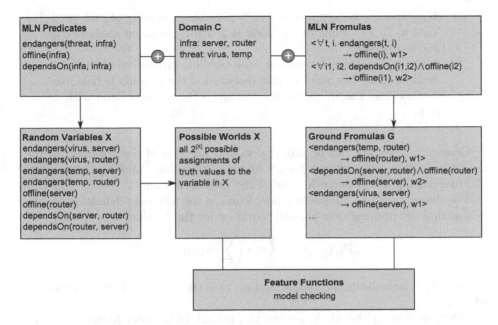

Fig. 1. The diagram describes the grounding of a Markov network. The grounded formulas G are generated by substituting each occurrence of every variable in the MLN Formulas with constants of the domain C. The possible worlds X are generated by giving all possible groundings of each predicate. Both the possible worlds X and the grounded formulas G are checked and provided with a value 1 if there are true and 0 otherwise. (Adapted from [7]).

but they do not need to, or in case of negative weights even should not, be satisfied. The probability of a possible world, one that satisfies all hard formulas, is proportional to the exponential sum of the weights of the soft formulas that are satisfied in that world. This corresponds to the common representation of Markov networks as log-linear model [6].

An MLN is a template for constructing a Markov network. Figure 1 illustrates the structure of a MLN. For each set of constants, there is a different Markov network, following the rules given in the MLN. Markov logic makes the assumption that different constants refer to different objects (unique name assumption) and the domain consists only of those constant and that no other objects (closed world assumption). An atom is a formula that consists of a single predicate and a grounding substitutes each occurrence of every variable in a formula with a constant. A set of grounded atoms is called a possible world.

An MLN L is a set of pairs $\langle F_i, w_i \rangle$, where F_i is a first-order logic formula and w_i is a real numbered weight [6]. The MLN L, combined with a finite set of constants $C = \{c_1, c_2, ...c_{|C|}\}$, defines a ground Markov network $M_{L,C}$ as follows:

1. $M_{L,C}$ has one binary node for each possible grounding of each predicate in L. The value of the node is 1 if the grounded atom is true and 0 otherwise.
2. $M_{L,C}$ contains one feature for each possible grounding of each formula F_i in L. The value of this feature 1 if the formula is true, and 0 otherwise. The weight of the feature is the w_i associated with F_i in L.

[6, p. 113]

Generally, a feature can be any real-valued function of the variables of the network. In this paper we use binary features, essentially making the value of the function equal to the truth value of the grounded atom.

The description as a log-linear model leads to the following definition for the probability distribution over possible worlds x for the Markov network $M_{L,C}$:

$$P(X = x) = \frac{1}{Z} exp\left(\sum_i w_i n_i(x) \right) \tag{1}$$

where Z is a normalization constant and $n_i(x)$ is the number of true groundings of F_i in x.

When describing the MLN we use the format $\langle first\ order\ formula, weight \rangle$. Hard formulas have infinite weights. If the weight is $+\infty$ the formula must always be true, if the weight is $-\infty$ it must always be false. A soft formula with weight 0 has equal probabilities for being satisfied in a world or not.

There are two types of inference with Markov logic: maximum a posteriori (MAP) inference and marginal inference. MAP inference finds the most probable world given some evidence. Marginal inference computes the posteriori probability distribution over the values of all variables given some evidence. We use marginal inference, which allows us to determine the probability distribution of the infrastructure variables for the offline predicate and thereby predict the future availability.

Most query engines require the input to be split into two parts: the formulas (also called program) and the known evidence data.

2.2 Availability

Achieving high availability, defined as up to 5 minutes unavailability per year, is a longstanding goal in the IT industry [8]. Continuous monitoring of availability is part of IT service management best practices like the Information Technology Infrastructure Library (ITIL) [5]. We define availability as the probability that a system is working properly and reachable. The availability of a system can be determined as follows:

$$Availability = \frac{Uptime}{Uptime + Downtime} \tag{2}$$

Unavailability is the inverse of availability:

$$Unavailability = 1 - Availability \tag{3}$$

We distinguish between measured availability and predicted availability. The measured availability of important infrastructure components and services is typically measured over a one-year time-frame. The predicted availability is an estimation how the availability will be, under the assumption of specific changes in the threat-landscape or the infrastructure. We use marginal inference in Markov logic networks to calculate the predicted availabilities in our approach.

3 Predicting Unavailability with Dependency Networks and MLNs

For the threat analysis, we need a dependency model, data on availability and threats. We show how this information can be combined and transformed into evidence for our Markov logic network. Afterwards we discuss the networks function.

3.1 Dependency Network for IT Infrastructures

The basis of our threat analysis is a dependency network. The dependency network models how the availability of one infrastructure component depends on that of other components.

We use this network to calculate how a new threat endangering one component propagates through the network and reduces the availability of other components. The nodes of the network are the high-level infrastructure components and services, for which availability information exists. There are three types of edges: Specific and generic dependencies are modeled as directed edges; redundancies are modeled as undirected edges.

A specific dependency means that a component needs another specific component and cannot be available without it. For example, an email service depends on the router and is unavailable if the router is unavailable.

A generic dependency means that a component needs at least one of a group of redundant components. For example, given two redundant servers realizing an email service, the email service is available if at least one of the servers is running. We model this with an edge between the email service node and each server node.

A redundancy edge means that two components provide the same functionality and one of them can, without manual reconfiguration, provide the work of both. It is possible to have more than two redundant components; in this case, they must be fully connected with redundancy edges. Furthermore, no component should have a redundancy edge to itself. We only consider fully redundant systems; redundancies that are more complex can be modeled with typed redundancies. An example for a dependency network can be seen in Figure 2 in Section 4.

The dependency network can be translated easily into evidence for the MLN. Each edge type translates into a predicate and each node translates into a constant. The symmetry of redundancy and the transitive behavior of the dependencies are modeled as formulas in the MLN program.

3.2 Markov Logic Network for IT Risk Management

Our Markov logic networks has three types of variables and six predicates. The different types of variables are `infra`[1] as the type of all infrastructure components and services, `threat` as the type of all threats and `float` is a numeric value. The predicate `specificDependency(infra, infra)` models that the first infrastructure component depends on the second infrastructure component. `genericDependency(infra, infra)` means that the first infrastructure component depends on the second infrastructure component or a redundant alternative. `redundancy(infra,infra)` models redundant components. `endangered(threat, infra, float)` expresses that a threat endangers an infrastructure component with a weight of `float`. `measuredUnavailability(infra, float)` encodes the measured unavailability as weight `float`, and `offline (infra)` states that a component is not available.

The only hidden predicate, a predicate without full evidence, is `offline` (`infra`). It is therefore the only predicate we query and whose variable distribution we determine through sampling. The variable distribution is used to determine the offline probability of an infrastructure component, i.e. the predicted unavailability.

All other predicates are observed, that means all grounded atoms that are not listed in the evidence are false. Each infrastructure component has an availability. If the availability is not specified explicitly the MLN sampling uses a weight of zero, roughly corresponding to an a priori availability of 0.5.

In its basic form, our MLN program comprises five formulas:

$$\langle \texttt{specificDependency(i1,i2)} \land \texttt{offline(i2)} \Rightarrow \texttt{offline(i1)}, \infty \rangle \qquad (4a)$$

$$\langle \texttt{genericDependency(i1,i2)} \land \texttt{redundancy(i2,i3)}$$
$$\land \texttt{offline(i2)} \land \texttt{offline(i3)} \Rightarrow \texttt{offline(i1)}, \infty \rangle \quad (4b)$$

$$\langle \texttt{redundancy(i1,i2)} \Rightarrow \texttt{redundancy(i2,i1)}, \infty \rangle \qquad (4c)$$

$$\langle \texttt{measuredUnavailability(i1,conf)} \Rightarrow \texttt{offline(i1)}, \texttt{conf} \rangle \qquad (4d)$$

$$\langle \texttt{endangered(t,i1,conf)} \Rightarrow \texttt{offline(i1)}, \texttt{conf} \rangle \qquad (4e)$$

Formula 4a is a hard formula that invalidates every world where infrastructure component `i2` is offline and infrastructure component `i1` is online, if there is a specific dependency between them.

Formula 4b does the same as Formula 4a for generic dependencies. Provided `i1` is generically dependent on `i2` and `i3`, which are redundant, it invalidates every world in which `i1` is online while `i2` and `i3` are offline.

Formula 4b supports only two redundant infrastructure components, but formulas for more than two redundant components can be constructed analogously.

---

[1] In the following we use type writer fonts like `infra` for statements in MLNs.

These analogous formulas need their own generic dependency predicate (e.g. genericDependencyTwo, genericDependencyThree, ...). This prevents that, for example, the formula for a two-component dependency influences the formula for three-component dependency. Though it is possible to create a first-order logic formula that works with any number of redundant components, not all MLN solvers support the full expressiveness of first-order logic. Hence, we chose this workaround for better solver support.

The hard Formula 4c models the symmetry of redundancy: if i1 is redundant to i2 then i2 is also redundant to i1.

Formulas 4d and 4e allow giving each evidence a separate weight. An evidence with measuredUnavailability("Server 1", -3) translates into ⟨ offline (" Server 1"), -3⟩. Formula 4d is used to assign an individual measured unavailability to each infrastructure component.

Formula 4e works analogously. The additional parameter threat t allows specifying more than one threat per infrastructure component. The last two formulas can be combined into one formula, but we think modeling is easier when not mixing single threats with estimated probabilities and quantitatively determined availabilities. The source-code for our MLN program is given in Appendix A.

The weights for the measured availabilities can be found manually by iteratively calculating the probabilities and correcting the weights. In some cases, finding the correct weights is not trivial [9], but there are efficient learning algorithms for MLNs [6].

The weights for new threats need to be estimated. We propose involving a domain expert in the estimation of how much the availability of the directly affected infrastructure component should be reduced. This allows us to learn a weight for the new threat and to determine how the new threat indirectly affects the availability of other components.

3.3   Summary of the Approach

We start by creating a dependency network of all major infrastructure components and services. We transform this network into evidence for our MLN program. We collect unavailability information for each node and use a learning algorithm to add the corresponding weights to the evidence. By adding threats, the resulting evidence can be used to determine the effect of a local threat to the whole network.

4   Case Study

A small case study demonstrates the usability of our solution. There exist several open-source inference engines for Markov logic networks, e.g. Alchemy[2], Tuffy[3], and RockIt[4]. We use RockIt for the calculations in our study.

---

[2] http://alchemy.cs.washington.edu
[3] http://hazy.cs.wisc.edu/hazy/tuffy
[4] https://code.google.com/p/rockit

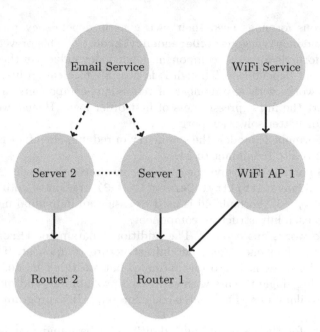

Fig. 2. The dependency network of the small IT infrastructure of our case study. Solid arrows indicate specific dependencies, dashed arrows symbolize generic dependencies and the dotted line represents a redundancy.

The base configuration of the dependency network (see Figure 2) has seven nodes: An Email Service is realized by two redundant servers Server 1 and Server 2. Each of the servers depends on its own router (Router 1 and Router 2, respectively). One of the two routers is used by a WiFi Access Point (AP), which offers a WiFi Service. The corresponding evidence is listed in Table 1, the MLN program can be found in the Appendix A. The infrastructure components and services have the measured unavailabilities given in column Scenario 1 in Table 2 and the corresponding, learned weights are shown in Table 3.

We can now add a new threat: Router 1 threatens to overheat because construction work cut off the normal airflow to the room. The predicate expressing this is endangered("Overheating", "Router 1", 3). By using marginal inference, we get the offline probabilities, which give us the predicted unavailabilities shown in column Scenario 2 in Table 2.

The threat increased the unavailability of Router 1 by 0.0095. This has the effect that the unavailability of WiFi AP 1, Server 1 and WiFi Service also increases by 0.0095. On the other hand, the unavailability of Email Service remains unaffected, because it can use Server 2, which depends on Router 2. The changes can be seen in Figure 3.

The cooling problem can only be solved through expensive additional construction work; therefore, other risk mitigation approaches should be investigated.

A cheap risk mitigation approach is to provide a second, redundant WiFi AP 2, which uses Router 2. We update the infrastructure model (Table 4) and

Table 1. The predicates for the dependency network of the base configuration

```
genericDependency("Email Service","Server 1")
genericDependency("Email Service","Server 2")
redundancy("Server 1","Server 2")
specificDependency("Server 1","Router 1")
specificDependency("Server 2","Router 2")
specificDependency("WiFi AP 1","Router 1")
specificDependency("WiFi Service","WiFi AP 1")
```

Table 2. The unavailabilities for the different scenarios of the case study. Scenario 1 is the base configuration, Scenario 2 is the base configuration with the overheating threat, Scenario 3 is the configuration with a second WiFi AP, and Scenario 4 is the configuration with a second WiFi AP and the overheating threat.

Component	Scenario 1 (measured unavailabilities)	Scenario 2 (predicted unavailabilities)	Scenario 3 (measured unavailabilities)	Scenario 4 (predicted unavailabilities)
Email Service	0.0010	0.0010	0.0010	0.0010
Router 1	0.0005	0.0100	0.0005	0.0099
Router 2	0.0010	0.0009	0.0010	0.0009
Server 1	0.0015	0.0110	0.0015	0.0109
Server 2	0.0020	0.0019	0.0020	0.0019
WiFi Service	0.0015	0.0110	0.0015	0.0015
WiFi AP 1	0.0010	0.0105	0.0010	0.0104
WiFi AP 2	-	-	0.0010	0.0010

set the unavailability for the new WiFi AP 2 equal to that of WiFi AP 1 (see Scenario 3 in Table 2). Again we use the MLN program from Appendix A and learn the corresponding weights (Table 3).

Now we can add again the threat endangered("Overheating", "Router 1", 3) and calculate the unavailabilities (see Scenario 4 in Table 2) with the help of marginal inference. The unavailability of Router 1 increases by 0.0094. The unavailability of Server 1 and WiFi AP 1 also increases again but this time the unavailability of the WiFi Service remains unaffected. The changes are also shown in Figure 3.

We can see that a second WiFi Access Point would successfully mitigate the risk for the WiFi Service.

The slightly different increase of the unavailability in the two scenarios has two reasons. First, the learning algorithm provides only an approximation of the correct weights for the unavailabilities. Second, the number of evidence (and thereby the number of possible worlds) changed between the two scenarios, but the weight of the threat remained the same. As can be seen in Figure 3, these effects are small enough to not influence the overall result.

The case study also demonstrates that the results of MLN marginal inference are not exactly the results one would expect from regular probability calculation.

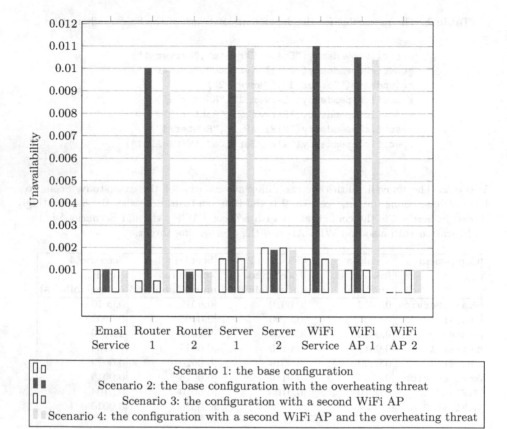

Fig. 3. The change of the unavailabilities in the different scenarios of our case study

However, as we demonstrate, the MLN calculation is well suited for the calculation of threat propagation.

5   Related Work

There exist alternative approaches that combine logic and probability (see [10] for an overview). Here we limit the discussion of related work to Bayesian logic programs (BLP) [11]. Because of the usage of Bayesian networks in combination with risk analysis [12], BLPs seem to be the most prevalent alternative to MLNs.

Bayesian logic programs aim at resolving some limitations of Bayesian networks, among others the essentially propositional nature of their representations. Therefore, Bayesian logic programs unify Bayesian networks with logic programming. Each Bayesian logic program represents a Bayesian network by mapping the atoms in the least Herbrand model, which constitutes the semantics of the logic program, to nodes of the Bayesian network.

Table 3. The learned weights for the measured unavailabilities in the base configuration

```
measuredUnavailability("Email Service",-6.907250)
measuredUnavailability("Router 1",6.933551)
measuredUnavailability("Router 2",0.001400)
measuredUnavailability("Server 1",-6.908549)
measuredUnavailability("Server 2",-6.905200)
measuredUnavailability("WiFi AP 1",-0.023739)
measuredUnavailability("WiFi Service",-7.590026)
```

Table 4. The predicates for the dependency network with a second WiFi AP.

```
genericDependency("Email Service","Server 1")
genericDependency("Email Service","Server 2")
genericDependency("WiFi Service","WiFi AP 1")
genericDependency("WiFi Service","WiFi AP 2")
redundancy("Server 1","Server 2")
redundancy("WiFi AP 1","WiFi AP 2")
specificDependency("Server 1","Router 1")
specificDependency("Server 2","Router 2")
specificDependency("WiFi AP 1","Router 1")
specificDependency("WiFi AP 2","Router 2")
```

A BLP computes the probability for one query from the known probabilities in the resolution to the query statement. In contrast, MLNs infer all probabilities from a given complete set of weights.

Furthermore, there exist efficient solvers for MLNs and they have been applied to a wide range of problems, for instance in requirements-driven root cause analysis [13] and data integration [14].

Another advantages of MLNs over other probabilistic logic approaches is that the Markov networks, constructed through the MLN, are undirected graphs. This has the effect that changing the weights at one node will influence the whole graph and thereby the results. Hence, it is more likely to find new relationships between elements that where not explicitly modeled. On the other side, this has the disadvantage that it is harder to isolate a single variable. Unlike BLPs [11], MLNs have very simple semantics while theoretically keeping the expressive power of first-order logic [6].

There are other approaches that use dependency networks to determine the global impact of a threat. The approach of Zambon et al. [15] focuses on downtime and temporal aspects but unlike our approach it is qualitative and considers only one threat at a time. The approach of Breu et al. [16] uses the number of attacks as the key quantitative concept and models each threat separately but does not take redundant components into account.

Table 5. The new learned weights for the configuration with a second WiFi AP.

```
measuredUnavailability("Email Service",-6.906300)
measuredUnavailability("Router 1",6.909860)
measuredUnavailability("Router 2",10.333070)
measuredUnavailability("Server 1",-6.905100)
measuredUnavailability("Server 2",-6.888114)
measuredUnavailability("WiFi AP 1",-7.600700)
measuredUnavailability("WiFi AP 2",-10.364995)
measuredUnavailability("WiFi Service",-6.500500)
```

6   Discussion

To our knowledge this paper presents the first application of Markov logic networks to risk management. We have shown that MLNs generally allow an automatic calculation of risks, exemplified by the probability of availability, in an IT infrastructure.

As described in the case study, our solution allows us to efficiently calculate how a threat affects an infrastructure network. We have demonstrated how the analysis can be used to compare changes in the infrastructure and thereby support the risk mitigation. Our approach has two major features. First, it employs a top-level model for the dependency network, which can be easily maintained and reused. Second, it uses the measured availabilities of the infrastructure components and thereby creates a quantitative infrastructure model without modeling every threat separately. This also has the advantage that the manual work for risk analysis is greatly reduced.

In most cases, risk assessments are performed regularly, e.g. every six month. At the same time, the link between availability and risk management is seldom used and technological support for IT risk management was identified as one area where improvement is needed [4].

Our approach enhances risk assessment by providing an automation and allowing reuse of earlier work. By using the availability measurements of the IT service management as quantitative input and provide results in the same way, we allow an easy communication of IT risk.

However, there are some limitations, caveats and lessons learned from using Markov logic networks, and in particular marginal inference in MLNs.

It is not possible to simply add or remove infrastructure components or services to or from an existing model. This is so because the weight of the new component or service influences the total weight of the model, which in turn affects the probabilities of all statements. In the current state of our solution, adding or removing a new infrastructure component requires relearning all weights.

Even though MLNs use a quite simple representation, modeling with them is not as straightforward as it may seem [7]. Each variable, every literal that involves a hidden predicate, in the MLN must have a weight. For instance in our case study this means that each node in the dependency network needs a `measuredUnavailability(infra, float)`. This requires an accurate specification of the MLN evidence. However, since the measurement of the availability is a best practice [5], the necessary data should be available.

Without an understanding of the normalization of weights and the log-linear model, the relationship between the weights and the resulting probabilities of the marginal inference can be counterintuitive. Changing the weight of a single formula shifts the relative weights of the possible worlds according to where the formula is true. This results in sometimes unexpected changes in probabilities of statements. Therefore, we usually learn the weights for the measured unavailabilities. While modeling with MLNs it is also important to have in mind that the weight of a soft formula does not directly correspond to a specific universal probability for this formula. The probability depends on the whole MLN and the modeled domain, including the number of individuals in this domain.

A limitation of existing implementations for marginal inference is their use of sampling algorithms to calculate the probabilities. To determine the effect of threats with very low probabilities, which are quite common in risk management, sampling requires a high number of iterations. Threats with very small probabilities can provide the problem that their frequency is so low that they do not influence the availability measurement of a component. These threats can still be added manually through the predicate `endangered(threat,infra, float)`. To our knowledge, there is no alternative to sampling as the exact computation is too complex to be done for larger networks. However, it has the advantage that it allows us to choose how much time to invest into the accuracy of the probabilities. We reduce the problem of sampling with low probability by using the measured unavailability, as combination of many small threats and thereby are able to aggregate them to larger numbers.

While there are different MLN solvers, to our knowledge none of them supports full first-order logic. Because of the undecidability of first-order logic, this will most likely not change.

7   Conclusion

We have demonstrated how Markov logic networks (MLN) can be used to calculate the expected availabilities of infrastructure components and services. Our solution uses a combination of a dependency network, measured availabilities and a new threat information as basis for this calculation. We obtain the evidence for the MLN by constructing a dependency network and learning the weights for the measured availabilities. By adding a new threat and using marginal inference, we can predict availabilities of IT components under different threat conditions. This allows a faster and more quantitative risk analysis, which is essential for today's threat landscape, than a manual analysis. We have focused our work on how threats indirectly affect the whole network. Future work is needed in differentiating the impact. Not all services are equally important for the organization and there are other kinds of impact than taking an IT component offline, for instance compromising it or reducing its efficiency. We plan to further improve the solution by integrating existing data sources to automatically generate the dependency network.

Acknowledgement. This work has been partially supported by the German Federal Ministry of Economics and Technology (BMWI) in the framework of the Central Innovation Program SME (Zentrales Innovationsprogramm Mittelstand - ZIM) within the project "Risk management tool for complex IT infrastructures".

We are thankful to Christian Meilicke for helpful feedback and support.

References

1. Kaplan, S., Garrick, B.J.: On the quantitative definition of risk. Risk Analysis 1(1), 11–27 (1981)
2. European Union Agency for Network and Information Security: Enisa threat landscape mid year 2013. Technical report, European Union Agency for Network and Information Security (2013)
3. IBM X-Force: Trend and risk report 2012. Technical report, IBM X-Force (2013)
4. Ernst & Young: Managing it risk in a fast-changing environment. Technical report, Ernst & Young (2013)
5. Cabinet Office: ITIL Service Design. TSO (The Stationery Office) (2011)
6. Richardson, M., Domingos, P.: Markov logic networks. Machine Learning 62(1-2), 107–136 (2006)
7. Jain, D.: Knowledge engineering with markov logic networks: A review. In: Beierle, C., Kern-Isberner, G. (eds.) Proceedings of Evolving Knowledge in Theory and Applications. 3rd Workshop on Dynamics of Knowledge and Belief (DKB-2011) at the 34th Annual German Conference on Artificial Intelligence, KI-2011, Berlin, Germany, October 4. Informatik-Bericht, vol. 361, pp. 16–30. Fakultät für Mathematik und Informatik, FernUniversität in Hagen (2011)
8. Gray, J., Siewiorek, D.: High-availability computer systems. Computer 24(9), 39–48 (1991)
9. Jain, D., Kirchlechner, B., Beetz, M.: Extending markov logic to model probability distributions in relational domains. In: Hertzberg, J., Beetz, M., Englert, R. (eds.) KI 2007. LNCS (LNAI), vol. 4667, pp. 129–143. Springer, Heidelberg (2007)
10. Braz, R., Amir, E., Roth, D.: A survey of first-order probabilistic models. In: Holmes, D.E., Jain, L.C. (eds.) Innovations in Bayesian Networks. Studies in Computational Intelligence, vol. 156, pp. 289–317. Springer, Heidelberg (2008)
11. Kersting, K., De Raedt, L.: Bayesian logic programs. CoRR cs.AI/0111058 (2001)
12. Weber, P., Medina-Oliva, G., Simon, C., Iung, B.: Overview on bayesian networks applications for dependability, risk analysis and maintenance areas. Engineering Applications of Artificial Intelligence 25(4), 671–682 (2012)
13. Zawawy, H., Kontogiannis, K., Mylopoulos, J., Mankovskii, S.: Requirements-driven root cause analysis using markov logic networks. In: Ralyté, J., Franch, X., Brinkkemper, S., Wrycza, S. (eds.) CAiSE 2012. LNCS, vol. 7328, pp. 350–365. Springer, Heidelberg (2012)
14. Niepert, M., Noessner, J., Meilicke, C., Stuckenschmidt, H.: Probabilistic-logical web data integration. In: Polleres, A., d'Amato, C., Arenas, M., Handschuh, S., Kroner, P., Ossowski, S., Patel-Schneider, P. (eds.) Reasoning Web 2011. LNCS, vol. 6848, pp. 504–533. Springer, Heidelberg (2011)

15. Zambon, E., Etalle, S., Wieringa, R.J., Hartel, P.H.: Architecture-based qualitative risk analysis for availability of it infrastructures. Technical Report TR-CTIT-09-35, Centre for Telematics and Information Technology University of Twente, Enschede (September 2009)
16. Breu, R., Innerhofer-Oberperfler, F., Yautsiukhin, A.: Quantitative assessment of enterprise security system. In: Jakoubi, S., Tjoa, S., Weippl, E.R. (eds.) Third International Conference on Availability, Reliability and Security, ARES 2008, pp. 921–928. IEEE Computer Society (2008)
17. Noessner, J., Niepert, M., Stuckenschmidt, H.: Rockit: Exploiting parallelism and symmetry for map inference in statistical relational models. In: des Jardins, M., Littman, M.L. (eds.) Proceedings of the Twenty-Seventh AAAI Conference on Artificial Intelligence, Bellevue, Washington, USA, July 14-18. AAAI Press (2013)

A   RockIt MLN

For our MLN, we use the syntax of RockIt [17]. RockIt expects first order formulas in conjunctive normal form (CNF). An online version of RockIt is available here: http://executor.informatik.uni-mannheim.de/systems/rockit/

```
*specificDependency(infra,infra)
*genericDependency(infra,infra)
*redundancy(infra,infra)
*endangered(threat,infra,float_)
*measuredUnavailability(infra, float_)
offline(infra)

!specificDependency(i1,i2) v !offline(i2) v offline(i1).
!genericDependency(i1,i2) v !redundancy(i2,i3) v !offline(i2)
  v !offline(i3) v offline(i1).
!redundancy(i1,i2) v redundancy(i2,i1).
conf: !measuredUnavailability(i1, conf) v offline(i1)
conf: !endangered(t,i1,conf) v offline(i1)
```

Automating Data Exchange in Process Choreographies

Andreas Meyer[1], Luise Pufahl[1], Kimon Batoulis[1], Sebastian Kruse[1], Thorben Lindhauer[1], Thomas Stoff[1], Dirk Fahland[2], and Mathias Weske[1]

[1] Hasso Plattner Institute at the University of Potsdam
{Andreas.Meyer,Luise.Pufahl,Mathias.Weske}@hpi.uni-potsdam.de,
Firstname.Lastname@student.hpi.uni-potsdam.de
[2] Eindhoven University of Technology
d.fahland@tue.nl

Abstract. Process choreographies are part of daily business. While the correct ordering of exchanged messages can be modeled and enacted with current choreography techniques, no approach exists to describe and automate the exchange of data between processes in a choreography using messages. This paper describes an entirely model-driven approach for BPMN introducing a few concepts that suffice to model data retrieval, data transformation, message exchange, and correlation – four aspects of data exchange. For automation, this work utilizes a recent concept to enact data dependencies in internal processes. We present a modeling guideline to derive local process models from a given choreography; their operational semantics allows to correctly enact the entire choreography from the derived models only including the exchange of data. We implemented our approach by extending the *camunda BPM platform* with our approach and show its feasibility by realizing all service interaction patterns using only model-based concepts.

Keywords: Process Modeling, Data Modeling, Process Choreographies, Data Exchange, BPMN, SQL.

1 Introduction

In daily business, organizations interact with each other, e.g., concluding contracts or exchanging information. Fig. 1 describes an interaction between a customer and a supplier with respect to a request for a quote. The customer sends the *request* to a chosen supplier which internally processes it and sends the resulting *quote* as response which then is handled internally by the customer. An interaction between business processes of multiple organizations via message exchange is called *process choreography* [32]. The industry

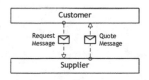

Fig. 1. Request for quote choreography

standard BPMN (Business Process Modeling and Notation) [20] provides the following concepts to model process choreographies. A *choreography diagram* describes the order of message *exchanges* between multiple participants from a global view, called *global choreography model*. The message exchanges are then refined into *send* and *receive activities* distributed over the different participants. This can be captured in *collaboration*

M. Jarke et al. (Eds.): CAiSE 2014, LNCS 8484, pp. 316–331, 2014.
© Springer International Publishing Switzerland 2014

diagrams describing how each participant's *public* process interacts with other participants [2], also called *local choreography model*. Deriving a local choreography from a global one is a non-trivial step; various techniques are required [7] including *locally enforcing* the order of globally specified message exchanges.

Typically, these two choreography models are used to globally agree on a contract about the messages exchanged and their order. In above example, both participants agreed that first the customer may send a request to the supplier which is then answered with a quote by the supplier. Based on the agreement, each participant has to implement its public process as a *private* process describing the executable part of this participant including the interactions with other participants as described in the choreography; this private process is called a *process orchestration* [13]. Existing approaches for deriving an orchestration for each participant from a choreography, such as the *Public-to-Private* approach [2], only cover the control-flow perspective of the contract: ensuring the correct *order* of messages. In the following, we address the correct *contents* of messages to achieve a correct *data exchange* that realizes the choreography.

Generally, organizations store their data in local databases that other choreography participants cannot access. These databases follow local data schemes which differ among the organizations. However, the interacting organizations want to exchange data and therefore have to provide the information to be sent in a format which is understood at the receiving side. Thus, an agreed exchange message format has to be part of the global contract mentioned above. For a successful process choreography, it has to be ensured that messages to be sent are provided correctly and that received messages are processed correctly *based on the global contract*. In more detail, three challenges arise:

C1—Data Heterogeneity. Interacting participants, such as our customer and supplier, each implement their own data schema for handling their private data. For sending a message to another participant, this local data has to be transformed into a message the recipient can understand. In turn, the received message has to be transformed into the local data schema to allow storing and processing by the recipient.

C2—Correlation. A participant may run *multiple instances* simultaneously. Therefore, messages arriving at the receiver side need to be correlated to the correct process instance to allow successful interaction.

C3—1:n Communication. In choreographies, there may be multiple participants of the same type, e.g., multiple suppliers, a customer sends a request for quote to. Thus, individual processes need to communicate with a multitude of (external) uniform participants.

Current choreography modeling languages such as BPMN do not provide concepts to solve C1-C3. Instead, each participant manually implements message creation and processing for their private process, which is error-prone, hard to maintain, and easily results in incompatibilities to other participants in the choreography.

In this paper, we describe a model-driven approach to automate the data exchange from process choreography models while maintaining existing control flow aspects to realize process choreographies. We utilize the industry standard BPMN and extend its choreography modeling by few but essential concepts for the data exchange. We describe a modeling guideline that shows how to utilize the new concepts for specifying details required to automate data exchange of a private orchestration model that is consistent to a public choreography model (the contract). We introduce operational semantics for the new modeling concepts which makes the orchestration models executable, and thus allows running the entire choreography purely model-based.

Thereby, we assume correctness of modeled choreographies, i.e., realizability [7], and correctness of data flow within each private process orchestration model, i.e., object life cycle conformance [14]. Further, we assume that all partners agreeing on the global contract, i.e., the structure of data objects, have the same understanding of the object's content, i.e., agree upon the co-domain for all data attributes. Following, no abnormal behavior of data exchanges and their control flow can occur.

The remainder of this paper is structured as follows. Section 2 discusses the requirements derived from above challenges. Subsequently, we explain the modeling guideline in Section 3 followed by the operational semantics allowing to execute the modeled choreographies directly from process model information in Section 4. In Section 5, we discuss our implementation and its feasibility for implementing all service interaction patterns purely model-based [3]. Section 6 is devoted to related work and Section 7 concludes the paper.

2   Requirements

The challenges C1-C3 described above give rise to specific requirements for automating data exchange in process choreography modeling and execution. We discuss these requirements and their possible realization in the following.

R1—Content of Message. Messages contain data of different types exchanged between participants. The involved participants have to commonly agree on the types of data and their format they want to exchange.

R2—Local Storage. The participants create and process data used for communication with other participants in their private processes. This needs to be stored and made available in their local databases.

R3—Message Provision. As the data provided in a message is local to the sender, the data must be adapted to the agreed format such that the recipient can interpret the message content.

R4—Message Routing. Multiple parties may wait for a message at a certain point in time. This requires to route the message to the correct recipient.

R5—Message Correlation. After being received by a participant, the message needs to be correlated to the activity instance which is capable to process the message content.

R6—Message Processing. Activities receiving messages have to extract data from the message and to transform it into the local data format usable within their processes.

Requirements R1, R2, R3, and R6 are basic features to realize C1; R4 and R5 originate in C3; and R5 also addresses C2.

Languages such as WSDL [27] use data modeling to specify message formats; we adopt these ideas to address R1. Requirements R2, R3, and R6 concern the processing of data in an orchestration. The approach in [16] allows to model and enact data dependencies in BPMN processes for create, read, update, and delete operations on multiple data objects – even in case of complex object relationships. For this, annotations on BPMN data objects are automatically transformed into SQL queries (R2). Further, data querying languages such as XQuery [30] allow to implement data transformations between a message and a local data model. In the following, we combine these approaches to specify message extraction (R3) and message storage (R6) in a purely model-based fashion. Languages such as BPEL [19] and BPMN [20] correlate a message to a process instances based on key attributes in the message; we adopt this idea to address R5. The next sections describe how to model process choreographies including details required to automate the data exchange so that data stored locally at the sender's side can be transmitted and stored in the receiver's local data model consistent with the global contract.

Requirement R4, the actual transmission of messages from sender to receiver, is abstracted from in choreography and process models and also not discussed in this paper. One can use standard technologies such as middleware or web services to realize the communication between the process engines of participants.

3 Modeling Guideline

This section introduces a few concepts that allow implementing the automatic data exchange of a process choreography in an entirely model-based approach. We present these concepts embedded in a modeling guideline for devising private orchestration models consistent to a public choreography model; Section 4 presents the execution semantics for our choreography models.

Figure 2 illustrates our modeling guideline which has a *global level*, where the public contract is defined, and a *local level*, where the local process implementations can be found. We assume that the choreography partners have already specified a collaboration diagram that shows how each participant's public process interacts with the other participants and ensures local enforceability of control-flow [2]; see Fig. 2 (top). To support data exchange between participants, we propose that this public contract is supplemented with a global data model in which the partners specify the business objects to

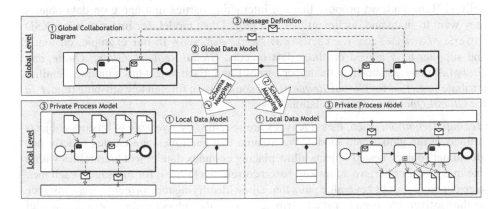

Fig. 2. Modeling guideline

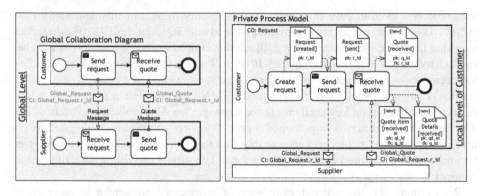

Fig. 3. Global choreography model and local process model of the customer

be exchanged; see Fig. 2 (top middle). Next, we follow and extend the P2P approach [2] to move from the global to the local level: each participant separately defines a local data model and a schema mapping between their local and the global data model and implements the private process conforming to their public process in the global collaboration diagram. Next, we describe the details of the global contract followed by the local level both along our modeling guideline.

On the global level, all choreography parties together define the following artifacts:

Global collaboration diagram: The global collaboration diagram describes the control flow layer of the choreography, i.e., it describes which messages are exchanged in which order on a conceptual level. Exemplary, the left part of Fig. 3 shows the collaboration diagram of the *Request for quote* choreography sketched in the introduction. It includes public processes with all necessary send and receive tasks for each participant, the customer and the supplier.

Global data model: Messages are used to exchange data. In choreography modeling languages such as WS-CDL [10] or BPEL4Chor [6], the data carried by a message is described technically by attribute names and data types for each message individually [27]. Instead, we propose that the interacting parties first agree on data objects they want to share and document this in a global data model, for instance using XSD (http://www.w3.org/standards/xml/schema). In our example, customer and supplier have agreed on three data objects, *Global_Request*, *Global_Quote*, and *Global_Articles*, as shown in the upper part of Fig.5. Each object has a unique identifier attribute (e.g., *r_id* for *Global_Request*) and some have a foreign key attribute (e.g., *r_id* for *Global_Quote*) to express relationships.

Message Definition: Then, message types are specified by *referring* to business objects defined in the global data model. We assume that each message carries exactly one global data object; nested objects allow placing complex data object hierarchies within one message. Further, we adopt key-based correlation [19, 20] for messages: each message contains a set of key/value pairs that allow identifying the correct process instance on the receiver side; each key is an attribute of some data object in the global data model. For example, *Request Message* of Fig. 3 (left) refers to the *Global_Request* object and

Quote Message refers to *Global_Quote* which has multiple *Global_Article* objects. A *Quote Message* will contain a *Global_Quote* object and all its *Global_Article* objects. Both messages use attribute *r_id* of *Global_Request* as correlation key.

Altogether, a message is declared as tuple $m = (name, CI, d)$, where $name$ is the message type, the correlation information $CI \subseteq K \times V$ is a set of key/value pairs, and d is the actual data object in the message. To model this tuple, BPMN must be extended as shown in the UML class in Fig. 3. Originally, a message contains a string identifying its name, i.e., message type. We add correlation information as a list of strings, each denoting one key/value pair, and the payload as data object.

Fig. 4. Message class

Then, each participant locally creates the following artifacts based on the global contract:

Local Data Model: Each participant defines a local data model which describes the classes of data objects handled by the private process. For example, the local data model of the *Customer* has four classes *Request*, *Quote*, *Quote Details*, and *Quote Item*; see Fig. 5 (bottom). We propose to also use the local data model to design the schema for the database where the objects are stored and accessed during the process execution. There are some requirements to the local data model wrt. the global data model as described next.

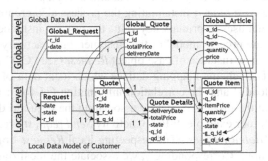

Fig. 5. Schema mapping for customer

Schema Mapping: A schema mapping defines how attributes of local classes map to attributes of global classes, and allows to automate a data transformation between global objects contained in messages and local objects. For this paper, we consider an attribute-to-attribute schema mapping which injectively maps each attribute of a global object to an attribute of a local object as shown in Fig. 5. Note that the attributes of object *Global_Quote* are distributed over objects *Quote* and *Quote Details*. The local implementation can hide private data in a local attribute by not mapping it to a global attribute (the mapping is not bijective), e.g., the *state* attributes of each local class. Local data model and schema mapping must ensure that primary and foreign keys are managed locally to avoid data inconsistency: when a local object can be created from a received global object, key attributes of the global object must map to non-key attributes of the local objects. For example, the local *Quote* shall be created from a *Global_Quote* object, thus *Quote* gets the attributes *g_q_id* and *g_r_id* to store the primary key *q_id* and the foreign key *r_id* of *Global_Quote* for local use. Typically, these keys are used for correlation.

Executable private process: Based on the global collaboration diagram, each participant designs their private process by enriching their public process with activities that

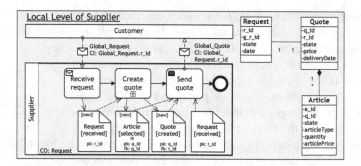

Fig. 6. Private process model and local data model of the supplier

are not publicly visible. In addition, each process (and each subprocess) gets assigned a *case object*; instantiating the process also creates a new instance of this case object that uses as primary key value the process instance id [16]. Fig. 3 (right) shows the private process model of the customer. First, activity *Create request* creates and prepares a new instance of case object *Request* (see "CO" in the top left corner of the process). The schema mapping defines which local data objects are required to derive the payload d and the correlation information CI for a message to be sent; this is included in the process model by associating the required data objects as input to the send task. In our example in Fig.3, activity *Send request* creates a *Request Message* containing a *Global_Request*. The respecting local *Request* object is associated to *Send request* as input. Correspondingly, we associate the local data objects into which the payload of a received message is transformed as output objects of a receive task. The last activity modeled in the customer process receives the *Quote Message*. The payload of this message is transformed into data objects *Quote*, *Quote Details*, and the multi-instance data object *Quote Item* all being associated as output to the receive task. The process designer has to specify whether the receive task creates new or updates existing data objects. We use the data annotations described in [16] to express operations and dependencies of local objects. In the given example, the message payload is used to create new data objects only as indicated by the identifier *new* in the upper part of each object. Local data schema, schema mapping, and private process *together* define the local choreography of the participant.

Fig.6 shows the private process model and the local data model of the second participant – the *Supplier*. Here, each attribute of a local class directly maps to a corresponding attribute with an equivalent name in the corresponding global class. For instance, attribute *price* of class *Global_Article* maps to to attribute *articlePrice* of class *Article*, attribute *r_id* of class *Global_Request* maps to attribute *g_r_id* of class *Request*, and so on. The private process has three activities: After receiving the *Global_Request*, which is stored as *Request* object in state *received*, the supplier processes the request and creates the *Quote*. Sending the *Global_Quote* message requires data objects *Quote* and *Article* to set the payload and *Request* to set the correlation identifier *Global_Request.r_id*.

This modeling guideline proposes a logical order in which the artifacts should be created based on dependencies between them. However, situations may arise where a different order (or iterations) are required. In any case, by refining the public process into a private one and by defining local data model and schema mapping as described, a process modeler always obtains a local choreography that is consistent with the global contract. In the next section, we show how to make the local choreography executable, thus achieving a correct implementation by design.

4   Executing Data-Annotated Process Choreographies

As discussed by the requirements of Section 2, exchanging a message requires the following 7 steps that we illustrate in Fig. 7 for the supplier sending a quote to the customer: (1) The required data objects are retrieved from the supplier's database (satisfying R2 of Section 2) and (2) transformed to the message (satisfying R1 & R3), which is (3) sent from the supplier and (4) received at the customer's side (satisfying R4). The received message is then (5) correlated to the corresponding activity instance (satisfying R5), where the message (6) gets transformed into data objects (satisfying R1 & R6) which are then (7) stored in the customer's database (satisfying R2 again).

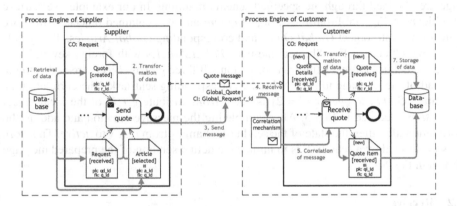

Fig. 7. Approach overview

We now present the operational semantics for the modeling concepts of Section 3 that automatically enact these steps from the local process model only. We first consider sending and receiving messages in Sections 4.1 and 4.2, respectively, followed by correlation handling in Section 4.3.

4.1   Send

According to the BPMN specification [20], each activity goes through various life cycle states including *inactive*, *ready*, *active*, *completing*, and *completed* in this order. Upon process instantiation, all activities are in state *inactive* and await enablement (state *ready*) taking place if the control flow proceeds to this activity *and* its input data is available.

Sending a message first requires all specified input data objects to be available to activate the send task. By Section 3, each send task has all required data objects as input data and availability can be checked via an automatically generated

SQL query [16]. For example, activity *Send quote* requires data object *Quote* in state *created* with primary key *q_id* and foreign key *r_id* pointing to object *Request*; the corresponding guard is (SELECT COUNT (q_id) FROM Quote WHERE r_id = $ID AND state = created) $\geq$ 1. This SQL query returns the number of *Quote* entries in the local database that are in state 'created' and related via foreign key *r_id* to the case object instance *Request* of the current process instance (identified by $ID); there has to be at least one [16]. For example, consider the database extract of Fig. 8a that shows four entries in the *Request*, *Quote*, and *Article* tables. If the current process instance has $ID = 6, then executing the SQL query returns 1, i.e., the required *Quote* is available. Availability is checked in this way for all input data objects.

If all input objects are available, the send task retrieves the data objects from the local database (step 1) and transforms them into the actual message (step 2). For retrieval, we adapt the SQL statements of [16] by replacing "SELECT COUNT ... $\geq$ 1" with "SELECT *". For example, object *Quote* is retrieved by SELECT * FROM Quote WHERE r_id = $ID AND state = created. All specified input objects are retrieved in this way. Then the global object and the correlation information of the message are obtained through the specified schema mapping. In our example, we retrieve all objects of Fig. 8a. From these, object *Quote* and its contained objects *Article* are transformed into object *Global_Quote* and corresponding *Global_Article*s. This yields the global objects of Fig. 8b, note the two *Global_Article*s with foreign key q_id = 30 to the *Global_Quote*. After transformation, all three global objects are added to the payload of the message to be sent by the corresponding sent task. The correlation information *Global_Request.r_id* = 21 is taken from attribute *g_r_id* of the local object *Request* as specified in Fig. 5. After completing the message creation and adding the correlation identifier, the state of the send task changes from *ready* to *active*. The work now performed by a send task is to initiate the actual sending of the prepared message shown in Fig. 8b.

4.2 Receive

After a received message has been correlated to the corresponding instance (see Section 4.3) it can be processed by basically reversing the two steps for sending a message. First, the objects in the message are transformed into the local data model (step 6 in Fig. 7) followed by storing them in the local database (step 7). A receive task can only receive a message when it is in state *active*; when it received the message it changes to state *completing*. In this activity state, the transformation and storage steps take place.

In our example, the received message of Fig. 8b is transformed via the schema mapping of Fig. 5: *Global_Quote* and its contained *Global_Article*s are mapped to a *Quote*, *Quote Details*, and multiple *Quote Items* as shown in Fig. 8c. Note that attributes in bold are private attributes that are not defined by the schema mapping (consider them empty for now). For instance, the local object *Quote* gets attributes *g_r_id* = 30 and *g_q_id* = 21 while attributes *state*, *r_id*, and *q_id* (in bold) are only set in the last step after *all* objects have been transformed.

The last step persists the transformed data objects in the local database based on the annotated output data objects of the receive task. For this, we use the approach of [16] for automatically deriving SQL queries for creating or updating

(a) Supplier database

Quote
- q_id = 30
- r_id = 6
- state = created
- price = 4149.75€
- deliveryDate = 13.12.2013

Article
- a_id = 16
- q_id = 30
- state = selected
- articleType = laptop
- quantity = 3
- articlePrice = 1349.95€

Article
- a_id = 17
- q_id = 30
- state = selected
- articleType = dvd spindle
- quantity = 10
- articlePrice = 9.99€

Request
- r_id = 6
- g_r_id = 21
- state = received
- date = 25.11.2013

— send ▸

(b) Message

Quote Message ✉ Global_Quote   CI: Global_Request.r_id = 21

Global_Quote
- q_id = 30
- r_id = 21
- totalPrice = 4149.75€
- deliveryDate = 13.12.2013

Global_Article
- a_id = 16
- q_id = 30
- type = laptop
- quantity = 3
- price = 1349.95€

Global_Article
- a_id = 17
- q_id = 30
- type = dvd spindle
- quantity = 10
- price = 9.99€

— receive ▸

(c) Customer database

Quote
- q_id = 53
- r_id = 21
- state = received
- g_r_id = 21
- g_q_id = 30

Quote Item
- qi_id = 41
- q_id = 53
- state = received
- type = laptop
- quantity = 3
- itemPrice = 1349.95€
- g_q_id = 30
- g_qi_id = 16

Quote Item
- qi_id = 42
- q_id = 53
- state = received
- type = dvd spindle
- quantity = 10
- itemPrice = 9.99€
- g_q_id = 30
- g_qi_id = 17

Quote Details
- qd_id = 32
- q_id = 53
- state = received
- totalPrice = 4149.75€
- deliveryDate = 13.12.2013

Fig. 8. Representation of one instance from the message flow shown in Fig. 7 where each object refers to one column in the corresponding database table named as the respecting object (cf. [16])

objects. In our example, all output objects of *Receive quote* are annotated with *[new]*, i.e., are newly created. The original approach of [16] only considers the annotations for primary key, foreign key, and state to generate the SQL query which would yield the query INSERT INTO Quote (q_id, r_id, state) VALUES (DEFAULT, $ID, received) for data object *Quote* ($ID identifies the current process instance). In this paper, we extend the query to include the information of the local data objects extracted from the received message. The complete query for the *Quote* object looks as follows: INSERT INTO Quote (q_id, r_id, state, g_r_id, g_q_id) VALUES (DEFAULT, $ID, received, 21, 30). For the multi-instance data object *Quote Item*, we generate two queries, one for each extracted local data object.

Fig. 8c visualizes the customer database after inserting all data objects extracted from the received message (for instance $ID=21). In this step, data objects have to be persisted in the right order to ensure the validity of key relations. In our example, the *Quote* object has to be stored first to ensure that the foreign key value for object *Quote Details* is known. This requires that key relationships do not form a cycle. Technically, we traverse the graph of dependencies between data objects starting at the root, e.g., first object *Quote*, then object *Quote Details*, and finally both *Quote Item* objects are inserted. When the graph is completely traversed, the receive task reaches the *completed* state.

Objects without annotation *[new]* are *updated* which happens analogously [15]. While the order of object processing is not important for updates, updates cannot be applied to data collections, i.e., multi-instance objects, because the objects in the message may be different from the objects stored locally. Assigning explicit global ids would solve this issue, but is out of scope for this paper. We also allow combinations of inserts and updates for one receive task, if the limitations of both operations are considered, i.e., insertion order for newly created objects and no update on data collections.

4.3 Correlation

Before a message can be handled, it must be assigned to its *receiving instance* which is also known as *correlation handling*. The standard approach is *key-based* correlation [19,20], where some attributes of the data model are designed as *correlation keys*.

An incoming message is correlated to a process instance when both store the same value for all correlation keys *in the message*; any two instances must be distinct on their correlation values. We first consider the case when an instance has all keys *initialized* already and then discuss *how* to initialize a key.

All keys initialized. Our approach refines key-based correlation by making correlation keys part of the global data model. On the one hand, each message $m = (name, CI, d)$ explicitly defines a number of correlations keys CI, where each key $d_2.a \in CI$ points to some attribute a of some global data object d_2 (not necessarily d). For example, the message of Fig. 8b has the correlation key *Global_Request.r_id* while its payload is of type *Global_Quote* (as specified in Fig. 3). On the other hand, each participant defines a local data model, where each correlation key attribute $d_2.a$ of m is mapped to a local attribute $f(d_2.a) = d_2'.b$ of some local data object d_2'. Each process instance $\$ID$ has its own case object instance and related object instances; message m correlates to $\$ID$ when the value of each $d_2.a \in CI$ matches the value of the corresponding $f(d_2.a)$ of some data object related to instance $\$ID$. For example, the *Customer* maps *Global_Request.r_id* to *Request.r_id* (see Fig. 5). Thus, the message of Fig. 8b can be correlated to a process instance where the case object has *Request.r_id* $= 21$.

Formally, the correlation information of a message $m = (name, CI, d)$ is a set $CI = \{(k_1, v_1), \ldots, (k_n, v_n)\}$ of key/value pairs, where each key $k_i = d_i.a_i$ is an attribute a_i of a global data object d_i. A participant's schema mapping f maps each key to a local attribute $f(d_i.a_i) = d_i'.a_i'$. The *value* of the correlation attribute $d_i'.a_i'$ can be extracted with respect to the case object c of the receiving instance $\$ID$ as follows. Object d_i' relates to c via foreign key relations. Thus, we can build an SQL query joining the tables that store d_i' and c, select only the entries where the primary key of c equals $\$ID$, and finally extract the value of attribute $d_i'.a_i'$; see [17]. Let $e(d_i'.a_i', c, \$ID)$ denote the results of this query. By ensuring that in the local data model the relations from c to d_i' are only 1:1, the extracted value $e(d_i'.a_i', c, \$ID) = v$ is uniquely defined. Now, m *correlates* to an instance $\$ID$ of a process with case object c iff for each $(k_i, v_i) \in CI$ holds $e(f(k_i), c, \$ID) = v_i$. This definition can be refined to not only consider the case object of the entire process, but also the case object and instance id of the scope that encloses the *active* task that can receive m.

Initializing correlation keys. When sending a message m, then its correlation keys are automatically *initialized* by extracting for each global correlation attribute k_i the corresponding value $e(f(k_i), c, \$ID) = v_i$ from the sender's local data model. Technically, this can be done in the same way as extracting the payload of m, see Section 4.1. From this point on, all process instances receiving a message with correlation key k_i have to agree on the value v_i. The only exception is when $e(f(k_i), c, \$ID) = \perp$ is still *undefined* at the receiving instance. By initializing the local attribute $f(k_i)$ to value v_i, we can make $\$ID$ a matching instance for m. Thus, we generalize the above condition: m *correlates* to an instance $\$ID$ of a process with case object c iff for each $(k_i, v_i) \in CI$ holds if $e(f(k_i), c, \$ID) \neq \perp$ then $e(f(k_i), c, \$ID) = v_i$. When receiving m, the local key attribute $f(k_i)$ can be initialized for $\$ID$ to value v_i by generating an SQL update statement as discussed in Section 4.2.

5 Evaluation

We implemented our approach by extending the *camunda Modeler*, a modeling tool supporting BPMN, and the *camunda BPM Platform*, a process engine for BPMN process models. The modeling tool was extended with the annotations for messages and data objects described in Section 3; message types of the global data model are specified in XSD and a simple editor allows to create an attribute-wise schema mapping from the global to the local data model. Once a private choreography model has been completed, the user can automatically generate XQuery expressions (http://www.w3.org/TR/xquery/) at the send and receive tasks to transform between local and global data model (Section 4). The engine was extended with a messaging endpoint for sending and receiving messages in XML format to correlate messages, to read and write local data objects by generating SQL queries from process models, and to process messages as described in Section 4. As the concepts in this paper, also our implementation does not address R4 (message routing); in particular if the receiving task is not in state *active* to receive the incoming message, the message will be discarded. Making the process layer compatible with error handling of the message transport layer is beyond the scope of this paper.

To demonstrate the feasibility of our approach, we implemented the *service interaction patterns* [3] which capture basic forms of message-based interaction. For the sake of brevity, we explain the central challenges and how they were solved in our approach; see [15] for details of our solutions.

(A) Single transmission, bilateral. Two participants A and B each send/receive one message; patterns *(P1:send)*, *(P2:receive)*, and *(P3:send/receive)* are affected. The challenges are to (1) generate and send a message, (2) to correlate a message based on an initialized or uninitialized key, and (3) to process a received message. Our running example in Fig. 3 shows how these challenges are solved.

(B) Single transmission, multilateral. Participant A sends/receives one message from multiple participants B1, B2, ..., each. The challenge in *(P4.racing incoming message)* is to receive only one message and discard others (solved by enabling the receive task only once). The challenge in *(P5.one-to-many send)* is to generate multiple messages with different correlation information for different recipients (solved by placing a send task in a multi-instance subprocess – each instance provides a unique id that is used as correlation identifier). The challenge in *(P6.one-from-many receive)* is to correlate multiple incoming messages (solved by using the same correlation key in all messages – the first message initializes the key and all subsequent messages are correlated accordingly). Pattern *(P7.one-to-many send/receive)* combines patterns P5 and P6 – its challenges are solved by combining solutions for P5 and P6.

(C) Multi-transmission interaction. Participant A directly exchanges multiple messages with one or more participants B1, B2, ... The challenge in *(P8.multi-response)* is to receive multiple replies for one request until a "stop" condition holds (solved by using the same correlation key in request and replies, the stop condition is limited to timeouts and "finalizing" message types). The challenge in *(P9.contingent request)* is to resend a request to a different recipient after no reply to a first request was received (solved by placing send/receive tasks in an iterative subprocess that produces a new correlation identifier in each iteration, and timer events to trigger a new iteration). The challenge

in *(P10.atomic multicast)* is to send a cancellation message to n recipients when less than m out of n recipients responded to a request (partially solved by placing send/receive tasks within a multi-instance subprocess with timeout gateways – the m out of n condition has to be defined manually).

(D) Routing. Participant B forwards messages from A to further participants C, D, ... which then send a reply to A directly. The challenge in *(P12.relayed request)* is to forward a correlation key of A to a participant C that can use the key in a reply to A (solved by making the correlation key part of the messages routed to C and by ensuring that each participant on the way can map the key to its local data model). The challenge in *(P13.dynamic routing)* is to forward a message to C or D based on the contents of a message sent by A (solved by using the attribute pattern A2 of [17] on an exclusive gateway that chooses between sending to C or sending to D). The challenge in *(P11.request w/ referral)* is to forward a message from A to some participant X whose URL is defined in the message (partially solved by defining the endpoint URL of X through a variable, the assignment to that variable from the contents of the message has to be defined manually).

Our implementation and the implemented patterns are available at *http://bpt.hpi.uni-potsdam.de/Public/BPMNData*.

6   Related Work

While briefly discussing approaches being related to the presented concepts, we focus on the communication between distributed partners, the transformation of data, and message correlation. The service interaction patterns discussed in [3] describe a set of recurrent process choreography scenarios occurring in industry. Thus, they are a major source to validate choreography support of a modeling language. Besides BPMN [20] as used in this paper as basis, there exist multiple solutions to cope with process choreographies. Most prominent are BPMN4Chor [5], Let's Dance [35], BPEL4Chor [6], and WS-CDL [29]. From these, only BPEL4Chor and WS-CDL realize operational semantics to handle message exchange by reusing respectively adapting the concepts defined in BPEL [19]. Though, message transformation to achieve interoperability between multiple participants is done with imperative constructs, i.e., the process engineer has to manually write these transformations and has to ensure their correctness. Additionally, BPEL4Chor and WS-CDL are not model-driven as the approach introduced in this paper.

Apart from process and service domains, distributed systems [24] describe the communication between IT systems via pre-specified interfaces similar to the global contract discussed in this paper. Usually, the corresponding data management is done by distributed databases [21] and their enhancements to data integration systems [12, 25] as well as parallel database systems [8] or is done by peer-to-peer systems [9, 26]. The database solution allows many participants to share data by working with a global schema which hides the local databases, but unlike our approach, the participants work on the same database or some replication of it. Peer-to-peer systems take the database systems to a decentralized level and include mechanisms to deal with very dynamic situations as participants change rapidly. In process choreographies, the participants are known and predefined such that a centralized solution as presented in this paper saves overhead as, in the worst case, the decentralized approach requires a schema mapping for each communication between two participants instead of only one mapping per participant to the global schema. The transformation of data between two participants can be achieved via schema mapping and matching [22,23], a mediator [33], an adapter [34], or ontology-based integration [4,18,31]. For instance, [4] utilizes OWL [28] ontologies, which are similar to our global data model, and mappings from port types to attributes via XPath expressions to transform data between web services. In this paper, we utilize schema matching due to the close integration of database support for data persistence.

Returning to the process domain, there exist fundamental works describing the implementation of process choreographies [1, 7] with [1] ensuring correctness for inter-process communication. These works only describe the control flow side although the data part is equally important as messages contain the actual artifacts exchanged. [11] introduces a data-aware collaboration approach including formal correctness criteria. They define the data exchange using data-aware interaction nets, a proprietary notation, instead of a widely accepted one as BPMN, the industry standard for process modeling, used as basis in this paper.

7 Conclusion

We presented an approach allowing to model and automate the data exchange of process choreographies entirely model-driven. Thereby, we utilized the industry standard BPMN and extended the model-driven data dependency enactment approach catered for process orchestrations with concepts for process choreographies. Based on challenges of data heterogeneity, correlation, and 1:n communication, we identified a set of six requirements covering the retrieval of data from the sender's local database, the data transformation into a global data schema all participants agreed upon, the correlation of a message to the correct activity instance, the transformation from the global to the receiver's local database schema, and the storage of the data there. The message routing between participants is out of scope of this paper by adapting existing technologies as, for instance, web services. In this paper, we describe a modeling guideline with the artifacts required to automatically execute the mentioned steps from these only. Furthermore, we describe the corresponding operational semantics and provide details about our implementation. Our approach has been implemented; we could implement all service interaction patterns of [3] except for dynamically setting URLs of recipients and evaluating data conditions over aggregations of data objects; both are outside the scope of this paper and deserve future work. Also the integration of process layer and message transport layer (in particular wrt. handling message transport errors) is outside the scope of this paper. The current approach only utilizes tasks to send and receive messages. However, BPMN also supports *message events* to which the discussed concepts could be applied as well by overcoming BPMN's limitation that events cannot transform and correlate data objects. In future work, we plan to provide an integrated formal verification technique for model-driven data enactment in process orchestrations and choreographies.

References

1. van der Aalst, W.M.P., Lohmann, N., Massuthe, P., Stahl, C., Wolf, K.: Multiparty contracts: Agreeing and implementing interorganizational processes. Comput. J. 53(1), 90–106 (2010)
2. van der Aalst, W.M.P., Weske, M.: The P2P approach to interorganizational workflows. In: Dittrich, K.R., Geppert, A., Norrie, M. (eds.) CAiSE 2001. LNCS, vol. 2068, pp. 140–156. Springer, Heidelberg (2001)
3. Barros, A., Dumas, M., ter Hofstede, A.H.M.: Service interaction patterns. In: van der Aalst, W.M.P., Benatallah, B., Casati, F., Curbera, F. (eds.) BPM 2005. LNCS, vol. 3649, pp. 302–318. Springer, Heidelberg (2005)
4. Bowers, S., Ludäscher, B.: An ontology-driven framework for data transformation in scientific workflows. In: Rahm, E. (ed.) DILS 2004. LNCS (LNBI), vol. 2994, pp. 1–16. Springer, Heidelberg (2004)
5. Decker, G., Barros, A.: Interaction modeling using BPMN. In: ter Hofstede, A.H.M., Benatallah, B., Paik, H.-Y. (eds.) BPM Workshops 2007. LNCS, vol. 4928, pp. 208–219. Springer, Heidelberg (2008)
6. Decker, G., Kopp, O., Leymann, F., Weske, M.: Bpel4chor: Extending bpel for modeling choreographies. In: ICWS, pp. 296–303. IEEE (2007)
7. Decker, G., Weske, M.: Interaction-centric modeling of process choreographies. Information Systems 36(2), 292–312 (2011)
8. DeWitt, D., Gray, J.: Parallel database systems: the future of high performance database systems. Communications of the ACM 35(6), 85–98 (1992)
9. Halevy, A.Y., Ives, Z.G., Suciu, D., Tatarinov, I.: Schema mediation in peer data management systems. In: Data Engineering, pp. 505–516. IEEE (2003)
10. Kavantzas, N., Burdett, D., Ritzinger, G., Fletcher, T., Lafon, Y., Barreto, C.: Web services choreography description language version 1.0. W3C candidate recommendation 9 (2005)
11. Knuplesch, D., Pryss, R., Reichert, M.: Data-aware interaction in distributed and collaborative workflows: Modeling, semantics, correctness. In: CollaborateCom, pp. 223–232. IEEE (2012)
12. Lenzerini, M.: Data integration: A theoretical perspective. In: Symposium on Principles of Database Systems, pp. 233–246. ACM (2002)
13. Mendling, J., Hafner, M.: From ws-cdl choreography to bpel process orchestration. Journal of Enterprise Information Management 21(5), 525–542 (2008)
14. Meyer, A., Polyvyanyy, A., Weske, M.: Weak Conformance of Process Models with respect to Data Objects. In: Services and their Composition, ZEUS (2012)
15. Meyer, A., Pufahl, L., Batoulis, K., Kruse, S., Lindhauer, T., Stoff, T., Fahland, D., Weske, M.: Data Perspective in Process Choreographies: Modeling and Execution. Tech. Rep. BPM-13-29, BPMcenter.org (2013)
16. Meyer, A., Pufahl, L., Fahland, D., Weske, M.: Modeling and Enacting Complex Data Dependencies in Business Processes. In: Daniel, F., Wang, J., Weber, B. (eds.) BPM 2013. LNCS, vol. 8094, pp. 171–186. Springer, Heidelberg (2013)
17. Meyer, A., Pufahl, L., Fahland, D., Weske, M.: Modeling and Enacting Complex Data Dependencies in Business Processes. Tech. Rep. 74, HPI at the University of Potsdam (2013)
18. Noy, N.F.: Semantic integration: a survey of ontology-based approaches. ACM Sigmod Record 33(4), 65–70 (2004)
19. OASIS: Web Services Business Process Execution Language, Version 2.0 (April 2007)
20. OMG: Business Process Model and Notation (BPMN), Version 2.0 (January 2011)
21. Özsu, M.T., Valduriez, P.: Principles of Distributed Database Systems. Springer (2011)
22. Rahm, E., Bernstein, P.A.: A survey of approaches to automatic schema matching. The VLDB Journal 10(4), 334–350 (2001)

23. Shvaiko, P., Euzenat, J.: A survey of schema-based matching approaches. In: Spaccapietra, S. (ed.) Journal on Data Semantics IV. LNCS, vol. 3730, pp. 146–171. Springer, Heidelberg (2005)

24. Tanenbaum, A.S., van Steen, M.: Distributed Systems: Principles and Paradigms. Prentice Hall (2006)

25. Tomasic, A., Raschid, L., Valduriez, P.: Scaling access to heterogeneous data sources with disco. IEEE Transactions on Knowledge and Data Engineering 10(5), 808–823 (1998)

26. Valduriez, P., Pacitti, E.: Data management in large-scale P2P systems. In: Daydé, M., Dongarra, J., Hernández, V., Palma, J.M.L.M. (eds.) VECPAR 2004. LNCS, vol. 3402, pp. 104–118. Springer, Heidelberg (2005)

27. W3C: Web Services Description Language (WSDL) 1.1 (March 2001)

28. W3C: OWL Web Ontology Language (February 2004)

29. W3C: Web Services Choreography Description Language, Version 1.0 (November 2005)

30. W3C: XQuery 1.0: An XML Query Language, 2nd edn. (December 2010)

31. Wache, H., Voegele, T., Visser, U., Stuckenschmidt, H., Schuster, G., Neumann, H., Hübner, S.: Ontology-based integration of information-a survey of existing approaches. In: IJCAI Workshop: Ontologies and Information Sharing, pp. 108–117 (2001)

32. Weske, M.: Business Process Management: Concepts, Languages, Architectures, 2nd edn. Springer (2012)

33. Wiederhold, G.: Mediators in the architecture of future information systems. Computer 25(3), 38–49 (1992)

34. Yellin, D.M., Strom, R.E.: Protocol specifications and component adaptors. ACM Transactions on Programming Languages and Systems (TOPLAS) 19(2), 292–333 (1997)

35. Zaha, J.M., Barros, A., Dumas, M., ter Hofstede, A.: Let's dance: A language for service behavior modeling. In: Meersman, R., Tari, Z. (eds.) OTM 2006. LNCS, vol. 4275, pp. 145–162. Springer, Heidelberg (2006)

Integrating the Goal and Business Process Perspectives in Information System Analysis

Marcela Ruiz[1], Dolors Costal[2], Sergio España[1], Xavier Franch[2], and Óscar Pastor[1]

[1] PROS Research Centre, Universitat Politècnica de València, Valencia, Spain
{lruiz,sergio.espana,opastor}@pros.upv.es
[2] GESSI Research Center, Universitat Politècnica de Catalunya (UPC), Barcelona, Spain
{dolors,franch}@essi.upc.edu

Abstract. There are several motivations to promote investment and scientific effort in the integration of intentional and operational perspectives: organisational reengineering, continuous improvement of business processes, alignment among complementary analysis perspectives, information traceability, etc. In this paper we propose the integration of two modelling languages that support the creation of goal and business process models: the *i** goal-oriented modelling method and Communication Analysis, a communication-oriented business process modelling method. We describe the methodological integration of the two modelling methods with the aim of fulfilling several criteria: i) to rely on appropriate theories; ii) to provide abstract and concrete syntaxes; iii) to provide scenarios of application; and iv) to develop tool support. We provide guidelines for using the two modelling methods in a top-down analysis scenario. We also present an illustrative case that demonstrates the feasibility of the approach.

Keywords: modelling language, requirements engineering, goal modelling, business process modelling, ontological analysis, metamodel integration.

1   Introduction

Organisations are aware of the importance of evolving to keep pace with changes in the market, technology, environment, law, etc. [1]. As a result, continuous improvement and reengineering have become common practices in information system engineering. Understanding organisations and their needs for change often requires several interrelated perspectives [2-3]. The information system engineering community has contributed a number of modelling languages that are typically oriented towards a specific perspective, requiring approaches to their integration [4].

In this paper, we focus on extending a business process perspective with intentional aspects of organisations. Business process modelling languages provide primitives to specify work practice (i.e. activities, temporal constraints and resources). Despite being widely accepted that processes are means to achieve organisational goals [5], process models give little attention to the strategic dimension [6]. The analysis, prioritization

M. Jarke et al. (Eds.): CAiSE 2014, LNCS 8484, pp. 332–346, 2014.

and selection of organisational strategies are the scope of intentional modelling languages, which focus on the business roles, their goals and their relationships.

Business processes and goals are intrinsically interdependent [7] and several works provide detailed arguments in favour of combining both perspectives: (i) An integrated approach allows understanding the motivation for processes [6]. (ii) In the opposite direction, goals may be used to guide process design [8]. (iii) Traceability is enhanced, which is necessary for enterprise management [9] and facilitates the sustainability of organisations [10]. (iv) It helps identifying cross-functional interdependencies during business change management, by supporting the identification of the goals for change and the analysis of the impact on processes [11] [8] [10].

We pursue this aim by integrating a goal-oriented and a business process-oriented modelling language. There are several criteria that one would expect from modelling language integration. Remarkably, we consider the following: (i) The languages to combine need to be formally described. (ii) The integration itself should be well founded in theory. (iii) It should clarify the scenarios where the integrated approach can be applied and provide some scenario-dependent guidelines. (iv) It should provide tool support. These criteria guide our research. A comparative review (see Section 2) reveals that proposals with similar aims do not fulfil one or several of the above-mentioned criteria, revealing that the challenge remains open.

This paper presents our steps from the problem investigation to the implementation of a modelling tool. We have chosen to integrate the languages proposed by $i*$ [3], a goal-oriented modelling method, and Communication Analysis (CA) [12], a communication-oriented business process modelling method. The reason to choose $i*$ is its expressiveness to specify dependencies, with which we intend to trace strategic motivations and processes. In the case of CA, we aim to get the most out of the communicational techniques in order to analyse business processes; it is not its notation what is important, but the underlying concepts and guidelines. Moreover, some current business process modelling suites use BPMN with a communicative approach. In addition, the authors have competence in these languages as to target the endeavour.

As a result, in this paper we present the following contributions:

- We report on the alignment between $i*$ and CA performed by means of ontological analyses and the investigation of overlapping concepts and semantic relations.
- We integrate the metamodels of both modelling languages, providing rationale for the design decisions, and we provide guidelines for a top-down modelling scenario.
- We describe an Eclipse-based tool that supports integrated modelling of $i*$ and CA.

We structure our research in terms of design science since it involves creating new artefacts and acquiring new knowledge. Our research methodology follows the engineering cycle as described by [13] (see Fig. 1). The second step corresponds to a method engineering effort; throughout the paper, we use the terminology in [14]. The resulting integrated method is exemplified by means of a running example that demonstrates the feasibility of the approach.

The paper is structured as follows. Section 2 defines the solution criteria and compares related works. Section 3 presents a running example and introduces the methods selected for integration. Section 4 presents our proposal for integrating $i*$ and CA. Section 5 presents guidelines for a top-down modelling scenario. Section 6 describes the modelling tool. Finally, Section 7 concludes with a discussion and future work.

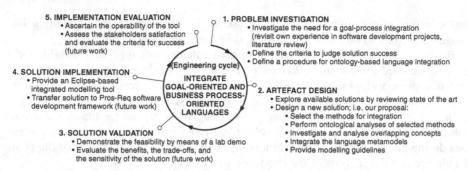

Fig. 1. Overview of the research methodology

2   Related Work

In the field of business process management, there are several related works that approach goal-oriented business process reengineering from diverse angles. We analyse these approaches based on the criteria mentioned in the introduction (see Table 1): (a) ontological foundation: none, just a conceptual framework, based on ontologies but no explicit alignment, ontology-based alignment; (b) metamodel integration: none, partial, complete; (c) modelling scenarios: top-down (from goal model to business process model), bottom-up (the other way round), iterative (switching back and forth among both models), evolution (business processes evolve as driven by goal models); (d) existence or not of tool support.

Some works focus on modelling the as-is system (reverse engineering). For instance, [15] proposes a goal elicitation method to deepen the understanding of current processes. The authors conclude that a suitable semantics and representation to relate goal and business process models is needed, which is a motivation for our proposal. [7] discusses the alignment of goal and process modelling methods (using Tropos and ARIS, respectively) and proposes a three-stage method to model the as-is system.

Other works focus on supporting the business process model evolution. [16] proposes a goal-based pattern definition language for business process evolution, where processes are trajectories in a space of all possible states, and goals are final states. [17] presents a formal approach to analysing the dependency of softgoals on processes; as a practical result, they enable modelling the evolution rationale.

Table 1. Summary of the review of the state of the art

Refs.	Ontological Foundation	Metamodel Integration	Modelling Scenario	Tool Support
[16]	Conceptual framework	N/A	Evolution	No
[15]	None	No	Top-down	No
[6]	Based on ontologies	No	N/A	No
[7]	Conceptual framework	No	Top-down	No
[11]	Conceptual framework	Complete	Iterative	No
[9]	None	No	Top-down	No
[8]	Conceptual framework	No	Top-down	No
[10]	Conceptual framework	No	N/A	No
[17]	Based on ontologies	No	Evolution	No
Ours	Ontologically aligned	Complete	Currently top-down Potentially may support the rest	Yes

Other works focus on modelling the to-be system (forward engineering). [8] presents an informal, seminal approach in which goals provide a basis for process definition. [11] defines a method that takes as input an as-is business process model and produces a to-be goal model and a to-be business process model.

Some of the above-mentioned works elaborate a conceptual framework to clarify definitions [7-8, 11, 16], and [17] even builds upon an existing ontology. However, none of them performs an ontological analysis to guide the integration of the modelling methods, which is our selected approach.

With regards to modelling language integration, [11] relies on EKD metamodels (both perspectives are integrated *a priori*) but, noticeably, none of the works report a proper, rigorous metamodel integration ([7] mentions it as future work, though).

We have taken the previous works as a reference and attempted to cover the gaps in terms of ontology-based analysis, metamodel integration and tool support (see last row in Table 1). Some works analyse semantic relations between goals and business processes [6, 9-10], what can be used as input for our guidelines definition. Similarly, the pattern-based approach in [16] could be adapted to the context of *i** and CA.

3   Running Example

In the rest of the paper we will use as running example the SuperStationery Co. case, a company that provides office material to its clients. The company acts as an intermediary: catalogued products are bought from suppliers and sold to clients. In this paper we focus on the intentional and operational aspects of sales management (acronym SALE). A relevant excerpt of the *i** model for the SuperStationery Co. case is shown in Fig. 2. We assume in the paper that the reader is familiar with *i**.

In this paper we will provide guidelines to support the transformation of such an *i** model into a CA model (i.e. a top-down scenario). CA is a requirements engineering method that analyses the communicative interactions between the information system (IS) and its environment [12]. Therefore, the method focuses on external IS functions: information acquisition and distribution. CA offers requirements structure and several modelling techniques: 1) the Communicative Event Diagram (CED) describes business processes from a communicational perspective; 2) the Event Specification Template allows the structuring of the requirements; and 3) Message Structure specifies description of new meaningful information that is conveyed to the information system in the event [18]. The CED (see Fig. 3) consists of communicative events (CE). A CE is an organisational action that is triggered as a result of a given change in the world. It is intended to account for that change by gathering information about it. A CE is structured as a sequence of actions that are related to information (acquisition, storage, processing, retrieval and/or distribution), which are carried out in a complete and uninterrupted way. CE are identified by the norms and guidelines referred as unity criteria (which act as modularity guidelines) [19]. In addition, CED consist of actors that trigger the CE and provide the input information (primary), actors who need to be informed of the occurrence of an event (receiver) and relationships to specify communicative interactions (ingoing/outgoing) and precedence relationships among CE.

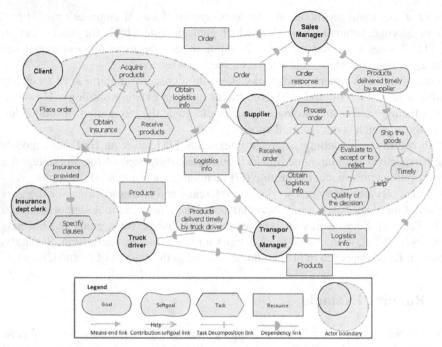

Fig. 2. Excerpt of an *i** model for the SuperStationery Co. case

4   Modelling Language Integration

In order to combine the process and intentional perspectives, we undertake a method engineering effort [14], where *i** and CA are considered method chunks. Note that the analysis of project situations is out of the scope of this paper. Instead, the focus is put in integrating the product and the process models of the methods. Taking the integration map proposed in [14] as reference method, Fig. 4 presents how we have operationalised each of its intentions, and points to the corresponding section.

4.1   Ontological Alignment between *i** and CA

Integrating the product models of two methods requires identifying pairs of concepts that have the same semantics, so as to later merge them. When the two product models have different terminology, as in the case of *i** and CA, Ralyté and Rolland suggest adapting the product models by means of name unification and transformation [14]. We have opted for ontological analysis, which is an equivalent strategy that offers strong theoretical foundations to method analysis and comparison. In an ontological analysis, the concepts of a method are mapped to the concepts of reference ontology. This is commonly used to assess to which extent the method covers the concepts of the ontology, and vice versa. Among other different possible options (e.g., BWW, Chisholm's, DOLCE, UFO, etc.), we have chosen FRISCO as reference ontology because we have already satisfactorily used it in previous analysis related to one of the two methods, CA [20].

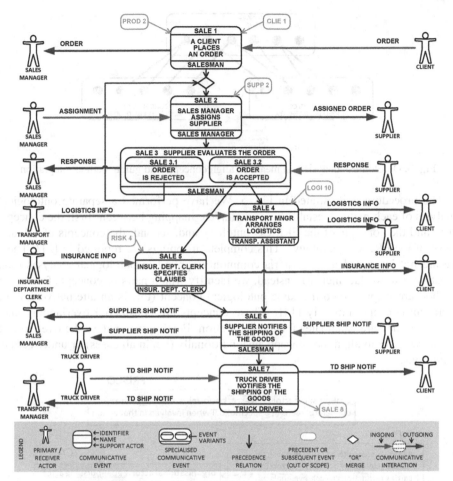

Fig. 3. Excerpt of a CA model for the SuperStationery Co. case

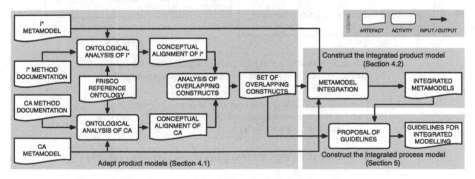

Fig. 4. Flow of modelling language integration

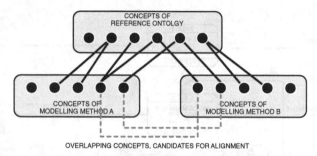

Fig. 5. Ontological analysis as a means to align concepts and guide method integration

The procedure is illustrated in Fig. 5. We have performed a separate ontological analysis of each method, establishing a complete mapping between: first, the concepts of *i** and the concepts of the FRISCO ontology and, second, the concepts of CA and those of the FRISCO ontology[1]. This complete mappings are reported in [21]. Then, we are not interested in the criteria commonly applied in ontological analyses (e.g. construct excess, laconicism). Instead, we identify which pairs of concepts from each method are mapped onto the same ontological concept (this is an alternative way of verifying concept similarity [14]). These concepts are considered overlapping and, therefore, they are candidates for the integration. Finally, we analyse the overlap and decide whether to align the concepts unconditionally (i.e. in all cases) or under certain conditions.

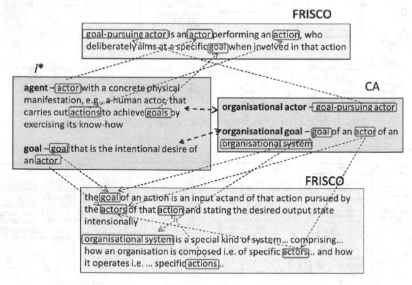

Fig. 6. Specific mappings for two pairs of overlapping concepts

---

[1] The *i**– FRISCO mapping was performed by the second author and revised by the fourth author. The CA – FRISCO mapping was performed by the third author and revised by the first author. Then all authors met to discuss the mappings, identify the candidate overlapping concepts and decide the alignment.

For the sake of illustration, Fig. 6 shows two examples of the type of reasoning process that has been applied during the ontological alignment. For instance, the method concepts *istar.agent* and *ca.organisational actor* map onto related FRISCO concepts (*frisco.goal-pursuing actor* is a specialisation of *frisco.actor*). Additionally, *istar.agent* is qualified as having physical manifestation and know-how; we interpret this additional qualification as compatible and also applicable to *ca.organisational actor*. Therefore, we consider the two method concepts as overlapping. Similarly, the method concepts *istar.goal* and *ca.organisational goal* map onto the same FRISCO concept (i.e. *frisco.goal*). Therefore, *istar.goal* and *ca.organisational goal* are overlapping concepts.

Table 2 summarises the overlapping concepts found in this analysis. Each row describes a pair of concepts that overlap. FRISCO mappings consist of FRISCO concepts (underlined) that are qualified when necessary. Table 2 also indicates the ontological alignments decided in view of the mappings (additional information of the methods was necessary). They are unconditional except in two cases. The CA method provides a set of unity criteria to identify and encapsulate communicative events that help to define them at an adequate level of modularity (see [19] for details). Therefore, an *istar.task* maps to a *ca.communicative event* only if it satisfies the unity criteria. An *istar.resource* maps to a *ca.message structure* only if it is informational (e.g. a delivery note). Hence, *istar.physical resource* does not map to *ca.message structure* (e.g. a pallet of boxes is not a message structure).

Table 2. Mappings of candidate overlapping concepts

i– FRISCO mapping		CA – FRISCO mapping		Alignment
i* concept	FRISCO mapping	CA concept	FRISCO mapping	
agent	actor with a concrete physical manifestation, for instance, a human actor, that carries out actions to achieve goals by exercising its know-how	organisational actor	goal-pursuing actor	equivalent
role	type of actors such that it characterizes the behaviour of agents	organisational role	type of goal-pursuing actors	equivalent
goal	goal that is an intentional desire of an actor	organisational goal	goal of an actor of an organisational system	equivalent
task	action that involves one actor in its pre-state and in its post-state	communicative event (CE)	composite transition	CE -> task / task -> CE (1)
resource	input actand of an action (if it is physical) or data that is the input actand of an action (if it is informational) such that an actor desires its provision and there are no open issues about how it will be achieved	message structure (MS)	type of messages; it is an input actand of a composite transition (i.e. the "communicative event")	MS -> resource / resource -> MS (2)

Alignment conditions: (1) task satisfies unity criteria (2) resource is informational

4.2 Metamodel Integration

To integrate *i** and CA metamodels, we analysed the alignment of concepts presented in Section 4.1. For each pair of aligned concepts we need to decide whether we keep both corresponding metaclasses (one of each modelling method) or just one metaclass. We provide some heuristics to make such decision and the implications of each choice (see Fig. 7.a for the starting point).

In some cases, the two concepts are totally equivalent, in the sense that their alignment is clear-cut (concepts in the first three rows in Table 2 fall into this category). In such cases, the simplest solution is to keep only one metaclass and it needs to be decided which of the two involved metaclasses is removed. Then, the relationships in which the removed metaclass participated need to be connected to the metaclass that is kept (see Fig. 7.b). In other cases, the alignment of two concepts is qualified with a condition specifying under which circumstances both concepts can be considered aligned (concepts in the last two rows of Table 2). Then, we propose to keep both metaclasses and create a relationship between them (see Fig. 7.c) to provide traceability in cases where the specific concepts are aligned. The application of these heuristics to our case is summarised in Table 3.

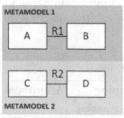 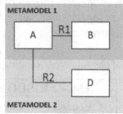 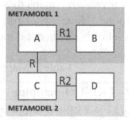

(a) Example of two meta-models to integrate (b) Integration of concepts totally equivalent (A≡C) (c) Integration of concepts aligned under specific conditions (A≅C)

Fig. 7. Deciding which metaclasses to keep

To create the integrated metamodel, we have departed from the *i** metamodel which is basically compliant to the *i** wiki version taken as reference in this work [22] and the CA metamodel [20]. Full description of the integrated metamodel is presented in [21].

Table 3. Metamodel integration

*i** meta-class	CA metaclass	Metaclasses kept	Rationale
AGENT	ORGANISATIONAL_ACTOR	AGENT	- Equivalent concepts
ROLE	ORGANISATIONAL_ROLE	ROLE	- *i** provides more
GOAL	GOAL	GOAL (from *i**)	detailed definition
TASK	COMMUNICATIVE_EVENT	Both	- Equivalent under specific conditions
RESOURCE	MESSAGE_STRUCTURE	Both	

5   Top-Down Scenario Guidelines and Illustration

We present our guidelines for a top-down scenario whose main purpose is to guide the mapping from *i** elements into CA elements. Other possible scenarios (e.g., bottom-up, iterative, evolutionary, etc.) are not considered in the paper, but it is worth to remark that the proposed FRISCO-based ontological mapping make possible the formulation of similar guidelines for these cases.

The following guidelines help to implement the mappings that we have identified at a metamodel level when departing from a specific *i** model to obtain a CA model. They indicate how to derive *ca.communicative events* and *ca.message structures* since these CA elements only map into *i** elements under specific conditions. As seen in the previous section, *ca.organisational actors*, *ca.organisational roles* and *ca.goals* are always mapped from *istar.agents*, *istar.roles* and *istar.goals*.

Due to the strategic focus of *i** models, some informational *istar.resources* or some *istar.tasks* that should map into *ca.message structures* or *ca.communicative events*, may not be explicitly represented if they do not add strategically relevant knowledge. The proposed guidelines provide advice not only on how to obtain CA elements from explicit *i** elements but also on how to derive CA elements from *i** elements that are not explicit but which existence can nevertheless be deduced from the model. For example, the existence of an implicit informational *istar.resource* Insurance info can be deduced from the istar.goal Insurance provided (see Fig. 2).

CA focuses on communicative interactions. Therefore, most guidelines involve *i** dependencies, because satisfying a dependency will require some type of interaction in general. Each type of dependum has an associated guideline except resource dependums in which informational and physical resources require different treatment.

Guideline 1 deals with the case of dependums that are informational resources which according to our metamodel alignment map into *ca.message structures*.

Guideline 1. The dependum of a dependency D maps into a message structure M if such dependum is an informational resource. In that case, D induces a communicative event C such that: (1) C's primary actor is D's dependee actor, (2) C's receiver actor is D's depender actor, (3) C's ingoing and outgoing interactions specify M, (4) if any of the SR elements of D's dependee and depender actors are tasks, they map into C.

In our SuperStationery Co. case, the resource Order of the dependency from Sales Manager to Client maps into the CA message structure Order (see ingoing interaction in Table 4). The dependency for the Order from the Sales Manager to the Client indicates that the communicative event A client places an order that allows the Client communicate the order to the Sales Manager is needed.

Table 4. Guideline 1 applied to dependency for Order from Sales Manager to Client

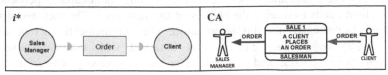

The rationale is that the *dependency* indicates that the *depender* expects to receive an information from the *dependee* and, therefore, a *communicative event* is needed to allow the *dependee* communicate that information to the *depender*.

The *ca.interface actor*, however, cannot be determined from the *i** model. It may coincide with the *primary actor* or not. It may even be an actor that does not appear in the *i** model at all because it is not strategically relevant. In the previous example the *ca.interface actor* Salesman does not appear in the *i** model.

Two *istar.tasks* i.e. one for the *dependee* and another for the *depender* may map into a single *communicative event*. The reason is that *i** provides a separate SR diagram for each actor and then the behaviour of a single *communicative event* with two involved actors appears distributed in two *istar.tasks* visualized into the boundary of the two actors. In our example, the task Place order in the Client SR maps into this new communicative event and a task of the Sales Manager SR (not shown in Fig. 2 for space reasons) also maps into it.

A dependency may be connected to SR elements which are not tasks indicating that the task of communicating the resource information is implicit in the *i** model.

Guideline 1 is also applied to the dependencies for Order (from the Supplier to the Sales Manager), Order response (from the Sales Manager to the Supplier) and Logistics Info (from Supplier and Client to the Transport Manager) to map to the communicative events SALE 2, SALE 3 and SALE 4 respectively (see Fig. 2 and Fig. 3).

The following group of guidelines deals with the rest of dependency types (i.e. where dependums are goals, tasks, softgoals or physical resources). Although these dependum types do not map directly into ca.message structures, they may indicate the existence of informational resources not explicit in the *i** model. We define an abstract guideline that yields to four actual guidelines (from guideline 2 to 5) depending on the type of dependum.

Abstract guideline. The dependum of a dependency D induces a message structure M if it is required that the dependee gives information to the depender about the intentional satisfaction of such dependum. In that case, D induces a communicative event C such that: (1) C's primary actor is D's dependee actor, (2) C's receiver actor is the D's depender actor, (3) C's ingoing and outgoing interactions specify M, (4) if any SR elements of D's dependee and depender actors are tasks, those tasks map into C.

We call this dependency an *informationable dependency*. The actual guidelines refine the notion of *intentional satisfaction* according to the type of the dependum.

Guideline 2. When the dependum is a goal, the notion of intentional satisfaction of the abstract guideline refines into attainment of this goal.

The informational resource mapping into the new *message structure* is implicit in the *i** model. In our example, the goal dependency for Insurance provided from the Client to the Insurance dept clerk is an informationable dependency because the client needs to receive the clauses of the insurance. The message structure Insurance info stands for this information. The communicative event Insur. Dept. clerk specifies clauses is obtained with communicative roles Insurance Dept Clerk and Client. The tasks Specify clauses (of the

`Insurance Dept Clerk`) and `Obtain Insurance` (of the `Client`) map into this event.

> **Guideline 3.** When the dependum is a task, the notion of <u>intentional satisfaction</u> of the abstract guideline refines into accomplishment of this task.

> **Guideline 4.** When the dependum is a softgoal, the notion of <u>intentional satisfaction</u> of the abstract guideline refines into level of satisfaction of this softgoal.

In our example, the softgoal dependency for `Products delivered timely by supplier` from the `Sales Manager` to the `Supplier` is an informationable dependency because the sales manager needs to be informed about the time when the products are shipped to supervise its timeliness. The message structure `Supplier ship notif` stands for this information. The communicative event `Supplier notifies the shipping of the goods` is obtained with communicative roles `Supplier` and `Sales Manager`. There is another informationable softgoal dependency for `Products delivered timely by truck driver` from the `Transport Manager` to the `Truck Driver`. The event `Truck Driver notifies the shipping of the goods` is obtained with communicative roles `Truck Driver` and `Transport Manager`.

> **Guideline 5.** When the dependum is a physical resource, the notion of <u>intentional satisfaction</u> of the abstract guideline refines into the provision of this physical resource.

The dependency for the physical resource `Products` from `Truck Driver` to `Supplier` leads to the creation of the communicative event `Supplier notifies the shipping of the goods`, which is merged with the notification that the `Supplier` gives to the `Sales Manager` (`SALE 6`). Thus, we add the receiver actor `Truck Driver` to `SALE 6`. Similarly, the dependency for `Products` from `Client` to `Truck Driver` leads to the addition of the receiver actor `Client` to `SALE 7`.

Finally, we provide two additional guidelines. Guideline 6 describes the derivation of information to be registered in the information system from an *istar.actor* and guideline 7 deals with ordering events in the CA model.

> **Guideline 6.** An actor about which relevant information has to be registered in the information system indicates that a communicative event and its corresponding message structure must be specified in order to register the actor information.

This guideline is only applied if the information about the actor is necessary. In our example, a message structure is required for `Client` in order to keep a registry of clients. Some of the information to be kept is: `VAT number`, `Client name`, `Telephone`, `Registration date`, `Client Addresses`. The communicative event `Clie 1` is also specified, it is not visible in Fig. 3 because it is part of another process, i.e. client registry.

In general, an *i** model does not provide information to deduce the ordering of the communicative events obtained from it, however if two chained dependencies with the same dependum appear in it then a precedence between the two mapped communicative events is implicitly induced. Guideline 7 stands for this case.

> **Guideline 7.** Two dependencies, D1 and D2, mapping into two communicative events C1 and C2, indicate that C1 precedes C2 in the communicative event diagram if:
> (1)   D1 and D2 have the same dependum
> (2)   the depender of D1 is the dependee of D2

In our example, there are two dependencies with the same dependum Order such that the Sales Manager is the depender in one and the dependee in the other. This indicates that the communicative event A client places an order where the Sales Manager receives the order must precede the event Sales Manager assigns supplier where the Sales Manager provides the order to the Supplier. Similarly, since there are two chained dependencies with the dependum Products, the event Supplier notifies the shipping of the goods must precede the event Truck driver notifies the shipping of the goods.

The internal structure of *ca.message* structures is not obtained by applying the guidelines because *i** models do not provide the details about the resources. It is necessary to explore organisational documents to obtain it.

6   Realising Goal and Process Integration: Prototype

A technological support for the integration of *i** and CA is necessary to carry out validations and future case studies. Although existing tools allow creating separate *i** and CA models, we intend to support the combined modelling.

We chose Eclipse (http://www.eclipse.org) as a technological platform. We used Eclipse Modelling Framework (http://www.eclipse.org/modeling/emf) and Graphical Modelling Framework (GMF, http://www.eclipse.org/modeling/gmp) to implement the metamodels and modelling tools for each method. We have followed a Model-Driven Architecture (MDA) [23] approach in order to develop a tool for both methods. This way, the handbooks of *i** and CA correspond to the Computation-Independent Model layer of MDA. The abstract syntax of both methods are represented by means of Platform-Independent Metamodels (PIMm), which correspond to Platform-Independent Model layer of MDA. According to these PIMm, we have specified the Platform-Specific Metamodels (PSMm) that are compliant with Eclipse. These PSMm corresponds to Platform-Specific Model layer of MDA. Finally, we defined the concrete syntax of both languages (graphical and textual appearance). The implemented tools correspond to the Code Model layer of MDA.

Previous works present a PSMm for CA models compliant with GMF [24].We adapted it based on the result of the metamodel integration (Section 4).

With respect to *i**, there are several metamodels available. We analysed the PIMm presented in [22] and we opted to maintain the most of its concepts, although it required some adaptations to account for the metamodel integration and make it GMF-compliant. To design the PSM metamodel for *i**, we have analysed three tool-oriented metamodels: the OpenOme metamodel [25], the metamodel presented by Giachetti [26], and the unified metamodel for *i** [27]. For further information and technical details about the prototype see [21].

7   Conclusions and Further Work

Given the existence of complementary perspectives in information system analysis, this work faces the challenge of integrating a goal-based and a business process-based modelling language. When attempting such task we had several criteria in mind: i) the languages should be described in a rigorous manner; ii) the integration should be theoretically underpinned; iii) the usage scenarios of the integrated language should be taken into consideration; and iv) tool support should be provided. We performed a review of related works, taking into account such criteria, to find out that there was indeed space for improvement. As a result, in this paper we undertake the integration of i* and Communication Analysis (CA). We have selected these languages for their expressiveness and their associated elicitation and specification techniques.

Following a design-science methodology, we created three new artefacts: 1) the ontological alignment between i* and CA, 2) the integrated metamodel, and 3) the guidelines for integrated modelling. For this purpose, we reported the ontological analysis of both languages. This analysis provided a sound theoretical foundation for integrating both modelling languages. Beyond supporting a conceptual reasoning, the analysis also facilitated making concrete decisions regarding metamodel integration; e.g., we selected one metaclass from a single language (removing the other) or we kept both depending on whether their associated concepts were totally equivalent or their alignment assumed a specific condition. We then integrated their metamodels, providing rationale for the design decisions. Moreover, we identified usage scenarios. In this paper we provided guidelines for top-down scenarios.

We have also developed an Eclipse-based tool to support the integrated modelling. We have taken into account the MDA layers and distinguished a platform-independent metamodel and a platform-specific metamodel, which involves techno-logical restrictions. This has facilitated clarifying the design rationale.

As a next step, we plan to provide guidelines for naming the CA elements and i* elements in order facilitate the traceability among the elements of the integrated models. In addition, we plan to confront top-down scenario so as to validate it (trade-off and sensitivity), transfer the solution to some of our industrial partners, and assess stakeholders' satisfaction. Also, we plan to provide guidelines to bottom-up, iterative and evolution scenarios.

Acknowledgements. This work has been supported by the Spanish MICINN PROS-Req (TIN2010-19130-C02-01, TIN2010-19130-C02-02); the Generalitat Valenciana ORCA (PROMETEO/2009/015); the FPI-UPV pre-doctoral grant; the European Commission FP7 Project CaaS (611351); and the ERDF structural funds.

References

1. Hammer, M., Champy, J.: Reengineering the corporation: a manifesto for business revolution. HarperCollins, New York (2003)
2. Henderson, J.C., Venkatraman, N.: Strategic alignment: leveraging information technology for transforming organizations. IBM Syst. J. 38(2-3), 472–484 (1999)
3. Yu, E.: Modelling Strategic Relationships for Process Reengineering, Department of Computer Science, University of Toronto (1995)

4. Zikra, I., Stirna, J., Zdravkovic, J.: Bringing Enterprise Modeling Closer to Model-Driven Development. In: Johannesson, P., Krogstie, J., Opdahl, A.L. (eds.) PoEM 2011. LNBIP, vol. 92, pp. 268–282. Springer, Heidelberg (2011)
5. Cardoso, E.C.S., Guizzardi, R.S.S., Almeida, J.P.A.: Aligning goal analysis and business process modelling: a case study in health care. IJBPIM 5(2), 144–158 (2011)
6. Yu, E., Mylopoulos, J.: From E-R to "A-R" - Modelling strategic actor relationships for business process reengineering. In: Loucopoulos, P. (ed.) ER 1994. LNCS, vol. 881, pp. 548–565. Springer, Heidelberg (1994)
7. Guizzardi, R.S.S., Guizzardi, G., Almeida, J.P.A., Cardoso, E.: Bridging the Gap between Goals, Agents and Business Processes, i* 2010: Hammamet, Tunisia
8. Kueng, P., Kawalek, P.: Goal-based business process models: creation and evaluation. Business Process Management Journal 3(1), 17–38 (1997)
9. Koliadis, G., Ghose, A.K.: Relating business process models to goal-oriented requirements models in KAOS. In: Hoffmann, A., Kang, B.-H., Richards, D., Tsumoto, S. (eds.) PKAW 2006. LNCS (LNAI), vol. 4303, pp. 25–39. Springer, Heidelberg (2006)
10. Morrison, E.D., et al.: Strategic alignment of business processes. In: WESOA (2011)
11. Kavakli, V., Loucopoulos, P.: Goal-driven business process analysis application in electricity deregulation. Information Systems 24(3), 187–207 (1999)
12. España, S., González, A., Pastor, Ó.: Communication analysis: A requirements engineering method for information systems. In: van Eck, P., Gordijn, J., Wieringa, R. (eds.) CAiSE 2009. LNCS, vol. 5565, pp. 530–545. Springer, Heidelberg (2009)
13. Wieringa, R.: Design science as nested problem solving. ACM DESRIST (2009)
14. Ralyté, J., Rolland, C.: An assembly process model for method engineering. In: Dittrich, K.R., Geppert, A., Norrie, M. (eds.) CAiSE 2001. LNCS, vol. 2068, p. 267. Springer, Heidelberg (2001)
15. Andersson, B., et al.: Towards a formal definition of goal-oriented business process patterns. Business Process Management Journal 11(6), 650–662 (2005)
16. Cardoso, E., et al.: A Method for Eliciting Goals for Business Process Models based on Non-Functional Requirements Catalogues. IJISMD 2(2) (2011)
17. Soffer, P., Wand, Y.: On the notion of soft-goals in business process modeling. Business Process Management Journal 11(6), 663–679 (2005)
18. González, A., Ruiz, M., España, S., Pastor, Ó.: Message Structures a modelling technique for information systems analysis and design. In: WER 2011 (2011)
19. Gonzalez, A., España, S., Pastor, O.: Unity criteria for business process modelling: A theoretical argumentation for a software engineering recurrent problem. In: RCIS 2009 (2009)
20. España, S.: Methodological integration of Communication Analysis into a model-driven software development framework, PhD thesis, UPV (2011)
21. Costal, D., et al.: Integration of i* and Communication Analysis, GESSI - UPC & PROS - UPV (2013), http://hci.dsic.upv.es/ca/CAiSE2014_TR.pdf
22. López, L., Franch, X., Marco, J.: Making Explicit Some Implicit i* Language Decisions. In: Jeusfeld, M., Delcambre, L., Ling, T.-W. (eds.) ER 2011. LNCS, vol. 6998, pp. 62–77. Springer, Heidelberg (2011)
23. OMG, MDA Guide, in How is MDA used? OMG. pp. 1–62 (2003)
24. Ruiz, M.: A model-driven framework to integrate Communication Analysis and OO-Method, Master thesis, Universitat Politècnica de València (2011)
25. OpenOME, an open-source requirements engineering tool, https://se.cs.toronto.edu/trac/ome/
26. Giachetti, G.: Supporting Automatic Interoperability in Model Driven Development Processes, PhD thesis, Universitat Politècnica de València (2011)
27. Santos, E., Silva, C., Alencar, F., Silva, M.J., Castro, J.: Towards a unified metamodel for i*. In: RCIS 2008 (2008)

Formalization of fUML: An Application to Process Verification

Yoann Laurent[1], Reda Bendraou[1], Souheib Baarir[1,2],
and Marie-Pierre Gervais[1,2]

[1] Sorbonne Universites, UPMC Univ Paris 06, UMR 7606, LIP6,
F-75005, Paris, France
[2] Universite Paris Ouest Nanterre La Défense, F-92001, Nanterre, France
first.last@lip6.fr

Abstract. Much research work has been done on formalizing UML Activity Diagrams for process modeling to verify different kinds of soundness properties (deadlock, unreachable activities and so on) on process models. However, these works focus mainly on the control-flow aspects of the process and have done some assumptions on the precise execution semantics defined in natural language in the UML specification. In this paper, we define a first-order logic formalization of fUML (Foundational Subset of Executable UML), the official and precise operational semantics of UML, in order to apply model checking techniques and therefore verify the correctness of fUML-based process models. Our formalization covers the control-flow, data-flow, resources, and timing dimensions of processes in a unified way. A working implementation based on the Alloy language has been developed. The implementation showed us that many kinds of behavioral properties not commonly supported by other approaches and implying multiple dimensions of the process can be efficiently checked.

Keywords: Formalization, Model-checking, fUML, Alloy.

1 Introduction

With the increasing complexity of processes, whatever their kind (i.e. business, software, medical, military), process modelers need adequate tooling support to simulate and to ensure their correctness before to use them in a real context. Recent studies reported a significant rate of errors in industrial process models [1,2]. Typical errors are deadlocks, unreachable activities, inefficient use of resources and timing problems.

UML Activity Diagrams (AD) are well-known for describing dynamic behavior and have been extensively used as a process modeling language (PML) [3,4,5]. UML is a standard with a good tooling support and AD allow the expression of most of the workflow patterns as identified by [6]. In order to verify UML-based process models, current state-of-the-art has already proposed some formalizations of the way an AD operates [7,8,9]. These formalizations are mandatory to apply model-checking techniques enabling an exhaustive and an automatic verification of their models. However, in the current UML specification [10], the operational semantics remains unclear, imprecise and ambiguous. This semantics

M. Jarke et al. (Eds.): CAiSE 2014, LNCS 8484, pp. 347–363, 2014.

is explained in *natural language* and dispersed through the specification. Due to this fact, the authors of these formalizations have done some assumptions on the precise operational semantics. As a consequence, the same process might be executed and verified differently from one tool into another, implying a *gap* between the semantics adopted respectively by each tool.

Recently, the OMG released fUML (Semantics of a Foundational Subset for Executable UML Models) [11], a new standard that precisely defines the execution semantics for a subset of UML 2.3 in a form of an *Execution Model* implemented in a virtual machine. However, even if the semantics is now clear and not subject to human interpretation, the semantics is not given in a formal way but in the form of pseudo Java-code. Therefore, it is not possible to straightforwardly apply model checking techniques.

In this paper, we define a formal model of fUML using first-order logic (FOL). The formalization addresses a subset of fUML encompassing only the concepts required for process modeling as identified in [3]. Current formalizations proposed in the literature focus mainly on the control-flow aspects of the process preventing to verify many kinds of properties related to data-flow, resources and timing constraints [12]. Therefore, our formalization covers both control and data-flow of the process through the use of the AD notations, and takes into account the associated organizational data such as resources and timing constraints. Then, we implement our formalization by using the Alloy modeling language [13] and we build a graphical tool on top of the implementation. The result of the verification is then graphically displayed on the process.

The rest of this paper is organized as follows. Section 2 presents the fUML standard and its execution semantics. Section 3 presents our FOL formalization of fUML. Section 4 gives an overview of interesting properties supported by our formalism. The implementation of the formalization and a case study are presented in Section 5. Finally, related work is addressed in Section 6 and Section 7 concludes by sketching some future perspectives of this work.

2   fUML

fUML is an OMG standard that precisely defines the execution semantics of a subset of UML 2.3. The standard defines a virtual machine in the form of pseudo Java-code, enabling compliant fUML models (i.e., UML models using only elements comprised in the fUML subset) to be executed. It can be decomposed in three main parts: (i) the abstract syntax represented by a subset of UML, mainly composed by the `Class Diagram` and most of the `Activity Diagram`; (ii) the Execution Model which defines the execution semantics of the abstract syntax and (iii) the model library which defines primitive types and behaviors (e.g. integer type and addition between two integers). In this section we give an overview of the Execution Model.

2.1   Execution Model

The Execution Model is itself a model, written in fUML, that specifies how fUML models are executed. The execution semantics adopted by fUML is quite similar

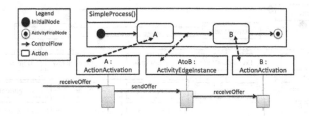

Fig. 1. Call between the UML elements within the Execution Model

to Coloured Petri Nets (CPN) and is based on the principle of offering and consuming object or control tokens between the different activity constituents.

To illustrate this concept, Figure 1 shows a simple process represented with an AD composed of one `InitialNode`, two `Action` nodes and an `ActivityFinalNode`. Each of these nodes are connected with a `ControlFlow` edge. The sequence diagram shows the corresponding calls between the nodes in the Execution Model. The diagram is a simplified version of what really happens during the execution and focuses on the interaction between elements. `ActionActivation` and `ActivityEdgeInstance` are the instantiation of the corresponding abstract syntax.

When the fUML virtual machine invokes this activity, it starts by inserting a token in each `InitialNode`. Then, the nodes with a token (i.e., the `InitialNode` in our example) *fire* (i.e., execute their own behavior) and *sendOffer* on each of their outputs `ControlFlow`. The `ControlFlow` is then able to call on its target node A to *receiveOffer*. When the node "A" receives an offer, it first checks if the prerequisites for its execution are satisfied, if yes, takes the offered tokens from the input control flows and fires. At the end of the firing operation, the node directly *sendOffer* on its outputs `ControlFlow`. The execution of an activity is then an extended chain of *sendOffer-receiveOffer-fire-sendOffer* calls between the activity constituents. When an `ActivityFinalNode` is reached or if there are no nodes still able to execute, the activity is terminated. Each abstract syntax element of an activity diagram has its own semantics. For example, a `DecisionNode` will offer a token only on one of its output edges determined during its fire execution.

Similarly to CPN, tokens positions and contents on the system represent the actual execution state. Since the goal of this paper is mainly on the verification of fUML-based process models, we focus on the formalization of the tokens game between the semantics elements of an UML AD. Note that we call "tokens game" the rules and conditions on which a token may pass through an edge to another node to form a complete execution.

3   Formalization of the fUML Tokens Game

In the following, we present our formalization of the fUML tokens game by defining the syntax of the langage and its semantics.

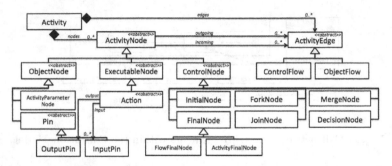

Fig. 2. Excerpt of the fUML Activity Diagram meta-model handled by our formalization

3.1 Syntax

Figure 2 shows an excerpt of the UML class diagram handled by our formalization. Here we concentrate only on those elements that are part of the fUML standard and useful for the definition of a process as identified in [3].

An `Activity` is a graph with three kinds of `ActivityNodes`: `ObjectNode`, `ControlNode` and `ExecutableNode`. An `ObjectNode` represents the data in a process, a `ControlNode` coordinates the execution flow and an `ExecutableNode` represents a node that can be executed, i.e. process action. There are two kinds of `ActivityEdge` to link the nodes: `ObjectFlow` and `ControlFlow`. `ObjectFlow` edges connect `ObjectNodes` and can have data passing along it. `ControlFlow` edges constrains the desired order of execution of the `ActivityNodes`. `ControlNode` can be used for parallel routing (`ForkJoin`), conditional routing (`DecisionNode`), synchronization (`JoinNode`) and merging multiple alternate flows (`MergeNode`). `InitialNode` and `AcitivityFinalNode` represent respectively the beginning and the end of an `Activity` while `FlowFinal` terminates a flow. `InputPin` and `OutputPin` are anchored to `Actions` to represent the required *input* data and the *output* data produced by the action. Similarly, an `Activity` can have multiple `ActivityParameterNode` to represent its data input and output. Thus, an `Activity` can represent a process by defining a coordinated sequencing set of actions using both control- and data-flow.

Formally, we consider three basic elements: *Control*, *Executable*, and *Object*.
- *Control* = {*fork*, *join*, *decision*, *merge*, *initial*, *activityFinal*, *flowFinal*} represents the different `ControlNode` types,
- *Executable* = {*action*} represents the `ExecutableNode` type,
- *Object* = {*activityParameter*, *outputPin*, *inputPin*} represents the `ObjectNode` type,
- *Types* = *Control* ∪ *Executable* ∪ *Object* represents the set of all types.

Thus, we introduce the notion of diagram as a vertex-labeled graph:

Definition 1. *A **Diagram** is a tuple $D = (V, E, Types, lab, lower, upper)$ such that:*
- *V is the set of vertices.*
- *$E \subseteq V \times V$ is the set of edges.*
- *$lab : V \mapsto Types$ is the labeling function associating to each vertice $v \in V$ a Types.*

- $lower/upper : V \mapsto \mathbb{N} \cup \{\epsilon\}$ *are functions that return, respectively, the* lower *and* upper *multiplicity of an object node.*

$$lower(v) \stackrel{def}{=} \begin{cases} n \in \mathbb{N} & \text{if } lab(v) \in Object \\ \epsilon & \text{otherwise} \end{cases}$$

The function upper *has the same definition.*

For a Diagram $D = (V, E, Types, lab, lower, upper)$, we introduce the following auxiliary functions that will help us to define formally an AD.

- $Vlab : Types \mapsto 2^V$ is the function that returns all the vertices of a type:

$$Vlab(t) \stackrel{def}{=} \{v \in V \mid lab(v) = t\}$$

- $incoming/outgoing : V \mapsto 2^E$ are functions that return, respectively, the incoming and outgoing edges of a node:

$$incoming(v) \stackrel{def}{=} \{(a, v) \in E \mid \forall a \in V\}$$
$$outgoing(v) \stackrel{def}{=} \{(v, a) \in E \mid \forall a \in V\}$$

- $source/target : E \mapsto V$ are functions that return, respectively, the source and target of an edge.

$$source(e) \stackrel{def}{=} \{s \in V \mid e = (s, t), \forall t \in V\}$$
$$target(e) \stackrel{def}{=} \{t \in V \mid e = (s, t), \forall s \in V\}$$

- $input/output : V \mapsto 2^V$ are functions that return, respectively, the input and output pins of an action node.

$$input(v) \stackrel{def}{=} \begin{cases} in \subseteq V & \text{if } lab(v) = action \wedge \forall v' \in in, lab(v') = inPin \wedge \\ & ((v, v') \in E \vee (v', v) \in E) \\ \emptyset & \text{otherwise} \end{cases}$$

$$output(v) \stackrel{def}{=} \begin{cases} out \subseteq V & \text{if } lab(v) = action \wedge \forall v' \in out, lab(v') = outPin \wedge \\ & ((v, v') \in E \vee (v', v) \in E) \\ \emptyset & \text{otherwise} \end{cases}$$

Now, we can define the notion of **Activity Diagram**. Actually, it is a **Diagram** with some additional structural constraints.

Definition 2. *An* **Activity Diagram** *is a Diagram,* $AD = (V, E, Types, lab, lower, upper)$, *with the following additional constraints:*

- *No node is disconnected:* $\forall v \in V, incoming(v) \neq \emptyset \vee outgoing(v) \neq \emptyset$.
- *The source and target of an edge are different:* $\forall e \in E, source(e) \neq target(e)$.
- *Initial nodes have no incoming edge:*

$$\forall v \in Vlab(initial) : incoming(v) = \emptyset$$

- *All activity final and flow final nodes have no outgoing edge:*

$$\forall v \in (Vlab(flowFinal) \cup Vlab(activityFinal)) : outgoing(v) = \emptyset$$

- *Pin nodes are connected to a unique pin node:*

$$\forall v \in Vlab(inPin) : |incoming(v) = \{(a, v) \in E \mid \forall a \in V\}| = 1 \wedge$$

$$\forall v \in Vlab(inPin), \forall e \in incoming(v), \forall a \in source(e) : lab(a) = outPin \wedge$$

$$\forall v \in Vlab(outPin) : |outgoing(v) = \{(v, a) \in E \mid \forall a \in V\}| = 1 \wedge$$

$$\forall v \in Vlab(outPin), \forall e \in outgoing(v), \forall a \in target(e) : lab(a) = inPin$$

- *The lower bound of an Object node is not greater than its upper bound:*

$$\forall v \in Vlab(Object) : lower(v) \leq upper(v)$$

- *The upper bound of an Object node is at least equal to one:*
$$\forall v \in Vlab(Object) : upper(v) \geq 1$$

Generally, a process is characterized by two main parts: the workflow and the associated organizational information. Here, the workflow is represented using UML AD. The organizational information is attached directly to the actions to give insight about the execution. This information is domain dependent. For instance, *software* processes might focus on the number of agents and their skills, while *medical* processes require instrumentation and drugs. Therefore, we define a process as an AD extended with most commonly used organizational information: resources and time. Note that the definition can be easily extended to take into account other domain dependent information.

Definition 3. *A **Process** is a tuple* $P = (V, E, Types, lower, upper, lab, Resource, Use, Timing)$ *where:*
- $(V, E, Types, lab, lower, upper)$ *forms an **Activity Diagram** s.t.:*
  - V *contains at least one initial node:* $\exists n \in V, lab(v) = initial.$
  - V *contains at least one activity final node:* $\exists n \in V, lab(v) = activity final.$
- *Resource is a finite set of resources,*
- $Use : V \mapsto 2^{Resource}$ *is the function that maps each action to a set of resources:*
$$Use(v) \stackrel{def}{=} \begin{cases} r \subseteq Resource & \text{if } lab(v) = action \\ \emptyset & \text{otherwise} \end{cases}$$
- $Timing : V \mapsto \mathbb{N} \cup \{\epsilon\}$ *is the function that associates to each action a time to perform it:*
$$Timing(v) \stackrel{def}{=} \begin{cases} v \in \mathbb{N} & \text{if } lab(v) = action \\ \epsilon & \text{otherwise} \end{cases}$$

3.2   Semantics

The semantics of our model follows the newly defined fUML standard [11]. We formalize the way the tokens transit between the nodes and edges that compose an fUML AD model. Moreover, to be able to reason about the timing constraints of the process, we extend the formalization with discrete clocks representing the time spent during the process execution.

The semantics of our formalism is based on the notions of *states*, *enabling* and *firing* of transitions (similar to those used in CPN).

State. A state formalizes the configuration on which the process is at any time of its execution.

Definition 4 (State). *A state of a process* $P = (V, E, Types, lower, upper, lab, Resource, Use, Timing)$ *is a tuple* $s = (m, gc, lc)$ *such that:*
- $m : V \cup E \mapsto \mathbb{N}$ *is the function, called marking, that associates to each node and edge a natural number.*
  - *for* $v \in V$, $m(v)$ *is the number of tokens,*
  - *for* $e \in E$, $m(e)$ *is the number of offers.*
- $gc \in \mathbb{N}$ *is the global discrete clock representing the current time spent on the process,*

– $lc : V \mapsto \mathbb{N} \cup \{\epsilon\}$ is the local discrete clock representing the current time spend on a given action:

$$lc(v) \overset{def}{=} \begin{cases} n \in \mathbb{N} & \text{if } lab(v) = action \\ \epsilon & \text{otherwise} \end{cases}$$

The set of all states of a process P is noted **States**.

Definition 5 (Initial State). An initial state $s_0 = (m_0, gc_0, lc_0)$ of the system is always defined as follows:

– All nodes own 0 token, except (i) the initial nodes which start with 1 token and (ii) the input activity parameter node which start with a number of tokens that varies between its lower and upper bounds:

$$m_0(v) = \begin{cases} 1 & \text{if } lab(v) = initial \\ n \in \{lower(v), ..., upper(v)\} & \text{if } lab(v) = activityParameter \wedge \\ & incoming(v) = \emptyset \\ 0 & \text{otherwise} \end{cases}$$

– The global clock is initialized to zero: $gc_0 = 0$.
– Local clocks are initialized to zero:

$$lc_0(v) = \begin{cases} 0 & \text{if } lab(v) = action \\ \epsilon & \text{otherwise} \end{cases}$$

Transition. The dynamic of a process, i.e. its execution, is defined through the notion of *transition*. To move from a state to another one, a transition is first *enabled* then *fired*. Therefore, the *enabling* notion corresponds to a precondition while the *firing* notion corresponds to a post-condition. We first define the enabling notion, and then formalize the firing concept.

Transition enabling. A transition is said to be *enabled* when some preconditions are met (to allow the firing of the transition). By abstracting the way the fUML Execution Model executes an AD, two cases can be distinguished: (i) a node is ready to execute; (ii) a node is ready to terminate. In our framework, these are represented by predicates **eStart** and **eFinish**, respectively. Also, note that the system can progress through time elapsing using the **eTime** predicate.

Let us consider a process $P = (V, E, Types, lower, upper, lab, Resource, Use, Timing)$ and a state $s = (m, gc, lc)$. To simplify our notation, we assume that s is implicitly available in the following enabling predicates.

1. **eStart** is the predicate that determines if a node v is ready to be executed. Its formal definition relies on the following auxiliary predicates.
   – The first condition corresponds to check if the node is not already executing (not owning tokens) and have incoming edges:

   $$pAll(v) \overset{def}{=} (m(v) = 0) \wedge incoming(v) \neq \emptyset$$

   – An *activity* node needs an offer on all of its incoming edges:

   $$pNode(v) \overset{def}{=} pAll(v) \wedge \bigwedge_{e \in incoming(v)} (m(e) > 0)$$

- An *action* node extends the behavior with input and output pins, so the number of offers on its incoming pins are also checked:

$$pAction(v) \overset{def}{=} pNode(v) \wedge \bigwedge_{e \in incoming(input(v))} (m(e) \geq lower(v))$$

- Unlike other activity nodes, a *merge* node needs at least one of its incoming edge to have an offer:

$$pMerge(v) \overset{def}{=} pAll(v) \wedge \bigvee_{e \in incoming(v)} (m(e) > 0)$$

Then, the enabling test corresponds to:

$$eStart(v) \overset{def}{=} \begin{cases} pAction(v) & \text{if } lab(v) = action \\ pMerge(v) & \text{if } lab(v) = merge \\ pNode(v) & \text{otherwise} \end{cases}$$

2. **eFinish** is the predicate that determines if a node is ready to terminate and relies on the following auxiliary predicates.
   - The node must own tokens:

$$haveTokens(v) \overset{def}{=} (m(v) > 0)$$

   - An *action* must have its local clock incremented at least until its defined timing:

$$pTiming(v) \overset{def}{=} (lc(v) \geq Timing(v))$$

Then, the enabling test to terminate a node corresponds to:

$$eFinish(v) \overset{def}{=} \begin{cases} haveTokens(v) \wedge pTiming(v) & \text{if } lab(v) = action \\ haveTokens(v) & \text{otherwise} \end{cases}$$

3. **eTime** determinates if the clocks can be increased. The clocks can be increased only during working time, i.e. when there is at least one action that is executing:

$$eTime() \overset{def}{=} \bigvee_{v \in V, lab(v) = action} ((m(v) > 0) \wedge (lc(v) < Timing(v)))$$

Transition firing. The firing of a transition and the effect it has on a state can be defined as follows. Also here, two cases have to be distinguished: (i) firing a transition on a node that can start; (ii) firing a transition on a node that can terminate and (iii) firing a transition to represent the elapsing time.

Let us consider a second state $s' = (m', gc', lc')$. **fStart**, **fFinish** and **fTime** express the constraints that must be satisfied to ensure that s' is a successor of s. **fStart** is a constraint related to a staring node (a node that satisfies the enabling predicate **eStart**), **fFinish** is a constraint related to a finishing node (a node that satisfies the enabling predicate **eFinish**), and **fTime** is a constraint related to the increasing of the clocks (if the current state satisfies the enabling predicate **eTime**). For simplification, we assume that s and s' are implicitly available in the following firing predicates.

We first introduce the predicate fz that constrains to equality the marking of all the vertices and edges of s and s', except the one given as parameter p:

$$fz(p \in (V \cup E)) \overset{def}{=} \bigvee_{v \in \{(V \cup E) \setminus p\}} (m'(v) = m(v))$$

1. **fStart** is based on the following auxiliary predicates.
   - An *activity* node is executed by adding a token on it and removing the offers from its incoming edges:

$$sNode(v) \stackrel{def}{=} (m'(v) = m(v) + 1) \wedge \bigwedge_{e \in incoming(v)} (m'(e) = m(e) - m'(v))$$
$$\wedge fz(v \cup incoming(v))$$

   - An *action* node requires some additional conditions due to the presence of input and output pins. Offers from the incoming edge of its input pin are consumed up to the maximum bound allowed by the multiplicity. Then, tokens are produced on the output pin between the lower and upper multiplicity bound:

$$sActionIPin(v) \stackrel{def}{=} \bigwedge_{\substack{i \in input(v), \\ inc \in incoming(i)}} ((\neg(upper(i) \geq m(inc)) \wedge m'(i) = m(inc))$$
$$\vee ((upper(i) \geq m(inc)) \wedge m'(i) = upper(i)))$$

$$sActionOPin(v) \stackrel{def}{=} \bigwedge_{o \in output(v)} (m'(o) \geq lower(o) \wedge m'(o) < upper(o))$$

$$sActionEdge(v) \stackrel{def}{=} \bigwedge_{\substack{e \in incoming(v) \\ \cup incoming(input(v))}} (m'(e) = m(e) - m'(v))$$

$$sAction(v) \stackrel{def}{=} (m'(v) = m(v) + 1) \wedge sActionIPin(v)$$
$$\wedge sActionOpin(v) \wedge sActionEdge(v)$$
$$\wedge fz(v \cup input(v) \cup output(v)$$
$$\cup incoming(v) \cup incoming(input(v)))$$

   - Unlike the other nodes, a *merge* node is executed by removing offers from only *one* of its incoming edges:

$$sMerge(v) \stackrel{def}{=} (m'(v) = m(v) + 1) \wedge (\bigvee_{\substack{e \in incoming(v), \\ m(e) > 0}} (m'(e) = m(e) - m'(v))$$
$$\wedge fz(e \cup v))$$

   Then, the transition firing, for a starting node, is characterized by:

$$fStart(v) \stackrel{def}{=} \begin{cases} sAction(v) & \text{if } lab(v) = action \\ sMerge(v) & \text{if } lab(v) = merge \\ sNode(v) & \text{otherwise} \end{cases}$$

2. **fFinish** is based of the following auxiliary predicates.
   - An *activity* node remove its owning tokens and offers it on all its outgoing edges:

$$fNode(v) \stackrel{def}{=} (m'(v) = m(v) - 1) \wedge \bigwedge_{e \in outgoing(v)} (m'(e) = m(e) + m(v))$$
$$\wedge fz(v \cup outgoing(v))$$

   - A *flowFinal* node removes its token but do not offer it:

$$fFlowFinal(v) \stackrel{def}{=} (m'(v) = m(v) - 1) \wedge fz(v)$$

- A *decision* node only offers its token only on one of its outgoing edges:

$$fDecision(v) \stackrel{def}{=} (m'(v) = m(v) - 1)$$
$$\wedge \bigvee_{e \in outgoing(v)} (m'(e) = m(e) + m(v) \wedge fz(v \cup e))$$

- An *action* node requires to reset its tokens on both its input and output pins, and offers its tokens on its outgoing edges and outgoing edges of its output pins. Moreover, its local clock is reinitialized to 0:

$$fActionPin(v) \stackrel{def}{=} \bigwedge_{p \in (output(v) \cup input(v))} (m'(p) = 0)$$

$$fActionEdge(v) \stackrel{def}{=} \bigwedge_{\substack{e \in (outgoing(v) \\ \cup outgoing(output(v)))}} (m'(e) = m(e) + m'(v))$$

$$fAction(v) \stackrel{def}{=} (m'(v) = m(v) - 1) \wedge fActionPin(v) \wedge fActionEdge(v)$$
$$\wedge (lc'(v) = 0) \wedge fz(v \cup input(v) \cup output(v)$$
$$\cup outgoing(v) \cup outgoing(output(v)))$$

Then, the transition firing, for a finishing node, is defined by:

$$fFinish(v) \stackrel{def}{=} \begin{cases} fFlowFinal(v) & \text{if } lab(v) = flowFinal \\ fDecision(v) & \text{if } lab(v) = decision \\ fAction(v) & \text{if } lab(v) = action \\ fNode(v) & \text{otherwise} \end{cases}$$

3. **fTime** increases the local clock of each action currently executing and increases the global clock as well:

$$fTime() \stackrel{def}{=} (gc' = gc + 1) \wedge \bigwedge_{\substack{v \in Vlab(action) \\ \wedge(m(v) > 0)}} (lc' = lc + 1) \wedge fz(\emptyset)$$

At this point we are able to define the complete transition (successor relation between states). Basically, when an activity final node is executed, or when there is no other node that can either start or terminate, the execution is over.

Definition 6 (Successor Relation). Let $P = (V, E, Types, lower, upper, lab, Resource, Use, Timing)$ be a process. Let $s = (m, gc, lc)$ and $s' = (m', gc', lc')$ be two states of P. s' is a successor of s, iff the predicate $transition(s, s')$ holds:

$$step(v) \stackrel{def}{=} (eStart(v) \wedge fStart(v))$$
$$\vee (eFinish(v) \wedge fFinish(v))$$
$$\vee (eTime() \wedge fTime())$$

$$transition(s, s') \stackrel{def}{=} \bigwedge_{v \in Vlab(activityFinal)} (m(v) = 0) \wedge \bigvee_{v \in V} (step(v))$$

Thus, to represent a process execution, we define the notion of trace:

Definition 7 (Trace). Let $P = (V, E, Types, lower, upper, lab, Resource, Use, Timing)$ be a process. A **Trace** is an ordered set of states denoted $\sigma = \langle s_0, s_1, ..., s_n \rangle \in States^*$ s.t.: $\forall i \in \mathbb{N}, transition(\sigma[i], \sigma[i+1])$ holds, where $\sigma[i]$ denotes the i-th state of the trace and s_0 is the initial state. The set of all trace is noted **Traces**.

4 Properties for Process Verification

To study the properties of the modelled process using our formalization we need a formal logic. Many logics exist and can express different kind of properties: Computation Tree Logic (CTL), Linear Temporal Logic (LTL), etc. In our case, almost all our properties can be handled using LTL.

LTL formulae are constructed from atomic propositions, logical operators $\vee$, $\wedge$, $\neg$, and temporal operators X (meaning "next"), G ("globally"), U ("until") and F ("eventually") [14]. In our formalism, atomic propositions are statical (related to the structure of the process) or dynamical, of the form $m(n)\ op\ v$ or $gc\ op\ v$ where $n \in V \cup E$, $op \in \{=, \neq, <, \leq, >, \geq\}$ and $v \in \mathbb{N}$.

Given a process $P = (V, E, Types, lower, upper, lab, Resource, Use, Timing)$ and an LTL property ϕ, we say that $P \models \phi$, iff $\forall \sigma \in \mathbf{Traces}, \sigma \models \phi$. It is worth noting that LTL semantics is defined over infinite traces. To treat the case of finite traces, we just used the so-called stuttering principle to extend a trace to an infinite one.

In the following, we give an overview of interesting properties that can be verified on a process and give some examples. Due to space restriction, we choose only some relevant constraints from each aspect of the process dimension. The goal here is to show the ability of our formalism to deal with a wide variety of process constraints rather than presenting them exhaustively.

Control-Flow. Control-flow analysis deals with questions like "does the process terminate?", "Is there any deadlock?", "Does TaskA ever happen?", etc. These properties are often referred as *soundness* properties [12] in the literature. Soundness tends to check some desirable properties such that a started process can always complete (*option to complete*).

- *Option to complete* can be checked by verifying that at least one ActivityFinalNode of the process is always executed:

$$F \left(\bigvee_{v \in Vlab(activityFinal)} (m(v) > 0) \right) \tag{1}$$

Data-Flow. The goal of data flow analysis [15] is to validate the process against different data problems such as *missing data*, i.e. when a data element needs to be accessed, but either it has never been created or it has been deleted without having been created again.

- *Missing data* can be checked by ensuring that when a node has offers on its control edges, it will finally have offers on its input pin:

$$G \left(\bigwedge_{v \in Vlab(action)} (pNode(v) \implies F(pAction(v))) \right) \tag{2}$$

Resources. Resources properties deal with resource problems like *missing resource*, i.e., when an activity requires a resource which may not be available.

- *Missing resource* can be checked by verifying that when an action is ready to start, there is no other action currently executing utilizing the same resource:

$$\bigwedge_{\substack{v \in Vlab(action), \\ r \in Resource, \\ r \in Use(v)}} \mathsf{G}\ (eStart(v) \implies (\bigwedge_{\substack{o \in Vlab(action), \\ o \neq v}} (r \in Use(o) \implies m(o) = 0))) \quad (3)$$

Time. The goal of timing properties is to answer questions like "Is it possible to finish the process *on time* whatever the path taken?".

- To check that the process can terminate before *max* time unit can be expressed by the following LTL property:

$$\mathsf{F}(\bigvee_{v \in Vlab(activityFinal)} (m(v) > 0) \land (gc > max)) \quad (4)$$

A counter-example to this formula means that at least one execution can terminate before *max* time unit. This answers the original property.

Business. While the other categories specify properties that must hold for all processes, business properties represent specific properties tailored to a given process. They play an important role since a process could be syntactically correct and valid against the precedent properties but still violates some business constraints. Business properties deal with questions like "does the ImportantAction is executed whatever the choice made during the execution?" or "Is ImportantArtefact (i.e., the goal of the process) always available at the end of the process?".

- Let $P = (V, E, Types, lower, upper, lab, Resource, Use, Timing)$ be a process. Let $actionA, actionB \in V, lab(ationA) = lab(actionB) = action$ be two action nodes and let $max \in \mathbb{N}$ be a natural representing the maximum time between the execution of two actions. To verify that when actionA is executed, actionB is always executed afterwards before *max* time units the property is expressed as follows:

$$\forall i \in \mathbb{N} : \mathsf{G}((m(\mathtt{actionA}) > 0 \land (gc = i)) \implies$$
$$\mathsf{F}((m(\mathtt{actionB}) > 0) \land (gc \leq max + i))) \quad (5)$$

Note that this constraint use infinite domain of integer which makes it not a standard LTL formula. However, we can turn it back to classical LTL formula by a simple modification of the treated model. For a sake of clarity, we do not burden the model and stick to our expression.

5   Implementation

We implement our formalization using the Alloy language [13]. It is is a declarative modeling language based on FOL and relational calculus for expressing complex structural and behavioral constraints. It is associated to a tool, called Alloy Analyzer: a constraint solver that provides fully automatic simulation and checking based on model-finding through SAT-solving (Satisfiability-solving).

On top of the formal framework implemented using Alloy, we have developed a prototype currently provided as an Eclipse EMF plugin. The main intent of

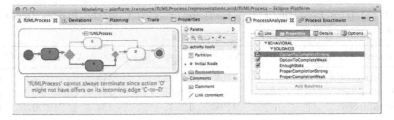

Fig. 3. Process Analyzer integrated inside our process environment, displaying a counter-example for the *option-to-complete* property

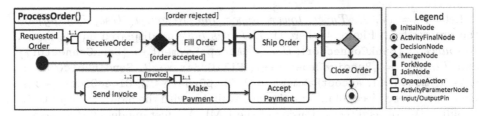

Fig. 4. ProcessOrder process represented as an fUML Activity Diagram

this prototype is to assist the modeler by automatically verifying fUML-based processes in the form of XMI Instances. It comes with a library of predefined properties ready to be checked, but also allows to add some common *business properties* through a graphical interface. The user only has to check in the interface the desired properties, and fill the parameter if required (e.g., maximum time to terminate the process). The *business properties* can be added through pre-defined templates, e.g. select the ActionA which must always be executed before ActionB. Figure 3 shows a screenshot of our tooling for process modeling and enactment emphasizing the process view and its analyzer. When the verification is performed, the path leading to the counter-example (if any) is highlighted in green for reachability properties, and in red otherwise.

5.1 Case Study

This section presents a case study on the Alloy implementation by checking the properties presented in section 4 on the ProcessOrder process from the UML specification [10]. This process simply proceeds the arrival of a new order and is visible on Figure 4.

To perform the verification, the process and the properties are translated into an Alloy specification. Then, this specification is given as input to the Alloy Analyzer which reduces the verification to a SAT problem. It is presented to a SAT solver (MiniSat among others) in a Conjunctive Normal Form (CNF) format. A CNF is a conjunction of clauses. Each clause represents a disjunction of variables. A satisfying assignement to a SAT problem consists of a boolean affectation to the variables such that all clauses are satisfied. Usually, the complexity of a SAT problem is measured by the number of clauses and variables.

Table 1. Metrics from the `Alloy Analyzer` executed on the `ProcessOrder` from Figure 4

PROPERTY	T. SEMANTICS	VARS	CLAUSES	CNF GEN.	SAT SOLVING	C.E.
(1) Control-flow		410k	1239k	31s	5s	no
(2) Data-flow		427k	1286k	27s	5s	no
(3) Resources		419k	1261k	33s	0.3s	no
(4) Time	✓	2361k	8716k	185s	3s	yes
(5) Business	✓	2385k	8716k	201s	199s	no

Let $P = (V, E, Types, lower, upper, lab, Resource, Use, Timing)$ be the process from Figure 4 where $(V, E, Types, lab)$ are displayed on the figure, $Resource = \{\texttt{BankConnector}\}$, $Use = \{\texttt{AcceptPayment} \mapsto \{\texttt{BankConnector}\}\}$ and $Timing = \{\texttt{ReceiveOrder} \mapsto 1, \texttt{FillOrder} \mapsto 2, \texttt{SendInvoice} \mapsto 1, \texttt{MakePayment} \mapsto 1, \texttt{AcceptPayment} \mapsto 2, \texttt{ShipOrder} \mapsto 3, \texttt{CloseOrder} \mapsto 1 \}$. Generally, these pieces of information are available with the model through UML Profiling [10] or as direct extension of the UML AD metamodel [3]. For sake of clarity, we do not propose some graphical representation of these data ($Resource$, Use and $Timing$) but directly give their formal representation.

Table 1 summarizes the obtained results. Column 1 represents the analyzed property from Section 4. For the "(4) time" property, we are using $max = 4$. Concerning the "(5) business" property, we choose the two actions `FillOrder` and `SendInvoice`, and $max = 6$. Columns 2 specifies if we are using the timed semantics for the verification. Due to the presence of the global and local clock ticks, a lot of extra states are introduced to support the properties related to the time. For efficiency reason, we also implemented a version of the semantics without these clocks on each state for the properties which are not relying on it. Columns 3 and 4 represent, respectively, the number of generated variables and clauses. Columns 5 and 6 represent, respectively, the time to generate the CNF and to solve the SAT problem. Columns 7 specifies the result of the verification, if there is any counter-example. All analyses were performed on a MacBook Air 2011 with Intel Core i5 processor and 4GB of RAM with Mavericks as OS.

These results highlight the effectiveness of our tool w.r.t. a concrete example. Actually, even if the whole generated SAT problems present a relatively high complexity (over 1 million clauses and over 410 thousand variables), the solving time is less than 1 minute for the untimed properties. The timed-related properties have a similar ratio in terms of clauses and variables but require few minutes due to the presence of extra states. Interested readers can download the complete Alloy formalization with the case study from our website[1].

6   Related Work

There is an extensive literature on verifying process models. A complete overview of the related work would be beyond the scope of this paper (see [12]). Therefore,

---

[1] `http://pagesperso-systeme.lip6.fr/Yoann.Laurent/`

we focus on the work directly relevant to this paper, namely formal verification approaches of UML AD.

Generally, the verification is based on mapping the process model into mathematical formalisms used to model systems such as automata, Petri Nets or process algebra. All of these formalisms have been investigated for the verification of UML AD. Jung et al. [16] propose a transformation from UML AD to Colored Petri Nets. Dong et al. [7] presents an approach for formalizing UML AD using π-calculus, a kind of computing models for representing concurrent systems and express the interactions between evolving processes. Eshuis et al. [8] check UML AD in the context of workflow modeling by translating the activity into the input language of NuSMV, a symbolic model checker. Guelfi et al. [9] propose a translation of UML AD extended with timing constraints into Promela (Process or Protocol Meta Language) in order to check behavioral properties with the model-checker SPIN. However, these works are not based on the new fUML standard and have done some assumptions on the precise operational semantics which creates tool-interoperability problems. Moreover, the semantics richness of these approaches are less complete than fUML, many simplifications have been carried out. While all of these approaches propose to check control-flow related properties, data-flow are not always considered and only [9] supports the timing constraints. Properties related to the resources are never supported.

Montogna et al. [17] propose an approach allowing the definition of a virtual machine for fUML in the $\mathbb{K}$-Framework, enabling the execution of models on a more formal definition than the current Java-based implementation. To the best of our knowledge, there is no temporal logic verification proposed.

Abdelhalim et al. [18] present an approach to manually map an fUML models into the process algebraic specification language CSP (Communicating Sequential Processes) and use the FDR (Failures-Divergences Refinement) model-checker to check if the model is deadlock free. When a deadlock is found, a counter-example trace which led to the deadlock is generated. Their formalization focuses only on the asynchronous communication between objects within fUML which has been guided by their case study.

To the best of our knowledge, our work is the first attempt to formalize the tokens game of the fUML standard to verify process models. If a comparison is made between the above-mentioned work, our approach is not relying on the semantics and concepts of the targeted formal language in terms of expressiveness, e.g. Petri Nets, instead of the modeling language. In these approaches, the assumption is made that the semantics choices made in these formal techniques are valid as well for UML AD.

7   Conclusion and Future Work

This paper proposes a first-order logic formalization of the newly defined fUML specification to verify fUML-based process models. The formalization is able to deal with the control- and data-flow, resources, and timing aspects of the process in a unified way. A tool implementation based on the Alloy modeling language has been successfully integrated in an Eclipse-based process environment. The tool is able to verify automatically a wide range of properties without the user's intervention and allows one to verify some *business* properties. Currently, the tool is under evaluation within the European MERgE project, which main goal is to develop and demonstrate innovative concepts and design tools addressing both "safety" and "security" concerns in development processes.

The case study and the tool proved the feasibility of our approach, however some improvements are already under realization. The first one consists in covering the formalization of more UML AD concepts that can be of interest for the modeling of more complex processes. Examples of such concepts are `DataStoreNode` (a buffer for non-transient data), `AcceptEventAction` and `SendSignalAction` (for dealing with events) and `StructuredActivity` (expansion, loop, conditional nodes). Moreover, we are working on extending the formalization to be *data-aware*. Currently, the contents of the tokens within the `ObjectNodes` are not taken into account. This prevents, for example, to express *guard* on edge to determine if the edge can be traversed. Some formalizations have taken some of these concepts into accounts [8]. However, much simplification has been done in comparison of the way fUML operates and only integers are considered. In fUML, each tokens can have a simple value type (integer, string, natural, boolean) or more complex `Classifier` type defined in a Class Diagram. Then, tokens are manipulated using the action nodes from the `IntermediateActions` package. This package defines the classical actions to create, read, suppress and modify tokens at runtime within the AD and formalizing such concepts is a non-trivial task. Finally, we are exploring optimizations techniques to treat the properties related to time in a more efficient way based on the expertise of well-known approaches such as timed automata.

Acknowledgments. This work was funded by the MERgE project (ITEA 2 Call 6 11011).

References

1. Mendling, J.: Empirical studies in process model verification. In: Jensen, K., van der Aalst, W.M.P. (eds.) Transactions on Petri Nets and Other Models of Concurrency II. LNCS, vol. 5460, pp. 208–224. Springer, Heidelberg (2009)
2. Mendling, J., Verbeek, H., van Dongen, B.F., van der Aalst, W.M., Neumann, G.: Detection and prediction of errors in epcs of the sap reference model. Data & Knowledge Engineering 64(1), 312–329 (2008)
3. Bendraou, R., Gervais, M.-P., Blanc, X.: UML4SPM: A UML2.0-based metamodel for software process modelling. In: Briand, L.C., Williams, C. (eds.) MoDELS 2005. LNCS, vol. 3713, pp. 17–38. Springer, Heidelberg (2005)
4. Bendraou, R., Jézéquel, J., Gervais, M., Blanc, X.: A comparison of six uml-based languages for software process modeling. IEEE Transactions on Software Engineering 36(5), 662–675 (2010)
5. Russell, N., van der Aalst, W.M., Ter Hofstede, A.H., Wohed, P.: On the suitability of uml 2.0 activity diagrams for business process modelling In: Proceedings of the 3rd Asia-Pacific Conference on Conceptual Modelling, vol. 53
6. van Der Aalst, W.M., Ter Hofstede, A.H., Kiepuszewski, B., Barros, A.P.: Workflow patterns. Distributed and Parallel Databases 14(1), 5–51 (2003)

7. Dong, Y., ShenSheng, Z.: Using π-calculus to formalize uml activity diagram for business process modeling. In: ECBS, pp. 47–54. IEEE (2003)
8. Eshuis, R.: Symbolic model checking of uml activity diagrams. TOSEM (2006)
9. Guelfi, N., Mammar, A.: A formal semantics of timed activity diagrams and its promela translation. In: APSEC. IEEE (2005)
10. OMG: Uml version 2.4.1 (2011), http://www.omg.org/spec/UML/
11. OMG: Fuml version 1.1 (2013), http://www.omg.org/spec/FUML/
12. van der Aalst, W., Van Hee, K., ter Hofstede, A., Sidorova, N., Verbeek, H., Voorhoeve, M., Wynn, M.: Soundness of workflow nets: classification, decidability, and analysis. Formal Aspects of Computing 23(3), 333–363 (2011)
13. Jackson, D.: Software Abstractions: logic, language and analysis. MIT Press (2011)
14. Pnueli, A.: The temporal logic of programs. In: 18th Annual Symposium on Foundations of Computer Science, pp. 46–57. IEEE (1977)
15. Trčka, N., van der Aalst, W.M.P., Sidorova, N.: Data-flow anti-patterns: Discovering data-flow errors in workflows. In: van Eck, P., Gordijn, J., Wieringa, R. (eds.) CAiSE 2009. LNCS, vol. 5565, pp. 425–439. Springer, Heidelberg (2009)
16. Jung, H.T., Joo, S.H.: Transformation of an activity model into a colored petri net model. In: TISC, pp. 32–37. IEEE (2010)
17. Motogna, S., Cr Ciun, F., Lazar, I.: Pârv: Formal definition of fuml in k-framework. Studia Universitatis Babes-Bolyai, Informatica 58(3) (2013)
18. Abdelhalim, I., Sharp, J., Schneider, S., Treharne, H.: Formal verification of tokeneer behaviours modelled in fUML using CSP. In: Dong, J.S., Zhu, H. (eds.) ICFEM 2010. LNCS, vol. 6447, pp. 371–387. Springer, Heidelberg (2010)

On the Elasticity of Social Compute Units

Mirela Riveni, Hong-Linh Truong, and Schahram Dustdar

Distributed Systems Group, Vienna University of Technology
{m.riveni,truong,dustdar}@infosys.tuwien.ac.at

Abstract. Advances in human computation bring the feasibility of utilizing human capabilities as services. On the other hand, we have witnessed emerging collective adaptive systems which are formed from heterogeneous types of compute units to solve complex problems. The recently introduced Social Compute Units (SCUs) present one type of these systems, which have human-based services as their core fundamental compute units. While, there is related work on forming SCUs and optimizing their performance with adaptation techniques, most of it is focused on static structures of SCUs. To provide better runtime performance and flexibility management for SCUs, we present an elasticity model for SCUs and mechanisms for their elastic management which allow for certain fluctuations in size, structure, performance and quality. We model states of elastic SCUs, present APIs for managing SCUs as well as metrics for controlling their elasticity with which it is possible to tailor their performance parameters at runtime within the customer-set constraints. We illustrate our contribution with an example algorithm.

Keywords: Social Compute Units, Elasticity, Adaptation, Collective Adaptive Systems.

1 Introduction

In recent years, new forms of collective adaptive systems(CASs) that consider heterogeneous types of compute units/resources(e.g., software services, human based services and smart-devices) have emerged [20]. These systems allow compute units to be flexibly added and/or removed from them, and different collectives can overlap with each other by utilizing each other's resources. Compute units within collectives are collaborative, manageable and may be given decision making responsibilities. With the advance of human computation [17] there is a possibility of forming CASs that include human-based services [21] as compute units. Social Compute Units(SCUs), introduced in [6], can be considered as one type of these collective adaptive systems. They are virtual compositions of individual human compute units, performing human computation tasks with a cloud-like behavior. SCUs are possible today because of the human resource pools that are provided by human computation platforms (e.g., crowdsourcing platforms, social networking platforms and expert networks), which have brought the possibility to investigate ways of utilizing human computation under the service oriented computing paradigm. However, due to the unpredictability of

M. Jarke et al. (Eds.): CAiSE 2014, LNCS 8484, pp. 364–378, 2014.

human behavior, human-based services bring considerable challenges in their management. This is especially the case with collective adaptive systems such as SCUs, where the ways to manage resources are obviously different and more complex than the management of crowd workers that work individually, and that of collaborations with fixed number of resources. In this context, traditional platforms that support virtual fixed-sized collaborations might not be as efficient as those that support SCUs with elastic capabilities that offer opportunities for variable resource numbers with variable scalable capabilities. There are several reasons for this. First, unexpected tasks might be generated at run-time which may require new type of elements with new type of capabilities. In fixed-resource collaborations, usually existing members need to learn these tasks and thus the work might be delayed and/or executed with lower quality. Next, there might be a human-compute unit that is temporarily misbehaving or its performance is degraded. Its exclusion would bring degradation of the collaboration and the performance of the collective, if another appropriate one is not employed in its place. Furthermore, due to badly planned delegations, it is often the case that some resources are overloaded while others are underutilized. The latter comes as a consequence of the problem of the reliance on human resource availability as one of the fundamental ones in social computing. In this context, the *willingness* of a human resource to execute a particular task at a specific time point is often overlooked. However, this is crucial for platforms supporting work that includes human computation because even if we assume that human resources can use "unlimited" software-based resources, e.g., using the cloud, human behavior is dynamic and highly unpredictable.

The aforementioned problems show that there is a need for management mechanisms to support elasticity by scaling in size and computing capabilities of SCUs in an elastic way. Authors in [8],[21] identify the underlying challenge in provisioning SCU elasticity to be the lack of techniques that enable proactive provisioning of human capabilities in a uniform way in large scale. Nevertheless, assuming the possibility of utilizing human-based services in a cloud-like way, systems should support runtime elastic coordination of collectives. To address the aforementioned issues, in this paper, we investigate and provide runtime mechanisms with the elasticity notion in mind, so that platforms would be able to provide *elastic capabilities of human-based compute units/SCUs*, that can be managed flexibly in terms of the number of resources, as well as their parameters such as cost, quality and performance time. Hence, our key contributions are:

- conceptualizing and modeling the SCU execution phase and states,
- defining SCU-elasticity properties and APIs,
- designing an SCU provisioning platform model with elastic capabilities.

The rest of this paper is organized as follows. In Section 2 we present a motivation example and discuss challenges in elasticity provisioning. In Section 3 we describe the SCU concept, model the execution mode of an SCU and present our platform for managing elastic SCUs. Section 4 illustrates the feasibility of our approach. We present related work in Section 5 and conclude the paper in Section 6.

2   Motivation, Background and Research Statement

Scenario. Let us consider a concrete scenario of a software development project e.g., for a health-care specific system, and assume that a software start-up company is engaged for its execution and completion. To deliver the end-artifact, these type of projects require diverse set of skills. Hence, in addition to the company employees, some specific parts of the project might need to be outsourced, e.g., to experts with experience in health-care but also to IT professionals with skills that the start-up is lacking. Hence, to solve the problem of skill deficiency, an SCU including human-based resources/services both from the software developing company but also "outside" experts is formed. The SCU utilizes software services for collaboration and task execution. On the other hand, the human-based services and the software services that they utilize are supported by an SCU provisioning and management platform that coordinates their performance.

The challenges that arise in this scenario come from the importance of performance and quality of results in paid expert units. A software solution needs to be delivered on time and in accordance with customer requirements and budget limitations. Fixed composite units with a known number of resources, including outsourced ones, often have problems with overloaded resources and may result in project delays with good quality or on time delivery of solutions with a lower quality than the desired ones. Problems such as those mentioned in the introduction also appear. However, with the availability of online resource-pools from human clouds [10], human-based services can be acquired and released from SCUs on demand, so as to best meet the customer performance and quality requirements. Hence, we assume that the "outside" experts for our software development SCU can be recruited from human clouds on demand. Under these assumptions and if the SCU supporting platform incorporates mechanisms that allow elasticity, an initial SCU will be able to adapt at runtime with respect to certain parameters, such as the number of its compute units, unit types, structure and performance. This can be particularly important in agile software development, where both the customer requirements and the development process evolve in an iterative way, and teams have high collaboration with the customer and are more responsive to change. Our hypothesis is that in consequence of these elastic capabilities, SCUs will provide higher efficiency at runtime. Thus, platforms that include mechanisms and techniques for runtime support of coordination of SCUs with elastic capabilities are crucial.

Background and Challenges. As aforementioned, our approach is based on the concept of *Social Compute Units* [6], which fundamentally represent virtual collective systems with human-based resources as compute units that are brought together to work on a common goal with a deadline. These compute units, can belong to an enterprise, they can be invoked from a crowdsourcing platform, an expert network or any platform that hosts pools of available resources for human (including social) computation. In relation to the work of the coauthors in [21], in this paper, we use the term Individual Compute Units (ICUs) for SCU members, which represent human-based services that can be programmed in a manner that they can execute tasks on-demand. Thus, an SCU is composed on request from a customer who defines requirements and sets constraints(e.g.,budget,deadline). It has its compute (performance) power, it can be programmed (managed) and is intended to work utilizing a collaboration platform hosted on the cloud. The behavior of an SCU is cloud-like, in the sense that its duration and performance depends on its goal, customer constraints as well as events generated during its execution.

Considerable related research focus has been put on formation algorithms [1],[13] and performance optimization within fixed teams. However, SCUs have a different nature than teams, as the SCU structures and capabilities can be programmed and SCU members can be elastically managed at runtime. Thus, even if some work for teams can be utilized, there is a research gap concerning SCU elasticity during the execution phase, in terms of resource numbers but also in terms of non-functional parameters(NFPs) such as cost, reliability, performance time etc. There has been a classification of human cloud platforms, where one category of platforms is said to be focused on project governance and complex coordination between resources [10], as opposed to crowdsourcing ones where the responsibility of project governance is not entirely on the platform. Examples of these type of platforms are TopCoder[1] and workio[2]. Even though these type of platforms can manage the lifecycle of collaborations, we argue that they lack the adaptation techniques and flexibility of resource management in terms of elasticity at runtime. For example, the pricing in these cases is not set by the customer like in crowdsourcing, rather the human-based services set their own prices. Thus, there is a possibility that with these models a collective of human resources can be automatically "programmed" so that if the number and type of resources changes the cost does not exceed the customer's total budget. This is one example of NFP elasticity in terms of cost. Consequently, identifying possible elastic operations that can be triggered at critical time points present important challenges for optimizing an SCUs performance. In the context of the aforementioned scenario and what lacks in current platforms, some of the research questions that we confront are:

- Given an initial formed SCU and a set of monitored team performance metrics, what are the set of actions that can enable SCU elastic capabilities, in situations when performance is degraded and violates a threshold value for a customer set constraint?
- When is optimization(e.g, load balancing) within an SCU not enough and a reorganization needed? Which tasks need to be reassigned, when and to whom(to a resource within/out of the SCU?

To sum up, this paper investigates the following fundamental challenge:*What are the mechanisms that a human computation system needs to deploy so as to provision SCUs with elastic capabilities, both in terms of resource scaling and in terms of variable properties?*

---

[1] http://www.topcoder.com/
[2] https://www.workio.com/

3   Social Compute Units and Elasticity

3.1   Elastic Social Compute Units

Elastic SCUs have elastic capabilities that can be triggered at runtime to tailor their performance to best fit client requirements at runtime. With human based resources being unpredictable and dynamic, their skills, price, interest and availability can change with time and within a specific context. However as stated in [6] the concept of SCU does not have a notion of elasticity in itself, thus an SCU provisioning platform which creates, deploys and supports the execution of SCUs needs to include mechanisms for scaling it up or down as needed, and as aforementioned, with this scale an SCUs performance parameters vary as well. These mechanisms should ensure that at each time point these parameters are within desired levels and comply with customer constraints. For our purposes, we conceptually define the elasticity of SCUs as follows:

Definition 1. *The Elasticity of Social Compute Units* *is the ability of SCUs to adapt at runtime in an automatic or semi-automatic manner, by scaling in size and/or reorganizing and rescheduling, such that the variations in the overall performance indicators such as capability, availability, effort, productivity and cost, at each point in time are optimal within the boundaries of the customer-set constraints.*

To support elasticity for SCUs, we identify as a prerequisite to have an execution model for an SCU, as previous work identifies SCU phases but do not go into details into its execution phase. An SCU lifecycle consists of the following stages: request, create, assimilate, virtualize, deploy and dissolve [6]. The elasticity mechanisms are needed after the virtualization stage, in the *execution phase*, which we model next.

3.2   SCU Execution Model

We denote a cloud of ICUs (e.g.,from online platforms and/or enterprise internal pool) as the universal set $R = \{r_1, r_2, r_3...r_n\}$, and the set of ICUs that are members of a particular SCU as $S = \{s_1, s_2, s_3...s_n\}$, where $S \subset R$. Let the set of tasks to be executed from a specific SCU be $T = \{t_1, t_2, t_3...t_n\}$. For each task $t_i \in T$, we denote the set of matching, appropriate and possible ICUs that can perform the task t_i as $P = \{p_1, p_2, p_3...p_n\}$, where $P \subset R$. Depending on constraints the following can be valid in different situations: $P \subset S^c$, $P \subset S$ or $P = S$. To provide elasticity, ICUs from S can be released and new ICUs from P can be added to S, therefore, $|S|$ might change at runtime. We model an ICU belonging to the cloud of ICUs R, with the following set of global properties, $ICU_{prop}^{gl} = \{Id_{icu}, skillset, reputation, price, state_{global}\}$. Moreover, an ICU from the perspective of the specific SCU of which it is a member, is modeled with its local properties, as $ICU_{prop}^{lscu} = \{Id_{scu}, ICU_{prop}^{gl}, state_{local},$ *productivity, trust*$\}$, where *reputation, state productivity,* and *trust* are aggregate metrics that we discuss further in this section.

States. An SCU in execution mode, at a specific time point τ, can be in one of the following action-states, $SCU_{state}(\tau) = \{running, suspending, resuming,$ $expanding, reducing, substituting, stopped\}$. These states are listed in Table 1. The mentioned states are basic/atomic ones and a combination of them makes a complex SCU execution state. For example, an SCU might be running but due to an adaptation action, at the same time multiple ICUs (a cluster of ICUs) within an SCU might be suspended, while a new ICU is being added in expanding state. In this case because *running, suspending* and *expanding* are all execution states of an SCU, then $running \wedge suspending \wedge expanding$ is also an SCU state. However, some states are mutually exclusive if they refer to the whole SCU and cannot be aggregated, i.e., an SCU cannot be in $running \wedge stopping$ state. If one of the atomic states refers to (a change in) individual or a cluster of ICUs, an SCU can be in $running \wedge extending$ state or for example an SCU can be in a $running \wedge reducing$ state. Thus, the aggregate states are valid in the context of the scope that a state-changing action takes place. Table 1 also shows the scope for which the state-changing actions are valid, in terms of the whole SCU, a cluster of ICUs, or ICUs only. The importance of the state of an SCU as a whole is tightly coupled with ICU states and is crucial when applying elastic strategies in two ways: 1) the state of the SCU can be a trigger for elastic operations on the SCU, and 2) it can be a desired result after applying these operations.

Table 1. Fundamental state alternatives of the SCU Execution phase

Trigger action	State	Scope	Triggering Role		
			Platform	Customer	ICU
Run	Running	SCU	√	√	
Suspend	Suspending	SCU/ICUcluster/ICU	√	√	√
Activate	Resuming	SCU/ICUcluster/ICU	√	√	√
Add	Expanding	ICUcluster/ICU	√	√	√
Exclude	Reducing	ICUcluster/ICU	√	√	√
Stop/Exclude/Add	Substituting	ICUcluster/ICU	√	√	√
Stop	Stopping	SCU	√	√	

SCU Elasticity Management. Table 1 shows ways of adaptation triggering: platform based, customer based and ICU based. To clarify, a platform that supports an SCU should have the mechanisms to support *all* of its execution states elastically. Thus all state-changing actions can be triggered in an automated way as shown in Table 1. Referring to our motivational scenario, in rare cases the customer could suspend the whole SCU of software development until he has consulted and decided for crucial changes. There are other triggering state-changing actions that the customer can also make(shown with light gray check signs). Table 1 also shows which state-changing actions can be most affected by communication and ICU feedback, which we illustrate in Section 4. We show an example for a software developing SCU in execution mode in Fig. 1. At a specific time point ICUs with *developer* skills are in running state while designers are suspended. Next, due to an event when expert information is needed(e.g.,health-care

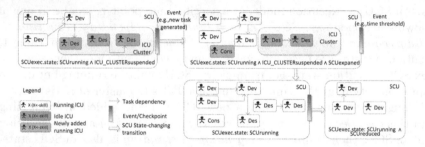

Fig. 1. An illustrative example of an SCU in execution: expanding and reducing states

information in our scenario), the SCU is expanded by including ICU with specific expertise and consultancy skills while a designer-ICU is resumed. At another time point each ICU is running, while before dissolving, the SCU is reduced as ICUs with designer and consultancy skills have finished their tasks. Adaptation actions on an SCU can change its execution model not only in terms of the state but also in terms of its execution structure. These changes are interdependent with task structure changes and ICU state changes.

Basic ICU and SCU Metrics. The decision to apply an elastic adaptation action depends on events that are triggered by two level monitoring of global and local metrics, namely to detect: 1) a violation of preset threshold values for overall SCU performance, and 2) which ICUs have affected the SCU's performance degradation. The focus of this paper is not to investigate extensive metrics, as many are context dependent. Thus, in this section we list and define some basic ones that we identify to be useful for SCUs at runtime.

Project Effort and *Productivity* have been listed as performance measures for software projects [12]. Modified versions of these metrics can be reused for SCUs on software and other goals. Thus, we define the *SCU Effort* as the sum of the average time spent by each ICU on each assigned task. The SCU task completion ratio, gives the fraction of completed tasks within those assigned. However this does not always mean that the results of all completed tasks are also

Table 2. Notation and description of basic ICU metrics and parameters

Metrics	Description
n_{req}	Number of willingness requests sent from the scheduler to an ICU
n_{ack}	Number of willingness acknowledgments sent to the scheduler by an ICU
n_{reasgn}	Number of tasks reassigned to an ICU
$n_{sucreasgn}$	Number of successfully executed reassigned tasks by an ICU
$n_{approved}(s_i)$	Total number of successfully executed/approved tasks for an ICU
$\tau(s_i, t_x)$	Processing time for task x executed by an ICU
$c(s_i, t_x)$	Cost for task x when executed by an ICU
$c(s_i^{nw}, t_x)$	Cost for task x when reassigned to a new ICU

approved. Thus, we also consider the number of valid or approved tasks, which we use for calculating the productivity of an SCU. We define *SCU Productivity* as the ratio of approved tasks to *SCU Effort*, giving an average number of tasks-per-time-unit value. The *SCU Reputation* is a weighted sum of the reputation score of each ICU regarding its expertise for the skill for which is included in the SCU. We model the *SCU Reputation* in this way because some ICUs in a specific SCU are more crucial than others by executing more critical tasks. We define the, $reputation(s_i)$ as a function of *(Success Rate, Approved Tasks, Timeliness, Reliability, SocialTrust)*. The *SCU Cost* is an aggregate sum of the cost of each ICU for each task according to its type and skill-type requirements. The metrics are given in Table 3, where $s_i \in S$ and $t_x \in T$. See Table 2 for notation on individual metrics, some of which we use in calculating those in Table 3. The described metrics are dynamic and a platform supporting elastic SCUs should be able to monitor and utilize them in runtime adaptation strategies.

From all that was discussed, we can now characterize the elastic profile of an SCU within time τ, as $SCU_{exec}(\tau) = \{SCU_{size}(\tau), SCU_{structure}(\tau), SCU_{state}(\tau), SCU_{effort}(\tau), SCU_{productivity}(\tau), SCU_{cost}(\tau), SCU_{reputation}(\tau)\}$.

Table 3. Example metrics of SCU performance

SCU Metrics	Definition
SCU Total Completed Tasks	$CT(scu_i) = \sum_{i=1}^{\|S\|} n_{completed}(s_i)$
SCU Approved Tasks	$AT(scu_i) = \sum_{i=1}^{\|S\|} n_{approved}(s_i)$
SCU Success Rate	$ST(scu_i) = AT(scu_i)/CT(scu_i)$
SCU Effort	$Effort(scu_i) = \frac{1}{CT(scu_i)} \sum_{s=1}^{\|S\|} \sum_{x=1}^{m} \tau(s_i, t_x)$
SCU Productivity	$Productivity(scu_i) = AT(scu_i)/Effort(scu_i)$
SCU Reputation	$Reputation(scu_i) = \sum_{i=1}^{\|S\|} w_{expertise} * reputation(s_i)$
SCU Cost	$Cost(scu_i) = \sum_{i=1}^{\|S\|} \sum_{x=1}^{m} c_{(s_i, t_x)}$

Elasticity APIs. To be able to provide SCU elasticity capabilities, which include ICUs having the aforementioned (and other domain-dependent) properties, we need to have common APIs for their description and management. Currently we develop APIs which we categorize in ICU-description APIs for manipulating ICU profiles, ICU-scheduling APIs for ICU management and elastic operations,

Table 4. Example API, abstract methods for ICU manipulation

Scheduling methods	Description
abstract AddICU()	adds an ICU to the SCU
abstract void SuspendICU(SCU scu)	brings an ICU to idle state, still included in the SCU
abstract void ExcludeICU(SCU scu)	excludes an ICU form the SCU
abstract void ResumeICU(SCU scu)	restart an ICU and its associated tasks
abstract void ReserveICU(Task t)	reserves an alternative ICU for an already assigned task
abstract void SubstituteICU()	substitutes an ICU with a reserved one
public List <ICU> getAllICUinSCU(SCU scu)	returns ICUs within the SCU
public List<ICU>getSuspendedICUs(SCU scu)	returns suspended ICUs within an SCU
public List<ICU>getIdleICUs(SCU scu)	returns idle ICUs in an SCU
public List<ICU>getReservedICUs(Task t)	maintains an ordered list of top appropriate ICUs for a certain task (ICUs might be in/out of the specific SCU)

and communication operations. Table 4 describes some specific methods that we develop to be utilized in strategies providing SCU elastic capabilities.

3.3   Elastic SCU Provisioning Platform

Figure 2 shows a model of our concept of an elastic SCU provisioning platform, that utilizing our SCU execution model, metrics and API is able to support elastic SCU management. Thus, the platform supports the following behavior: a customer/SCU consumer submits a project/request with multiple tasks to it. When submitting tasks and request for SCU formation, the client specifies functional and non-functional ICU requirements such as: skill, reputation and cost. In addition he specifies overall SCU constraints, such as total budget and deadline. The platform integrates an SCU formation component with ICU selection/ranking algorithms. The resource selection and initial task assignment is not in our focus. The SCU creation/formation component's output is an initial SCU created by selecting ICUs from human cloud providers. This SCU is "fed" to a *controller*-a component that hosts monitoring and adaptation algorithms utilizing APIs for elasticity control, which provide SCU runtime management. The challenge of this component, is to monitor and adapt the SCU in accordance to customer set constraints, such that the SCU gives the maximum performance and quality within the preset boundaries for time related, cost and quality related indicators. Different scheduling and ICU management algorithms can be plugged into the platform, which would support the SCU during its lifecycle.

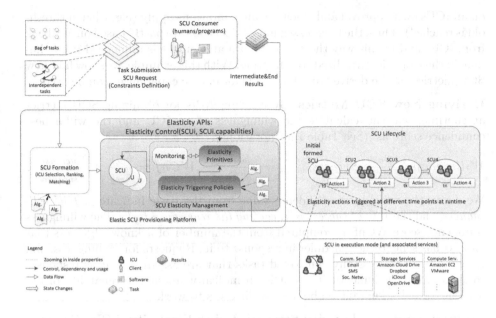

Fig. 2. Conceptual platform model supporting elastic SCUs

4   Illustrating Example

In this section we show the benefit of having explicit state management, metrics and elasticity for supporting elastic SCU. We present the way our framework can simplify the complexity of the development of elasticity strategies for SCUs. Typically, an elasticity strategy for an SCU is a domain-specific problem. In the following, we illustrate how an *ICU Feedback-based elastic SCU management strategy* can be implemented.

As ICUs within an SCU are inherently dynamic and unpredictable, we cannot always fully rely on the system-based availability information concerning an ICU and fully automated task assignment and scheduling might not always be the most suitable approach, especially when there is a possibility of unexpected generation of tasks at runtime. Hence, we propose an SCU adaptation strategy that uses ICU acknowledgments for their *willingness* to work on specific tasks. More specifically, these acknowledgments are sent in response to system requests for availability guarantees for the execution of tasks that need reassignment. This strategy supports elasticity in the sense that it departs from the idea that a customer knows in advance which and how many ICUs will contribute and the final cost for his "project". However, the customer budget is kept within its limits as the cost may vary within these limits, just as the size and structure of the assembled SCU may vary with time until the final result is returned.

Our example of elastic SCU mechanism is a semi-automatic task scheduling strategy where part of the coordination for task re-assignment is delegated to ICUs. With this approach a task is being re-assigned to a more available ICU, on an ICUs own approval and when certain conditions apply (e.g, when a threshold is reached). Thus, the task reassignment decisions are partly based on feedback from ICUs and in this way the elastic SCU management is influenced from "human in the loop" decentralized coordination. With this example, we show how new SCU metrics can be derived and how APIs for elastic capabilities can be used.

Deriving New SCU Metrics. By utilizing APIs for obtaining SCU metrics at runtime, one can calculate the willingness of an ICU and the willingness confidence score as: (See Table I for notations):

$$Willingness = \frac{n_{ack}}{n_{req}}, Success_{reasgn} = \frac{n_{sucreasgn}}{n_{reasgn}}, WCnf = \frac{n_{ack}}{n_{req}} \times \frac{n_{sucreasgn}}{n_{reasgn}}.$$

We derive the willingness confidence value from the basic indicators, *ICU willingness,* and the *rate of success in executing the reassigned tasks.* The willingness confidence score WCnf, is computed from the number of acknowledgments that an ICU has sent to the scheduler in response to its Requests for Willingness, and the number of successfully completed tasks that are assigned to it as responses to these acknowledgments. Thus, it is an indicator about the reliability of the alternative ICUs guarantee about its willingness to work.

Programming an Elasticity Strategy Using Elasticity APIs. Considering worker willingness, provides a way to measure and control the unpredictability/reliability of ICUs by asking them for task-execution guarantees because it provides a way to compare their "statements" with their actual behavior. This is what the value of *Willingness Confidentiality* indicates.   In this strategy we assume that each incoming task is assigned to the ICU at the top of a ranked list which is returned by a ranking algorithm, and references to the first x most appropriate ICUs from the ranked list are stored as reserves/alternatives for each task. The algorithm can be summarized with the following steps:

1. When a preset threshold, related to a task which is already assigned to the most appropriate ICU matching the requirements is reached, e.g.,the tasks waiting-time in an ICUs task-queue, the scheduler sends a request for execution willingness to the next top x number of ICUs that it has references to (reserves from the initial ranked list), which at the same time are idle, or their task queues are smaller than that of the ICU to which the task was initially assigned. With this request for willingness, it notifies them that there is a task that they can work on. This request is a resource availability-check; it is a request for a resource's *willingness* to work on a specific task as a form of a worker-side commitment or guarantee that the task will be executed by it.

2. Each ICU that receives this request and is ready and wishes to work on the task then sends the scheduler a willingness acknowledgment(Ack)/feedback to this request.

3. The scheduling component reassigns the task on threshold to the alternative resource that has sent a willingness acknowledgment and that is idle or has the smallest task queue. Priority is given to less loaded ICUs that are already members of the SCU.

Algorithm 1. Task-reassignment with ICU-side assurance

Require: scuTasks for SCU
Require: customer constraints on NFP
 1: **for all** tasks in T **do**
    rank matching ICUs and return the first 10 appropriate
 2:     $P \leftarrow getReservedICUList(Taskt)$ ▷ store reserve ICUs
 3:     assign task t to top ranked ICUs r
 4:     **if** r is not an element in SCU **then** do
 5:         $SCU \leftarrow addICU()$ ▷ add ICU r to SCU x and update its profile
 6:     **if** $task.taskQueueTime == task.timeThreshold$ **then** do
 7:         **if** $r == idle$ **then** do
 8:             $SCU \leftarrow removeICU()$ ▷ reduction: remove ICU r from SCU
 9:         **for all** ICU in P **do**
10:             $getICUState(ICUICUid)$
11:             **if** ICU_ STATE==idle AND $icuReserve.tQueue() < r.tQueueSize()/2$
    then do
12:                 $willingnessReqMessage()$
13:             **for all** $icuReserve.sentAck == true$ in ascending order of
    $icuResource.taskQueue$ **do**
14:                 **if** resource belongs in SCU **then** do
15:                     $substituteICU()$ ▷ re-assign task to SCU member and update its
    profile
16:                     **break**
17:                 $substituteICU()$ ▷ re-assign task to external ICU and update its
    profile
18:             $SCU \leftarrow addICU()$ ▷ expansion: include resource y in SCU

When multiple reserve ICUs send acknowledgments that they are ready to execute the task, the reassignment decision is made based on the information from the Acks combined with monitoring information about their task queues and logged information about the WCnf score. This type of scheduling combines the freedom of choosing tasks that workers have in crowdsourcing environments, with policy based assignment of tasks. It is these ICU-side guarantees that are combined with task queue analysis, that can avoid problems such as *delegation sinks*. We outline the steps of this strategy in Alg 1. Alternatively, the request for willingness can be sent immediately after the task's initial assignment so that when a threshold is reached the scheduler only checks the task queues of ICUs.

Executing an Elasticity Strategy. We implemented the algorithm using methods described in the API section. We created tasks with different skill requirements and modeled an ICU with a single skill for simplicity, and assigned each of them different costs. When a decision is made about which tasks are going to be reassigned to which ICU, the new cost calculation includes the prices of each of the new ICUs, as follows:

$$Cost_{adapt}(scu_i) = Cost_{previous}(scu_i) - \sum_{i=1}^{m}\sum_{x=1}^{j} c(s_i, t_x) + \sum_{i=1}^{m}\sum_{x=1}^{j} c(s_i^{nw}, t_x),$$

where $Cost_{adapt}(scu_i) \leq Allowed\ Budget$. Due to space limitations and to the fact that it is not our goal to show how good this strategy is, we provide a supplement material[3].

Generally, the results show that SCU productivity raises with the number of ICUs and the same effort, while it declines if the effort is high for a low number of tasks and a small number of ICUs.

5   Related Work

Resource Management and Adaptation. Work on a retainer model for crowdsourcing environments and examples of its application are presented in [4],[3]. The model is designed for recruiting guaranteed workers by paying them a small additional amount, and in this way keeping them in reserve and in ready state for handling real-time tasks. The similarity of our ICU-feedback based strategy is in that our scheduler keeps references to the top x number of resources that are previously ranked as most suitable for a specific task. Hence, these resources are the reserve resources in our approach. However, the difference in our approach is that no prior payment is made for reservation of these resources, rather the scheduler sends them a notification asking for feedback for their willingness to execute a task that is already assigned to another resource but for which a threshold is reached. Our model is not concerned with initial task assignment and it is not intended for crowdsourcing tasks, although ICUs may be invoked from a crowdsourcing platform. Authors of [15] present a programming language and framework called CrowdLang for systems that incorporate human computation, and what is of interest to us is that they provide cross-platform integration of resources, in this way making a human cloud possible. There is a considerable amount of work conducted on adaptation and more interestingly on self-adaptation strategies. For example, authors in [16] have presented an architecture that includes a self-adaptation framework for service-oriented collaboration systems. The part that this work relates to, is their approach on identifying worker misbehavior patterns (e.g., as a result of uncontrolled task delegations) and providing a solution of reassigning tasks to other alternative resources by taking into account their task-queue size. Our strategy differs from theirs in that tasks are not delegated if ICUs are not willing to accept tasks. Rather, the task reassignment is managed with *consent* from alternative ICUs. [9] describes a delegation model and related algorithms that concern trust updates. The authors mention adoption as a process where the delegation is initiated by the "delegatee". Our algorithm stands in between delegation and adoption.

Collaborative Communities and Teams. The concept of the SCU that we utilize in our work is presented by one of the coauthors in [6]. However, while this is the fundamental work introducing the SCU, it describes its life-cycle and does not go into details into the SCU execution phase as this was not its aim. This is tackled in [19], where researchers have looked into a specific case of incident management to investigate how SCUs and their evolution(adaptation) perform better

---

[3] dsg.tuwien.ac.at/research/viecom/prototypes/viecas

over traditional process management. Resource discovery in crowdsourcing and team formation strategies and algorithms have been the subject of investigation in many works, such as [1], [2], [14], [13],[5]. The algorithms in these works can be utilized for SCU formation and some also for ICU selection when an SCU needs to be extended. Task executing collaboration models and runtime collaborations are also investigated in works such as [18]. However, the mentioned works focus on fixed teams without elasticity assumptions.

Elasticity. The notion of elasticity is treated in several domains and contexts and has especially gained importance with the advance of cloud computing. In [8] authors discuss the reasons, challenges and their approach toward virtualizing humans and software under the same service-based model that will enable elastic computing in terms of scaling both software and human resources. The concept of elasticity in Cloud computing, is being extended to concepts like application [22] and process [7] elasticity, e.g., in [7], the authors identify resource, cost and quality elasticity as being crucial in modeling processes in service oriented computing. Mechanisms and a middleware to support scaling services in and out from applications utilizing SaaS are presented in [11].

6   Conclusion

Our research focus in this work was to provide mechanisms for effective provisioning of SCUs with elastic capabilities and their efficient runtime management. We have modeled an SCU at runtime and provided exemplary algorithm that utilizes operations for provisioning of elastic capabilities. We have shown that platforms supporting human computation in collective collaborations are more reliable by working based on the elasticity concept of scalability in terms of both resources and their parameters. Our future work includes further development of an SCU execution framework, which will include the presented model, metrics, API and algorithms so as to be able to deploy our approach in real environments.

Acknowledgments. This work is supported by the Vienna PhD School of Informatics (http://www.informatik.tuwien.ac.at/teaching/phdschool) and by the EU FP7 FET SmartSociety project(http://www.smart-society-project.eu/) under the Grant agreement n.600854.

References

1. Anagnostopoulos, A., Becchetti, L., Castillo, C., Gionis, A., Leonardi, S.: Power in unity: forming teams in large-scale community systems. In: CIKM, pp. 599–608 (2010)
2. Anagnostopoulos, A., Becchetti, L., Castillo, C., Gionis, A., Leonardi, S.: Online team formation in social networks. In: Proceedings of the 21st International Conference on World Wide Web, WWW 2012, pp. 839–848. ACM, New York (2012)
3. Bernstein, M.S., Brandt, J., Miller, R.C., Karger, D.R.: Crowds in two seconds: enabling realtime crowd-powered interfaces. In: Proceedings of the 24th Annual ACM Symposium on User Interface Software and Technology, UIST 2011, pp. 33–42. ACM, New York (2011)

4. Bernstein, M.S., Karger, D.R., Miller, R.C., Brandt, J.: Analytic methods for optimizing realtime crowdsourcing. CoRR abs/1204.2995 (2012)
5. Dorn, C., Dustdar, S.: Composing near-optimal expert teams: A trade-off between skills and connectivity. In: Meersman, R., Dillon, T.S., Herrero, P. (eds.) OTM 2010. LNCS, vol. 6426, pp. 472–489. Springer, Heidelberg (2010)
6. Dustdar, S., Bhattacharya, K.: The social compute unit. IEEE Internet Computing 15, 64–69 (2011)
7. Dustdar, S., Guo, Y., Satzger, B., Truong, H.L.: Principles of elastic processes. IEEE Internet Computing 15(5), 66–71 (2011)
8. Dustdar, S., Truong, H.L.: Virtualizing software and humans for elastic processes in multiple clouds- a service management perspective. IJNGC 3(2) (2012)
9. Hexmoor, H., Chandran, R.: Delegations and Trust. International Journal of Computational Intelligence, Theory and Practice 3(2), 95–108 (2008)
10. Kaganer, E., Carmel, E., Hirschheim, R., Olsen, T.: Managing the human cloud. MITSloan Management Review 54(2), 23–32 (2013)
11. Kapuruge, M., Han, J., Colman, A., Kumara, I.: ROAD4SaaS: Scalable business service-based saaS applications. In: Salinesi, C., Norrie, M.C., Pastor, Ó. (eds.) CAiSE 2013. LNCS, vol. 7908, pp. 338–352. Springer, Heidelberg (2013)
12. Kasunic, M.: A Data Specification for Software Project Performance Measures: Results of a Collaboration on Performance Measurement. Technical report. Carnegie Mellon University, Software Engineering Institute (2008)
13. Lappas, T., Liu, K., Terzi, E.: Finding a team of experts in social networks. In: Proceedings of the 15th ACM SIGKDD International Conference on Knowledge Discovery and Data Mining, KDD 2009, pp. 467–476. ACM, New York (2009)
14. Lopez, M., Vukovic, M., Laredo, J.: Peoplecloud service for enterprise crowdsourcing. In: 2010 IEEE International Conference on Services Computing, pp. 538–545 (2010)
15. Minder, P., Bernstein, A.: Crowdlang: programming human computation systems. Technical report (JAN (2012)
16. Psaier, H., Juszczyk, L., Skopik, F., Schall, D., Dustdar, S.: Runtime behavior monitoring and self-adaptation in service-oriented systems. In: Proceedings of the 2010 Fourth IEEE International Conference on Self-Adaptive and Self-Organizing Systems, SASO 2010, pp. 164–173. IEEEComputerSociety, Washington, DC (2010)
17. Quinn, A.J., Bederson, B.B.: A taxonomy of distributed human computation
18. Sagar, A.B.: Modeling collaborative task execution in social networks. In: Potdar, V., Mukhopadhyay, D. (eds.) CUBE, pp. 664–669. ACM (2012)
19. Sengupta, B., Jain, A., Bhattacharya, K., Truong, H.-L., Dustdar, S.: Who do you call? Problem resolution through social compute units. In: Liu, C., Ludwig, H., Toumani, F., Yu, Q. (eds.) Service Oriented Computing. LNCS, vol. 7636, pp. 48–62. Springer, Heidelberg (2012)
20. SmartSociety: Hybrid and diversity-aware collective adaptive systems: When people meet machines to build a smarter society, http://www.smart-society-project.eu/ FP7 FET,EU Funded Project (accessed: December 20, 2013)
21. Truong, H.-L., Dustdar, S., Bhattacharya, K.: Programming hybrid services in the cloud. In: Liu, C., Ludwig, H., Toumani, F., Yu, Q. (eds.) Service Oriented Computing. LNCS, vol. 7636, pp. 96–110. Springer, Heidelberg (2012), http://dblp.uni-trier.de/db/conf/icsoc/icsoc2012.html#TruongDB12
22. Zhang, X., Kunjithapatham, A., Jeong, S., Gibbs, S.: Towards an elastic application model for augmenting the computing capabilities of mobile devices with cloud computing. Mob. Netw. Appl. 16(3), 270–284 (2011)

Open-Source Databases: Within, Outside, or Beyond Lehman's Laws of Software Evolution?

Ioannis Skoulis, Panos Vassiliadis, and Apostolos Zarras

Dept. of Computer Science and Engineering
University of Ioannina (Hellas)
{iskoulis,pvassil,zarras}@cs.uoi.gr

Abstract. Lehman's laws of software evolution is a well-established set of observations (matured during the last forty years) on how the typical software systems evolve. However, the applicability of these laws on databases has not been studied so far. To this end, we have performed a thorough, large-scale study on the evolution of databases that are part of larger open source projects, publicly available through open source repositories, and report on the validity of the laws on the grounds of properties like size, growth, and amount of change per version.

Keywords: Schema evolution, software evolution, Lehman's laws.

1 Introduction

Software evolution is the change of a software system over time, typically performed via a remarkably difficult, complicated and time consuming process, software maintenance. In an attempt to understand the mechanics behind the evolution of software and facilitate a smoother, lest disruptive maintenance process, Meir Lehman and his colleagues introduced a set of rules in mid seventies [1], also known as the *Laws on Software Evolution* (Sec. 2). Their findings, that were reviewed and enhanced for nearly 40 years [2], [3], have, since then, given an insight to managers, software developers and researchers, as to *what* evolves in the lifetime of a software system, and *why* it does so. Other studies ([4], [5], [6] to name a few significant ones) have complemented these insights in this field, typically with particular focus to open-source software projects.

In sharp distinction to traditional software systems, database evolution has been hardly studied throughout the entire lifetime of the data management discipline. This deficit in our knowledge is disproportional to the severity of the implications of database evolution, and in particular, of database schema evolution. A change in the schema of a database may immediately drive surrounding applications to crash (in case of deletions or renamings) or be semantically defective or inaccurate (in the case of information addition, or restructuring). Overall, schema evolution threatens the syntactic and semantic validity of the surrounding applications and severely affects both developers and end-users. Given this

M. Jarke et al. (Eds.): CAiSE 2014, LNCS 8484, pp. 379–393, 2014.

importance, it is only amazing to find out that in the past 40 years of database research, only three(!) studies [7], [8] and [9] have attempted a first step towards understanding the mechanics of schema evolution. Those studies, however, focus on the statistical properties of the evolution and do not provide details on the actual events, or the mechanism that governs the evolution of database schemata.

In this paper, *we perform the first large-scale study of schema evolution in the related literature. Specifically, we study the evolution of the logical schema of eight databases, that are parts of publicly available, open-source software projects.* To achieve the above goal, we have collected, cleansed and processed the available versions of the database schemata for the eight case studies. Moreover, we have extracted the changes that have been performed in these versions and, finally, we have come up with the respective datasets that can serve as a foundation for future analysis by the research community (Sec. 3). Concerning the applicability of Lehman's laws to open-source databases, our results show that *the essence of Lehman's laws holds*: evolution is not about uncontrolled growth; on the contrary, there appears to be a stabilization mechanism that employs perfective maintenance to control the otherwise growing trend of increase in information capacity of the database (Sec. 4). Having said that, we also observe that the growth mechanisms and the change patterns are quite different between open source databases and typical software systems.

2   Lehman Laws of Software Evolution in a Nutshell

Meir M. Lehman and his colleagues, have introduced, and subsequently amended, enriched and corrected a set of rules on the behavior of software as it evolves over time [1], [2], [3]. Lehman's laws focus on *E-type systems*, that concern "software solving a problem or addressing an application in the real-world" [2]. The main idea behind the laws of evolution for E-type software systems is that their *evolution is a process that follows the behavior of a feedback-based system.* Being a feedback-based system, the evolution process has to balance (a) *positive feedback*, or else the need to adapt to a changing environment and grow to address the need for more functionality, and, (b) *negative feedback*, or else the need to control, constrain and direct change in ways that prevent the deterioration of the maintainability and manageability of the software. In the sequel we list the definitions of the laws as they are presented in [3], in a more abstract form than previous versions and with the benefit of retrospect, after thirty years of maturity and research findings.

(I) **Law of Continuing Change.** An E-type system must be continually adapted or else it becomes progressively less satisfactory in use.

(II) **Law of Increasing Complexity.** As an E-type system is changed its complexity increases and becomes more difficult to evolve unless work is done to maintain or reduce the complexity.

(III) **Law of Self Regulation.** Global E-type system evolution is feedback regulated.

(IV) Law of Conservation of Organisational Stability. The work rate of an organisation evolving an E-type software system tends to be constant over the operational lifetime of that system or phases of that lifetime.

(V) Law of Conservation of Familiarity. In general, the incremental growth (growth ratio trend) of E-type systems is constrained by the need to maintain familiarity.

(VI) Law of Continuing Growth. The functional capability of E-type systems must be continually enhanced to maintain user satisfaction over system lifetime.

(VII) Law of Declining Quality. Unless rigorously adapted and evolved to take into account changes in the operational environment, the quality of an E-type system will appear to be declining.

(VIII) Law of Feedback System. E-type evolution processes are multi-level, multi-loop, multi-agent feedback systems.

Before proceeding with our study, we present a first apodosis of the laws, taking into consideration both the wording of the laws, but most importantly their accompanying explanations [3].

An E-Type software system continuously changes over time (I) obeying a complex feedback-based evolution process (VIII). On the one hand, due to the need for growth and adaptation that acts as positive feedback, this process results in an increasing functional capacity of the system (VI), produced by a growth ratio that is slowly declining in the long term (V). The process is typically guided by a pattern of growth that demonstrates its self-regulating nature: growth advances smoothly; still, whenever there are excessive deviations from the typical, baseline rate of growth (either in a single release, or accumulated over time), the evolution process obeys the need for calibrating releases of perfective maintenance (expressed via minor growth and demonstrating negative feedback) to stop the unordered growth of the system's complexity (III). On the other hand, to regulate the ever-increasing growth, there is negative feedback in the system controlling both the overall quality of the system (VII), with particular emphasis to its internal quality (II). The effort consumed for the above process is typically constant over phases, with the phases disrupted with bursts of effort from time to time (IV).

3   Experimental Setup of the Study

Datasets. We have studied eight database schemata from open-source software projects. *ATLAS*[1] is a particle physics experiment at CERN, with the goal of learning about the basic forces that have shaped our universe – famously known for the attempt on the Higgs boson. *BioSQL*[2] is a generic relational model covering sequences, features, sequence and feature annotation, a reference taxonomy, and ontologies from various sources such as GenBank or Swissport. *Ensembl* is

---

[1] http://atlas.web.cern.ch/Atlas/Collaboration/

[2] http://www.biosql.org/wiki/Main_Page

a joint scientific project between the European Bioinformatics Institute (EBI)[3] and the Wellcome Trust Sanger Institute (WTSI)[4] which was launched in 1999 in response to the imminent completion of the Human Genome Project. The goal of Ensembl was to automatically annotate the three billion base pairs of sequences of the genome, integrate this annotation with other available biological data and make all this publicly available via the web. *MediaWiki*[5] was first introduced in early 2002 by the Wikimedia Foundation along with Wikipedia, and hosts Wikipedia's content since then. *Coppermine*[6] is a photo gallery web application. *OpenCart*[7] is an open source shopping cart system. *PhpBB*[8] is an Internet forum package. *TYPO3*[9] is a free and open source web content management framework.

Dataset Collection and Processing. A first collection of links to available datasets was made by the authors of [9], [10][10]; for this, these authors deserve honorable credit. We isolated eight databases that appeared to be alive and used (as already mentioned, some of them are actually quite prominent). For each dataset we gathered as many schema versions (DDL files) as we could from their public source code repositories (cvs, svn, git). We have targeted main development branches and trunks to maximize the validity of the gathered resources. *We are interested only on changes of the database part of the project as they are integrated in the trunk of the project.* Hence, we collected all the versions of the database, committed at the trunk or master branch, and ignored all other branches of the project.

We collected the files during June 2013. For all of the projects, we focused on their release for MySQL (except ATLAS Trigger, available only for Oracle). The files were then processed by sequential pairs from our tool, Hecate, that allows the detection of (a) changes at the attribute level, and specifically, attributes inserted, deleted, having a changed data type, or participation in a changed primary key, and (b) changes at the relation level, with relations inserted and deleted, in a fully automated way. Hecate, was then used to give us (a) the differences between two subsequent committed versions, and (b) the measures we needed to conduct this study – for example, the *size of the schema* (in number of tables and attributes), the total number of changes for each transition from a version to the next, which we also call *heartbeat*, or the *growth* assessed as the difference in the size of the schema between subsequent versions. *Hecate, along with all the data sets and our results are available at our group's public repository* https://github.com/DAINTINESS-Group.

---

[3] https://www.ebi.ac.uk/
[4] https://www.sanger.ac.uk/
[5] https://www.mediawiki.org/wiki/MediaWiki
[6] http://coppermine-gallery.net/
[7] http://www.opencart.com
[8] https://www.phpbb.com/
[9] http://typo3.org/
[10] http://data.schemaevolution.org

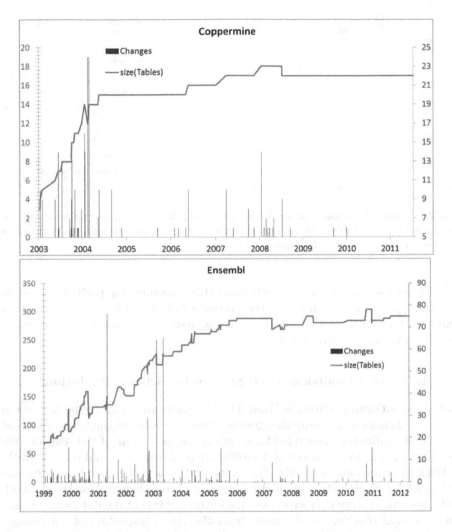

Fig. 1. Combined demonstration of heartbeat (number of changes per version) and schema size (no. of tables) for Coppermine and Ensemble. The left axis signifies the amount of change and the right axis the number of tables.

4   Assessing the Laws for Schema Evolution

The laws of software evolution where developed and reshaped over forty years. Explaining each law in isolation from the others is precarious as it risks losing the deeper essence and inter-dependencies of the laws [3]. To this end, in this section, we organize the laws in three thematic areas of the overall evolution management mechanism that they reveal. The first group of laws discusses the existence of a feedback mechanism that constrains the uncontrolled evolution of software. The second group discusses the properties of the growth of the system,

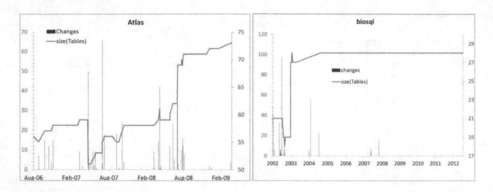

Fig. 2. Combined demonstration of heartbeat (number of changes per version) and schema size (no. of tables) for Atlas and BioSQL. The left axis signifies the amount of change and the right axis the number of tables.

i.e., the part of the evolution mechanism that accounts for positive feedback. The third group of laws discusses the properties of perfective maintenance that constrains the uncontrolled growth, i.e., the part of the evolution mechanism that accounts for negative feedback.

4.1   Is There a Feedback-Based System for Schema Evolution?

Law of Continuing Change (Law I). The main argument of the first law is that the schema continuously changes over time. To validate the hypothesis that the law of continuing change holds, we study the heartbeat of the schema's life (see Fig. 1 and 2 for a combined demonstration of heartbeat and schema size).

With the exception of BioSQL that appeared to be "sleeping" for some years and was later re-activated, in all other cases, we have changes (sometimes moderate, sometimes even excessive) over the entire lifetime of the database schema. An important observation stemming from the visual inspection of our change-over-time data, is that the term *continually* in the law's definition is challenged: *we observe that database schema evolution happens in bursts, in grouped periods of evolutionary activity, and not as a continuous process*! Take into account that the versions with zero changes are versions where either commenting and beautification takes place, or the changes do not refer to the information capacity of the schema (relations attributes and constraints) but rather, they concern the physical level properties (indexes, storage engines, etc) that pertain to performance aspects of the database.

Can we state that this stillness makes the schema "unsatisfactory" (referring back to the wording of the first law by Lehman)? We believe that the answer to the question is negative: since the system hosting the database continues to be in use, user dissatisfaction would actually call for continuous growth of the database, or eventual rejection of the system. This does not happen. On the other hand, our explanation relies on the reference nature of the database in terms of software architecture: if the database evolves, the rest of the code, which is basically using the database (and not vice versa), breaks!

Overall, if we account for the exact wording of the law, we conclude that the law partially holds.

Law of Feedback System (Law VIII). The wording of Law VIII refers to the existence of a self-stabilizing feedback mechanism that governs evolution. Its experimental evaluation typically refers to the possibility of demonstrating adherence to a basic formula of feedback, by estimating the size of the system (here: in terms of number of relations) accurately – i.e., with small error compared to the actual values. The formula typically used [2] is: $\widehat{S}_i = \widehat{S}_{i-1} + \frac{\overline{E}}{\widehat{S}_{i-1}^2}$, where $\widehat{S}$ refers to the estimated system size and $\overline{E}$ is a model parameter approximating effort (actually obtained as the average value of a set of past assessments of E).

Related literature [2] suggests computing $\overline{E}$ as the average value of individual E_i, one per transition. Then, we need to estimate these individual effort approximations. [2] suggests two formulae that we generalize here as follows: $E_i = \frac{s_i - s_\alpha}{\sum_{j=\alpha}^{i-1} \frac{1}{s_j^2}}$, where s_i refers to the actual size of the schema at version i and α refers to the version from which counting starts. Specifically, [2] suggests two values for α, specifically (i) 1 (the first version) and (ii) s_{i-1} (the previous version).

We now move on to discuss what seems to work and what not for the case of schema evolution. We will use the OpenCart data set as a reference example; however, all datasets demonstrate exactly the same behavior.

First, we assessed the formulae of [2]. In this case, we compute the average $\overline{E}$ of the individual E_i over the entire dataset. We employ four different values for α, specifically 1, 5, 10, and n, with n being the entire data set size, and depict the result in Fig. 3, where the actual size is represented by the blue solid line. The results indicate that the approximation modestly succeeds in predicting an overall increasing trend for all four cases, and, in fact, all four approximations targeted towards predicting an increasing tendency that the actual schema does not demonstrate. At the same time, all four approximations fail to capture the individual fluctuations within the schema lifetime.

A better estimation occurred when we realized that back in 1997 people considered that the parameter $\overline{E}$ was constant over the entire lifetime of the project; however, later observations (see [3]) led to the revelation that the project was split in phases. So, for every version i, we compute $\overline{E}$ as an average over the last τ E_j values, with small values for τ (1/5/10).

As we can see in Fig. 3, *the idea of computing the average $\overline{E}$ with a short memory of 5 or 10 versions produced extremely accurate results. This holds for all data sets.* This observation also suggests that, if the phases that [3] mentioned actually exist for the case of database schema, they are really small and a memory of 5-10 versions is enough to produce very accurate results.

Overall, *the evolution of the database schema appears to obey the behavior of a feedback-based mechanism, as the schema size of a certain version of the database can be accurately estimated via a regressive formula that exploits the amount of changes in recent, previous versions.*

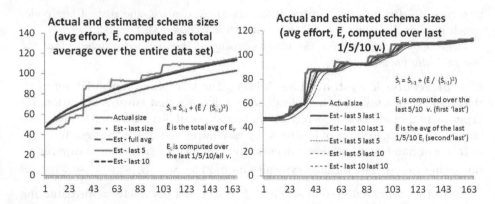

Fig. 3. Actual and estimated schema size via a total (left) and a bounded (right) average of individual E_i for OpenCart; the x-axis shows the version id

Law of Self-Regulation (Law III). Whereas the law simply states that the evolution of software is feedback regulated, its experimental validation in the area of software systems is typically supported by the observation of a recurring pattern of smooth expansion of the system's size(a.k.a. "baseline" growth), that is interrupted with releases of perfective maintenance with size reductions or with releases of growth. Moreover, due to a previous wording of the law (e.g., see [2]) that described change to follow a normal distribution, the experimental assessment included the validation of whether growth demonstrates oscillations around the average value [1,2,3].

Size. The evolution of size can be observed in Fig. 1 and 2. We have to say that we simply do not detect the same behaviour that Lehman did (contrast Fig. 1, 2 to the respective figures of articles [1] and [2]): in sharp contrast to the smooth baseline growth that Lehman has highlighted, the evolution of the size of the studied database schemata provides a landscape with a large variety of *sequences of the following three fundamental behaviors.*

- In all schemata, we can see periods of increase, especially at the beginning of their lifetime or after a large drop in the schema size. This is an indication of positive feedback, i.e., the need to expand the schema to cover the information needs of the users.
- In all schemata, there are versions with drops in schema size. Those drops are typically sudden and steep and usually take place in short periods of time. Sometimes, in fact, these drops are of significantly larger size than the typical change. We can safely say that the existence of these drops in the schema size indicate perfective maintenance and thus, the existence of a negative feedback mechanism in the evolution process.
- In all schemata, there are periods of stability (i.e., size stays still, or –near-still).

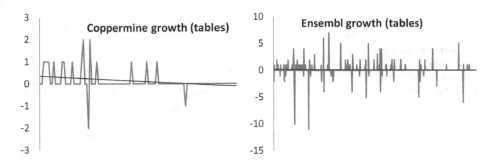

Fig. 4. Growth for Coppermine and Ensembl (over version id, concealed for fig. clarity); the slowly dropping solid line shows the linear interpolation of the values

Growth. Growth (i.e., the difference in the size between two subsequent versions) in all datasets has the following broad characteristics (Fig. 4, 6). In terms of tables, in most cases, growth is small (typically ranging within 0 and 1), and moderately small when it comes to attributes. We *have too many occurrences of zero growth*, typically iterating between small non-zero growth and zero growth. Due to perfective maintenance, we also have negative values of growth (less than the positive ones). We do not have a constant flow of versions where the schema size is continuously changing; rather, we have small spikes between one and zero. Thus, we have to state that the growth comes with *a pattern of spikes*. Due to this characteristic, *the average value is typically very close to zero (on the positive side) in all datasets, both for tables and attributes*. There are *few cases of large change* too; we forward the reader to Law V for a discussion of their characteristics.

We would like to put special emphasis to the observation that *change is small*. In terms of tables, growth is mostly bounded in small values. This is not directly obvious in the charts, because they show the ripples; however, almost all numbers are in the range of [-2..2] – in fact, mostly in the range [0..2]. Few abrupt changes occur. In terms of attributes, the numbers are higher, of course, and depend on the dataset. Typically those values are bounded within [-20,20]. However, the deviations from this range are not many.

In the course of our deliberations, we have observed a pattern common in all datasets: *there is a Zipfian model in the distribution of frequencies*. Observe Fig. 5 that comes with two parts, both depicting how often a growth value appears in the attributes of Ensemble. The x-axis keeps the delta size and the y-axis the number of occurrences of this delta. In the left part we include zeros in the counting (343 occurrences out of 528 data points) and in the right part we exclude them (to show that the power law does not hold only for the most popular value). We observe that there is a small range of deltas, between -2 and 4 that takes up 450 changes out of the 528. This means that, despite the large outliers, change is strongly biased towards small values close to zero.

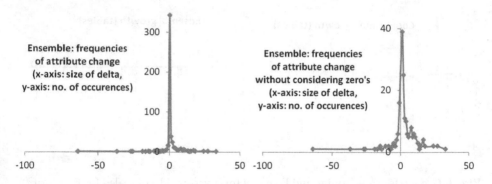

Fig. 5. Frequency of change values for Ensembl attributes

Despite the fact that change does not follow the pattern of baseline smooth growth of Lehman and the fact that change obeys a Zipfian distribution with a peak at zero, we have to say that the presence of feedback in the evolution process is evident; thus the law holds.

4.2 Properties of Growth for Schema Evolution

Law of Continuing Growth (Law VI). The sixth law of continuing growth requires us to verify whether the information capacity of the system (schema size) continuously grows. In all occasions, the schema size increases in the long run (Fig. 1, 2). We frequently observe some shrinking events in the timeline of schema growth in all data sets. However, *all data sets demonstrate the tendency to grow over time*. However, we also have differences from the traditional software systems that the law studies: as with Law I, the term "continually" is questionable. As already mentioned (refer to Law III and Fig. 1, 2), change comes with frequent (and sometimes long) periods of *stability*, where the size of the schema does not change (or changes very little).

Therefore we can conclude that *the law holds, albeit modified to accommodate the particularities of database schemata.*

Law of Conservation of Familiarity (Law V). A first question, of central interest for the fifth law's intuition is: "What happens after excessive changes? Do we observe small ripples of change, showing the absorbing of the change's impact in terms of corrective maintenance and developer acquaintance with the new version of the schema?" An accompanying question, typically encountered in the literature, is: "What is the effect of age over the growth and the growth ratio of the schema?" Is it slowly declining, constant or oblivious to age? Again, we would like to remind the reader on the properties of growth, discussed in Law III of self-regulation: the changes are small, come with spike patterns between zero and non-zero deltas and the average value of growth is very close to zero.

Concerning the ripples after large changes, we can detect several patterns. Observe Fig. 6, depicting attribute growth for the MediaWiki dataset. Due to

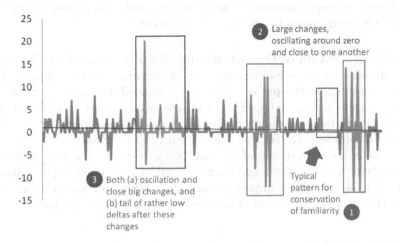

Fig. 6. Different patterns of change in attribute growth of Mediawiki (over version-id, concealed for fig. clarity)

the fact that this involves the growth of attributes, the phenomena are amplified compared to the case of tables. Reading from right to left, we can see that there are indeed cases where a large spike is followed by small or no changes (case 1). However, within the small pool of large changes that exist overall, it is quite frequent to see sequences of large oscillations one after the other, and quite frequently being performed around zero too (case 2). In some occurrences, we see both (case 3).

Concerning the effect of age, we do not see a diminishing trend in the values of growth; however, *age results to a reduction in the density of changes and the frequency of non-zero values in the spikes. This explains the drop of the average value in almost all the studied data sets* (Fig. 4): the linear interpolation drops; however, this is not due to the decrease of the height of the spikes, but due to the decrease of their density.

The heartbeat of the systems tells a similar story: typically, change is quite more frequent in the beginning, despite the fact that existence of large changes and dense periods of activities can occur in any period of the lifetime. Fig. 1 and 2 clearly demonstrate this by combining schema size and activity. This trend is typical for almost all of the studied databases (with phpBB being the only exception, demonstrating increased activity in its latest versions with the schema size oscillating between 60 and 63 tables).

Concerning the validity of the law, we *believe that the law is possible but not confirmed.* The law states that the growth is constrained by the need to maintain familiarity. However, the peculiarity of databases, compared to typical software systems, is that there are other good reasons to constrain growth: (a) a high degree of dependence of other modules from the database, and, (b) an intense effort to make the database clean and organized. Therefore, conservation of familiarity, although important cannot solely justify the limited growth. The extent of the contribution of each reason is unclear.

Law of Conservation of Organizational Stability (Law IV). To validate the hypothesis that the law of conservation of organizational stability holds, we need to establish that the project's lifetime is divided in phases, each of which (a) demonstrates a constant growth, and, (b) is connected to the next phase with an abrupt change. Moreover, abrupt changes should occur from time to time and not all the time (resulting in extremely short phases).

If we focus on the essence of the law, we can safely say that it does not hold. The heartbeats of Fig. 1 and 2 and the arbitrary sequencing of spikes and stability (Fig. 4, 6) make it impossible to speak about constant growth, even in phases. The open-source nature of our cases plays a role to that too.

4.3   Perfective Maintenance for Schema Evolution

Law of Increasing Complexity (Law II). The law states that complexity increases with age, unless effort is taken to prevent this – nevertheless, the law does not prescribe a clear assessment method for its validity. The rationale behind verifying the law dictates the observation of (a) an increasing trend in complexity of a software system, battled by (b) a perfective maintenance activity that attempts to reduce it and demonstrated by drops in the system size and rate of expansion. As there is no precise definition and measurement of complexity in the law, different metrics have been employed (coupling, cyclomatic complexity, etc. – see [6] for a review). Unfortunately, as most of these metrics are non-applicable to the case of databases, we take a definition already found in Lehman [1]: *complexity is defined as the number of modules handled (in our case tables added or modified) over the absolute value of growth per transition.* This formula approximates how much effort has been invested in expanding the system over the actual difference achieved (large values demonstrate too much effort for too small change).

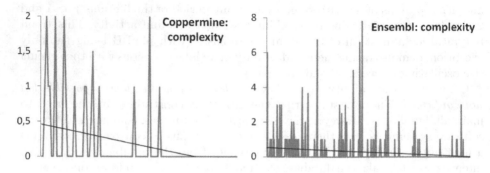

Fig. 7. Complexity for Coppermine and Ensembl (over version-id, concealed for clarity)

Related literature typically speaks for increasing complexity [1], [2], [3], [6], although there have been counterarguments for the case of open source software [5]. In our case, *in all the datasets but Biosql, complexity, as defined in the previous paragraph, does not increase* (Fig. 7). The phenomenon must be coupled with the drop in change density (Law V) and although we cannot provide undisputable explanation, we offer the synergy of two causes: (a) the increasing dependence of the surrounding code to the database that makes developers more cautious to perform schema changes as they incur higher maintenance costs, and, (b) the success of the perfective maintenance, which results in a clean schema, requiring less corrective maintenance in the future.

Although we cannot confirm or disprove the law based on undisputed objective measurements, we have indications that the second law partially holds, albeit with completely different connotations than the ones reported by Lehman for typical software systems: in the case of database schemata, complexity, when measured as the fraction of expansion effort over actual growth, drops.

Law of Declining Quality (Law VII). The seventh law postulates that quality declines with age unless the system is rigorously adapted to its external environment. Lehman and Fernandez-Ramil [3] avoid both (a) a definition of quality "the definition, measurement, modelling and monitoring of software quality-related characteristics are very dependent on application, organisation, product and process characteristics and goals", and, (b) giving any other support to the law than a logical proof: as the system expands over time, its complexity rises and thus the addressing of user requirements and removal of defects becomes more and more difficult, unless work is done to confront the phenomenon ("the decline in software quality with age, appears to relate to a growth in complexity that must be associated with ageing").

We have already demonstrated that the rationale behind complexity increase is not supported by our observations. At the same time, we cannot assess schema quality with undisputed means. Therefore, we cannot confirm or disprove the law based on undisputed objective measurements.

5 Discussion

In this section, we summarize fundamental *observations* and *patterns* that have been detected in our study. We intentionally avoid the term *law*, as we do not have unshakeable evidence for their explanation. Apart from the *empirical grounding*, due a very large amount of datasets that obey the same patterns (which we believe we have fairly attained), we would require an undisputed *rationalized grounding*, that can be obtained via a clear explanation of the underlying mechanism that guides them, also established on measured, undisputed data.

Feedback-Based Behavior for Schema Evolution. *As an overall trend, the information capacity of the database schema is enhanced – i.e., the size grows in the long term (VI). The existence of perfective maintenance is evident in almost all datasets with the existence of relation and attributes removals, as well* *as observable drops in growth and size of the schema (sometimes large ones). In fact, growth frequently oscillates between positive and negative values (III). The schema size of a certain version of the database can be accurately estimated via a regressive formula that exploits the amount of changes in recent, previous versions (VIII).* Based on the above, we can state that the essence of Lehman's laws applies to open-source databases too: *Schema evolution demonstrates the behavior of a feedback-regulated system, as it obeys the antagonism between the need for expanding its information capacity to address user needs and the need to control the unordered expansion, with perfective maintenance.*

Observations Concerning the Heartbeat of Change. *The database is not continuously adapted, but rather, alterations occur from time to time, both in terms of versions and in terms of time (I). Change does not follow patterns of constant behaviour (IV). Age results in a reduction of the density of changes to the database schema in most cases (V).*

Schema Growth Is Small (Observations): *Growth is typically small in the evolution of database schemata, compared to traditional software systems (III). The distribution of occurrences of the amount of schema change follows a Zipfian distribution, with a predominant amount of zero growth in all data sets. Plainly put, there is a very large amount of versions with zero growth, both in the case of attributes and in the case of tables. The rest of the frequently occurring values are close to zero, too. The average value of growth is typically close to zero (although positive) (III) and drops with time, mainly due to the drop in change density (V).*

Threats to Validity. We start with a *fundamental inquiry*: are databases E-type systems, so that this research is meaningful in the first place? Despite a fundamental difference (as databases involve information and not functional capacity), databases, closely resemble E-type systems as they address the real problem of query answering, come with their own user community (developers, DBA's), and act as fairly independent modules in information systems. Concerning the *external validity* of our study, its context concerns *the study of the evolution of the logical schema of databases in open-source software*. We avoid generalizing our findings to databases operating in closed environments and we stress that our study has focused only on the logical structure of databases, avoiding physical properties (let alone instance-level observations). Overall, we believe we have provided a safe, representative experiment with a significant number of schemata, having different purposes in the real world and time span (from rather few (40) to numerous (500+) versions). Our findings are generally consistent (with few exceptions that we mentioned). Concerning *internal validity* and cause-effect relationships, we avoid directly relating age with phenomena like the dropping density of changes or the size growth; on the contrary, we attribute the phenomena to a confounding variable, perfective maintenance actions, which we anticipate to be causing the observed behavior. When it comes to *construct validity*, all the measures we have employed are accurate, consistent with the metrics used in the related literature and appropriate for assessing the law to which they are employed. The only exceptions to this statement are Laws II and VII dealing with the complexity and the quality of the schemata. Both terms are very general and the related database literature does not really provide adequate metrics other than size-related (which we deem too simple for our purpose); our own measurement of complexity requires deeper investigation. Therefore, the undisputed assessment of these laws remains open.

Future Work. The extension of the study to more datasets, possibly non-relational too, and the study of databases in closed environments for large periods of time, are possible roads for future research. Concerning the current findings of our study, the detailed understanding of the feedback mechanism, especially when it comes to ageing and complexity (Law II) as well as patterns of growth (Laws III and V), or patterns in the heartbeat of the evolution, are open issues worth investigating.

Acknowledgment. This research has been co-financed by the European Union (European Social Fund - ESF) and Greek national funds through the Operational Program "Education and Lifelong Learning" of the National Strategic Reference Framework (NSRF) - Research Funding Program: Thales. Investing in knowledge society through the European Social Fund.

References

1. Belady, L.A., Lehman, M.M.: A model of large program development. IBM Systems Journal 15(3), 225–252 (1976)
2. Lehman, M.M., Ramil, J.F., Wernick, P., Perry, D.E., Turski, W.M.: Metrics and laws of software evolution - the nineties view. In: 4th IEEE International Software Metrics Symposium (METRICS 1997), p. 20 (1997)
3. Lehman, M.M., Fernandez-Ramil, J.C.: Rules and Tools for Software Evolution Planning and Management. In: Software Evolution and Feedback: Theory and Practice. John Wiley and Sons Ltd. (2006) ISBN-13: 978-0-470-87180-5
4. Xing, Z., Stroulia, E.: Analyzing the evolutionary history of the logical design of object-oriented software. IEEE Trans. Software Eng. 31(10), 850–868 (2005)
5. Fernández-Ramil, J., Lozano, A., Wermelinger, M., Capiluppi, A.: Empirical studies of open source evolution. In: Software Evolution, pp. 263–288 (2008)
6. Xie, G., Chen, J., Neamtiu, I.: Towards a better understanding of software evolution: An empirical study on open source software. In: 25th IEEE International Conference on Software Maintenance (ICSM 2009), Edmonton, Alberta, Canada, pp. 51–60 (2009)
7. Sjøberg, D.: Quantifying schema evolution. Information and Software Technology 35(1), 35–44 (1993)
8. Papastefanatos, G., Vassiliadis, P., Simitsis, A., Vassiliou, Y.: Metrics for the prediction of evolution impact in etl ecosystems: A case study. J. Data Semantics 1(2), 75–97 (2012)
9. Curino, C., Moon, H.J., Tanca, L., Zaniolo, C.: Schema evolution in wikipedia: toward a web information system benchmark. In: Proceedings of ICEIS 2008. Citeseer (2008)
10. Curino, C.A., Moon, H.J., Zaniolo, C.: Graceful database schema evolution: the prism workbench. Proceedings of the VLDB Endowment 1, 761–772 (2008)

Schema Independent Reduction
of Streaming Log Data

Theodoros Kalamatianos and Kostas Kontogiannis

National Technical University of Athens
Dept. of Electrical and Computer Engineering
Athens, 15780, Greece
{thkala,kkontog}@softlab.ntua.gr

Abstract. Large software systems comprise of different and tightly interconnected components. Such systems utilize heterogeneous monitoring infrastructures which produce log data at high rates from various sources and in diverse formats. The sheer volume of this data makes almost impossible the real- or near real-time processing of these system logs. In this paper, we present a log schema independent approach that allows for the real time reduction of logged data based on a set of filtering criteria. The approach utilizes a similarity measure between features of the incoming events and a set of filtering features we refer to as beacons. The similarity measure is based on information theory principles and uses caching techniques so that infinite log data streams and log data schema alterations can be handled. The approach has been applied successfully on the KDD-99 intrusion detection benchmark data set.

Keywords: software engineering, log analysis, log filtering, information theory.

1   Introduction

Large software systems consist of many interconnected components. The operation of such systems is usually monitored by specialized applications that emit a wealth of information in the form of event logs. In this context, a challenging task is to understand in a tractable manner what operations are performed by the system at any given time, in order not only to understand how the system operates, but also to identify situations where the system is performing unscheduled or unexpected tasks. To date, most dynamic analysis approaches are applied off-line, but for most practical applications a real-time on-line analysis is preferred. However, the sheer volume of the emitted logged data makes such an on-line analysis non tractable. The objective is thus to devise log filtering techniques that allow for the selective reduction of logged data according to specific filtering criteria. The filtering criteria can be set by the administrators and relate to specific hypotheses or analyses that need to be tested or performed.

In this paper we propose an on-line, schema independent approach that is based on information theory principles to calculate log event similarity with

M. Jarke et al. (Eds.): CAiSE 2014, LNCS 8484, pp. 394–408, 2014.

the purpose of analyzing and appropriately grouping streaming events that are emitted by a system's monitoring infrastructure. The technique consists of three main steps. In the first step, which can be performed off-line, a collection of significant log features or "beacons" are selected by the user or by an automated process (e.g. a data mining process), as being significant to a use case or to a possible type of system incident. Such beacon features may be unsuccessful login attempts to a particular server, a warning for a failed transaction, transaction requests arriving at a high frequency from a group of servers, or a performance degradation alert. Beacon features are then used to generate user defined *beacon events*. In the second step of the process, event similarity values are computed between the beacon events and the incoming events in the log data set. The similarity scores are computed by comparing attribute values that are weighted by an information content coefficient. For example, if an attribute value is constant across all logged events, then this attribute value should not be considered as important for the computation of an overall similarity between two events. The result of the second step is an overall similarity value for each event with the beacon event set as a whole. In the third step of the process, a threshold is selected and events that exhibit an aggregated similarity value with the beacon set that is above the threshold value, are considered as a cohesive collection of events that correspond to a use case or an incident.

The proposed approach has three notable advantages over existing dynamic analysis approaches. First, it is schema independent and it is, therefore, readily available for collections of logged data that are emitted by different monitoring components and not conforming to the same schema or format. This eliminates the need for event schema merging or mapping, a process that is often too computationally expensive to be performed for on-line analysis. Second, the proposed approach does not require a training data set, a requirement for most approaches that are based on machine-learning techniques. Rather, the proposed approach is based on the on-line adaptive re-calculation of an information content coefficient for each attribute value, allowing thus the similarity score to be automatically adapted as the system evolves or its operational profile changes. Finally, it can be applied to streaming log data, permitting real time analysis, in contrast to most log analysis techniques that analyze stored logged data in an off-line manner.

This paper is organized as follows: Section 2 presents related work. Section 3 presents the event model. Section 4 discusses the event similarity measure and the selection of the filtered output. Section 5 presents implementation considerations, Section 6 presents experimental results, while Sections 7 and 8 provide related discussion and conclude the paper.

2   Related Work

Dynamic program analysis has been extensively used to understand the behavior of software systems. Bruegge et al. [1] proposed a framework to support dynamic analysis by source code instrumentation of systems written in C/C++. Männistö et al. [2] proposed the tool SCED, for modeling dynamic properties of object oriented systems. Both tools require access to the source code, which might not always be the case.

In the area of data set filtering, in [3] two different data filtering and noise reduction techniques are discussed. The first is based on multiple-partitioning filtering while the second is based on iterative partitioning filtering. In [4] a technique that allows for the discovery of processes by analyzing event logs is proposed, while in [5] a log analysis technique has been used to evaluate the evolution of business models by comparing known model templates to actual models. In [6] a domain independent approach is proposed for log reduction. The main difference between the proposed approach and the one presented in [6] is that the approach discussed here uses information theory for event similarity calculation and that it can be applied in streaming log data.

In the field of log analysis by event feature reduction, [7] discusses a technique using Latent Semantic Indexing for log reduction and filtering so that root cause analysis can be tractable for systems emitting large volumes of log data. In [8] a technique to identify event features important for dynamic analysis and, in particular, intrusion detection is presented. The reduced feature sets allow for more tractable analysis to be performed. Compared to our approach, the work in [8] is fine tuned for intrusion detection and aims to reduce features as opposed to events. In [9] the Enhanced Support Vector Decision Function technique is used for selecting important features in log entries to support intrusion detection analysis. In [10] a technique based on the maximization of conditional information and weak dependence is proposed for the selection of important features in data collections. In [11] an information theoretic approach that selects an optimal set of attributes by removing irrelevant and redundant features is presented. Similarly, in [12] a hybrid approach for feature selection based on information theory as well as filter and wrapper models is presented. In [13] a two phase approach for network intrusion detection that is based on feature reduction and reasoning using fuzzy clustering and the Dempster-Shafer theory is proposed.

Overall, the main differences of our work with the related work presented in this section are that our approach is domain and schema independent and it does not require training data sets. Furthermore, it can be applied on real-time streaming data, thus allowing for on-line analysis.

3   Event Modelling

3.1   Static Event Model

Each event e_i of the input stream $\mathcal{E} = \{e_1, e_2, \ldots e_{N_E}\}$ is defined as a set of pairs that consist of an attribute $a_j \in \mathcal{A}$ and its associated value $v_{j,i}$. More specifically, each event e_i in the input stream is defined as:

$$e_i = \{< a_j, v_{j,i} >: 1 \leq i \leq |\mathcal{E}|, 1 \leq j \leq |\mathcal{A}|\} \tag{1}$$

where $\mathcal{A} = \{a_1, a_2, \ldots a_{N_A}\}$ is the set of all attributes a_j appearing in the events of the input stream. If an event e_i does not have an attribute a_j we simply consider the value for this particular attribute to be NULL. This notation can be used to represent any acyclic tree-like structure, such as those commonly generated by system utilities (e.g. XML, JSON), while it can be easily stored in a database, such as MongoDB.

It should be noted that this approach is particularly effective when used with *structured* data, with its precision increasing as the detail of the representation increases. While free-form attribute string values can still be used as input to the low-level primitive value distance metric calculation, several approaches have been proposed (e.g [14], [15]) to extract schema information from log files.

3.2 Stream Model

The implicit insertion of NULL values allows each attribute a_j to be defined as a stream S_{a_j} of its values $v_{j,i}$: $S_{a_j} = \{v_{j,1}, v_{j,2}, \ldots v_{j,N_E}\}$. Therefore the event stream can be viewed as a collection of discrete time series, one for each attribute, that are evolving in parallel.

The proposed approach is most effective when each attribute is an independent variable with no correlation to other attributes. Redundant information in the input stream may skew the results of the process by incorrectly emphasizing certain values, while reducing the perceived importance of others. The problem of normalizing redundant information streams has been studied extensively. For example, several feature selection techniques have been proposed (e.g. [10], [8]) and can be used as a pre-processing stage to remove redundant features.

4 Event Analysis and Filtering

4.1 Beacon Event Set Compilation

The first phase of the proposed process involves the compilation of a cohesive beacon event set $\mathcal{B} = \{b_1, b_2, \ldots b_{N_B}\}$ that serves as the filtering criterion. These events can be selected directly from the input stream or can be drafted by the operator, as a collection of *pseudo-events*, by combining features and values that the operator considers important or of interest. The system requires no information on the actual selection process, which allows the use of opaque third-party utilities.

4.2 Similarity Computation

In order to compute a similarity measure of each event in the input stream with the beacon set, we propose a three stage process. The results of each stage are fed to the next one, creating a hierarchical process that is described bellow.

Stage 1. The first stage involves the dynamic determination of the importance that an attribute or a value carries in the evaluation of a final overall similarity measure. For example, an attribute for which its value is constant throughout the input stream does not carry any significant *information content* for the computation, while attribute values that vary may carry higher *information content*. This allows a low-level similarity metric for primitive values (e.g. strings), typically described as $dist : \mathcal{E} \times \mathcal{E} \times \mathcal{A} \to \mathcal{R}$, to be used as the basis of an event-level similarity measure.

More specifically, the proposed approach attempts to determine which attributes and attribute values offer the best event *selectivity* with regard to a specific beacon set. For this purpose, a statistical similarity measure based on information theory is introduced. Each attribute a_j is considered an independent discrete random variable with an alphabet V_j of N_{V_j} possible symbols (values).

According to information theory, the entropy H of an independent variable X is a measure of the average information content of each sample of X. Likewise, the information content I is a metric of the *importance* of a variable as a whole. If X is a discrete time series of N samples with an alphabet of n symbols and a probability mass function of $p(X)$, we have:

$$H(X) = E(-log_r p(X)) = -\sum_{i=1}^{n} p(x_i) log_r p(x_i) \qquad (2)$$

$$I(X) = -\sum_{i=1}^{N} log_r p(x_i) = N \cdot H \qquad (3)$$

The probability $p(x_i)$ of a symbol is equal to its relative frequency within the time series. Specializing formula 3 using the individual attribute value frequencies, it is therefore possible to compute the information content of a specific attribute value $v_{j,i}$, as well as that of a discrete attribute a_j as a whole:

$$I(v_{j,i}) = -n_{j,i} \cdot log_r \frac{n_{j,i}}{N_E} \qquad (4)$$

$$I(a_j) = -\sum_{i=1}^{N_{V_j}} (n_{j,i} \cdot log_r \frac{n_{j,i}}{N_E}) \qquad (5)$$

The selectivity offered by each event attribute is in direct relation to the information content of the equivalent time series. Conceptually, highly repetitive attributes, such as domain-specific constants, have a limited use as *distinguishing features* between events, but they also exhibit a relatively low entropy that can be used to reduce their participation in the event comparison process. Furthermore, attributes with extreme diversity, e.g. unique identifiers, tend to skew the similarity metric, since they have a high information content despite being of limited value for determining similarity. To offset this issue, the information content $I(v_{j,i})$ contributed by each specific *attribute value* is taken into account in relation to the information content $I(a_j)$ of that particular attribute as a whole. This leads to the following definition of the *information content fractions* $IF(a_j)$ and $IF(v_{j,i})$ for an attribute and an attribute value respectively:

$$IF(a_j) = \frac{I(a_j)}{\sum_{j}^{N_A} I(a_j)} \qquad (6)$$

$$IF(v_{j,i}) = \frac{I(v_{j,i})}{I(a_j)} \tag{7}$$

The information content fraction is a dimensionless quantity in the $[0,1]$ range. Using it as a coefficient lessens the impact of attribute values with low overall contribution. This is especially effective for attributes with high diversity: a large number of discrete values means that each specific value has a minuscule contribution to the overall information content on its own. The resulting IF fraction will be relatively low, reducing the skew normally caused by high-diversity attributes. Using this principle, a similarity metric $SV_{i,b,j}$ can be defined for the attribute a_j values of input event e_i and beacon event b as follows:

$$SV_{i,b,j} = IF(v_{j,b}) \cdot IF(v_{j,i}) \cdot dist(i,b,j) \tag{8}$$

Stage 2. At the second stage we compute a weight W_{a_j} for each attribute a_j in the input stream $\mathcal{E}$. This attribute-specific weight is affected by the information content of the attribute and the particular contribution of its specific values in the beacon event set. This enhances the effect of less frequent values that are common within the beacon event set and may, therefore, be a distinguishing feature for the selection process.

$$W_{a_j} = I(a_j) \cdot \prod_{b \in \mathcal{B}} IF(v_{j,b}) \tag{9}$$

Stage 3. The final stage contains the evaluation of a similarity measure between two events and leverages that measure to compare each input stream event with the beacon set as a whole.

Lin [16] offers a formal definition of the concept of similarity, based on three basic intuitive tenets: (a) the more commonality two objects share, the more similar they are; (b) the more differences two objects have, the less similar they are and; (c) two identical objects should always reach the maximum similarity.

Using a weighted mean to leverage the per-attribute similarity values from the previous stages to an event-level metric $SE_{i,b}$ satisfies all three basic conditions. Additionally, it allows the attribute-level weights which are not bounded to form a bounded metric with the same range as the primitive correlation metrics:

$$SE_{i,b} = \frac{\sum_{j=1}^{N_A}(W_{a_j} \cdot SV_{i,b,j})}{\sum_{j=1}^{N_A} W_{a_j}} \tag{10}$$

The final computation involves the determination of an overall similarity SB_i of an input event with the beacon set as a whole. To procure a similarity metric between a single event and an *event set* using a metric defined between single events, it becomes necessary to reexamine the three basic principles mentioned above. More specifically, the requirement for a maximum similarity result on identical inputs is no longer satisfiable since sets and single items are not directly comparable. Our prototype implementation uses an arithmetic mean, averaging the similarities calculated for the input event with each beacon event:

$$SB_i = E(SE_{i,b}) = \frac{\sum_{b \in \mathcal{B}} SE_{i,b}}{N_B} \qquad (11)$$

4.3   Filtered Event Group Selection

Conceptually, for the reduced event set we aim to select those events with the highest similarity values. Providing a *threshold* for that selection, however, is not trivial. Real-time streams are unbounded with regard to space and impose certain latency constraints, while the amount of information that is known a priori is limited. Therefore an *adaptive* threshold selection method should be used for the last phase of the process.

In our approach, the resulting event group is computed using a dynamic threshold, which is determined by detecting significant gaps in the distribution of similarity values. More specifically, a *sketch* of the cumulative distribution function (CDF) of the similarity values is formed in constant space and time, and is updated and examined periodically as the input stream is processed. Using a rough derivative computation it is possible to detect plateaus in the CDF, which typically separate similarity value clusters. A heuristic algorithm is then used to select an appropriate threshold, by taking into account the distances between the highest valued clusters, their size and their position within the similarity value range. Similar techniques based on sub-linear data sketches have been used for approximate percentile determination on real time streams ([17], [18]).

5   Design and Implementation Considerations

5.1   Adaptivity of the Proposed Approach

Adaptivity to Schema Changes. The prototype implementation is completely domain agnostic, with no *a priory* knowledge of the domain or the event schema. As such, it operates on the inherent assumption that only part of the actual schema has been considered at any given time. An incoming event may contain a number of previously unseen attributes that expand the existing view of the schema of the monitored domain. Each new attribute is essentially treated as a time series that only contained *null* values until its time of emergence.

However, for most event domains and monitoring systems it is reasonable to assume a *fixed number of attributes*. Therefore, the set of attributes that are known to the system at runtime will gradually converge towards a constant set, with few or no new additions after a sufficient amount of time.

Information Content Aging. Typical statistical algorithms are generally targeted at data *sets* and not well suited for streaming input:

1. Common set-based metrics exhibit a form of *inertia* as the number of recorded data points increases. New data has a decreasing effect as time passes, gradually reducing the adaptability of the system to zero.
2. Cumulative metrics, e.g. the mean and standard deviation, suffer from numerical range and precision issues when implemented trivially on a computer.

To avoid these issues, the proposed system makes use of algorithms that *devalue* older data points with the passage of time. Daneshgaran et al. [19] provide an information theoretic definition of aging, while Cormode et al. ([20]) describe a generic exponential decay model for aggregate metrics.

Our prototype implementation synchronizes using input events as a *time reference* and ignores any other perception of time. As a result, the decay model used for the aging process, is a simple step-wise decay model. For each *cycle*, the information content currently recorded for all attributes and attribute values is multiplied by a positive *decay* coefficient no greater than 1:

$$I_{aged,t+1} = decay \cdot I_t + (I_{t+1} - I_t) \tag{12}$$

The decay coefficient should be selected with regard to the monitored system, most notably its event rate and other temporal characteristics. Typical values for the *decay* coefficient during experimentation were in the $[0.95, 1)$ range.

5.2   Space Complexity and Object Replacement Algorithms

Since real-time systems have no known limit for the length of the input stream, their space complexity should be constant, or at most sub-linear, with respect to the size of the input. For this reason, it is necessary to *approximate* the operation of the similarity determination algorithm in a space-efficient manner. From the mathematical formulas at its foundation it is clear that the values with the least impact are those with the lowest contribution of information content. Therefore, a potential approximation involves limiting the volume of retained metadata by eliminating the entries that correspond to low-impact values.

Taking the effects of the aging process into account, one can intuitively identify the low-impact values as those that (a) are infrequent or (b) have not appeared recently in the input stream. Selecting items based on frequency and recency is essentially the purpose of *object replacement algorithms*, more commonly known as *caching algorithms*. The main intent of a caching subsystem is to use a predetermined amount of space to store results of past requests, replacing old or infrequent entries when necessary. Therefore, we can use such replacement algorithms to provide a hard limit for the space usage of the proposed system.

For our prototype implementation, we selected the *Adaptive Replacement Cache* [21] algorithm, due to its simplicity and overall performance. It provides a good balance between recency and frequency, while also being resistant to pathological behaviors and able to adapt to its input. Moreover, it has excellent runtime performance and does not need external tuning that would require domain-specific knowledge.

5.3   Runtime Performance

In order to ensure the scalability of the system for monitoring large infrastructures, several approaches to parallelization are available:

- *Attribute-level parallelization*, where each processor handles a subset of the attributes within each event, based on the assumption that each attribute is a completely independent time series.
- *Beacon-level parallelization*, where the comparison of an input event with each beacon event is handled by a separate processor.
- *Event level parallelization*, where the input events are distributed to a large number of processing nodes using an appropriate load-balancing scheduler.

These methods are generally orthogonal and can therefore be employed simultaneously if necessary. The prototype implementation, supports the first two methods and is able to achieve a sustainable throughput of several thousand events per second, when making full use of a 4-processor personal computer.

6   System Evaluation

For the evaluation of the proposed algorithm we used a data set generated within the scope of a competition that was held in conjunction with KDD99, the Fifth International Conference on Knowledge Discovery and Data Mining. The KDD99 data set [22] is a derivative of the DARPA Intrusion Detection Evaluation 1999 data set. As such, KDD99 events represent traffic within a computer network, while specific security breaches are attempted. The data set features about 4.8 million events and 41 distinct attributes, of both continuous and discrete types. In addition, the KDD99 data set contains embedded classification data for each event, which can serve as a *reference* for the evaluation of the quality metrics of any selection method. This alleviates the need for domain-specific tools or manual intervention for the creation of the *golden standard* against which our system will be evaluated.

The prototype implementation was written in the Java programming language and tested extensively in streaming mode. For each experiment, the used beacon events were selected randomly from a specific attack type, with the rest of the events that belong to the same attack type being the expected result.

6.1   Similarity Metric Evaluation

To evaluate the quality of the similarity metric, it is necessary to examine its selectivity between matching and non-matching events. Intuitively, an acceptable metric would provide results with clear *separation* between potential matches and the rest of the input, allowing the selection of the matching results by means of a simple similarity threshold. Ideally, the separating space would also not contain any noise in the form of infrequent errant values, although their

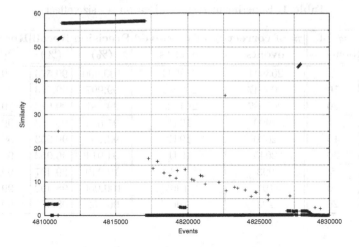

Fig. 1. Similarity values for a part of the input stream with two clusters of potential matches

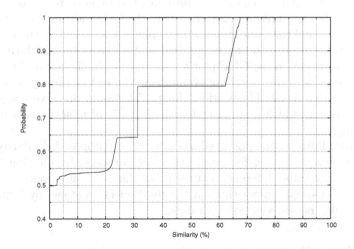

Fig. 2. Cumulative distribution function for the produced similarity values

effect on the overall accuracy of the system would be negligible and they could be filtered-out relatively easily using a variety of methods.

Fig.1 illustrates the aforementioned similarity gap for the events from a small range of the input stream. The plotted values were produced using a beacon set of 20 events that match the *neptune* attack type from the KDD99 data set. The input set contains two event clusters of the same type in this particular range, in the subranges [4810961 − 4817099] and [4827760 − 4827959]. The corresponding similarity values rise from a baseline of about 5 − 10% to values in the 40 − 60% range, with virtually no noise in the range from approximately 20% to 40%, thus being in complete accordance with the golden standard.

Table 1. Experiment results - Beacon set size effect

Test	# of beacons	# of correct events	# of retrieved events	Precision (%)	Recall (%)	Reduction (%)
neptune	5	203941	203941	100.000	99.573	79.606
neptune	10	203947	203941	99.997	99.573	79.605
neptune	20	205087	204023	99.481	99.613	79.491
back	5	1999	1941	97.099	96.953	99.800
back	10	2070	1941	93.768	96.953	99.793
back	20	2045	1941	94.914	96.953	99.796
teardrop	5	993	198	19.940	99.497	99.900
teardrop	10	196	196	100.000	98.492	99.980
teardrop	20	203	196	96.552	98.492	99.980

Fig.2 depicts a plot of the cumulative distribution function (CDF) of the similarity for the same scenario, calculated over a range of $1,000,000$ events. The CDF of the similarity essentially provides the ratio of rejected events for each possible selection threshold. Sharp rises in the CDF indicate the existence of a tight cluster around the same value, while a plateau is caused by the lack of any data points in the corresponding range. In Fig.2 a gap in the similarity values, indicated by a plateau in the CDF plot for similarities in the approximate range of $31 - 63\%$, separates the matching events from the rest of the input stream. A rather conservative threshold selection of e.g. 35% would preserve roughly 20% of the input stream, which is congruent with the ratio of *neptune*-type events in the same range.

Both figures illustrate the potential usability of the proposed similarity metric as a *distinguishing criterion* for event selection purposes. In addition, the significant similarity value difference between matching and non-matching events allows the use of simpler algorithms in the final selection stage, by limiting the need for complex noise-reduction techniques.

6.2   Quality of Results

An accepted technique of assessing an information retrieval process is the measurement of *precision* and *recall* values. For our system, recall is more important than precision, since recall is critical for ensuring that the technique does not discard matching events, especially in a streaming environment where the recovery of such events might not be possible. However, precision still remains an important quality, since it relates to the reduction effected upon the size of the input, which is the final purpose of the proposed system.

For the evaluation process, the prototype implementation was subjected to a series of experiments, a subset of which is presented in table 1. Table 1 contains results from experiments performed over a range of $1,000,000$ events for three different event types and for a variable beacon event set size. The selected

Table 2. Experimental results - Effect of noise in the beacon set

Test	Beacon noise (%)	# of retrieved events	# of correct events	Precision (%)	Recall (%)	Reduction (%)
neptune	10	204027	204021	99.997	99.612	79.597
neptune	20	204810	204021	99.615	99.612	79.519
neptune	30	204027	204021	99.997	99.612	79.597
neptune	40	205260	204798	99.775	99.992	79.474
neptune	50	206266	204733	99.257	99.960	79.373
back	10	2070	1941	93.768	96.953	99.793
back	20	5433	1941	35.726	96.953	99.457
back	30	44540	1929	4.331	96.354	95.546
back	40	77757	1904	2.449	95.105	92.224
back	50	497826	1985	0.399	99.151	50.217
teardrop	10	389445	199	0.051	100.000	61.056
teardrop	20	497395	199	0.040	100.000	50.261
teardrop	30	497395	199	0.040	100.000	50.261
teardrop	40	497395	199	0.040	100.000	50.261
teardrop	50	497395	199	0.040	100.000	50.261

scenarios cover a significant event frequency range, with *neptune*-type events comprising about 20% of the input, while *back* and *teardrop* events correspond to 0.2% and 0.02% respectively. Despite this variation, the system reliably manages to retrieve over 95% of the requested events, with a precision that typically lies in the range of 90 − 95%. The system is able to produce acceptable results with as low as 5 beacon events, which makes it usable by human operators without the aid of additional tools. Varying the size of the beacon event set, does not generally appear to have a consistently significant effect, although in most cases we observed that larger sets resulted in a slightly higher amount of noise. The *teardrop* event type, however, is a notable exception, due to the relatively limited cohesion and higher diversity that characterizes its members. As a result, a larger beacon event set is required to allow the system to reliably establish which features characterize the *teardrop* events, as evidenced by the low precision calculated for the 5-event beacon set. In addition the small size of the *teardrop* event set aggravates the effects of any factor that negatively affects the precision of the system.

6.3 Stability Assessment

To assess the stability of the system we considered its behavior with respect to the presence of random noise in the beacon event set. The evaluation is particularly important, since in real-life cases it is not always possible to define a beacon event set with absolute precision. Table 2 illustrates the experimental results of randomly selected noisy events in the beacon set. Low amounts (e.g. 10%) of

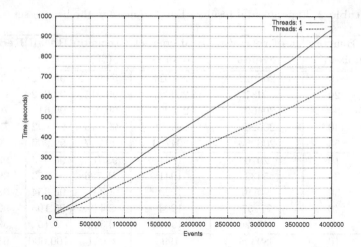

Fig. 3. Processing time versus input size for a variable number of worker threads

noise do not generally have a significant impact, while higher amounts may have a negative effect on precision with the recall being mostly unaffected. On the other hand, event types with limited cohesion, such as the *teardrop* type, are far more susceptible to the negative effects of noise, since the beacon events feature a certain amount of noise themselves. It should be noted that these comments are only valid in the case of *random* noise. The effects of cohesive erroneous events in the beacon set are more severe, with the system generally selecting events that match either the requested or the erroneous event set.

6.4 Runtime Performance

The runtime performance of the prototype implementation was evaluated from several aspects, in order to assess the feasibility of its deployment in production environments. On a mid-range personal computer with four processor cores, the throughput of the system was macroscopically stable and typically well in excess of 5,000 events/second, with 10,000 events/second being attainable for smaller beacon event sets. The use of multiple worker threads provided a notable performance increase, as seen in Fig.3, although the prototype had not been adequately optimized for multiple processors. Last, the system had quite reasonable memory requirements, being able to process the KDD99 data set with less than 96 MB of heap memory available to the Java VM.

7   Discussion

The proposed approach is mainly intended as an efficient schema-independent initial-approach analysis tool. As such, several assumptions were made which can potentially create situations where the system will misbehave:

Each attribute is examined in isolation: The potential usefulness of *combinations* of attribute values is not examined. Addressing this issue in a domain-agnostic manner requires the use of adaptive methods to avoid the introduction of operations with exponential complexity in relation to the combination size.

The system examines each event independently: No temporal relationships are established between events or attribute values. In general the detection of systematic transitions is considered to be beyond the scope of this system, for complexity and performance reasons.

The information content determination algorithm does not take value proximity into account: In some cases it makes sense to consider as equivalent attribute values which happen to be in close numerical or lexicographical proximity.

However, the event selection approach presented in this paper is more flexible than rule-based filters, as it does not require any domain knowledge and can adapt to the input stream.

8 Conclusion

In order for on-line tractable analysis of log data streams to be performed, we should first devise techniques that allow for the selective reduction of the volume of the data that needs to be considered for each analysis. In this paper, we have presented an approach that allows for the on-line selection of logged events that are highly cohesive with respect to a particular feature set. The feature set is used to compile a set of user defined events we refer to as beacon event set. The proposed approach is based on information theory to compute a similarity measure between incoming events and the beacon set, and is schema independent. The result is a highly reduced collection of incoming events that are highly related to specific system behavior. Results obtained from the KDD99 benchmark data set indicate that the approach can tractably reduce the size of events that need be considered with respect to some important system activity such as intrusion attempts, while maintaining high recall and precision levels. Possible future work includes the extension of the approach to handle combinations of attributes for computing event similarity, the incorporation of an attribute reduction pre-processing phase so that further performance enhancements can be possible, and the investigation of techniques for adaptive threshold selection. This work has been supported by CA Labs and CA Technologies UK.

References

1. Bruegge, B., Gottschalk, T., Luo, B.: A framework for dynamic program analyzers. SIGPLAN Notices 28(10), 65–82 (1993)
2. Koskimies, K., Männistö, T., Systä, T., Tuomi, J.: SCED: a tool for dynamic modelling of object systems. University of Tampere, Dept. of Computer Science, Report A-1996, vol. 4, p. 199 (1996)
3. Khoshgoftaar, T.M., Rebours, P.: Improving software quality prediction by noise filtering techniques. Journal of Computer Science and Technology 22(3), 387–396 (2007)

4. Goedertier, S., De Weerdt, J., Martens, D., Vanthienen, J., Baesens, B.: Process discovery in event logs: An application in the telecom industry. Applied Soft Computing 11(2), 1697–1710 (2011)
5. Agrawal, R., Gunopulos, D., Leymann, F.: Mining process models from workflow logs. In: Schek, H.-J., Saltor, F., Ramos, I., Alonso, G. (eds.) EDBT 1998. LNCS, vol. 1377, pp. 467–483. Springer, Heidelberg (1998)
6. Kalamatianos, T., Kontogiannis, K., Matthews, P.: Domain independent event analysis for log data reduction. In: IEEE Conference on Computers, Software and Applications, pp. 225–232. IEEE (2012)
7. Zawawy, H., Kontogiannis, K., Mylopoulos, J.: Log filtering and interpretation for root cause analysis. In: 2010 IEEE International Conference on Software Maintenance (ICSM), pp. 1–5 (2010)
8. Zargar, G.R., Kabiri, P.: Identification of effective network features for probing attack detection. In: First International Conference on Networked Digital Technologies, NDT 2009, pp. 392–397 (2009)
9. Zaman, S., Karray, F.: Features selection for intrusion detection systems based on support vector machines. In: 6th IEEE Consumer Communications and Networking Conference, CCNC 2009, pp. 1–8. IEEE (2009)
10. Fleuret, F.: Fast binary feature selection with conditional mutual information. The Journal of Machine Learning Research 5, 1531–1555 (2004)
11. Last, M., Kandel, A., Maimon, O.: Information-theoretic algorithm for feature selection. Pattern Recognition Letters 22, 799 (2001)
12. Sebban, M., Nock, R.: A hybrid filter/wrapper approach of feature selection using information theory. Pattern Recognition 35(4), 835–846 (2002)
13. Chou, T.S., Yen, K.K., Luo, J.: Network intrusion detection design using feature selection of soft computing paradigms. International Journal of Computational Intelligence 4(3), 196–208 (2008)
14. Xu, W., Huang, L., Fox, A., Patterson, D., Jordan, M.I.: Detecting large-scale system problems by mining console logs. In: Proceedings of the ACM SIGOPS 22nd Symposium on Operating Systems Principles, pp. 117–132. ACM (2009)
15. Nagappan, M., Vouk, M.A.: Abstracting log lines to log event types for mining software system logs. In: 2010 7th IEEE Working Conference on Mining Software Repositories (MSR), pp. 114–117. IEEE (2010)
16. Lin, D.: An information-theoretic definition of similarity. In: 15th International Conference on Machine Learning, vol. 1, pp. 296–304 (1998)
17. Zhang, Q., Wang, W.: A fast algorithm for approximate quantiles in high speed data streams. In: 19th International Conference on Scientific and Statistical Database Management, p. 29. IEEE (2007)
18. Cormode, G., Korn, F., Muthukrishnan, S., Srivastava, D.: Space-and time-efficient deterministic algorithms for biased quantiles over data streams. In: Proceedings of the 25th ACM SIGMOD, pp. 263–272 (2006)
19. Daneshgaran, F., Mondin, M.: Information aging. In: Proceedings of IEEE International Symposium on Information Theory, p. 38 (1997)
20. Cormode, G., Tirthapura, S., Xu, B.: Time-decayed correlated aggregates over data streams. Statistical Analysis and Data Mining 2(5-6), 294–310 (2009)
21. Megiddo, N., Modha, D.: ARC: a self-tuning, low overhead replacement cache. In: Proceedings of the 2nd USENIX Conference on File and Storage Technologies, pp. 115–130 (2003)
22. The Knowledge Discovery & Data Mining Cup 1999 Data, http://kdd.ics.uci.edu/databases/kddcup99/kddcup99.html

Automatization of the Stream Mining Process

Lovro Šubelj, Zoran Bosnić, Matjaž Kukar, and Marko Bajec

University of Ljubljana, Faculty of Computer and Information Science,
SI-1001 Ljubljana, Slovenia
{lovro.subelj,zoran.bosnic,matjaz.kukar,marko.bajec}@fri.uni-lj.si

Abstract. The problem this paper addresses is related to *Data Stream Mining* and its automatization within *Information Systems*. Our aim is to show that the expertise which is usually provided by data and data mining experts and is crucial for problems of this kind can be successfully captured and computerized. To this end we observed data mining experts at work and in discussion with them coded their knowledge in a form of an expert system. The evaluation over four different datasets confirms the automatization of the stream mining process is possible and can produce results comparable to those achieved by data mining experts.

Keywords: data mining, stream mining, expert system.

1 Introduction

With emergence of pervasive distributed computing environments, such as cell phones and sensor networks, the data production has enormously increased [8]. In such environments, data are frequently seen as continuous infinite streams, which cannot be stored for later use. The storage and processing characteristics of streams do not allow for the application of conventional techniques for data analysis and mining; instead, specialized approaches are required that are capable of timely analysis and efficient memory usage. Data stream mining received a lot of attention among researchers and a lot of aspects have already been investigated and resolved [2,13].

The approaches that are available today offer a reasonable trade-off between predictive accuracy and timely responsiveness and can be efficiently used to handle various practical situations [8]. However, data mining requires a deep understanding of the problem domain and data (provided by domain experts) and processing techniques (algorithms, their usage and optimization) that can be employed to perform the analysis (provided by data mining experts). This necessity to employ data and domain experts is recognized as an important obstacle which limits the usage of the data stream mining approaches in practice [9].

In this paper we focus on automatization of the data stream mining process. We do this by capturing and storing the knowledge that the experts employ in various steps of the stream mining process. The main steps of our approach include: (1) the acquisition of the client's requirements and main data properties, (2) the selection of methods that best match the given problem, (3) the setting

M. Jarke et al. (Eds.): CAiSE 2014, LNCS 8484, pp. 409–423, 2014.

and trimming methods' parameters, and (4) learning from the method application on the given problem. We carefully analyzed and discussed the above steps over four case studies with two selected experts. As a result we developed an expert system that fully automatizes the stream mining process. We show that the stream mining of a reasonable quality can be performed using only a minimal domain knowledge and without involvement of data mining experts. This is an important finding which reveals that the stream mining can become more widely used within information systems dealing with streams of data.

The paper is structured as follows: Section 2 briefly explains the related work, Section 3 the expert system, and Section 4 the evaluation. The conclusion is given in Section 5.

2   Related Work

We relate our work to the two relevant sub-fields of machine learning: (1) the field of incremental learning, which deals with the complexity of this task, and (2) the field of meta-learning, which focuses on automatically relating algorithm performance to the characteristics of the data and prior domain knowledge. In the following we review the important works in the both fields.

2.1   Data Stream Processing and Its Complexity

A data stream consists of an ordered sequence of examples, which arrive online. Examples of such applications include sensor measurements, financial applications, telecommunication and network transactions, and others. To achieve processing in real time, the examples are read only once, processed and then discarded or archived. If the example is archived, it has to be stored in memory, which is relatively small compared with the potentially unbounded size of the whole data stream. Several works [2,8] discuss characteristics of data streams and emphasize the following:

- stream mining is performed by sliding window techniques which maintain only the most recent examples in the stream;
- batch processing approaches are inadequate due to the fast processing requirements and the inability to store all past data. They have to be replaced with incremental approaches;
- adaptivity to changes in data is important due to potentially changing data distributions. Since the sequence of examples is not independent and the examples are generated by non-stationary distributions, the target concept may gradually change over time (concept drift) [5];
- summarization, sampling and synopsis techniques are required to compress data and store their statistics; and
- queries over streams cannot be evaluated precisely and are approximated.

Different research directions stem from the listed set of challenges, e.g., proposing learning algorithms for supervised and unsupervised learning [4], improving

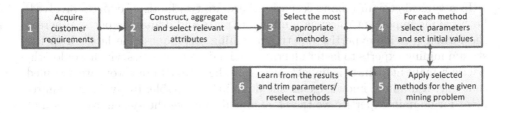

Fig. 1. Main activities in the stream mining process

their accuracy [13], performing queries over transient examples in a stream [2], sampling over data streams, dealing with concept drift [8], and others. The diversity of the former challenges illustrates the complexity of the decisions that need to be taken by users.

2.2 Meta-modeling of Algorithm Performance

Meta-learning focuses on modeling relationship between characteristics of a problem domain and the learning algorithm performance [6]. To predict the performance, the meta-learning algorithm records the past empirical performance of different learning algorithms along with the attributes that describe the problem domain. Choosing these meta-attributes appropriately is a challenge in this field; they can be based either on the data parameters (e.g., data set size, number of attributes, class distributions etc.) or the parameters of the particular underlying learning algorithm [1]. An alternative to automatic construction of meta-learning knowledge is to construct them manually.

Related meta-learning based approaches include stacked generalization [16], which is considered a form of meta-learning because the transformation of the training set conveys information about the predictions of the base-learners; selecting a learning algorithm for each individual test example based on the algorithm's performance exhibited in the example's neighborhood [11]; and inductive transfer of learned knowledge across domains or tasks [12].

Both mentioned fields of the related work motivate us to develop an experimental automated stream mining system that addresses the challenges of the incremental learning and uses meta-modeling to facilitate automation of parameter-setting tasks. Our wishful goal is to enable the non-data mining experts to use the proposed system and achieve comparable performance to the performance of algorithms used by field experts.

3   Expert System

3.1   Stream Mining Process

As emphasized in the introduction, the goal of our research was (a) to capture the expert knowledge of stream mining experts and (b) to formalize this knowledge within an expert system for the automatization of the stream mining process.

In a typical stream mining scenario, there are two kinds of experts involved, both having important roles: data mining experts and domain experts. Whereas the former provide expertise on stream mining techniques, the latter help the stream mining experts to faster identify crucial data properties which would otherwise remain hidden. It is important to note here that in our work we assumed that only a minimal knowledge on the domain is available; by avoiding requirement for domain expertise we therefore aimed to make the system as general as possible. Based on the above limitation and discussion with two stream mining experts we constructed a simplified stream mining process, shown in Figure 1 (explanation in the following). In this process we identified three main areas where the expert knowledge is most important, which are:

- the construction, aggregation and selection of relevant attributes (Figure 1, Activity 2);
- the selection of most appropriate stream mining methods based on problem and data description (Figure 1, Activity 3); and
- setting and re-setting of stream mining methods' parameters (Figure 1, Activities 4 and 6).

In the following sections we first explain the minimal domain knowledge that is required in order to mine streams (with or without experts). Then we describe the activities within the stream mining process where the mining expertise is the most beneficial and explain how these activities were implemented within our expert system.

3.2   Minimal Required Knowledge

For an expert or an expert system some minimal required prior knowledge (RK) is beneficial to make reasonably informed decisions and recommendations:

RK1. *Client's subjective preferences*: requirements such as transparency, visualization possibilities, ability to explain and evaluate results in terms of confidence or reliability. Fulfilling these requirements dictates the choice of stream mining methods;

RK2. *Client's objective preferences*: requirements for data stream predictors. *How will performance be measured? What is a required response time? Should responses be available at any time, even if they are not perfect? What are the time spans of interest? What is the frequency of predictions?* For example, the client might request that every day at 6:00 AM we produce predictions of certain parameters for the next 6, 12 and 24 hours;

RK3. *Known data stream properties*: number of attributes, attribute types, attribute values, distribution of values, frequency of data generation, sparse (e.g., unstructured text) or dense (e.g., sensor) data; and

RK4. *Known data stream mining problem properties*: also based on client's preferences and determines the necessary stream mining paradigm, i.e., prediction of parameter values (both discrete-classification and continuous-regression), anomaly detection, detection of recurrent and/or irregular patterns, and concept drift detection (fundamental changes in data stream generation process).

Initial recommendations of the stream mining experts are produced by consideration of RK1–RK4 without looking into the data stream, which is assumed not to be available at this point. This activity (requirements acquisition) is not yet implemented in our expert system and thus has to be performed manualy in discussion with the client. In future, we intend to develop wizard-based interfaces that will allow clients to provide requirements and domain knowledge directly to the system, i.e., without any involvement of the experts.

3.3   Choosing Appropriate Stream Mining Methods

After acquiring the main client preferences (RK1 and RK2) and data properties (RK3), a stream mining expert selects a set of methods that best match the given problem. This is typically done by considering the importance of different methods' characteristics for the client. The following characteristics are considered as the most important and included in the discussion:

- *Transparency* reflects experts' opinion on how readable and transparent will be the generated model for end-users;
- *Visualization* describes possibilities for visual representation of the model;
- *Explanation* refers to model's abilities to automatically explain its predictions and allow users to assess them;
- *Reliability* describes model's abilities to automatically estimate reliability of its predictions, as well as to allow users to assess them;
- *Response* is an estimate of model's expected response time, both in terms of model updates (training) and model predictions. Normally, shorter response times go hand in hand with lower performance; and
- *Performance* is an estimate of model's performance (in terms of established performance measures, such as mean squared error, classification accuracy, κ statistic etc.).

In our expert system, we first filter the available stream mining methods and select only a subset that best matches client's requirements and domain description. Later, during stream mining we on-line evaluate the selected methods on real data and further refine their selection, if necessary. The knowledge that we acquired from the experts and used to filter out the methods that best match the client's requirements, is summarized in the Table 1 (for classification methods only, due to lack of space).

Our system supports 12 classifiers (methods for predicting a discrete class attribute), 9 regressors (methods for predicting a continuous class attribute) and 5 clustering algorithms from WEKA, MOA and IBLStreams toolkits [7,3,15]. For classification we use: BAYES: a simple Naive Bayesian classifier; RULES: decision rules with Naive Bayes classifiers; TREE: a Hoeffding tree with information gain split criterion; ENSMB: a weighted ensemble with Hoeffding trees; BOOST: AdaBoost boosting approach based; KNN: simple nearest neighbors; and META: a

Table 1. Descriptive properties of data stream mining methods for classification methods. The symbols in the table denote: high importance (+), medium importance (○), low importance (−).

	Transparency	Visualization	Explanation	Reliability	Response	Performance
BAYES	○	○	+	+	+	+
TREE	+	+	+	+	○	○
KNN	○	○	○	○	−	○
RULES	○	○	+	○	○	○
ENSMB	−	−	○	○	−	+
BOOST	−	−	○	○	−	+

meta approach with all above based on κ statistic. For regression we use: KNN: nearest neighbors with linear regression; RULES: adaptive model rules regression; TREE: a Hoeffding regression tree with options; ADDIT: stochastic gradient boosting; DISCT: discretization based approach; SVM: support vector machines based; and META: meta approach with all above based on *MSE*.

3.4 Setting and Trimming Stream Mining Methods' Parameters

In a stream mining experiment the stream mining experts start by setting some reasonable parameter values. When data arrives, the experts observe methods' performance and experiment with their parameters. The choice and magnitude of parameter changes is based on experts' experience and intuition and is difficult to formalize.

For our initial experiments, the experts provided parameter values that were expected to provide reasonable performance of the selected methods. Some parameters (e.g., initial window size) were set according to expected frequency of data generation (RK3), required timespans and frequency of predictions (RK3), thus, to include all possible natural and human cycles. For each of the chosen data stream mining methods, experts also identified a small number of parameters that were sensible to further tune to increase methods' performance.

For the automatization of this activity (Figure 1, Activities 4–6), we initially set the parameters to their default values and then tune them based on the methods' performance. While the first step is rather trivial (the default values are typically suggested by the methods' authors), the second one is much more complicated, as it requires a learning system. We implemented such a system that executes data mining methods in a batch and tunes their parameters on recent subsets of data in order to optimize performance indicators (κ statistic or mean squared error). When the improvement of tuned performance compared with the online performance is statistically significant, the parameter values are applied also within the production (online) stream mining methods. In contrast to the manual parameter setting, where stream mining experts work only with a subset of parameters, the expert system deals with all the parameters in parallel. In addition, if some of the initially selected methods significantly decline in their expected performance, they are terminated and possibly replaced with others.

Please note that the herein described online parameter tuning feedback loop is still a work in progress, and its results are not included in this paper.

3.5   Construction, Aggregation and Selection of Relevant Attributes

Data preprocessing, cleaning and filtering, attribute construction, aggregation, and subset selection, are very important for successful data mining. Many methods are prone to perform poorly when using irrelevant and noisy attributes. While some data mining methods implement constructive induction of attributes [10], they are very complex and time consuming and therefore inappropriate for stream mining. Data expert knowledge (if available) can be used to construct more relevant general attributes; however, for data streams, temporal aggregations are relatively straightforward.

In the observed experiments the stream mining experts started with the application of some basic data preprocessing techniques, such as imputation of missing values detection and imputation of outliers, and adaptive normalization of continuous values. For the supervised stream mining problems, they extended the data with a class attribute lagged by one time step and by the size of the prediction window. They proceeded with attribute aggregation, mostly based on prior data knowledge and their experience.

In our system, we include all basic data preprocessing techniques that are described above. We also provide lagged class attributes, and descriptive statistics, such as the average, mode and others. Temporal attribute aggregation is based on online implementations of discrete and continuous distributions that allow on-the-fly construction of different attributes (e.g., lagged, minimum, average, mode, median, randomly sampled etc.). Stream mining experts defined several periods, based upon natural and human cycles (e.g., hourly, daily, weekly, monthly, yearly). In conjunction with expected frequency of data generation (RK3) we automatically generate aggregate and lagged attributes, such as (for an hourly cycle) data reading an hour ago and hourly cyclic attributes (i.e., sine and cosine with an hourly period).

3.6   Architecture of the Stream Mining Expert System

Figure 2 illustrates the high-level architecture of our proposed system. The system in the figure has two inputs: (1) domain description and user requirements (denoted with ②) and (2) a data stream itself (denoted with ①). Knowledge base consists of decision rules and tables that were elicited from data mining experts. We use it for initial method and parameter selection, selection of evaluation protocol with respect to the stream properties, and on-line parameter trimming (denoted with ③ and ④). These entries are continuously refined during stream mining by including better parameter settings produced by meta learner (denoted with ⑥ and ⑦).

A selected subset of appropriate stream mining methods (utilizing WEKA, MOA, and IBLStreams toolkits) is run in parallel for a given data stream (denoted with ⑨). The induced stream models are evaluated in the model evaluator

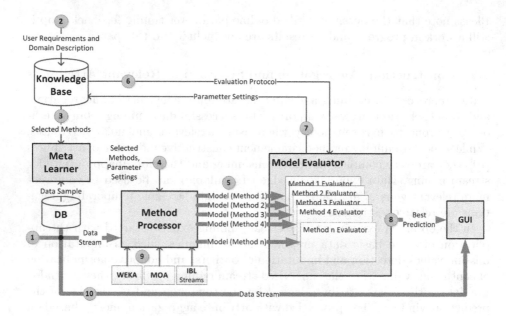

Fig. 2. Expert system high-level architecture

(denoted with ⑤). Its function is twofold: (1) to assist meta learner's feedback loop in order to select better methods and their parameters, and (2) to provide the best current model's results (usually a prediction) to GUI (denoted with ⑧).

3.7 Meta Learner

In our stream mining expert system, as depicted in Figure 2, the *meta learner* component plays a crucial part. It is used for both initial selection of applicable stream mining methods and their parameter setting and optimization of stream mining methods' parameters during execution.

Initially, a subset of methods is selected, based upon client's requirements and domain description. For this purpose, expert knowledge encoded in the knowledge base is used. An example of encoded knowledge used for method selection is shown in Table 1. When a subset of methods $M = \{M_1, M_2, \ldots, M_n\}$ is selected, they are also assigned a set of default parameters (part of the knowledge base), and a set of tunable[1] parameters with their tuning range (both default parameters and sensible tuning range are also parts of the knowledge base).

For the purpose of parameter optimization, for each method M_i we run several instances M_{ij} in parallel with slightly (randomly) perturbed tunable parameters. All method instances M_{ij} are run in parallel on the same data stream. Further parameter optimization is performed with fairly standard genetic algorithm approach [14]. The interval for production of fitness values is determined from client's required timespans and frequency of predictions (RK3).

---

[1] Note that not all parameters can be tuned during method's execution. An example is changing neural network's topology.

For the purpose of genetic operators parameter values are Gray-encoded within the tuning range with resolution of 10 bits. Standard crossover and mutation operators are used in conjunction with tournament selection. Besides this we also use twofold elitist approach. For the next generation we always save the currently best instance $M_{i\,\max j}$ and the instance with default parameter settings M_{i0}. When performance of the currently best instance is significantly ($p < 0.01$) better than the performance of the instance M_i0 with default parameters, the new set of parameters is forwarded (see ④ in Figure 2) from the method processor into the knowledge base alongside with the domain description.

Our current approach assumes that we have enough resources available to run several method instances in parallel (in total possibly hundreds of instances). We intend to explore also a resource-scarce scenario when for each method M_i we will have only a single instance for parameter tuning. It will work on windowed samples and serially optimize parameter values.

3.8 Integration within an Information System

From the information system engineering point of view, such an expert system, once developed, can be reused in various contexts and information systems. Its integration within an information system that deals with data streams and requires the stream prediction, is straightforward due to a very clear interface - the data stream is routed to the expert system for the mining and the predicted stream with the measure of confidence is sent back.

4 Empirical Analysis

4.1 Experimental Framework

We adopt standard statistics for measuring the performance of classifiers: the classification accuracy (CA), Cohen's κ (Kappa) statistic, geometric mean of recall and precision denoted F-score, and Rand index. We evaluate regression algorithms with the mean absolute error (MAE), mean absolute percentage error ($MAPE$), root mean squared error ($RMSE$) and Pearson correlation coefficient. All statistics are computed using a sliding window of the most recent examples.

Additionally, for comparing the performance of two particular classifiers A and B, we use the Q-statistic:

$$Q_{A,B} = \log_2 \frac{CA_A + 1}{CA_B + 1}.$$

When $Q_{A,B} > 0$, classifier A performs better that B (and vice-versa).

4.2 Experimental Datasets

The stream mining tool was analyzed on four datasets from real-world problems (Table 2). First two datasets were used to test the system's classification performance and the remaining two were used to test the regression prediction performance. The datasets were fed to the stream mining methods in temporal order of learning examples. Short description of these datasets is as follows:

Table 2. Temporal datasets used in the analysis. (Hz/3600 is the frequency of the data in examples per hour, while Δ is the size of the prediction window.)

	Dataset	Attributes	Examples	Hz/3600	Δ
Classification	Airline flight delays (2008)	$8 + 1$	21600	≈ 10	0
	Electricity market price (~1996)	$6 + 1$	17520	2	0
Regression	Electric energy consumption	$1 + 1$	16200	1	24
	Solar energy forecast (1994-2007)	$16 + 1$	5113	24^{-1}	0

- **Flight delay prediction within the USA.** The dataset[2] was published at the Data Expo Competition in 2009 and represents an actual non-stationary streaming real-world problem. It contains flight arrival and departure details for all the commercial flights within the USA between 1987 and 2008. The goal is to predict a flight delay based on the available attributes that include *date and time, carrier id, flight number, actual elapsed time, origin, estination, distance,* and *diverted*;
- **Electricity market price in New South Wales.** The dataset was collected from the Australian New South Wales Electricity Market. In this market, prices are affected by demand and supply of the market; they are set every five minutes. The dataset contains 45,312 instances. The attribute set consists of one temporal and five other attributes (*price, demand, transfer, day, period*), and a binary class that specifies whether the price is higher than the moving average of the last day. We supplemented the dataset with attributes that describe daily and weekly periodic cycles;
- **Electric energy consumption of Portugal.** The prediction goal is to continuously predict the electricity load demand for a certain region of Portugal for the next day, based on a stream of measurements that arrive in one hour intervals. Examples contain only one temporal attribute. We constructed additional attributes that describe daily, weekly and yearly periodic cycles; and
- **Solar energy forecast for Oklahoma.** The "Solar energy forecast for Oklahoma" dataset deals with predicting the average daily incoming solar energy at 98 Oklahoma Mesonet sites based on data between 1997 and 2004. The solar energy was directly measured by a pyranometer at each Mesonet site every 5 minutes and summed from the sunrise to 23:55 UTC of the date listed in each column. Numerical prediction data include predictions of 11 ensemble members for various time steps.

4.3   Results and Discussion

To objectively evaluate our approach, we performed the experiments in the following three iterations:

---

[2] http://stat-computing.org/dataexpo/

Table 3. Classification performance for prediction of the **airline flight delays within the USA**: classification accuracy (CA), (Kappa) statistic, F-score, and Rand index. Statistics are computed with a sliding window of 10000 examples.

Algorithm		κ	CA	F	$Rand$
System	META	**0.1562**	**57.81%**	**0.5781**	**0.5781**
	RULES	0.1526	57.71%	0.5755	0.5771
Expert	BAYES	0.1455	57.28%	0.5728	0.5728
	ENSMB	0.1449	57.25%	0.5725	0.5725
Best on raw data		0.1381	56.91%	0.5691	0.5691

1. As a baseline approach, we utilized our stream mining system without any expert system support and measured the results. Only raw streaming data without any preprocessing and attribute aggregation were used. We selected the results of the best performing stream mining algorithm (selected from those described in Section 3.3) as the reference point for the following iterations. These results are denoted with "Best on raw data" in Tables 3–6.
2. In the next step we executed tests by fully involving the stream mining experts in method selection, attribute aggregation, parameter setting and trimming. The obtained results are denoted with "Expert" in Tables 3–6; we consider them as the golden standard of what our expert system can optimally achieve.
3. In the last iteration, we repeated the experiments using a support of the proposed expert system. Expert system's results are denoted with "System" in Tables 3–6.

The results for each of four used datasets are shown in tables, which show the results of our expert system (System) with respect to the baseline approach

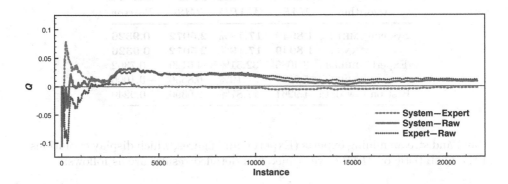

Fig. 3. Q-statistic for comparing three prediction systems for the **airline flight delays within the USA**. Positive values of the curve denote better performance of algorithm A in pair A–B.

Table 4. Classification performance for prediction of the **electricity market price in New South Wales**: classification accuracy (*CA*), (Kappa) statistic, *F*-score, and Rand index. Statistics are computed with a sliding window of 10000 examples.

Algorithm		κ	*CA*	*F*	*Rand*
System	META	0.5271	76.49%	0.7650	0.7649
	BOOST	**0.5287**	**76.61%**	**0.7660**	**0.7661**
Expert	ENSMB	0.4540	72.81%	0.7283	0.7281
	TREE	0.4333	71.70%	0.7174	0.7170
Best on raw data		0.2494	62.80%	0.6273	0.6280

Table 5. Regression performance for prediction of the **electricity consumption of Portugal**: mean absolute error (*MAE*), mean absolute percentage error (*MAPE*), root mean squared error (*RMSE*) and Pearson correlation coefficient. Statistics are computed with a sliding window of 8760 examples.

Algorithm		*MAE*	*MAPE*	*RMSE*	*Pearson*
System	META	82.79	8.73%	122.96	0.9339
	KNN	**81.54**	**8.58%**	**121.27**	**0.9357**
Expert	DISCT	111.17	12.01%	148.39	0.9044
	ADDIT	167.78	19.68%	206.66	0.8023
Best on raw data		326.75	38.49%	388.90	−0.0124

Table 6. Regression performance for prediction of the **solar energy forecast for Oklahoma**: mean absolute error (*MAE*), mean absolute percentage error (*MAPE*), root mean squared error (*RMSE*) and Pearson correlation coefficient. Statistics are computed with a sliding window of 1000 examples, while *MAE* and *RMSE* are in 10^6.

Algorithm		*MAE*	*MAPE*	*RMSE*	*Pearson*
System	META	**1.8949**	**17.19%**	**2.5072**	**0.9326**
	KNN	**1.8949**	**17.19%**	**2.5072**	**0.9326**
Expert	RULES	3.4086	32.51%	4.6129	0.7362
	TREE	5.8087	57.19%	6.8556	−0.1006
Best on raw data		1.9261	17.87%	2.6390	0.9240

(Raw) and stream mining experts (Expert), and figures, which display evolutions of the *Q*-statistic or *MAPE* over time. The detailed results are as follows:

- **Flight delay prediction within the USA.** The results are shown in Table 3 and Figure 3. We can observe that the results for System outperform the Expert (green curve), while in the long run the Expert slightly prevails. Both System and Expert perform better than Raw.

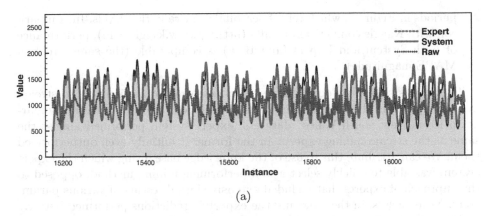

(a)

Fig. 4. Predictions of three systems on the **electricity consumption of Portugal**. Note that the results for System and Expert overlap.

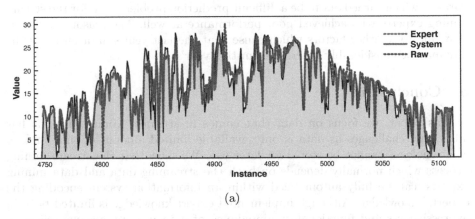

(a)

Fig. 5. Predictions of three systems on the **solar energy forecast for Oklahoma** (the values are in 10^6). Note that the results for System and Expert overlap.

- **Electricity market price in New South Wales.** The results are shown in Table 4. We can observe that in this case System performs slightly worse than Expert, while both perform considerably better than Raw.
- **Electric energy consumption of Portugal.** The results are shown in Table 5 and Figure 4. As with the previous dataset, we can observe that System performs slightly worse than Expert, while both perform considerably better than Raw. We can also notice weekly periods in Figure 4, which reflect different electricity demands on weekends.
- **Solar energy forecast for Oklahoma.** The results are shown in Table 6 and Figure 5. We can observe that System initially performs slightly worse than Expert, while in the long run the difference is negligible. However, neither performs considerably better than Raw. We can also notice yearly

periods in Figure 5, which reflect seasonal solar radiation levels. In comparison with Kaggle competition results (http://www.kaggle.com), performance of both System and Expert (and Raw) is comparable (the same order of MAPE magnitude).

The results show that our expert system often performs similarly to stream mining experts. In the "Airline flight delay prediction" and the "Electricity market price in New South Wales" datasets, expert system performed almost the same as the stream mining experts, in the former it initially even outperformed them. We can attribute this to use of the knowledge base, using which the expert system was able to quickly select a well-performing mining method, opposed to the approach of experts that included extensive initial testing of various parameters. Nevertheless, in the long run, the experts' predictions performed better.

The expert system performed better that the baseline approach (best streaming method on raw data), as we expected, in three out of four datasets. It achieved poor performance only on the "Solar energy forecast for Oklahoma" dataset, which turned out to be a difficult prediction problem even for the stream mining experts who achieved poor performance as well. The reason for this is that due to weather factors which cause that the last year's data on the same day may be considerably different from this year's.

5   Conclusion

In this paper, we focus on data that comes in streams. Mining streams has additional challenges as data is only available limited amount of time and — as a whole — cannot be stored for later use. We show that the stream mining process which normally depends on both the streaming data and data mining experts, can be fully automatized within an information system encoding the experts' knowledge. Although implemented expert knowledge is limited both in expressiveness and functionality, abundance of data in data streams seems to largely compensate this gap, as in the long run, experts' and expert system's performance is (at least in our experiments) quite similar.

In our work we wished to emphasize that solving data mining problems typically requires involvement of individuals with expertise in data mining techniques and approaches. This alone puts some limitations on the application of data mining in business practice as such knowledge is rarely available among employees and needs to be outsourced. Besides the obvious financial limitations (such expertise is costly), and, especially in stream mining, there is an ongoing need for experts' involvement due to data streams' dynamic nature. Therefore, each data mining problem needs to be tackled independently as there seems to be no general solution. The above indicates that the data mining is not fully exploited in business environments and computerized within their supporting information systems. This is a pity, since many information systems today have access to immense amounts of current and historical data.

The results of our study show that the stream mining expertise has become routinized enough to be captured in a form of explicit knowledge and thus computerized. We believe that this represents an important finding which might impact the level of possible automatization of problems known from the *Big Data, Internet of Things* and similar domains.

References

1. Aha, D.W.: Generalizing from case studies: A case study. In: Proceedings of the International Conference on Machine Learning (MLC 1992), Aberdeen, Scotland, pp. 1–10 (1992)
2. Babcock, B., Babu, S., Datar, M., Motwani, R., Widom, J.: Models and issues in data stream systems. In: Proceedings of the ACM SIGMOD-SIGACT-SIGART Symposium on Principles of Database Systems (PODS 2002), Madison, WI, USA, pp. 1–16 (2002)
3. Bifet, A., Holmes, G., Kirkby, R., Pfahringer, B.: MOA: Massive online analysis. J. Mach. Learn. Res. 11, 1601–1604 (2010)
4. Cormode, G.: Conquering the divide: Continuous clustering of distributed data streams. In: Proceedings of the International Conference on Data Engineering (ICDE 2007), Istanbul, Turkey, pp. 1036–1045 (2007)
5. Gama, J., Medas, P., Castillo, G., Rodrigues, P.P.: Learning with drift detection. In: Bazzan, A.L.C., Labidi, S. (eds.) SBIA 2004. LNCS (LNAI), vol. 3171, pp. 286–295. Springer, Heidelberg (2004)
6. Gama, J., Brazdil, P.: Characterization of classification algorithms. In: Pinto-Ferreira, C., Mamede, N.J. (eds.) EPIA 1995. LNCS, vol. 990, pp. 189–200. Springer, Heidelberg (1995)
7. Hall, M., Frank, E., Holmes, G., Pfahringer, B., Reutemann, P., Witten, I.H.: The WEKA data mining software: An update. SIGKDD Explorations 11(1), 10–18 (2009)
8. Hulten, G., Spencer, L., Domingos, P.: Mining time-changing data streams. In: Proceedings of the ACM SIGKDD International Conference on Knowledge Discovery and Data Mining (KDD 2001), San Francisco, CA, USA, pp. 97–106 (2001)
9. Kriegel, H.-P., Borgwardt, K.M., Kröger, P., Pryakhin, A., Schubert, M., Zimek, A.: Future trends in data mining. Data Min. Knowl. Discov. 15(1), 87–97 (2007)
10. Matheus, C.J., Rendell, L.A.: Constructive induction on decision trees. In: Proceedings of the International Joint Conference on Artificial Intelligence (IJCAI 1989), Detroit, MI, USA, pp. 645–650 (1989)
11. Merz, C.J.: Dynamical selection of learning algorithms. In: Learning from Data: Artificial Intelligence and Statistics, pp. 281–290. Springer (1996)
12. Pratt, L., Jennings, B.: A survey of connectionist network reuse through transfer. In: Learning to Learn, pp. 19–43. Springer (1998)
13. Rodrigues, P.P., Gama, J., Bosnic, Z.: Online reliability estimates for individual predictions in data streams. In: Proceedings of the IEEE International Conference on Data Mining Workshops (ICDMW 2008), Pisa, Italy, pp. 36–45 (2008)
14. Rossi, A.L.D., Soares, C., Carvalho, A.C.P.L.F.: Bioinspired parameter tuning of MLP networks for gene expression analysis: Quality of fitness estimates vs. Number of solutions analysed. In: Köppen, M., Kasabov, N., Coghill, G. (eds.) ICONIP 2008, Part II. LNCS, vol. 5507, pp. 252–259. Springer, Heidelberg (2009)
15. Shaker, A., Hüllermeier, E.: IBLStreams: a system for instance-based classification and regression on data streams. Evolving Systems 3(4), 235–249 (2012)
16. Wolpert, D.H.: Stacked generalization. Neural Networks 5(2), 241–259 (1992)

Matching User Profiles Across Social Networks

Nacéra Bennacer[1], Coriane Nana Jipmo[1],
Antonio Penta[2], and Gianluca Quercini[1]

[1] Supélec E3S,
3, rue Joliot-Curie, 91190 Gif-sur-Yvette (France)
{nacera.bennacer,coriane.nanajipmo,gianluca.quercini}@supelec.fr
[2] Università di Torino
Corso Svizzera 185, Torino (Italy)
penta@di.unito.it

Abstract. *Social Networking Sites*, such as Facebook and LinkedIn, are
clear examples of the impact that the Web 2.0 has on people around the
world, because they target an aspect of life that is extremely important
to anyone: social relationships. The key to building a social network is the
ability of finding people that we know in real life, which, in turn, requires
those people to make publicly available some personal information, such
as their names, family names, locations and birth dates, just to name a
few. However, it is not uncommon that individuals create multiple profiles in several social networks, each containing partially overlapping sets
of personal information. Matching those different profiles allows to create a global profile that gives a holistic view of the information of an
individual. In this paper, we present an algorithm that uses the network
topology and the publicly available personal information to iteratively
match profiles across n social networks, based on those individuals who
disclose the links to their multiple profiles. The evaluation results, obtained on a real dataset composed of around 2 million profiles, show that
our algorithm achieves a high accuracy.

1 Introduction

A social network is a set of individuals and their relationships. In a broader sense,
the term social network also refers to a website, such as Facebook and LinkedIn,
which enables individuals to create a personal page, or *profile*, and to stay in
contact with their acquaintances. The key to building a social network is the
ability of finding people that we know in real life, which in turn requires those
people to make publicly available on their profiles some personal information,
such as their names, family names, locations and birth dates, just to name a
few. Several surveys showed that Social Networking Services (SNSs) users tend
to share many of their personal data, including sensitive information, such as
home addresses and phone numbers [1–3].

However, it is not uncommon that an individual creates multiple profiles in
different SNSs, each disclosing sets of personal information that are unlikely to
be identical, though they might overlap. Indeed, profile information might not be

M. Jarke et al. (Eds.): CAiSE 2014, LNCS 8484, pp. 424–438, 2014.

updated regularly and are not necessarily created at the same time. Moreover, the differences between two profiles of an individual might reflect the fact that they are created in SNSs that target different aspects of the individual life. For instance, information on the career of individuals are more likely to be found on their LinkedIn profiles than Facebook's, as LinkedIn is mainly used for professional networking. As a result, finding a person based on a limited knowledge of her personal information might require several manual searches across social networks, which is obviously annoying and time-consuming. It would be useful to create a global profile that provides a holistic view of the personal information of an individual by automatically integrating all her profiles. This calls for efficient methods for automatically determining the profiles that an individual owns across different SNSs, which is the focus of our paper. We say that two profiles *match* if they are owned by the same individual.

In this paper, we present an algorithm that matches profiles across n distinct social networks by using the network topology and the personal information that are publicly available in the profiles. The algorithm first selects a candidate set of profile pairs that are likely to match; this selection exploits the fact that some links between profiles referring to the same individual already exist, as explicitly disclosed in the profiles themselves. Next, the algorithm applies a set of rules that compare the values of the *profile attributes* (such as names, family names, usernames) to determine the pairs that match. Finally, the algorithm uses the newly found matches to retrieve more candidates and further determine other matches in an iterative way. The key contributions of our paper are the following:

- We define sets of rules that use the values of a limited set of attributes to determine whether two profiles match. Unlike the existing rule-based approaches (i) we consider that all attributes are equally important, which relieves us from assigning each attribute an empirical and, inevitably, arbitrary weight and (ii) we study the combined contribution of the different attributes, when used in the same rule.
- Our algorithm matches new profiles in a iterative way, which means that the new found matches are used to discover new matches. Moreover, the discovered matches are propagated by transitive closure across all considered social networks. To the best of our knowledge, no existing method is iterative in this sense.
- We evaluate our algorithm on four real social networks, namely Flickr, Live-Journal, Twitter and YouTube, which combined form a graph composed of around 2 million nodes and more than 17 million links. On this dataset, our algorithm achieves a precision of 94%. No existing approach is evaluated on such a big dataset.

The remainder of the paper is organized as follows. We survey the research work that is related to ours in Section 2 and we introduce basic concepts and notation in Section 3. Section 4 is the central part of the paper, in which we detail our algorithm, which is then thoroughly evaluated in Section 5. Section 6 concludes the presentation.

2   Related Work

Numerous solutions have been proposed to the problem that we study in this paper. Interestingly, two of them focus only on the username of an individual as a way to match different profiles, based on the observation that individuals tend to use the same or a similar username across distinct social networks [4, 5]. Although in our evaluation we confirm this observation, we also consider other attributes, in order to match profiles of individuals who choose to use unrelated usernames.

The use of the attributes to match profiles across distinct social networks has been largely investigated [6–12]. Two approaches describe each pair of profiles as a vector of scores, which represent the similarity between the values of the attributes, and use machine learning techniques to determine whether they match [9, 10]. While the results are promising, both approaches need a training set, which is not easy to determine. In fact, a careful analysis of the available data is necessary to create a training set that is representative of all possible situations where profile pairs match or not. Moreover, a model trained on a given pair of social networks might not be generalizable to other networks, which implies that a training set should be created for each network pair. Some social networks allow the exportation of profiles that are described with the Friend of a Friend ontology (FOAF); the advantage is that standard Semantic Web techniques, such as OWL reasoning, can be used to match profiles [8, 12]. However, these techniques are applied to a limited set of attributes, and in particular to those, such as the email, that are likely to identify uniquely an individual. Similarly to us, Carmagnola et al. determine the profile attributes that are more likely to identify uniquely an individual, by assigning them an *importance factor* [6]. The importance factor is used to weight the similarity score that is computed between two profiles that have similar attributes. Our approach goes a step further and uses the pairs of profiles that are found to match to iteratively discover new matches. Moreover, our evaluation is based on a real large social internetwork, while theirs uses different closed user-adaptive systems. The key difference is that in Web social networks often individuals are reluctant to disclose their real identities, while in closed user-adaptive systems they feel that their privacy is less threatened; as a result, data in social networks are likely to be erroneous and messy, which constitutes a real challenge. Some researchers also propose the computation of semantic similarity between profile attributes [7, 11]. Although these approaches are original, they provide little (50 user profiles [11]) or no evaluation.

Some authors proposed to go beyond the profile attributes and investigated the possibility of using the network properties [13–16]. The approach proposed by Buccafurri et al. considers that two nodes are similar, and therefore likely to refer to the same individual, if they have similar usernames and the nodes to which they are connected are recursively similar [14]. This approach presents two major drawbacks. First, profiles associated with dissimilar nicknames are ignored and discarded with no further analysis, although they might very well refer to the same person; second, the discovered associations between profiles are not used to re-iterate the algorithm and discover new associations. Our approach overcomes these two limitations. Besides considering the network structure, Jain et al. also propose to use of the content that an individual publishes in the form of short texts [15]. This approach has the merit of exploring the use of the content and the shared connections to match profiles. However, the experiments reveal that this information is not very effective alone, as only 4 out of 543 profiles are matched correctly. We found an elegant approach that combines profile attributes and network by using conditional random fields [13]. The key advantage is that it is robust to the absence of profile and/or network information and therefore can also be applied to cases where no profile information is available except the network, although with a significant drop in recall. The disadvantage is that the proposed model needs training data, which, as recalled before, might not be easy to find. Finally, Narayanan et al. consider the case of anonymized networks where little or no profile attributes are available and only the network structure can be exploited [16]. They propose a method that first selects a small set of seed profiles in both networks that are highly likely to belong to the same individual. Then, new matchings are propagated iteratively by using the seed. This is similar in spirit to our approach. However, since they only use the network structure the accuracy of their approach is quite low compared to ours.

Finally, social aggregators, such as *FriendFeed* [17] or *Plaxo* [18], provide a platform for people to manage their own profiles but they make no attempt at automatically discovering profiles linked to an individual across social networks. *Spokeo* [19] seems to be quite accurate in finding personal information from different sources (not necessarily social networks), but it shows its limits when it comes to aggregating them. To the best of our knowledge, there is no existing tool that is able to automatically match profiles across social networks.

3   Background

We define a *social internetwork* as a collection of n distinct social networks and we model it as a directed graph. Its nodes correspond to the profiles of the individuals or, with an abuse of language, to the individuals themselves. A *profile* consists of a set of attributes (such as username, name, email address), which are usually described in a Web page created by an individual, and a *uri*, identifying that page on the Web. A link in a social internetwork connects either two profiles within the same social network, in which case we call it a *friendship link*, or two profiles that refer to the same individual in two different social networks, and we call it a *cross-link*.

Formally, a social internetwork with n social networks is a directed labelled graph defined as follows:

$$\mathcal{G} = < \bigcup_{i=1}^{n} V_i \, , \bigcup_{i=1}^{n} E_i \, , \bigcup_{1, i \neq j}^{n} E_{i,j} >$$

where:

- V_i is the node set of the social network i. Since the social networks are distinct, $V_i \cap V_j = \emptyset, \forall i, j, \ i \neq j$. Each node v_i is the profile of an individual in the social network i. A is the set of the attributes defined in a profile, while $P_a(v_i)$ denotes the value(s) of the attribute $a \in A$ in the profile v_i.
- E_i is the set of friendship links, which are identified by the label $friend$. Each link $(v_i^1, friend, v_i^2)$ represents a friendship link from the individual v_i^1 to the individual v_i^2 within the social network i.
- $E_{i,j}$ is the set of cross-links, which are identified by the label me. Each link (v_i, me, v_j) represents a cross-link between two profiles v_i and v_j owned by the same individual in the social networks i and j, $i \neq j$. By definition, this type of link is symmetrical and transitive. For instance, Bob might indicate in his Flickr profile, represented by the node v_f, the uri of the page of his profile LiveJournal, represented by the node v_l, and in this page he declares the uri of the page of his profile Twitter, represented by the node v_t. In this case, $E_{f,l} = \{(v_f, me, v_l), (v_l, me, v_f)\}$, $E_{t,l} = \{(v_t, me, v_l), (v_l, me, v_t)\}$ and $E_{t,f} = \{(v_t, me, v_f), (v_f, me, v_t)\}$.

The problem of matching the profiles that are owned by the same individual across social networks is the problem of discovering the missing cross-links in a social internetwork and is formalized as follows:

Input: $\mathcal{G} = < \bigcup\limits_{i=1}^{n} V_i \ , \ \bigcup\limits_{i=1}^{n} E_i \ , \ \bigcup\limits_{1, i \neq j}^{n} E_{i,j} >$

Output: $\mathcal{G}' = < \bigcup\limits_{i=1}^{n} V_i \ , \ \bigcup\limits_{i=1}^{n} E_i \ , \ \bigcup\limits_{1, i \neq j}^{n} E_{i,j} \ \bigcup\limits_{1, i \neq j}^{n} D_{i,j} >$ with

$D_{i,j} = \{(v_i, me, v_j) | v_i \in V_i, v_j \in V_j, 1 \leq i \neq j \leq n, (v_i, me, v_j) \notin E_{i,j}\}$

$D_{i,j}$ is the set of the discovered cross-links between the social networks i and j.

4 Our Approach

A first intuitive solution to our problem is to compare each pair of profiles (v_i, v_j), which are not connected via a cross-link, for each pair of networks (i, j), $1 \leq i \neq j \leq n$. However, this amounts to analyse $\sum_{i,j} |V_i| \times |V_j| - |E_{i,j}|$ pairs of nodes, which is not feasible when social networks are large, as it is usual the case. Based on this observation, our matching approach goes through two steps:

- **Candidate selection.** A subset of profile pairs is selected which are likely to represent the same individual and are therefore candidate profiles for the matching approach. The candidates are identified based solely on the topology of the graph.
- **Cross-links determination.** The pairs of profiles that are deemed to correspond to the same individual are identified among the selected candidates. The determination is based on a set of rules which compare the attribute values of the candidate pairs.

The two steps are iterated until no new cross-links can be determined. The remainder of this section describes both steps in greater detail.

4.1   Candidate Selection

The selection of the candidates is based on the observation that a small percentage of individuals own multiple accounts, but they tend to be connected with friends who also have multiple profiles; moreover, when two friends have both multiple profiles, they are frequently friends in multiple networks [8]. Therefore, we consider as candidates the friends of the same individual across different social networks. More specifically, if $\exists (v_i, me, v_j) \in E_{i,j}$, $v_i' \in friend(v_i), v_j' \in friend(v_j)$ then (v_i', v_j') is a candidate, where :

$$friend(v_i) = \{v_i' | (v_i', friend, v_i) \vee (v_i, friend, v_i') \in E_i\}$$

represents the set of the profiles of the friends of an individual v_i. The set of candidates, denoted $C_{i,j}$, for the social networks i and j is formally defined as follows:

$$\{(v_i', v_j') | \exists v_i' \in friend(v_i) \wedge v_j' \in friend(v_j) \wedge (v_j, me, v_i) \in E_{i,j} \wedge (v_i', me, v_j') \notin E_{i,j}\}$$

4.2   Cross-links Determination

Once the candidate set $C_{i,j}$ is created for a social network pair (i, j), we need a method to determine if a pair of candidate profiles (v_i, v_j) represents the same individual. More precisely, we need to determine the set of cross-links $D_{i,j}, \forall i, j, i \neq j$. We introduce the attributes that we use in our approach and then we detail the rules that allow the determination of the new cross-links, as well as the algorithm that we defined.

The Attributes. In all major social networks the values of some attributes are publicly accessible as per default privacy policy and/or left accessible by the individuals. It is therefore natural to analyse these data to establish new cross-links between i and j.

Based on the observations by Krishnamurthy et al., who identified a set of attributes that are generally publicly available in 12 of the most important social networks [20], we focus our attention on the following: *username*, *name* (which includes first name and last name), *email*, and *links* to other Web pages.

Username. Denoted as u, the username is always publicly accessible, as it is the only way to uniquely identify an individual within a social network, and is generally a part of the URL of the web page that hosts the profile. Studies have shown that individuals tend to use the same username, or a similar one, when registering different profiles [4, 5]. In order to determine the similarity of two usernames, we chose the *Levenshtein* distance d_{lev}, which is the minimum number of single character edits (insertion, deletion and substitution), as several studies have revealed that is quite effective in capturing the variations in the usernames chosen by the individuals [4, 5, 14]. The similarity of two usernames

u_1 and u_2 is computed as $1 - \frac{d_{lev}(u_1,u_2)}{max(l(u_1),l(u_2))}$, where $l(u_i)$ is number of characters of $u_i, i = 1, 2$. The Levenshtein distance between the username *cospics* of the Flickr profile at www.flickr.com/photos/cospics and the username *cos* of the LiveJournal profile at www.livejournal.com/users/cos/profile is 4, because we need to suppress the substring "pics", composed of four characters, to obtain the second username from the first. As a result, their similarity is 0.43. To determine whether two usernames are similar or not, we empirically define a threshold θ_u, whose value is discussed in Section 5.

Name. Denoted as n, the first and family name are also present in most of the networks we came across, but their values cannot be trusted as much as the usernames. Indeed, in some social networks, such as LiveJournal, the profile of a person is almost entirely public and consequently individuals do not feel confident in revealing their real names. Moreover, names are often ambiguous, and do not generally identify uniquely an individual. As a result, we do not expect the name of an individual to reveal many profile matches, if not in combination with other attributes. The similarity of two names n_1 and n_2 is computed with the *Jaccard* similarity measure as $\frac{|N_1 \cap N_2|}{|N_1 \cup N_2|}$, where N_1 and N_2 are the sets of the words that compose n_1 and n_2 respectively. For example, if n_1 is "Barack Obama" and n_2 is "Barack Hussein Obama", then $N_1 = \{Barack, Obama\}$, $N_2 = \{Barack, Hussein, Obama\}$ and their similarity is $\frac{2}{3}$. The reason why we select the Jaccard measure instead of the Levenshtein distance is that generally social networks do not force their individuals to specify their first names before the last names. Moreover, some individuals might specify their middle names in a profile, while omitting them in another. Therefore, a comparison between "Barack Obama" and "Obama Barack" would give a Levenshtein distance of 10, although the two strings are equivalent, while Jaccard gives score 1. Similarly to the username, we define a threshold θ_n to determine whether two names are similar.

Email. Denoted as e, *email* is a multi-valued attribute whose values correspond to the different email addresses disclosed by an individual. The email address is a very sensitive attribute, because it could identify uniquely a person. If two profiles are associated with the same email address, there are high chances that the two profiles refer to the same individual. It is certainly possible that two individuals share the same email address, as in the case of people that work within the same organization. But these are particular cases, and in general email addresses can be trusted. The only problem is that only a small percentage of people grant public access to their email addresses. In order to compare the values of the attribute e of two profiles, we need to determine whether one of the email addresses of a profile is identical to one of the email address of the other profile. In this case, the similarity score is 1, otherwise it is 0.

Links to other Web pages. This is a multi-valued attribute whose different values correspond to different URLs of Web pages. We distinguish between two types of links, those to Web pages that describe online profiles in social networks (denoted as s), and those to other Web pages (denoted as w). We aim at investigating the contribution of the two attributes separately. Indeed, the former are likely to indicate the links to the different social network profiles that an individual owns, which might indicate a cross-link in our graph. On the other side, the links to other Web pages are links to resources that an individual wants to share and does not necessarily identify the individual. The similarity score for s (respectively, w) for a profile pair is 1 if one of the values of s (resp., w) of one profile is identical to one of the values of s (resp., w) of the other profile. In this paper, we limit ourselves to determine whether the values of the attribute s or w for two profiles have at least a URL in common without analysing the content of these pages.

Another attribute that is worth considering is the location, whose values are often publicly accessible in different social networks. However, the location name poses some challenges, such as their ambiguity, which fall out of the scope of this paper. For this reason, we leave the use of this attribute for future work.

The Rules. In order to determine whether two profiles v_i et v_j refer to the same individual, we defined a set of rules based on the attributes introduced above. Each rule considers the contribution of one or several attributes. We assume that the higher the number of attributes that match, based on the defined similarity measures, the higher the probability for two profiles to refer to the same individual. We therefore define the *order* k of a rule as the number of attributes that the rule uses. The rule with the highest confidence is the one that uses all the attributes ($k = |A|$). The rules with the lowest confidence are those that use just one attribute ($k = 1$).

Let $match(P_a(v_i), P_a(v_j))$ be the predicate which is true when the values of the attribute a match for the profiles v_i and v_j, based on the similarity measure defined for the attribute a. A rule with the order k, or $k-$rule, $\mathcal{R}^k$ is defined as follows:

$$\mathcal{R}^k(v_i, v_j) = \begin{cases} \bigwedge_{a \in A} match(P_a(v_i), P_a(v_j)) & \text{if } k = |A| \\ \bigvee_{B \in [A]^k} \bigwedge_{a \in B} match(P_a(v_i), P_a(v_j)) & \text{if } 1 \leq k < |A| \end{cases}$$

where $[A]^k$ is the set of all subsets of A with k elements.

Therefore, if $\bigvee_{1 \leq k \leq |A|} \mathcal{R}^k(v_i, v_j)$ is true, then v_i and v_j are considered to refer to the same individual. If for one pair of candidate profiles (v_i, v_j) at least one rule $\mathcal{R}^k(v_i, v_j)$ is *true*, then no rule with order $l < k$ is applied. In the worst case, for (v_i, v_j) no rule is true, in which case the two profiles are considered to refer to two distinct individuals. When there is a rule $\mathcal{R}^k(v_i, v_j)$ which is *true*, the pair (v_i, v_j) is added to $D_{i,j}$, meaning that a new cross-link is discovered.

4.3   The Algorithm

We here detail the procedure that adds missing cross-links to a social inter-network $\mathcal{G}$ with n distinct social networks (cf. Algorithm 1). For each pair of social networks i and j in $\mathcal{G}$, the set $C_{i,j}$ of candidate profile pairs is computed

(Line 3), as described in Section 4.1. Next, the k−rules are applied to each candidate (v_i, v_j) by decreasing order, starting with $k = |A|$, until either one is true or none applies (Lines 5 through 7). If one rule is verified, a cross-link is added between v_i and v_j (Line 8).

Algorithm 1. The algorithm to match profiles across n social networks

---

Data: $\mathcal{G} =< \bigcup\limits_{i=1}^{n} V_i , \bigcup\limits_{i=1}^{n} E_i , \bigcup\limits_{1,i\neq j}^{n} E_{i,j} >$

Result: $\mathcal{G}' =< \bigcup\limits_{i=1}^{n} V_i , \bigcup\limits_{i=1}^{n} E_i , \bigcup\limits_{1,i\neq j}^{n} E_{i,j} \bigcup\limits_{1,i\neq j}^{n} D_{i,j} >$

1 **foreach** *social network pair* (i,j) **do** $D_{i,j} \leftarrow \emptyset$;
2 **foreach** *social network pair* (i,j) **do**
3 $\quad$ $C_{i,j} \leftarrow candidateSelection(\mathcal{G}, i, j)$ $newCl \leftarrow false$;
4 $\quad$ **while** $C_{i,j} \neq \emptyset$ **do**
5 $\quad\quad$ **foreach** $(v_i, v_j) \in C_{i,j}$ **do**
6 $\quad\quad\quad$ $k \leftarrow |A|$;
7 $\quad\quad\quad$ **while** $\neg \mathcal{R}^k(v_i, v_j) \wedge k \geq 1$ **do** $k \leftarrow k-1$;
8 $\quad\quad\quad$ **if** $k > 0$ **then** $D_{i,j} \leftarrow D_{i,j} \cup (v_i, v_j)$; $newCl \leftarrow true$;
9 $\quad\quad$ **if** $newCl$ **then** $C_{i,j} \leftarrow candidateSelection(\mathcal{G}', i, j)$;
10 $\quad\quad$ **else** $C_{i,j} \leftarrow \emptyset$;
11 $\quad$ $transitiveClosure(\mathcal{G}')$;

Once all pairs of candidate profiles are processed, the newly discovered cross-links are used to get new candidates (Line 9), on which the algorithm applies again the rules, and this is iterated until no more candidates can be found ($C_{i,j} = \emptyset$). Finally, before considering the next pair of social networks, the discovered cross-links are propagated over the n social networks by transitive closure (Line 11).

The example depicted in Figure 1 represents a social internetwork composed of four social networks. The arrows represent the friendship links, while the black dashed lines are the existing cross-links, that the algorithm uses to find the candidates. The algorithm starts from the pair of profiles of Lisa in Flickr and LiveJournal. The candidate set is the result of the Cartesian product between the set of the friends of Lisa in Flickr (Bob, Mark and Alice) and the set of friends of Lisa in LiveJournal (Alice and Ben). After applying the rules to the candidate set, the algorithm unveils a cross-link between the profiles of Alice in Flickr and LiveJournal, which is represented as a dotted line. By transitive closure, three more cross-links are found, represented as dash-dotted lines.

Complexity. Let (i, j) be a pair of social networks.
The selection of candidates (Line 3, for the first iteration, Line 9, for the others) costs $T_S = \sum_{(v_i, v_j) \in D_{i,j}} |friends(v_i)| \times |friends(v_j)|$ ($D_{i,j} = E_{i,j}$ for the first iteration). We observe that in our dataset, the number of cross-links $|D_{i,j}| <<$ $min(|V_i|, |V_j|)$; moreover, each node has 74 friends on average (the degree of a node ranges from 1 to 18305). As a result, the cost of selecting the candidates

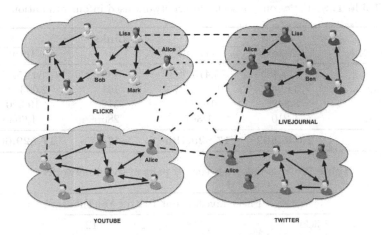

Fig. 1. Description of the algorithm on a small social internetwork. Continuous lines are friendship links, dashed lines are the existing cross-links. Cross-links established after applying the rules are dotted. Cross-links established by transitive closure are dash-dotted.

(and the number of candidates $|C_{i,j}|$ itself) is much smaller than $|V_i| \times |V_j|$, which would be the cost of considering all possible pairs of nodes. The cost of applying all rules on one candidate (Line 7) is $\sum_{k=1}^{|A|} \binom{|A|}{k} \times k \times \alpha$, α being the cost of the comparison of the values of one attribute. Since $k \leq |A|$, this cost is bounded by $r = \alpha \times |A| \times (2^{|A|} - 1)$. The cost of applying all rules to all candidates (Lines 5-7) is $T_R = r \times O(|C_{i,j}|)$. Therefore, the cost of Lines 4-9 is $p \times (T_S + T_R)$, where p is the number of times Lines 4 - 9 are repeated. Finally, the transitive closure (Line 11) cost is $O(|V| \times |E_c|)$, where $|V|$ (respectively, $|E_c|$) is the number of nodes (respectively, cross-links) in the social internetwork. Since $|E_C| << |V|$, this amounts to $O(|V|)$.

5   Evaluation Results

In order to evaluate our approach, we considered the dataset used by Buccafurri et al. in their experiments [14]. The original dataset includes a social internetwork with four social networks, namely LiveJournal, Flickr Twitter and YouTube [1]. The graph is composed of 93,169 nodes, 145,580 friendship links and 462 cross-links. We note that the number of cross-links declared by Buccafurri et al. [14] is 745, but this also includes duplicate links, which we removed.

After a careful analysis of the data, we found that many *friend* links were missing between a large number of nodes, probably because they were added after the internetwork was crawled. Moreover, the only available profile attribute is

---

[1] http://www.ursino.unirc.it/pkdd-12.html

Table 1. Statistics on the social internetwork used in our evaluation

Network	Nodes	Links		
		friend	*me*	Total
Flickr	1,814,405	15,415,083	189	154,152,72
LiveJournal	211,045	2,093,737	161	2,093,898
Twitter	8,842	19,008	312	19,320
YouTube	1,210	1,367	286	1,653
Total	**2,035,502**	**17,529,195**	**474**	**17,529,669**

Table 2. Cross-links between all pairs of social networks

Network	Flickr	LiveJournal	Twitter	YouTube
Flickr	–	148	29	12
LiveJournal	148	–	11	2
Twitter	29	11	–	272
YouTube	12	2	272	–

the username. For this reason, we updated the internetwork by obtaining the missing information using the API of the four SNSs under evaluation. While we were at that, we also enriched the graphs by adding new nodes that are linked via a *friend* link to the existing nodes. As a result, we obtained a much larger internetwork, whose properties are shown in Table 1. In total, we have more than 2 million nodes, more than 17 million links and 474 cross-links after transitive closure. We note that the cross-links are sparse, compared to the friendship links. The number of cross-links between each pair of networks is detailed in Table 2.

In the implementation of our approach, the social internetwork is stored in a Neo4j database[2], which is particularly indicated to handle large graphs.

5.1 Evaluation of the Rules

We observe that the accuracy of our algorithm might degrade if cross-links are established between pairs of profiles that do not match. In fact, the algorithm determines at each iteration the missing cross-links based on those discovered at the previous iterations. Therefore, the set of rules that we described in Section 4.2 need to be highly effective in determining whether any two profiles match.

In this section, we describe a first evaluation that aims at identifying the attributes that are the most relevant, as well as tuning the thresholds of the approximate similarity measures that we defined in Section 4.2 to compare the profile attributes. To this extent, we consider Flickr and LiveJournal, the two largest networks in our dataset. We arbitrarily set to 0.7 the thresholds θ_u and θ_n for the similarity measures that compare the usernames and names respectively, and we run only the first iteration of our algorithm.

---

[2] www.neo4j.org/

Table 3. Evaluation of the rules on Flickr and LiveJournal $\theta_u = 0.7$ and $\theta_n = 0.7$

Rule	Attributes	ratio of $|\mathcal{M}|\%$	$\frac{|C|}{|\mathcal{M}|}\%$	$\frac{|W|}{|\mathcal{M}|}\%$	$\frac{|U|}{|\mathcal{M}|}\%$
	$\{u\}$	83.09	60.39	30.19	9.42
	$\{n\}$	3.21	42.72	54.55	2.73
$\mathcal{R}^1$	$\{s\}$	2.92	100.00	0.00	0.00
	$\{w\}$	2.19	96.00	2.00	2.00
	Total	**91.41**	**61.85**	**29.42**	**8.73**
	$\{u,s\}$	3.21	100	0	0
	$\{u,w\}$	2.07	99.09	0	0.91
$\mathcal{R}^2$	$\{u,n\}$	1.93	92.42	1.52	6.06
	$\{n,s\}$	0.26	100	0	0
	$\{n,w\}$	0.18	100	0	0
	Total	**7.65**	**97.71**	**0.38**	**1.91**
	$\{u,n,s\}$	0.55	100	0	0
$\mathcal{R}^3$	$\{u,w,n\}$	0.32	100	0	0
	$\{u,w,s\}$	0.03	100	0	0
	Total	**0.91**	**100**	**0**	**0**
$\mathcal{R}^4$	$\{u,n,w,s\}$	0.03	100	0	0
	Total	**0.03**	**100**	**0**	**0**
	Grand total	**100**	**64.95**	**26.93**	**8.12**

Table 3 shows the results for each rule $\mathcal{R}^k$ that is verified by at least one candidate. The second column shows the set of attributes used by each rule; we recall from Section 4.2 that u, n, s and w refer to the attributes username, name, link to a social network profile and link to a web page respectively. We note that the attribute e (email) does not contribute to any rule, which is due to the fact that the value for this attribute is almost never disclosed in both profiles of the candidate pairs; this is why the rule $\mathcal{R}^5$ does not appear in the table. In total, the algorithm retrieves 16,000 candidates and determines a set $\mathcal{M}$ of 3,424 cross-links. As shown in the third column, 91.41% verify a 1−rule, 7.65% verify a 2−rule, 0.91% verify a 3−rule and 0.03% verify a 4−rule. The results clearly show that only a small percentage of profile pairs verify a k−rule, with $k \geq 2$, and the vast majority verifies a 1−rule, which indicates that in the selected networks the information disclosed by the individuals have little overlapping. We note also that the attribute username is present in a large number of rules verified by the profile candidates.

In order to evaluate the accuracy of the rules, we determined a ground truth by tagging each cross-link $(v_f, me, v_l) \in \mathcal{M}$ as either *correct*, if v_f and v_l match, or *incorrect*, if they do not match, or *undetermined*, if no decision can be taken. To this extent, we split set $\mathcal{M}$ into four equal-size independent subsets, one for each author of this paper, who had to assign the proper tag to each cross-link, based on a visual inspection of the profile web pages of the individuals concerned. Most of the time the information on the profile web pages were enough to determine whether two profiles referred to the same individual; however, in some cases the information are so scarce that no conclusive evidence as to whether the two profiles match can be found. In order to avoid errors in the ground truth, which would inevitably invalidate the results of our evaluation, we introduced the tag *undetermined*, which we assigned to all cross-links that we could not determine with certainty either as *correct* or *incorrect*. As a result, we determined three subsets of $\mathcal{M}$: (i) C, the set of the cross-links tagged as *correct*; (ii) W, the set of the cross-links tagged as *incorrect* and (iii) U, the set of the cross-links tagged as *undetermined*. The *precision*, computed as $P = \frac{|C|}{|\mathcal{M}|}$, is reported in the fourth column while the *error rate* is shown in the fifth column. It took approximately 300 hours in total to tag all the cross-links in $\mathcal{M}$. Since this work was split among 4 people, it took 10 days to have the ground truth available. We note that while this is acceptable for the preliminaries results that we discuss in this paper, we are aware that it is not feasible for the larger scale experiments that we are organizing. We will involve more evaluators and we will make sure that each cross-link is tagged by more than one person; the agreement among the evaluators on the assigned tags, which can be computed by using the Pearson correlation coefficient, will be a solid evidence that the ground truth is error-free, or, at least, contains a negligible amount of errors.

As for the $1-$rules, those that show the highest error rate (30.19% and 54.55% respectively) are the ones that use u and n. On the other hand, the $1-$rules that have the highest precision (100% and 96% respectively) are the ones that use s and w, which confirms our intuition that the attribute link to other profiles is highly relevant. We also note that the rules that combine at least two attributes, including those that use n and u, achieve a precision between 92% et 100%. This confirms our hypothesis that the more the attributes that match, the higher the probability that two profiles refer to the same individual.

We further studied the two $1-$rules that achieve a high error rate and we raised the value of thresholds θ_u and θ_n. While the precision significantly improves for the $1-$rule that uses u, no significant change is observed for the $1-$rule that uses n. This undeniably shows that a even high similarity of two names is not alone a good indicator that two profiles refer to the same individual. As a matter of fact, n is not only ambiguous, but also sensitive, which implies that very often an individual omits it or provides a fake name in order not to reveal her identity. This is evident by just looking at any two profiles belonging to the same individual in our dataset. Most of those that we came across disclose names that are partially or completely different across the two profiles.

5.2 Evaluation of the Algorithm and Comparison

Based on the discussion in the previous section, we discarded the $1-$rule that uses the attribute name and we set to 0.9 the value of θ_u. We run our algorithm on the four social networks of the dataset, namely Flickr, LiveJournal, Twitter and YouTube. The algorithm terminated after four iterations and discovered 2,788 new cross-links: 1,053 after the first iteration, 1,005 after the second, 654 after the third and 76 after the fourth. The precision is 94% with 2% of error rate and 4% of undetermined.

We first compare our algorithm against the one proposed by Buccafurri et al. [14], as we built our dataset on top of theirs. As explained above, we considerably enriched their dataset by adding new nodes and friendship links (but no new cross-link); as a result, we evaluated our algorithm on a much larger social internetwork. Their evaluation consists in selecting 160 cross-links that are given as input to their algorithm, which discovers 22 new cross-links across the four social networks with a precision of 85%. Thus, their algorithm discovers a considerably lower number of cross-links than ours, which is likely to be due to the iterative nature of our algorithm.

Finally, we compare our algorithm against the approach proposed by Malhotra et al. [9], which uses machine learning techniques. Similarly to our algorithm, they consider multiple attributes, such as username and name, but they ignore the network topology. They train four classifiers to determine whether two profiles match. Their model, applied to a real world scenario, which includes two social networks, namely LinkedIn and Twitter, achieves an accuracy of 64% [9]. No information is given on the number of discovered cross-links, nor the number of considered profile pairs.

6   Concluding Remarks

In this paper, we presented an algorithm to match profiles of individuals across several social networks by using the network topology and the personal information that are publicly available in the profiles. We thoroughly evaluated the algorithm on a large dataset of four real social networks, which constitutes a real challenge, because data are likely to be erroneous and messy. The evaluation showed the robustness of our algorithm, as it achieves a high precision (94%). We also presented a comparison against two existing approaches and discussed the results. We note that our algorithm relies on the attributes whose values are publicly available on the profiles of the individuals. It would be interesting to further explore the use of the network topology to generalize the algorithm to networks where the attribute values are anonymized. Moreover, we are currently fetching data from other social networks, to evaluate our algorithm on a mix of heterogeneous kinds of networks. Finally, we are migrating our dataset to the newest version of Neo4j and optimizing the code of the algorithm to fully take advantage of the new features of Neo4j. The time performance of the optimized code will be thoroughly assessed.

References

1. Gross, R., Acquisti, A.: Information Revelation and Privacy in Online Social Networks. In: Proceedings of the 2005 ACM Workshop on Privacy in the Electronic Society, WPES 2005, pp. 71–80. ACM, New York (2005)

2. Little, L., Briggs, P., Coventry, L.: Who Knows about Me?: An Analysis of Age-related Disclosure Preferences. In: Proceedings of the 25th BCS Conference on Human-Computer Interaction, BCS-HCI 2011, pp. 84–87. British Computer Society, Swinton (2011)
3. Stutzman, F.: An Evaluation of Identity-Sharing Behavior in Social Network Communities. iDMAa Journal 3(1) (2006)
4. Perito, D., Castelluccia, C., Kaafar, M.A., Manils, P.: How Unique and Traceable Are Usernames? In: Fischer-Hübner, S., Hopper, N. (eds.) PETS 2011. LNCS, vol. 6794, pp. 1–17. Springer, Heidelberg (2011)
5. Zafarani, R., Liu, H.: Connecting Corresponding Identities across Communities. In: Third International AAAI Conference on Weblogs and Social Media (2009)
6. Carmagnola, F., Cena, F.: User Identification for Cross-system Personalisation. Inf. Sci. 179, 16–32 (2009)
7. Cortis, K., Scerri, S., Rivera, I., Handschuh, S.: Discovering Semantic Equivalence of People Behind Online Profiles. In: Proceedings of the Resource Discovery (RED) Workshop. ESWC (2012)
8. Golbeck, J., Rothstein, M.: Linking Social Networks on the Web with FOAF: A Semantic Web Case Study. In: AAAI, vol. 8, pp. 1138–1143 (2008)
9. Malhotra, A., Totti, L., Meira, W., Kumaraguru, P., Almeida, V.: Studying User Footprints in Different Online Social Networks. In: International Workshop on Cybersecurity of Online Social Network, ACM ASONAM 2012 (2012)
10. Motoyama, M., Varghese, G.: I Seek You: Searching and Matching Individuals in Social Networks. In: Proceedings of the Eleventh International Workshop on Web Information and Data Management, pp. 67–75. ACM (2009)
11. Raad, E., Chbeir, R., Dipanda, A.: User Profile Matching in Social Networks. In: 2010 13th International Conference on Network-Based Information Systems (NBiS), pp. 297–304. IEEE (2010)
12. Rowe, M.: Interlinking Distributed Social Graphs. In: Linked Data on the Web Workshop, WWW (2009)
13. Bartunov, S., Korshunov, A., Park, S., Ryu, W., Lee, H.: Joint Link-attribute User Identity Resolution in Online Social Networks. In: SNA-KDD Workshop (2012)
14. Buccafurri, F., Lax, G., Nocera, A., Ursino, D.: Discovering Links among Social Networks. In: Flach, P.A., De Bie, T., Cristianini, N. (eds.) ECML PKDD 2012, Part II. LNCS, vol. 7524, pp. 467–482. Springer, Heidelberg (2012)
15. Jain, P., Kumaraguru, P., Joshi, A.: @i Seek 'fb.me': Identifying Users Across Multiple Online Social Networks. In: WWW (Companion Volume), pp. 1259–1268 (2013)
16. Narayanan, A., Shmatikov, V.: De-anonymizing Social Networks. In: 30th IEEE Symposium on Security and Privacy, pp. 173–187. IEEE (2009)
17. FriendFeed, http://friendfeed.com
18. Plaxo, http://www.plaxo.com
19. Spokeo, http://www.spokeo.com
20. Krishnamurthy, B., Wills, C.E.: On the Leakage of Personally Identifiable Information via Online Social Networks. In: Proceedings of the 2nd ACM Workshop on Online Social Networks, pp. 7–12. ACM (2009)

Indexing and Efficient Instance-Based Retrieval of Process Models Using Untanglings

Artem Polyvyanyy[1], Marcello La Rosa[1,2], and Arthur H.M. ter Hofstede[1,3]

[1] Queensland University of Technology, Brisbane, Australia
[2] NICTA Queensland Lab, Brisbane, Australia
[3] Eindhoven University of Technology, Eindhoven, The Netherlands
{artem.polyvyanyy,m.larosa,a.terhofstede}@qut.edu.au

Abstract. Process-Aware Information Systems (PAISs) support executions of operational processes that involve people, resources, and software applications on the basis of *process models*. Process models describe vast, often infinite, amounts of *process instances*, i.e., workflows supported by the systems. With the increasing adoption of PAISs, large process model *repositories* emerged in companies and public organizations. These repositories constitute significant information resources. Accurate and efficient retrieval of process models and/or process instances from such repositories is interesting for multiple reasons, e.g., searching for similar models/instances, filtering, reuse, standardization, process compliance checking, verification of formal properties, etc. This paper proposes a technique for *indexing* process models that relies on their alternative representations, called *untanglings*. We show the use of untanglings for retrieval of process models based on process instances that they specify via a solution to the *total executability problem*. Experiments with industrial process models testify that the proposed retrieval approach is up to three orders of magnitude faster than the state of the art.

1 Introduction

The Information Systems discipline studies different ways in which information can be processed, often algorithmically using process modeling practices. Workflow management systems, business process management systems, and enterprise information systems are examples of Process-Aware Information Systems (PAISs) [1]. PAISs support executions of operational processes on the basis of *process models* that are usually expressed in languages such as the Web Services Business Process Execution Language (WS-BPEL) or the Business Process Model and Notation (BPMN). For example, Fig. 1 shows a BPMN model that describes various scenarios for handling travel quote requests.

Process models describe vast amounts of executions, or *process instances*, for handling similar scenarios. The number of instances captured in a process model is exponential in the number of decisions that one can take when executing the model. This number explodes with respect to the amount of tasks that can be executed simultaneously in a model. Moreover, a model can describe an *infinite* number of instances, in case of loops.

As it becomes increasingly common for organizations to adopt the process-oriented approach to model and execute their routines, organizations often end up managing

M. Jarke et al. (Eds.): CAiSE 2014, LNCS 8484, pp. 439–456, 2014.
© Springer International Publishing Switzerland 2014

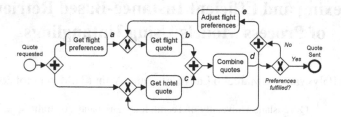

Fig. 1. A BPMN model for handling travel quote requests

repositories that comprise up to thousands of process models. For example, Suncorp, the Australian insurer, maintains a repository of more than 3,000 models [2,3].

Process model repositories are immense information resources. In order to reduce this *information overload*, one should be striving for automated retrieval systems. Accurate and efficient retrieval of information about process instances that are stored in process model repositories is interesting for several reasons, including:

- o *Reuse/redesign.* When developing new or modifying existing process models, one can reuse information that is contained in process model repositories [4], e.g., by retrieving process models that specify process instances of interest.
- o *Compliance.* Process models are subject to constraints enforced by regulations and/or laws, often referred to as *compliance rules*. Effective compliance checking requires the retrieval of information about process instances [5].
- o *Standardization.* Standard process models are exemplar models that should be used as references [6]. These models encode best practices for handling similar process instances across several models in a repository. The starting point of a process model standardization initiative often deals with identification of similar process models, i.e., those models that capture identical or similar process instances.

For example, an organization can issue a *compliance rule* which checks that in every travel handling scenario it is never possible that both tasks "*Get flight preferences*" and "*Adjust flight preferences*" occur together. This rule can be triggered to avoid internal adjustments of travel preferences. In this case, the model in Fig. 1 must be retrieved as one that violates the rule. Alternatively, one may want to redesign routines so that every time flight and hotel quotes are processed, there is also an option to propose a quote for renting a car. To implement this intent, one can start by retrieving all models that describe instances in which both tasks "*Get flight quote*" and "*Get hotel quote*" occur.

The contribution of this paper is threefold. First, it proposes an index data structure that is tailored towards efficient retrieval of process models based on information about process instances. The index is due to an alternative representation of models, called *representative untanglings*. The unique characteristics of this index allow for a novel querying experience. Second, it demonstrates this novel querying experience using *query primitives* that take the form of an extended version of the classical *executability* problem [7], called the *total executability* problem. Given a model and a set of tasks as input, the total executability problem deals with deciding if the model describes at least one instance in which all tasks from the given set occur. Among other applications, a solution to the total executability problem can be used to implement the above illustrated retrieval scenarios. Third, it suggests an efficient solution to the total executability problem using representative untanglings. Experiments with industrial models show up to three orders of magnitude speed up compared to the state of the art.

The rest of the paper is organized as follows: Sect. 2 positions our research in the light of related work. Next, Sect. 3 provides preliminary notions. Sect. 4 describes a novel index data structure. Sect. 5 exemplifies the use of this index for querying process model repositories. Sect. 6 reports on the performance measurements of a prototype that implements the developed querying technique. Finally, Sect. 7 concludes the paper.

2 Related Work

Querying deals with retrieving information that is relevant to a given *information need* from a collection of *information resources*. In case of process model querying, information resources are process models (*structural information*) as well as process instances that these process models describe (*behavioral information*).

There exist various techniques to query process model repositories based on structural information, cf. [2,3,8,9,10]. Given a query specified as a structural pattern, or a structural template with wildcards, these techniques are capable of retrieving process models which are formalized as structures that match the pattern, or fit the template. First, indexing techniques are employed to filter the repository by obtaining a set of candidate models that fit the indexed features of the query. Second, graph isomorphism or graph-edit distance techniques [11] are applied to identify the models from the candidate set that score an exact match, or are sufficiently similar, to the query. In contrast, we propose a technique that retrieves process models based on behavioral information.

Other techniques retrieve process models based on *abstractions* of behavioral information, cf. [12,13]. They accept loss of behavioral information, and consequently decrease in precision and recall, as the price for efficient retrieval. Our retrieval technique is *precise* and *sensitive*, i.e., it always retrieves *all and only* models that match the query.

Model checking is a technique that can be used to verify various properties of process models [7]. This technique usually proceeds by constructing an alternative representation of a model and then uses this representation for efficient verification. Model checking can be used to implement precise and sensitive process model retrieval that is based on behavioral information. Indeed, behavioral information needs can be expressed as properties to be verified. Similar to model checking, our technique makes retrieval decisions based on alternative representations of process models. Unlike in model checking, once constructed, our representations can be reused much more often than those employed for model checking purposes, as model checking usually relies on a fresh artifact for verification of every new property. This reuse of untanglings yields significant performance gains when querying process model repositories.

3   Preliminaries

This section introduces formalisms that will be used to support subsequent discussions.

3.1   Petri Nets and Net Systems

Petri nets are a well-established formalism for modeling distributed systems, e.g., PAISs. For many high-level process modeling languages, including WS-BPEL and BPMN, there exist mappings to the Petri net formalism [14]. The benefits of such mappings are twofold: (i) rigorous definition of an execution semantics of a high-level language, and (ii) reuse of the mathematical theory of Petri nets for analysis of process models.

This section introduces the basic Petri net terminology and notations.

Definition 3.1 (Petri net). A *Petri net*, or a *net*, is an ordered triple $N := (P,T,F)$, where P and T are finite disjoint sets of *places* and *transitions*, respectively, and $F \subseteq (P \times T) \cup (T \times P)$ is a *flow* relation.

A *node* $x \in P \cup T$ is an *input* (an *output*) node of a node $y \in P \cup T$ iff $(x,y) \in F$ $((y,x) \in F)$. By $\bullet x$ $(x\bullet)$, $x \in P \cup T$, we denote the *preset* (the *postset*) of x – the set of all input (output) nodes of x. For a set of nodes $X \subseteq P \cup T$, $\bullet X := \bigcup_{x \in X} \bullet x$ and $X\bullet := \bigcup_{x \in X} x\bullet$. A node $x \in P \cup T$ is a *source* (a *sink*) node of N iff $\bullet x = \varnothing$ $(x\bullet = \varnothing)$. Given a net $N := (P,T,F)$, by $Min(N)$ $(Max(N))$ we denote the set of all source (all sink) nodes of N. For technical convenience, we require all nets to be T-restricted. A net N is *T-restricted* iff the preset and postset of every transition is non-empty, i.e., $\forall\, t \in T : \bullet t \neq \varnothing \neq t\bullet$.

We distinguish between observable and silent transitions of a net via the notion of a *labeled* net because we shall define our query primitives on observable behavior.

Definition 3.2 (Labeled net). A *labeled net* is a tuple $N := (P,T,F,\mathcal{T},\lambda)$, where (P,T,F) is a net, $\mathcal{T}$ is a set of labels, where $\tau \in \mathcal{T}$ is a special label, and $\lambda : T \to \mathcal{T}$ is a function that assigns to each transition in T a *label* in $\mathcal{T}$.

If $\lambda(t) \neq \tau$, where $t \in T$, then t is *observable*; otherwise, t is *silent*.

The execution semantics of Petri nets is based on states and state transitions and is best perceived as a 'token game'. A state of a net is represented by a *marking*, which describes a distribution of *tokens* on the net's places.

Definition 3.3 (Marking of a net). A *marking*, or a *state*, of a net $N := (P,T,F)$ is a relation $M : P \to \mathbb{N}_0$ that assigns to each place $p \in P$ a number $M(p)$ of *tokens* in p.[1]

In the sequel, we shall often refer to a marking M as to the multiset containing $M(p)$ copies of place p for every $p \in P$.[2] A *net system* is a Petri net at a certain state/marking.

Definition 3.4 (Net system). A *net system*, or a *system*, is an ordered pair $S := (N,M)$, where N is a net and M is a marking of N.

In the graphical notation, a common practice is to visualize places as circles, transitions as rectangles, the flow relation as directed edges, and tokens as black dots inside assigned places; see Fig. 2 for an example of a net system visualization.

---

[1] $\mathbb{N}_0$ denotes the set of all natural numbers including zero.

[2] We shall write $[p_1, p_1, p_2]$ to denote the marking that puts two tokens at place p_1, one token at place p_2, and no tokens elsewhere.

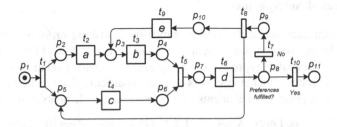

Fig. 2. A net system that captures the semantics of the BPMN model in Fig. 1

Whether a transition is *enabled* at a given marking depends on the tokens in its input places. An enabled transition can *occur*, which leads to a new marking of the net.

Definition 3.5 (Semantics of a system). Let $S := (N,M)$, $N := (P,T,F)$, be a system.

- o A transition $t \in T$ is *enabled* in S, denoted by $S[t\rangle$, iff every input place of t contains at least one token, i.e., $\forall p \in \bullet t : M(p) > 0$.
- o If a transition $t \in T$ is enabled in S, then t can *occur*, which leads to a *step* from S to $S' := (N,M')$ via t, where M' is a fresh marking such that $M'(p) := M(p) - \mathbf{1}_F((p,t)) + \mathbf{1}_F((t,p))$, for each $p \in P$, i.e., t 'consumes' one token from every input place of t and 'produces' one token for every output place of t.[3]

By $S[t\rangle S'$, we denote the fact that there exists a step from S to S' via t. Note that Fig. 2 shows the labeled net system that formalizes the execution semantics of the BPMN model in Fig. 1. Empty rectangles denote silent transitions. Rectangles with labels inside denote observable transitions. These labels refer to the short names shown next to task nodes in Fig. 1; e.g., the full label of transition t_2 in Fig. 2 is "*Get flight preferences*".

A net system induces a set of its *instances* (in the context of Petri nets usually referred to as *occurrence sequences*) and *reachable markings*.

Definition 3.6 (Occurrence sequence). Let $S_0 := (N,M_0)$ be a net system.

- o A sequence of transitions $\sigma := t_1 \ldots t_n$, $n \in \mathbb{N}_0$, of N is an *occurrence sequence* in S_0 iff there exists a sequence of net systems $S_0, S_1 \ldots S_m$, $m = n$, such that for every position i, $i \geq 1$, in σ it holds that $S_{i-1}[t_i\rangle S_i$; we say that σ *leads* from S_0 to S_m.
- o A marking M is *reachable* in S_0 iff there exists an occurrence sequence σ in S_0 that leads from S_0 to (N,M).

Given a net system S, by $\Sigma(S)$ and $[S\rangle$, we denote the set of all occurrence sequences and the set of all reachable markings in S, respectively. A net system $S := (N,M)$, $N := (P,T,F)$, is *n-bounded*, or *bounded*, iff there exists a number $n \in \mathbb{N}_0$ such that for every reachable marking M' in S and for every place $p \in P$ it holds that the amount of tokens at p is at most n, i.e., $\forall M' \in [S\rangle \forall p \in P : M'(p) \leq n$. It is easy to see that the set of all reachable markings in a bounded net system is finite.

---

[3] $\mathbf{1}_F$ denotes the characteristic function of F on the set $(P \times T) \cup (T \times P)$.

3.2   Processes of Net Systems

Occurrence sequences suit well when it comes to describing *orderings* of transition occurrences. In this section, we present *processes* of net systems [15]. One can rely on processes to adequately represent *causality* and *concurrency* relations on transition occurrences. A process of a net system is a net of a particular kind, called a *causal net*, together with a mapping from elements of the causal net to elements of the net system.

Definition 3.7 (Causal net). A net $N := (B,E,G)$ is a *causal* net iff: (i) for every $b \in B$ it holds that $|\bullet b| \le 1$ and $|b \bullet| \le 1$, and (ii) N is acyclic, i.e., G^+ is irreflexive.[4]

Elements of E are called *events*, whereas elements of B are called *conditions* of N. Two nodes x and y of a causal net $N := (B,E,G)$ are *causal* iff $(x,y) \in G^+$. Nodes x and y are *concurrent* iff $(x,y) \notin G^+$ and $(y,x) \notin G^+$. Finally, a *cut* of a causal net is a maximal (with respect to set inclusion) set of its pairwise concurrent conditions.

One can utilize events of causal nets to represent transition occurrences.

Definition 3.8 (Process, adapted from [15])
A *process* of a system $S := (N,M)$, $N := (P,T,F)$, is an ordered pair $\pi := (N_\pi, \rho)$, where $N_\pi := (B,E,G)$ is a causal net and $\rho : B \cup E \to P \cup T$ is such that:

- $\rho(B) \subseteq P$ and $\rho(E) \subseteq T$, i.e., ρ preserves the nature of nodes,
- $M = m(\rho, Min(N_\pi))$, where $m(\rho,D)(p) := |\rho^{-1}(p) \cap D|$, $D \subseteq B$, for each $p \in P$, and
- for every event $e \in E$ and for every place $p \in P$ it holds that
  $$1_F((p,\rho(e))) = |\rho^{-1}(p) \cap \bullet e| \text{ and } 1_F((\rho(e),p)) = |\rho^{-1}(p) \cap e \bullet|,$$
  i.e., ρ respects the environment of transitions.[5]

Let $\pi := (N_\pi, \rho)$ be a process of a net system S. It is known that every cut of N_π encodes a reachable marking in S.

Theorem 3.9 (Cuts and reachable markings, cf. [15, Theorem 3.5])
Let $\pi := (N_\pi, \rho)$, $N_\pi := (B,E,G)$, be a process of a net system S. If $C \subseteq B$ is a cut of N_π, then $M := m(\rho,C)$ is a reachable marking in S.

Fig. 3 shows two processes of the net system in Fig. 2. When visualizing processes, conditions $c_i, c_i' \ldots$ refer to place p_i; e.g., for the process in Fig. 3(b) it holds that $\rho(c_5) = \rho(c_5') = p_5$, where p_5 is a place in Fig. 2. Similarly, we assume events $e_i, e_i' \ldots$ to refer to transition t_i; e.g., $\rho(e_4) = \rho(e_4') = t_4$ for the process in Fig. 3(b). Observe that we distinguish between shapes of events that correspond to silent transitions and those that correspond to observable ones only for clarity. Fig. 3(b) shows a process and four cuts of its causal net N_π. Each cut is defined as a set of conditions that intersect with the respective dashed line. For example, cut D_1 is defined as the set of conditions $\{c_3, c_6\}$. Note that cuts D_{min} and D_{max} are equal to $Min(N_\pi)$ and $Max(N_\pi)$, respectively. Moreover, both cuts D_1 and D_{max} encode the same marking $m(\rho, D_1) = [p_3, p_6] = m(\rho, D_{max})$, which is a reachable marking in the net system in Fig. 2, for instance via occurrence sequences $t_1 t_4 t_2$ or $t_1 t_2 t_4 t_3 t_5 t_6 t_7 t_8 t_9 t_4$. Finally, it is easy to see that the set of all processes of the net system in Fig. 2 is *infinite*.

---

[4] R^+ denotes the transitive closure of a binary relation R.
[5] $\rho(X) := \{\rho(x) \mid x \in X\}$ and $\rho^{-1}(z) := \{y \in Y \mid \rho(y) = z\}$, where X is a subset of ρ's domain Y.

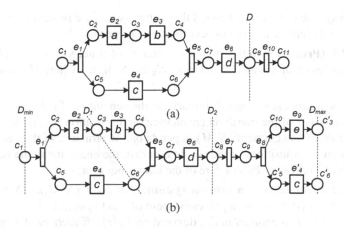

Fig. 3. Two processes of the net system in Fig. 2

4   Indexing

This section proposes to use untanglings of process models, or more precisely of the corresponding net systems, as data structures that improve the speed of retrieving process instances stored in process model repositories. Similar to database indexes, untanglings require the use of additional storage space to maintain the extra copy of data. However, at this additional cost, they can be used to quickly discover requested process instances without having to iterate over all instances, of which there can be infinitely many.

An *untangling* of a net system is a set of its processes. A process of a system is a static model that describes a *finite* portion of its occurrence sequences, cf. Sect. 3.2. For example, in [16], Jörg Desel suggests to enhance a causal net N_π of a process $\pi := (N_\pi, \rho)$ of a system $S := (N, M)$ with a marking M_π that puts one token at every source condition of N_π and no tokens elsewhere. Then, every occurrence sequence in the fresh system (N_π, M_π) *represents* (via mapping ρ) an occurrence sequence in S. E.g., consider the net system S_π composed of the causal net in Fig. 3(b) and a marking that puts one token at condition c_1 and no tokens elsewhere. Then, occurrence sequence $e_1 e_2 e_3 e_4 e_5 e_6 e_7 e_8 e_9 e'_4$ in S_π represents occurrence sequence $\rho(e_1)\rho(e_2)\rho(e_3)\rho(e_4)\rho(e_5)\rho(e_6)\rho(e_7)\rho(e_8)\rho(e_9)\rho(e'_4) = t_1 t_2 t_3 t_4 t_5 t_6 t_7 t_8 t_9 t_4$ in the net system in Fig. 2. Observe that in this way S_π represents six occurrence sequences of the net system in Fig. 2.

The number of occurrence sequences that are represented in a single process explodes with respect to the amount of its pairwise concurrent events. This hints at the fact that processes are highly suitable for indexing occurrence sequences. Still, it is easy to see that one might often need an *infinite* number of processes to represent — as per the above proposed intuition — all occurrence sequences in a system; e.g., consider the net system in Fig. 2. Clearly, every index must be finite. To this end, we rely on an *enhanced* interpretation of processes, which allows treating a process as a static model that can represent an *infinite* number of occurrence sequences. This enhanced interpretation is formalized in the notion of a *process set system*, where every process set system can be seen as a semantic union of elementary models, called *process systems*.

A *process system* is an abstract model that suggests a way a process of a system can encode a possibly infinite number of occurrence sequences.

Definition 4.1 (Process system). A *process system* of a net system $S := (N, M_0)$ induced by a process π of S is an ordered triple $\mathcal{S}_\pi := (N, M, \pi)$, where M is a marking of N.

The semantics of process systems – similarly to the semantics of net systems, cf. Definition 3.5 – consists of the transition enablement and transition occurrence rules. The enablement rule of a net system (N, M) depends on the structure of the net N, i.e., on tokens in presets of transitions of the net. In contrast, the enablement rule of a process system (N, M, π) relies on the structure of the causal net of π.

Definition 4.2 (Semantics of a process system). Let $\mathcal{S}_\pi := (N, M, \pi)$, $N := (P, T, F)$, $\pi := (N_\pi, \rho)$, $N_\pi := (B, E, G)$, be a process system of a net system S.

- A transition $t \in T$ is *enabled* in $\mathcal{S}_\pi$, denoted by $\mathcal{S}_\pi[t\rangle$, iff there exist a cut $C \subseteq B$ of N_π and an event $e \in E$ such that $M = m(\rho, C)$, $\bullet e \subseteq C$, and $t = \rho(e)$.
- If a transition $t \in T$ is enabled in $\mathcal{S}_\pi$ then t can *occur*, which leads to a *step* from $\mathcal{S}_\pi$ to $\mathcal{S}'_\pi := (N, M', \pi)$, where M' is a fresh marking such that $(N, M)[t\rangle(N, M')$.

According to Theorem 3.9, if $C \subseteq B$ is a cut of a causal net $N_\pi := (B, E, G)$ taken from a process (N_π, ρ) of a system $S := (N, M)$, then $m(\rho, C)$ is a reachable marking in S. Moreover, it is easy to see that, in general, if $D \subseteq B$ is a subset of conditions, $e \in E$ is an event, and $\bullet e \subseteq D$, then transition $t := \rho(e)$ is enabled in N at the marking $m(\rho, D)$; this follows from the fact that ρ preserves the nature of nodes and environment of transitions. Thus, a process system $\mathcal{S}_\pi := (N, M, \pi)$, $\pi := (N_\pi, \rho)$, restricts the semantics of the net system (N, M) to those reachable markings that are induced by cuts of N_π and to those transition occurrences that are captured by events of N_π.

Similar to net systems, a sequence of transitions σ is an *occurrence sequence* in a process system $\mathcal{S}_\pi$ if σ is empty or the first transition in σ is enabled in $\mathcal{S}_\pi$ and an occurrence of a transition from σ in $\mathcal{S}$ (except of an occurrence of the last transition in σ) leads to a process system that enables the next transition in σ. We accept that a process π of a net system $S := (N, M)$ *represents* all those occurrence sequences in S which are also occurrence sequences in the process system (N, M, π).

As an example consider a process system $\mathcal{S}_\pi := (N, M, \pi)$, where (N, M) is the net system in Fig. 2 and $\pi := (N_\pi, \rho)$, $N_\pi := (B, E, G)$, is the process in Fig. 3(b). It holds that $\mathcal{S}_\pi$ enables transition t_1. Indeed, for cut D_{min} of N_π and event e_1, refer to Fig. 3(b), we have $m(\rho, D_{min}) = [p_1] = M$, $\{c_1\} = \bullet e_1 \subseteq D_{min} = \{c_1\}$, and $\rho(e_1) = t_1$. An occurrence of t_1 leads to a step from $\mathcal{S}_\pi$ to the process system $(N, [p_2, p_5], \pi)$. It is easy to see that a sequence of transitions $t_1 \, t_4 \, t_2 \, t_3 \, t_5 \, t_6$ is an occurrence sequence in $\mathcal{S}_\pi$ which leads to the process system $\mathcal{S}'_\pi := (N, [p_8], \pi)$. Observe that $\mathcal{S}'_\pi$ enables transition t_7 only, whereas the net system $(N, [p_8])$ enables transitions t_7 and t_{10}; recall that N is the net in Fig. 2. There exists only one cut in Fig. 3(b) that induces marking $[p_8]$; this is cut D_2. Finally, it is only event e_7 for which it holds that $\bullet e_7 \subseteq D_2$ and $\rho(e_7) = t_7$. Observe that process system $\mathcal{S}_\pi$ represents *infinitely* many occurrence sequences in the net system in Fig. 2; this is due, for instance, to the fact that the process system $(N, [p_3, p_6], \pi)$ enables transition t_3 via cut D_1. Moreover, $\mathcal{S}_\pi$ represents infinite occurrence sequences; those in which transitions $t_3 \ldots t_9$ can occur infinitely often.

Every process system has its natural boundaries on what portion of process instances it can describe. *Process set systems* aim to overcome these boundaries.

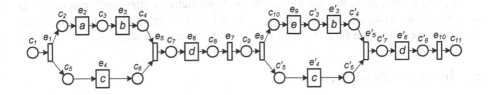

Fig. 4. A process of the net system in Fig. 2

Definition 4.3 (Process set system)
A *process set system* of a net system $S := (N, M_0)$ induced by a set of processes Π of S is an ordered triple $S_\pi := (N, M, \Pi)$, where M is a marking of N.

The semantics of a process set system $S := (N, M, \Pi)$ is 'composed' of all the semantics of individual process systems that are induced by processes in Π.

Definition 4.4 (Semantics of a process set system)
Let $S := (N, M, \Pi)$, $N := (P, T, F)$, be a process set system.
  - A transition $t \in T$ is *enabled* in S, denoted by $S[t\rangle$, iff there exists a process $\pi \in \Pi$ such that $(N, M, \pi)[t\rangle$.
  - If a transition $t \in T$ is enabled in S, then t can *occur*, which leads to a *step* from S to $S' := (N, M', \Pi')$, where M' is a fresh marking such that $(N, M)[t\rangle(N, M')$ and $\Pi' := \{\pi \in \Pi \mid (N, M, \pi)[t\rangle\}$.

As an example consider a process set system $S := (N, M, \{\pi_1, \pi_2\})$, where (N, M) is, again, the net system in Fig. 2, and π_1 and π_2 are the processes in Figs. 3(a) and 3(b), respectively. The sequence of transitions $t_1 t_2 t_3 t_4 t_5 t_6$ is an occurrence sequence in S which leads to the process set system $S' := (N, [p_8], \{\pi_1, \pi_2\})$; again, a sequence of transitions σ is an occurrence sequence in a process set system S if the first transition in σ is enabled in S and an occurrence of a transition from σ in S (except that of the last transition) leads to a process set system that enables the next transition in σ. Transitions t_7 and t_{10} are enabled in S'. Transition t_7 is enabled due to cut D_2 and event e_7 in π_2. Transition t_{10} is enabled due to cut D and event e_{10} in π_1. An occurrence of t_{10} in S' leads to the process set system $(N, [p_{11}], \{\pi_1\})$, which does not enable any transition.

The process set system $(N, M, \{\pi_1, \pi_2\})$ from the example above represents a big portion of the occurrence sequences in (N, M). Still, it fails to represent all of them. E.g., it does not represent occurrence sequences in which both t_7 and t_{10} occur. A *representative untangling* of a net system S is a collection of its processes that induces a process set system which represents *all* the occurrence sequences in S.

Definition 4.5 (Representative untangling). An untangling Π (i.e., a set of processes) of a net system $S := (N, M)$ is *representative* if every occurrence sequence in S is also an occurrence sequence in the process set system (N, M, Π).

In [17], we demonstrated that: (i) one can always construct a finite representative untangling of a bounded net system, and (ii) a net system S and a process set system S of S induced by a representative untangling of S are *occurrence net equivalent* [18], i.e., they are two different specifications of exactly the same distributed system.

In [17], we proposed the first algorithm for constructing representative untanglings of bounded net systems. Given the net system in Fig. 2 as input, this algorithm returns two processes shown in Figs. 3(a) and 4 as its representative untangling.

5   Instance-Based Retrieval

A representative untangling of a system S is another specification that represents *all and only* occurrence sequences in S. This section shows how one can employ the unique characteristics of representative untanglings to engineer a process model querying technique. To this end, Sect. 5.1 proposes the *total executability* problem and its efficient solution in terms of representative untanglings, whereas Sect. 5.2 uses this solution to formulate basic *query primitives*.

5.1   Executability

Given a net system $S := (N,M)$, $N := (P,T,F)$, and a set of transitions $U \subseteq T$, the classical *executability* problem deals with deciding whether *some* transition in U can ever be 'executed' (can occur) in S. It is a fundamental problem in concurrency theory, e.g., a solution to the executability problem can help deciding *reachability* and *safety* [7].

Definition 5.1   (Executability, cf. [7])
A net system $S := (N,M)$, $N := (P,T,F)$, *can execute some transition* in $U \subseteq T$ iff there exist an occurrence sequence σ in S and a transition $t \in U$ such that t occurs in σ.

One can solve the executability problem of a system using its representative untangling.

Lemma 5.2   (Executability)
Let Π be a representative untangling of a net system $S := (N,M)$, $N := (P,T,F)$. Then, S can execute some transition in $U \subseteq T$ iff there exist a process $\pi := (N_\pi,\rho)$, $N_\pi := (B,E,G)$, in Π, a transition $t \in U$, and an event $e \in E$ for which it holds that $\rho(e) = t$.

The proof of Lemma 5.2 is similar to the proof of correctness of a solution to the *total executability* problem that is proposed below.

For example, according to Lemma 5.2, one can decide that the net system S in Fig. 2 describes an occurrence sequence that contains transition t_3 using event e_3 of process π in Fig. 3(a) for which it holds that $\rho(e_3) = t_3$. Moreover, one can use π to generate sample occurrence sequences that contain t_3; these are occurrence sequences in a process system of S induced by π that contain t_3, e.g., $t_1 t_2 t_4 t_3$ is one such sequence.

The executability problem is a *decision problem* on the level of process instances and as such can be naturally applied to formulate queries for searching process models and/or process instances. E.g., a query that relies on a solution to the executability problem can be formulated as follows: "Find all process models that describe a process instance in which a given transition occurs." Alternatively, one can search for exemplary process instances in which a given task occurs. Clearly, one can answer both these questions efficiently using representative untanglings and the result of Lemma 5.2.

In fact, representative untanglings can be used to efficiently solve an extended version of the classical executability problem. As we shall see, this solution broadens the applicability of representative untanglings when searching process model repositories.

Given a net system $S := (N,M)$, $N := (P,T,F)$, and a set of transitions $U \subseteq T$, the *total executability* problem deals with deciding whether there exists an occurrence sequence in S which contains *all* the transitions in U.

Definition 5.3 (Total executability)
A net system $S := (N,M)$, $N := (P,T,F)$, *can execute all transitions* in $U \subseteq T$ iff there exists an occurrence sequence σ in S such that every transition $t \in U$ occurs in σ.

The total executability problem can be solved using representative untanglings. The proof of correctness of this solution relies on the next corollary.

Corollary 5.4 (Processes and occurrence sequences). Let $\pi := (N_\pi,\rho)$, $N_\pi := (B,E,G)$, be a process of a net system S. Then, there exists an occurrence sequence σ in S such that for every event $e \in E$ it holds that transition $\rho(e)$ occurs in σ.

Please note that Corollary 5.4 is a special case of Lemma 1 in [16]. Finally, the solution to the total executability problem proceeds as follows.

Lemma 5.5 (Total executability). *Let Π be a representative untangling of a net system $S := (N,M)$, $N := (P,T,F)$. Then, S can execute all transitions in $U \subseteq T$ iff there exists a process $\pi := (N_\pi,\rho)$, $N_\pi := (B,E,G)$, in Π such that for every transition $t \in U$ there exists an event $e \in E$ for which it holds that $\rho(e) = t$.*

Proof. We prove each direction of the statement separately.
($\Rightarrow$) *Proof by construction.* Assume that S can execute all transitions in U. According to Definition 5.3, there exists an occurrence sequence σ in S such that every transition $t \in U$ occurs in σ. Then, according to Definition 4.4 and Definition 4.5, there exists a process $\pi := (N_\pi,\rho)$, $N_\pi := (B,E,G)$, in Π such that σ is an occurrence sequence in the process system (N,M,π). Thus, for every transition in σ there exists an event $e \in E$ for which it holds that $\rho(e) = t$.
($\Leftarrow$) *Proof by contradiction.* Assume that there exists a process $\pi := (N_\pi,\rho)$, $N_\pi := (B,E,G)$, in Π such that for every transition $t \in U$ there exists an event $e \in E$ of N_π for which it holds that $\rho(e) = t$, but S cannot execute all transitions in U. According to Corollary 5.4, there exists an occurrence sequence σ in S such that for every event $e \in E$ it holds that transition $\rho(e)$ occurs in σ and, hence, every transition $t \in U$ occurs in σ. We reached a contradiction. ∎

For instance, according to Lemma 5.5, one can decide that the net system S in Fig. 2 describes an occurrence sequence that contains transitions t_3, t_7, and t_9 using events e_3, e_7, and e_9 of process π in Fig. 4 for which it holds that $\rho(e_3) = t_3$, $\rho(e_7) = t_7$, and $\rho(e_9) = t_9$. This conclusion is due to the process system S_π of S induced by π; e.g., $t_1 \ldots t_9$ is one of infinitely many occurrence sequences in S_π that contains all the three transitions.

The total executability problem can be solved efficiently using untanglings.

Proposition 5.6. *Given a representative untangling Π of a net system $S := (N,M)$, $N := (P,T,F)$, and a set of transitions $U \subseteq T$, the following problem can be solved in linear time in the size of Π: To decide if S can execute all transitions in U.*

The proof of Proposition 5.6 is due to Lemma 5.5. Clearly, one can solve the total executability problem by visiting each event of the representative untangling once. Hence, representative untanglings can be used to efficiently retrieve process models and/or exemplary process instances in which all tasks from a given set of tasks occur. Note that, in general, the existence of certain tasks in a process model does not imply the fact that this model describes a process instance in which all these tasks occur; this is due to conflicting process instances and/or behavioral anomalies, like *deadlocks* [19].

5.2   Query Primitives

This section proposes query primitives that are founded on the definition of the (total) executability problem. The basic construct for all the subsequently proposed primitives is a predicate that given a labeled system S and a set of labels L tests if there exists an occurrence sequence σ in S such that some transitions that are labeled with labels in L occur in σ. This basic predicate can be specialized into four tests:

- CanOccurOne(labeled system S, set of labels L) := $\exists\,\sigma \in \Sigma(S)\,\exists\,l \in L : l \in \sigma$;[6]
  The CanOccurOne predicate tests if there exists an occurrence sequence in S which contains at least one transition labeled with some label in L.
- CannotOccurOne(labeled system S, set of labels L) := $\forall\,\sigma \in \Sigma(S)\,\forall\,l \in L : l \notin \sigma$;
  The CannotOccurOne predicate tests if there does not exist an occurrence sequence in S which contains at least one transition labeled with some label in L.
- CanOccurAll(labeled system S, set of labels L) := $\exists\,\sigma \in \Sigma(S)\,\forall\,l \in L : l \in \sigma$;
  The CanOccurAll predicate tests if there exists an occurrence sequence in S which for every label l in L contains a transition labeled with l.
- CannotOccurAll(labeled system S, set of labels L) := $\forall\,\sigma \in \Sigma(S)\,\exists\,l \in L : l \notin \sigma$;
  The CannotOccurAll predicate tests if there does not exist an occurrence sequence in S which for every label l in L contains a transition labeled with l.

For example, one can find all process models that describe a process instance in which task "*Obtain flight price*" occurs by selecting every model K (from a given repertoire of models) for which test CanOccurOne(S,{"*Obtain flight price*"}) evaluates to true, where S is a labeled net system that corresponds to K (refer to Sect. 3.1 for details).

   Process model repositories often suffer from inconsistent usage of labels, i.e., semantically similar tasks might 'wear' different labels, e.g., "*Get flight quote*" and "*Obtain flight price*". Consequently, the search procedure that is exemplified above will not retrieve the process model in Fig. 1, which can be accepted as a model that matches the query semantically. To address this issue, we 'expand' the predicates. In information retrieval, a *query expansion* is a process of reformulating a *seed query* to improve effectiveness of search results. Every label that is used as input to one of the above proposed seed predicates can be expanded to a set of semantically similar labels, e.g., using the approach in [20]. Accordingly, the predicates get reformulated as follows:

- CanOccurOneExpanded(labeled system S, set of sets of labels $\mathcal{L} := \{L_1 \ldots L_n\}$) :=
  $\exists\,\sigma \in \Sigma(S)\,\exists\,L \in \mathcal{L}\,\exists\,l \in L : l \in \sigma$; The CanOccurOneExpanded predicate tests if there exist an occurrence sequence σ in S and a set of labels L in $\mathcal{L}$ such that σ contains a transition labeled with some label in L.
- CannotOccurOneExpanded(labeled system S, set of sets of labels $\mathcal{L} := \{L_1 \ldots L_n\}$)
  := $\forall\,\sigma \in \Sigma(S)\,\forall\,L \in \mathcal{L}\,\forall\,l \in L : l \notin \sigma$; The CannotOccurOneExpanded predicate tests

---

[6] It holds that $l \in \sigma$ iff there exists a transition in σ that is labeled with l.

if there do not exist an occurrence sequence σ in S and a set of labels L in $\mathcal{L}$ such that σ contains a transition labeled with some label in L.

○ CanOccurAllExpanded(labeled system S, set of sets of labels $\mathcal{L} := \{L_1 \ldots L_n\}$) := $\exists \sigma \in \Sigma(S) \, \forall L \in \mathcal{L} \, \exists \, l \in L : l \in \sigma$; The CanOccurAllExpanded predicate tests if there exists an occurrence sequence σ in S such that for every set of labels L in $\mathcal{L}$ it holds that σ contains a transition labeled with some label in L.

○ CannotOccurAllExpanded(labeled system S, set of sets of labels $\mathcal{L} := \{L_1 \ldots L_n\}$) := $\forall \sigma \in \Sigma(S) \, \exists \, L \in \mathcal{L} \, \forall \, l \in L : l \notin \sigma$; The CannotOccurAllExpanded predicate tests if there does not exist an occurrence sequence σ in S such that for every set of labels L in $\mathcal{L}$ it holds that σ contains a transition labeled with some label in L.

For instance, if one is interested in process instances (or models) in which tasks "*Obtain flight price*" and "*Obtain hotel price*" (or semantically similar tasks) occur together, one can start by constructing sets of similar labels, e.g., $L_1 := \{$"*Obtain flight price*","*Get flight quote*"$\}$ and $L_2 := \{$"*Obtain hotel price*","*Get hotel quote*"$\}$. Then, the model in Fig. 1 is a match to the query CanOccurAllExpanded($S,\{L_1,L_2\}$), where S, again, is the net system in Fig. 2. Indeed, the model in Fig. 1 describes process instances in which both tasks "*Get flight quote*" and "*Get hotel quote*" occur. Finally, the model in Fig. 1 can be ranked as one that is less relevant to the query as some other model that is retrieved based on labels "*Obtain flight price*" and "*Obtain hotel price*", as these labels were initially provided as input, cf. [20] for further details on how results can be ranked.

The above proposed predicates explore all possible configurations of the (total) executability problem and the suggested query expansion principle. These predicates are provided for the sake of completeness. However, only *three* (out of the total of eight) checks specify distinct computation patterns. Indeed, every CannotOccurXY, X $\in$ {'One','All'}, Y $\in$ {'','Expanded'}, predicate is the negation of the CanOccurXY check. CanOccurOneExpanded(S, $\mathcal{L}$) can be implemented via CanOccurOne(S, $\bigcup_{L \in \mathcal{L}} L$). Note that two out of the three remaining predicates can be expressed in terms of the third one, i.e., CanOccurOne(S, L) := $\bigvee_{l \in L}$ CanOccurAll($S,\{l\}$) and CanOccurAllExpanded (S, $\{L_1 \ldots L_n\}$) := $\bigvee_{L \in \{\{l_1 \ldots l_n\} \mid l_1 \in L_1, \ldots, l_n \in L_n\}}$ CanOccurAll(S,L). However, these two last definitions imply multiple CanOccurAll checks which require multiple (and as it turns out unnecessary) traversals of representative untanglings.

Because of Proposition 5.6, the CanOccurAll(S, L) test can be accomplished in linear time in the size of a representative untangling Π of S; one has to verify if Π contains a process which for every label l in L contains an event that describes an occurrence of a transition labeled with l. Similarly, because of Lemma 5.2, when evaluating the CanOccurOne(S, L) predicate one needs to search for a process in Π which contains an event that describes an occurrence of a transition labeled with some label in L. Finally, because of Lemma 5.5, in order to fulfill the CanOccurAllExpanded($S, \mathcal{L}$) predicate, there should exist a process in Π that for every set of labels L in $\mathcal{L}$ contains an event which describes an occurrence of a transition labeled with some label in L. For all the above checks it suffices to perform a single traversal of a representative untangling of S.

6   Evaluation

The proposed querying approach has been implemented and is publicly available as part of the jBPT initiative [21]. Using this implementation, we conducted an experiment to assess the performance of the approach in terms of querying time and accuracy of results. The experiment was performed on a computer with a dual core Intel CPU with 2.26 GHz, 4GB of memory, running Windows 7 and SUN JVM 1.7 (with standard allocation of memory). To eliminate load time from the measures, each test was executed six times, and we recorded average times of the second to sixth executions.

The study was conducted on a collection of 448 bounded systems that model processes from financial services, telecommunications, and other domains. These systems were selected from a larger collection of 735 models [19]; systems that do not model concurrency were filtered out as they do not suffer from the state space explosion problem and can be handled efficiently using structural analysis methods.

The study is subdivided into two stages. First, representative untanglings of all systems from the data set are constructed — the *indexing stage*. Then, the resulting untanglings are employed for efficient validation of queries — the *querying stage*.

An extensive experiment that assesses the performance of the indexing stage is reported in [17]. This experiment can be downloaded and reproduced.[7] Next, we summarize basic measures on constructing representative untanglings of the 448 systems. The indexing stage requires 2.72s. Hence, on average, a representative untangling is constructed in 6.06ms; the minimal and maximal construction times are 0.58ms and 221ms, respectively. The average duplication factor, i.e., the average number of times the size of an untangling is larger than the size of its corresponding system (in the number of nodes), is 3.54.

Once constructed, representative untanglings are stored and reused for querying purposes. Table 1 reports average times (in microseconds) of performing CanOccurOne and CanOccurAll checks. The first two columns report on the characteristics of the model collection by providing information on the number 'n' of systems within a given 'Size' range (measured as the number of nodes). The number of labels used as input to queries ranged from one to five (see the second row and columns three to twelve in the header of the table). Each value is measured as the average time of executing 100 random queries. For example, the value of 9.36 in the third row and fifth column in Table 1 reports the average time (in microseconds) of performing CanOccurOne checks for the input of three random labels over 44 systems, each of size within the range from 101 to 150 nodes; in total, 4400 different queries were checked to obtain this

Table 1. Average times of checking query primitives (in microseconds)

Net systems		CanOccurOne (μs)					CanOccurAll (μs)				
Size	n	1	2	3	4	5	1	2	3	4	5
1–50	221	1.56	0.93	0.88	0.87	0.84	2.43	1.9	1.9	2.4	2.36
51–100	164	4.27	3.5	3.23	3.06	2.88	7.13	7.17	7.35	7.19	7.39
101–150	44	12.1	10.5	**9.36**	8.87	7.23	22	20.3	20.6	21.7	23.7
151–200	9	25.4	34.8	18.5	16.9	13.6	35	41.2	43.7	46.3	46.2
201–250	7	53.3	49.6	32.7	23	19.8	69	92.6	87.5	100.6	94.2
251–300	3	221.6	147.2	133.8	89.5	81.2	353.9	372	505.9	390.7	424.4
1–300	448	6.35	4.75	4.31	3.72	3.3	10.1	10.3	11.3	11.1	11.4

---

[7] http://code.google.com/p/jbpt/wiki/UntanglingsExperiment

average value. The last row in the table shows average times of performing queries over all systems in the collection; these are plotted in Fig. 5(a). One can observe a quasi-linear dependency between the average time of performing a single check and the size of the set of labels provided as input. The average values for `CanOccurOne` checks show a negative slope. Indeed, as the size of the input set of labels increases, the chance of discovering an occurrence sequence that includes at least one transition labeled with a label from the input set of labels increases as well. On the other hand, more labels in the input sets of `CanOccurAll` queries lead to slower checks as more conditions need to be satisfied.

Table 2 shows average querying times (columns two to seven) and compares accuracy of retrieved results with label filtering techniques (columns eight to thirteen). The first column lists sizes of input sets of labels; we also vary the sizes of sets used as inputs to `CanOccurAllExpanded` checks. For instance, the value of 7.32 in the second row and fifth column in Table 2 is the average time (in milliseconds) of querying 448 systems using the `CanOccurAllExpanded` primitive for an input set that contains two sets, each composed of three labels. Average querying times report on a quasi-linear dependency with the size of the input set of labels, cf. Fig. 5(b).

When searching for process models, one often starts by performing a filtering step, e.g., filtering out those models that do not contain tasks with labels of interest [9,10]. Afterwards, computation intensive methods, either structural or behavioral, cf. Section 2, are applied to a much smaller (pre-selected) collection of models. Query primitives from Section 5.2 can improve effectiveness of existing filtering techniques. To verify this experimentally, we implemented filtering primitives that 'mimic' the primitives from Section 5.2; these fresh primitives analyze process models rather than process instances. For instance, the filtering counterpart of the `CanOccurOne` check from Section 5.2 verifies if a given process model contains a task labeled with some label from a given set of labels. In Table 2, columns eight to thirteen report average numbers of retrieved systems over 100 random queries using both types of primitives. For example, 2.7/6.67 in the third row and eleventh column reports that, on average, the behavioral version of the `CanOccurAllExpanded` primitive retrieved 2.7 systems while the structural version retrieved 6.67 systems. The additional systems selected by analyzing models rather than

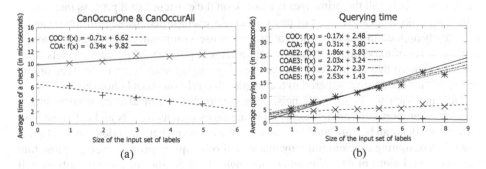

Fig. 5. (a) Average times of performing one check, and (b) average querying times (over 448 systems); COO stands for `CanOccurOne`, COA—`CanOccurAll`, and COAEn, $n \in 2..5$, stands for `CanOccurAllExpanded`, where n is the size of each set in the input set of sets of labels.

Table 2. Average times of querying a collection of 448 systems (in milliseconds) and average numbers of retrieved systems (using behavioral/structural querying)

Query size	Query time (ms)		CanOccurAllExpanded				Net systems retrieved (using behavioral/structural querying)		CanOccurAllExpanded			
	COO	COA	2	3	4	5	COO	COA	2	3	4	5
1	2.48	4.03	5.45	5.05	4.22	3.71	32.5/33.6	32.5/33.6	67.8/70.7	90.2/93.5	119.2/124	131.8/136.5
2	2.02	4.53	7.82	**7.32**	7.05	6.69	68.8/72.6	1.23/2.84	5.74/9.47	15.8/21.8	22.4/34.8	31.3/42.3
3	2.09	4.86	9.75	9.76	9.56	9.28	90.8/94.1	0.16/0.54	1.4/2.64	**2.7/6.67**	4.51/10.4	9.78/19.3
4	1.73	5	11.1	11.2	11.7	11.7	102/106.2	0.01/0.05	0.13/0.62	0.54/2.55	2.84/5.87	4.13/10.2
5	1.46	5.25	12.9	13.4	13.4	13.5	138.6/144.5	0/0.01	0.02/0.16	0.15/1	0.67/2.95	1.39/6.95
6	1.32	5.22	14	14.5	15	15.5	148.8/154.4	0/0.01	0.02/0.13	0.05/0.47	0.17/1.61	0.55/3.7
7	1.48	6.83	18.8	19.2	20.3	21.4	183.5/189.6	0/0	0/0.02	0.02/0.32	0.04/0.98	0.28/2.54
8	1.21	5.96	17.9	18.6	19.4	20.6	194.2/200.5	0/0	0/0.01	0.02/0.25	0.05/0.67	0.09/1.8

(*) COO and COA stand for CanOccurOne and CanOccurAll, respectively

their instances are false positives in the situation when one is interested in systems that describe instances in which given transitions occur together.

Finally, we experimented with a behavioral querying approach that relies on the *model checking* technique described in [7]. Model checking of our query primitives requires, on average, 4ms (based on an implementation that uses Uma[8]). Though this is approximately 2ms faster than constructing a representative untangling (see above), untanglings can be reused for checking query primitives over any combination of labels, i.e., a single untangling of a system fits all, while a fresh model checking exercise has to be performed for every fresh combination of labels. Note that the time of 4ms, which is required to perform a single model checking exercise, is often comparable with the average time of performing a query over 448 systems that we report in Table 2.[9]

7   Conclusion

This paper proposed a technique for instance-based retrieval of process models from process model repositories. The technique relies on the use of an index, called a representative untangling, which is optimized towards accurate and efficient retrieval of process instances. The use of this index is exemplified via a family of query primitives that are founded on the extended version of the classical executability problem. The basic construct for all the primitives is a check on the existence of a process instance in which all tasks from a given set of tasks occur. As exemplified, these primitives can be effectively applied in practice, e.g., for process reuse, compliance, and standardization. Finally, a set of experiments conducted on a large repository of process models from practice showed that during retrieval the use of our index leads to an up to three orders of magnitude speed-up compared to techniques that rely on model checking.

Our approach works on Petri nets. This means that it can also be used to check behavioral properties of models defined in languages such as BPMN and EPCs, so long as these models can be translated to Petri nets. We envision that our index can be of great use when designing efficient implementations of other query primitives, e.g., those that explore the relations of *causality* and *concurrency* [22]. Studies of these primitives will

---

[8] http://service-technology.org/uma/

[9] All the experiments reported in this section can be downloaded and reproduced: http://code.google.com/p/jbpt/wiki/QueryingExperiment

contribute to the maturity of process model query languages, e.g., BPMN-Q [9] and APQL [23]. Another avenue for future work is to evaluate the perceived usefulness of behavioral querying with end users.

Acknowledgments. This work is partly funded by the ARC Linkage Project LP110100252. NICTA is funded by the Australian Government (Department of Broadband, Communications and the Digital Economy) and the Australian Research Council through the ICT Centre of Excellence program.

References

1. Dumas, M., van der Aalst, W.M.P., ter Hofstede, A.H.M.: Process-Aware Information Systems: Bridging People and Software Through Process Technology. Wiley (2005)
2. Dumas, M., García-Bañuelos, L., La Rosa, M., Uba, R.: Fast detection of exact clones in business process model repositories. IS 38(4), 619–633 (2013)
3. Jin, T., Wang, J., La Rosa, M., ter Hofstede, A.H.M., Wen, L.: Efficient querying of large process model repositories. CII 64(1), 41–49 (2013)
4. Awad, A., Sakr, S., Kunze, M., Weske, M.: Design by selection: A reuse-based approach for business process modeling. In: Jeusfeld, M., Delcambre, L., Ling, T.-W. (eds.) ER 2011. LNCS, vol. 6998, pp. 332–345. Springer, Heidelberg (2011)
5. Governatori, G., Sadiq, S.: The Journey to Business Process Compliance. In: Handbook of Research on BPM, pp. 426–454. IGI Global (2009)
6. Tregear, R.: Business Process Standardization. In: Handbook on Business Process Management: Part II, pp. 307–327. Springer (2010)
7. Esparza, J., Heljanko, K.: Unfoldings – A Partial-Order Approach to Model Checking (2008)
8. Beeri, C., Eyal, A., Kamenkovich, S., Milo, T.: Querying business processes. In: VLDB, pp. 343–354. ACM (2006)
9. Awad, A., Sakr, S.: On efficient processing of BPMN-Q queries. CII 63(9), 867–881 (2012)
10. Yan, Z., Dijkman, R., Grefen, P.: FNet: An index for advanced business process querying. In: Barros, A., Gal, A., Kindler, E. (eds.) BPM 2012. LNCS, vol. 7481, pp. 246–261. Springer, Heidelberg (2012)
11. Dijkman, R.M., Dumas, M., van Dongen, B.F., Käärik, R., Mendling, J.: Similarity of business process models: Metrics and evaluation. IS 36(2), 498–516 (2011)
12. Jin, T., Wang, J., Wen, L.: Querying business process models based on semantics. In: Yu, J.X., Kim, M.H., Unland, R. (eds.) DASFAA 2011, Part II. LNCS, vol. 6588, pp. 164–178. Springer, Heidelberg (2011)
13. Kunze, M., Weidlich, M., Weske, M.: Behavioral similarity – A proper metric. In: Rinderle-Ma, S., Toumani, F., Wolf, K. (eds.) BPM 2011. LNCS, vol. 6896, pp. 166–181. Springer, Heidelberg (2011)
14. Lohmann, N., Verbeek, E., Dijkman, R.: Petri net transformations for business processes – A survey. In: Jensen, K., van der Aalst, W.M.P. (eds.) ToPNoC II. LNCS, vol. 5460, pp. 46–63. Springer, Heidelberg (2009)
15. Goltz, U., Reisig, W.: The non-sequential behavior of Petri nets. IANDC 57(2/3) (1983)
16. Desel, J.: Validation of process models by construction of process nets. In: van der Aalst, W.M.P., Desel, J., Oberweis, A. (eds.) Business Process Management. LNCS, vol. 1806, pp. 110–128. Springer, Heidelberg (2000)
17. Polyvyanyy, A., La Rosa, M., Ouyang, C., ter Hofstede, A.H.M.: Untanglings: A novel approach to analyzing concurrent systems (2013), http://eprints.qut.edu.au/56455/

18. van Glabbeek, R.J., Vaandrager, F.W.: Petri net models for algebraic theories of concurrency. In: de Bakker, J.W., Nijman, A.J., Treleaven, P.C. (eds.) PARLE 1987. LNCS, vol. 259, pp. 224–242. Springer, Heidelberg (1987)
19. Fahland, D., Favre, C., Koehler, J., Lohmann, N., Völzer, H., Wolf, K.: Analysis on demand: Instantaneous soundness checking of industrial business process models. DKE (5) (2011)
20. Awad, A., Polyvyanyy, A., Weske, M.: Semantic querying of business process models. In: EDOC, pp. 85–94. IEEE Computer Society (2008)
21. Polyvyanyy, A., Weidlich, M.: Towards a compendium of process technologies: The jBPT library for process model analysis. In: CAiSE Forum. CEUR, vol. 998 (2013)
22. Polyvyanyy, A., Weidlich, M., Conforti, R., La Rosa, M., ter Hofstede, A.H.M.: The 4C spectrum of fundamental behavioral relations for concurrent systems. In: Kindler, E. (ed.) PETRI NETS 2014. LNCS, vol. 8489, pp. 210–232. Springer, Heidelberg (2014)
23. ter Hofstede, A.H.M., Ouyang, C., La Rosa, M., Song, L., Wang, J., Polyvyanyy, A.: APQL: A process-model query language. In: Song, M., Wynn, M.T., Liu, J. (eds.) AP-BPM 2013. LNBIP, vol. 159, pp. 23–38. Springer, Heidelberg (2013)

Predictive Monitoring of Business Processes

Fabrizio Maria Maggi[1], Chiara Di Francescomarino[2],
Marlon Dumas[1], and Chiara Ghidini[2]

[1] University of Tartu, Liivi 2, 50409 Tartu, Estonia
{f.m.maggi,marlon.dumas}@ut.ee
[2] FBK-IRST, Via Sommarive 18, 38050 Trento, Italy
{dfmchiara,ghidini}@fbk.eu

Abstract. Modern information systems that support complex business processes generally maintain significant amounts of process execution data, particularly records of events corresponding to the execution of activities (event logs). In this paper, we present an approach to analyze such event logs in order to predictively monitor business constraints during business process execution. At any point during an execution of a process, the user can define business constraints in the form of linear temporal logic rules. When an activity is being executed, the framework identifies input data values that are more (or less) likely to lead to the achievement of each business constraint. Unlike reactive compliance monitoring approaches that detect violations only after they have occurred, our predictive monitoring approach provides early advice so that users can steer ongoing process executions towards the achievement of business constraints. In other words, violations are predicted (and potentially prevented) rather than merely detected. The approach has been implemented in the ProM process mining toolset and validated on a real-life log pertaining to the treatment of cancer patients in a large hospital.

Keywords: Predictive Process Monitoring, Recommendations, Business Constraints, Linear Temporal Logic.

1 Introduction

The execution of business processes is generally subject to internal policies, norms, best practices, regulations, and laws. For example, a doctor may only perform a certain type of surgery if this is preceded by a pre-operational screening, while in a sales process, an order can be archived only after that the customer has confirmed receipt of all ordered items. We use the term *business constraint* to refer a requirement imposed on the execution of a process that separates compliant from non-compliant behavior [20].

Compliance monitoring is an everyday imperative in many organizations. Accordingly, a range of research proposals have addressed the problem of monitoring business processes with respect to business constraints [15,14,16,26,13,19,4,10,5,28]. Given a process model and a set of constraints – expressed, e.g., in temporal logic – these techniques provide a basis to monitor ongoing executions of a process (a.k.a. *cases*) in order to assess whether they comply with the constraints in question. However, these monitoring approaches are *reactive*, in that they allow users to identify a violation only *after*

M. Jarke et al. (Eds.): CAiSE 2014, LNCS 8484, pp. 457–472, 2014.

it has occurred rather than supporting them in *preventing* such violations in the first place.

In this setting, this paper presents a novel monitoring framework, namely *Predictive Business Process Monitoring*, based on the continuous generation of predictions and recommendations on what activities to perform and what input data values to provide, so that the likelihood of violation of business constraints is minimized. At any point during the execution of a business process, the user can specify a business constraint using Linear Temporal Logic (LTL). Based on an analysis of execution traces, the framework continuously provides the user with estimations of the likelihood of achieving each business constraint for a given ongoing process execution. The proposed framework takes into account the fact that predictions often depend both on: (i) the sequence of activities executed in a given case; and (ii) the values of data attributes after each activity execution in a case. For example, for some diseases, doctors may decide whether to perform a surgery or not, based on the age of the patient, while in a sales process, a discount may be applied only for premium customers.

The core of the proposed framework is a method to generate predictions of business constraint fulfillment. Specifically, the technique estimates for each enabled activity in an ongoing case, and for every data input that can be given to this activity, the probability that the execution of the activity with the corresponding data input will lead to the fulfillment of the business constraint. In line with the principle of considering both control-flow and data, the proposed technique proceeds according to a two-phased approach. Given an ongoing case in which certain activities are enabled, we first select from the set of completed execution traces, those that have a prefix "similar" to the (uncompleted) trace of the ongoing case (control-flow matching). Next, for each selected trace, we produce a *data snapshot* consisting of a value assignment for each data attribute up to its matched prefix. Given a business constraint, we classify a data snapshot as a positive or a negative example based on whether the constraint was eventually fulfilled in the completed trace or not. In this way, we map the prediction task to a classification task, wherein the goal is to determine if a given data snapshot leads to a business constraint fulfillment and with what probability. Finally, we solve the resulting classification task using decision tree learning, i.e., we produce a decision tree to discriminate between fulfillments and violations. The decision tree is then used to estimate the probability that the business constraint will be achieved, for each possible combination of input attribute values.

The proposed framework can be applied both for prediction and recommendation. For prediction, the decision tree is used to evaluate the probability for the business constraint to be satisfied for a given combination of attribute values. For recommendation, the decision tree is used to select combinations of attribute values that maximize the probability of the business constraint being satisfied. The predictive monitoring framework has been implemented in the ProM toolset for process mining. The framework has been validated using a real-life log (provided for the 2011 BPI challenge [1]) pertaining to the treatment of cancer patients in a large Dutch academic hospital.

The remainder of the paper is structured as follows. Section 2 introduces a running example. Section 3 introduces concepts pertaining to LTL and decision trees. Section 4 presents the predictive monitoring framework and its implementation. Section 5 discusses the validation on a real-life log. Finally, Section 6 discusses related work and Section 7 draws conclusions and perspectives.

2   Running Example

During the execution of a business process, process participants cooperate to satisfy certain business constraints. At any stage of the process enactment, decisions are taken aimed at achieving the satisfaction of these constraints. Therefore, it becomes crucial for process participants to be provided with predictions on whether the business constraints will be achieved or not and, even more, to receive recommendations about the choices that maximize the probability of satisfying the business constraints.

Fig. 1 shows a BPMN model of a business process we will use as running example. It describes how a patient is nursed according to the instructions of a doctor. During the process execution, the doctor has to make decisions on therapies and on the doses of medicines to be administered to the patient. The process starts when the patient provides the doctor with lab test results. Based on the tests, the doctor formulates a diagnosis. Then, the doctor has to decide the therapy to prescribe. The therapy can be a surgery, a pharmacological therapy or a manipulation. In case of a pharmacological therapy, the doctor has also to prescribe the quantity of medicine the patient has to assume.

In this scenario, historical information about past executions of the process could be used to support the doctor in making decisions by providing him or her with predictions about the (most likely) iter of the disease and recommendations about the best choices to be made in order to guarantee the patient recovery. The approach presented in this paper aims at supporting process participants in their decisions by providing them with predictions about the satisfaction of their constraints and, in case they can influence the process with their decisions, by recommending them the best choices to be made to satisfy their business constraint.

In our example, the constraint the doctor wants to satisfy could be that every diagnosis is eventually followed by the patient recovery. By exploiting data related to the clinical history of other patients with similar characteristics, our technique aims at providing the process participants with predictions about whether the patient will recover or not. In addition, whenever the doctor has to make decisions (e.g., prescribe the type of therapy or choose the dose of a medicine), recommendations are provided about the options for which it is more likely that the patient will recover.

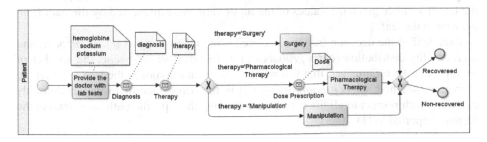

Fig. 1. A simple process describing the medical treatment management

3 Background

In this section, we first introduce the language used for the business constraint definition (LTL), and we then provide an overview on decision tree learning.

3.1 LTL

In our proposed approach, a business constraint can be formulated in terms of LTL rules, as LTL (and its variations) is classically used in the literature for expressing business constraints on procedural knowledge [21]. LTL [23] is a modal logic with modalities devoted to describe time aspects. Classically, LTL is defined for infinite traces. However, when focusing on the compliance of business processes, we use a variant of LTL defined for finite traces (since business process are supposed to complete eventually).

We assume that events occurring during the process execution fall in the set of atomic propositions. LTL rules are constructed from these atoms by applying the temporal operators X (next), F (future), G (globally), and U (until) in addition to the usual boolean connectives. Given a formula φ, $X\varphi$ means that the next time instant exists and φ is true in the next time instant (strong next). $F\varphi$ indicates that φ is true sometimes in the future. $G\varphi$ means that φ is true always in the future. $\varphi U\psi$ indicates that φ has to hold at least until ψ holds and ψ must hold in the current or in a future time instant.

In the context of the running example, examples of relevant business constraints formulated in terms of LTL rules include:

- $\varphi_0 = G(\text{``diagnosis''} \to F(\text{``recovered''}))$,
- $\varphi_1 = F(\text{``tumor marker } CA - 19.9\text{''}) \vee F(\text{``ca} - 125 \text{ using meia''})$,
- $\varphi_2 = G(\text{``CEA} - \text{tumor marker using meia''} \to F(\text{``squamous cell carcinoma using eia''}))$,
- $\varphi_3 = (\neg\text{``histological examination} - \text{biopsies nno''}) U(\text{``cytology} - \text{ectocervix} - \text{''})$,
- $\varphi_4 = F(\text{``histological examination} - \text{big resectiep''})$, and
- $\varphi_5 = (\neg\text{``histological examination} - \text{biopsies nno''}) U(\text{``squamous cell carcinoma using eia''})$.

3.2 Decision Tree Learning

Decision tree learning uses a decision tree as a model to predict the value of a target variable based on input variables (features). Decision trees are built from a set of training dataset. Each internal node of the tree is labeled with an input feature. Arcs stemming from a node labeled with a feature are labeled with possible values or value ranges of the feature. Each leaf of the decision tree is labeled with a class, i.e., a value of the target variable given the values of the input variables represented by the path from the root to the leaf.

Each leaf of the decision tree is associated with a class support (*class support*) and a probability distribution (*class probability*). *Class support* represents the number of examples in the training set, that follow the path from the root to the leaf and that are correctly classified; *class probability* (*prob*) is the percentage of examples correctly classified with respect to all the examples following that specific path, as shown in the formula reported in (1).

$$prob = \frac{\#(corr\_class\_leaf\_examples)}{\#(corr\_class\_leaf\_examples + incorr\_class\_leaf\_examples)} \quad (1)$$

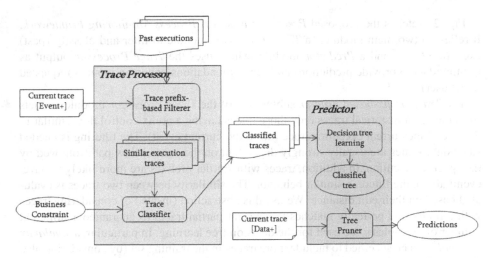

Fig. 2. *Predictive Business Process Monitoring Framework*: architectural overview

One of the most used decision tree learning algorithms is the C4.5 algorithm [24]. C4.5 relies on the normalized information gain to choose, for each node of the tree, the feature to be used for splitting the set of examples. The feature with the highest normalized information gain is chosen to make the decision.

4   Approach

In this section, we present the details of the proposed approach, which combines different existing techniques ranging from clustering approaches to decision tree learning, to provide predictions, at runtime, about the fulfillments of business constraints in an execution trace. In the following sections, we provide an overview of the approach and of the more specific implementation.

4.1   General Approach

Before presenting the approach proposed in this paper, some assumptions should be made. First, we assume that a set of historical execution traces of the process is available from which we can extract information about how the process was executed in the past. Based on the information extracted from the historical traces, we can provide predictions and recommendations for a running execution trace. Second, we assume that the underlying business process should be in some way non-deterministic or, at least, the mechanisms that guide the decisions taken during the process execution should not be known by the user. Any recommendation or prediction would be useless if the process participant already knows how the process develops given the input data values provided (we can think to a doctor who may not know about new therapies, or to a company providing services that does not know about the behaviors of its customers). Third, we assume that data used in the process are globally visible throughout the whole process.

Fig. 2 sketches the proposed *Predictive Business Process Monitoring Framework*. It relies on two main modules: a *Trace Processor* module to filter and classify (past) execution traces and a *Predictor* module, which uses the *Trace Processor* output as training data to provide predictions and recommendations (when an input is requested to the user).

The *Trace prefix-based Filterer* submodule of the *Trace Processor* module extracts from the set of historical traces only those traces having a prefix control flow similar to the one of the current execution trace (up to the current event). The filtering is needed since data values are usually strongly dependent on the control flow path followed by the specific execution. In addition, traces with similar prefixes are more likely to have, eventually in the future, a similar behavior. The similarity between two traces is evaluated based on their edit distance. We use this abstraction (instead of considering traces with a prefix that perfectly matches the current partial trace) to guarantee a sufficient number of examples to be used for the decision tree learning. In particular, a *similarity threshold* can be specified to include more traces in the training set (by considering also the ones that are less similar to the current trace).

Each (historical) trace is identified with a *data snapshot* containing the assignment of values for each attribute in the corresponding selected prefix. The traces (the data snapshots) of the training set are classified by the *Trace Classifier* submodule based on whether, in each of them, the desired business constraint is satisfied or not. The constraint is expressed in terms of a set of LTL formulas. In the case of our running example, the constraint "whenever a diagnosis is performed, then the patient will eventually recover" can be represented in LTL through formula φ_0 reported in Section 3.1.

Formulas have to be satisfied along the whole execution trace. Four possible cases can occur at evaluation time:

- the formula is permanently violated: the prediction is trivial (non-satisfied);
- the formula is permanently satisfied: the prediction is trivial (satisfied);
- the formula is temporary violated/satisfied: the prediction should be able to indicate whether the formula will be satisfied or not in the future.

Once the relevant traces and, therefore, the corresponding data snapshots, are classified, they are passed to the *Decision tree learning* module, in charge to derive the learned decision tree with the associated class support and probability. Fig. 3 shows a decision tree related to our running example: the number of data training examples (with values of the input variables following the path from the root to each leaf) respectively correctly and non-correctly classified is reported on the corresponding leaf of the tree. For example, for values "Joint dislocation" and "Pharmacological therapy", the resulting class is the formula satisfaction ("yes"), with 2 examples of the training set following the same path correctly classified and 1 non-correctly classified, i.e., with a class probability $prob = \frac{2}{2+1} = 0.66$.

All the data values assigned in the past, are supposed to be known by the predictor system at the current execution point of the trace. The tree can hence be pruned by removing all the branches corresponding to known values. The pruning algorithm returns either a unique path (and a unique class) or a subtree of the original tree, according to whether the system is used as predictor (the values of all the tree attributes are known) or as a recommender (there are attributes in the tree that are still unknown), respectively.

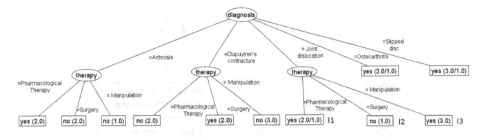

Fig. 3. Example decision tree

In the latter case, leaves are ranked according to the associated class probability. The conditions on the values of the unknown attributes corresponding to the leaves with the highest rankings are returned to the user as recommendations.

For example, consider the case in which a diagnosis ("Joint dislocation") and a therapy ("Pharmacological therapy") have been given by the doctor. The *Predictor* will consider only the path from the root to leaf l_1 (pruning all the other branches) and will predict the satisfaction of the formula with a probability class $prob = 0.66$ (see Fig. 3). We can also consider the case in which a diagnosis has already been made (e.g., "Joint dislocation"), but no therapy has been prescribed yet. Then, all the branches corresponding to other values of the diagnosis attribute (i.e., "Arthrosis", "Dupuytren's contracture", "Osteoarthritis", "Slipped disc") can be pruned. Only the subtree corresponding to the branch "Joint dislocation" is analyzed and, since no other attribute is known, the class probability of each leaf computed. As shown in Fig. 3, the three leaves have the following classes and class probabilities:

- l_1: satisfied with $prob_{l1} = \frac{2}{2+1} = 0.66$
- l_2: non-satisfied with $prob_{l2} = \frac{1}{1} = 1$
- l_3: satisfied with $prob_{l3} = \frac{3}{3+0} = 1$

The system will hence recommend "Manipulation" ($prob_{l3} = 1$).

Note that, if we consider as a feature of the decision tree the next activity to be executed, our framework is also able to recommend which activity should be performed next to maximize the probability of satisfying a business constraint.

4.2 Implementation

The approach has been implemented in the ProM process mining toolset. ProM provides a generic Operational Support (OS) environment [2,29] that allows the tool to interact with external workflow management systems at runtime. A stream of events coming from a workflow management system is received by an OS service. The OS service is connected to a set of OS providers implementing different types of analysis that can be performed online on the stream. Our *Predictive Business Process Monitoring Framework* has been implemented as an OS provider.

Fig. 4 shows the entire architecture. The OS service receives a stream of events (including the current execution trace) from a workflow management system and forwards

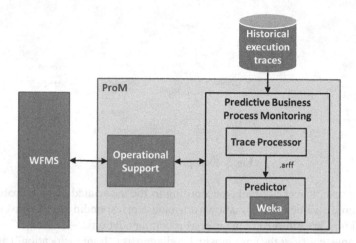

Fig. 4. *Predictive Business Process Monitoring Framework*: implemented architecture

it to the *Predictive Business Process Monitoring Framework* that returns back predictions and recommendations. The OS service sends these results back to the workflow management system.

For the implementation of the *Predictor*, we rely on the WeKa J48 implementation of the C4.5 algorithm, which takes as input a .arff file and builds a decision tree. The .arff file contains a list of typed variables (including the target variable) and, for each trace prefix (i.e., for each data snapshot), the corresponding values. This file is created by the *Trace Processor* and passed to the *Predictor*. The resulting decision tree is then analyzed to generate predictions and recommendations.

5   Experimentation

We have conducted a set of experiments by using the BPI challenge 2011 [1] event log. This log pertains to a healthcare process and, in particular, contains the executions of a process related to the treatment of patients diagnosed with cancer in a large Dutch academic hospital. The whole event log contains $1,143$ cases and $150,291$ events distributed across 623 event classes (activities). Each case refers to the treatment of a different patient. The event log contains domain specific attributes that are both case attributes and event attributes in addition to the standard XES attributes.[1] For example, *Age*, *Diagnosis*, and *Treatment code* are case attributes and *Activity code*, *Number of executions*, *Specialism code*, and *Group* are event attributes.

In our experimentation, first, we have ordered the traces in the log based on the time at which the first event of each trace has occurred. Then, we have splitted the log in two parts. We have used the first part (80% of the traces) as training set, i.e., we have used these traces as historical data to derive predictions. We have implemented a log replayer to simulate the execution of the remaining traces (remaining 20%) and send them as an event stream to the OS service in ProM (test set).

---

[1] XES (eXtensible Event Stream) is an XML-based standard for event logs proposed by the IEEE Task Force on Process Mining (www.xes-standard.org).

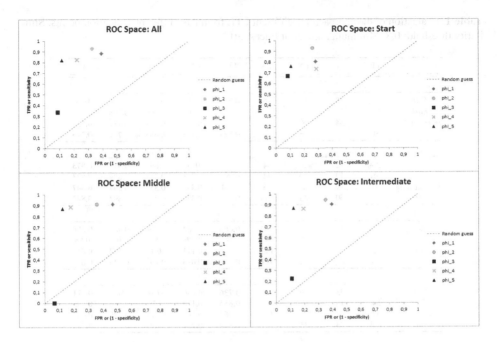

Fig. 5. ROC spaces drawn for different LTL formulas and different evaluation points. Similarity threshold: 0.8; Minimum number of traces: 30.

We defined 5 business constraints corresponding to a subset (from φ_1 to φ_5) of the LTL rules reported in Section 3.1. This set of rules, indeed, allows us to exercise all the LTL constructs while investigating possibly real business constraints. We have asked for a prediction about each of the defined business constraints in different evaluation points during the replay of each trace in our test set. In particular, we have considered as evaluation points the initial event (start event) of each trace, an early event (i.e., an event located at about 1/4 of each trace), and an intermediate event (i.e., an event located in the middle of each trace).

As well as a similarity threshold (see Section 4.1), the implemented OS provider allows the user to specify a minimum number of traces to be used in the training set. In this way, if the threshold does not guarantee a sufficient number of examples, further traces are considered from the set of historical traces with a similarity with the current execution trace lower than the specified threshold. In a first experiment, we have considered a similarity threshold of 0.8 and a minimum number of traces of 30.

For evaluating the effectiveness of our approach, we have used the ROC space analysis. In particular, we have classified predictions in four categories, i.e., *i*) true-positive (T_P: positive outcomes correctly predicted); *ii*) false-positive (F_P: negative outcomes predicted as positive); *iii*) true-negative (T_N: negative outcomes correctly predicted); *iv*) false-negative (F_N: positive outcomes predicted as negative). The *gold standard* used as reference is the set of all true positive instances. In our experiments, we can easily identify the true positive instances. Indeed, if we are asking for a prediction at a certain point in time during the replay of a trace, we can understand if the prediction is correct by replaying the trace until the end.

Table 1. Evaluation of the approach for different LTL formulas, different evaluation points. Similarity threshold: 0.8; Minimum number of traces: 30.

	TP	FP	FN	TN	TPR	FPR	PPV	F1	ACC
φ_1									
Start	46	18	11	46	0.807	0.281	0.718	0.76	**0.76**
Early	73	37	7	42	0.912	0.468	0.663	0.768	**0.723**
Intermediate	75	34	8	52	0.903	0.395	0.688	0.781	**0.751**
All	194	89	26	140	0.881	0.388	0.685	0.771	**0.743**
φ_2									
Start	104	12	8	34	0.928	0.26	0.896	0.912	**0.873**
Early	101	19	10	34	0.909	0.358	0.841	0.874	**0.823**
Intermediate	110	19	7	35	0.94	0.351	0.852	0.894	**0.847**
All	315	50	25	103	0.926	0.326	0.863	0.893	**0.847**
φ_3									
Start	8	13	4	140	0.666	0.084	0.38	0.484	**0.896**
Early	0	11	9	148	0	0.06	0	0	**0.88**
Intermediate	2	18	7	143	0.222	0.111	0.1	0.137	**0.852**
All	10	42	20	431	0.333	0.088	0.192	0.243	**0.876**
φ_4									
Start	53	33	19	82	0.736	0.286	0.616	0.67	**0.721**
Early	54	18	7	83	0.885	0.178	0.75	0.812	**0.845**
Intermediate	57	22	9	92	0.863	0.192	0.721	0.786	**0.827**
All	164	73	35	257	0.824	0.221	0.691	0.752	**0.795**
φ_5									
Start	55	10	17	85	0.763	0.105	0.846	0.802	**0.838**
Early	52	13	11	94	0.825	0.121	0.8	0.812	**0.858**
Intermediate	61	14	9	100	0.871	0.122	0.813	0.841	**0.875**
All	168	37	37	279	0.819	0.117	0.819	0.819	**0.857**

To draw a ROC space, we need two metrics, i.e., the *true positive rate (TPR)*, represented on the y axis, and the *false positive rate (FPR)*, represented on the x axis. The TPR (or recall) defines how many positive outcomes are correctly predicted among all positive examples available:

$$TPR = \frac{T_P}{T_P + F_N}. \tag{2}$$

On the other hand, the FPR defines how many negative outcomes are predicted as positive among all negative examples available:

$$FPR = \frac{F_P}{F_P + T_N}. \tag{3}$$

We have classified predictions for each LTL rule φ_i, and, therefore, each of them is represented as one point in the ROC space. In Fig. 5, we show four spaces drawn by classifying the evaluation points by position (start, early, intermediate). In the figure, we also show the results obtained by considering all the evaluation points together. Note that the best possible prediction method would yield a point in the upper left corner of the ROC space, representing 100% sensitivity (no false negatives) and 100% specificity (no false positives). A completely random guess would give a point along a diagonal line from the left bottom to the top right corners. Points above the diagonal represent good classification results, points below the line poor results.

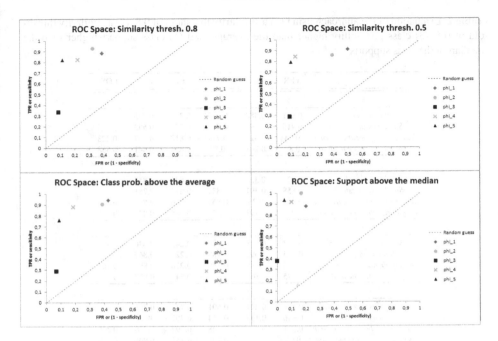

Fig. 6. Comparison of ROC spaces drawn using (1) a similarity threshold of 0.8, (2) a similarity threshold of 0.5, (3) class probability higher than the average, and (4) class support higher than the median of the class supports.

The ROC space analysis highlights that for φ_1, φ_2, φ_4, and φ_5 our OS provider was able to discriminate well between positive and negative outcomes.[2] The results for φ_3 are less good since the number of positive examples for this formula is extremely low and the discovered decision tree overfits.

In general, the position in a trace in which we ask for a prediction does not affect significantly its reliability. In the presented scenario, in which case attributes are available since before the initial event occurs, this is true also for the initial event. Nevertheless, in case of overfitting, there is more variability. Table 1 shows that our results are good also in terms of *positive predictive value (PPV)*, or precision, indicating how many positive outcomes are correctly predicted among all the outcomes predicted as positive:

$$PPV = \frac{T_P}{T_P + F_P}, \tag{4}$$

in terms of *harmonic mean* of precision and recall:

$$F_1 = 2 \cdot \frac{PPV \cdot TPR}{PPV + TPR}, \tag{5}$$

---

[2] Note that, in some cases, the OS provider does not return any prediction. This is due to the fact that, when one of the features reported in the decision tree is an enumeration (and this is the case for several attributes in the considered log), it can happen that not all the possible values of the feature are included in a path from the root to a leaf of the decision tree. Therefore, it is not possible to do any prediction about the behavior of executions in which the feature has one of these values.

Table 2. Evaluation of the approach using (1) a similarity threshold of 0.8, (2) a similarity threshold of 0.5, (3) class probability higher than the average, and (4) class support higher than the median of the class supports

	TPR	FPR	PPV	F1	ACC	LOSS
φ_1						
Similarity thresh. 0.8	0.881	0.388	0.685	0.771	**0.743**	-
Similarity thresh. 0.5	0.915	0.498	0.612	0.734	**0.693**	-
Class prob. above the average	0.94	0.429	0.714	0.812	**0.767**	0.223
Support above the median	0.88	0.201	0.83	0.854	**0.841**	0.508
φ_2						
Similarity thresh. 0.8	0.926	0.326	0.863	0.893	**0.847**	-
Similarity thresh. 0.5	0.858	0.391	0.831	0.844	**0.781**	-
Class prob. above the average	0.903	0.39	0.851	0.876	**0.818**	0.294
Support above the median	1	0.171	0.971	0.985	**0.974**	0.519
φ_3						
Similarity thresh. 0.8	0.333	0.088	0.192	0.243	**0.876**	-
Similarity thresh. 0.5	0.285	0.092	0.188	0.227	**0.864**	-
Class prob. above the average	0.285	0.07	0.176	0.218	**0.897**	0.167
Support above the median	0.375	0	1	0.545	**0.977**	0.559
φ_4						
Similarity thresh. 0.8	0.824	0.221	0.691	0.752	**0.795**	-
Similarity thresh. 0.5	0.846	0.132	0.754	0.797	**0.86**	-
Class prob. above the average	0.881	0.186	0.728	0.797	**0.838**	0.206
Support above the median	0.92	0.1	0.793	0.851	**0.905**	0.518
φ_5						
Similarity thresh. 0.8	0.819	0.117	0.819	0.819	**0.857**	-
Similarity thresh. 0.5	0.794	0.101	0.807	0.801	**0.862**	-
Class prob. above the average	0.761	0.089	0.809	0.784	**0.86**	0.23
Support above the median	0.938	0.053	0.938	0.938	**0.942**	0.53

and in terms of accuracy. Accuracy is particularly important in our context since it indicates how many times a prediction was correct:

$$ACC = \frac{T_P + T_N}{T_P + F_P + T_N + F_N} \qquad (6)$$

Note that the accuracy value is good also in case of overfitting (formula φ_3).

In a second experiment, we used a lower similarity threshold (0.5) and, again, a minimum number of traces equal to 30. The results for this experiment (for all the evaluation points together) are reported in Table 2 and in Fig. 6. This experiment shows that generating predictions based on a higher number of historical traces not always improves the quality of the results. This is due to the fact that, even if we are considering a larger training set, this set also includes traces that are quite dissimilar from the current trace, thus producing misleading results.

One way of assessing the reliability or "goodness" of a prediction is to use its *class probability*. In Table 2 and in Fig. 6, we show the results obtained by filtering out predictions with a class probability that is lower than the average. Table 2 also reports the prediction loss (LOSS), i.e., the percentage of predictions lost when filtering out predictions with a low class probability. This experiment shows that considering only predictions with a high class probability not always improves the quality of the results, though the percentage of predictions lost is not high (about 20%).

Another way of evaluating the reliability of a prediction is to consider its class support. In Table 2 and in Fig. 6, we show the results obtained by filtering out predictions with support lower than the median of the supports. In this case, although the cut of predictions is high (more than half of the predictions are filtered out), there is a clear improvement in all the considered metrics: in the ROC dimensions, in the F-measure as well as in the average accuracy of the predictions.

In summary, the evaluation shows that the proposed approach is feasible and provides accurate predictions (and hence recommendations). Results seem overall not to be affected by the position of the evaluation point, thus demonstrating that the approach works well even when few variables are known. Support seems to be an important factor influencing the results, i.e., the more evidences we have in the training set, the more accurate are the produced predictions. If on the one hand this highlights the need to have adequate training sets, on the other it also shows that sacrificing outlier predictions, it is possible to obtain very accurate results (accuracy around 0.9).

6 Related Work

In the literature, there are some works that provide approaches for generating predictions and recommendations during process execution and are focused on the time perspective. In [3,2], the authors present a set of approaches based on annotated transition systems containing time information extracted from event logs. The annotated transition systems are used to check time conformance while cases are being executed, predict the remaining processing time of incomplete cases, and recommend appropriate activities to end users working on these cases. In [9], an ad-hoc predictive clustering approach is presented, in which context-related execution scenarios are discovered and modeled through state-aware performance predictors. In [25], the authors introduce a method for predicting the remaining execution time of a process based on stochastic Petri nets.

There are several works focusing on generating predictions and recommendations to reduce risks. For example, in [7], the authors present a technique to support process participants in making risk-informed decisions, with the aim of reducing the process risks. Risks are predicted by traversing decision trees generated from the logs of past process executions. In [22], the authors propose an approach for predicting of time-related process risks by identifying (using statistical principles) indicators observable in event logs that highlight the possibility of transgressing deadlines. In [27], the authors propose an approach for Root Cause Analysis based on classification algorithms. After enriching a log with information like workload, occurrence of delay and involvement of resources, they use decision trees to identify the causes of overtime faults.

An approach for prediction of abnormal termination of business processes has been presented in [11]. Here, a fault detection algorithm (local outlier factor) is used to estimate the probability of a fault to occur. Alarms are provided to early notify probable abnormal terminations to prevent risks rather than simply react to them. In [6], Castellanos et al. present a business operations management platform equipped with time series forecasting functionalities. This platform allows for predictions of metric values on running process instances as well as for predictions of aggregated metric values of future instances (e.g., the number of orders that will be placed next Monday). Predictive monitoring focusing on failures and quality has also been applied to real case studies (e.g., in transportation contexts [18,8]).

A key difference between these approaches and our technique is that they rely either on the control-flow or on the data perspective for making predictions at runtime, whereas we take both perspectives into consideration. In addition, the purpose of our recommendations is different. We provide recommendations neither to reduce risks nor to satisfy/discover timing constraints. We aim instead at maximizing the likelihood of satisfying business constraints expressed in the form of LTL rules.

7 Conclusion

This paper presented a framework for predictive business process monitoring based on the estimation of probabilities of fulfillment of LTL rules at different points during the execution of a case. The framework takes into account both the sequencing of activities as well as data associated to the execution of each activity. A validation of the framework using a real-life log demonstrates that recommendations generated based on the framework have a promising level of accuracy when sufficient support is available.

Increased accuracy could be achieved by extending the technique along two directions. First, the proposed technique matches the trace of an ongoing case against prefixes of completed traces based on edit distance. While this is a well-known measure of similarity and suitable as a first step in this study, other approaches could be considered, including trace similarity measures based on occurrences of n-grams, counts of activities and activity pairs, and other relevant features that have been studied in the context of trace clustering [17]. In a similar vein, discriminative sequence mining techniques [12] could be applied in order to extract prefix patterns that are associated with fulfillment of a given business constraint. These patterns can also be taken as input in the prediction. Secondly, we have considered the use of decision trees to build the classifier. With larger number of attributes, which might be encountered in richer logs, decision trees are likely to exhibit lower accuracy due to their inherent weaknesses when dealing with large feature sets. In this context, other classification techniques, such as random forests or sparse logistic regression are possible alternatives.

Acknowledgments. This work is partly funded by ERDF via the Estonian Centre of Excellence in Computer Science and by the European Union Seventh Framework Programme FP7-2013-NMP-ICT-FOF (RTD) under grant agreement 609190 - "Subject-Orientation for People-Centred Production".

References

1. 3TU Data Center: BPI Challenge 2011 Event Log (2011), doi:10.4121/uuid:d9769f3d-0ab0-4fb8-803b-0d1120ffcf54
2. van der Aalst, W.M.P., Pesic, M., Song, M.: Beyond process mining: From the past to present and future. In: Pernici, B. (ed.) CAiSE 2010. LNCS, vol. 6051, pp. 38–52. Springer, Heidelberg (2010)

3. van der Aalst, W.M.P., Schonenberg, M.H., Song, M.: Time prediction based on process mining. Inf. Syst. 36(2), 450–475 (2011)
4. Beheshti, S.-M.-R., Benatallah, B., Motahari-Nezhad, H.R., Sakr, S.: A query language for analyzing business processes execution. In: Rinderle-Ma, S., Toumani, F., Wolf, K. (eds.) BPM 2011. LNCS, vol. 6896, pp. 281–297. Springer, Heidelberg (2011)
5. Birukou, A., D'Andrea, V., Leymann, F., Serafinski, J., Silveira, P., Strauch, S., Tluczek, M.: An integrated solution for runtime compliance governance in SOA. In: Maglio, P.P., Weske, M., Yang, J., Fantinato, M. (eds.) ICSOC 2010. LNCS, vol. 6470, pp. 122–136. Springer, Heidelberg (2010)
6. Castellanos, M., Salazar, N., Casati, F., Dayal, U., Shan, M.-C.: Predictive business operations management. In: Bhalla, S. (ed.) DNIS 2005. LNCS, vol. 3433, pp. 1–14. Springer, Heidelberg (2005)
7. Conforti, R., de Leoni, M., La Rosa, M., van der Aalst, W.M.P.: Supporting risk-informed decisions during business process execution. In: Salinesi, C., Norrie, M.C., Pastor, Ó. (eds.) CAiSE 2013. LNCS, vol. 7908, pp. 116–132. Springer, Heidelberg (2013)
8. Feldman, Z., Fournier, F., Franklin, R., Metzger, A.: Proactive event processing in action: a case study on the proactive management of transport processes. In: DEBS (2013)
9. Folino, F., Guarascio, M., Pontieri, L.: Discovering context-aware models for predicting business process performances. In: Meersman, R., Panetto, H., Dillon, T., Rinderle-Ma, S., Dadam, P., Zhou, X., Pearson, S., Ferscha, A., Bergamaschi, S., Cruz, I.F. (eds.) OTM 2012, Part I. LNCS, vol. 7565, pp. 287–304. Springer, Heidelberg (2012)
10. Holmes, T., Mulo, E., Zdun, U., Dustdar, S.: Model-aware monitoring of SOAs for compliance. In: Service Engineering, pp. 117–136. Springer (2011)
11. Kang, B., Kim, D., Kang, S.H.: Real-time business process monitoring method for prediction of abnormal termination using knni-based lof prediction. Expert Syst. Appl. (2012)
12. Lo, D., Cheng, H.: Lucia: Mining closed discriminative dyadic sequential patterns. In: Proc. of EDBT, pp. 21–32. Springer (2011)
13. Ly, L.T., Rinderle-Ma, S., Knuplesch, D., Dadam, P.: Monitoring business process compliance using compliance rule graphs. In: Meersman, R., Dillon, T., Herrero, P., Kumar, A., Reichert, M., Qing, L., Ooi, B.-C., Damiani, E., Schmidt, D.C., White, J., Hauswirth, M., Hitzler, P., Mohania, M. (eds.) OTM 2011, Part I. LNCS, vol. 7044, pp. 82–99. Springer, Heidelberg (2011)
14. Maggi, F.M., Westergaard, M., Montali, M., van der Aalst, W.M.P.: Runtime verification of LTL-based declarative process models. In: Khurshid, S., Sen, K. (eds.) RV 2011. LNCS, vol. 7186, pp. 131–146. Springer, Heidelberg (2012)
15. Maggi, F.M., Montali, M., Westergaard, M., van der Aalst, W.M.P.: Monitoring business constraints with linear temporal logic: An approach based on colored automata. In: Rinderle-Ma, S., Toumani, F., Wolf, K. (eds.) BPM 2011. LNCS, vol. 6896, pp. 132–147. Springer, Heidelberg (2011)
16. Maggi, F.M., Montali, M., van der Aalst, W.M.P.: An operational decision support framework for monitoring business constraints. In: de Lara, J., Zisman, A. (eds.) Fundamental Approaches to Software Engineering. LNCS, vol. 7212, pp. 146–162. Springer, Heidelberg (2012)
17. de Medeiros, A.K.A., Guzzo, A., Greco, G., van der Aalst, W.M.P., Weijters, A.J.M.M.T., van Dongen, B.F., Saccà, D.: Process mining based on clustering: A quest for precision. In: ter Hofstede, A.H.M., Benatallah, B., Paik, H.-Y. (eds.) BPM Workshops 2007. LNCS, vol. 4928, pp. 17–29. Springer, Heidelberg (2008)
18. Metzger, A., Franklin, R., Engel, Y.: Predictive monitoring of heterogeneous service-oriented business networks: The transport and logistics case. In: SRII (2012)
19. Montali, M., Pesic, M., van der Aalst, W.M.P., Chesani, F., Mello, P., Storari, S.: Declarative specification and verification of service choreographiess. TWEB 4(1) (2010)

20. Pesic, M., van der Aalst, W.M.P.: A Declarative Approach for Flexible Business Processes Management. In: Eder, J., Dustdar, S. (eds.) BPM Workshops 2006. LNCS, vol. 4103, pp. 169–180. Springer, Heidelberg (2006)
21. Pesic, M., Schonenberg, H., van der Aalst, W.M.P.: Declare: Full support for loosely-structured processes. In: Proc. of EDOC, pp. 287–300 (2007)
22. Pika, A., van der Aalst, W.M.P., Fidge, C.J., ter Hofstede, A.H.M., Wynn, M.T.: Predicting deadline transgressions using event logs. In: La Rosa, M., Soffer, P. (eds.) BPM Workshops 2012. LNBIP, vol. 132, pp. 211–216. Springer, Heidelberg (2013)
23. Pnueli, A.: The temporal logic of programs. In: SFCS, pp. 46–57 (1977)
24. Quinlan, J.R.: C4.5: Programs for Machine Learning. M. Kaufmann Publishers Inc (1993)
25. Rogge-Solti, A., Weske, M.: Prediction of remaining service execution time using stochastic petri nets with arbitrary firing delays. In: Basu, S., Pautasso, C., Zhang, L., Fu, X. (eds.) ICSOC 2013. LNCS, vol. 8274, pp. 389–403. Springer, Heidelberg (2013)
26. Santos, E.A.P., Francisco, R., Vieira, A.D.: F.R. Loures, E., Busetti, M.A.: Modeling business rules for supervisory control of process-aware information systems (2012)
27. Suriadi, S., Ouyang, C., van der Aalst, W.M.P., ter Hofstede, A.H.M.: Root cause analysis with enriched process logs. In: La Rosa, M., Soffer, P. (eds.) BPM Workshops 2012. Lecture Notes in Business Information Processing, vol. 132, pp. 174–186. Springer, Heidelberg (2013)
28. Weidlich, M., Ziekow, H., Mendling, J., Günther, O., Weske, M., Desai, N.: Event-based monitoring of process execution violations. In: Rinderle-Ma, S., Toumani, F., Wolf, K. (eds.) BPM 2011. LNCS, vol. 6896, pp. 182–198. Springer, Heidelberg (2011)
29. Westergaard, M., Maggi, F.M.: Modeling and verification of a protocol for operational support using coloured petri nets. In: Kristensen, L.M., Petrucci, L. (eds.) PETRI NETS 2011. LNCS, vol. 6709, pp. 169–188. Springer, Heidelberg (2011)

What Shall I Do Next?

Intention Mining for Flexible Process Enactment

Elena V. Epure[1, 2], Charlotte Hug[1], Rebecca Deneckère[1], and Sjaak Brinkkemper[2]

[1] Centre de Recherche en Informatique, Université Paris I Panthéon-Sorbonne, France
{charlotte.hug,rebecca.deneckere}@univ-paris1.fr
[2] Department of Information and Computing Sciences, Utrecht University, the Netherlands
{E.V.Epure,S.Brinkkemper}@uu.nl

Abstract. Besides the benefits of flexible processes, practical implementations of process aware information systems have also revealed difficulties encountered by process participants during enactment. Several support and guidance solutions based on process mining have been proposed, but they lack a suitable semantics for human reasoning and decisions making as they mainly rely on low level activities. Applying design science, we created *FlexPAISSeer*, an *intention mining* oriented approach, with its component artifacts: 1) *Intent-Miner* which discovers the intentional model of the executable process in an unsupervised manner; 2) *IntentRecommender* which generates recommendations as intentions and confidence factors, based on the mined intentional process model and probabilistic calculus. The artifacts were evaluated in a case study with a Netherlands software company, using a Childcare system that allows flexible data-driven process enactment.

Keywords: intention mining, process mining, flexible processes, process aware information systems, process recommendations.

1 Introduction: Intention Mining

Process Aware Information Systems (PAIS) form a category of information systems, highly adopted by organizations, defined by van der Aalst as "software systems that manage and execute operational processes involving people, applications, and/or information sources on the basis of process models" [3]. In flexible PAISs which support process changes and variations as result of the external and internal environment, the primacy of humans has been highly acknowledged [8, 18, 26]. The agency characteristic of process participants, entailing their freedom of decision making during process enactments becomes thus central as it impacts the process outcomes. For instance, let's consider an e-commerce application: when a net surfer adds a product to his basket, several choices are offered: he can select another product, handle his basket, create his customer account etc. Following the flexibility of the studied process, the decision making complexity can increase rapidly. An experienced process participant who is highly aware of the process is able to make a better decision about the action to execute next under specific constraints or how to model a process fragment at run-time. In contrast, this can

M. Jarke et al. (Eds.): CAiSE 2014, LNCS 8484, pp. 473–487, 2014.

be very challenging for a less experienced process participant or for a process participant who faces a very dynamic and complex process environment [2, 23, 26]. If the resulting problem-prone situation is ignored, the adoption of flexible processes can instead have a negative impact on organizations.

Consequently, in this paper, we focus on tackling the difficulties of process participants when enacting flexible processes in PAISs by proposing *FlexPAISSeer*, a solution based on *intention mining* [12]. A PAIS enables the process discovery in a bottom-up manner by capturing events during enactment. Practically, this is realized by process mining, whose main goal is "to discover, monitor and improve real processes" by transforming the event logs data in valuable knowledge [3]. The mining result is most often a process model. Additionally, process mining has been used as a key technology in several approaches to support process participants during enactment [1, 22, 26]. While these solutions integrate process mining successfully, we consider the recommendations semantically not rich enough to support effective decision making meaning *effective criteria identification, development, and analysis of alternatives* [13]. The recommendations are formulated based on the mined process models which are frequently represented as control flows of low level activities. Therefore, to semantically enrich the recommendations, the mined process models must be enriched.

Through intention mining, we have the ambitious goal of extending process mining with a more suitable perspective for supporting humans in decision making, by mining the intentional process model from event logs and by using it for providing recommendations as intentions and confidence factors. We consider the intention a higher abstraction and a logical grouping of activities which captures their hidden goal: what the user wanted/want to achieve by following those activities. Human behavior is intentional by nature. Hence, making decisions based on intentions is closer to his natural reasoning mechanism. This topic has been extensively discussed in philosophy [4, 10], artificial intelligence [7, 16] and various areas of information systems, as requirements and enterprise engineering [15, 17, 18, 25, 31], and data mining [5, 27].

Once the process participant adopts an intention, he acts accordingly to achieve it [4]. Hence, the event log contains data about his intention. The research objectives regarding the unsupervised intention mining technique are: *the identification of the data which provides information about intentions* and *the identification of the intentional cluster of events associated with an intention and its naming*. We propose a general definition of *IntentMiner*, applicable for multiple systems while we also identify domain-specific aspects as the cost function in clustering and the intention naming. We propose *IntentRecommender* to *predict a set of intentions* based on the process model and the process participant trace, *each having associated a confidence factor*: a numerical value *aggregating the probability of the past occurrence of the full or partial sequence of intentions* (the trace and each predicted intention).

We used design science [11] collaborating with 42windmills, a software company located in Leiden, the Netherlands. We chose this research method as it addresses the relevance and acceptance of our created artifacts in the application domain. Accordingly, this paper is organized as follows: Section 2 describes the *FlexPAISSeer* approach and its artifacts design, Section 3 presents the artifacts development and demonstration in the case study context, Section 4 details the artifacts evaluation. Finally, Section 5 presents the conclusions and future works.

2   FlexPAISSeer: Enactment Support in Flexible PAISs

We identified the problem situation could be best tackled with a knowledge management approach. Thus, we chose the knowledge management cycle proposed by Wiig [28] for the FlexPAISSeer design which distinguished four phases: *Build* knowledge, *Hold* knowledge, *Pool* knowledge and *Use* knowledge.

IntentMiner is the central component of the *Build* and *Hold* knowledge phases. It consists of the intention mining technique that creates and embeds knowledge as follows: it mines all the existing event logs and generates the *intentional process model* enriched with meta-data regarding the frequencies of various process instances (steps 9, 4, 10-11 in Fig. 1); *IntentMiner* also transforms the current process instance in the *intentional process instance* to feed *IntentRecommender*, and uses it for updating the *intentional process model* (steps 1-5 in Fig. 1).

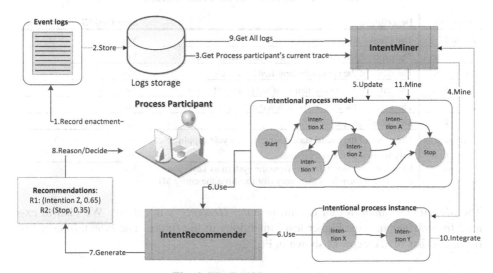

Fig. 1. FlexPAISSeer approach

IntentRecommender is the central component for the *Pool* knowledge phase: it assembles and reconstructs the intentional process instance and the process model as recommendations composed of *intentions* and *confidence factors* (steps 6-7 in Fig. 1). The *Use* knowledge phase concerns the *Process Participant* who can decide to enact considering the given recommendations (steps 8). However, the recommendations are not enforced, the Process Participant being free to enact the process differently when required by the situation at hand.

Further, we present *IntentMiner* and *IntentRecommender* with a focus on our design decisions and algorithms. The design decisions were created based on extensive literature review and interviews with the company before and during the project [9].

2.1   IntentMiner

The main design goal of *IntentMiner* is to discover the intentional process model from the traces of the process participants, by both mining their intentions and the flow between these intentions. We group these design decisions in the following categories: input-related and algorithm-related design decisions.

The *input-related design* focuses on the identification of the relevant data for mining the intentional process, a logging mechanism and a data extraction mechanism. After analyzing other process mining techniques [3], we decided to structure the event logs as in Table 1. Moreover, the mechanism extracting the data from the data source should produce event logs compliant with the XES standard for storing and exchanging logs [3] as it is the most used in the process mining domain.

Table 1. The definition of the event structure

Attribute	Description	Standard XES extension
Event Id	The event's unique identifier	Yes
Originator	The process participant's identifier (username or user Id)	Yes
Operation	The name of the operation identified by a verb	Yes
Timestamp	The date and time information of the produced event	Yes
Entity	The name of the entity type handled in the event	No
Trace Id	The trace's unique identifier	Yes
Lifecycle Transition	The name of the event' state during its lifecycle (applicable only for non-momentary events)	Yes
Process Context	Extra information, extracted from the system as key/value, relevant for intentions discovery (for example the entity Id)	No

The *algorithm-related design* is built to mine *elementary* intentions. We plan to extend *IntentMiner* to mine higher level intentions in the future. The *IntentMiner* algorithm consists of six steps, as shown in Fig. 2.

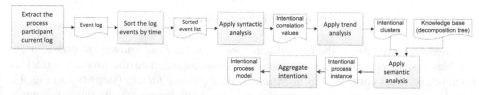

Fig. 2. The *IntentMiner* algorithm steps

We explain the *IntentMiner* algorithm by means of a semi-formal presentation. A full example is shown in section 3.2. Let P be the set of process participants for a specific PAIS. An intention I is said to be *elementary* if there exists a set of activities $A_I = \{a_1, a_2... a_t\}$, executed by a process participant $p \in P$ such that their *consecutive execution* leads to the achievement of I and only I.

Each activity $a_i \in A$ is associated to an event $e_i \in E$ which is logged during its execution. Thus, we define the *intentional cluster* as the set of events $C_I = \{e_1, e_2... e_t\}$ logged during the consecutive execution of their corresponding activities $A_I = \{a_1, a_2... a_t\}$, which leads to the achievement of the elementary level intention I.

Let L be *a log of events ordered by time*, recorded *for a process participant* $p \in P$. Practically, L represents a series of events corresponding to a series of activities which were executed for realizing a series of intentions. Therefore, the log can be transformed in a series of intentional clusters $L = \{C_{Ik}: C_{Ik}$ identifies I_k, for every k, $1 \leq k \leq n\}$. Consequently, the first goal of the *IntentMiner* algorithm is to mine the intentional clusters and to extract the associated intention out of each cluster.

As mentioned earlier, each event e is described by a set of attributes, $AT_e = \{at_{ek}:$ for some k, $1 \leq k \leq m\}$. This data, contained in the event structure, gives information about the realized intention. We define the *intentional correlation* as a function [23] applied on two consecutive events for quantifying the similarity with regard to the unknown intention I: $f(at_i, at_{i+1}) = \sum_{i=1..m} \alpha_k * g(at_{e_ik}, at_{e_{i+1}k})$, e_i, $e_{i+1} \in L$ where $g(at_{e_ik}, at_{e_{i+1}k}) = 1$ if $at_{e_ik} \equiv at_{e_{i+1}k}$, 0 otherwise and $0 \leq \alpha_k \leq 1$. The coefficient α_k is introduced to differentiate the contribution of two attributes to the total correlation value. For example, two consecutive events that refer to the same *entity instance* have a much stronger correlation than two events that refer to the same *entity type*.

This introduces the third step of the algorithm: discovering the intentional clusters [24] with **syntactic analysis** which consists in the application of the function f on each pair of consecutive events belonging to the input log L. In this way, the log is transformed in a series of intentional correlation values. Then, the normalization of the series is realized by subtracting from each correlation value the minimum correlation value discovered in the set, until this minimum becomes null.

The fourth step is the **trend analysis** built on the observation that the progressive achievement of the intention [4, 7] is captured by the trend in the correlation values as follows: an *increasing trend* marks the progressive realization of an intention while a *change in trend* from increasing to decreasing or a *null correlation* value delineates two intentions. We analyzed multiple event logs of different applications and observed that two consecutive events belonging to an intention had a similar process context and a higher correlation value. Contrarily, if two events were triggered as a result of achieving two different intentions, they had different process context and a low or null correlation value. The result is the discovery of the intentional clusters.

Once the intentional clusters are identified, the further step is the intention extraction and naming by applying the **semantic analysis** [20] for each C_{Ik}, $1 \leq k \leq n$. A predefined knowledge base is created as a decomposition tree (see example in Fig. 4) populated with a starting set of known intentions and activities. The activities are always positioned in leaves and they could belong to multiple intentions. An intention could be standalone or a sub-intention of another intention (high level intention). The extracted intention for a cluster is the one on the *lowest level in the tree* that covers the *maximum number of known activities* of that cluster. The first implication is that an intention can be discovered even if not all activities are known in the knowledge base. The second implication is that a cluster could represent a different intention which is not yet known and stored in the knowledge base. An expert as a process administrator being responsible for process definition and implementation should review the mined process instance and the intentional clusters to decide if the knowledge base should be updated with new intentions or activities. The flow between intentional clusters describes the *flow between intentions*, thus obtaining the *intentional process instance*.

The final step is the ***aggregation*** of the mined process instance in the intentional process model: new mined intentions and transitions are added, and the transitions frequencies are increased. Thus, we obtain the updated intentional process model (step 5 in Fig. 1) that is further used by *IntentRecommender* for providing up-to-date recommendations to the process participants.

2.2   IntentRecommender

The leading design decision of *IntentRecommender* was to provide recommendations at *the intentional level* as we considered it could offer a more effective support to process participants in making decisions. This enables a more effective support for the identification of the decision criteria, the developing of the decision alternatives and the analysis of the decision alternatives.

The second design decision was to provide recommendations according to the *as-is intentional process model*, discovered by *IntentMiner* instead of using a pre-defined process model which might not be exactly followed by the process participants in practice. Moreover, *IntentMiner* transforms the process participant's partial trace of events in a flow of intentions which is given as input to *IntentRecommender* and is also used for *updating* the intentional process model.

The third design decision was to provide recommendations that contain information about the behavior of *other process participants* in a similar or identical process enactment situation, through *a confidence factor* [6]. The confidence factor is a numerical value attached to the recommendation, which quantifies *the match* and *the frequency* of the current process participant log based on the known process data.

Providing recommendations starting from a flow of intentions $F = \{I_1 \rightarrow \ldots \rightarrow I_n\}$, $n \geq 1$ is a matter of prediction, having, as prior knowledge, the intentional process model. A recommendation is the next predicted intention, $I_{predicted}$, which has attached the confidence factor $CF_{Ipredicted}$. We focus further on describing the two main parts of *IntentRecommender*: the prediction and the confidence factor computation.

The *prediction* is the identification of the next intentions based on the input flow of intentions, F, and the process model. *IntentRecommender* consists of three steps:

- **Discover the set of intentions**, $SI_{predicted}$, that are directly reachable from the last intention I_n, $n \geq 1$ of the flow F: $SI_{predicted} = \{I_{predicted} : I_n \rightarrow I_{predicted}, n \geq 1$ *exists in the intentional process model*$\}$.
- For each $I_{predicted} \in SI_{predicted}$, **create the set of predecessors** consisting of the intentions found in the flow, sorted by time in descending order, $P_{Ipredicted} = \{I_n \ldots I_1\}$ $n \geq 1$. However, there are two possible issues. First, the path described by F cannot be fully found in the intentional process model. In this case, $P_{Ipredicted}$ is modified to contain only those intentions which describe an existing flow to $I_{predicted}$ in the intentional process model: $P_{Ipredicted} = \{I_n \ldots I_k\}$, $n, k \geq 1$ *and* $I_k \rightarrow \ldots \rightarrow I_n \rightarrow I_{predicted}$ *exists in the intentional process model*. Second, an intention could appear several times in $P_{Ipredicted}$. In this case, the interpretations could be: (i) an intention was among its list of predecessors, thus influencing its future occurrence; or (ii) the flow exposed different ways of achieving that intention. By invoking Occam's razor [18], which

specifies that the model with the simple assumptions should be selected, we chose the interpretation (ii). This implies another constraint on $P_{Ipredicted}$: each intention in the sequence of predecessors must be *unique* and *different* from $I_{predicted}$.

- For each $I_{predicted} \in SI_{predicted}$, **compute the confidence factor** $CF_{Ipredicted}$ (1) having the possibility to tune it through the coefficients α and β, $0 \leq \alpha, \beta \leq 1$. The process administrator can decide the frequency of a certain path is more important through α's value, or the match of a certain path is more important, through β's value.

$$CF_{Ipredicted} = \alpha * P(\{I_{predicted}\} + P_{Ipredicted}) + \beta * L(\{I_{predicted}\} + P_{Ipredicted}) / L(F) \qquad (1)$$

$$P(\{I_{predicted}\} + P_{Ipredicted}) = Probability\ of\ I_k \rightarrow \ldots \rightarrow I_n \rightarrow I_{predicted}\ n,\ k\geq 1\ occurs \qquad (2)$$

$$L(\{I_{predicted}\} + P_{Ipredicted}) = n - k + 2 = Length\ of\ I_k \rightarrow \ldots \rightarrow I_n \rightarrow I_{predicted}\ n,\ k\geq 1 \qquad (3)$$

$$L(F) = n = Length\ of\ I_1 \rightarrow I_2 \rightarrow \ldots \rightarrow I_n \qquad (4)$$

Every time a new process instance is mined, *IntentMiner* updates the tree T_I of each intention I with all the paths that lead to it and their frequencies. Based on the data maintained in T_I we compute the probabilities. The tree has a specific structure: a full discovered process instance that describes a path to I is stored in a leaf; then this path is recursively decomposed in shorter paths to I by removing one intention from the tail until there is nothing left to be removed. For example, let's consider *IntentMiner* discovers the following process instance: $I_1 \rightarrow I_2 \rightarrow \ldots \rightarrow I_k \rightarrow \ldots \rightarrow I_n$. The tree corresponding to the intention I_k is updated as follows: the leaf node $n_1 = I_1 \rightarrow I_2 \rightarrow \ldots \rightarrow I_k$ is created, then a new node $n_2 = I_2 \rightarrow \ldots \rightarrow I_k$ is created and linked to n_1 and so on until the root $r = I_k \rightarrow null$ is reached. During the path decomposition, it might happen that a node is already in the tree in which case only the link is created and the node frequency is incremented. Considering, $\#T_I$ the total number of mined paths that lead to the intention I, we have:

$$P(\{I_{predicted}\} + P_{Ipredicted}) = Frequency(\{I_{predicted}\} + P_{Ipredicted}) / \#T_{Ipredicted} \qquad (5)$$

We compute the confidence factor (1) by using (2-5) and create the recommendation. The computation is realized for each intention of $SI_{predicted}$ (step 7 in Fig. 1).

3   The Demonstration of FlexPAISSeer

3.1   Case Study of an Enterprise Software Product

To demonstrate the validity of our *FlexPAISSeer* approach, we conducted a revelatory single case study [30]. We selected the case company considering its suitability (the support of flexible processes through its software product): the Childcare system developed by 42windmills used by several child day care centers in the Netherlands. Childcare is created with the company's main product: a platform which generates software following a model driven approach. The platform together with a Web-based application designer enables the customers to design, preview, generate, re-design and deploy a wide variety of business applications.

Even if some processes of the created business application can be automated, most of them are flexible, being enacted in a data-centered, human-driven manner. In a data-centered approach, the elements that influence the process enactment are entities, entity attributes and entity relationships (as shown in Fig. 3). A transition in the process enactment is triggered by a change in the entity state through user forms [23]. An exploratory interview reported that the high Childcare's complexity combined with the flexible processes support created problems: inexperienced process partici-pants often enacted inefficiently the processes or made mistakes because of the scena-rio complexity.

To ensure the research reliability, construct and internal validity, we defined a case study protocol beforehand and we used multiple sources of evidence which were care-fully documented in a case study database. We conducted exploratory interviews with the CTO, the Childcare consultant and the platform architect to deepen the under-standing of the problem the company was facing, to study more thoroughly the tech-nical aspects of the product and to validate the suitability of the proposed solution. The external validity, concerning the generalization of the results, is more difficult to guarantee after a single-case study. However, given the generic type of the administra-tive application and the standard technology employed, we can consider the case settings as a good representative for an enterprise software product [29].

We developed prototypes for both *IntentMiner* and *IntentRecommender* using Mi-crosoft C#.NET language, Visual Studio 2012 and Microsoft SQL Server 2005. We choose these technologies to ensure an easier integration of the artifacts with the company's product. Though generic, the prototypes are not officially released as they must be integrated and some parts still need improvements.

3.2   IntentMiner's Demonstration

IntentMiner is demonstrated for the *Request child care* process. In Fig. 3, we present a partial entity model involved in the registration process. As mentioned, the enactment of the Childcare's processes is based on the entity states transitions.

Fig. 3. Entities involved in the registration process

In Table 2a, we present a possible process instance of the *Request child care* process. We defined the intentional correlation function (used in Table 2b) to take into account the following event attributes: the trace Id (for Childcare being the Child entity Id), the entity type and the entity Id (which is stored as contextual information):

$$f(e_i, e_{i+1}) = 0.5 * g(EntityId_{e_i}, EntityId_{e_{i+1}}) + 0.3 * g(EntityType_{e_i}, EntityType_{e_{i+1}}) + 0.2 * g(TraceId_{e_i}, TraceId_{e_{i+1}})$$

The intentional correlation for each pair of consecutive events is calculated (*syntactic analysis*, Table 2b). According to the defined rules of trend analysis, the intentional clusters are formed (*trend analysis*, Table 2c).

Table 2. Exemplification of the *IntentMiner* algorithm

(a) Extract process participant log and sort by timestamp	$E_1 \rightarrow e_2 \rightarrow e_3 \rightarrow e_4 \rightarrow e_5 \rightarrow e_6 \rightarrow e_7$ e_1: Read the list of Child entities e_2: Read the Child entity with Id C1 e_3: Update the Child entity with Id C1	e_4: Read the list of Child entities e_5: Read the Child entity with Id C2 e_6: Read the list of Parent entities e_7: Read the list of Child Picker entities
(b) Apply syntactic analysis	$f(e_1, e_2) = 0.5*0 + 0.3*1 + 0.2*0 = 0.3;$ $f(e_2, e_3) = 0.5*1 + 0.3*1 + 0.2*1 = 1;$ $f(e_3, e_4) = 0.5*0 + 0.3*1 + 0.2*0 = 0.3;$	$f(e_4, e_5) = 0.5*0 + 0.3*1 + 0.2*0 = 0.3;$ $f(e_5, e_6) = 0.5*0 + 0.3*0 + 0.2*0 = 0;$ $f(e_6, e_7) = 0.5*0 + 0.3*0 + 0.2*0 = 0;$
(c) Apply trend analysis	$C_{11} = \{e_1, e_2, e_3\}$ $C_{12} = \{e_4, e_5\}$ $C_{13} = \{e_6\}$ $C_{14} = \{e_7\}$ e_1 and e_2 have a correlation higher than 0 and are grouped in C_{11}. The correlation of e_3 with e_2 is higher than its correlation with e_4, thus e_3 is added to C_{11} too. The first change in trend is identified (the decrease from 1 to 0.3) so C_{12} is formed, to which e_4 is added. Further, the correlation of e_5 with e_4 is higher than its correlation with e_6 so e_5 is added to C_{12}. The change in trend (the decrease from 0.3 to 0) marks the creation of C_{13} consisting of e_6. Finally, because the correlation of e_6 with e_7 is zero, C_{14} consisting of e_7 is built.	
(d) Apply semantic analysis	I_1 (Update Child entity) $\rightarrow$ I_2 (Read Child entity) $\rightarrow$ I_3 (Read Parent entities) $\rightarrow$ I_4 (Read ChildPicker entities)	

Once we discover the intentional clusters, we identify the intention associated with each of them (*semantic analysis*, Table 2d). For this, we pre-defined a knowledge base during the Childcare analysis. For each entity type, a decomposition tree based on Fig. 4 was created. The intention composition is generic for all the Childcare entities because of the software's nature, being model driven generated.

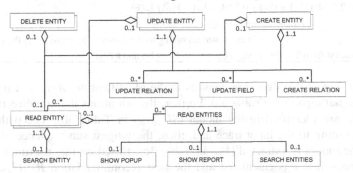

Fig. 4. Intention composition for semantic analysis

The tree contains five elementary intentions (Create entity, Read entity, Read entities, Update entity, and Delete entity) and seven activities (Update relation, Update field, Create relation, Search entity, Search entities, Show popup and Show report).

3.3   IntentRecommender's Demonstration

The *IntentRecommender* algorithm is also demonstrated further. The inputs consist of the intentional process model in Table 3, and the trees associated to each intention (discovered with *IntentMiner*). The process relates to the Childcare registration, as only this part was mined during the experiments. When the process participant invokes *IntentRecommender*, the input trace is extracted. The intentional process instance does not necessary match the intentional process model as our goal is process discovery and not conformance checking [3].

Table 3. Recommendation algorithm – running example

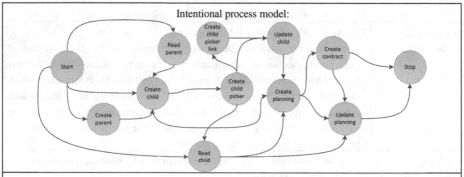

(a) Process participant's intentional process instance:
F: I_{t1} (Read parent list) → I_{t2} (Read parent) → I_{t3} (Create child) → I_{t4} (Create child picker)

(b) Discover the set of intentions directly reachable from the last intention, I_{t4}:
$SI_{predicted}$ = { I_{p1} (Create child picker link), I_{p2} (Update child), I_{p3} (Read child) }

(c) Compute the confidence factor exemplified for I_{p3} (Read child) :
P_{Ip3} = { I_{t4}, I_{t3}, I_{t2} } CF_{Ip3} = $0.5 * P (\{I_{p3}\} + P_{Ip3}) + 0.5 * L (\{I_{p3}\} + P_{Ip3}) / L (F)$ $= 0.5 * P (I_{p3} \leftarrow I_{t4} \leftarrow I_{t3} \leftarrow I_{t2}) + 0.5 * 3 / 4$ where $P (I_{p3} \leftarrow I_{t4} \leftarrow I_{t3} \leftarrow I_{t2})$ is calculated according to the formula (5), considering the information extracted from T_{Ip3} (Frequency ($I_{p3} \leftarrow I_{t4} \leftarrow I_{t3} \leftarrow I_{t2}$) and $\#T_{Ip3}$)

The first step of the algorithm consists in the identification of the last intention of the process participant: I_{t4} (Table 3a). Further, the intentions that are directly reachable from I_{t4} are identified in the model ($SI_{predicted}$ in Table 3b). The path to I_{p3} is formed according to the input trace and, then, the longest sub-sequence of this path found in the model is extracted (P_{Ip3} in Table 3c). Based on this maximal sequence, the confidence factor is calculated and the first recommendation R_3: (I_{p3}, CF_{Ip3}) is formulated. We repeat step (c) for the other left intentions – I_{p1} and I_{p2}, in a similar manner.

4   Preliminary Evaluation of FlexPAISSeer

The evaluation of the artifacts consisted in an experiment with 10 participants, interacting with Childcare [9]. Previous experience was not required, though we provided a tutorial about the application usage in advance. The participants had to be able to express themselves in English and to have basic computer skills. An experiment lasted around two hours and consisted of two parts. In the first part, we evaluated *IntentMiner*. The process participants were asked to perform different tasks while they were verbalizing their intentions in the presence of the interviewer. The second part focused on the *IntentRecommender*'s evaluation through structured interviews.

4.1   IntentMiner's Evaluation

We evaluated *IntentMiner* following the Confusion matrix approach, built on the concept of instances classification, realized by a classifier system [14]. In our context, the classifier system was *IntentMiner* and the instance was the discovery/existence of an intention. An intention discovery was classified as positive when *IntentMiner* discovered it from event logs and negative otherwise (*Classified instance*, Table 4). An intention existence was positive if the process participant confirmed he had that intention and negative otherwise (*Actual instance*, Table 4).

Table 4. Confusion matrix for intention mining

		Classified instance	
Results of the case study		*Negative*: an intention I is not discovered	*Positive*: an intention I is discovered
Actual instance	*Negative*: the process participant does not have the intention I	#TN (the number of *true negative* instances): **0**	#FP (the number of *false positive* instances): **47**
	Positive: the process participant has the intention I	#FN (the number of *false negative* instances): **3**	#TP (the number of *true positive* instances): **105**

The participants verbalized 108 intentions out of which 105 (#TP) were correctly discovered by *IntentMiner* and 3 (#FN) were not. *IntentMiner* discovered 152 intentions out of which 47 (#FP) were negative as the process participants did not have those intentions. The number of true negative instances was always 0. Since a process participants had no intention and did not act accordingly, there were no logs based on which the intention could be mined.

Given an intention discovered by *IntentMiner*, the **average precision (Precision = #TP / (#TP + #FP))** of *being correct* was **0.69**. Furthermore, *IntentMiner* mined the process participants' intentions in **0.97** cases. This was measured by the **average recall (Recall = #TP / (#TP + #FN))**. These results are very satisfactory for a first time use of our *unsupervised* intention mining technique. Khodabandelou et al. [12] reported an average recall of 0.93 and an average precision of 0.97 for their *supervised* intention mining technique based on Hidden Markov Models. The precision was considerably better given the fact the classifier was trained in advance.

For getting more insights into how we could improve *IntentMiner*, we analyzed thoroughly each log and noticed two recurring issues. First, *IntentMiner* discovered several intentions even if the activities behind them were not intended for that, but for higher intentions. For example, *Explore the Childcare application* was mined as reading different entities. Second, several activities were triggered by the system on behalf of the process participant thus were mined as process participant's intention. Every time a new *Child* entity was created, an empty *ChildPicker* entity was also created by the system; these events were mined as two separate intentions but in reality it was only one intention: *Create Child entity.*

In conclusion, the functional requirements of *IntentMiner* were completely satisfied as proved by its usage without errors in the experiments. *IntentMiner* can be used for mining intentional processes but a further review of the results by the process administrator is required as they might not be completely precise.

4.2   IntentRecommender's Evaluation

Unit tests were used for validating the *IntentRecommender* functionality. The non-functional evaluation of *IntentRecommender* was reduced to the following phases:

1. The non-functional evaluation of *IntentMiner* as the quality of the produced output (used as input for *IntentRecommender*) influences the quality of the recommendations. This was covered in section 4.1.
2. The analysis of the perceived effectiveness of recommendations as intentions and confidence factors on decision making support by the process participants.

The second phase consisted in a *structured interview based on a questionnaire*. It had various conceptual scenarios inspired from Childcare which required the process participants to make decisions. Besides, there were also general and confidence factors-related questions. The hypotheses guiding the evaluation of *IntentRecommender* were:

H1: The recommendations given as intentions improve the support for decision making by improving the support for *the criteria identification*.
H2: The recommendations given as intentions improve the support for decision making by improving the support for *the alternatives formulation*.
H3: The recommendations given as intentions improve the support for decision making by improving the support for *the alternatives analysis*.
H4: The confidence factors included in the *recommendations* improve the support for decision making.

In the first scenario, without any recommendations, the participants were asked to identify what they believed they should do next. The participants identified the high level intention (to update the child planning) without problems. When asked to give details about the specific process steps, they were able to cover only a part of them (even if they were revealed in the tutorial provided in the beginning). After the first set of recommendations as activities was given, most of the participants chose the option that was aligned with their previously identified intention except for two: one changed his intention from updating the child to updating the planning and the other stated that his new decision was based on the confidence factors.

After the intention behind the recommended set of activities was revealed, 9 of 10 participants agreed that the decision making was easier in that case motivating the answer as follows: the intention helped to clarify the activities to be performed, helped to validate an intention adopted in advance and provided information about the context. One participant disagreed with the added value by invoking the efficiency in following activities without reasoning about intentions (step by step guidance).

Consequently, it was shown that the recommendations as intentions improved the support for the criteria selection (*H1*) in two ways: *by the intention realization* when the process participants adopted the suggested intention and made the decision accordingly; *by the intention validation* when the process participants checked if the suggested intention was the same with the one they already formulated in their mind.

The aim of the next scenario was to compare the decision making support when recommendations were given as intentions and then as activities. 7 of 10 participants found the set of recommendations given as intentions helpful for supporting the decision making while 3 disagreed: two preferred a step by step guidance and one found it hard to make the decision because there were too many recommendations in the set. Analyzing the collected data, we noticed that most of the participants wanted support in interacting with the application and *preferred the recommendations as intentions* to recommendations as activities. Thus, *H2 and H3 seemed to be supported*.

The final questions were focused on the confidence factors. 6 of 10 participants disagreed that the numerical values attached to each recommendation influenced their decision. The main invoked reason was that there was no re-assurance the other participants enacted the process more efficiently or more effectively, to follow their behavior. Nevertheless, the other 4 participants agreed with the usefulness of the confidence factors and mentioned that their decision was influenced completely (following the others behavior) or partially (checking if the others reasoned similarly) by this. Consequently, *H4 could not be verified* based on the existing data.

5   Conclusion and Future Works

In this paper, our main goal was to create an improved approach for supporting process participants during flexible processes enactment, by offering recommendation based on an intentional process model. As process mining captures accurately how real life processes are enacted, we created *IntentMiner* to discover intentional process models automatically from event logs. The intentional process model was integrated in *IntentRecommender*, which after the evaluation in a case study, demonstrated its contribution to the problem solving. To sum up with, we consider the largest contribution of this research is the thorough study of the intentionality in the context of process enactment and its integration with process mining.

We intend to improve the evaluation of this approach as the evaluation of the artifacts was realized for only one case study with 10 participants. According to Yin [30] a more accurate evaluation should include at least 3 case studies. We will then conduct more case studies including other software products in different organizational settings. With more participants, we could do quantitative evaluation too.

IntentMiner can be improved to mine more accurately the intentions. The semantic analysis can be supported by ontologies and semantic annotations of the event logs which should also enable the mining of the non-functional intentions. Moreover, other machine learning algorithms for clustering can be explored, as self-organizing maps or genetic algorithms. *IntentMiner* in its current form requires several adaptations for being re-used by other applications (selection of event attributes relevant for the syntactic analysis, redefinition of the correlation function according to the selected event attributes, adaptation of the hierarchy of intentions for semantic analysis). These changes – triggered by specific cases – should be formalized in a method and supported by a tool to ease future adaptations. The intentional process models produced by *IntentMiner* are not as flexible as Map intentional process models [25]. We do not consider parallel intentions and refinement of intentions. Producing more complex intentional process models is one of our next steps. A ProM plugin for *IntentMiner* and *IntentRecommender* should be further developed. Official XES extensions also have to be proposed to integrate the concepts of process context and entity (Table 1).

Finally, *IntentRecommender* can be extended with an inference mechanism based on the Dynamic Bayesian Network [21], a more suitable probabilistic model for processes. This would allow an intention to be in its list of predecessors when calculating the confidence factors. The prototype should be released in a stable version and integrated in a PAIS to allow its runtime evaluation.

References

1. van der Aalst, W.M.P.: Decision Support Based on Process Mining. In: International Handbooks Information System, pp. 637–657 (2008)
2. van der Aalst, W.M.P., Pesic, M., Schonenberg, H.: Declarative Workflows: Balancing Between Flexibility and Support. In: Computer Science - R&D, pp. 99–113 (2009)
3. van der Aalst, W.M.P.: Process Mining: Discovery, Conformance and Enhancement of Business Processes. Springer (2011)
4. Bratman, M.E.: Intention, Plans, and Practical Reason. Cambridge University Press (1999)
5. Chen, Z., Lin, F., Liu, H., Liu, Y., Ma, W.-Y., Wenyin, L.: User Intention Modeling in Web Applications Using Data Mining. Journal of World Wide Web Internet And Web Information Systems 5(3), 181–191 (2002)
6. Cleger-Tamayo, S., Fernández-Luna, J.M., Huete, J.F., Tintarev, N.: Being Confident about the Quality of the Predictions in Recommender Systems. In: Serdyukov, P., Braslavski, P., Kuznetsov, S.O., Kamps, J., Rüger, S., Agichtein, E., Segalovich, I., Yilmaz, E. (eds.) ECIR 2013. LNCS, vol. 7814, pp. 411–422. Springer, Heidelberg (2013)
7. Cohen, P.R., Levesque, H.: Intention is choice with commitment. Journal of Artificial Intelligence 42(2), 213–261 (1990)
8. Ellis, C.A., Kim, K.: Process aware information systems: a human centered perspective. In: Dong, G., Lin, X., Wang, W., Yang, Y., Yu, J.X. (eds.) APWeb/WAIM 2007. LNCS, vol. 4505, pp. 39–49. Springer, Heidelberg (2007)
9. Epure, E.V., Hug, C., Deneckere, R., Brinkkemper, S.: Intention-mining: A solution to process participant support in process aware information systems. Technical report. Department of Information and Computing Sciences, Utrecht University (2013)
10. Fishbein, M., Ajzen, I.: Belief, Attitude, Intention, and Behavior: An Introduction to Theory and Research. Addison-Wesley, Reading (1975)
11. Hevner, A.R., March, S.T., Park, J., Ram, S.: Design Science in Information Systems Research. MIS Quarterly 28(1), 75–105 (2004)
12. Khodabandelou, G., Hug, C., Deneckère, R., Salinesi, C.: Supervised intentional process models discovery using Hidden Markov models. In: IEEE RCIS, pp. 1–11. IEEE (2013)
13. Klein, G.A., Orasanu, J., Calderwood, R., Zsambok, C.E.: Decision making in action: Models and methods. Ablex Publishing (1993)
14. Kohavi, R., Provost, F.: On Applied Research in Machine Learning. Applications of Machine Learning and the Knowledge Discovery Process 30(2), 127–132 (1998)
15. Kueng, P., Kawalek, P.: Goal-Based Business Process Models: Creation and Evaluation. Journal of Business Process Management 3(1), 17–38 (1997)

16. Lacey, N., Hexmoor, H., Beavers, G.: Planning at the intention level. In: FLAIRS 2002, pp. 8–12. AAAI Press (2002)
17. van Lamsweerde, A., Letier, E.: From object orientation to goal orientation: A paradigm shift for requirements engineering. In: Wirsing, M., Knapp, A., Balsamo, S. (eds.) RISSEF 2002. LNCS, vol. 2941, pp. 325–340. Springer, Heidelberg (2004)
18. Lee, J., Kim, H., Seo, W., Kim, K., Kim, C.H.: Condition-based process patterns for modeling of human processes in Knowledge-intensive Business Services. Journal of Expert Systems with Applications 38, 4025–4038 (2011)
19. MacKay, D.J.C.: Information Theory, Inference and Learning Algorithms. Cambridge University Press (2003)
20. de Medeiros, A.K.A., Pedrinaci, C., van der Aalst, W.M.P., Domingue, J., Song, M., Rozinat, A., Norton, B., Cabral, L.: An Outlook on Semantic Business Process Mining and Monitoring. In: Meersman, R., Tari, Z. (eds.) OTM-WS 2007, Part II. LNCS, vol. 4806, pp. 1244–1255. Springer, Heidelberg (2007)
21. Murphy, K.: Dynamic Bayesian Networks: Representation, Inference and Learning. UC Berkeley, Computer Science Division (2002)
22. Petrusel, R., Stanciu, P.L.: Making Recommendations for Decision Processes Based on Aggregated Decision Data Models. In: Abramowicz, W., Kriksciuniene, D., Sakalauskas, V. (eds.) BIS 2012. LNBIP, vol. 117, pp. 272–283. Springer, Heidelberg (2012)
23. Reichert, M., Weber, B.: Enabling Flexibility in Process-Aware Information Systems - Challenges, Methods, Technologies. Springer (2012)
24. Rokach, L.: A survey of Clustering Algorithms. In: Data Mining and Knowledge Discovery Handbook, pp. 269–298 (2010)
25. Rolland, C., Prakash, N., Benjamen, A.: A Multi-Model View of Process Modelling. Journal of Requirements Engineering 4(1), 169–187 (1999)
26. Schonenberg, H., Weber, B., van Dongen, B.F., van der Aalst, W.M.P.: Supporting flexible processes through recommendations based on history. In: Dumas, M., Reichert, M., Shan, M.-C. (eds.) BPM 2008. LNCS, vol. 5240, pp. 51–66. Springer, Heidelberg (2008)
27. Song, I., Diederich, J.: Intention extraction from text messages. In: Brauer, W. (ed.) GI 1973. LNCS, vol. 1, pp. 330–337. Springer, Heidelberg (1973)
28. Wiig, K.M.: Case Study Research: Design and Methods. Journal of Knowledge Management 1(1), 6–14 (1997)
29. Xu, L., Brinkkemper, S.: Concepts of Product Software. European Journal of Information Systems 16(5), 531–541 (2007)
30. Yin, R.K.: Case Study Research: Design and Methods. Sage Publications (2009)
31. Yu, E.S.K.: Towards modelling and reasoning support for early-phase requirements engineering. In: IEEE Int. Symp. on Requirements Engineering, pp. 226–235. IEEE (1997)

Using Reference Domain Ontologies to Define the Real-World Semantics of Domain-Specific Languages

Victorio A. de Carvalho[1,2], João Paulo A. Almeida[1], and Giancarlo Guizzardi[1]

[1] Ontology & Conceptual Modeling Research Group (NEMO)
Federal University of Espírito Santo (UFES), Vitória, ES, Brazil
[2] Research Group in Applied Informatics, Informatics Department,
Federal Institute of Espírito Santo (IFES), Colatina, ES, Brazil
{Victorio,gguizzardi}@ifes.edu.br, jpalmeida@ieee.org

Abstract. This paper proposes a principled approach to the definition of real-world semantics for declarative domain-specific languages. The approach is based on: (i) the explicit representation of the admissible states of the world through a reference domain ontology (which serves as semantic foundation for the domain-specific language), (ii) a representation of the valid expressions of a domain-specific language (to determine the abstract syntax of the language), and (iii) the rigorous definition of the relation between the abstract syntax and the reference domain ontology (to define the real-world semantics of the language). These three elements of the approach are axiomatized in three corresponding logic theories, enabling a systematic treatment of real-world semantics, including formal tooling to support language design and assessment.

Keywords: Ontology, Metamodel, Domain-Specific Language, Semantics.

1   Introduction

Conceptual modeling is generally considered a fundamental activity in information systems engineering [1], and comprises the use of diagrammatic languages for communication, understanding and problem solving regarding a universe of discourse. The effectiveness of a conceptual modeling language to support the aforementioned tasks is strongly related to the language's *domain appropriateness*, i.e., to the language's ability to express the relevant characteristics of the domain at hand, as discussed by a number of authors [2, 3].

A language designer must, therefore, understand the phenomena (or domain) that should be covered by the language and propose symbolic structures that will empower prospective language users to efficiently carry out certain tasks concerning the represented phenomena.

This requires the design of a language with some form of 'correspondence between its constructs and things in the external world' [4]. We call such a correspondence *real-world semantics*, following [5]. Consider for example a domain-specific language to describe genealogical relations. A real-world semantics for this language would provide meaning for the various language constructs in terms of parenthood or

M. Jarke et al. (Eds.): CAiSE 2014, LNCS 8484, pp. 488–502, 2014.

ancestry relations between persons, thereby enabling its expressions (or models) to be used as a vehicle to talk about parenthood or ancestry between persons of interest.

Although essential to language design and semantic interoperability tasks, the *real-world semantics* is often defined only informally for modeling languages. As a consequence, no systematic treatment of real-world semantics is possible, and the designer must face semantic issues with little methodological support. In this paper, we address this gap by proposing a principled approach to real-world semantics definition for declarative domain-specific languages. This approach is based on: (i) the explicit representation of the admissible states of the world through a reference domain ontology (which serves as semantic foundation for the domain-specific language), (ii) a representation of the valid expressions of a domain-specific language (to determine the abstract syntax of the language), and (iii) the rigorous definition of the relation between the abstract syntax and the reference domain ontology (to define the real-world semantics of the language). These three elements are axiomatized in three corresponding logic theories, enabling a systematic treatment of real-world semantics, including formal tooling to support language design and assessment.

From the methodological perspective, the approach promotes the separation of concerns enabling designers to handle semantic issues separately from other language design concerns. By defining the semantics of a language in terms of a reference domain ontology, the language designers explicitly account for the language's ability to represent domain features truthfully [6].

Although some of us have defended in [6] that the abstract syntax of a language should ideally be isomorphic to an ontology underlying the language, this would only apply to a particular kind of (ideal) language intended to represent complete knowledge about a domain. This is not always feasible or desirable due to pragmatic and language design issues. Thus, in this paper we relax the stringent isomorphism requirement, supporting thus a more flexible relation between language metamodels and reference ontologies.

The remainder of the paper is structured as follows: section 2 discusses the notion of reference domain ontology contrasting it with the notion of language metamodels; section 3 discusses our approach to define real-world semantics for domain-specific languages; section 4 introduces our running example, defining a reference domain ontology for genealogy; section 5 defines the syntax of a domain-specific language to capture genealogy trees, specifying a semantics for this DSL based on the ontology described earlier; section 6 shows the use of formal tools to analyze the language in the light of some properties defined in our approach; section 7 presents some additional reflections on ontologies, metamodels and the real-world semantics definition; section 8 discusses related work and section 9 presents conclusions and future work.

2   Reference Domain Ontologies and Language Metamodels

An ontology can be defined as a set of entities acknowledged by a theory or system of thought [7]. In the original definition of formal ontology in philosophy, the "set of entities" in question refer to domain-independent categories such as object, quality, relation, event, type, situation, among others. In a modern jargon, these are termed

Foundational Ontologies [8, 9]. In contrast, in computer science (in a tradition which can be traced back to Hayes' seminal paper [10]), ontologies are specifications, i.e., particular engineering artifacts meant to represent "sets of entities" of a different nature, namely, those entities whose existence is countenanced by a *conceptualization* of a particular area of application or knowledge (e.g., law, cell biology, chemistry, software engineering). These are termed *domain ontologies* [8].

In the past 15 years, an increasingly large number of domain ontologies have been constructed in a number of domains. As discussed in depth in [6], domain ontologies can play an important role in the evaluation, (re)design and interoperability of domain-specific conceptual modeling languages informing the axiomatisation for their abstract syntax and formal semantics and guiding the design of pragmatically more efficient systems of visual concrete syntax. However, in order to play this role, these ontologies must be constructed as *reference ontologies*, i.e., they must be constructed with the sole objective of making the best possible description of a certain domain or portion of reality, capturing a shared conceptualization of that specific domain. In particular, these ontologies should be able to formally characterize the exact world states which are deemed admissible by that conceptualization[1]. Furthermore, as the author demonstrates in [6], in order to systematically achieve this desiderata, domain ontologies should be constructed with the support of a proper foundational ontology. In this sense, a foundational ontology, determines all possible world states according to fundamental ontological commitments (relating to notions of space, time, object, event, action, etc.). A domain ontology aligned with a foundational ontology, defines a subset of these states selecting only those admissible in a specific domain, as shown in Fig. 1 (for a foundational ontology and two overlapping domain ontologies).

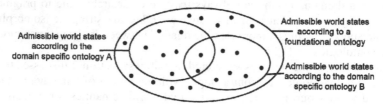

Fig. 1. Sets of admissible world states according to different domain ontologies

Language metamodels are often captured in frame-based languages (such as UML, MOF, Ecore) and enriched with additional constraints in order to define syntactic rules of the language that cannot be captured directly in the frame-based language. Examples of language used to define such syntactic constraints include OCL and first-order logic. In the remainder of this paper, we use the term "abstract syntax" referring to the syntactic rules implicit in the metamodel as well as those additional constraints.

Fig. 2 illustrates the role of a language's abstract syntax. It defines the set of syntactically valid models of a language, as a subset of all possible models that can be instantiated from metamodels expressible in a given language (such as, e.g., Ecore).

---

[1] A further analysis of the relation between ontologies and conceptualizations is outside the scope of this paper. We refer the reader to [**Error! Reference source not found.**], which accounts for this relation.

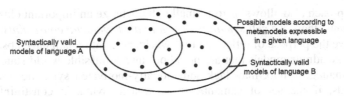

Fig. 2. Sets of language expressions according to different metamodels

Note that Fig. 1 and Fig. 2 are analogous with the important difference that, while Fig. 1 concerns states of the world deemed admissible by reference domain ontologies, Fig. 2 concerns symbolic expressions deemed syntactically valid in domain-specific languages. In our approach, we represent both reference domain ontologies and a language's abstract syntax through logic theories. Although represented in a similar fashion, the logic theories have clear and distinct roles. A reference domain ontology should aim solely at describing phenomena of reality representing a certain conceptualization and is not influenced by language design issues. The logic theory that captures a reference ontology quantifies over real-world entities. In contrast, a metamodel (and additional constraints) should define a language syntax capable of meeting information demands about phenomena of reality for some specific task. Thus, it quantifies over symbolic expressions (instead of real-world entities).

3   An Approach for Real-World Semantics Definition

In order to provide real-world semantics for a domain-specific language, we relate the valid models of the language to corresponding world states that are deemed admissible by a reference domain ontology. Since both language syntax and reference domain ontologies are axiomatized into logic theories, that task can be accomplished with a third logic theory that quantifies over symbolic expressions and world states at the same time. The resulting relation is depicted schematically in Fig. 3.

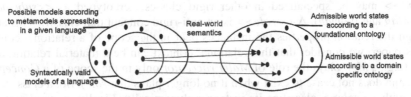

Fig. 3. Real-world semantics definition

By formalizing the correspondence between language models and world states, we can characterize an important property of a language: we say that a *language has a well-defined real-world semantics according to a reference ontology* iff each of its (syntactically-correct) models is about (at least one) admissible world according to the ontology. A language that fails to have this property is one that allows the definition of meaningless models, i.e., models with no correspondence to the phenomena they intend to represent. We consider it thus a minimum semantic requirement[2].

---

[2] The choice of reference domain ontology is clearly important in this process. This is discussed in section 7.

This approach also allows us to formally characterize an important class of syntactic constraints, those we call *semantically-motivated syntactic constraints*. These constraints have the purpose of reflecting real-world rules into a language abstract syntax. If a language admits models that are not about any admissible world state, it suggests that the language syntax may lack semantically-motivated syntactic constraints. In other words, if the set of semantically-motivated syntactic constraints is strong enough, the language can be said to have a well-defined real-world semantics. Conversely, if we suppose that a language has a well-defined real-world semantics, then all its semantically-motivated syntactic constraints should be entailed by the remainder of the unified theory, i.e. by the semantic mapping axioms in tandem with the ontology axioms. This means that the ontology axioms may be used to shape the definition of the language, in particular, helping in abstract syntax definition.

To illustrate the approach and its implications, we present an example to show how the three logic theories are combined to accomplish real-world semantic definition. We show the use of the Alloy formal method [11] to guarantee that the unified theory is consistent and to identify which syntactic constraints are semantically-motivated.

4   A Reference Domain Ontology in Genealogy

This section presents an ontology in the genealogy domain which will be used later to define the semantics of a domain-specific language. Our approach to present this ontology is to illustrate it with an OntoUML diagram [8], and then present the axioms that are not implied by this diagram.

OntoUML specializes the UML class diagram by differentiating various categories of classes according to taxonomy of types in the Unified Foundational Ontology (UFO) [8]. In an OntoUML diagram some ontological distinctions of UFO are represented as stereotypes. A class with a <<*kind*>> stereotype applies necessarily to its instances (e.g., instances of *Person* cannot cease to be so without ceasing to exist) and provides a uniform principle of identity for them. A class stereotyped as <<*kind*>> may be specialized in other rigid classes stereotyped as <<*subkind*>> (e.g., *Man* and *Woman*). A <<*role*>> is an anti-rigid concept that classifies instances through the relation properties the instances bear in the scope of a relational context. In this paper, we consider that this relational context can be a material relation or an event (e.g., a *Man* plays the role of *MaleProcreator* only in the scope of a *Conception* event, and does not cease to exist when it no longer plays that *role*). So, a class stereotyped with <<*role*>> classifies its instances dynamically. Finally, a <<*phase*>> is an anti-rigid concept that defines a partition of a <<*kind*>> depending on one or more of its intrinsic properties (e.g., a *Person* can be said to be in either of the two *phases*: *LivingPerson* or *DeceasedPerson*). Fig. 4 depicts the OntoUML diagram that illustrates the main concepts of the ontology.

The proposed domain reference ontology defines that the (biological) ancestry relationships are derived from *Conception* events. It is based on the stance that human beings are products of instantaneous *Conception* events, which occur when a human male sperm unites with a human female oocyte egg. Thus, each human being (*Person*) is the product of a *Conception* event. For the sake of simplicity, we consider that, in the case of identical multiple siblings, several *Conceptions* occur at the same time boundary. In addition to the *Person* who plays the role of *Offspring* (the product of the *Conception*) two other *Persons* participate in a *Conception* event, namely: *(i)* a *Man*, playing the role of *MaleProcreator* and *(ii)* a *Woman* on the role of *FemaleProcreator*. We assume that the product of the *Conception* event is considered a *LivingPerson* (i.e., a fetus is a living person even before its birth). On the other hand, both *LivingPersons* and *DeceasedPersons* may participate in a *Conception* as procreators (i.e., the ontology considers the possibility of artificial insemination).

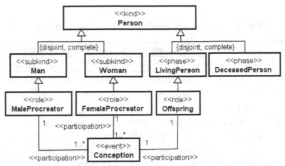

Fig. 4. A domain ontology about genealogy in OntoUML

We formalize the ontology as a theory in many-sorted first-order logic, quantifying over possible states of the world and entities that may exist (objects) or occur (events). Thus, we assume two disjoint sets of entities: a set W of worlds and a set U of entities that are typed by the classes present in the OntoUML diagram. In order to represent the dynamic of the change in world states, we use a predicate $next(w_1,w_2)$ which holds between a world w_1 and all the world states that follow it in time. We consider *next* represents an asymmetric, irreflexive, transitive and completely ordered relation (i.e. a strict total order relation) between worlds. We further assume: (i) A binary predicate for each *kind, subkind* and *phase* from the OntoUML diagram, namely, *Person(w,p)*, *Man(w,p)*, *Woman(w,p)*, *LivingPerson(w,p)* and *DeceasedPerson(w,p)* (e.g. *Person(w,p)* holds if an entity p is an instance of *Person* and exists in a world w); (ii) A binary predicate representing the *Conception* event (e.g. *Conception(w,c)* holds if c is an occurrence of *Conception* that happens in the time boundary of a world w), and; (iii) A ternary predicate for each *Role* from the OntoUML diagram, namely, *isMaleProcreator(w,c,p)*, *isFemaleProcreator(w,c,p)* and *isOffspring(w,c,p)* (e.g. *isOffspring (w,c,p)* holds if an entity p is an instance of *Person* and an entity c is an instance of *Conception*, the person p plays the role of *Offspring* in the context of the *Conception* c and both, c and p, exist in a world w).

For the sake of brevity, the axioms implied by the OntoUML diagram (classes' rigidity, lower and upper bound for cardinality constraints, specialization relations) are omitted. Those not expressed by the OntoUML diagram are presented in Table 1.

Axioms A1 and A2 determines that every *Person* must play the role of *Offspring* of one *Conception* event in which two other *Persons* play the role of *Procreators,* except for the case of the first *Persons* considered to exist (the "original" persons). We assume that these *Persons* come into existence in the same world. The origin of these *Persons* is outside the scope of this ontology (as it is neutral with respect to accounts of the origin of humans such as biological evolution, theological creation).

Axioms A6 and A7 state that the *Man* and the *Woman* who play the roles of procreators in a *Conception* event are considered, respectively, the *father* and the *mother* of the person who plays the role of *Offspring* in such event. Thus, we can infer that every "non-original" *Person* has exactly one father and exactly one mother. Axiom A9 defines the ancestry relationship based on the parenthood relation (defined in A8). Thus, the ontology defined here precisely defines the ancestry relationships explaining the concepts of *parent* and *ancestor* in terms of the concept of *Conception* event.

Table 1. Axioms not implied by the OntoUML diagram

A1	A *Person* who plays the role of *Offspring* in a world does not exist in previous worlds.
	$\forall w{:}W,\ \forall p,c{:}U\ (isOffspring(w, c, p) \rightarrow \neg \exists w'{:}W(next(w', w) \wedge Person(w', p)))$
A2	If a *Person* exists in a world w and it does not exist in any world previous to w then this *Person* plays the role of *Offspring* in w or he/she is an "original" person(i.e., there are no persons in worlds previous to w).
	$\forall w,w'{:}W,\ \forall p{:}U\ ((next(w', w) \wedge Person(w,p) \wedge\ \neg Person(w', p)) \rightarrow$ $\quad (\exists c{:}U\ (isOffspring(w, c, p)) \vee \neg \exists p'{:}U\ (Person(w', p'))))$
A3	Once a *Person* exists in a world w, it will exist in all worlds subsequent to w.
	$\forall w,w'\ {:}W,\ \forall p{:}U(((Person(w, p) \wedge next(w, w')) \rightarrow Person(w', p))$
A4	A *Person* cannot simultaneously play the roles of *Procreator* and *Offspring*.
	$\forall w{:}W,\ \forall c,p{:}U\ (isOffspring(w, c, p) \rightarrow$ $\quad \neg \exists c'{:}U\ (isFemaleProcreator(w, c', p) \vee isMaleProcreator(w, c', p)))$
A5	A *LivingPerson* eventually becomes a *DeceasedPerson*.
	$\forall w{:}W,\ \forall p{:}U\ (LivingPerson(w, p) \rightarrow \exists w'{:}W(next(w, w') \wedge DeceasedPerson(w', p)))$
A6	If a person is a *DeceasedPerson* in a world it remains a *DeceasedPerson* in all subsequent worlds.
	$\forall w,\ w'{:}W,\ \forall p{:}U\ ((DeceasedPerson(w, p) \wedge next(w, w')) \rightarrow DeceasedPerson(w', p))$
A7	The father of a person *y* is the person *x* who played the role of *MaleProcreator* in the *Conception* in which *y* played the role of *OffSpring*.
	$\forall w{:}W,\ \forall x,y{:}U\ (FatherOf(w, x, y) \leftrightarrow \exists w'{:}W, \exists c{:}U(((w'{=}w) \vee next(w', w)\ ) \wedge$ $\quad isOffspring(w', c, y) \wedge isMaleProcreator(w', c, x)))$
A8	The mother of a person *y* is the person *x* who played the role of *FemaleProcreator* in the *Conception* in which *y* played the role of *OffSpring*.
	$\forall w{:}W,\ \forall x,y{:}U\ (MotherOf(w, x, y) \leftrightarrow \exists w'{:}W, \exists c{:}U(((w'{=}w) \vee next(w', w)) \wedge$ $\quad isOffspring\ (w', c, y) \wedge isFemaleProcreator(w', c, x)))$
A9	A person *x* is a parent of a person *y* iff *x* is *y's* father or mother
	$\forall w{:}W,\ \forall x,y{:}U\ (ParentOf(w, x, y) \leftrightarrow(FatherOf(w, x, y) \vee MotherOf(w, x, y)))$
A10	A person *x* is ancestor of a person *y* iff *x* is parent of *y* or *x is* ancestor of *y's* parent.
	$\forall w{:}W,\ \forall x,y{:}U\ (AncestorOf(w, x, y) \leftrightarrow$ $\quad ParentOf(w, x, y) \vee(\exists z{:}U(ParentOf(w, z, y) \wedge AncestorOf(w, x, z)))$

5   A DSL to Represent Genealogy Trees – Syntax and Semantics

In this section, we define the abstract syntax of a DSL for describing genealogy trees, and later we define the semantics for this language in terms of the genealogy ontology presented in the previous section.

5.1   Abstract Syntax Definition

Considering that a genealogy tree aims to map the ancestry of a given person, a DSL for representing genealogy trees must provide constructs to represent persons and to represent parenthood. Fig. 5 depicts the metamodel of such a DSL represented in Ecore. From now on we will refer to this language as *DSL1*. The names of metamodel elements are prefixed with "M" to avoid confusion with the ontology concepts.

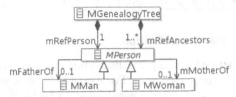

Fig. 5. A metamodel for representing genealogical trees (*DSL1*)

In the depicted metamodel, the *MGenealogyTree* class represents the genealogy tree itself. An *MGenealogyTree* is composed by instances of *MPerson*. The *MPerson* construct represents persons in a genealogy tree. The *MPersons* that compose a *MGenealogyTree* are divided into two groups according to their role in the tree: (i) one *MPerson*, identified by the *mRefPerson* association, represents the person whose ancestry is modeled by the tree, called the reference person of the tree; (ii) the other *MPersons* that composes the tree are referenced by the *mRefAncestors* association and represent the ancestors of the reference person. An *MPerson* may be associated with one *MMan* through an *mFatherOf* relation. In turn, an *mMotherOf* relation may be used to associate an *MPerson* with an *MWoman*. The *mFatherOf* and the *mMotherOf* constructs represent the parenthood relationships between the represented persons.

We define the language's abstract syntax with a theory in many-sorted first-order logic, quantifying over well-formed instances of the metamodel and over all possible instances of the language constructs. Thus, we assume two disjoint sets of symbolic entities: a set M of well-formed models (instances of the top-level container *MGenealogyTree*), and a set P of instances of *MMan* and *MWoman*. We further assume: (i) Binary predicates to represent the *mRefPerson* and the *mRefAncestors* containment relations, namely *mRefPerson(m,p)* and *mRefAncestor(m,p)* (e.g. *mRefPerson(m,p)* holds if an entity *p* is the reference person of a model *m*); (ii) Binary predicates to represent the constructs *MMan* and *MWoman*, namely *MMan(m,p)* and *MWoman(m,p)* (e.g. *MMan(m,p)* holds if an entity *p* is an instance of *MMan* and is part of a model *m*), and; (iii) Ternary predicates to represent *mFatherOf* and *MMotherOf* relations, namely *MFatherOf(m,a,b)* and *MMotherOf(m,a,b)* (e.g. *MFatherOf(m,a,b)* holds if, in a model m∈M, an instance *a* of *MMan* is associated to an *MPerson b* through a *mFatherOf* relation). For the sake of brevity, we omit here syntactic constraints that are implied by the metamodel (cardinality constraints, specialization relations).

The syntactic constraints not implied by the metamodel are shown in Table 2. The constraint C1 is a helper defining the *MAncestorOf* relation deriving it from *MFatherOf* and *MMotherOf* relations. The C2 constraint guarantees that a genealogy tree is all connected. C3 ensures that there are no ancestry cycles in a tree. Finally, C4 defines that the father and the mother of the *MRefPerson* must be represented.

Table 2. Syntactic constraints for *DSL1* (not implied by the metamodel)

C1	∀m:M, ∀a,b:P (MAncestorOf(m, a, b) ↔ MFatherOf(m, a, b) ∨ MMotherOf(m, a, b) ∨ ∃c:P((MFatherOf(m, c, b) ∨ MMotherOf(m, c, b)) ∧ MAncestorOf(m, a, c))
C2	∀m:M, ∀a,b:P ((MRefPerson(m, a) ∧ MRefAncestor(m, b)) → MAncestorOf(m, b, a))
C3	∀m:M, ∀a,b,c:P (MAncestorOf(m, a, b) → ¬ MAncestorOf(m, b, a))
C4	∀m:M, ∀a:P (MRefPerson(m, a) →∃b,c:P (MFatherOf(m, b, a) ∧ MMotherOf(m, c, a))

5.2   Real-World Semantics Definition

The syntax we have defined in the previous section is silent with respect to the various semantic issues for genealogy trees. For example, it does not define whether the language represents biological or legal parenthood (or both), if an (unborn) fetus may be represented in a model as a person, if a deceased person may be represented. These issues are the object of the language's real-world semantics, which we will define here as a logic theory binding the reference ontology and the abstract syntax.

Considering that a *DSL1* model aims to represent information about a set of admissible world states according to the genealogy ontology, the predicate *isAbout(m,w)* relates a model *m* in *DSL1* to an admissible world according to the ontology. When a model *m* represents information about a world *w*, the model elements may denote elements that exist in the world states. Thus, to represent the relation between an instance of a language construct and an instance of a real-world entity we define the predicate *refersTo(e,u)* that holds if an instance of a syntactic element *e* ∈ P refers to an instance of real-world entity *u* ∈ U. Table 3 shows the axioms that formalize the definition of the predicate *isAbout*, thereby characterizing the real-world semantic definition formally.

Table 3. Defining Real-World Semantics for *DSL1*

S1	∀m:M, ∀w:W (isAbout(m, w) → ∀a:P (MMan(m, a) → ∃!x:U(Man(w, x) ∧ refersTo(a, x))))
S2	∀m:M, ∀w:W (isAbout(m, w) → ∀a:P (MWoman(m, a) → ∃!x:U(Woman(w, x) ∧ refersTo(a, x))))
S3	∀m:M, ∀w:W (isAbout(m, w) → ∀a,b:P(MFatherOf (m,a,b) →∃!x,y:U (FatherOf(x,y) ∧ refersTo(a,x) ∧ refersTo(b,y))))
S4	∀m:M, ∀w:W (isAbout(m,w) → ∀a,b:P(MMotherOf (m,a,b) →∃!x,y:U (MotherOf(x,y) ∧ refersTo(a,x) ∧ refersTo(b,y))))
S5	∀m:M, ∀w:W((∀a:P (MMan(m,a) → ∃!x:U(Man(w,x) ∧ refersTo(a,x))) ∧ ∀a:P (MWoman(m,a) → ∃!x:U(Woman(w,x) ∧ refersTo(a,x)))∧ ∀a,b:P(MFatherOf (m,a,b) →∃!x,y:U (FatherOf(x,y) ∧ refersTo(a,x) ∧ refersTo(b,y))) ∧ ∀a,b:P(MMotherOf (m,a,b) →∃!x,y:U (MotherOf(x,y) ∧ refersTo(a,x) ∧ refersTo(b,y)))) → isAbout(m,w))

S1 relates the *MMan* construct to the ontology concept of *Man*, defining that if we have a model *m* which aims to describe a portion of a world *w* and there is in such model an instance *a* of the *MMan* construct then *a* must refer to a *Man x* which exists in *w*. S2 is similar to S1 dealing with the relation between the *MWoman* construct and the concept of *Woman*. S3 states that if, in a model *m*, there is a *MFatherOf* relation between an instance *a* of *MMan* and an instance *b* of *MPerson*, then there must be, in the world *w*, a *FatherOf* relation between the *Man x* referred by *a* and the *Person y* referred by *b*. S4 places a similar statement on the relation between *MMotherOf* and *MotherOf*. Thus, S1-S4 define necessary conditions to predicate that a model *m* in *DSL1* is about a world *w*.

S5 states that if all *MMan* constructs that exist in *m* refers to instances of *Man* that exist in *w*, all *MWoman* constructs that exist in *m* refers to instances of *Woman* that exist in *w*, all *mFatherOf* relations that exist in the *m* refers to instances of *FatherOf* relations that exist in *w*, and all *mMotherOf* relations that exist in the *m* refers to instances of *MotherOfRelation* that exist in *w*, then the model *m* *isAbout* the world *w*. Thus, S5 defines the sufficient conditions to predicate that a model *m* in *DSL1* is about a world *w*.

6   Language Analysis

We have used Alloy to analyze some properties of *DSL1*. Alloy is a structural modeling language based on first-order logic [11]. A software framework named Alloy Analyzer supports model simulation and consistency checking assuming the *small scope hypothesis* in order to ensure tractability [11].

To enable the analysis, we have represented the three logic theories in three Alloy modules. The module corresponding to the genealogy ontology was derived automatically using the transformation from OntoUML to Alloy [12]. The module corresponding the *DSL1* metamodel (presented in Fig. 5) was derived following the systematic patterns defined in [13]. In this way, we have ensured the correspondence between the Alloy specifications and the models presented in Figures 4 and 5. The module representing the real-world semantics definition refers to the two previous modules, allowing us to verify that the combined specification is consistent.

In order to automatically verify which of the syntactic constraints are semantically-motivated, we have added the assumption that for every model *m* there is at least one world *w* such that *isAbout(m,w)* holds, i.e. we have assumed that the language has a *well-defined real-world semantics*. Then, we have verified each syntactic constraint as an assertion. When no counter-example is found, the Alloy Analyzer guarantees that, within a bounded scope, the assertion (in this case the tested syntactic constraint) is entailed by the remainder of the specification (in this case the semantic axioms in tandem with the ontology axioms). Thus, we can conclude the tested syntactic constraint is *semantically-motivated*.

Using this method, we have found that the syntactic constraint C3 (Table 2) is *semantically-motivated*. In fact, C3 reflects, in *DSL1* abstract syntax, the rule that ancestry cycles are not allowed by the ontology. Note that, assuming that for every model *m* there is at least one world *w* such that *isAbout(m,w)* holds, C3 is entailed by the ontological axioms A1, A2, A4, A7, A8, A9 and A10 in tandem with the semantic axioms S3 and S4. Thus, considering the abstract syntax in isolation, if C3 were missing there would be syntactically valid expressions of *DSL1* with no semantics.

Applying the same method, we have concluded that the syntactic constraints C2 and C4 are not *semantically-motivated*. Indeed, they are concerned with representation characteristics of genealogy trees and are not necessitated by the ontology (C2 guarantees that a genealogy tree is all connected and C4 defines the father and the mother of the *mRefPerson* must be represented). Consequently, the syntactic constructs *mRefPerson* and *mRefAncestors,* used in those constraints, are not mapped into ontological concepts by the *DSL1* real-world semantics definition. Another consequence is that these two constraints can be omitted and/or altered without affecting the *DSL1* real-world semantics as long the resulting theory is still consistent. This again can be checked automatically.

The minimum and maximum cardinality constraints of the *mFatherOf* and the *mMotherOf* relations were also analyzed (both are defined with 0..1 multiplicity on the metamodel). The analysis reveals that the maximum cardinality constraint is *semantically-motivated*. This is because the maximum cardinality constraint reflects the ontological rule that every *Person* has at most one father and one mother. The analysis also reveals that the minimum cardinality constraint is not semantically-motivated. This reflects a choice of the designer of *DSL1* to allow models in which a person is represented omitting her father and/or mother. The ontology, in turn, states that all *Persons* must have exactly one father and one mother (with the exception of the "original persons" which do not have parents).

This divergence between the ontological rules and syntactic constraints is a consequence of the fact that the language allows incomplete models with respect to the world states. In the genealogy case, it is reasonable to imagine that no one has information about all his ancestors. On the other hand, the ontology ought to describe a conceptualization of the reality and shall not be influenced by pragmatic issues, as the need to foresee a lack of information. It is worth noticing that this difference on constraints does not lead to inconsistencies on the *DSL1* semantics definition using the referred domain ontology. According to the semantic axiom S1, every *MMan* in a model must refer to a *Man* that exists in the worlds described by that model. So, if a model in *DSL1* presents an instance *m* of *MMan* with no *mFatherOf* association we can infer that the *Man* referred to by *m* has a *Father* which is not represented in the model or he is an "original" *Person*. No syntactic or semantic inconsistences arise.

7   Discussion

Our running example illustrates how the different purposes of reference domain ontology and language metamodel affect their definition. On the one hand, the domain ontology accounts for the parenthood and ancestry relationships in terms of participations in *Conception* events. On the other hand, since the language only aims at *representing* the parenthood relationship (instead of aiming at *grounding* the concept of parenthood), the *DSL1* metamodel represents the concepts of *MotherOf* and *FatherOf* as primitive syntactic constructs, not including constructs to represent *Conception* events. In this example we can observe that, the real-world semantics definition explicitly settles that *MotherOf* and *FatherOf* represent the biological notions of parenthood (as grounded on *Conception* events). This is of course a particular worldview or conceptualization (or to be more precise, a particular ontological commitment) which is reflected by the ontology.

Furthermore, considering that it is assumed here unnecessary to know if a person is alive or not in the context of a genealogy tree specified in *DSL1* and aiming to reduce the language complexity (another example of pragmatic issue that may influence DSL metamodels) the concepts of *LivingPerson* and *DeceasedPerson* have no counterpart in the language metamodel. Thus, the approach of using a domain ontology to define the language semantics allowed us to clearly specify the worldview underlying the language without creating a counterpart construct for each real-world concept.

We should finally note that, when selecting a domain reference ontology to define the semantics of a language one must carefully analyze the suitability of assuming the underlying conceptualization as provider of the language real-world semantics. According to our ontology, a person exists as a result of the *Conception* event in which it plays the role of *Offspring*. So, even a fetus is considered a person. Since we have used this ontology as a basis to define *DSL1's* real-world semantics, this has the consequence that fetuses may appear in a genealogy tree. If this is considered undesirable by language designers, a domain ontology that would provide a distinction between a fetus and a person who is already born would be required. (This could possibly be a refinement of the ontology used in this paper).

8   Related Work

Our investigation was initially motivated by the apparent confusion involving the relation between ontologies and language metamodels in the literature. Some authors (e.g. [14]) posit that the origin of this confusion may be the fact that both are often depicted with the same or similar languages, such as variants of frame-based languages (of which UML in an example). There are many works in the literature (e.g. [6], [15], [16]) that point to similarities and differences between these two concepts and explore their relations. It is worth to note that various authors propose different criteria to distinguish ontology from metamodel, which indicates that this is still an open issue in the literature.

For example, Bezivin et al. [17] and Atkinson [18] suggest that the distinction between ontologies and model engineering artefacts (such as metamodels) is primarily a matter of technical space. As we have shown here, ontologies and metamodels play clear distinct roles in language engineering. Thus, while they can be harmonized into the same overall framework eliminating accidental differences from technical spaces (as we have done here with axiomatic logic theories) they serve different yet complementary purposes.

The integration of modeling languages is the focus of [16]. The authors argue that most existing integration approaches are metamodel-based, and that they face some difficulties because (domain) "concepts can be hidden in a metamodel". Then the authors propose a semi-automatic process to refactor metamodels into ontologies to reveal those hidden concepts. The defined patterns are based on the fact that "in a metamodel not necessarily all modeling concepts are represented as first-class citizens". While the presented patterns are shown to be useful, we argue that the semantic issues are more complex than what can be addressed by metamodel refactoring, which does not address explicitly choices concerning the semantics of language elements.

In [15] the authors discuss the use of ontologies, models and metamodels in model-driven engineering (MDE). They present a proposal for the role of ontologies in meta-pyramid of MDA. This proposal argues that role of ontologies is to describe the existing world and the domain of the system while the role of system models is to specify and control the system under study. They allude to a relation between real-world objects and software objects at M0 ("is described by"). However, they position ontologies at M1 and do not elaborate on a possible relation between reference ontologies and language metamodels (at M2). We believe this is an important gap in their ontology-aware meta-pyramid for MDE, which we address in this paper.

The work of Ciocoiu and Nau [19] also consider the problem of providing semantics for declarative languages based on ontologies. Similarly to our approach, they show that information in language expressions may be incomplete or partial, and that a mapping to a domain ontology will reveal assumptions that are implicit in language expressions. Differently from our approach, they focus on language translation, and not on implications for the language engineering effort.

Finally, we believe that the work described in this paper has implications beyond language design and could also be applied to the area of database design. In particular, we believe that the so-called "semantic integrity constraints" in database systems literature is analogous to what we have called semantically-motivated syntactic constraints. According to [20], the purpose of semantic integrity constraint in database systems is "to avoid database states for which no correspondence can exist in the real world". While great importance has been given to the management of "semantic integrity constraints" in database systems, little attention has been devoted to the design and validation of such constraints. It is said intuitively, in the literature, that they reflect the universe of discourse but no guidelines are given on how to discover the necessary constraints or how to control their quality. Thus, the data modeler (not unlike the language designer) must face semantic issues (e.g., the definition of "semantic integrity constraints") with little methodological support. We believe our work has implications to the design of database systems, in that it could account for "semantic integrity constraints" as semantically-motivated syntactic constraints. Given that we could quantify over temporal aspects and histories (instead of world states only) the approach can be extended to cover both the so-called static and dynamic constraints.

9   Conclusions and Future Work

In this paper we have discussed a principled approach to define the real-world semantics for declarative domain-specific languages in terms of a reference domain ontology. We illustrated our approach with a running example, describing a domain ontology and using it to define the real-world semantics of a DSL. It allowed us to show clear examples of how reference ontologies and language metamodels differ.

We have argued for a strict separation of concerns distinguishing the role of reference ontologies and language metamodels, separating syntactic and semantic concerns and then linking them explicitly and precisely. A clear separation of concerns allows us to apply suitable modeling disciplines to each of the tasks at hand: understanding and capturing a domain conceptualization (a concern of ontology engineering) and dealing with abstract syntax design (a concern of language engineering).

Our approach is grounded on the fact that the relation between a language and reality is always mediated by a certain conceptualization [21]. If nothing is said about the conceptualization underlying a language, each language user may interpret a model based on his/her own concepts about reality. Thus, the formal definition of a language real-world semantics is essential to empower language's users to efficiently communicate about reality.

Besides its importance to avoid misunderstandings in a communication process, the explicit real-world semantics representation may bring some additional benefits to language's designers and users: (i) the real-world rules formalized by the ontology inform language design (e.g. guiding the definition of constructs and syntactic constraints); (ii) the explicit real-world semantic definition allows systematic evaluation of truthfulness of a language with respect to a specific domain conceptualization; (iii) reasoning may be used to infer some information not represented (explicitly) in the models using the semantic mapping and the ontological axioms.

Moreover, by formally characterizing the syntactic constraints, ontology axioms and semantic definition, our approach forms a basis for DSL design automation. Leveraging the existing transformations from OntoUML to Alloy, we have shown that it is possible to automatically verify which of the syntactic constraints are semantically-motivated. Without these constraints the language would produce models with no meaning. We believe the formal approach discussed here can be used to support more advanced evaluation of DSL semantics, systematizing the application of the ontological analysis approach discussed in [6]. We also intend to use the presented approach to enable the semantic interoperation of languages in multi-viewpoint modeling. Another challenge is to define a step-by-step ontology-driven DSL design approach. These are topics for further investigation.

Finally, the availability of a reference domain ontology greatly simplifies the task of the language designer. However, we should emphasize that our approach does not presuppose the development of a specific reference ontology with the sole purpose of supporting the design of a particular language. Ideally, the effort invested in the design of a reference ontology should be compensated by its reuse in a number of applications, e.g., the design of several languages, (semantic) language interoperability, database construction and integration, etc. A number of challenges concerning methodological implications of our approach remain open for further investigation, including guidelines for choosing a reference domain ontology suitable to define the real-world semantics of a DSL and guidelines for developing reusable ontologies.

Acknowledgments. This research is funded by the Brazilian Research Funding Agencies CAPES and CNPq (grants number 310634/2011-3, 311578/2011-0 and 485368/2013-7).

References

1. Olivé, A.: Conceptual Modeling of Information Systems. Springer (2007)
2. Weber, R.: Ontological Foundations of Information Systems. Coopers & Lybrand (1997)
3. Grice, H.P.: Logic and conversation. In: Cole, P., Morgan, J. (eds.) Syntax and Semantics, vol. 3, pp. 43–58. Academic Press, New York (1975)
4. Davis, R., Shrobe, H., Szolovits, P.: What is a knowledge representation? AI Magazine, Spring (1993)
5. Sheth, A.P., Kashyap, V.: So far (schematically) yet so near (semantically). In: Proc. of the IFIP WG 2.6 Database Semantics Conference on Interoperable Database Systems (1992)

6. Guizzardi, G.: On ontology, ontologies, conceptualizations, modeling languages, and (meta) models. In: Vasilecas, O., Eder, J., Caplinskas, A. (eds.) Databases and Information Systems IV, pp. 18–39. IOS Press, Amsterdam (2007)
7. Lowe, E.J.: Ontology. In: Honderich, T. (ed.) The Oxford companion to philosophy, p. 670. Oxford University Press (2005)
8. Guizzardi, G.: Ontological Foundations for Structural Conceptual Models. University of Twente, Enschede, The Netherlands (2005)
9. Guarino, N.: Formal ontology and information systems. In: Proceedings of International Conference on Formal Ontology in Information Systems (FOIS), pp. 3–15. IOS Press (1998)
10. Hayes, P.: The Naïve Physics Manifesto. In: Ritchie, D. (ed.) Expert Systems in Microeletronics age, pp. 242–270. Edinburgh University Press (1978)
11. Jackson, D.: Software Abstractions: Logic, Language and Analysis. The MIT Press (2006)
12. Benevides, A.B., Guizzardi, G., Braga, B.F.B., Almeida, J.P.A.: Validating Modal Aspects of OntoUML Conceptual Models Using Automatically Generated Visual World Structures. Journal of Universal Computer Science 16, 2904–2933 (2011)
13. Anastasakis, K., Bordbar, B., Georg, G., Ray, I.: On Challenges of Model Transformation from UML to Alloy. Software & Systems Modeling 9, 69–86 (2010)
14. Ruiz, F., Hilera, J.R.: Using ontologies in software engineering and technology. In: Calero, C., Ruiz, F., Piattini, M. (eds.) Ontologies for Software Engineering and Software Technology, pp. 49–102. Springer, Berlin (2006)
15. Aßmann, U., Zschaler, S., Wagner, G.: Ontologies, meta-models, and the model-driven paradigm. In: Calero, C., Ruiz, F., Piattini, M. (eds.) Ontologies for Software Engineering and Software Technology, pp. 249–273. Springer, Berlin (2006)
16. Kappel, G., Kapsammer, E., Kargl, H., Kramler, G., Reiter, T., Retschitzegger, W., Schwinger, W., Wimmer, M.: Lifting metamodels to ontologies: A step to the semantic integration of modeling languages. In: Wang, J., Whittle, J., Harel, D., Reggio, G. (eds.) MoDELS 2006. LNCS, vol. 4199, pp. 528–542. Springer, Heidelberg (2006)
17. Bézivin, J., et al.: An M3-neutral infrastructure for bridging model engineering and ontology engineering. In: Proc. of the First International Conference on Interoperability of Enterprise Software and Applications, pp. 159–171. Springer (2005)
18. Atkinson, C.: On the unification of MDA and web-based knowledge representation technol-ogies. In: 1st International Workshop on the Model-Driven Semantic Web (2004)
19. Ciocoiu, M., Nau, D.: Ontology-Based Semantics. In: Proceedings of the Seventh International Conference on Principles of Knowledge Representation and Reasoning (2000)
20. Türker, C.: Semantic Integrity Constraints in Federated Database Schemata. Dissertations in Database and Information Systems, vol. 63. Infix-Verlag, Sankt Augustin (1999)
21. Baldinger, K.: Semantic Theory: Towards a Modern Semantics. Palgrave Macmillan (1980)

Dual Deep Instantiation
and Its ConceptBase Implementation

Bernd Neumayr[1], Manfred A. Jeusfeld[2], Michael Schrefl[1],
and Christoph Schütz[1]

[1] Johannes Kepler University Linz, Austria
{neumayr,schrefl,schuetz}@dke.uni-linz.ac.at
[2] University of Skövde, Sweden
manfred.jeusfeld@acm.org

Abstract. Application integration requires the consideration of instance data and schema data. Instance data in one application may be schema data for another application, which gives rise to multiple instantiation levels. Using deep instantiation, an object may be deeply characterized by representing schema data about objects several instantiation levels below. Deep instantiation still demands a clear separation of instantiation levels: the source and target objects of a relationship must be at the same instantiation level. This separation is inadequate in the context of application integration. Dual deep instantiation (DDI), on the other hand, allows for relationships that connect objects at different instantiation levels. The depth of the characterization may be specified separately for each end of the relationship. In this paper, we present and implement set-theoretic predicates and axioms for the representation of conceptual models with DDI.

Keywords: Conceptual Data Modeling, Metamodeling, Deep Characterization, Powertypes.

1   Introduction

Conceptual modeling for application integration and the accompanying data interchange must consider both schema data, such as classes and associations, and instance data, such as objects and links. What is represented as instance data in one application may be represented as schema data in another application. For example, in an application for managing a mobile phone catalog, a class MobilePhone is instantiated by objects representing particular mobile phone models, such as SamsungGS4. In an application for managing an inventory of mobile phones, the same phone model may be represented by a class SamsungGS4 which is instantiated by objects representing individual mobile phones, such as SarahsPhone. In a compact and integrated representation, a single model element, e.g., SamsungGS4, should represent both: an individual object, e.g., the mobile phone model SamsungGS4, and a class, e.g., individual phones of model SamsungGS4.

M. Jarke et al. (Eds.): CAiSE 2014, LNCS 8484, pp. 503–517, 2014.

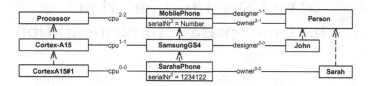

Fig. 1. From Deep Instantiation to Dual Deep Instantiation

Such a *schema/instance duality* is inherent to conceptual models with Deep Instantiation (DI) [4]. DI extends the traditional notion of instantiation with the concept of potency: each attribute of a class may have a potency that specifies at how many instantiation levels below the class the attribute is to be instantiated. For example, in Fig. 1, MobilePhone has an attribute serialNr with a potency of *2* which is to be instantiated by the instantiations, e.g., SarahsPhone, of its instantiations, e.g., SamsungGS4.

A schema/instance duality is also inherent to relationships in conceptual models with DI. For example, a cpu relationship between phone model SamsungGS4 and processor model Cortex-A15 is, first, an instantiation of the cpu relationship between Processor and MobilePhone and, second, acts as schema for relationships between individual phones, such as SarahsPhone, and individual processors of type Cortex-A15.

The flexibility, however, of modeling with DI is restricted by the tenets of *strict metamodeling*: DI only allows relationships between objects at the same level [3–5, 9]. A common problem with strict metamodeling is illustrated by the following situation which cannot be represented. Every instantiation of MobilePhone has a designer being a person. Likewise, every instantiation of an instantiation of MobilePhone, e.g., SarahsPhone, has an owner which is also a person.

Dual Deep Instantiation (DDI) lifts the restrictions of strict metamodeling. DDI, unlike traditional DI, distinguishes between source potency and target potency. DDI relationships may connect objects at different instantiation levels. Every relationship has both a source and target potency to separately indicate the depth of characterization for both sides of the relationship. For example, MobilePhone relates to Person, first, via a relationship owner with a source potency of *2* and a target potency of *1*, and, second, via a relationship designer with a source potency of *1* and a target potency of *1*. Relationship owner is to be instantiated between instantiations of instantiations of MobilePhone, such as SarahsPhone, and instantiations of Person. Relationship designer is to be instantiated between instantiations of MobilePhone, such as SamsungGS4, and instantiations of Person.

This paper introduces a concise set-theoretic formalization of "basic" DDI (Sect. 2). Section 3 extends basic DDI by object specialization resulting in the full axiomatic specification of DDI. The running mobile phone example motivates the constructs throughout sections 2 and 3. The implementation (Sect. 4) shows the satisfiability of the DDI axioms under the Datalog semantics of ConceptBase [12, 14]. We have created a collection of sample DDI models that show the absence of redundancy in the DDI axiom system. The implementation also shows that the consistency checking for DDI models can be automated at run time. Section 5 reviews related work before we conclude with a summary.

2   Basics of Dual Deep Instantiation

We first discuss the setting in which DDI is introduced and then formally describe the modeling primitives of DDI, auxiliary predicates, axioms checking well-formedness of DDI models, and consistent instantiation. Table 1 contains the full DDI specification, which we elaborate in the text by referring to the line numbers (No. 1 – No. 31), with the part relating to specialization (No. 17 – No. 27) being explained in Sect. 3. The formal description is illustrated by a sample DDI model depicted in Fig. 2. We also discuss criticism of the DI approach and relate DI and DDI to modeling using the powertype pattern.

DDI is introduced in a setting that extends the following class-instance model (of the ER model or UML) to arbitrary instantiation levels:

1. Entity sets (classes) are related by binary relationship sets (associations), where one end of the relationship is generally referred to as source and the other end as target role. For conciseness of presentation, we omit role names and depict/denote sources at the left and targets at the right hand side.
2. Entities (instances) of entity sets are related by relationship occurrences (links), whereby a corresponding relationship set must exist between their entity sets, i.e., a relationship set r between two entity-sets x and y acts - considered as function and inverse - as two referential integrity constraint, a domain constraint for the source and a range-constraint for the target.
3. Relationships occurrences (links) and relationship sets (associations) carry a label, which is the same for the relationship occurrence and the relationship set to which it belongs.
4. Values are treated as objects, and consequently, attributes as relationships.

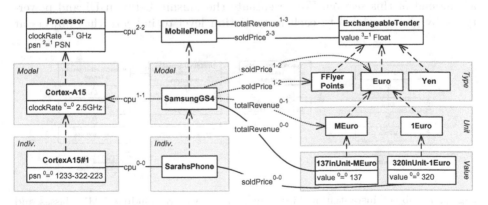

Fig. 2. Modeling a Mobile Phone Catalog and Inventory using DDI

A DDI model contains a set of objects, O (No. 1), which are organized in instantiation hierarchies with an arbitrary number of instantiation levels, where $in(x, y)$ expresses that x is an instantiation of y (No. 5). For sake of the later extension to specialization, we introduce for the time being *member* and *isa* as synonym to *in* (No. 9 and No. 11). Object x is called an n-member of y if x is gained by n times of instantiation from y, or it is a 0-member of y if $x = y$ (No. 10). We synonymously say x is at the n-th instantiation level of y if x is a n-member of y and we say x is a $i..j$-member of y if x is a n-member of y with $i \leq n \leq j$, and x is a *-member of y if x is an n-member of y with an arbitrary n ('x is a *-member of y' is equivalent to $isa^*(x, y)$).

Objects in DDI combine aspects of classes and of instances. An object acts as hook for the definition of instance data and schema data about objects in the instantiation subtree rooted in the object, tying together descriptions about objects at different instantiation levels. Objects further down in the instantiation tree instantiate and specialize these data. In this regard, instantiation hierarchies combine aspects of classification hierarchies and of generalization hierarchies.

Example 1 (Objects). Object SarahsPhone (see Fig. 2) is an instantiation of SamsungGS4 which is an instantiation of MobilePhone. SamsungGS4 is at the first instantiation level (is a 1-member) of MobilePhone and SarahsPhone is at the second instantiation level (is a 2-member) of MobilePhone. Now, looking at the instantiation hierarchy rooted in object ExchangeableTender: object Euro is an instantiation of ExchangeableTender and represents the Euro currency, a particular type of exchangeable tender, object MEuro represents a particular unit of Euro and is at the second instantiation level of ExchangeableTender, and, finally, object 137inUnit-MEuro is an instantiation of MEuro and represents a particular value in a particular unit of the Euro currency and is at the third instantiation level of ExchangeableTender.

We will now discuss the kinship between deep instantiation and powertypes [7], not taking into account DDI relationships and, thus, talking of DI objects instead of DDI objects; we will come back to DDI relationships and powertypes at the end of this section. We accentuate the kinship between DI and powertypes by giving a label to each instantiation level to indicate that objects at

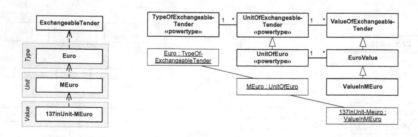

Fig. 3. DI object instantiation hierarchy (left) and corresponding UML classes and objects (right), disregarding DDI relationships

some instantiation level are in a 1-to-1 relationship to instances of the class related to that level. For example (see Fig. 3), the instantiation levels of ExchangeableTender are labeled Type, Unit, and Value. These levels are related to classes arranged in a cascaded powertype pattern: TypeOfExchangeableTender is powertype of UnitOfExchangeableTender which in turn is powertype of ValueOfExchangeableTender. The DI object ExchangeableTender can be regarded as a multi-faceted construct that represents these three classes. Likewise, instantiation between DI objects is multi-faceted. For example, the instantiation of DI object ExchangeableTender to Euro represents the instance-of relationship between Euro and TypeOfExchangeableTender as well as the specialization of UnitOfExchangeableTender and ValueOfExchangeableTender to UnitOfEuro and EuroValue, respectively. Note: labels and sortals associated with levels are outside the set-theoretic formalization of DDI and are thus omitted in Table 1.

Coming back to the set-theoretic formalization of DDI: We impose two restrictions on object instantiation. First, acyclic instantiation (No. 12) is a basic assumption of the DDI approach. Second, the restriction to single instantiation (No. 13) is mainly due to space limitations. The extension to multiple instantiation/inheritance is ongoing research.

Relationships in DDI combine aspects of relationship occurrences (links) and relationship sets (associations). An a^{i-j} relationship (where i is the *source potency*, j the *target potency*, and a the *relationship label*) between *source object* x and *target object* y is a multi-faceted construct. It represents, first, a link between x and y, and, second, can be further instantiated between $0..i$-members of x in the source role and $0..j$-members of y in the target role, and represents, in this regard, a set of multiple associations, one association for each combination of possible source and target instantiation levels. An a^{0-0} relationship cannot be further instantiated. We say, a relationship between source object x and target object y instantiates a relationship between source object c and target object d if they have the same relationship label and x is a *-member of c and y is a *-member of d.

Relationships at more abstract instantiation levels implicitly impose *domain and range referential integrity constraints* on relationships at more concrete instantiation levels. An intermediary relationship (i.e., a relationship that instantiates another relationship and can itself be further instantiated) refines these constraints. This is akin to the redefinition of associations in the UML (see [6] for an in-depth treatment) where associations are refined with regard to association ends. To allow a similar flexiblity in DDI, relationships are asserted by three kinds of so-called *A-facts* (No. 6): DR-facts (No. 4) which express associated domain and range constraints (No. 7, No. 8), R-facts (No. 2) which express an associated range constraint (No. 7), and D-facts (No. 3) which express an associated domain constraint (No. 8). In the visual illustration of DDI, DR-facts are depicted by solid lines, R-facts and D-facts by dotted arcs directed to the target object or the source object, respectively. We demand that each relationship label is introduced with a single unique DR-fact (No. 14) such that all other relationships with that relationship label are instantiations thereof.

Table 1. DDI modeling primitives, predicates, well-formedness and consistency rules

---

DDI Core: Modeling Primitives and Predicates

Sorts & Asserted Predicates:
(1) O: objects, $\mathbb{N}$: natural numbers including 0, L: relationship labels
(2) $R \subseteq O \times \mathbb{N} \times L \times \mathbb{N} \times O$
(3) $D \subseteq O \times \mathbb{N} \times L \times \mathbb{N} \times O$
(4) $DR \subseteq O \times \mathbb{N} \times L \times \mathbb{N} \times O$
(5) $in \subseteq O \times O$

Auxiliary Predicates:
(6) $A(x,i,a,j,y) :\Leftrightarrow R(x,i,a,j,y) \vee DR(x,i,a,j,y) \vee D(x,i,a,j,y)$
(7) $R'(x,i,a,j,y) :\Leftrightarrow R(x,i,a,j,y) \vee DR(x,i,a,j,y)$
(8) $D'(x,i,a,j,y) :\Leftrightarrow D(x,i,a,j,y) \vee DR(x,i,a,j,y)$
(9) $member(x,c) :\Leftrightarrow in(x,c)$
(10) $nmember(x,c,n) :\Leftrightarrow (n = 0 \wedge x = c) \vee$
     $\exists m \exists d : ((n = m + 1) \wedge nmember(x,d,m) \wedge member(d,c))$
(11) $isa(x,c) :\Leftrightarrow in(x,c)$

Well-formedness Criteria and Syntactic Restrictions:
(12) $isa^+(x,c) \rightarrow x \neq c$
(13) $in(x,c) \wedge in(x,d) \rightarrow c = d$
(14) $A(x,i,a,j,y) \wedge A(s,k,a,l,t) \rightarrow \exists c \exists m \exists n \exists d : DR(c,m,a,n,d) \wedge$
     $isa^*(x,c) \wedge isa^*(s,c) \wedge isa^*(y,d) \wedge isa^*(t,d)$
(15) $A(x,i,a,j,y) \wedge A(s,k,a,l,t) \wedge isa^+(x,s) \rightarrow j \leq l$
(16) $A(x,i,a,j,y) \wedge A(s,k,a,l,t) \wedge isa^+(y,t) \rightarrow i \leq k$

DDI with Specialization: Additional Modelling Primitives and Predicates

Additional Asserted Predicate:
(17) $spec \subseteq O \times O$

Auxiliary Predicates (Additions and Redefinitions):
(18) $member(x,c) :\Leftrightarrow \exists s \exists d : spec^*(x,s) \wedge in(s,d) \wedge spec^*(d,c)$
(19) $nmember(x,c,n) :\Leftrightarrow (n = 0 \wedge spec^*(x,c)) \vee$
     $\exists m \exists d : ((n = m + 1) \wedge nmember(x,d,m) \wedge member(d,c))$
(20) $isa(x,c) :\Leftrightarrow in(x,c) \vee spec(x,c)$
(21) $concrete(x) :\Leftrightarrow \nexists y : spec(y,x)$

Well-formedness Criteria and Syntactic Restrictions:
(22) $in(x,c) \rightarrow concrete(c)$
(23) $spec(x,s) \wedge spec(x,z) \rightarrow s = z$
(24) $spec(x,s) \rightarrow \nexists c : in(x,c)$
(25) $A(x,i,a,j,y) \wedge A(s,k,a,l,t) \wedge spec^+(x,s) \rightarrow \neg spec^+(t,y)$
(26) $R'(x,i,a,j,y) \wedge R'(x,i,a,j,t) \rightarrow \neg spec^+(y,t)$
(27) $D'(x,i,a,j,y) \wedge D'(s,i,a,j,y) \rightarrow \neg spec^+(x,s)$

Consistent Instantiation and Specialization:

(28) $A(x,i,a,j,y) \wedge A(c,k,a,l,d) \wedge nmember(x,c,n) \rightarrow n = k - i$
(29) $A(x,i,a,j,y) \wedge A(c,k,a,l,d) \wedge nmember(y,d,n) \rightarrow n = l - j$
(30) $A(x,i,a,j,y) \wedge R'(c,k,a,l,d) \wedge (j \leq l) \wedge isa^*(x,c)$
     $\rightarrow \exists d' : R'(c,k,a,l,d') \wedge isa^*(y,d')$
(31) $A(x,i,a,j,y) \wedge D'(c,k,a,l,d) \wedge (i \leq k) \wedge isa^*(y,d)$
     $\rightarrow \exists c' : D'(c',k,a,l,d) \wedge isa^*(x,c')$

Example 2 (Relationships). Relationship label cpu is introduced with relationship cpu^{2-2} between Processor and MobilePhone and expresses that relationships labeled cpu may exist only between 0..2-members of Processor in the source role and 0..2-members of MobilePhone in the target role. This relationship, being asserted as a DR-fact, imposes domain and range constraints: 0..2-members of Processor may be related by relationships labeled cpu only to 0..2-members of MobilePhone and vice versa. This relationship is instantiated by relationship cpu^{1-1} between Cortex-A15 and SamsungGS4 which relates 0..1-members of Cortex-A15 to 0..1-members of SamsungGS4. This relationship, being asserted as a D-fact, imposes only a domain constraint but no range constraint: 0..1-members of SamsungGS4 in the target role may be related only to 0..1-members of Cortex-A15 in the source role, but 0..1-members of Cortex-A15 may still be related to other 0..2-members of MobilePhone. This relationship is in turn instantiated by relationship cpu^{0-0} between CortexA15#1 and SarahsPhone, which is not further instantiated. Relationship label totalRevenue is introduced with relationship $totalRevenue^{1-3}$ between MobilePhone and ExchangeableTender. It expresses that relationships labeled totalRevenue may exist only between 0..1-members of MobilePhone and 0..3-members of ExchangeableTender. This relationship is instantiated by $totalRevenue^{0-1}$ between SamsungGS4 and MEuro, which expresses that the total revenue with mobile phone model SamsungGS4 is given only in unit 'millions of Euros'. This relationship is in turn instantiated by relationship $totalRevenue^{0-0}$ between SamsungGS4 and 137inUnit-MEuro.

The *potency reduction* axioms (No. 28, No. 29) state that potencies of relationships need to be consistent with the number of instantiation steps in related object instantiation hierarchies. We first look at source potencies: If object x is an n-member of object c and both are source of a relationship labeled a with source potency i and k, respectively, then the difference between i and k must be equal to n which is the number of instantiation steps between x and c (No. 28). The same needs to hold analogously for target potencies (No. 29). For example, $totalRevenue^{1-3}$ between MobilePhone and ExchangeableTender is instantiated consistently by $totalRevenue^{0-1}$ between SamsungGS4, which is a 1-member of MobilePhone, and MEuro, which is a 2-member of ExchangeableTender.

The DDI approach requires a *local stratification* of relationships (No. 15, No. 16) to ensure that every relationship is direct instantiation of at most one other relationship. Local stratification is far more flexible than *strict metamodeling* and still reduces the overall complexity of the approach and avoids potential conflicts of domain and range constraints due to multiple instantiation. We first look at local stratification with regard to target potencies (No. 15): If object s is source of a relationship labeled a with target potency l, then *-members of s must not be source of a relationship with the same label a and a target potency higher than l. The same needs to hold, in the opposite direction, for source potencies (No. 16). For example, this holds for relationship $soldPrice^{0-0}$ between SarahsPhone and 320inUnit-1Euro, which is direct instantiation of exactly one relationship, namely $soldPrice^{1-2}$ between SamsungGalaxyS4 and Euro.

This would not be the case, if there also were a relationship soldPrice$^{0-3}$ between SarahsPhone and ExchangeableTender.

An object may be source of multiple relationships that only differ in the target object and are identical with regard to relationship label and potencies. The range and/or domain restriction imposed by multiple such relationships is given by their union, i.e., a lower-level relationship must instantiate any one of these! For example, object SamsungGS4 is source of soldPrice$^{1-2}$ relationships with target objects FFlyerPoints and Euro to indicate that SamsungGS4 phones may be paid for in frequent flyer points or in Euro. Consider range restrictions (No. 30): If for a (i,j)-potency relationship labeled a with source x and target y there is a range-restricting relationship labeled a with a source object c that is the same as or is an ancestor of x and a target potency l that is higher or equal to j, then c must be source of some range-restricting relationship, which the former relationship instantiates. Domain restrictions (No. 31) work analogously.

The representation of DI using the powertype pattern (see Fig. 3) can be extended to also cover DDI relationships, but one need to take recourse to additional, annotated constraints in OCL that reflect that relationships at higher

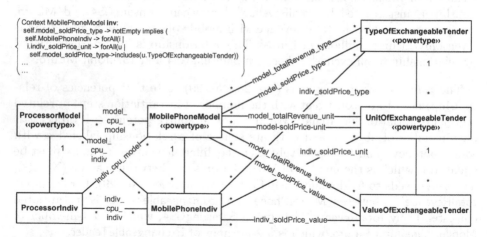

Fig. 4. Alternative representation in UML of the instantiation levels of root objects (Processor, MobilePhone, and ExchangeableTender) of Fig. 2 using the powertype pattern. Class names, e.g., ProcessorModel, are constructed from the names of root objects, e.g., Processor, and the labels of instantiation levels, e.g., Model. Root relationships (cpu$^{2-2}$, totalRevenue$^{1-3}$, and soldPrice$^{2-3}$) are each represented by multiple associations to represent their possible instantiations at different levels. Association names, e.g., model_cpu_indiv, are constructed from relationship labels, e.g., cpu, and labels of connected instantiation levels, e.g., Model and Indiv. The shown OCL constraint represents the domain and range restriction imposed by DDI relationships labeled soldPrice between source objects at level model and target objects at level type (in UML to be represented as instances of association model_soldPrice_type) on relationships labeled soldPrice between levels indiv and unit (in UML to be represented as instances of association indiv_soldPrice_unit). To represent the semantics of DDI, such an OCL constraint is necessary for each possible combination of instantiation levels of relationships.

levels act as schema for relationships at lower levels (see Fig. 4). The semantic modeling construct DDI, in contrast, keeps schema and associated constraints at one place and implicitly captures involved constraints, a key characteristic of semantic data models [10].

3   DDI with Object Specialization

In this section we investigate the interplay between dual deep instantiation and object specialization and extend the axiomatic specification of DDI accordingly (Table 1, No. 17 – No. 27).

DDI objects at the same instantiation level may be organized in specialization hierarchies, where $spec(x, y)$ expresses that object x is a specialization of object y (No. 17). The idea of specialization hierarchies in DDI is to factor out common features of objects at the same level to a joint more general object at that level. Features of an object are inherited unchanged by its specializations, unless overridden. We say, an object is *concrete* if it has no specializations (No. 21) and *abstract* otherwise. To simplify the approach we assume that only concrete objects are instantiated (No. 22), a restriction that is akin to the *abstract superclass rule* [11]. Further, we only consider single specialization (No. 23) and assume that an object that is an instantiation of an object may not be at the same time a specialization of some object (No. 24).

The predicates *isa*, *member*, and *nmember* are redefined to also cover specialization hierachies. We say x *isa* y if x is an instance of y or x specializes y (No. 20). We say x is a member of y if x relates to y by a chain of *isa* with exactly one instantiation step (No. 18). We say x is an n-member of y if x relates to y by a chain of *isa* with n instantiation steps (No. 19).

Example 3. Euro and Yen in Fig. 5 are *concrete* types of exchangeable tender. They are made specializations of Currency, which is an *abstract* type of exchangeable tender. MEuro and 1Euro are members of Euro as well as of Currency, and

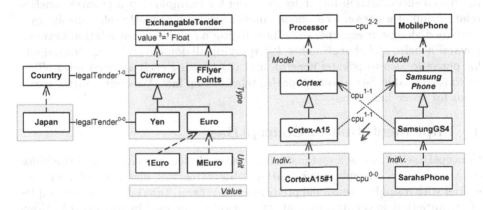

Fig. 5. DDI with Object Specialization   **Fig. 6.** Cross-over of Relationships

2-members of ExchangeableTender. Euro is a 0-member of itself and of Currency
and a 1-member of ExchangeableTender. Relationship label legalTender is introduced with relationship legalTender$^{1-0}$ between Country and Currency to express
that only types of exchangeable tender that are specializations of Currency can
be legal tender in individual countries. Yen is the legal tender in Japan.

The *local stratification* requirement is extended to exclude also a "cross-over"
of several relationships with the same label with respect to the specialization
hierarchies of their source and target objects (No. 25) as depicted in Fig. 6.
Further, to ensure that the represented range constraints for an object with
the same target potency are redundancy free, they need to be to orthogonal
target objects (two objects are ortogonal if they are not in a direct or indirect
specialization relationship) in a specialization hierarchy (No. 26). This holds
analogously for domain constraints (No. 27).

Consistent instantiation and specialization has already been defined in a way
(No. 30, No. 31) through the use of *isa* to cover both, instantiation and specialization. Inherited facts may be overridden but in a co-variant manner, such that
any relationship facts in which a source object participates meets the range constraints of its ancestors with regard to instantiation and specialization (No. 30)
and conversely, any relationship fact in which a target objects participates meets
the domain constraints of its *isa*-ancestors (No. 31). While the notation of these
axioms do not explicitly distinguish between instantiation and specialization,
any DDI model must differentiate between them: predicate *in* corresponds to
an element-set relation, and predicate *spec* to a subset-superset relation. The
potency reduction axioms (No. 28, No. 29) ensure that on instantiation, source
or target potencies of relationships, are accordingly reduced, but stay the same
on specialization. Thus, axioms No. 30 and No. 31 can take this as given and
need not discriminate between instantiation and specialization. For example, the
target potencies of legalTender are both 0 for Currency and its specialization Yen,
but source potencies are reduced from 1 to 0 because Japan is an instantiation
of Country.

The presented base model can be extended to relationships that are organized in a specialization-hierarchy to model for example that a privatePhoneNo-
relationship of a person to a phone number is also a phoneNo-relationship, by -
explained along our example - (1) introducing a specialization relation between
privatePhoneNo and phoneNumber, (2) applying all domain and range constraints
for phoneNo also to privatePhoneNo, and (3) treating each asserted privatePhoneNo relationship fact also as phoneNo relationship fact. We omit a furter treatment for space limitations.

4   Implementation in ConceptBase

ConceptBase [12, 14] is a metamodeling system based on Datalog and the Telos
data model [21]. All explicit information (objects, classes, metaclasses) are represented with a single extensional predicate P(id,from,label,to). The principles
of instantiation, specialization and attribution are defined by axioms [13]. However, they lack the DDI notion of potency. The implementation strategy is to

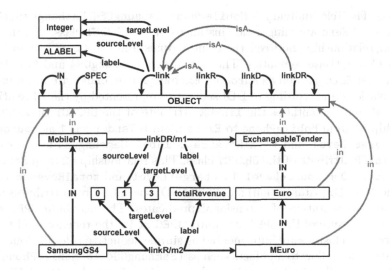

Fig. 7. Classes (and an instantiation) for the representation of the DDI model in Telos

create first a Telos metamodel to store DDI models. Secondly, the DDI predicates are defined by deductive rules. Finally, the DDI axioms are encoded as integrity constraints. The result is a prototypical environment for storing and analyzing the consistency of DDI models.

Figure 7 illustrates the OBJECT class and its attributes for the representation of DDI in Telos. The *in* and *spec* predicates from the DDI model translate into the IN and SPEC attributes of the OBJECT class, which are represented by arrows with the respective label. The *A* predicate from the DDI model translates into the link attribute of the OBJECT class. In ConceptBase, attributes are essentially relationships between objects and it is possible to define attributes for the relationships themselves, similar to association class in UML. The link attribute of the OBJECT class has a label (ALABEL) as well as an integer number for the source potency (sourceLevel) and the target potency (targetLevel). Similarly, attributes (or relationships) may specialize other attributes (or relationships). The linkD, linkR, and linkDR attributes of the OBJECT class specialize the link attribute. These attributes represent the *D*, *R*, and *DR* predicate, respectively; the link attribute derives from these predicates. The following Telos frame defines OBJECT including derived attributes:

```
OBJECT with
  attribute
    link: OBJECT; linkDR: OBJECT; linkD: OBJECT; linkR: OBJECT;
    IN: OBJECT;  SPEC: OBJECT;
    predD: OBJECT; predR: OBJECT;
    SPEC_t: OBJECT; SPEC_rt: OBJECT;
    ISA: OBJECT
end
```

Besides the illustration of the DDI metamodel in Telos, Fig. 7 illustrates an example instantiation which represents part of a mobile phone product catalog. The Telos individuals MobilePhone, SamsungGS4, ExchangeableTender, Euro, and MEuro are "linguistic" instances of the OBJECT class, i.e., the instantiation relationships between these individuals and the OBJECT class bear the usual ConceptBase semantics. The individuals SamsungGS4 and MobilePhone, MEuro and Euro, as well as Euro and ExchangeableTender are in an instantiation relationship according to DDI semantics represented by the IN relationship. MobilePhone instantiates the linkDR attribute of the OBJECT class. This relationship m1 from MobilePhone to ExchangeableTender has 1 as sourceLevel, 3 as targetLevel, and totalRevenue as label. SamsungGS4 also instantiates the linkDR attribute of the OBJECT class. This relationship m2 from SamsungGS4 to Euro has 0 as sourceLevel, 1 as targetLevel, and totalRevenue as label.

The IN (DDI instantiation) and SPEC (DDI specialization) attributes are used for the representation of extensional predicates. The attribute SPEC_t is the transitive closure of the SPEC attribute, SPEC_rt its the reflexive and transitive closure. The closures are implemented as simple deductive rules in ConceptBase. The attributes allow to add facts such as (SamsungGS4 IN MobilePhone) to the database as well as to define rules and constraints imposed on them. Distinguish the DDI instantiation fact with label IN from the Telos instantiation fact, e.g., (SamsungGS4 in OBJECT), which represents the DDI model within Telos. The predicates of the DDI model (Sect. 2) are implemented by deductive rules in ConceptBase. For example, the following deductive rule represents the *isa* defined by formula (20) in Table 1:

```
forall x,y/OBJECT (x SPEC y) or (x IN y) ==> (x ISA y)
```

Whereas the *nmember* predicate of the DDI model translates to a function, the $A(x, s, a, t, y)$ predicate requires a Telos formalization that uses the Ai(x, link, m) predicate provided by ConceptBase which returns an instance m of the link attribute of object x:

```
A(x,s,a,t,y) :<=> exists m/OBJECT!link Ai(x,link,m) and To(m,y) and
                        (m label a) and (m sourcelevel s) and (m targetlevel t)
```

The axioms of the DDI model are transcribed using the formula for the A predicate of the DDI model. The DDI axioms become integrity constraints in ConceptBase. As an example consider the translation of axiom (28) in Table 1:

```
forall x,y,c,d/OBJECT a/ALABEL i,j,k,l,n/Integer mx,mc/OBJECT!link
Ai(x,link,mx) and To(mx,y) and (mx label a) and (mx sourcelevel i) and (mx targetlevel j) and
Ai(c,link,mc) and To(mc,d) and (mc label a) and (mc sourcelevel k) and (mc targetlevel l) and
(n = NMEMBER(x,c)) ==> (n = k - i)
```

A large portion of the predicates in the formula are due to the mechanic expansion of the quinary predicate A. The function NMEMBER recursively computes the number of DDI instantiations between two objects. It is compared with the arithmetic expression k - i.

ConceptBase offers a validation of axioms within the expressiveness of a Datalog-neg [1] fixpoint model. An axiom represented as a constraint – or formally, a rule that derives inconsistency – can be violated by a given database state, i.e. an example DDI model. Around 50 example models were created to validate the non-trivial satisfiability of the axioms under Datalog semantics. The examples also showed that the implementation of DDI coincided with the behavior that we expected. The tested example models include the examples used in this paper. In order to demonstrate that the DDI axioms are free of redundancy, we provide for each axiom a an example "negative" DDI model that violates a but no other axiom. Besides the validation, the implementation was also used in the evolution of the DDI axioms: a revised set of axioms can be checked against the given example DDI models to analyze the resulting behavior. All example DDI models, the full DDI implementation, and further documentation are available online at `http://conceptbase.cc/ddi`.

5   Related Work

VODAK [15] was the first system to introduce what was later called deep instantiation/characterization [8, 17]. The capability of deep instantiation was achieved by VODAK in that objects where in parallel to types also organized into classes and meta-classes. Meta-classes defined own-types, instance-types and instance-instances-types, basically representing a cascading structure of what later became known as *power type* design pattern [8]. Type instantiation is between an object and its class's instance type and is inferred from the functional association of an object to a class to provide for a lossless and redundancy-free representation of functional data dependencies according to database design theory. Different to DDI, the semantics of the relationships between objects at different instantiation levels was captured behaviorally by methods attached to types and not by implicit constraints as in DDI.

Telos [21] and its implementation *ConceptBase* [12, 14] support a loose form of deep characterization. An attribute may be instantiated recursively many times and thereby acts as referential integrity constraint for its direct and indirect instances. The Telos axiomatization, however, does not specify the depth of characterization and attributes carry only a range but no domain constraint.

Deep instantiation [4] extends the approach of VODAK to an arbitrary number of instance^n-types, but rather than explicitly introducing types, attributes receive a potency number indicating to which implicit instance^n-type they belong. Deep instantiation was complemented by a Java implementation [16]. The discussion of deep instantiation of connectors, (relationships) [3, 9] focuses on their graphical rendering and is limited to strict metamodeling [5]. The modeling language Nivel [2] provides a formal semantics for deep instantiation. Materialization [24] is akin to deep instantiation and allows for deep characterization by introducing different types of attribute propagation. Similar to deep instantiation, materialization focuses on attributes and not on bi-directional relationships.

MetaDepth [18, 20] is a meta-modelling tool that incorporates deep instantiation. The practical experiences with MetaDepth [19] fit well with our own findings. They also recognized the need to relate objects at different meta-levels and do so by *deep references*. However, this novel modeling construct is not elaborated in detailed and only described informally. Further, deep references in MetaDepth are uni-directional instead of bi-directional relationships as known from the E/R model or from associations in the UML, consequently they only carry a range referential integrity constraint but no domain constraint.

M-Objects and M-Relationships [22] achieve deep characterization by a hierarchy of named concretization (instantiation) levels. Different to DDI, with m-relationships it is not possible to separately refine domain or range constraints and they do not come with an implementation that allows for automatic consistency checking. A comparison with different techniques for deep characterization, then called 'multi-level abstraction', is given in [23].

This paper contributes to the state of the art in deep characterization by providing a simple, formal representation and associated consistency axioms that cover (i) DDI with instantiation and specialization, (ii) domain or range redefinition of DDI relationships as it is known for UML associations, (iii) DDI model restrictions that on the one hand lift the requirement of global stratification through strict-meta modelling but on the other hand ensure local stratification (as explained in Sect. 2), and (iv) associated consistency checks for instantiation and specializaton with multiple dominating domain- or range constraints. This paper further contributes to the debate [7] about the ontological adequacy of deep instantiation by clearly differentiating (see Sect. 2) between the multi-faceted instantiation-of relationship between DDI objects at different instantiation levels and the instance-of relationship between an object and its class.

6   Conclusion

We have introduced the semantic modeling primitive DDI along a small running example, integrating different applications, a mobile phone catalog and associated inventories for different phone models. We have demonstrated that DDI allows for a concise representation of integrity constraints without need to take recourse to sophisticated constraint annotations. We currently work on extending the DDI approach to specialization of relationships as shortly exemplified in Sect. 3 and on introducing cardinality constraints at multiple instantiation levels.

References

1. Abiteboul, S., Hull, R.: Data functions, datalog and negation. SIGMOD Rec. 17(3), 143–153 (1988)
2. Asikainen, T., Männistö, T.: Nivel: a metamodelling language with a formal semantics. Software and System Modeling 8(4), 521–549 (2009)
3. Atkinson, C., Gutheil, M., Kennel, B.: A flexible infrastructure for multilevel language engineering. IEEE Trans. Software Eng. 35(6), 742–755 (2009)
4. Atkinson, C., Kühne, T.: The Essence of Multilevel Metamodeling. In: Gogolla, M., Kobryn, C. (eds.) UML 2001. LNCS, vol. 2185, pp. 19–33. Springer, Heidelberg (2001)
5. Atkinson, C., Kühne, T.: Profiles in a strict metamodeling framework. Sci. Comput. Program. 44(1), 5–22 (2002)

6. Costal, D., Gómez, C., Guizzardi, G.: Formal semantics and ontological analysis for understanding subsetting, specialization and redefinition of associations in UML. In: Jeusfeld, M., Delcambre, L., Ling, T.-W. (eds.) ER 2011. LNCS, vol. 6998, pp. 189–203. Springer, Heidelberg (2011)
7. Eriksson, O., Henderson-Sellers, B., Ägerfalk, P.J.: Ontological and linguistic meta-modelling revisited: A language use approach. Information & Software Technology 55(12), 2099–2124 (2013)
8. Gonzalez-Perez, C., Henderson-Sellers, B.: A powertype-based metamodelling framework. Software and System Modeling 5(1), 72–90 (2006)
9. Gutheil, M., Kennel, B., Atkinson, C.: A Systematic Approach to Connectors in a Multi-level Modeling Environment. In: Czarnecki, K., Ober, I., Bruel, J.-M., Uhl, A., Völter, M. (eds.) MODELS 2008. LNCS, vol. 5301, pp. 843–857. Springer, Heidelberg (2008)
10. Hull, R., King, R.: Semantic database modeling: survey, applications, and research issues. ACM Comput. Surv. 19(3), 201–260 (1987)
11. Hürsch, W.L.: Should superclasses be abstract? In: Tokoro, M., Pareschi, R. (eds.) ECOOP 1994. LNCS, vol. 821, pp. 12–31. Springer, Heidelberg (1994)
12. Jarke, M., Gallersdörfer, R., Jeusfeld, M.A., Staudt, M., Eherer, S.: ConceptBase - a deductive object base for meta data management. J. Intell. Inf. Syst. 4(2), 167–192 (1995)
13. Jeusfeld, M.A.: Complete list of O-Telos axioms (2005), http://merkur.informatik.rwth-aachen.de/pub/bscw.cgi/d1228997/O-Telos-Axioms.pdf
14. Jeusfeld, M.A., Jarke, M., Mylopoulos, J. (eds.): Metamodeling for Method Engineering. MIT Press, Cambridge (2009)
15. Klas, W., Schrefl, M.: Metaclasses and Their Application - Data Model Tailoring and Database Integration. Springer (1995)
16. Kühne, T., Schreiber, D.: Can programming be liberated from the two-level style: multi-level programming with deepjava. In: Gabriel, R.P., Bacon, D.F., Lopes, C.V., Jr., G.L.S. (eds.) OOPSLA, pp. 229–244. ACM (2007)
17. Kühne, T., Steimann, F.: Tiefe Charakterisierung. In: Rumpe, B., Hesse, W. (eds.) Modellierung. LNI, vol. 45, pp. 109–119. GI (2004)
18. de Lara, J., Guerra, E.: Deep meta-modelling with METADEPTH. In: Vitek, J. (ed.) TOOLS 2010. LNCS, vol. 6141, pp. 1–20. Springer, Heidelberg (2010)
19. de Lara, J., Guerra, E., Cobos, R., Moreno-Llorena, J.: Extending deep meta-modelling for practical model-driven engineering. Comput. J. 57(1), 36–58 (2014)
20. de Lara, J., Guerra, E., Cuadrado, J.S.: Model-driven engineering with domain-specific meta-modelling languages. In: Software & Systems Modeling, pp. 1–31 (2013)
21. Mylopoulos, J., Borgida, A., Jarke, M., Koubarakis, M.: Telos: Representing knowledge about information systems. ACM Trans. Inf. Syst. 8(4), 325–362 (1990)
22. Neumayr, B., Grün, K., Schrefl, M.: Multi-Level Domain Modeling with M-Objects and M-Relationships. In: Link, S., Kirchberg, M. (eds.) APCCM. CRPIT, vol. 96, pp. 107–116. ACS, Wellington (2009)
23. Neumayr, B., Schrefl, M., Thalheim, B.: Modeling techniques for multi-level abstraction. In: Kaschek, R., Delcambre, L. (eds.) The Evolution of Conceptual Modeling. LNCS, vol. 6520, pp. 68–92. Springer, Heidelberg (2011)
24. Pirotte, A., Zimányi, E., Massart, D., Yakusheva, T.: Materialization: A Powerful and Ubiquitous Abstraction Pattern. In: Bocca, J.B., Jarke, M., Zaniolo, C. (eds.) VLDB, vol. 0605, pp. 630–641. Morgan Kaufmann (1994)

An Adapter-Based Approach to Co-evolve Generated SQL in Model-to-Text Transformations

Jokin García[1], Oscar Díaz[1], and Jordi Cabot[2]

[1] Onekin Research Group, University of the Basque Country (UPV/EHU),
San Sebastian, Spain
{jokin.garcia,oscar.diaz}@ehu.es
[2] Atlanmod, Ecolé des Mines de Nantes - INRIA, Nantes, France
jordi.cabot@inria.fr

Abstract. *Forward Engineering* advocates for code to be generated dynamically through model-to-text transformations that target a specific platform. In this setting, platform evolution can leave the transformation, and hence the generated code, outdated. This issue is exacerbated by the perpetual beta phenomenon in Web 2.0 platforms where continuous delta releases are a common practice. Here, manual co-evolution becomes cumbersome. This paper looks at how to automate —fully or in part—the synchronization process between the platform and the transformation. To this end, the transformation process is split in two parts: the stable part is coded as a MOFScript transformation whereas the unstable side is isolated through an adapter that is implicitly called by the transformation at generation time. In this way, platform upgrades impact the adapter but leave the transformation untouched. The work focuses on DB schema evolution, and takes *MediaWiki* as a vivid case study. A first case study results in the upfront cost of using the adapter paying off after three releases *MediaWiki* upgrades.

1 Introduction

The changing nature of DB schemas has been a constant concern since the inception of DBs. Software consuming data is dependent upon the structures keeping this data, i.e. the DB schema. Such software might refer to relational views [5], data mappings (i.e. describing how data instances of one schema correspond to data instances of another) [15] or application code [4]. But, what if this software is not directly coded but generated? The popularity of Model-Driven Forward Engineering (FE) is making code generation go mainstream. Key gears of this infrastructure are *Model-to-Text (M2T)* transformations as supported by *Acceleo*[1][2]. M2T transformations (hereafter referred to as just "transformations") obtain "the text" (i.e. the software code akin to a target platform) from a model, i.e. an abstract representation of the solution (a.k.a. Platform Independent Model). As any other application, the generated "text" is fragile upon

---

[1] http://www.eclipse.org/acceleo/ or *MOFScript*.
[2] http://modelbased.net/mofscript/

M. Jarke et al. (Eds.): CAiSE 2014, LNCS 8484, pp. 518–532, 2014.

changes on the underlying platform, i.e. "the text" should co-evolve with the platform. Traditionally, this is achieved at "the text" level [4]. FE opens a different way: co-evolving *not* the generated code but the transformation that generates this code. This is the research question we tackle, i.e. how changes in the DB schema can be propagated to the transformation.

We turn the issue of keeping the application and the DB schema in sync, into one of maintaining the consistency between the code generators (i.e. the transformation) and the DB schema. Despite the increasing importance of FE, this issue has been mostly overlooked. This might be due to understanding that traditional co-evolution techniques can be re-used for transformations as well. After all, transformations are just another kind of applications. However, existing strategies for application co-evolution assume that either the generated SQL script is static or the trace for DB changes is known (and hence, can later be replicated in the application) [4]. However, these premises might not hold in our scenario. Rationales follow:

- transformations do not *specify* but *construct* SQL scripts. The SQL script is dynamically generated once references to the input model are resolved. This specificity of transformations makes it necessary to do the adaptation dynamically after the transformation engine has resolved the references but before it prints the result to the output file. As a result, solutions proposed for "static" scenarios are hardly applicable in this context.
- the trace for DB changes might be unknown. The DB schema and the transformation might belong to different organizations (i.e. there exist an *external* dependency from the transformation to the schema). This rules out the possibility of tracking schema upgrades to be later replicated into the transformation. External dependencies are increasingly common with the advent of the Web 2.0, and the promotion of open APIs and open-source platforms such as Content Management Systems (e.g. *Alfresco*), Wiki engines (e.g. *MediaWiki*) or Blog engines (e.g. *WordPress*). Here, the application (i.e. the portal, the wiki or the blog) is developed on top of a DB schema that is provided by a third party (e.g. the *Wikimedia* foundation).

We had to face the aforementioned scenarios ourselves when implementing *Wiki-Whirl* [10], a Domain-Specific Language (DSL) built on top of *MediaWiki*. *Wiki-Whirl* is interpreted, i.e. a *WikiWhirl* model (an expression described along the *WikiWhirl* syntax) delivers an SQL script that is enacted. The matter is that this *SQL* script goes along the *MediaWiki* DB schema. If this schema changes, the script might break apart. Since *MediaWiki* is part of the *Wikimedia Foundation*, we do not have control upon what and when *MediaWiki* releases are delivered. And release frequency can be large (the perpetual-beta effect) which introduces a heavy maintenance burden upon *WikiWhirl*. This paper describes how we faced this issue by applying the adapter pattern to transformations. That is, data manipulation requests (i.e. insert, delete, update, select) are re-directed to the adapter during the transformation. The adapter outputs the code according to the latest schema release. In this way, the main source of instability (i.e. schema upgrades) is isolated in the adapter. The paper describes the adapter architecture, a case study and a cost analysis to characterize the settings that can benefit from this approach. We start by framing our work within the literature in DB schema evolution.

2   Related Work

This section frames our work within the abundant literature in DB schema evolution. The aim is *not* to provide an exhaustive list but just some representative examples that serve to set the design space (for a recent review refer to [5]). For our purposes, papers on schema co-evolution can be classified along two dimensions: the target artifact to be co-evolved, and the approach selected to do so. As for the former dimension, the target artifact includes data and applications. As for **data**, upgrading the schema certainly forces to ripple those changes to the corresponding data (e.g. tuples). The strategy used in [7] is for designers to express schema mappings in terms of queries, and then use these queries to evolve the data between the DB schemas. On the other hand, **applications** consuming data are dependent upon the structures keeping this data. Applications might include DB views [5], data mappings [15] or application code [4]. Our work focuses on a specific kind of applications: transformations.

The second dimension tackles the mechanisms used to approach the aforementioned co-evolution scenarios. First, **Application Programming Interfaces** (APIs). This technique allows programs to interface with the DB through an external conceptual view (i.e. the API) instead of a logical view (i.e. the SQL data-manipulation language over the DB schema). This technique is investigated in [3] where they introduce an API which aims at providing application programs with a conceptual view of the relational DB. The second technique is the use of **rewriting methods**. Here, the approach is to replace sub-terms of a formula with other terms. In our setting, this formula can stand for a DB view or data mapping expression (a.k.a. Disjunctive Embedded Dependencies). A rewriting algorithm reformulates a query/mapping upon an old schema into an equivalent query/mapping on the new schema. An example is described in [5]. Next, **DB views** are also used to support co-evolution. Views ensure logical data independence whereby the addition or removal of new entities, attributes, or relationships to the conceptual schema should be possible without having to rewrite existing application programs. Unfortunately, solutions based on views cannot support the full range of schema changes [11]. Finally, **wrappers** enclose artifacts to keep the whole ecosystem functioning. Upon upgrades on the DB schema, the artifact to be wrapped can be either the schema itself or the legacy applications. The first approach is illustrated by [4] where the new schema is encapsulated through an API. The wrapper converts all DB requests issued by the legacy application into requests compliant with the new schema. Alternatively, wrappers can be used to encapsulate the legacy applications. In this case, wrappers act as mediators between the application requests and the DB system. Wrappers for reusing legacy software components are discussed in [12] and [13].

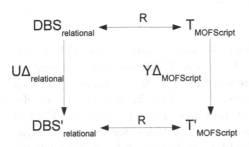

Fig. 1. Artifacts involved in unidirectional co-evolution. R denotes the consistency relationship. (Adapted from [1]).

Our approach can be characterized as being wrapper based. Since the DB schema is beyond our grasp, the wrapper necessarily sits upon the legacy application. However and unlike previous studies, we do not wrap the application itself but the generator (i.e. the transformation) so that the resultant application (i.e. the SQL script) is already tuned to the new DB schema. By working at a higher level (i.e. the transformation), we factor out the adaptation strategy to account for the set of applications handled by the transformation. Figure 1 depicts the main artifacts involved: $DBS_{relational}$ is the original DB schema; T_{M2T} is the original legacy application (i.e., the version of the transformation that co-existed with the original DB); $DBS'_{relational}$ is the new DB schema; T'_{M2T} is the new target artifact; $U\Delta_{relation}$ is the update applied to the original source[3]; $Y\Delta_{M2T}$ is the target update resulting from the coevolution.

$U\Delta_{relation}$ can be obtained by recording the changes upon $DBS_{relational}$ while the user edits it [4]. However, in our setting this is not always possible since the schema belongs to a third party. Alternatively, an update can be computed using a homogeneous artifact comparison operator, which takes an original version of an artifact and its new version, and returns an update connecting the two. This is our approach. Now, we could obtain transformation update (i.e. $Y\Delta_{M2T}$) out of $U\Delta_{relation}$. We propose transformations to be engineered for evolution. Therefore, a transformation is conceived as a pair (S,N) where S denotes the stable part, and N stands for the no-stable part. The no-stable part is supported through an adapter. Therefore, $Y\Delta_{M2T}$ denotes the update to be conducted in the adapter. Therefore, this work presents an architecture to compute adapter updates (i.e. $Y\Delta_{M2T}$) out of differences between DB schema models (i.e. $U\Delta_{relation}$). Our vision is for the adapter to be domain-agnostic, and hence, reusable in other domains. We envisage transformation adapters to play a role similar to DBMS drivers. A DBMS driver shelters applications from the heterogeneity of DBMS. The driver translates the application's data queries into commands that the DBMS understands. Likewise, a transformation adapter seeks to isolate the transformation from changes in the DB schema. As long as these changes are domain agnostic (e.g. the way to face attribute rename is domain independent) then, the adapter can be re-used by the community. Our solution is available in *www.onekin.org/downloads/public/Batch_MofscriptAdaptation.rar*

---

[3] An **update** is a function that takes an artifact as input, and returns the updated artifact as output, e.g. $DBS'_{relational} = U\Delta_{relational}(DBS_{relational})$.

3 Case Study

This section outlines the *WikiWhirl* project [9] and the challenges posed by its external dependency with the *MediaWiki* DB schema. Wikis are main exponents of collaborative editing where users join forces towards a common goal (e.g. writing an article about a topic). It comes as no surprise that wikis promote an article-based view as opposed to a holistic view of the wiki content. As a result, APIs and GUIs of wiki engines favor operations upon single articles (e.g. editing and discussing the article's content) while overlooking operations on the wiki as a whole (e.g. rendering the wiki's structure or acting upon this structure by splitting, merging or re-categorizing articles). To amend this, *WikiWhirl* abstracts wiki structure in terms of mindmaps, where refactoring operations (*WikiWhirl* expressions) are expressed as reshapes of mindmaps. Since wikis end up being supported as DBs, *WikiWhirl* expressions are transformed into SQL scripts. Figure 2 shows a snippet of a *WikiWhirl* transformation: a sequence of SQL statements with interspersed dynamic parts that query the input model (i.e. the *WikiWhirl* expression). These statements built upon the DB schema of *MediaWiki*, and in so doing, create an external dependency of *WikiWhirl* w.r.t. *MediaWiki*. In a $4\frac{1}{2}$ year period, the *MediaWiki* DB had 171 schema versions [6]. According to [6], the number of tables has increased from 17 to 34 (100% increase), and the number of columns from 100 to 242 (142%). This begs the question of how to make *WikiWhirl* coevolve with the *MediaWiki* upgrades. Table 1 compares four options in terms of the involvement (i.e. time and focus) and the required technical skills.

```
1 texttransformation FreeMind2MediaWiki (in ww:"www.onekin.org/wikiwhirl",
2     in diff: "http://www.eclipse.org/emf/compare/diff/1.1",
3     in Ecore: "http://www.eclipse.org/emf/2002/Ecore") {
4     var timestamp : String = "('%Y%m%d%k%i%s')"
5     var categoryTitle : String = wikiRes2.title
6     var userId: String = "1"
7         [...]
8   ww.Categorize::categorize_sql(){
9       println("UPDATE page set page_touched = " + timestamp +
10      " where page_namespace = 14 and page_title = '" + categoryTitle + "';")
11      println("INSERT into recentchanges (rc_timestamp, rc_cur_time, rc_user,
12      rc_user_text, rc_namespace, rc_title, " + "rc_comment, rc_new, rc_cur_id,
13      rc_this_oldid, rc_last_oldid, rc_type, rc_old_len, rc_new_len, rc_deleted)
14      VALUES (" + timestamp + ", " + timestamp + ", " + userId + ", '" + userName +
15      "', " + namespace + ", '" + pageTitle + "', '" + comment + "', 0, pageId, " +
16      lastRevisionId + ", " + pageRevisionId + ", 0, " + pageLen + ", " + pageLen +
17      " - " + categoryTitle.size() + " - " + "[[Categoy:]]".size() + ", 0);")
18  }   [...]
```

Fig. 2. A *WikiWhirl* transformation snippet. The transformation constructs the SQL statements dynamically from the input model, i.e. the *WikiWhirl* expression (e.g. *categortyTitle* in line 10, *pageTitle* in line 15, etc)

Option 1: Manually Changing the Generated Code. The designer detects that the new release impacts the generated code, and manually updates this code. This approach is discouraged in Forward Engineering outside the protected areas, since subsequent regenerations can override the manual changes. On the upside,

Table 1. Alternatives to manage platform evolution

Approach	Involvement	Skills	Infrastructure skills
manually changing the generated code	High	SQL	default
manually changing the transformation	High	SQL, MOFScript	default
automatically changing the transformation	Low	SQL, ATL	ATL Injectors, ATL metamodel, SQL schema Injectors, Model differentiation
automatically *adapting* the transformation	Low	SQL	SQL schema Injectors, Model differentiation

this approach acts directly on the generated code, so only SQL skills are required to accomplish the change.

Option 2: Manually Changing the Transformation. For sporadic and small transformations, this might be the most realistic option. However, frequent platform releases and/or SQL-intensive transformations make this manual approach too cumbersome and error-prone to be conducted in a regular basis. The user needs to know both the platform language (e.g. SQL) and the transformation language (e.g. *MOFScript*). No additional infrastructure is introduced.

Option 3: Automatically Changing the Transformation. The idea is to inject the transformation into a model and next, use a *Higher-Order Transformation* (HOT) [14] to upgrade it. HOTs are used to cater for transformation variability in Software Product Lines [8]. Variability is sought to generate code for different platforms, different QoS requirements, language variations, or target frameworks. The approach is to define "aspects" (i.e. variability realizations) as higher-order transformations, i.e. a transformation whose subject matter is another transformation. Using aspect terminology, the *pointcuts* denote places in a transformation that may be modified by the high-order transformation (HOT). *Advices* modify base transformations through additional transformation code to be inserted before, after, or to replace existing code. Likewise, we could rephrase schema co-evolution as a "variability-in-time" issue, and use HOTs to isolate schema upgrades. Unfortunately, the use of HOTs requires of additional infrastructure: (1) a metamodel for the transformation language at hand, and (2) the appropriate injector/extractor to map from the *MOFScript* code to the *MOFScript* model, and vice versa. The availability of these tools is not always guarantee. For instance, *MOFScript* has both an injector and an extractor. However, *Acceleo* lacks the extractor. Another drawback is generality. It could be possible to develop a HOT for the specific case of *WikiWhirl*. But we aim at the solution to be domain-agnostic, i.e. applicable to no matter the domain meta-model. Unfortunately, HOTs find difficulties in resolving references to the base transformation's input model where its metamodel is unknown at compile time (i.e. where the HOTs is enacted). Moreover, this approach requires additional infrastructure: (1) SQL schema injectors that obtain a model out of the textual description of the DB schema and (2), a model differentiation tool that spots the differences among two schema models. This infrastructure is domain-independent.

Option 4: Automatically Adapting the Transformation. The transformation is engineered for change, i.e. variable concerns (i.e SQL scripts) are moved outside the transformation into the adapter. The user does not need to look at the transformation (which is kept unchanged) but at the generated code. SQL skills are sufficient. At runtime, the transformation invokes the adapter instead of directly generating the DB code (i.e. the SQL script). This brings two important advantages. First, and unlike the HOT option, the issue of resolving references to the base transformation's input model, does not exist, as references are resolved at runtime by the transformation itself. Second, this solution does not require the model representation of the transformation (i.e. injectors for the transformation are not needed). On the other side, this approach requires, as option 3, SQL schema injectors and a model differentiation tool.

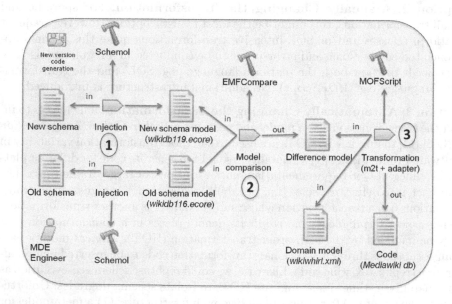

Fig. 3. A generic co-evolution process, exemplified for the WikiWhirl case study

Figure 3 outlines the different steps of our proposal. First, DB schemas (i.e. *New schema, Old Schema*) are injected as *Ecore* artifacts (step 1); next, the schema difference is computed (i.e. *Difference model*) (step 2); finally, this schema difference feeds the adapter used by the transformation (i.e. *MOFScript program*). *MOFScript* is a template-based code generator that uses *print* statements to generate code and language instructions to retrieve model elements. Our approach mainly consists of replacing the *print* statements with invocations to

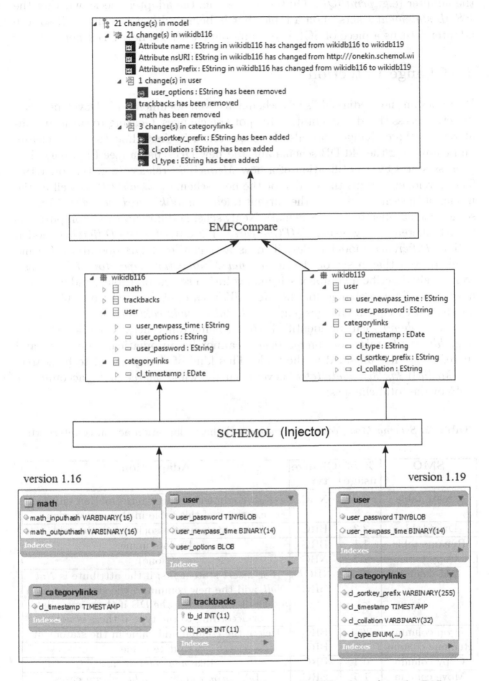

Fig. 4. Injection: from catalog tuples (those keeping the DB schema) to the Difference model

the adapter (e.g. *printSQL*). On the invocation, the adapter checks whether the *<SQL statement>* acts upon a table that is being subject to change. If so, the adapter returns a piece of SQL code compliant with the new DB schema.

4   Change Detection

Upgrades on the MediaWiki's DB schema are well documented [4]. Developers can directly access this documentation to spot the changes. Gearing towards automatization, these changes can also be ascertained by installing the new release, and comparing the old DB schema and the new DB schema (see Figure 4). The process starts by a notification of a new *MediaWiki* release (e.g. version 1.19). The developer obtains the model for the new schema (*wikidb119*) as well as the model of the schema used in the current release of *WikiWhirl* (*wikidb116*) using some schema injector (e.g. Schemol). Next, schema differences are computed as model differences (e.g. using *EMFCompare*). The output is the *Difference* model.

The *Difference* model is described as a sequence of DB operators. Curino et al. proved that a set of eleven *Schema Modification Operators (SMO)* can completely describe a complex schema evolution scenario. Table 2 indicates the frequency of these change for the *MediaWiki* case, elaborated from [6]. Fortunately, most frequent changes (e.g. *'create table'*, *'add column'*, *'drop column'* or *'rename column'*) can be identified from schema differences. Complex changes (e.g. *'distribute table'* or *'merge table'*) cannot be automatically detected and therefore are not included in the table. This kind of changes tend to be scarce. For *MediaWiki*, *'distribute table'* never occurred while *'merge table'* accounts for 1,5% of the total changes.

Table 2. *Schema Modification Operators* and their adaptation action counterparts

SMO	% of usage	Change type	Adaptation
Create table	8.9	NBC	New comment in the transformation on the existence of this table in the new version
Drop table	3.3	BRC	Delete statement associated to the table
Rename table	1.1	BRC	Update name
Copy table	2.2	NBC	(None)
Add column	38.7	NBC/ BRC	For *insert* statements: if the attribute is *Not Null*, add the new column in the statement with a default value (from the DB if there is available or according to the type if there is not)
Drop column	26.4	BRC	Delete the column and value in the statement
Rename column	16	BRC	Update name
Copy column	0.4	BRC	Like *add column* case
Move column	1.5	BRC	Like *drop column* + *add column* cases

---

[4] http://www.mediawiki.org/wiki/Manual:Database_layout

5   Change Propagation

Schema changes need to be propagated to the generated code through the transformation. The transformation delegates to the adapter how the SQL command
ends up being supported in the current DB schema. That is, *MOFScript's print*
is turned into the adapter's *printSQL* (e.g. *"printSQL (<SQL statement>)"*).
On invocation, the adapter checks whether the SQL statement acts upon a table
that is subject to change (i.e. appears in the *Difference* model). If so, the adapter
proposes an adaptation action to restore the consistency. This adaptation action
depends on the kind of change. Similar to other co-transformation approaches
(e.g. [2]), changes are classified as *(i) Non Breaking Changes (NBC)*, i.e., changes
that do not affect the transformation; *Breaking and Resolvable Changes (BRC)*,
i.e., changes after which the transformations can be automatically co-evolved;
and *Breaking and Unresolvable Changes (BUC)*, i.e., changes that require human intervention to co-evolve the transformation. Based on this classification,
different contingency actions are undertaken: no action for NBC, automatic co-
evolution for BRC, and assisting the user for BUC. Table 2 describes this typol-
ogy for DB changes, the usage percentage of each change for *MediaWiki* [6], and
the adaptation counterpart.

```
 1  printSQL(statement: String){
 2    [...]
 3    var tableName : String = java("org.gibello.zql.ZqlParser",
 4    "getTableName", statement , CLASSPATH );
 5    diff.objectsOfType(diff.RemoveModelElement)->forEach
 6    (rme:diff.RemoveModelElement | rme.rightParent.name=tableName){
 7      var paramsRemoveColumn:List;
 8      paramsRemoveColumn.add(statement);
 9      paramsRemoveColumn.add(rme.rightParent.name);
10      paramsRemoveColumn.add(rme.leftElement.name);
11      println("#"+statement);
12      println(java("org.gibello.zql.ZqlParser", "removeColumn",
13      paramsRemoveColumn, CLASSPATH) + ";");
14    }
15    [...]
16  }
```

Fig. 5. The adapter. A *printSQL* function that handles the *"remove column"* case.

Implementation wise, the adapter has two inputs: the *Difference* model and
the model for the new schema (to obtain the full description of new attributes,
if applicable). The ZQL open-source SQL parser was used[5] to parse SQL statements to Java structures. This parser was extended to account for adaptation
functions to modify the statements (e.g. *removeColumn*) and support functions
(e.g. *getTableName*). Figure 5 provides a glimpse of the adapter for the case
"remove column". It starts by iterating over the changes reported in the *Difference* model (line 5). Next, it checks (line 6) that the deleted column's table
corresponds with the table name of the statement (retrieved in lines 3-4). Then,
all, the statement, the table name and the removed column are added to a list of
parameters (lines 7-10). Finally, the adapter outputs an SQL statement without

---

[5] http://zql.sourceforge.net/

```
 1  INSERT into categorylinks (cl_from, cl_to, cl_sortkey, cl_timestamp) VALUES
 2    (@pageId, 'Softwareproject','Housse_Testing',
 3    (DATE_FORMAT(CURRENT_TIMESTAMP(), '%Y%m%d%k%i%s'));
 4  INSERT into trackbacks (tb_name, tb_title, tb_url, tb_ex, tb_id, tb_page) VALUES
 5    ('trackback1', 'title', 'http://blog/post', '', '', '');
 6  INSERT into user (user_id, user_name, user_real_name, user_password,
 7    user_newpassword, user_newpass_time, user_email, user_options, user_touched,
 8    user_token, user_email_token_expires, user_registration, user_editcount) VALUES
 9    ('1', 'Jokin', 'Jokin Garcia', 'c7c105fac2d29c1f420865f9e50b4ab3', '', NULL,
10    'jokin.garcia@ehu.es', 'quickbar=1', '20110902144454',
11    'd863a16e41accc0acb8323a15373129b', '', '20070718151421', '1360'));
```

```
 1  INSERT into categorylinks (cl_from,cl_to,cl_sortkey,cl_timestamp,cl_type) VALUES
 2    (@pageId, 'Softwareproject','Housse_Testing',
 3    (DATE_FORMAT(CURRENT_TIMESTAMP(), '%Y%m%d%k%i%s'), 'page');
 4  #WARNING: Deleted table trackbacks
 5  #INSERT into trackbacks (tb_name, tb_title, tb_url, tb_ex, tb_id, tb_page) VALUES
 6  #  ('trackback1', 'title', 'http://blog/post', '', '', '');
 7  #WARNING: Deleted column user_options in table user
 8  #INSERT into user (user_id, user_name, user_real_name, user_password,
 9  #  user_newpassword, user_newpass_time, user_email, user_options, user_touched,
10  #  user_token, user_email_token_expires, user_registration, user_editcount) VALUES
11  #  ('1', 'Jokin', 'Jokin Garcia', 'c7c105fac2d29c1f420865f9e50b4ab3', '', NULL,
12  #  'jokin.garcia@ehu.es', 'quickbar=1', '20110902144454',
13  #  'd863a16e41accc0acb8323a15373129b', '', '20070718151421', '1360'));
14  INSERT into user (user_id, user_name, user_real_name, user_password,
15    user_newpassword, user_newpass_time, user_email, user_touched,
16    user_token, user_email_token_expires, user_registration, user_editcount) VALUES
17    ('1', 'Jokin', 'Jokin Garcia', 'c7c105fac2d29c1f420865f9e50b4ab3', '', NULL,
18    'jokin.garcia@ehu.es', '20110902144454',
19    'd863a16e41accc0acb8323a15373129b', '', '20070718151421', '1360'));
```

Fig. 6. MediaWiki 1.16 generated script *versus* MediaWiki 1.19 generated script. Since the MOFScript code keeps constant, differences are due to the adapter. The adapter also intermingles comments (#) to ease user inspection.

the removed column, using a function with the list of parameters that modifies the expression (lines 12-13). The adaptation process is enacted for each *SQLprint* statement, regardless of whether the very same statement has been previously processed or not. Though this penalizes efficiency, the frequency and the time at which this process is conducted make efficiency a minor concern.

Back to our sample case, the SQL script in Figure 6 is the result of enacting the generation process with *wikidiff_v16v19* as the *Difference* model. Once references to the variables and the model elements have been resolved, MOFScript's *printSQL* statements invoke the adapter. The adapter checks whether either the tables or the attributes of the *printSQL* statement are affected by the upgrade (as reflected in the *Difference* model) and applies the appropriate adaptation (see table Table 2). Specifically, the *Difference* model *wikidiff_v16v19* reports:

1. the introduction of three new attributes in the *categorylinks* table, namely, *cl_type*, *cl_sortkey_prefix* and *cl_collation*. Accordingly, the adapter generates *SQL* insert/update statements where new attributes which are 'Not Null' are initialized with their default values (lines 1-4 below);
2. the deletion of tables *math* and *trackback*. This causes the affected *printSQL* statements to output nothing (i.e. the old output is left as a comment) (lines 5-7 below);
3. the deletion of attribute *user_options* in the *user* table. Consequently, the affected *printSQL* statements, output the SQL but removing the affected attributes (lines 14-18 below). In addition, a comment is introduced to note this fact (lines 8-13 below).

6   Assessment

Table 3. Co-evolving *WikiWhirl* from *MediaWiki* 1.16 to *MediaWiki* 1.19. Effort estimated in terms of the number of *MOFScript* instructions affected.

Version	#Add column	#Impacts on WikiWhirl	#Drop column	#Impacts on WikiWhirl
1.17	1	3	0	0
1.18	0	0	1	1
1.19	2	11	1	0

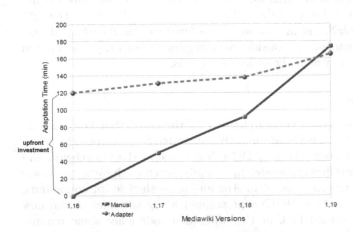

The net value of an adapter is given by the cost savings that occur to accommodate each DB release minus the development cost of the adapter. These savings are expected from *Breaking and Resolvable Changes (BRC)* since (1) they are amenable to be automated, and (2) they account for the majority of the change. Next paragraphs provide some figures for BRCs, comparing the manual vs the adapter-based approach. To this end, we conducted an assessment on the cost of migrating a *WikiWhirl*'s *MOFScript* transformation from version 1.16 to version 1.17 of the *MediaWiki* DB schema. Table 3 provides some figures of the schema changes and their impact. The experiment was conducted by 8 PhD students who were familiarized with SQL, *MOFScript* and *Ant* [6] (4 for the manual and 4 for the assisted).

Fig. 7. Accumulative costs of keeping *WikiWhirl* and *MediaWiki* in sync. Comparison of the manual (continuous line) and the assisted approach (dotted line).

Manual Propagation

Subjects conducted two tasks: (1) identifying changes between the two versions from the documentation available in the *MediaWiki* web pages, and (2), adapting manually the transformation. The following equation resumes the main costs:

---

[6] http://ant.apache.org/

$$Manual\ Cost = D + P\ *\ \#Impacts$$

being D: the time estimated for detecting whether the new *MediaWiki* release impacts the transformation, P: the time needed to **P**ropagate a single change to the *MOFScript* code, and *#Impacts:* the number of instructions in the transformation **I**mpacted by the upgrade.

The Experiment. D very much depends on the documentation available. For *MediaWiki*, designers should check the website[7], navigate through the hyperlinks, and collect those changes that might impact the code. The experiment outputted an average of 38' for $D_{MediaWiki}$, which is not very high due to the subjects being already familiarized with the *MediaWiki* schema. Next, the designer peers at the code, updates it, and checks the generated code. Subjects were asked to provide a default value for the newly introduced columns. On average, this accounts for 4' for a single update (i.e. $P_{BRC} = 4$'). Since the 1.17 upgrade impacted 3 *MOFScript* instructions, this leads to a total cost of 50' (i.e. $38 + 4*3$). The execution time is considered negligible in both the manual and the assisted options since it is in the order of seconds.

Assisted Propagation

Subjects conducted two tasks: (1) configuration of the batch that launches the assisted adaptation, and (2), verification of the generated SQL script. The batch refers to a macro that installs the new DB release, injects the old schema and new schema, obtains the difference model, and finally, executes the adapter-aware *MOFScript* code. This macro is coded in *Ant* and some shell script commands. Running this macro outputs a *MOFScript* snippet along the lines of the new DB schema. Designers should look at this upgraded code since some manual intervention might still be needed. For instance, the introduction of new columns might also involve the assignment of a value that might not coincide by the one assigned by the adapter. Likewise, column deletion, though not impacting the transformation as such, might spot some need for the data in the removed column to be moved somewhere else. Worth noticing, the designer no longer consults the documentation but relies on the macro to spot the changes in the *MOFScript*. We assume, the comments generated by the adapter are expressive enough for the designer to understand the change (Figure 6). On this basis, the designer has to verify the proposed adaptation is correct, and amend it, if appropriate. The following equation resumes the main costs:

$$Assisted\ Cost = C + V\ *\ \#Impacts$$

being C: the time needed to **C**onfigure the batch; V: the time needed to **V**erify that a single automatically adapted instruction is correct and to alter it, if applicable.

The Experiment. It took an average of 5' for the subjects to configure the macro (mainly, file paths) to the new DBMS release. As for V, it took an average

---

[7] http://www.mediawiki.org/wiki/Manual:Database_layout

of 6' for users to check the *MOFScript* code. Therefore, the assisted cost goes up to 11'.

Similar studies where conducted for other *MediaWiki* versions. Figure 7 depicts the accumulative costs of keeping *WikiWhirl* and *MediaWiki* in sync. Actually, till version 1.16 all upgrades were handled manually. Ever since, we resort to the macro to spot the changes directly on the generated *MOFScript* code. Does the effort payoff? Figure 7 shows the breakeven. It should be noted that subjects were already familiarized with the supporting technologies. This might not be the case in other settings. Skill wise, the manual approach is more demanding on *MOFScript* expertise while it does not require *Ant* knowledge. Alternatively, the assisted approach requires some knowledge about *Ant* but users limit themselves to peer at rather than to program *MOFScript* transformations.

The cost reduction rests on the existence of an infrastructure, namely, the adapter and the macro. The adapter is domain-agnostic, and hence, can be reused in other domains. On these grounds, we do not consider the adapter as part of the development effort of the *WikiWhirl* project in the same way that DBMS drivers are not included as part of the cost of application development. However, there is a cost of familiarizing with the tool, that includes the configuration of the batch macro (e.g. DB settings, file paths and the like). We estimated this accounts for 120' (reflected as the upfront investment for the assisted approach in Figure 7). On these grounds, the breakeven is reached after the third release.

7   Conclusions and Future Work

The original contribution of this paper is to address, for a specific case study, the issue of transformation co-evolution upon DB schema upgrades. The suitability of the approach boils down to two main factors: the DB schema stability and the transformation coupling (i.e. the number of SQL instructions in the *MOFScript* code). If the DB schema stability is low (i.e. large number of releases) and the transformation coupling is high, the cost of keeping the transformation in sync, increases sharply. In this scenario, we advocate for a preventive approach where the transformation is engineered for schema stability: *MOFScript's 'print'* is substituted by the adapter's *'printSQL'*. The adapter, using general recovery strategies, turns SQL statements based on the *old* schema into SQL statements based on the *new* schema.

That said, this approach presupposes that the impact of DB schema changes are confined to the SQL statements without affecting the logic of the transformation itself. In our experience, this tends to be the case for medium-size upgrades. However, substantial changes in the DB schema might require changing the transformation logic. This is certainly outside the scope of the adapter. Next follow-on includes to generalize this approach to other settings where schema evolution is also an issue such as ontologies or XML schemas.

Acknowledgements. This work is co-supported by the Spanish Ministry of Education, and the European Social Fund under contract TIN2011-23839 *(Scriptongue).* Jokin enjoyed a pre-doctoral grant from the Basque Government under the "Researchers Training Program".

References

1. Antkiewicz, M., Czarnecki, K.: Design space of heterogeneous synchronization. In: Lämmel, R., Visser, J., Saraiva, J. (eds.) GTTSE 2007. LNCS, vol. 5235, pp. 3–46. Springer, Heidelberg (2008)
2. Cicchetti, A., Di Ruscio, D., Eramo, R., Pierantonio, A.: Automating Co-evolution in Model-Driven Engineering. In: Enterprise Distributed Object Computing Conference (2008)
3. Cleve, A., Brogneaux, A.F., Hainaut, J.L.: A conceptual approach to database applications evolution. In: Parsons, J., Saeki, M., Shoval, P., Woo, C., Wand, Y. (eds.) ER 2010. LNCS, vol. 6412, pp. 132–145. Springer, Heidelberg (2010)
4. Cleve, A., Hainaut, J.: Co-transformations in database applications evolution. In: Lämmel, R., Saraiva, J., Visser, J. (eds.) GTTSE 2005. LNCS, vol. 4143, pp. 409–421. Springer, Heidelberg (2006)
5. Curino, C., Moon, H.J., Deutsch, A., Zaniolo, C.: Automating the database schema evolution process. VLDB J. 22(1), 73–98 (2013)
6. Curino, C.A., Tanca, L., Moon, H.J., Zaniolo, C.: Schema evolution in wikipedia: toward a web information system benchmark. In: ICEIS (2008)
7. Miller, R.J., Hernandez, M.A., Haas, L.M., Yan, L., Ho, H.C.T., Fagin, R., Popa, L.: The clio project: managing heterogeneity. SIGMOD Rec. 30(1), 78–83 (2001)
8. Oldevik, J., Haugen, Ø.: Higher-order transformations for product lines. In: SPLC, pp. 243–254. IEEE Computer Society (2007)
9. Puente, G., Díaz, O., Azanza, M.: Refactoring affordances in corporate wikis: a case for the use of mind maps. Enterprise Information Systems, 1–50 (2013)
10. Puente, G., Díaz, O.: Wiki refactoring as mind map reshaping. In: Ralyté, J., Franch, X., Brinkkemper, S., Wrycza, S. (eds.) CAiSE 2012. LNCS, vol. 7328, pp. 646–661. Springer, Heidelberg (2012)
11. Ra, Y.G.: Relational schema evolution for program independency. In: Das, G., Gulati, V.P. (eds.) CIT 2004. LNCS, vol. 3356, pp. 273–281. Springer, Heidelberg (2004), http://dx.doi.org/10.1007/978-3-540-30561-3_29
12. Sneed, H.M.: Encapsulation of legacy software: A technique for reusing legacy software components. Annals of Software Engineering 9(1-4), 293–313 (2000)
13. Thiran, P., Hainaut, J.L., Houben, G.J., Benslimane, D.: Wrapper-based evolution of legacy information systems. ACM Trans. Softw. Eng. Methodol. 15(4), 329–359 (2006)
14. Tisi, M., Jouault, F., Fraternali, P., Ceri, S., Bézivin, J.: On the use of higher-order model transformations. In: Paige, R.F., Hartman, A., Rensink, A. (eds.) ECMDA-FA 2009. LNCS, vol. 5562, pp. 18–33. Springer, Heidelberg (2009)
15. Velegrakis, Y., Miller, J., Popa, L.: Preserving mapping consistency under schema changes. The VLDB Journal 13(3), 274–293 (2004)

Mining Predictive Process Models
out of Low-level Multidimensional Logs

Francesco Folino, Massimo Guarascio, and Luigi Pontieri

National Research Council of Italy (CNR),
via Pietro Bucci 41C, I87036 Rende (CS), Italy
{ffolino,guarascio,pontieri}@icar.cnr.it

Abstract. Process Mining techniques have been gaining attention, especially as concerns the discovery of predictive process models. Traditionally focused on workflows, they usually assume that process tasks are clearly specified, and referred to in the logs. This limits however their application to many real-life BPM environments (e.g. issue tracking systems) where the traced events do not match any predefined task, but yet keep lots of context data. In order to make the usage of predictive process mining to such logs more effective and easier, we devise a new approach, combining the discovery of different execution scenarios with the automatic abstraction of log events. The approach has been integrated in a prototype system, supporting the discovery, evaluation and reuse of predictive process models. Tests on real-life data show that the approach achieves compelling prediction accuracy w.r.t. state-of-the-art methods, and finds interesting activities' and process variants' descriptions.

Keywords: Business Process Analysis, Data Mining, Prediction.

1 Introduction

Process Mining techniques aim at extracting useful information from historical process logs, possibly in the form of descriptive or predictive process models, which can support the analysis, design, and improvement of business processes. An emerging research stream [1,9,4] concerns the induction of models for predicting a given performance measure for new cases at run time.

Originally focused on workflow systems, Process Mining research has been moving towards less structured processes, possibly featuring a wide variety of behaviors and many low-level tasks. This calls for enhancing classical approaches with the capability to capture diverse execution scenarios (a.k.a. "process variants"), and to map log events to high-level activity concepts [3], in order to prevent the construction of useless models giving a cumbersome and undergeneralized view of process behavior.

The need of providing expressive process views is also witnessed by the proliferation of works on activity abstraction [12,11,7] and on log clustering [14,9,4], as well as by recent efforts to model different process variants and their link to

M. Jarke et al. (Eds.): CAiSE 2014, LNCS 8484, pp. 533–547, 2014.

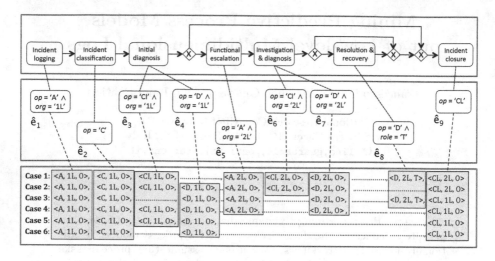

Fig. 1. A simplified Incident Management scenario: unknown high-level tasks (top), low-level event log (bottom), and data-driven event classes (middle)

environmental factors [13]. Some works also tried to combine trace clustering and activity abstraction, in order to build expressive process models, with different process variants represented via high-level tasks (or sub-processes, at different levels of aggregation/abstraction) [10,8,6].

Unfortunately, most of these methods assume that the log events are mapped to well defined process tasks, which is not true in many real-life collaborative work environments (such as issue tracking systems, or transaction systems), where lots of data are yet stored (in the form of event/case attributes) that might well help model/predict system behaviour.

Example 1. As an example scenario, consider the simplified version of the ITIL's "Incident Management" process (inspired to [3]) at the top of Figure 1. Assume that none of the high-level process tasks appear in the execution traces (like those at the bottom of the figure), where each event just stores low-level information as a triple $\langle op, org, role \rangle$. Specifically, attribute op, which encodes rather generically the operation performed, can take one of the following values: A (allocating the incident to someone), C (classifying the incident), D (describing the incident or its solution), CI (associating the incident with a configuration item) and CL (closing the incident). Attribute org tells which organizational entity the executor belongs to: 1L (early intervention) and 2L (second level team). Finally, the stored executor role can be either O (*operator*) or T (technician).   ◁

In the log of lowly structured processes, like those above, none of the event attributes fully capture the semantics of all performed actions. In such a case, abstracting each event as a fixed combination of multiple attributes is likely to yield overfitting models, seeing as a very high number of distinct state/activity representations may be produced, most of which just cover a bunch of log events.

Conversely, simple event abstraction strategies (consisting in replacing each log event with the associated task or executor or them both) tend to be adopted in the area of predictive process mining, where the combination of model induction and automated activity abstraction has not been investigated so far.

Contribution To overcome the above limitations, we state the prediction of process performances as the search for an enhanced kind of performance model, consisting of three components: *(a)* an event classification function, for abstracting each low-level event into an event class, regarded as a distinct activity type (rather than as a subprocess or macro-activity, as in [12,11,7]); *(b)* a trace classification function, for discriminating among different process variants, based on case data; and *(c)* a collection of state-aware predictors, each associated with one process variant. The event classification function is meant to partition all (low-level) log events into clusters, like those in the middle layer of Figure 1, each associated with a classification rule (over event attributes). Analogous rules (over case attributes) can be found to partition all process traces into execution classes. Such a model supports the forecast of the analyzed performance measure on an ongoing process case τ via three logical steps: *(i)* each τ's event is abstracted by the event classification function; *(ii)* the obtained abstract trace is assigned to a process variant through the trace classification function and *(iii)* the predictor of the selected variant is eventually used to predict the performance of τ.

A discovery algorithm is presented in the paper for inducing both classification functions by way of a co-clustering scheme (extending the logics-based framework of *predictive clustering* [5]), prior to building a local predictor for each trace cluster. Besides enjoying compelling prediction accuracy (w.r.t. current methods, combined with usual log abstractions), in real-life application cases the approach managed to recognize relevant activity patterns at the right abstraction level. Moreover, the descriptive nature of the discovered classification rules (expressed in terms of event/trace data) can help comprehend process behaviors, and how its performances depend on both context factors and activity patterns.

Organization. The rest of the paper is structured as follows. After introducing some preliminary concepts in Section 2, we present, in Section 3, our solution approach and a prototype system implementing it. An empirical analysis on two real-life case studies is then discussed in Section 4, before drawing some concluding remarks and future work directions.

2 Preliminaries

Let us denote by E and $\mathcal{T}$ the universes of all possible events and (both fully unfolded and partial) traces, respectively, for the process under analysis – as usual, we assume that a *trace* is recorded for each process instance (a.k.a "case"), encoding the sequence of *events* happened during its enactment. For our purposes, an event $e \in E$ is regarded as a tuple storing a case identifier and a timestamp, denoted by $case(e)$ and $time(e)$, as well as a vector $prop(e)$ of data properties, in some given space of event attributes. For example, in structured process management settings (like those handled by WfMSs), any event keeps information on both the task performed and the executor. However, as discussed above, this does not happen in many flexible BPM environments (e.g., issue/project management systems), where the tasks are not precisely conceptualized, or they just represent generic operations (e.g., update a document or exchange a message).

For each trace $\tau \in \mathcal{T}$, let $\tau[i]$ be the i-th event of τ, and let $\tau(i) \in \mathcal{T}$ be the *prefix* trace consisting of its first i events, for $i = 1 \mathbin{..} len(\tau)$, where $len(\tau)$ is the number of events stored in τ. Moreover, let $prop(\tau)$ be a vector of data properties associated with any trace $\tau \in \mathcal{T}$, possibly including "environmental" variables characterizing the state of the BPM system (as proposed in [9]).

A *log* L (over $\mathcal{T}$) is a finite subset of $\mathcal{T}$, while the *prefix set* of L, denoted by $\mathcal{P}(L)$, is the set of all prefix traces that can be extracted from L. Finally, $events(L)$ indicates the set of all events stored in (some trace of) L.

Let us denote by $\lambda : \mathcal{T} \to \mathbb{R}$ the (unknown) performance measure (targeted by our predictive analysis) that virtually assigns a performance value to any (possibly partial) trace – for the sake of concreteness, and w.l.o.g., λ is assumed to range over real numbers. Two examples of such a measure are the remaining processing time and steps of a trace, i.e. the time and steps, respectively, needed to complete the respective process enactment.

A (predictive) *Process Performance Model (PPM)* is a model estimating the performance value of any process instance, based only on its current trace. Such a model can be viewed as a function $\tilde{\lambda} : \mathcal{T} \to \mathbb{R}$ that approximates λ all over the trace universe — including the prefix traces of unfinished enactments. Discovering such a model is an induction problem, where a given log L is used as a training set, and the λ is known for each (sub-)trace $\tau \in \mathcal{P}(L)$.

In order to focus on relevant facets of events, current approaches rely all on some abstraction functions such as those defined below (similarly to [1,9]).

Definition 1 (Event/Trace Abstraction). Let $\mathcal{T}$ be a trace universe, and E be its associated event universe. Let $\hat{E} = \{\hat{e}_1, \ldots, \hat{e}_k\}$ be a given set of abstract event representations. An *event abstraction function* $\mathcal{E} : E \to \hat{E}$ is a function mapping each event $e \in E$ to $\mathcal{E}(e) \in \hat{E}$, based on e's properties. Moreover, the trace abstraction function $abs^{\mathcal{E}} : \mathcal{T} \to \mathbb{N}^n$ is defined as follows: $abs^{\mathcal{E}}(\tau) = \langle\ count(\hat{e}_1, \tau), \ldots, count(\hat{e}_k, \tau)\ \rangle$, where $count(\hat{e}_i, \tau) = |\{\ i \in \{1, \ldots, len(\tau)\} \mid \mathcal{E}(\tau[i]) = \hat{e}_i\ \}|$, for any trace $\tau \in \mathcal{T}$. $\qquad\square$

For example, let τ_1 be the complete trace associated with the first case (Case 1) in the log of Figure 1, and let $\mathcal{E}_{op}$ be an event abstraction function that replaces each event with its first field op. Then, by applying function $abs^{\mathcal{E}_{op}}$ to the (prefix) traces $\tau_1(1)$, $\tau_1(2)$, $\tau_1(3)$ and $\tau_1(4)$, four tuples are obtained, which encode the multi-sets $[\mathtt{A}]$, $[\mathtt{A}, \mathtt{C}]$, $[\mathtt{A}, \mathtt{C}, \mathtt{CI}]$, and $[\mathtt{A}^2, \mathtt{C}, \mathtt{CI}]$, respectively.

More expressive trace abstraction schemes can be defined, as in [1], which take account for the ordering of events, and possibly discard less recent ones (according to a horizon threshold). However, such an issue is not considered in this work, which mainly aims at studying how a given (even simple) trace abstraction scheme can be enhanced through ad-hoc event/trace clustering methods.

Based on such trace abstractions, an annotated finite state machine ("AFSM") can be derived as in [1], where each node corresponds to one abstract trace representation (produced by $abs^{\mathcal{E}}$) and stores an estimate for the target measure, while each transition is labelled with an event abstraction (produced by $\mathcal{E}$). Alternatively, classic regression methods can be used to extract a PPM from a propositional encoding of the log, like that in Definition 1.

Basic PPM learning methods were recently hybridized with Predictive Clustering techniques [5], which partition a data set into clusters, while assuming that all data instances own two kinds of features: *target* attributes (to be predicted), and *descriptive* attributes (used to define logical splits). Specifically, such a clustering procedure was combined with the AFSM method [9] and standard regression methods [4], with context data used as descriptive trace attributes.

3   Approach and Implementation

Clearly, the effectiveness of current performance mining approaches strongly depends on the capability of the event abstraction function $\mathcal{E}$ to focus on those properties of log events that are really connected with the behavior (and performances) of the process at hand. Unfortunately, the common solution of abstracting each event into a task's and/or an executor's label does not fit the case of logs storing fine grain records (corresponding to low-level and generic operations), where none of the event properties is suitable for making an effective event abstraction. For instance, in the case of Example 1, considering just the kind of operation performed leads to excessive information loss. Conversely, defining abstract activities as the mere combination of multiple properties (e.g., regarding each distinct triple in Example 1 as an activity) may yield a cumbersome and ineffective representation of process states (as proven empirically in our experimentation). On the other hand, many real-life tracing systems keep lots of context information for each process case, which may be used to build precise and articulated performance prediction models like those in [9].

In order to fully exploit the variety of (events' and cases') data stored in a process log, we try to build an expressive performance model for the process, hinging on two interrelated classification models: one allowing to grasp the right level of abstraction over log events, and the other encoding the business rules that determine each variant. A precise definition of such a model is given below.

Definition 2 (CCPM). Let L be a log, over an event (resp., trace) universe E (resp., $\mathcal{T}$). Then, a *Co-Clustering Performance Model* (CCPM) for L is a triple of the form $M = \langle \mathcal{C}_E, \mathcal{C}_{\mathcal{T}}, \Lambda \rangle$, where: *(i)* $\mathcal{C}_E : E \to \mathbb{N}$ is a partitioning function over E; *(ii)* $\mathcal{C}_{\mathcal{T}} : \mathcal{T} \to \mathbb{N}$ is a partitioning function over $\mathcal{T}$; and *(iii)* $\Lambda = \langle \lambda_1, \ldots, \lambda_q \rangle$ is a list of PPMs, all using $\mathcal{C}_E$ as event abstraction function, such that q is the number of clusters produced by $\mathcal{C}_{\mathcal{T}}$, and λ_i is the model of the i-th cluster, for $i \in \{1, \ldots, q\}$. The overall prediction function encoded by M (denoted by the same symbol M, for shortness) is: $M(\tau) = \lambda_j(\tau)$, where $j = \mathcal{C}_{\mathcal{T}}(\tau)$. $\square$

Conceptually, a forecast for any new process instance τ can be made with the help of such a model, in three steps: *(i)* an abstract representation of τ is obtained

Input: A log L (over some trace universe $\mathcal{T}$) with an associated target measure λ,
    max. iterations' number $maxIter \in \mathbb{N}$, min. (relative) loss reduction $\gamma \in (0,1]$,
    max. number $maxCl_E, maxCl_T \in \mathbb{N} \cup \{\infty\}$ of (events', resp. traces') clusters,
    min. cluster coverages $\sigma \in (0,1]$ (for both events and traces).
Output: A CCPM model for L (fully encoding λ all over $\mathcal{T}$).
Method: Perform the following steps:
  1 set $\mathcal{C}_T^{(0)} := \{L\}$; $\mathcal{C}_E^{(0)} := \{events(L)\}$; $Err^{(0)} := \infty$; $k := 0$;
  2 **do**
  3    $k := k+1$;
  4    $EV := \mathcal{V}_E(L, \mathcal{C}_T^{(k-1)})$; // *build an e-view for L w.r.t. $\mathcal{C}_T^{(k-1)}$ (cf. Def. 4)*
  5    $\mathcal{C}_E^{(k)} := \mathtt{minePCM}(EV, \sigma, maxCl_E)$; // *induce a novel event clustering model*
  6    $TV := \mathcal{V}_T(L, \mathcal{C}_E^{(k)})$; // *build a t-view for L w.r.t. $\mathcal{C}_E^{(k)}$ (cf. Def. 3)*
  7    $\mathcal{C}_T^{(k)} := \mathtt{minePCM}(TV, \sigma, maxCl_T)$; // *induce a novel trace clustering model*
  8   let $Err^{(k)} = Loss(\mathcal{C}_E^{(k)}, \mathcal{C}_T^{(k)}, L)$; // *estimate current prediction error*
  9    $improved := Err^{(k-1)} - Err^{(k)} \leq \gamma^{(k)} \times Err^{(k-1)}$;
10 **while** $k \leq maxIter$ **and** $improved$;
11 **if** $improved$ **then** $\mathcal{C}_T := \mathcal{C}_T^{(k)}$; $\mathcal{C}_E := \mathcal{C}_E^{(k)}$;
12   **else** $\mathcal{C}_T := \mathcal{C}_T^{(k-1)}$; $\mathcal{C}_E := \mathcal{C}_E^{(k-1)}$;
13 let $TC = \langle \hat{t}_1, \ldots, \hat{t}_q \rangle$ be the list of trace clusters produced by $\mathcal{C}_T$ on $\mathcal{P}(L)$;
14 **for each** $\hat{t}_i$ in TC **do**
15    $\lambda_i := \mathtt{minePPM}(\hat{t}_i, \mathcal{C}_E)$;
16 **end**
17 **return** $\langle \mathcal{C}_E, \mathcal{C}_T, \langle \lambda_1, \ldots, \lambda_q \rangle \rangle$

Fig. 2. Algorithm CCD

in the form of a vector (as specified in Definition 1) that summarizes both its context data and structure, with each event abstracted into an event class via $\mathcal{C}_E$; *(ii)* τ is assigned to a trace cluster (representing a particular execution scenario for the process) via function $\mathcal{C}_T$; *(iii)* the predictor of the chosen cluster is used to make a forecast for τ, by providing it with $abs^{\mathcal{C}_E}(\tau)$. The functions $\mathcal{C}_E$ and $\mathcal{C}_T$, encoding two different classification models (defined over descriptive attributes), are hence exploited to abstract raw log events into high-level classes, and to discriminate among different process variants, respectively.

3.1 Solution Algorithm

In principle, one might seek an optimal CCPM for a given log L by trying to minimize some suitable loss measure (comparing the actual performance of each trace with the corresponding estimate). By contrast, in order to avoid prohibitive computation times across such a large search space, we rephrase the discovery problem into two simpler ones: *(1)* find a locally optimal pair of classification functions $\mathcal{C}_E$ and $\mathcal{C}_T$, and *(2)* derive a collection of cluster-wise PPM predictors.

Our solution approach is summarized in Figure 2 as an algorithm, named CCD ("Co-Clustering based Discovery"). Since the quality of the trace clustering model $\mathcal{C}_T$ strongly depends on the chosen abstraction function $\mathcal{C}_E$, and vice versa, we regard the first subproblem as a co-clustering one, were an optimal partition must be found for both traces and events. This problem is approached via an iterative alternate-optimization scheme, where, at each iteration k, updated versions of the two partitioning functions are computed, denoted by $\mathcal{C}_E^{(k)}$ and $\mathcal{C}_T^{(k)}$, until no satisfactory loss reduction (w.r.t. the previous iteration) is achieved. Notice that, for efficiency reasons, any loss $Err^{(k)}$ is measured by accounting for the distribution of performances in each "co-cluster" as follows: $Loss(\mathcal{C}_T, \mathcal{C}_E, L) = \sum_{\tau \in \mathcal{P}(L)} [\lambda(\tau) - avg(\{\lambda(\tau'') \mid \mathcal{C}_T(\tau'') = \mathcal{C}_T(\tau)$ and $\mathcal{C}_E(\tau''[len(\tau'')]) = \mathcal{C}_E(\tau[len(\tau)])\})]^2$.

Each model $\mathcal{C}_E^{(k)}$ is induced, via function minePCM, from an "event-oriented" view ($e\text{-}view$) EV of the input log, which encodes both event data and a series of performance measurements, computed on current trace clusters. The discovered event clustering $\mathcal{C}_E^{(k)}$ is then used, as a novel event abstraction method, to provide minePCM with a "trace-oriented" view ($t\text{-}view$) TV of the log, in order to eventually induce an updated trace partitioning $\mathcal{C}_T^{(k)}$. In this way, any novel trace clustering takes advantage of the most recent definition of event classes, and vice versa, according to a reinforcement learning scheme. Both kinds of views are formally defined below.

Definition 3 (T-View). Let L be a log, and $\mathcal{C}_E$ be a partitioning function defined over $events(L)$. Then, a $t\text{-}view$ for L w.r.t. $\mathcal{C}_E$, denoted by $\mathcal{V}_T(L, \mathcal{C}_E)$, is a relation containing, for each trace $\tau \in \mathcal{P}(L)$, a tuple $z_\tau = prop(\tau) \oplus abs^{\mathcal{C}_E}(\tau) \oplus \langle \lambda(\tau) \rangle$, where $\oplus$ stands for tuple concatenation. For any such tuple z_τ, $prop(\tau)$ and $abs^{\mathcal{C}_E}(\tau)$ are considered as descriptive features, while $\lambda(\tau)$ is the associated (unidimensional) target. $\qquad\square$

Definition 4 (E-View). Let L be a log, $\mathcal{C}_T$ be a (trace) partitioning function over $\mathcal{P}(L)$, and $\{\hat{t}_1, \ldots, \hat{t}_q\}$ be the clusters which $\mathcal{C}_T$ ranges over (with $\hat{t}_i = \{\tau \in \mathcal{P}(L) \mid \mathcal{C}_T(\tau) = i\}$ for $i \in \{1 \ldots q\}$). Then, an $e\text{-}view$ for L w.r.t. $\mathcal{C}_T$, denoted by $\mathcal{V}_E(L, \mathcal{C}_T)$, is a relation consisting of a tuple $z_e = prop(e) \oplus \langle val(e, \hat{t}_1), \ldots, val(e, \hat{t}_q) \rangle$ for each $e \in events(L)$, where $\oplus$ still denotes tuple concatenation, and, for any $i \in \{1, \ldots, q\}$, it is:

$$val(e, \hat{t}_i) = \begin{cases} \text{NULL, if } \nexists \, \tau \in \hat{t}_i \text{ s.t. } prop(\tau[len(\tau)]) = prop(e); \\ avg(\{\lambda(\tau) \mid \tau \in \hat{t}_i \text{ and } prop(\tau[len(\tau)]) = prop(e) \}), \text{ otherwise.} \end{cases}$$

For any tuple z_e, all the fields in $prop(e)$ are regarded as descriptive attributes, and $\langle val(e, \hat{t}_1), \ldots, val(e, \hat{t}_q) \rangle$ as its associated (multidimensional) target. $\qquad\square$

Provided with such propositional views, function minePCM is meant to induce a logics-based partitioning function, by applying some predictive clustering procedure to the given (target and descriptive) data. Details on how this function was implemented in our prototype system can be found in the following subsection.

Once an (locally) optimal pair of event and trace clusterings has been found, each cluster predictor λ_i, for $\in \{1, \ldots, n\}$, is eventually computed by providing function minePPM with all the traces assigned to the cluster, and with the event abstraction function $\mathcal{C}_E$. To this end, the function converts $\hat{t}_i$ in its t-view w.r.t. $\mathcal{C}_E$, prior to applying some suitable regression method to it.

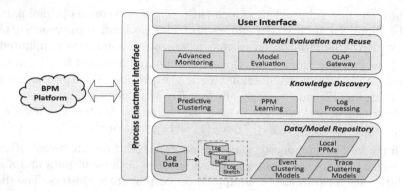

Fig. 3. Conceptual architecture of the developed prototype system

Notice that the auxiliary parameters of algorithm CCD are meant to give the analyst some control on both computation times ($maxIter$, γ) and the complexity of the discovered model ($maxCl_E$, $maxCl_T$). However, whatever setting is used, the algorithm is guaranteed to terminate, since the loss measure must decrease at each iteration ($\gamma > 0$), and the number of event/trace classification functions is finite. Notably, in a wide series of tests, the computation naturally finished in a few steps (less than $maxIter$), by just fixing $\gamma = 0$.

3.2   Implementation Issues and Prototype System

Functions minePPM and minePCM The current implementation of minePPM follows the method proposed in [5] for inducing a PCT (Predictive Clustering Tree), a logics-based predictive clustering model where the cluster assignment function is encoded in terms of decision rules (over descriptive attributes). Basically, such a model is built via a top-down partitioning scheme, where the log is split recursively, while selecting each time a descriptive attribute that locally minimizes the (weighted) average of the variances of the newly generated clusters — i.e. the 2-norm distances between the centroid of each new cluster and all instances in it. To curb the growth of the tree, an F-test based stopping criterion is used, possibly combined with a user-given upper bound to the total number clusters.

The current implementation of function minePCM just relies applying one of the two following standard regression methods to a propositional log view like that in Definition 1): the regression-tree induction algorithm *RepTree* and the *k-NN* procedure *IB-k*, both available in the popular Weka library [15].

System Prototype. The approach has been integrated into a prototype system, featuring the conceptual architecture in Figure 3, whose two lower layers leverage some core functionalities of the Process Mining framework ProM [2].

Basically, the bottommost layer is responsible for storing both historical process logs, and the different kinds of views extracted from them, as well as the different kinds of models composing each discovered CCPM models. All data mining and transformation mechanisms used in our approach are implemented in

Table 1. Summary features of the two application scenarios (including the associated event/trace attributes used in the tests)

Scenario	#events	#cases	Event Attributes	Trace Attributes	Target
Harbor	21484	5336	movType, shift, area_from, area_to, vehicleType, block_from, block_to	service_in, service_out, imo, line_in, line_out, size, height, vessel_in, containerType, reefer, carrierType_in, carrierType_out, prevCall, nextCall, outOfGauge, prevCountry, nextCountry	remaining time
Bug	8661	2283	assignee, blocks, component, hardware, priority, product, resolution, os, severity, status	comments, votes, severity, QA, classification, component, URL, reporter, keywords, resolution, product, assignee, priority, status, hardware, flags	remaining steps

the *Knowledge Discovery* layer, which supports the discovery of a new CCPM, in a interactive and iterative manner, based on the computation scheme of algorithm CCD. In particular, the *Predictive Clustering* and *PPM Learning* modules implement the functions minePCM and minePPM functions, respectively.

All models discovered out of a process log (i.e., traces' and events' clustering models, and the PPM models of each trace cluster) are made available to the *Model Evaluation and Reuse Layer*, which, in particular, provides the user with an easily-readable report, including the error metrics considered in our tests. The *OLAP Gateway* module is meant to reorganize historical log data into different aggregated views, in order to possibly support OLAP-like analyses.

Thanks to its predictive nature, each discovered CCPM can be used to configure a forecasting service for the process it was discovered for, to estimate (at run time and step-by-step) the performance outcome of any new instance of the process. Besides pure performance prediction, the *Advanced Monitoring* module supports the anticipated notification of Service Level Agreement (SLA) violations, whenever a process instance is estimated to fail a given quality requirement, previously established for one of the performance measures associated with the process.

4   Experiments

In order to assess the validity our approach, we conducted a series of tests on the logs of two real process management systems: the operational system of a maritime hub, and bug-tracking system. For readability purposes, Table 1 summarizes some features of both scenarios, indicated hereinafter as *harbor* and *bug*, respectively. Notice that a few trace attributes (e.g., comments and votes, in the *Bug* scenario) are not really known at the very beginning of a case. Clearly, such properties can be used to dynamically (re-)assign a process case to a trace cluster only if they have already taken a value. Anyway, as any trace clustering returned by our approach is ensured to cover the entire universe of traces at any step of its unfolding, each process instance falls into one of the trace clusters.

Three variants of the CCD algorithm were studied in our tests, which differ in the implementation of function minePPM: CCD-RT, using the regression-tree induction algorithm *RepTree* [15]; CCD-IBK, based on the *IB-k* procedure implemented in Weka [15]; and CCD-AVG, where each cluster predictor just returns the average performance in the cluster — the last method just serves as a baseline and quantifies co-clustering loss. In all cases, a fixed setting was used for the auxiliary parameters: $maxIter{=}20$, $\gamma{=}0$, $\sigma{=}1\%$, and $maxCl_E{=}maxCl_T{=}50$. Notice that we bounded the number of event/traces to have handier process models and speed up the computation, at the cost of low precision loss (at least for CCD-RT and CCD-IBK), with respect the default setting $maxCl_E{=}maxCl_T{=}\infty$.

For the sake of comparison, besides using the two base regressors mentioned above (denoted by RT and IBK) as baselines, we tested the FSM-based method in [1] (here named AFSM), the CATP algorithm of [9] (which reuses AFSM), and two variants of the approach in [4], denoted by as AATP-IBK and AATP-RT, using IBK and RepTree, respectively, as base learners. We remark that all competitors lack automated mechanisms for abstracting log events (into activity/action entities), and hence need the application of some a-priori event abstraction function. Conversely, all of the tested methods but AFSM can take advantage of case data.

Three standard error metrics have been used to evaluate prediction accuracy: *root mean squared error (rmse)*, *mean absolute error (mae)*, and *mean absolute percentage error (mape)*. For the sake of significance, all the error results reported next were computed via 10 fold cross-validation and averaged over 10 trials. Moreover, a statistical test was applied to check whether the methods performed really different. Specifically, for each error metrics, we used a paired two-tail Student's *t*-test to compare the outcomes of each method with those of the most precise one (i.e. the one achieving the lowest average error on that metric), at two different confidence levels: 95% and 99%. We then considered a method as almost equivalent to (resp., substantially worse than) the best performer if it did not differ at the 95% level (resp., it did differ at the 99% level) from the latter.

4.1 Tests on the *Harbor* Scenario

This scenario pertains the handling of containers in a maritime terminal, where a series of logistic activities are performed and traced for each container passing through the harbor. As mentioned in Example 1, each log event stores, by way of event attributes, different aspects of the logistics (move) actions performed on a container, including the followings: *(i)* the source and destination position it was moved between, in terms of yard's blocks (block_from and block_to, respectively) and areas (area_from and area_to, respectively) *(ii)* the kind of operation performed (movType), ranging over **MOV**e, **DR**ive to **B**ring, **DR**rive to **G**et, **LOAD**, **DIS**charge, **SHu**Ffle, **OUT**; *(iii)* the type of instrument used (vehicleType), ranging from cranes to straddle-carriers and multi-trailers.

Trace attributes convey instead different properties of the handled container, ranging from the previous and next ports (prevCall and nextCall), and their associated countries (prevCountry and nextCountry), to several physical features (e.g., size and height). Like in [9], for each container, we also considered,

Table 2. Prediction results on the *harbor* scenario: errors made (over remaining times) by CCD and several competitors. For each metrics, the **best** outcome is reported in bold and underlined, while all methods **nearly equivalent** to the best one, and those *neatly worse* than it (according to T-test) are shown in bold and in italics, respectively.

Predictors		Error Measures		
Approach	*Methods*	rmse	mae	mape (%)
Algorithm CCD (Fig. 2)	CCD-IBK	**26.57±8.11**	**5.39±8.11**	**15.00±11.34**
	CCD-RT	**25.39±8.38**	**5.95±0.91**	**10.17±10.61**
	CCD-AVG	*28.58±11.44*	*8.27±1.44*	*38.10±15.86*
Competitors with the given (1-attribute) event abstraction *EA1*	AATP-IBK [4]	31.93±12.50	*7.04±1.20*	*63.62±5.65*
	AATP-RT [4]	29.95±9.67	*8.76±1.31*	*66.32±14.80*
	AFSM [1]	*80.46±11.93*	*30.74±1.40*	*279.15±26.72*
	CATP [9]	31.53±8.33	*8.35±0.60*	*58.26±26.96*
	IBK [15]	*33.66±9.37*	*7.64±0.89*	*72.50±9.85*
	RT [15]	*30.28±8.91*	*8.36±0.77*	*69.67±8.70*
Competitors with the given (5-attribute) event abstraction *EA2*	AATP-IBK [4]	*54.38±7.98*	*16.66±2.00*	*288.55±44.82*
	AATP-RT [4]	*43.84±8.08*	*16.58±1.08*	*144.19±46.31*
	AFSM [1]	*75.31±16.68*	*25.27±2.77*	*53.95±20.27*
	CATP [9]	*56.21±11.68*	*20.25±1.73*	*85.56±34.64*
	IBK [15]	*54.02±5.97*	*16.50±1.42*	*290.54±28.76*
	RT [15]	*43.33±6.04*	*15.59±0.76*	*205.06±48.89*

as a sort of environmental variables, the hour (resp., week-day, month) when it arrived, and the total number of containers ("workload") in the port at that time. The list of all events' and traces' attributes can be found in Table 1.

While our approach doesn't need any preliminary event abstraction/labelling, and it can deal with raw (multi-dimensional) event tuples, an event abstraction criterion must be defined prior to applying any other method. Two different solutions were used to this purpose in our tests: *(EA1)* abstracting each container-handling event with just the associated move type (namely, MOV, DRB, etc.); and *(EA2)* using the combination of the former five event attributes in Table 1.

Prediction Accuracy Results. Table 2 reports the (average and standard deviation for the) errors made by our methods and the competitors/baseline ones, when trying to predict the remaining processing time over a sample of 5336 containers, all exchanged with ports of the Mediterranean sea in the first third of 2006. Clearly, when faced with the challenge of dealing with complex events, according to setting *S2*, all competitors exhibit a neat worsening of results, w.r.t. the case where they were just made focus on the kinds of moves performed (setting *S1*). In fact, we verified empirically that this is the best possible single-attribute event abstraction for the given log — i.e. worse results are obtained by previous methods when abstracting the events via any other single attribute. Moreover, all base learners IBK, RT and AFSM seem to improve when embedded in a trace clustering scheme (see AAPT-IB, AAPT-RT and CATP, respectively). However, the best achievements are clearly obtained by our methods CCD-IBK and CCD-RT. Besides confirming the ability of our approach to find an effective abstraction over raw events, these results show its superiority to the two-phase (i.e. event abstraction, followed by model induction) strategy commonly used in the field of process mining, often relying on manually defined activities.

Table 3. Some event clusters (left) and trace clusters (right) returned by running CCD-RT on the *harbor* scenario with $\sigma = 0.01$, and $maxCl_E = maxCl_T = 50$. Incidentally, in this specific test the algorithm discovered 12 event clusters and 48 trace clusters. Cluster sizes are expressed as percentages (of all log events/traces).

id	condition	size
$\hat{e}_1$	area_to $\in \{C,BFS,SR\} \wedge$ area_from $\in \{A\text{-}NEW,T,B\text{-}NEW,\dots\}$	12%
$\hat{e}_2$	area_to $\in \{C,BFS,SR\} \wedge$ area_from $\in \{C,CR,A,\dots\}$	5%
$\hat{e}_3$	area_to $\in \{CR,BITTE\}$	17%
$\hat{e}_4$	area_to $\in \{MTR,T,GT,\dots\}$	12.7%
$\hat{e}_9$	area_to $\in \{A\text{-}NEW,A,B\text{-}NEW,\dots\} \wedge$ movType $= MOV \wedge$ area_from $\in \{A\text{-}NEW,A,BITTE,\dots\}$	11%
$\hat{e}_{12}$	area_to $\in \{A\text{-}NEW,A,B\text{-}NEW,\dots\} \wedge$ movType $\in \{OUT,DRG,LOAD,DRB,$ $DIS,SHF\} \wedge$ area_from $\in \{A\text{-}NEW,A,BITTE,\dots\}$	6%

id	condition	size
$\hat{t}_{20}$	$count(\hat{e}_1) \leq 0 \wedge count(\hat{e}_3) \leq 0 \wedge$ $count(\hat{e}_4) \leq 0 \wedge count(\hat{e}_9) > 0 \wedge$ nextCountry $\in \{BG,BE,KR,\dots\} \wedge$ service_OUT $\in \{ME3,GBX,\dots\}$	6%
$\hat{t}_{33}$	$count(\hat{e}_1) \leq 0 \wedge count(\hat{e}_2) \leq 0 \wedge$ $count(\hat{e}_3) \leq 0 \wedge count(\hat{e}_4) \leq 0 \wedge$ $count(\hat{e}_9) \leq 0 \wedge count(\hat{e}_{12}) \leq 0 \wedge$ nextCountry $\in \{GE,HR,TN,\dots\} \wedge$ service_OUT $\in \{AEC,GAX,\dots\} \wedge$ line_OUT $\in \{CPP,CPS,SEN,\dots\}$	4%
$\hat{t}_{44}$	$count(\hat{e}_1) \leq 0 \wedge count(\hat{e}_3) \leq 0 \wedge$ $count(\hat{e}_4) \leq 0 \wedge count(\hat{e}_9) \leq 0 \wedge$ nextCountry $\in \{GR,ES,AE,\dots\} \wedge$ service_OUT $\in \{EEX,BSS,\dots\} \wedge$ line_OUT $\in \{MSK,APL,HLL,\dots\} \wedge$ prevCountry $\in \{LB,SY,BE,EG,DZ\}$	2%

Qualitative Results. Table 3 summarizes some of the classification (i.e. partitioning) rules appearing in both clustering functions discovered with our approach (precisely, with CCD-RT) on the harbor scenario. Notice that these rules are quite easy to interpret and validate, and provide the analyst with a useful description of process behavior (besides supporting accurate predictions). In particular, the event clusters in the table confirm that performance-relevant activity patterns cannot be captured by just one of the event properties, nor by a fixed combination of them. Interestingly, indeed, while some event clusters just correspond to a subset of destination areas, some others also depend on the source area, or even further on the kind of move performed. On the other hand, the descriptions of trace clusters let us reckon the presence of different execution scenarios, linked to both context factors (e.g., the country of the previous/next port, or the line/service planned to bring the container) and to some of the discovered event clusters (hence playing as high-level activity patterns).

4.2 Tests on the *Bug* Scenario

As a second testing scenario, we analyzed the Eclipse project's bug repository, developed with the *Bugzilla* bug-tracking system (see *http://www.bugzilla.org*).

Essentially, each bug in the repository is associated with several fields (here regarded as trace attributes), which keep information, e.g., on: who reported the bug (reporter); who it has been allocated to (assignee); the affected software module (component, product, version, hardware); its severity and priority levels; its status and resolution. the number of comments written about the bug (comments). Almost all these fields can be updated as long as a bug evolves. In particular, the status of a bug can take one of the following values: *unconfirmed, new, assigned, resolved, verified, reopened,* and *closed.*

Table 4. Prediction results on the *bug* scenario: errors made (over remaining steps) by CCD and several competitors. The **best** result is in bold and underlined, methods **nearly equivalent** to the best one are in bold, those *neatly worse* than it in italics.

Predictors		Error Measures		
Approach	*Methods*	rmse	mae	mape (%)
Algorithm CCD (Fig. 2)	CCD-IBK	**1.369±0.666**	**0.448±0.111**	**0.167±0.010**
	CCD-RT	**1.345±0.658**	0.496±0.101	*0.210±0.008*
	CCD-AVG	*1.440±0.666*	0.578±0.118	0.197±0.005
Competitors, provided with ad-hoc defined activity labels	AATP-IBK [4]	**1.369±0.446**	0.472±0.143	**0.176±0.020**
	AATP-RT [4]	1.381±0.723	0.566±0.128	0.767±0.134
	AFSM [1]	1.463±0.818	0.590±0.164	0.779±0.035
	CATP [9]	1.404±0.839	0.578±0.175	0.684±0.041
	IBK [15]	1.392±0.848	0.484±0.164	0.555±0.041
	RT [15]	1.499±0.787	0.637±0.154	0.873±0.020

The **resolution** of a resolved bug can be: *fixed, duplicate, works-for-me, invalid,* or *won't-fix.*

As to log events, the history of a bug is kept in Bugzilla as by way of update records, possibly grouped in "bug activities", each of which gathers all changes made within a single access session. In order to let our propositional mining methods capture "simultaneous" updates, we encoded each bug activity a into an event having as many attributes as the number of (modifiable) bug fields, such that each attribute stores either *(i)* the new value assigned to the corresponding field, if it was really modified in a, or *(ii) null,* otherwise.

In order to provide the competitors with abstracted events, we tried different combinations of bug fields as possible activity labels, and empirically found that the best solution for them consists in only focusing on the changes made to the **status** (and to the **resolution** field, if modified "contemporaneously"), or to the **assignee**. In the former case, the activity label just encoded the new value assigned, without keeping any information about the person to whom a bug was (re-)assigned. The resulting abstract events look like the following activity labels: **status:=new**, **status:=resolved + resolution:=fixed**, **status:=verified**, etc., Δ**assignee** (simply indicating a generic change to the **assignee** field).

Prediction results. The tests were performed on a subset of the bugs created from January 1st, 2012 to April 1st, 2013, such that they were fixed at least once, but not opened and closed in the same day. Moreover, we filtered out all events (i.e. bug activities) that did not refer any of the fields **status**, **resolution**, and **assignee**. The resulting log consists of 2283 traces, with lengths (i.e. nr. of events) ranging from 2 to 25. Prediction errors on the *bug* scenario are reported in Table 4. Despite the fact that it was not provided with any suggestion on how events should be abstracted, our approach reached excellent prediction results (except when using the naïve regressor CCD-AVG), neatly better than all competitors, with the exception of AATP and, partially, of IBK.

Qualitative results. The models in Table 5 confirm that our approach really managed to automatically extract a suitable abstract representation for the given log events, which looks indeed very similar to the one defined for optimally

Table 5. All event clusters (left) and some of the 50 trace clusters (right) found by algorithm CCD on the *bug* scenario, with $\sigma = 0.01$, and $maxCl_E = maxCl_T = 50$

id	condition	size
$\hat{e}_1$	status = *closed*	47%
$\hat{e}_2$	status = *verified*	2%
$\hat{e}_3$	status $\in$ {*resolved,new*} $\wedge$ resolution = *fixed*	38%
$\hat{e}_4$	status $\in$ {*resolved,new*} $\wedge$ resolution $\in$ {*worksforme,invalid*}	1%
$\hat{e}_5$	status = *assigned*	8%
$\hat{e}_6$	status = *reopened*	4%

id	condition	size
$\hat{t}_1$	$count(\hat{e}_1) > 0 \wedge$ comments $> 6 \wedge$ component $\in$ {*build, foundation,*...}	1%
$\hat{t}_{22}$	$count(\hat{e}_1) \leq 0 \wedge 5 <$comments$\leq 15 \wedge$ $count(\hat{e}_2) \leq 0 \wedge count(\hat{e}_3) > 0$ component $\in$ {*DBWS, Graphiti,*...}	4%
$\hat{t}_{47}$	$count(\hat{e}_1) \leq 0 \wedge count(\hat{e}_3) \leq 0 \wedge$ $count(\hat{e}_5) \leq 0 \wedge$ comments $\leq 10 \wedge$ product $\in$ {*Xtend, Aether, Jetty,*...} $\wedge$ component $\in$ {*Xpand, Debugger,* ...}	3%

applying the competitors, Indeed, the `status` and `resolution` attributes have been fully exploited for discriminating among event classes. Trace clusters seem to depend mainly on the number of comments associated with bugs, and on the component and/or product affected — as well as on some of the discovered event classes, here playing as high-level performance-relevant activity patterns.

5   Discussion and Conclusions

The method proposed in this paper enhances current process mining approaches for the analysis of business process performances in different respects. First of all, it removes the common assumption that all traced event logs refer explicitly (or can be easily mapped to) well defined process tasks, and allows to automatically replace the formers with high-level activity types, capturing performance behaviors at the right level of abstraction.

Empirical findings from two real application scenarios proved that the approach can achieve compelling prediction accuracy with respect to state-of-the-art process-mining methods, even when these latter are provided with a manual definition of process activities, carefully specified by an expert. We believe that prediction accuracy could be improved further by resorting to more powerful regression methods for inducing cluster-wise PPMs, in place of the straightforward ones used in our current implementation. Moreover, the descriptive power of logical event/trace partitioning rules, beside allowing for a quick validation and evaluation of the discovered models, can really help the analyst better comprehend the behavior of the process, and the way its performances depend on both context factors and activity patterns.

As to efficiency, the approach seems to work well in practice. Indeed, in the two scenarios discussed above, at most 6 co-clustering iterations were needed to find a solution (with σ=1% and $maxCl_E$=$maxCl_T$=50), and our approach only took 3.6 times longer than the quickest among the competitors — excluding IBK, which performs no real learning task. This ratio only became 5.4 when no finite upper bound was set for the numbers of clusters.

As future work, we plan to extend the expressive power of our event/trace classification models, and to integrate advanced regression methods for learning cluster predictors, as well as to implement our discovery approach as a ProM [2]'s plugin, and to refine the OLAP-oriented capabilities of our prototype system.

Acknowledgments. The work was partially supported by the Italian Ministry of Education, Universities and Research (MIUR), under project *FRAME*.

References

1. van der Aalst, W.M.P., Schonenberg, M.H., Song, M.: Time prediction based on process mining. Information Systems 36(2), 450–475 (2011)
2. van Dongen, B.F., de Medeiros, A.K.A., Verbeek, H.M.W(E.), Weijters, A.J.M.M.T., van der Aalst, W.M.P.: The ProM framework: A new era in process mining tool support. In: Ciardo, G., Darondeau, P. (eds.) ICATPN 2005. LNCS, vol. 3536, pp. 444–454. Springer, Heidelberg (2005)
3. Baier, T., Mendling, J.: Bridging abstraction layers in process mining by automated matching of events and activities. In: Daniel, F., Wang, J., Weber, B. (eds.) BPM 2013. LNCS, vol. 8094, pp. 17–32. Springer, Heidelberg (2013)
4. Bevacqua, A., Carnuccio, M., Folino, F., Guarascio, M., Pontieri, L.: A data-driven prediction framework for analyzing and monitoring business process performances. In: ICEIS 2013, Revised Selected Papers (to appear)
5. Blockeel, H., Raedt, L.D.: Top-down induction of first-order logical decision trees. Artificial Intelligence 101(1-2), 285–297 (1998)
6. Bose, R.P.J.C., Verbeek, H.M.W., van der Aalst, W.M.P.: Discovering hierarchical process models using prom. In: CAiSE Forum (Selected Papers), pp. 33–48 (2011)
7. Jagadeesh Chandra Bose, R.P., van der Aalst, W.M.P.: Abstractions in process mining: A taxonomy of patterns. In: Dayal, U., Eder, J., Koehler, J., Reijers, H.A. (eds.) BPM 2009. LNCS, vol. 5701, pp. 159–175. Springer, Heidelberg (2009)
8. Ekanayake, C.C., Dumas, M., García-Bañuelos, L., La Rosa, M.: Slice, mine and dice: Complexity-aware automated discovery of business process models. In: Daniel, F., Wang, J., Weber, B. (eds.) BPM 2013. LNCS, vol. 8094, pp. 49–64. Springer, Heidelberg (2013)
9. Folino, F., Guarascio, M., Pontieri, L.: Discovering context-aware models for predicting business process performances. In: Meersman, R., et al. (eds.) OTM 2012, Part I. LNCS, vol. 7565, pp. 287–304. Springer, Heidelberg (2012)
10. Greco, G., Guzzo, A., Pontieri, L.: Mining taxonomies of process models. Data & Knowledge Engineering 67(1), 74–102 (2008)
11. Günther, C.W., Rozinat, A., van der Aalst, W.M.P.: Activity mining by global trace segmentation. In: Rinderle-Ma, S., Sadiq, S., Leymann, F. (eds.) BPM 2009. LNBIP, vol. 43, pp. 128–139. Springer, Heidelberg (2010)
12. Liu, D., Shen, M.: Workflow modeling for virtual processes: an order-preserving process-view approach. Information Systems 28, 505–532 (2003)
13. Milani, F., Dumas, M., Matulevičius, R.: Decomposition driven consolidation of process models. In: Salinesi, C., Norrie, M.C., Pastor, Ó. (eds.) CAiSE 2013. LNCS, vol. 7908, pp. 193–207. Springer, Heidelberg (2013)
14. Song, M., Günther, C.W., van der Aalst, W.M.P.: Trace clustering in process mining. In: Ardagna, D., Mecella, M., Yang, J. (eds.) BPM 2008 Workshops. LNBIP, vol. 17, pp. 109–120. Springer, Heidelberg (2009)
15. Witten, I.H., Frank, E.: Data Mining: Practical Machine Learning Tools and Techniques, 2nd edn. Kaufmann Publishers Inc. (2005)

Mining Event Logs to Assist the Development of Executable Process Variants

Nguyen Ngoc Chan[1], Karn Yongsiriwit[2], Walid Gaaloul[2], and Jan Mendling[3]

[1] Université de Lorraine, Loria UMR 7503, France
[2] Telecom SudParis, Samovar UMR 5157, France
[3] Institute for Information Business
Wirtschaftsuniversität Wien (WU Vienna), Austria

Abstract. Developing process variants has been proven as a principle task to flexibly adapt a business process model to different markets. Contemporary research on variant development has focused on conceptual process models. However, process models do not always exist, even when process logs are available in information systems. Moreover, process logs are often more detailed than process models and reflect more closely to the behavior of the process. In this paper, we propose an activity recommendation approach that takes into account process logs for assisting the development of executable process variants. To this end, we define a notion of neighborhood context for each activity based on logs, which captures order constraints between activities with their occurrence frequency. The similarity of the neighborhood context between activities provides us then with a basis to recommend activities during the process of creating a new process model. The approach has been implemented as a plug-in for ProM. Furthermore, we conducted experiments on a large collection of process logs. The results indicate that our approach is feasible and applicable in real use cases.

Keywords: process mining, business process design, neighborhood context, context matching.

1 Introduction

A process variant is an adjustment of a business process to flexibly adapt the business model to a specific context. Enterprises or organizations usually need to support many variants of the same process due to constraints from regulations, geography, religion, etc. For example, car rental companies, such as Hertz, Avis or Sixt, need to customize their reservation process to follows laws in a country or culture of a region. Suncorp, one of the largest Australian insurance group, has developed more than 30 different variants of the process of handling an insurance claim [32].

In recent years, there have been many efforts on facilitating the development of business process variants such as (i) using available reference models to be individualized to fit the requirements [14, 31], or (ii) finding existing similar models to inspire the new process design [4, 15, 35]. However, the design with

M. Jarke et al. (Eds.): CAiSE 2014, LNCS 8484, pp. 548–563, 2014.

reference models is still labor-intensive, which is often the cause for error-prone and time-consuming design [3]. Meanwhile, recommending entire process models costs much computation time, especially when the number of activities is large. Large models are also not handy for a designer who needs to pick a specific piece of functionality from them. In this context, it is desirable to recommend only a small but well-selected set of activities in order to help the designer.

Prior research has emphasized the advantages of recommendations during process model design [11–13, 21]. However, business process models do not always exist in large-scale information systems such as ERP, CRM, or workflow management systems [1], even when process logs are available. Executable process models also require detailed technical activities to be recommended, while conceptual process models often describe processes in a coarse-granular way [6]. Moreover, process models do not explicitly show the importance of activities or connection flows, which can be a valuable parameter to compute more precisely the similarity between two activities. Meanwhile, this information is recorded in process event logs in the form of traces and their frequency.

In this paper, we propose an approach that builds upon process event logs for making activity recommendations during the development of executable process variants. We examine the relation between activities based on their execution order and frequency as recorded in logs. We define the notion of a *neighborhood context* of an activity as a fragment of the log-based model that contains the considered activity and relations to its neighbors. Relations between activities and their occurrence frequency provide the basis for the computation of the similarity between activities. In the process design phase, this similarity is used to recommend activities which might be closely related to the one that has just been added to the model.

The rest of the paper is organized as follows. Section 2 presents an example that motivates our approach. Section 3 continues with the process model and the neighborhood context graph extracted from logs. Section 4 defines the recommendation approach. Section 5 presents the implementation and experimental results. Section 6 discusses related work before Section 7 concludes the paper.

2   Motivating Example

Consider a process designer who is about to develop a new variant of a liability claim process of an insurance company (inspired from[28]). She starts her work by either retrieving an existing process or quickly designing a new one based on her experiences (Fig. 1): first, some data related to the claim is registered (cf. activity A), and then a full check is performed (B). Afterwards, the claim will be evaluated (D), and then it is either rejected (F) or approved (E and G). Finally, the case is archived and closed (H).

To develop a new variant, the designer may need recommendations for certain positions of the current process. Our approach assist her by providing recommended activities for at each selected position. For example, in Fig. 2, K is recommended for A, C is recommended for B and so on. These recommendations possibly help her easily have new ideas to design a new process variant, for instance, as given in Fig. 3.

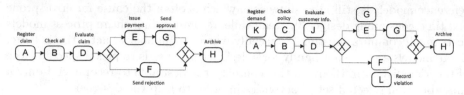

Fig. 1. Initial design   **Fig. 2.** Activity recommendation

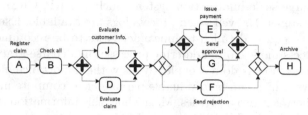

Fig. 3. A new variant

Table 1. Event logs of the liability claim process ([28])

Traces	Log traces	Repeat
1	ACDGEH	
2	ABDFH	
3	ABDEGH	
4	ABDFH	trace 2
5	ACDGEH	trace 1
6	ABDGEH	
7	ACDFH	

Table 2. Event logs of a customer subscription process

Traces	Log traces	Repeat
1	KBJFH	
2	KBJGH	
3	KBJFH	trace 1
4	KBJFH	trace 1
5	KBJGH	trace 2

Recommendations for each activity are made based on their similarity. The computation of this similarity can be based on process event logs even when a a-priori process model is not available.

To elaborate the steps to recommendations in our approach, we use the example of a liability claim process within an insurance company that was presented in [28] and another example of a customer subscription process. Table 1 and Table 2 present the process event logs of these processes. Each process instance is recorded as a *trace*. Each trace is a sequence of activities, which presents their execution order within a process instance. In a trace, the following activity (activity on the right) is performed after the followed activity (activity on the left). For example, consider a trace $\sigma = ABCD$, activity B is performed after activity A and before activity C. The third column of Table 1 and Table 2 presents the repetition of a trace that was previously executed.

In the following, we present an approach to build log-based business process models based on process event logs. These models provide the basis for defining a notion of activity neighborhood context, which we utilize for computing the similarity between activities.

3 Exploiting Activity Neighborhood Context from Logs

In this section, we present the log-based business process and the neighborhood context that are captured from business process logs. We firstly present some definitions related to business process logs (section 3.1). Then, we present definitions of the log-based business process (section 3.2) and the activity neighborhood context (section 3.3).

3.1 Preliminaries

According to [1] and [29], a business process log is defined as follows.

Definition 1 (Log trace, business process log, L). *Let A be a set of activities. A^* denotes the set of finite sequences over A and $\sigma = a_1 a_2 \ldots a_n \in A^*$ is a log trace. $L \in \mathcal{P}(A^*)$ is a business process log[1].*

As explained in [1, 29], a business process log does not consider the repetition of a trace. For example, in Table 1, L includes only traces 1, 2, 3, 6 and 7. Traces 4 and 5 are excluded by L as they repeat traces 2 and 1. In our approach, we extend Definition 1 to define the *full* business process log (see Definition 2) that includes all log traces.

Definition 2 (Full business process log, L^*). *A full business process log is the business process log that includes all executed traces. The full business log is denoted by L^*, $L^* \in \mathcal{P}^*(A^*)$. $L \subseteq L^*$.*

For example, in Table 1, L^* includes all traces from 1 to 7. In Table 2, L^* includes all traces from 1 to 5, while L includes only trace 1 and 2.

Definition 3 (Log-based ordering relation, $>_L$). *Let L be a business process log over A, i.e., $L \in \mathcal{P}(A^*)$. Let $a, b \in A$. $a >_L b$ iff $\exists \sigma = a_1 a_2 \ldots a_n$, $i \in \{1, 2, \ldots, n-1\}$: $\sigma \in L \land a_i = a \land a_{i+1} = b$.*

For example, from the logs given in Table 1, we have $A >_L B$, $A >_L C$, $C >_L D$, $B >_L D$, and so on.

3.2 Log-Based Business Process

The sequence of activities in a log trace $\sigma = a_1 a_2 \ldots a_n \in A^*$ presents their ordering relations. A relation between an activity a_i and its followed activity a_{i+1} in the trace σ, $1 \leq i \leq n-1$ can be presented as a *directed edge* from a_i

---

[1] $\mathcal{P}(A^*)$ is the power set of A^*, i.e., $L \subseteq A^*$.

to a_{i+1}. The activity relations in a business process log L can be presented as a weighted directed graph where the edge's weight presents the number of times that the edge was repeated in the log L. This graph is called *log-based business process graph* (Definition 4).

Definition 4 (Log-based business process graph). *A log business process graph is a weighted directed graph* $G_L = (V_L, E_L, w)$ *built from a business process log* $L^* \in \mathcal{P}^*(A^*)$ *where:*

- $V_L = A = \{a_1, a_2, \ldots, a_n\}$,
- $E_L = \{(a_i, a_j) \in A \times A : a_i >_L a_j\} \subseteq A \times A$,
- w *is a weight function from* E_L *to* N:

$$w: \quad E_L \quad \longrightarrow \quad N$$
$$(a_i, a_j) \quad \mapsto \quad |a_i >_L a_j|$$

$|a_i >_L a_j|$ *is number of times that* $a_i >_L a_j$ *comes about in the log* L^*
$w(a_i, a_j) = 0$ *if* $\nexists \sigma = a_1 a_2 \ldots a_n, k \in \{1, 2, \ldots, n-1\} : a_k = a_i \wedge a_{k+1} = a_j$

For example, the log-based business process graphs of the event logs given in Table 1 and Table 2 are depicted in Fig. 4. The weight of each flow is the number of times that the flow is executed. It is emphasized by the arrow's thickness.

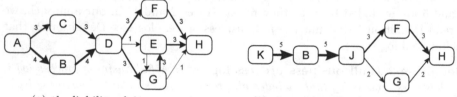

(a) the liability claim process   (b) the customer subscription process

Fig. 4. Log-based business process graphs

The log-based graph presents the execution of a business process in reality, regardless its conceptual model. The weights of edges present their execution frequency which indicates the strength of relations between activities. In the following, we present our approach to build the neighborhood context of an activity based on these relations.

3.3   Log-Based Neighborhood Context

We define the log-based neighborhood context as a directed labeled graph that presents the shortest path from an activity to its neighbors. Intuitively, the closeness between activities is presented by the paths connecting them. The shortest path between activities presents their closest relation. The log-based neighborhood context of an activity presents the best relations between the activity and its neighbors.

In a log-based neighborhood context graph, each vertex is associated to a number that indicates the shortest path length from it to the associated activity. Vertexes that have the same shortest path length are considered to be located on the same *layer* around the associated activity. Thus, we name the number associated to each activity in a neighborhood context graph *layer number*. The layer number of an activity a is denoted by $l(a)$. The area limited between two adjacent layers is called *zone*. The edge connecting two vertexes in a neighborhood context graph belongs to a zone as the vertexes are on the same or adjacent layers. We assign to each edge a number, so-call *zone number*, which determines the zone that the edge belongs to.

The edge connecting a_j, a_k in the neighborhood context graph of an activity a_i is assigned a zone number $z(a_j, a_k) = min(l(a_j), l(a_k)) + 1$. This means, if a_j and a_k are located on two adjacent layers, the edge (a_j, a_k) will belongs to the zone limited by $l(a_j)$ and $l(a_k)$. In the case that a_j and a_k are located on the same layer, the edge connecting them belongs to the outer zone of their layer, which is limited by layers $l(a_j)$ and $l(a_j) + 1$.

Definition 5 (Activity neighborhood context graph). *The neighborhood context graph of an activity a_i, denoted by $G_C(a_i)$, is an extension of the log-based graph $G_L = (V_L, E_L, w)$ with vertex layer numbers and edge zone numbers. The layer number of a vertex a_j, denoted by $l(a_j)_{G_C(a_i)}$, is the shortest path length from a_j to a_i and the zone number of an edge (a_j, a_k), denoted by $z(a_j, a_k)_{G_C(a_i)}$, has value $min(l(a_j)_{G_C(a_i)}, l(a_k)_{G_C(a_i)}) + 1$:*

1. $l(a_j)_{G_C(a_i)} = ShortestPathLength(a_j, a_i)$,
2. $z(a_j, a_k)_{G_C(a_i)} = min(l(a_j)_{G_C(a_i)}, l(a_k)_{G_C(a_i)}) + 1$, $a_j >_L a_k \vee a_k >_L a_j$.

For example, the neighborhood context graphs of activity D and J in Fig. 4 are depicted in Fig. 5.

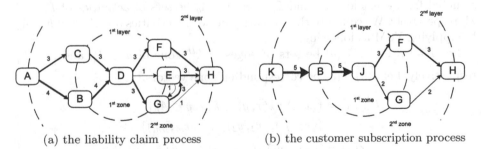

(a) the liability claim process   (b) the customer subscription process

Fig. 5. Neighborhood context graphs of the given event logs

Definition 6 (k^{th}-neighbor). *a is the kth-neighbor of b, iff $l(a)_{G_C(b)} = k$. Set of kth-neighbors ($k \geq 1$) of an activity a_i is denoted by $N^k(a_i)$. $N^k(a_i) = \{a_j : l(a_j)_{G_C(a_i)} = k\}$.*

For example, in Fig. 4a, $N^1(A) = \{B, C\}$, $N^2(A) = \{D\}$, $N^3(A) = \{F, E, G\}$, $N^1(D) = \{C, B, F, E, G\}$, $N^2(D) = \{A, H\}$, $N^3(D) = \varnothing$, and so on.

4   Activity Recommendation Based on Neighborhood Context Matching

The layer number and the zone number in a neighborhood context graph present the closeness between activities, while the weights of edges in the log-based graph present the strength of their relations. In this section, we detail our approach with log-based neighborhood context matching and activity recommendation.

4.1   Neighborhood Context Matching

To compute the matching between two neighborhood contexts, we (1) compute the matching of their edges in each zone, (2) multiply this matching with a zone-weight value and (3) sum up the matching in all zones.

We apply the vector space model (VSM) to compute the matching of edges in each zone of two neighborhood context graphs. VSM is a common technique used in Information Retrieval to compute the similarity between two items. It presents items in vectors and compute their similarity based on the cosine of the angle between the two corresponding vectors. In our approach, we present each zone as a vector of which elements are edges and values are their corresponding weights. Then, we align elements that connect the same activities in the same layers. Next, we present these vectors in the same space by filling 0 values in corresponding positions of the unaligned elements. Finally, we compute the cosine value of these two zone-vectors.

Particularly, in the first zone, we match the edges that connect the two associated activities to the same activities in the first layer. To formalize our computation, we define the two associated activities as *root activities* and name them r_0.

Concretely, assume that P_p and P_q are two log-based business processes constructed from event logs L_p and L_q. Let A_p, A_q be sets of activities of P_p and P_q respectively. We compute the similarity between activities $a \in A_p$ and $b \in A_q$ by applying VSM as following.

Let $E_{P_p}^k(a)$ and $E_{P_q}^k(b)$ be sets of edges in k^{th}-zone of $a \in P_p$ and $b \in P_q$ respectively. Let $\overrightarrow{e(a)}$, $\overrightarrow{e(b)}$ be corresponding zone vectors.

$$E_{P_p}^k(a) = \{(x,y) : z(x,y) = k, x,y \in A_p\}$$
$$= \{(x_1,y_1),(x_2,y_2),\ldots,(x_m,y_m)\}$$
$$\overrightarrow{e(a)} = (w(x_1,y_1),w(x_2,y_2),\ldots,w(x_m,y_m))$$
$$E_{P_q}^k(b) = \{(e,f) : z(e,f) = k, e,f \in A_q\}$$
$$= \{(e_1,f_1),(e_2,f_2),\ldots,(e_n,f_n)\}$$
$$\overrightarrow{e(b)} = (w(e_1,f_1),w(e_2,f_2),\ldots,w(e_n,f_n))$$

Let $N_c^{k-1}(a,b)$ and $N_c^k(a,b)$ be the sets of common neighbors of a and b on layers $k-1$ and k, $k > 0$. We have:

$$N_c^{k-1}(a,b) = N_{P_p}^{k-1}(a) \cap N_{P_q}^{k-1}(b)$$

$$N_c^k(a,b) = N_{P_p}^k(a) \cap N_{P_q}^k(b)$$

As we define the two associated activities as *root activities* and name them r, we have: $N_{P_p}^0(a) = a = r_0$, $N_{P_q}^0(b) = b = r_0$ and $N_c^0(a,b) = r_0$.

Let E_c^k be the set of common edges of a and b in k^{th}-zone.

$$E_c^k = \{(r,t) : (r \in N_c^{k-1}(a,b), t \in N_c^k(a,b)| r >_{L_p} t \wedge r >_{L_q} t)$$
$$\cup (r \in N_c^k(a,b), t \in N_c^{k-1}(a,b)| r >_{L_p} t \wedge r >_{L_q} t)\}$$
$$= \{(r_1,t_1),(r_2,t_2),\dots,(r_m,t_m)\}$$

Let $\overrightarrow{e_c(a)}$, $\overrightarrow{e_c(b)}$ be vectors of weights of these common edges.

$$\overrightarrow{e_c(a)} = (w(r_1,t_1), w(r_2,t_2),\dots,w(r_z,t_z)),(r_i,t_i) \in E_L(A_p), 1 \leq i \leq z$$

$$\overrightarrow{e_c(b)} = (w(r_1,t_1), w(r_2,t_2),\dots,w(r_z,t_z)),(r_i,t_i) \in E_L(A_q), 1 \leq i \leq z$$

By applying VSM, the similarity between a and b in the kth zone is given by Equation. 1.

$$M^k(a,b) = \frac{\overrightarrow{e_c(a)} \cdot \overrightarrow{e_c(b)}}{|\overrightarrow{e(a)}| \times |\overrightarrow{e(b)}|} \qquad (1)$$

For example, we have: the common neighbors of D and J in the 1st-layer are $N_c^1(D,J) = \{F,G,B\}$. So, $\overrightarrow{e_c(D)} = (w(D,F), w(D,G), w(B,D)) = (3,3,4)$, $\overrightarrow{e_c(J)} = (w(J,F), w(J,G), w(B,J)) = (3,2,5)$ and their matching in the 1st-zone is:

$$M^1(D,J) = \frac{3 \times 3 + 3 \times 2 + 4 \times 5}{\sqrt{3^2 + 1^2 + 3^2 + 3^2 + 4^2} \times \sqrt{3^2 + 2^2 + 5^2}} = 0.86$$

In the 2nd-zone, we have the common edges of these two context graphs are: (F,G) and (G,H). So, their matching in this zone is:

$$M^2(D,J) = \frac{3 \times 3 + 1 \times 2}{\sqrt{3^2 + 4^2 + 3^2 + 3^2 + 1^2 + 1^2 + 3^2} \times \sqrt{5^2 + 3^2 + 2^2}} = 0.24$$

The behavior of an activity is strongly reflected by the connections to its closet neighbors. Therefore, we propose to consider a zone weight in our matching. Concretely, as the zone-weight has to have greater values in smaller k^{th} connection zone, we propose to assign the zone-weight a value computed by a polynomial function which is $w_j^z = \dfrac{k+1-j}{k}$, where j is the zone number ($1 \leq j \leq k$), k is the number of considered zones around an associated activity. The closest zone to the associated activity has a weight 1 and the farthest zone has a weight $\dfrac{1}{k}$. The final matching formula improved with the zone weight consideration is given in Equation 2.

$$M^*(a,b) = \frac{2}{k+1} \times \sum_{i=1}^{k} \frac{k+1-i}{k} \times M^i(a,b) \qquad (2)$$

For example, the matching between the neighborhood contexts of D and J (in 2 zones) with zone weights is:

$$M^*(D, J) = \frac{2}{3} \times (M^1(D, J) + \frac{1}{2} \times M^2(D, J)) = \frac{2}{3} \times (0.86 + \frac{1}{2} \times 0.24) = 0.65$$

4.2   Activity Recommendation

The neighborhood context graph presents the interactions between the associated activity and its neighbors in layers. It can infer the behavior of the associated activity. Therefore, the matching between neighborhood context graphs exposes the similarity between the associated activities. In our approach, the higher the matching value is, the more similar the activities are. Basically, the steps to make recommendations based on log-based neighborhood context matching are:

1. We represent the business execution logs in a log-based graph. This graph contains relations between activities and their weight values.
2. For each activity in the log-based graph, we build a neighborhood context graph which contains the closet relations between the associated activity and its neighbors. In a neighborhood context graph, activities are presented in layers and relations between them are presented in zones.
3. We compute the matching between neighborhood context graphs using vector space model. This matching presents the similar between two corresponding activities in terms of relations to their neighbors.
4. Finally, for a selected activity, we sort other activities in descending order of similarity and pick up top-n activities for recommendation.

4.3   Computational Complexity

In our approach, only the connection flows connecting common neighbors in two adjacent layers are taken into account for the matching computation. So, by using queues (data structure) to store the common neighbors and track them from the nearest layers to the furthest layers, *we avoid the redundant checking of unrelated neighbors*. On the other hand, the number of activities as well as the number of common neighbors in a log-based business process are not great[2], our algorithm can run fast in computing the neighborhood context matching of two activities. The worst case of this algorithm's computation time is $\mathcal{O}(n_A \times n_P \times n \times k)$, where n_A is the number of activities, n_P is the number of business processes, n is the maximum number of common activities located on a layer and k is the number of considered layers. The worst case only happens when all the business processes in the system are entirely matched. In addition, the performance of the algorithm can be improved by processing the neighborhood context matching periodically off-line.

---

[2] On making statistics on the public dataset used in our experiment, we have that in average, there are 11.36 services in a business process (section 5).

5   Implementation and Experiments

To validate our approach, we implement a tool that generates recommendations based on business process logs. We also perform experiments on a large public dataset shared by the IBM Business Integration Technologies (BIT) team. Details of our implementation (section 5.1) and experiments (section 5.2) are presented as follows.

5.1   Implementation

We implemented an activity recommendation plug-in and integrated it into ProM. This plug-in interacts with either a database or log files to retrieve recommendations for each selected activity in the ProM interface. This application[3] was developed to validate our approach as a proof of concept.

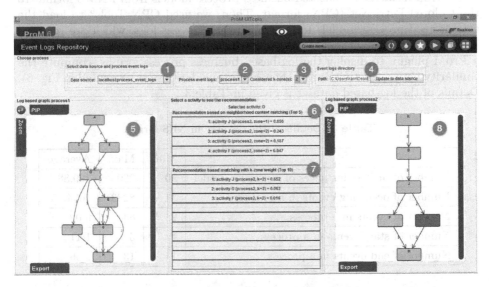

Fig. 6. A screen shot of the log-based activity recommendation application

The screen-shot of our application is shown in Fig. 6. It includes of 8 areas. Areas 1 and 4 allow selecting event log resources, which can be either from a database or a log files directory. The designer selects a working process in area 2 and specifies a zone number to be considered by the algorithm in area 3. The working process is shown in area 5. The designer can select an activity in the working process to obtain recommendations. Area 6 shows the top-5 recommended activities *without zone-weight* in the computation. Meanwhile, area 7 shows the top-10 recommended activities *with zone-weight* consideration. If the designer selects a recommended activity in area 6 or 7, this activity and its involved process will be shown in area 8 (the selected activity is highlighted).

---

[3] Published at: http://www-inf.it-sudparis.eu/SIMBAD/tools/LogRec/

5.2   Experiments

A big challenge of our approach is the availability of real business process logs. We attempted to search and contact other research groups for both public and private logs. However, process event logs are not published or they are not under a disclosure agreement. There are very few logs that are shared for the competition of the BPI challenge[4]. But they are not usable in our approach as they are just logs of one business process while we need logs of several different processes.

We performed experiments on logs generated from real business processes. Data of these processes were shared by the IBM Business Integration Technologies (BIT) team. This dataset includes 735 different processes in Petri net Markup Language (PNML) format. These processes are designed for insurance, banking, customer relationship, as well as construction and automotive supply chain domains [20].

We transformed the collected business process models from PNML format to the Colored Petri Net (CPN) format. Then, we used CPN Tools[5] to load the transformed process models to generate process event logs, which are resulted in XES files. Finally, these log files were imported by our application, which is a ProM plugin, to display the log-based business process graphs, compute the similarity between activities and show recommendations (as presented in Fig. 6). Details of the log-based dataset is given in Table 3.

Table 3. Details of the dataset in XES format

	Min.	Max.	Average
Number of process instances of a process model	50	299	189.88
Number of occurring events in a process	31	8283	1004.15
Number of events in a process	2	64	9.02
Number of start events in a process	1	5	1.11
Number of end events in a process	1	13	2.56

We perform two experiments to evaluate the *feasibility* and the *accuracy* of our approach. In the first experiment, we vary the kth-zone values from 1 to 5 and make statistics on the number of recommended activities for each selected activities. Fig. 7 shows the percentage of activities that have at least 1 recommended activity with the similarity value is greater than 0, 0.5 and 0.8.

Concretely, we obtained that more than 76.56% activities that have at least one similarity value greater than 0 with k varies from 1 to 5. With $k = 1$, we obtained 53.68% activities with similarity value greater than 0.5 and 23.31% activities with similarity value greater than 0.8. These results show that our approach can provide recommendations for a majority activities as we can retrieve

---

[4] http://www.win.tue.nl/bpi/

[5] CPN Tools is an application to generate synthetic process event logs from models described in CPN format. It is available at: http://cpntools.org/

similar activities for more than 3/4 number of activities in average. It means that our approach is *feasible* and can be applied in real use-cases.

In the second experiment, we evaluate the accuracy of our approach based on *Precision* and *Recall* metrics. As our approach takes into account neighborhood contexts instead of activity identifiers, we consider activity identifiers as ground-truth data in computing Precision and Recall. Concretely, consider a selected activity a in a log-based business process P. Assume that a appears in n

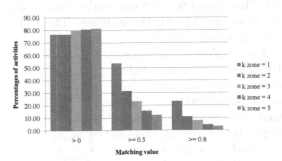

Fig. 7. Percentage of activities that have at least one recommended activity with the similarity value greater than 0, 0.5 and 0.8

log-based business processes. The recommendations for this selected position consist of l activities, in which $t(t \leq l)$ activities are a. Precision and Recall of these recommendations are given by Equation 3.

$$Precision = \frac{t}{l}; \qquad Recall = \frac{t}{n} \qquad (3)$$

The primary objective of the experiment is to retrieve a *small* share of activities that are likely *irrelevant* (high precision). It is of secondary importance to retrieve the full range of potentially relevant activities (moderate recall) in order to avoid the designer being overwhelmed.

In our experiment, we computed the Precision and Recall with l (number of activities recommended for each selected activity) equal to 1, 4, 7 and 10. We performed the experiment with k^{th}-zone=1 and on activities that appear in at least 2, 5, 7 and 10 different business processes.

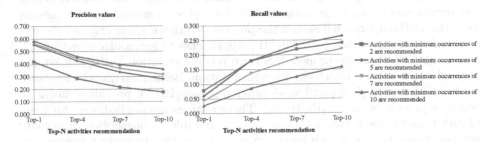

Fig. 8. Precision and Recall values of activities that are occurrence in at least 2, 5, 7 and 10 different processes, k^{th}-zone=1 and l is equal to 1, 4, 7 and 10

Fig. 8 shows that we obtained good Precision values (from 0.42 to 0.59) in case of recommending 1 activity for each selected activity. These values decrease when we increase the number of recommended activities. On the other hand, activities that appear in more processes will have greater Precision values. It also shows that the Recall values increase when l (or top-N) changes from 1 to 10. This means that we can retrieve more relevant activities when the number of recommended activities increases. The highest Recall value in our experiment is 0.264 when l=10.

Fig. 9 shows the average Precision and Recall values of our approach with different k^{th}-zone values. It shows that our approach achieved much better results than an approach that generates recommendations randomly (in average, 8.6 times greater the Precision value and 17.4 times greater the Recall value).

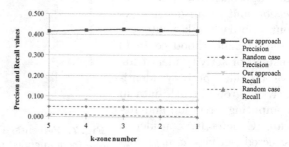

Fig. 9. Average Precision and Recall values with different zone layers

The Precision and Recall values showed that our approach retrieve not only the *right activities* but also *new relevant activities* for each selected position and the number of new activities increases when the number of recommended activities increases. These results showed that our approach can be applied in real use-cases as we can provide the designer the flexibility in using existing process fragments or designing new process variants.

6   Related Work

Computing the similarity of two process models first requires the definition of a mapping between the activities using automatic matching techniques [17]. Principles for matching process models have been integrated in the ICoP framework [33] and extended with semantic matching techniques [23]. Applications in the area of supporting process model design adopt such semantic techniques, as for instance the approach based on the process descriptor space [25] and the recommendation approach reported in [21]. Approaches to harmonize structure [27] and labels [24] were also proposed. Service recommendation [9, 10] can be also applied in the context of activity recommendation. Behavioral abstractions such as trace adjacency [5, 36] and weak order relations[19, 34] provide a means to compare process behavior [15, 16, 22]. These notions are applied, e.g., for identifying connections between actions [30] comparable to our notion of activity neighborhood. Our approach builds on this observation to make recommendations for executable processes. In addition, we focus on process fragments instead of the entire model. We recommend activities instead of process models and we do not face the computational complexity problem.

In our previous work [11–13], we exploited activity relations in process models and we did not take into account the occurrence frequency of activities. In this work, we realize that knowledge from process logs can be also utilized for process design by applying process mining techniques. Different techniques have been defined for automatically discovering whole models from logs, e.g. [1, 18, 26]. The automatic matching between event logs and process models is discussed in [6] showing that logs on the execution level are often much more detailed than models. The challenge of process mining is the observation that process models often turn out to be overwhelmingly complex, so-called spaghetti models [2]. The approach reported in this paper helps to present correlations between activities in a context-specific way, which allows us to hide the complexity of the behavior. Hidden knowledge in process event logs are discovered for assisting business process design. In this way, we complement log-based recommendation approaches to support process designers at runtime [7] or at configuration time [8].

7 Conclusion

In this paper, we addressed the challenge of supporting the designer during the act of modeling, even in cases where no comparable process models exist. We present an approach that effectively utilizes knowledge extracted from business process logs for recommending activities. This approach is based on a notion of activity neighborhood and a corresponding calculation of similarity. The approach has been implemented as a plug-in for ProM and evaluated using generated log data of 735 processes from practice.

In future work, we aim to extend the similarity calculation with other properties of an activity such as descriptions, actors, resources and dependencies. We also plan to integrate our neighborhood matching technique with a specific query language to help to retrieve activities that have similar contexts based on a requested activity context.

References

1. van der Aalst, W., Weijters, T., Maruster, L.: Workflow mining: Discovering process models from event logs. Knowl. and Data Eng. (9), 1128–1142 (2004)
2. van der Aalst, W.M.P.: Process Mining - Discovery, Conformance and Enhancement of Business Processes, pp. 1–352. Springer (2011)
3. van der Aalst, W., Lohmann, N., La Rosa, M., Xu, J.: Correctness ensuring process configuration: An approach based on partner synthesis. In: Hull, R., Mendling, J., Tai, S. (eds.) BPM 2010. LNCS, vol. 6336, pp. 95–111. Springer, Heidelberg (2010)
4. van der Aalst, W.M.P., de Medeiros, A.K.A., Weijters, A.J.M.M.T.: Process equivalence: Comparing two process models based on observed behavior. In: Dustdar, S., Fiadeiro, J.L., Sheth, A.P. (eds.) BPM 2006. LNCS, vol. 4102, pp. 129–144. Springer, Heidelberg (2006)
5. Bae, J., Liu, L., Caverlee, J., Zhang, L.-J., Bae, H.: Development of distance measures for process mining, discovery and integration. Int. J. Web Service Res. 4(4), 1–17 (2007)
6. Baier, T., Mendling, J.: Bridging abstraction layers in process mining by automated matching of events and activities. In: Daniel, F., Wang, J., Weber, B. (eds.) BPM 2013. LNCS, vol. 8094, pp. 17–32. Springer, Heidelberg (2013)

7. Barba, I., Weber, B., Valle, C.D., Ramirez, A.J.: User recommendations for the optimized execution of business processes. Data Knowl. Eng. 86, 61–84 (2013)
8. Buijs, J.C.A.M., van Dongen, B.F., van der Aalst, W.M.P.: Mining configurable process models from collections of event logs. In: Daniel, F., Wang, J., Weber, B. (eds.) BPM 2013. LNCS, vol. 8094, pp. 33–48. Springer, Heidelberg (2013)
9. Chan, N.N., Gaaloul, W., Tata, S.: Web services recommendation based on user's behavior. In: ICEBE, pp. 214–221 (2010)
10. Chan, N.N., Gaaloul, W., Tata, S.: A web service recommender system using vector space model and latent semantic indexing. In: AINA, pp. 602–609 (2011)
11. Chan, N.N., Gaaloul, W., Tata, S.: Composition context matching for web service recommendation. In: SCC, pp. 624–631 (2011)
12. Chan, N.N., Gaaloul, W., Tata, S.: Context-based service recommendation for assisting business process design. In: Huemer, C., Setzer, T. (eds.) EC-Web 2011. LNBIP, vol. 85, pp. 39–51. Springer, Heidelberg (2011)
13. Chan, N.N., Gaaloul, W., Tata, S.: Assisting business process design by activity neighborhood context matching. In: Liu, C., Ludwig, H., Toumani, F., Yu, Q. (eds.) ICSOC 2012. LNCS, vol. 7636, pp. 541–549. Springer, Heidelberg (2012)
14. Curran, T., Keller, G., Ladd, A.: SAP R/3 business blueprint: understanding the business process reference model, Upper Saddle River, NJ, USA (1998)
15. Dijkman, R., Dumas, M., García-Bañuelos, L.: Graph matching algorithms for business process model similarity search. In: Dayal, U., Eder, J., Koehler, J., Reijers, H.A. (eds.) BPM 2009. LNCS, vol. 5701, pp. 48–63. Springer, Heidelberg (2009)
16. Dijkman, R.M., van Dongen, B.F., Dumas, M., García-Bañuelos, L., Kunze, M., Leopold, H., Mendling, J., Uba, R., Weidlich, M., Weske, M., Yan, Z.: A short survey on process model similarity. In: Seminal Contributions to Information Systems Engineering. Springer (2013)
17. Ehrig, M., Koschmider, A., Oberweis, A.: Measuring similarity between semantic business process models. In: Conceptual Modelling 2007, APCCM 2007. CRPIT, vol. 67, pp. 71–80. Australian Computer Society (2007)
18. Engel, R., van der Aalst, W., Zapletal, M., Pichler, C., Werthner, H.: Mining inter-organizational business process models from edi messages: A case study from the automotive sector. Advanced Inf. Sys. Engineering (2012)
19. Eshuis, R., Grefen, P.W.P.J.: Structural matching of bpel processes. In: ECOWS 2007, pp. 171–180. IEEE Computer Society (2007)
20. Fahland, D., Favre, C., Jobstmann, B., Koehler, J., Lohmann, N., Völzer, H., Wolf, K.: Instantaneous soundness checking of industrial business process models. In: Dayal, U., Eder, J., Koehler, J., Reijers, H.A. (eds.) BPM 2009. LNCS, vol. 5701, pp. 278–293. Springer, Heidelberg (2009)
21. Hornung, T., Koschmider, A., Lausen, G.: Recommendation based process modeling support: Method and user experience. In: Li, Q., Spaccapietra, S., Yu, E., Olivé, A. (eds.) ER 2008. LNCS, vol. 5231, pp. 265–278. Springer, Heidelberg (2008)
22. Kunze, M., Weske, M.: Metric trees for efficient similarity search in large process model repositories. In: Muehlen, M.z., Su, J. (eds.) BPM 2010 Workshops. LNBIP, vol. 66, pp. 535–546. Springer, Heidelberg (2011)
23. Leopold, H., Niepert, M., Weidlich, M., Mendling, J., Dijkman, R., Stuckenschmidt, H.: Probabilistic optimization of semantic process model matching. In: Barros, A., Gal, A., Kindler, E. (eds.) BPM 2012. LNCS, vol. 7481, pp. 319–334. Springer, Heidelberg (2012)
24. Leopold, H., Smirnov, S., Mendling, J.: On the refactoring of activity labels in business process models. Inf. Syst. 37(5), 443–459 (2012)

25. Lincoln, M., Golani, M., Gal, A.: Machine-assisted design of business process models using descriptor space analysis. In: Hull, R., Mendling, J., Tai, S. (eds.) BPM 2010. LNCS, vol. 6336, pp. 128–144. Springer, Heidelberg (2010)

26. Maggi, F.M., Bose, R.P.J.C., van der Aalst, W.M.P.: Efficient discovery of understandable declarative process models from event logs. In: Ralyté, J., Franch, X., Brinkkemper, S., Wrycza, S. (eds.) CAiSE 2012. LNCS, vol. 7328, pp. 270–285. Springer, Heidelberg (2012)

27. Polyvyanyy, A., García-Bañuelos, L., Dumas, M.: Structuring acyclic process models. Inf. Syst. 37(6), 518–538 (2012)

28. Rozinat, A., Mans, R.S., Song, M., van der Aalst, W.M.P.: Discovering colored petri nets from event logs. Int. J. Softw. Tools Technol. Transf (1), 57–74 (2007)

29. Schonenberg, H., Weber, B., van Dongen, B.F., van der Aalst, W.M.P.: Supporting flexible processes through recommendations based on history. In: Dumas, M., Reichert, M., Shan, M.-C. (eds.) BPM 2008. LNCS, vol. 5240, pp. 51–66. Springer, Heidelberg (2008)

30. Smirnov, S., Weidlich, M., Mendling, J., Weske, M.: Action patterns in business process model repositories. Computers in Industry (2012)

31. Stephens, S.: Supply chain operations reference model version 5.0: A new tool to improve supply chain efficiency and achieve best practice. In: Information Systems Frontiers pp. 471–476 (December 2001)

32. van der Aalst, W.M.P.: Configurable services in the cloud: Supporting variability while enabling cross-organizational process mining. In: Meersman, R., Dillon, T.S., Herrero, P. (eds.) OTM 2010. LNCS, vol. 6426, pp. 8–25. Springer, Heidelberg (2010)

33. Weidlich, M., Dijkman, R., Mendling, J.: The iCoP framework: Identification of correspondences between process models. In: Pernici, B. (ed.) CAiSE 2010. LNCS, vol. 6051, pp. 483–498. Springer, Heidelberg (2010)

34. Weidlich, M., Mendling, J., Weske, M.: Efficient consistency measurement based on behavioral profiles of process models. IEEE Trans. Soft. Eng. 37, 410–429 (2011)

35. Yan, Z., Dijkman, R., Grefen, P.: Fast business process similarity search with feature-based similarity estimation. In: Meersman, R., Dillon, T.S., Herrero, P. (eds.) OTM 2010. LNCS, vol. 6426, pp. 60–77. Springer, Heidelberg (2010)

36. Zha, H., Wang, J., Wen, L., Wang, C., Sun, J.: A workflow net similarity measure based on transition adjacency relations. Computers in Industry 61(5), 463–471 (2010)

An Extensible Framework for Analysing Resource Behaviour Using Event Logs

Anastasiia Pika[1], Moe T. Wynn[1], Colin J. Fidge[1], Arthur H.M. ter Hofstede[1,2],
Michael Leyer[3], and Wil M.P. van der Aalst[2,1]

[1] Queensland University of Technology, Brisbane, Australia
{a.pika,m.wynn,c.fidge,a.terhofstede}@qut.edu.au
[2] Eindhoven University of Technology, Eindhoven, The Netherlands
w.m.p.v.d.aalst@tue.nl
[3] Frankfurt School of Finance and Management, Frankfurt am Main, Germany
m.leyer@fs.de

Abstract. Business processes depend on human resources and managers must regularly evaluate the performance of their employees based on a number of measures, some of which are subjective in nature. As modern organisations use information systems to automate their business processes and record information about processes' executions in event logs, it now becomes possible to get objective information about resource behaviours by analysing data recorded in event logs. We present an extensible framework for extracting knowledge from event logs about the behaviour of a human resource and for analysing the dynamics of this behaviour over time. The framework is fully automated and implements a predefined set of behavioural indicators for human resources. It also provides a means for organisations to define their own behavioural indicators, using the conventional Structured Query Language, and a means to analyse the dynamics of these indicators. The framework's applicability is demonstrated using an event log from a German bank.

Keywords: Process mining, resource behaviour indicators, employee performance measurements.

1 Introduction

Human resource management is an important function in any organisation. Human behaviour is considered to be "unequivocally the single most important element that can affect project success" [17]. Hence, having accurate information about how an employee performs their required tasks can be very valuable in evaluating that employee's performance. Knowledge about past actions of resources can also assist in forecasting how a resource might perform in the future.

Modern companies use information systems to automate their business operations. Details about such business operations (i.e., business processes) are usually recorded in logs, including information about the activity being performed, the time at which it was performed and the person responsible for carrying it out.

M. Jarke et al. (Eds.): CAiSE 2014, LNCS 8484, pp. 564–579, 2014.

Fig. 1. Our three-step approach for resource behaviour analysis

Our research aims to make use of information recorded in event logs to extract knowledge about the behaviour of a resource over time.

Process mining focuses on analysing business processes using data available in event logs [20]. Recently, ways have been proposed for analysing certain aspects of resource behaviour via such logs, e.g., to extract social networks [16,21] or organisational models [16]. However, these methods usually look at resource behaviour from an organisational, rather than individual, perspective and they do not consider the fact that a resource's behaviour can change over time.

Here we present an extensible software framework that allows organisations to extract knowledge about the behaviour of their employees from event logs, including how their behaviour has changed over time. Our approach consists of three steps, shown in Figure 1. (1) For various dimensions of resource behaviour, such as skills, utilisation, preferences, productivity and collaboration, we define a set of Resource Behaviour Indicators (RBIs) which are discoverable from event logs. The framework enables the definition of new RBIs as necessary via Structured Query Language (SQL) [5] statements. (2) We extract from an event log a time series that reflects the evolution of each RBI over time. (3) We analyse the time series using established methods such as time series charts with trends, outlier detection, change point detection, and time series comparison.

Knowledge extracted using the framework can provide valuable insights for resource performance evaluation, e.g., for rewards and recognition as well as for risk management. For example, a manager could see that an employee is getting involved in more complex tasks or is getting faster when executing certain tasks. A manager can also discover that an employee's workload is abnormally high at the end of each quarter, which could result in delays or low-quality outputs. The framework has been implemented as a plug-in within the process mining framework, ProM, and evaluated using data from a real-life event log.

2   Related and Previous Work

The performance of human resources with respect to business processes can be seen from two perspectives [14]. (1) Descriptive measures, i.e., how the performance of a resource is actually observed. (2) Normative measures, i.e., what the performance of a resource should be. Evaluation of an individual employee's performance is an important factor for companies because individuals are the smallest entity in the company who perform the work. However, performance indicators are typically defined on an aggregate level, e.g., company, department or process teams [11]. There is little literature on individual measures and only a few measures have been described [10,18]. Our approach also uses indicators to measure human resource performance, but we focus on individual resources and present an extensible framework which allows new measures to be defined.

Some techniques that can extract knowledge about certain aspects of resource behaviour from event logs have been proposed in the process mining area: Van der Aalst et al. proposed a method for extracting social networks [16,21]; Song et al. proposed techniques for mining organisational models [16]; Nakatumba et al. investigated the effect of resource workload on service times [9]; and Huang et al. proposed a few measures for resource preference, availability, competence and cooperation and demonstrated how these measures can be used [4]. In our own earlier work, we showed how process risk indicators can be used to detect the risk of case delays [12,13]. Some of these previous risk indicators were related to the behaviour of resources. We showed that the involvement of certain resources in a case or a high resource workload can result in case delays. Bose et al. proposed a generic framework for detecting concept drifts in business processes and defined features that characterise control-flow perspective [1]. By contrast, we focus here on understanding the evolving behaviour of individual resources over time and develop an extensible framework that can identify trends, anomalies and changes in resource behaviours.

3   Approach

To extract knowledge about resource behaviour we follow the three major steps depicted in Figure 1: defining RBIs (Section 3.1); extracting RBI time series from event logs (Section 3.2); and analysing RBI time series (Section 3.3). Our approach is based on the analysis of event log data, hence the quality of the data is crucial for getting meaningful results.

3.1   Defining Resource Behaviour Indicators

Our first challenge concerns the kinds of resource behaviour we wish to measure. This will vary depending of the reasons for the analysis. For example, if we wish to gain insights into the performance of an employee, we may look at their workload, their average duration to execute tasks, the number of interactions with other employees, etc. Thus, relevant employee behaviour depends on a particular context. In a specific situation there may be many indicators of interest [10]. Based on the literature we propose here the following general categories.

1. Skills [18]: *What can a resource do?*
2. Utilisation [10]: *What is a resource actually doing?*
3. Preferences [4,19]: *What working behaviour does a resource often demonstrate?*
4. Productivity [8]: *How good is a resource at what it does?*
5. Collaboration [4,21]: *How does a resource work with other employees?*

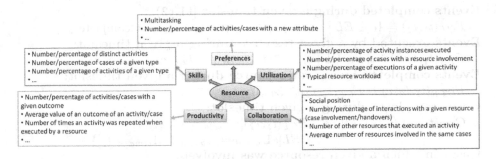

Fig. 2. Categories of resource behaviour and RBIs

Within these five categories, we present a set of RBIs which can be drawn from typical event logs (depicted in Figure 2). Some predefined RBIs are generic while others are only relevant in specific contexts. Though these pre-defined RBIs can provide useful insights about resource behaviour, we recognise that managers may be interested in other indicators that reflect the specifics of their organisations. Therefore, the framework supports the definition of new RBIs.

Definitions. An *event log EL* consists of a set of events $e \in \mathcal{E}$. Events are characterised by different attributes. Let $\{caseid, task, type, time, resource\}$ be *basic* event attributes, i.e., we assume that we can retrieve the values of these attributes for each event. We assume that *start* and *complete* event types are recorded for each activity. Such an event log can be treated as a relation whose relation scheme is specified by the set of event attributes. Similarly, a *case log CL* consists of a set of cases $c \in \mathcal{C}$ that are characterised by attributes. A case is uniquely identifiable by the case attribute *caseid*. A case log can also be treated as a relation whose relation scheme is specified by the set of case attributes. Events and cases can have other attributes (e.g., *outcome*, *cost*, etc.). Most of our pre-defined RBIs only require basic event and case attributes. We also show examples of RBIs that require richer data to be recorded. The value of attribute a of event e is denoted as e_a and the value of attribute a of case c is denoted as c_a. We derive from the basic event log case attribute *case_duration* (the time difference between the timestamps of the last and the first event in a case). The following event attributes are also derived from a basic event log: *task_duration* (the time difference between corresponding activity *complete* and *start* events), *workload* (the number of work items that are assigned to or started but not completed by a resource executing an event at the moment of event execution) and *workload_duration* (the time period during which the resource's workload has not changed). If a resource is involved in multiple processes that are recorded in separate logs, we assume that preprocessing is performed and logs are merged ensuring that case identifiers in the combined log are unique.

Let R be a set of resources, A be a set of activities, t_1 and t_2 be the beginning and the end of a given time slot and r be a given resource. We define the following functions that are later used in RBI definitions.

Events completed during a given timeslot [t1,t2):
$$E_{CT}(t_1, t_2) \triangleq \{e \in EL \mid e_{time} \geq t_1 \land e_{time} < t_2 \land e_{type} = \text{'complete'}\}$$
Events executed by a given resource during a given timeslot:
$$E_{TR}(t_1, t_2, r) \triangleq \{e \in EL \mid e_{time} \geq t_1 \land e_{time} < t_2 \land e_{resource} = r\}$$
Events completed by a given resource during a given timeslot:
$$E_{CTR}(t_1, t_2, r) \triangleq E_{CT}(t_1, t_2) \cap E_{TR}(t_1, t_2, r)$$
Cases completed during a given timeslot:
$$C_{CT}(t_1, t_2) \triangleq \{c \in C \mid \exists e \in E_{CT}(t_1, t_2)[e_{caseid} = c_{caseid}] \land$$
$$\nexists e1 \in EL[e1_{caseid} = c_{caseid} \land e1_{time} > t_2]\}$$
Cases in which a given resource was involved:
$$C_R(r) \triangleq \{c \in C \mid \exists e \in EL[e_{caseid} = c_{caseid} \land e_{resource} = r]\}$$
Cases in which a given resource was involved during a given timeslot:
$$C_{TR}(t_1, t_2, r) \triangleq \{c \in C \mid \exists e \in E_{TR}(t_1, t_2, r)[e_{caseid} = c_{caseid}]\}$$

Below we discuss RBIs in each of the categories of resource behaviour. Due to space limitations we provide formal definitions for only a small selection of pre-defined RBIs, the rest are briefly described in text.

1. Skills: *What can a resource do?* Resources within an organisation have different capabilities and they tend to acquire new skills in different paces. Knowledge about resource capabilities is needed for more precise resource scheduling [4,18], resource performance evaluation and for resource development planning. For the RBIs in this category we assume that a resource is capable of performing those activities it has performed in the past. Hence, we can find out from an event log how a resource's skills are developing over time. These RBIs reflect only "demonstrated" skills, i.e., we cannot see from a log that a resource is capable of performing some activity if it has never performed it. RBI "Distinct activities" is relevant in the working environments where new employees are involved in few tasks, they learn new skills and are involved in more tasks over time (e.g., in fast food restaurants). Looking at the types of cases executed by a resource one can find out, for example, that the resource is getting involved in more complex cases over time.

> **Distinct Activities:** The number of distinct activities completed by a given resource, r, during a given timeslot, t_1 to t_2.
> $$Distinct\_Activities(t_1, t_2, r) \triangleq |\{task \in A \mid$$
> $$\exists e \in E_{CTR}(t_1, t_2, r)[e_{task} = task]\}|$$

> **Case types:** The number of cases with a given property (e.g., *complexity*) completed during a given timeslot in which a given resource was involved (requires case type attributes to be recorded in a log).
> $$Complex\_Cases(t_1, t_2, r) \triangleq |\{c \in C_{CT}(t_1, t_2) \cap C_R(r) \mid$$
> $$c_{complexity} = \text{'complex'}\}|$$

Other RBIs defined in this category include: the percentage of distinct activities completed, the number of activity completions with a given property, and the percentage of activity or case completions with a given property.

2. Utilisation: *What is a resource actually doing?* Utilisation RBIs reflect how active a resource is without considering the quality of its outputs. They are inspired by manufacturing measures, e.g., the number of units produced [10].

> **Activity completions:** The number of activity instances completed by a given resource during a given time slot.
> $$Activity\_Completions(t_1, t_2, r) \triangleq |E_{CTR}(t_1, t_2, r)|$$

> **Case completions:** number of cases completed during a given time slot in which a given resource was involved.
> $$Case\_Completions(t_1, t_2, r) \triangleq |C_{CT}(t_1, t_2) \cap C_R(r)|$$

We have also defined RBIs for: the percentage of activity instances completed, number and percentage of completions of a given activity, percentage of completed cases in which a resource was involved, and typical resource workload.

3. Preferences *What working behaviour does a resource often demonstrate?* Resources have different working preferences and styles that may affect their performance and overall process outcomes [19]. For example, they may prefer execution of certain activities [4], working on multiple tasks, executing similar tasks or taking risks.

> **Multitasking:** The percentage of active time when a given resource is involved in more than one activity.
> $$Multitasking(t_1, t_2, r) \triangleq \sum_{\{e \in E_{TR}(t_1, t_2, r) | e_{workload} > 1\}} e_{workload\_duration} / \sum_{\{e \in E_{TR}(t_1, t_2, r) | e_{workload} > 0\}} e_{workload\_duration}$$

> **New Attributes:** The number of times a resource completed a task during a given timeslot with a new value of a given attribute, e.g., *sum* (reflects propensity to execute new hence risky tasks).
> $$New\_Attributes(t_1, t_2, r, sum) \triangleq |\{e \in E_{CTR}(t_1, t_2, r) \mid \nexists e1 \in EL$$
> $$[e1_{sum} = e_{sum} \wedge e1_{time} < e_{time}]\}|$$

4. Productivity *How good is a resource at what it does?* RBIs in this category reflect a resource's results, e.g., in terms of timeliness, costs or quality of outputs (assuming cost and quality information is recorded in the event log). We defined here RBIs for: the number/the percentage of activities/cases completed with a given outcome in which a resource was involved, average value of a given outcome for a given activity or a case completed by a resource, and the number of times when a given activity was repeated when completed by a resource.

> **Activity Outcomes:** The percentage of activities completed during a given time slot by a given resource with a given outcome (e.g., *duration*).
> $$In\_Time\_Activities(t_1, t_2, r, dur) \triangleq$$
> $$|\{e \in E_{CTR}(t_1, t_2, r) \mid e_{task\_duration} < dur\}| / |\{e \in E_{CTR}(t_1, t_2, r)\}|$$

Case outcomes: The percentage of cases completed during a given time slot with a given outcome (e.g., *cost*) in which a given resource was involved (requires case attribute *cost* to be recorded).

$Overbudget\_Cases(t_1, t_2, r, cost) \triangleq$

$$|\{c \in C_{CT}(t_1, t_2) \cap C_R(r) \mid c_{cost} > cost\}| \ / \ |C_{CT}(t_1, t_2) \cap C_R(r)|$$

5. Collaboration *How does a resource work with other employees?* Collaborative aspects of resource behaviour are important as people are more often involved in teamwork nowadays. RBIs in this category can help us to learn about resource's collaboration patterns with a particular resource or to get insights about his overall social position within an organisation.

Social position: The percentage of resources involved in the same cases with a given resource during a given time slot.

$Social\_Position(t_1, t_2, r) \triangleq$

$$|\{r_1 \in R \mid \exists c \in C_{TR}(r_1) \cap C_{TR}(r)\}| \ / \ |\{r_1 \in R \mid \exists c \in C_{TR}(r_1)\}|$$

Interactions with a given resource: The number of cases completed during a given time slot in which two given resources were involved.

$Interactions\_With\_A\_Resource(t_1, t_2, r_1, r_2) \triangleq$

$$|C_{CT}(t_1, t_2) \cap C_R(r_1) \cap C_R(r_2)|$$

We have also defined collaboration RBIs for: the number of other resources that executed a given activity, the average number of resources involved in the same cases with a given resource, and the number of handovers with a given resource.

3.2 Extracting RBI Time Series from Event Log

The value of an RBI at a particular point in time is not very useful unless it is being compared with some other values. For such comparisons, we extract RBI time series as the second step. This consists of RBI values extracted for a given period of time, e.g., per day, week, month, etc, for a particular resource. The user selects a starting time point, time series sampling rate and a number of time slots. Selection of the time series sampling rate is an important step that can affect the analysis results. It is a well-known problem often discussed in the literature [6]. When choosing sampling rate for RBI time series one should consider process characteristics (e.g., process granularity) and the type of analysis one is interested in. For example, if a manager is interested in checking whether or not an employee is less productive on Mondays, daily RBI values are needed, rather than weekly or monthly.

Let $RBI_n(t_1, t_2)$ denote the value of an RBI n during a time slot (t_1, t_2); TS_{start} be the starting time point; $TS_{slotsize}$ be the sampling rate; TS_{size} be the number of time slots; $Start(t)$ and $End(t)$ are functions that return the beginning and the end of a timeslot for a given time t correspondingly. Then an RBI time series can be defined as:

$$TS_{RBI_n} \triangleq \{(RBI_n(Start(t), End(t)), t) \mid$$
$$t \in \{TS_{start} + i * TS_{slotsize} \mid i \in \{0, 1, \ldots, TS_{size} - 1\}\}\}$$

We use here the following pre-defined functions for the beginning and the end of a time slot: $Start(t) = t$ and $End(t) = t + TS_{slotsize}$. We also provide an interface for users to define their own functions. This gives flexibility to use different time series sampling methods, e.g., defining overlapping time slots.

3.3 Analysing RBI Time Series

During the third step, we analyse the extracted RBI time series and visualise the results. Our framework generates time series charts accompanied by trend lines. It can also automatically detect change points and outliers and provides a means for time series comparisons. Hence, one can compare RBI values for different resources or compare RBI values against benchmark values.

Time series charts alone accompanied by trend lines can give many interesting insights about the dynamics of resource behaviour. For example, a manager can see when the number of cases handled by a resource has increased or decreased significantly or a resource is handling an abnormally higher or lower number of tasks during certain periods. While charts are simple and powerful tools for time series analysis, they are not very convenient when the amount of available data is large. If a manager is doing periodic performance reviews for multiple employees and is interested in multiple RBIs it may be necessary to check hundreds of charts. To facilitate this, we enable the use of automatic techniques for time series analysis such as the detection of change points [15], outliers detection [22] and time series comparison [7].

One way to make time series analysis efficient is automatic detection of significant changes. One would like to know if such changes have occurred and the points in time when they did so. The problem of change point detection has received significant attention and many methods have been developed. Most of the existing change point detection techniques make certain assumptions about the distribution of the data, however recently a few non-parametric methods have been proposed [3,15]. As we do not know the distributions of RBIs in advance, we advocate using such methods. A user can choose non-parametric tests to detect changes in location (Mann-Whitney), in scale (Mood) or to detect arbitrary distributional changes (Kolmogorov-Smirnov, Cramer-von-Mises) [15]. Alternative approach would require learning the distribution of the data and using an appropriate change point detection test.

Detecting outliers in RBI time series (i.e., points in time when RBI values significantly deviate from typical values) can be helpful in problem investigations. For example, a high resource workload during specific points in time may explain case delays. Many outlier detection techniques have been proposed in different research fields. We use an outlier detection method that fits the distribution of the observations and detects observations which are unlikely to be generated by this distribution [22].

The time series analysis methods described above allow the analysis of how the behaviour of a resource has evolved over time. Another way to evaluate performance of a resource using RBIs is to compare its behaviour with the behaviour of other resources. This allows us to quickly identify those resources

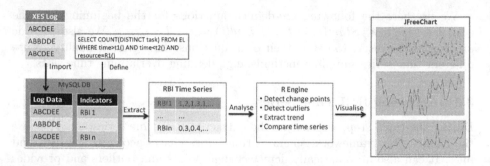

Fig. 3. Overview of the plug-in for analysing resource behaviour

whose behaviour significantly differs from others (e.g., over-performing or under-performing employees). To compare RBI time series we recommend using the non-parametric Mann-Whitney U-test [7].

However, typical event logs do not contain complete information about the behaviour of a resource, hence the meaning of an RBI can be subject to interpretation. In addition, the existence of certain change points may not provide an explanation regarding the root causes behind such changes. Let's consider as an example RBI "typical duration of a given activity completed by a given resource". If we detect that a resource is getting faster when executing a particular activity, this may mean that the resource is getting more efficient as it becomes more experienced in carrying out such an activity or it could mean that the resource is doing a hasty and possibly poor job.

4 Validation

This section first describes the implementation of our approach as a plug-in of the process mining framework ProM[1] and then presents the practical insights gained from testing the framework with an event log from a German bank.

4.1 Implementation

Figure 3 depicts the main functionality of our plug-in. An input to the plug-in is an XES event log. XES is a standard format for event log data[2]. Event log data is then converted and stored in a MySQL[3] database. Tables EL and CL are created that contain event and case attributes correspondingly. Pre-defined RBIs are stored in the database as views. The plug-in provides an interface that allows users to define their own RBIs using SQL. We adopted SQL for this purpose because it is standardised, unambiguous, and widely-used, although

---

[1] http://www.promtools.org/prom6/
[2] http://www.xes-standard.org/
[3] http://www.mysql.com/

other formalised languages could also have been used, most notably 'set builder' (a.k.a. 'set comprehension') mathematical notation. To define a new RBI a user needs to provide an SQL statement characterising the value of the RBI per a given time slot. Table 1 shows an example of an RBI definition. When defining RBIs users can use pre-defined parameters implemented as functions ($t1()$,$t2()$ and $R1()$ in Table 1). They can also define their own parameters by providing parameter names and data types, and functions that return the values of the parameters will be created automatically and can be used in definitions of RBIs.

Table 1. Example of definition of an RBI using SQL

RBI "Distinct activities"	$Distinct\_Activities(t_1, t_2, r) \triangleq$
	$|\{task \in A \mid \exists e \in E_{CTR}(t_1, t_2, r)[e_{task} = task]\}|$
SQL definition	SELECT COUNT (DISTINCT $task$) FROM EL WHERE $time \geq t1()$
	AND $time < t2()$ AND $resource = R1()$ AND $type =$ 'complete'

To start the analysis a user needs to select a resource whose behaviour is to be analysed, the RBIs of interest, a time period and time series sampling rate. Optionally the user can define functions that return the beginning and the end of a time slot for a given point in time. Based on these inputs the plug-in will extract time series for the RBIs. The user then selects methods of time series analysis and provides corresponding input parameters.

For statistical analysis of RBI time series we use R[4] whose functionality is accessed from the plug-in using JRI Java/R Interface[5]. To detect change points we use the CPM framework that implements many popular parametric and non-parametric tests and is implemented as R package cpm[6]. The framework allows control over the level of changes that are detected by choosing the value of parameter ARL0, the "average number of observations between false-positive detections assuming that no change has occured" [15]. Higher values of ARL0 allow detection of only significant changes. For outlier detection we use the R package $extremevalues$[7] that implements Van der Loo's outlier detection methods [22]. For time series comparison we use R's $wilcox$ method[8] that implements the Mann-Whitney U-test [7] and for trend fitting we use R's lm method[9]. The results of the analysis are visualised using the JFreeChart library[10].

---

[4] http://www.r-project.org/
[5] http://rforge.net/JRI/
[6] http://cran.r-project.org/web/packages/cpm/vignettes/cpm.pdf
[7] http://cran.r-project.org/web/packages/extremevalues/extremevalues.pdf
[8] http://stat.ethz.ch/R-manual/R-patched/
library/stats/html/wilcox.test.html
[9] http://stat.ethz.ch/R-manual/R-devel/library/stats/html/lm.html
[10] http://www.jfree.org/jfreechart/

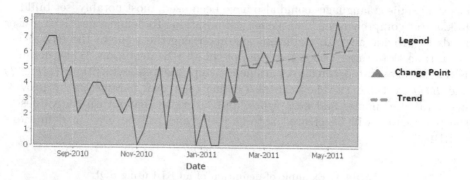

Fig. 4. The number of distinct activities completed by resource R9

4.2   Analysing the Behaviours of Resources in a German Bank

In this section we demonstrate how the framework can be used to analyse resource behaviour by applying the techniques to an actual event log. An event log which describes a loan application process in a German bank was used in this experiment. The log has the following characteristics:
- Number of cases: 1731; log duration: 43 weeks;
- Number of activities: 25; number of resources: 220;
- Average case duration: 18.7 days; average number of resources in a case: 4.

The resources can also be involved in other processes, however, the organisation allows resources to spend up to 85% of their time on this loan application process. Hence, all results discussed in this section reflect resource behaviour in just one process but it can be considered as a representative set of data for the analysis. We selected the ten most frequent resources in the log (referred to here as R1–R10) for our analysis. In our experiments we used two different values of the time slot size: one week and one day. We looked at the daily values of an RBI "number of activity instances completed" for the ten resources. We found that some resources tend to complete slightly more activities in the middle of the week than on Mondays and Fridays while others do not display any differences within a week. In all experiments described below, the time slot size was one week. We show below RBIs from each resource behaviour category as examples.

Figure 4 depicts time series for the RBI "Number of distinct activities completed by a resource" extracted for resource R9. We can observe that the values of the RBI were decreasing until January 2011, but starting from February 2011 resource R9 began executing more distinct tasks. The plug-in was able to identify this change point using the Mann-Whitney test for identifying changes in location, as depicted by the triangle shape in Figure 4. Changes in resource behaviour can affect organisational performance. Automatic identification of such changes can help managers to take timely actions.

To demonstrate the resource utilisation indicators we used as examples the RBIs "Number of cases completed in which a given resource was involved" and "Percentage of cases completed in which a given resource was involved".

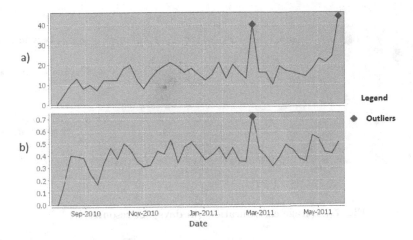

Fig. 5. Number (a) and percentage (b) of cases completed in which R1 was involved

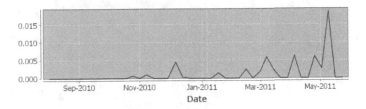

Fig. 6. Percentage of active time when resource R7 is involved in more than one activity

Figure 5(a) shows that during two weeks (in February and May 2011) an abnormal number of cases were completed in which resource R1 was involved (marked as diamond shapes). In Figure 5(b) is the percentage of cases completed in which R1 was involved and we can see only one outlier (in February 2011). All outliers were identified by the plug-in. We can conclude that the reason for the higher number of cases processed by resource R1 in May 2011 was a higher case arrival rate, as the percentage is not abnormal, while the higher number of case completions in February 2011 cannot be explained in a similar manner. Abnormal resource workload can be a cause of process delays or low-quality outputs. Further investigations may help to discover reasons for such behaviour and conduct any corrective or preventive actions if necessary.

We also analysed the behaviour of the RBI "Multitasking" for these ten resources and found that all of them were involved in multiple activities on only rare occasions. Figure 6 depicts multitasking preferences for resource R7. Although we can observe a slight increase in tendency to multitask over time the percentage of time when the resource is working on more than one activity is very small (no more than 2% of the resource's active time).

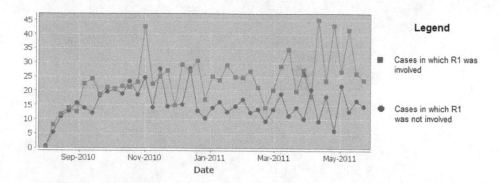

Fig. 7. Average case duration (in days) for resource R1

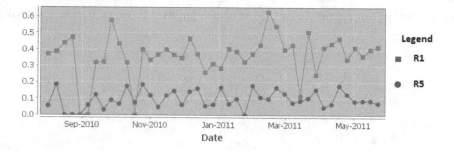

Fig. 8. Percentage of resources involved in the same cases with a given resource

Figure 7 demonstrates the performance of the productivity RBI "Average duration of a case in which a given resource was involved" for resource R1. We can observe that starting from November 2010 the average duration of cases in which resource R1 was involved is higher (typically around 25 days) when compared with the average duration of cases in which resource R1 was not involved (typically around 15 days). A conclusion one may draw from this is that R1 is a source of case delays. Alternatively it is possible that R1 is an expert who is usually involved in more complex and lengthy cases.

Figure 8 shows the percentage of resources that are involved in the same cases with a particular resource. We can see, for example, that during a week resource R1 interacts in different cases with approximately 40% of all resources involved in the process during that week, while resource R5 typically interacts with 5–15% of resources involved in the process. This RBI reflects the social position of a resource within the organisation. A high number of interactions with other employees often means that a resource has a higher influence in an organisation [4]. We can also see in Figure 8 that the social positions of the two resources did not change significantly during the period of analysis.

Having analysed the behaviours of the ten most frequent resources in the log we can see that most of the resources are active during the period of analysis and their behaviours did not change significantly. We saw that some resources are getting faster in execution of some tasks (e.g. R3) and some are often involved in long-running cases (e.g. R1). We learned that some resources do not process cases with high loan amounts requested. These are only few examples illustrating knowledge discovered from the log. Managers can use this knowledge to evaluate the performance of these resources and to plan their future workload and development. Identified outliers (e.g., in Figure 5) show behavioural anomalies that could have affected the process performance. Further investigation is required in order to understand their causes and consequences. It can provide insights for improving the process performance in the future. We showed that behaviour of some RBIs can have different interpretations as the event log does not contain all information about resource behaviour. However, such RBIs can still provide valuable insights to managers as the managers may be able to interpret the RBIs using their own knowledge of the process. Automatic analysis of time series can help a manager quickly gain insights about the dynamics of resource behaviour, e.g., to get all RBIs where changes in behaviour have occurred. One can also find those resources whose behaviour significantly differs from others.

5 Conclusions

Human resources are responsible for carrying out business processes, however their actions can have both positive and negative impacts on organisational performance. Having objective knowledge about the behaviour of these resources will assist managers to evaluate their performance, to investigate issues and to apply appropriate rewards or mitigation actions.

In this paper we presented an automated, extensible framework for the analysis of the dynamics of resource behaviour using event logs. The framework can be used to measure and track resource's skills, utilisation, preferences, productivity and collaboration. As a starting point for such analysis we proposed a set of indicators for each category of resource behaviour. Our framework also provides an interface to define new RBIs. For each RBI, we extract a time series, analyse its dynamics and visualise the results.

The current framework concentrates on measurements for individual RBIs and any interdependencies among indicators are not considered. Hence, an extension of this work will be to combine several RBIs to a single performance measure. For this purpose we can use Data Envelopment Analysis – a non-parametric efficiency measurement method developed by Charnes et al. [2]. Another possible extension of this work is using the results of the analysis to enrich event logs with knowledge about resource behaviour.

We have applied the framework to a real event log and demonstrated that it can extract knowledge about resource behaviour. We have shown how our framework can be used to analyse various aspects of behaviour and demonstrated the different types of analysis that can be applied. We also explained how this analysis can help in evaluating a resource's performance and in identifying resource-related issues.

References

1. Bose, J.C.R.P., van der Aalst, W.M.P., Zliobaite, I., Pechenizkiy, M.: Dealing with concept drifts in process mining. IEEE Transactions on Neural Networks and Learning Systems, PP(99) (2013)
2. Charnes, A., Cooper, W.W., Rhodes, E.: Measuring the efficiency of decision making units. European Journal of Operational Research 2(6), 429–444 (1978)
3. Hawkins, D.M., Deng, Q.: A nonparametric change-point control chart. Journal of Quality Technology 42(2), 165–173 (2010)
4. Huang, Z., Lu, X., Duan, H.: Resource behavior measure and application in business process management. Expert Systems with Applications 39(7), 6458–6468 (2012)
5. International Organization for Standardization /International Electrotechnical Commission. Information technology - Database languages - SQL (ISO/IEC 9075:2011) (2011)
6. Lijffijt, J., Papapetrou, P., Puolamäki, K.: Size matters: Finding the most informative set of window lengths. In: Flach, P.A., De Bie, T., Cristianini, N. (eds.) ECML PKDD 2012, Part II. LNCS, vol. 7524, pp. 451–466. Springer, Heidelberg (2012)
7. Mann, H.B., Whitney, D.R.: On a test of whether one of two random variables is stochastically larger than the other. The Annals of Mathematical Statistics 18(1), 50–60 (1947)
8. Murphy, P.: Service performance measurement using simple techniques actually works. Journal of Marketing Practice: Applied Marketing Science 5(2), 56–73 (1999)
9. Nakatumba, J., van der Aalst, W.M.P.: Analyzing resource behavior using process mining. In: Rinderle-Ma, S., Sadiq, S., Leymann, F. (eds.) BPM 2009. LNBIP, vol. 43, pp. 69–80. Springer, Heidelberg (2010)
10. Neely, A., Gregory, M., Platts, K.: Performance measurement system design: a literature review and research agenda. International Journal of Operations & Production Management 25(12), 1228–1263 (2005)
11. Nudurupati, S.S., Bititci, U.S., Kumar, V., Chan, F.T.S.: State of the art literature review on performance measurement. Computers & Industrial Engineering 60(2), 279–290 (2011)
12. Pika, A., van der Aalst, W.M.P., Fidge, C.J., ter Hofstede, A.H.M., Wynn, M.T.: Predicting deadline transgressions using event logs. In: La Rosa, M., Soffer, P. (eds.) BPM Workshops 2012. LNBIP, vol. 132, pp. 211–216. Springer, Heidelberg (2013)
13. Pika, A., van der Aalst, W.M.P., Fidge, C.J., ter Hofstede, A.H.M., Wynn, M.T.: Profiling event logs to configure risk indicators for process delays. In: Salinesi, C., Norrie, M.C., Pastor, Ó. (eds.) CAiSE 2013. LNCS, vol. 7908, pp. 465–481. Springer, Heidelberg (2013)
14. Rao, D.S.P., O'Donnell, C.J., Battese, G.E., Coelli, T.J.: An introduction to efficiency and productivity analysis. Springer (2005)
15. Ross, G.J., Adams, N.M.: Two nonparametric control charts for detecting arbitrary distribution changes. Journal of Quality Technology 44(2), 102–116 (2012)
16. Song, M., van der Aalst, W.M.P.: Towards comprehensive support for organizational mining. Decision Support Systems 46(1), 300–317 (2008)
17. Thevendran, V., Mawdesley, M.J.: Perception of human risk factors in construction projects: an exploratory study. International Journal of Project Management 22(2), 131–137 (2004)

18. Thompson, G.M., Goodale, J.C.: Variable employee productivity in workforce scheduling. European Journal of Operational Research 170(2), 376–390 (2006)
19. van der Aalst, W.M.P.: Business process simulation revisited. In: Barjis, J. (ed.) EOMAS 2010. LNBIP, vol. 63, pp. 1–14. Springer, Heidelberg (2010)
20. van der Aalst, W.M.P.: Process Mining: Discovery, Conformance and Enhancement of Business Processes. Springer, Berlin (2011)
21. van der Aalst, W.M.P., Reijers, H.A., Song, M.: Discovering social networks from event logs. Computer Supported Cooperative Work (CSCW) 14(6), 549–593 (2005)
22. van der Loo, M.P.J.: Distribution based outlier detection for univariate data: discussion paper 10003. Statistics Netherlands (2010)

Extracting Facets from Lost Fine-Grained Categorizations in Dataspaces

Riccardo Porrini[1,2], Matteo Palmonari[1], and Carlo Batini[1]

[1] DISCo, University of Milano-Bicocca
Viale Sarca, 336/14, 20126, Milan, Italy
{matteo.palmonari,carlo.batini}@disco.unimib.it
[2] 7Pixel s.r.l.
Via Lanzoni 13, 27010, Giussago (PV), Italy
riccardo.porrini@trovaprezzi.it

Abstract. Categorization of instances in dataspaces is a difficult and time consuming task, usually performed by domain experts. In this paper we propose a semi-automatic approach to the extraction of facets for the fine-grained categorization of instances in dataspaces. We focus on the case where instances are categorized under heterogeneous taxonomies in several sources. Our approach leverages Taxonomy Layer Distance, a new metric based on structural analysis of source taxonomies, to support the identification of meaningful candidate facets. Once validated and refined by domain experts, the extracted facets provide a fine-grained classification of dataspace instances. We implemented and evaluated our approach in a real world dataspace in the eCommerce domain. Experimental results show that our approach is capable of extracting meaningful facets and that the new metric we propose for the structural analysis of source taxonomies outperforms other state-of-the-art metrics.

Keywords: dataspaces, web data integration, taxonomy integration, facet extraction.

1 Introduction

The *dataspace* abstraction describes data integration architectures that deal with large heterogeneous data, which are partially unstructured, possibly sparse and characterized by high dimensionality [6]. Differently from traditional data integration architectures, where data from local sources are consistently integrated in a global view after their schemas are aligned, pay-as-you-go data integration is needed in dataspaces: data are more and more integrated along time, as more effective data access features are required [11].

Data integration methodologies inspired by dataspace principles are widely adopted for industry-scale Web data integration because of the amount and heterogeneity of source instances to be integrated [5]. Several examples of Web data integration systems can be found in the eCommerce domain. *Price Comparison Engines* (PCEs) integrate a very large number of heterogeneous product *offers*

M. Jarke et al. (Eds.): CAiSE 2014, LNCS 8484, pp. 580–594, 2014.

(i.e., dataspace instances) from many different e-marketplaces providing search and browsing features over the integrated information. Through PCE front-ends, end-users compare different eMarketplaces product offerings in terms of price and/or product features. Many PCEs such as Google Shopping [1], PriceGrabber [2] and Amazon [3] have been developed, which differ in terms of coverage and effectiveness of search and browsing features.

Category-based and *facet-based* browsing are two examples of data access features that many PCEs aim to deliver to their users. These features require the creation and maintenance of categorizations respectively based on *taxonomies*, i.e., hierarchies of product categories such as "Mobile Phones" or "Wines", and *facets*, i.e., sets of mutually exclusive coordinate terms that belong to a same concept (e.g., "Grape: Barolo, ..., Cabernet", ..., "Type: Red Wine, ..., White Wine") [19,21]. A *global taxonomy* is used to annotate all the instances in the dataspace with a coarse-grained categorization, which helps end-users to rapidly recall the "family" of instances they are interested in. Facets can be used within a specific (global) taxonomy category, to annotate instances in the dataspace with a fine-grained categorization, which helps end-user to rapidly recall instances with specific characteristics (e.g., "Grape: Barolo", "Type: Red Wine"). Facet-based categorizations can be also useful in relation to Search Engine Optimization because facets indexed by search engines can bring more traffic to the PCEs' websites.

Unfortunately, facet creation and maintenance is an extremely time and effort consuming task in PCEs, which is left to manual work of domain experts. The definition of meaningful facets at large scale requires a deep understanding of the salient characteristics of dataspace instances (e.g., wines are characterized by grape, type, provenance, and so on) for a large number of diverse product categories. As a result, while a *global taxonomy* is used in most of PCEs[4], many PCEs provide only few generic facets (e.g., "Price Range" and "Merchant") and others provide a richer set of facets but only for a limited amount of popular product categories.

In this paper we propose an approach to automatic facet extraction in dataspaces, which is aimed to support domain experts in creating and maintaining significant facets associated with global categories. Our approach leverages the information already present in the dataspace, namely (i) taxonomies used to classify instances in the data sources and (ii) mappings established from source taxonomies to the global taxonomy of the dataspace, to suggest meaningful facets for a given global category. Unlike the global taxonomy, which has to cover instances from very diverse domains, source taxonomies are often specialized in certain domains (e.g., "Wines"). Domain experts map specific categories in source taxonomies (e.g., "Barolo") to generic categories in the global taxonomy (e.g., "Wines"). The idea behind our approach consists in reusing the

---

[1] http://www.google.com/shopping
[2] www.pricegrabber.com/
[3] http://amazon.com/
[4] See, e.g., http://www.google.com/basepages/producttype/taxonomy.en-US.txt

fine-grained categories that occur in several source taxonomies mapped to the global taxonomy (e.g., "Barolo","Cabernet"), to extract a set of relevant facets for a given global category (e.g., "Grape: Barolo, ..., Cabernet", ..., "Type: Red Wine, ..., White Wine").

Our approach incorporates an automatic facet extraction algorithm that consists of three steps: *extraction* of potential facet values (e.g., "Cabernet"); *clustering* of facet values into sets of mutually exclusive terms (e.g., "Bordeaux", "Cabernet", "Chianti"); *labeling* of clusters with meaningful labels (e.g., "Grape"). The algorithm is based on structural analysis of source taxonomies and on *Taxonomy Layer Distance*, a novel metric introduced to evaluate the distance between mutually exclusive categories in different taxonomies. Experiments conducted to evaluate the approach show that our algorithm is able to extract meaningful facets that can then be refined by domain experts. In addition, since our approach extracts facets from source categorizations, the annotation of the dataspace instances with the extracted facets is straightforward, supporting facet-based browsing.

The paper is organized as follows. The problem of facet extraction is defined and explained in Section 2. Our approach to facet extraction is described in Section 3 and the evaluation is discussed in Section 4. Related work is presented in Section 5. Section 6 draws conclusions and discusses future work.

2   Problem Definition and Domain Example

A *facet* can be defined as "a clearly defined, mutually exclusive, and collectively exhaustive aspect, property, or characteristic of a class or specific subject" [19]. As input to our problem, we assume that there exists a global taxonomy used in the dataspace and a set of mappings from leaf categories in source taxonomies to leaf global categories. We assume that the mappings have many-to-one cardinality, i.e., many categories in each source taxonomy are mapped one global category. Observe that mappings of this kind can be easily extracted in any dataspace where instances are categorized using one source taxonomy category and one global taxonomy category.

In the following paragraph we summarize the terminology used in the rest of the paper, along with a precise description of the problem of Facet Extraction.

Source Taxonomy: a source taxonomy consists of a partially ordered set S of source categories s.

Global Taxonomy: a global taxonomy consist of a partially ordered set G of global categories g.

Leaf-to-leaf Category Mapping: a leaf-to-leaf (leaf for brevity) category mapping $m : g \leftarrow s$ is a correspondence from a leaf category s of some source taxonomy S to a global leaf category g. The semantics of a leaf mapping from s to g is that instances that are classified under s at the source can be classified under g once they enter the dataspace.

Facet: a facet F^g for a global category g is a finite set of values $v_1, ..., v_n$ (e.g., {"Red Wine", "White Wine"}) associated with a label; conceptually, a facet

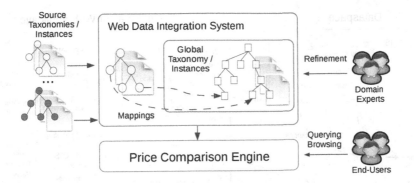

Fig. 1. Conceptual architecture of a Price Comparison Engine

label for a facet F^g briefly describes the concept of reality that facet values refer to (i.e., "Wine Type").

Facet Extraction Problem: given a global leaf category g, a set of mappings M from source categories $s_1, \ldots, s_n$ to g in the form $g \leftarrow s_1, \ldots, g \leftarrow s_n$, extract a set $\mathcal{F}^g$ of facets F^g, each one associated with a label.

As introduced in Section 1, the Facet Extraction problem is common in PCEs. The dataspace of a PCE consists of offers (i.e., the dataspace instances) coming from many eMarketplaces (i.e., the data sources). The conceptual architecture of a PCE is sketched in Figure 1. Each eMarketplace categorizes offers using a own source taxonomy. Source instances are integrated within the dataspace by specifying mappings from a large population of (often domain specific) source taxonomies to a global taxonomy. Mappings are defined and maintained by domain experts with the aid of (semi) automatic algorithms. To size the problem, we provide some figures about the dataspace of one of the most popular PCE on the Italian market. TrovaPrezzi[5] integrates many times per day 7 millions product offers from about 3900 eMarketplaces. Over more than 10 years of activity, more than 1 million of leaf mappings have been specified from source categories to more than 500 global categories.

3   Facet Extraction

The semi-automatic approach to facet extraction proposed in this paper is sketched in Figure 2 and is aimed to support domain experts who are in charge of maintaining classifications and mappings within a dataspace. Domain experts trigger the facet extraction process for a specified global category using a Web interface. An automatic facet extraction algorithm suggests a set of facets to domain experts, who inspect, validate and refine the result of the automatic extraction algorithm, deciding which facets will be part of the dataspace.

---

[5] www.trovaprezzi.it

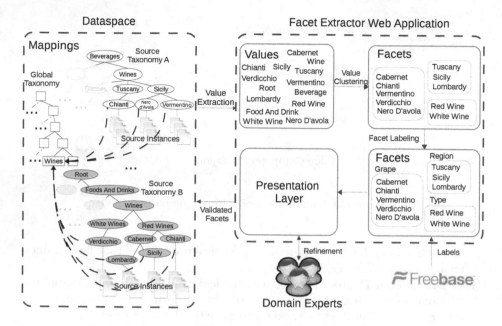

Fig. 2. Overview of the proposed approach to facet extraction

The automatic facet extraction algorithm at the core of the proposed approach is inspired by the following principle: the specialized taxonomies used in data sources contain information that can be analyzed to extract a set of significant facets for a global taxonomy category. The facet extraction algorithm extracts the set of facets $\mathcal{F}^g$ for a global category g using a three-phase process:

1. **Value Extraction:** A set of normalized facet values is produced by case lowerization, special characters removal and stemming of all the source categories mapped to g.
2. **Value Clustering:** Facet values are clustered together into facets according to source taxonomies structural analysis. Since we look for facets of mutual exclusive values, we admit facets containing at least two values. Thus, values that cannot be added to any facet (i.e., clusters of one element) are discarded.
3. **Facet Labeling:** Facets are labelled using external knowledge sources.

The third phase of the facet extraction process is aimed to suggest labels to domain experts' who can accept the suggestion or change the label. We assume that all the taxonomies are lexicalized in a same language. However, our approach does not depend on a particular language: frequency and structural-based principles are used to select and cluster facet values; state-of-the-art Natural Language Processing techniques available in nearly any language are used for facet value normalization; external knowledge sources like the one we used for facet labeling are now available in several languages.

3.1   Value Extraction

During this phase we identify the set of facet values that are frequently used for categorization at the sources. In order to identify such values for a global category g we rely on existing mappings to g. For each source taxonomy S we form the set N_S^g of values occurring as names of source categories mapped to g and all their ancestors in the respective source taxonomy. The level of detail of source taxonomies can be different in each source taxonomy, thus ancestors' names are included in N_S^g to consider every possible significant value. The set N_S^g for a global category g and a source taxonomy S is defined as $N_S^g = \{s \mid \exists\, g \leftarrow s \text{ or } \exists\, g \leftarrow s', \text{ with } s \in S \text{ and } s' \text{ is a descendant of } s\}$.

The set V_S^g of normalized values is obtained by applying case lowerization, special characters removal and stemming to N_S^g. As far as stemming is concerned, we use Hunspell Stemmer[6] to normalize values' terms with respect to their singular form. Hunspell stemmer is based on language dependent stemming rules that are available for most of languages. Normalized values are then unioned together to form the set V^g of facet values for a global category g. In this phase, duplicated values are removed. The set V^g of unique values for a global category g over all the n source taxonomies is $V^g = \bigcup_{i=1}^n V_{S^i}^g$.

After normalization and unioning, a simple ranking function is applied to V^g. Unique values are ranked according to their frequency over the all sets $V_{S^i}^g$. Intuitively, the more a value occurs as source category name mapped to the global category g, the higher rank it will get. Based on this ranking we reduce V^g to the set V_k^g of the top k frequent values. The rationale behind this choice is to keep only those values that are more commonly used across many independent and heterogeneous sources and thus are likely to be more relevant for the fine-grained classification of dataspace instances. The set V_k^g of the top frequent values produced by this phase represents the input for the next phase. In addition, we keep track of the (possibly) many source categories to which each value $v \in V_k^g$ correspond. In this way, the annotation of the dataspace instances with facet values extracted by the algorithm is straightforward.

Example. Given the two taxonomies A and B in Figure 2, for the global category "Wines", $N_A^{wines} = \{$ "Beverages", "Wines", "Tuscany", "Chianti", "Sicily", "Nero d'Avola", "Vermentino"$\}$ and $N_B^{wines} = \{$ "Root", "Food And Drinks", "Wines", "White Wines", "Verdicchio", "Red Wines", "Cabernet", "Lombardy", "Sicily", "Chianti"$\}$. After normalization, values from N_A^{wines} and N_B^{wines} form the set of unique values $V^{wines} = \{$ "Root", "Beverage", "Food And Drink", "Wine", "Lombardy", "Cabernet", "Tuscany", "Chianti", "Sicily", "Vermentino", "Nero d'Avola", "White Wine", "Verdicchio", "Red Wine"$\}$.

3.2   Value Clustering

Values in V_k^g are clustered to form the set of facets $\mathcal{F}^g$. We aim at clustering together all values that are more likely to be coordinate values of a same

---

[6] http://hunspell.sourceforge.net/

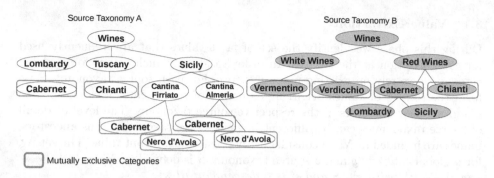

Fig. 3. An example of mutually exclusive source categories

characteristic. As an example, suppose that we get $V_k^{wines} = \{$"Cabernet", "Chianti", "Lombardy", "Sicily"$\}$. An ideal clustering should be $F_1^g = \{$"Cabernet", "Chianti"$\}$ and $F_2^g = \{$"Lombardy", "Sicily"$\}$ because each facet refers to a same characteristic (i.e., the wine's grape variety and the origin Italian region).

In order to discover the set $\mathcal{F}^g$ of facets over V_k^g we make use of the DB-SCAN *density-based* clustering algorithm [4]. DBSCAN clusters together values within a maximum distance threshold ϵ and satisfying a cluster density criterion and discards as noise values that are distant from any resulting cluster. DBSCAN algorithm requires in input the minimum cardinality of expected clusters $minPoints$ and the maximum distance threshold ϵ. We set $minPoints$ to 2 and empirically find the best value for ϵ (see Section 4). Finally, DBSCAN does not require a number of expected clusters as input. We use DBSCAN for several reasons. We deal with heterogeneous taxonomies, thus we cannot make any assumption about the shape of clusters (i.e. facets) and we must employ clustering techniques that incorporate the notion of noise. Otherwise, clustering algorithms requiring the expected number of clusters as input are not suitable (e.g. KMeans) since the number of facets to detect is not known in advance.

In order to use the DBSCAN clustering algorithm it is crucial to provide an effective distance metric between the values. We propose a distance metric that considers near those values that refer to a same characteristic of instances, according to a taxonomic structural criterion. We now formally define the proposed distance metric, starting from the principle that it aims at capturing: source categories mutual exclusivity.

Source Category Mutual Exclusivity Principle. We recall from Section 2 that a facet is "a clearly defined, mutually exclusive, and collectively exhaustive aspect, property, or characteristic of a class or specific subject" [19]. The Source Category Mutual Exclusivity principle (SCME) states that the more two values refer to mutually exclusive categories, the more they should be grouped together into the same facet. Given two source categories s_1 and s_2, their occurrence as siblings indicates that s_1 and s_2 are mutually exclusive (e.g., "Lombardy" and "Sicily" in Figure 3). SCME is a *structural* principle: it takes source taxonomies structure into account by considering reciprocal relationships among categories.

Taxonomy Layer Distance. We propose a distance metric that captures the SCME principle by considering sibling relationships between source categories, or more generally, the co-occurrence of categories on a same taxonomy layer. Given a taxonomy S, a taxonomy *layer* l^S of S is the set of all categories that are at the same distance from the taxonomy root. For example, the set {"Lombardy", "Tuscany", "Sicily"} is a layer for taxonomy A in Figure 3. At large scale, categories occurring on same taxonomy layers are likely to be mutually exclusive since they usually represent partitions of the set of entities categorized under the considered taxonomy. Considering co-occurrences on the same taxonomy layer represents a good way to capture the SCME principle: the more two values v_1 and v_2 co-occur at the same layer across all source taxonomies, the more they should be clustered together and thus the less they are distant from each other.

We compute the Taxonomy Layer Distance (TLD) between two values v_1 and v_2 by counting their co-occurrences on the same taxonomy layer and scaling it by their nominal occurrences across all source taxonomies. Computing TLD is equivalent to computing the Jaccard Distance between the two sets of taxonomy layers where two values v_1 and v_2 occur, respectively. Given a value v and a source taxonomy S we define the set L_v^S of layers containing v in S as $L_v^S = \{l^S \mid v \in l^S\}$ (a category can occur in more than one layer). The overall set L_v of layers containing v is computed by unioning all layers across all n source taxonomies as $L_v = \bigcup_{i=1}^n L_v^{S_i}$. Then we compute the Jaccard Distance between L_{v_1} and L_{v_2}:

$$\text{TLD}(v_1, v_2) = 1 - \frac{|L_{v_1} \cap L_{v_2}|}{|L_{v_1} \cup L_{v_2}|} \qquad (1)$$

Example. Given the two source taxonomies from Figure 3 and values "Cabernet" and "Chianti", we first compute layers containing "Cabernet" and "Chianti":
$l_1^A = \{$"Cabernet", "Chianti", "Cantina Firriato", "Cantina Almeria"$\}$
$l_2^A = \{$"Cabernet", "Nero d'Avola"$\}$
$l_1^B = \{$"Vermentino", "Cabernet", "Verdicchio", "Chianti"$\}$
The set of layers containing "Cabernet" and "Chianti" are:
$L_{Cabernet} = L_{Cabernet}^A \cup L_{Cabernet}^B = \{l_1^A, l_2^A, l_1^B\}$
$L_{Chianti} = L_{Chianti}^A \cup L_{Chianti}^B = \{l_1^A, l_1^B\}$
Then, we compute the distance between "Chianti" and "Cabernet" as:

$$\text{TLD}(\text{"Cabernet"}, \text{"Chianti"}) = 1 - \frac{|L_{Cabernet} \cap L_{Chianti}|}{|L_{Cabernet} \cup L_{Chianti}|} = 1 - \frac{2}{3} = \frac{1}{3}$$

3.3 Facet Labeling

During the labeling phase a semantically meaningful label is attached to each facet F^g discovered in the value clustering phase. Ideally, each label should shortly describe the characteristic to which the values of a facet are likely to refer. For example, if we consider two facets $F_1^g = \{$"Cabernet", "Chianti"$\}$ and $F_2^g = \{$"Italy", "France"$\}$, meaningful labels can be "Grape Variety" and "Country", respectively. Conceptually, labeling each facet means responding to the following question: "to which concept of reality do values of facet F^g refer?".

In order to answer this question, we reconcile each facet value to entities from the Freebase[7] multilingual knowledge base. Given a facet F^g, we submit each facet value of F^g as a keyword query to the Freebase Search Web service[8]. This API performs keyword search over Freebase entities and returns a list of entities ranked by relevance. We select the entity type of the top k ranked entities returned by the keyword search API. We pick as label the most frequent type returned by the Freebase Search API for all facet values in F^g.

4   Evaluation

The core idea of our proposed approach to facet extraction is that we group facet values according to a structural criterion (i.e., TLD). We focus on evaluating the facet value clustering phase. Our goal is to show that TLD effectively captures the SCME principle and supports domain experts in facets definition. To the best of our knowledge there are no distance metrics for taxonomies that explicitly aim at capturing the SCME principle. However, structural similarity metrics that consider path distance between categories within a taxonomy are good candidates to compare our work to. Intuitively, the more two source categories co-occur in the same source taxonomy path (i.e. they are similar to some degree according to structural similarity metrics) from the root to a leaf, the less they are mutually exclusive and the more they should be clustered into different facets (i.e., the clustering algorithm should consider them distant from each other).

We compare TLD with two known structural concept similarity metrics, namely Leacock and Chodorow [9] (LC) and Wu and Palmer [22] (WP) metrics. Both LC and WP achieve high effectiveness results in determining the similarity of concepts within the WordNet taxonomy [16]. LC measures the similarity between two taxonomy categories by considering the shortest path between them and scaling it by the depth of the taxonomy. Similarly, WP measures the similarity between two categories by considering the distance from their nearest common ancestor and the distance of the nearest common ancestor from the taxonomy root. We adapted LC and WP to the case of multiple taxonomies. More specifically, given two values v_1 and v_2 we evaluate their LC and WP similarities for each source taxonomy where v_1 and v_2 co-occur and we take the mean similarity as the final distance value.

4.1   Gold Standard

We created a gold standard from the real world TrovaPrezzi Italian PCE dataspace. We chose ten TrovaPrezzi global categories and ran the Values Extraction phase over them. We presented the set of top k frequent values to TrovaPrezzi domain experts, who found that relevant facet values generally appear among the top 100 ranked values. Thus we choose $k = 100$ as cardinality of the set of

---

[7] http://www.freebase.com/

[8] https://developers.google.com/freebase/v1/search-overview

extracted facet values. Facet values were manually grouped together by a domain expert from TrovaPrezzi mapping team and facets were then validated by other domain experts in order to ensure their correctness. As we expected, some of the values were discarded by domain experts as they could be added to any existing facet.

Gold Standards' global categories cover different domains and a relevant portion of the overall dataspace of the PCE, that is 688 source taxonomies and 22594 leaf mappings. For each source taxonomy an average of about 33 mappings have been specified. Moreover, for 322 source taxonomies mappings to more than one global category have been specified. Notice that all the data upon which we created the gold standard are lexicalized in Italian. Our approach to facet extraction is language independent, thus results that we present in following sections are comparable to others obtained considering different languages. For sake of clarity, we provide examples translated to English.

4.2   Evaluation Metrics

We evaluate our facet extraction approach from two different perspectives: facet value effectiveness and value clustering effectiveness. This kind of evaluation campaign has been previously used to evaluate several facet extraction algorithms [8,3]. We introduce the notation we will use in the rest of the section. Given a global category g, we denote with $\mathcal{V}^g$ the set of discovered facet values (i.e. values that have not been classified as noise by the algorithm). We denote with $\mathcal{V}^g_*$ the set of gold standard facet values (i.e., values not classified as noise by domain experts). Lastly, we denote with $\mathcal{F}^g_*$ the set of manually discovered facets (i.e., the gold standard for the global category g), which is compared to the set $\mathcal{F}^g$ of automatically discovered facets.

Value Effectiveness. In our proposed approach noisy values are discarded. In order to evaluate the ability of our technique to filter noisy values out we compare sets $\mathcal{V}^g$ and $\mathcal{V}^g_*$, using Precision (P), Recall (R) and F-Measure (F_1). All these metrics do not take clustering effectiveness into account.

Value Clustering Effectiveness. We evaluate clustering effectiveness using several standard clustering quality metrics, that are Purity (P^*), Normalized Mutual Information (NMI^*), Entropy (E^*), and F-Measure for clustering (F^*). One remark about the usage of these evaluation metrics is that the set of facet values clustered by our approach is different from the set of facet values grouped by humans (i.e., $\mathcal{V}^g \neq \mathcal{V}^g_*$). We may fail in including meaningful values into some clusters, or we may mistakenly include noisy values into some facets. Clustering quality metrics cannot handle these cases. Thus, we modify facets in $\mathcal{F}^g$ by (1) removing all noisy values and by (2) adding to $\mathcal{F}^g$ as single value facets all gold standard values that have been automatically classified as noise. These adjustment ensures that $\mathcal{V}^g = \mathcal{V}^g_*$ and thus clustering quality metrics can be used properly. With this adjustment, facet value effectiveness is not considered.

Table 1. Effectiveness of TLD, LC and WP metrics

	Value Effectiveness			Clustering Effectiveness				Quality
	P	R	F_1	F^*	NMI^*	Purity	E^*	PRF^*
LC_n	0.359	0.447	0.370	0.403	0.603	**0.308**	**0.243**	0.359
LC_q	0.394	0.953	0.537	0.666	0.709	0.220	0.685	0.531
WP	0.377	**0.984**	0.525	0.682	0.714	0.210	0.744	0.520
TLD	**0.416**	0.901	**0.541**	**0.719**	**0.746**	0.286	0.416	**0.558**

Overall Quality. In order to evaluate the overall effectiveness of our approach, we aggregate facet value precision P, facet value recall R and clustering F-measure F^* into an overall quality measure. The PRF^* measure combines P, R and F^* by means of an armonic mean:

$$PRF^* = \frac{3 * P * R * F^*}{R * P + P * F + P * R} \qquad (2)$$

4.3   Experimental Results

We conducted several experiments, comparing clustering performance of TLD, LC and WP metrics. We recall from Section 3.2 that the DBSCAN algorithm used for clustering is configured with a maximum distance threshold ϵ. Optimal values of ϵ depend on the used distance metric, and influence clustering performance. The tuning of ϵ can be driven by two orthogonal factors: overall quality (i.e., PRF^*) and the number of discovered clusters. High values of ϵ (i.e., quality oriented configuration) can lead to better overall quality, but fewer discovered clusters (i.e., the clustering algorithm will tend to group values into one single cluster). Lower values of ϵ (i.e., cluster number oriented configuration) can lead to lower quality, but more discovered clusters. We found that quality oriented and cluster number oriented configurations generally coincide except for LC. In the following section we refer to quality oriented configuration of LC as LC_q while we indicate with LC_n the corresponding cluster number oriented configuration. Since optimal configurations for WP and TLD coincide we omit pedices for them. Moreover, due to space limitation we include only the mean value of metrics computed across all gold standard categories.

Table 1 presents results of our experiments. TLD is more effective in finding relevant facet values and discarding noisy ones, as indicated by an higher F_1. The ability of effectively discarding noisy values substantially reduces domain experts' effort in validating discovered facets. LC_q and WP obtain almost perfect value recall, but substantially lower precision. Thus, they do not effectively support domain experts. Moreover, TLD achieves best performance according to quite all clustering effectiveness metrics, with the exceptions of purity and entropy for LC_n. Clusters discovered by LC_n contain more homogeneous values, in the sense that they have been manually classified as belonging to the same gold standard group. However, LC_n achieves better purity and entropy at the cost of discarding most of the values as noise, thus sacrificing overall quality.

Table 2. Number of groups discovered by TLD, LC, and WP for each source category, compared to the gold standard

	$|\mathcal{F}_*^g|$	LC_q	LC_n	WP	TLD
Dogs and Cats Food	3	1	5	1	7
Grappe, Liquors, Aperitives	1	1	5	1	6
Wines	3	1	1	1	6
Beers	2	6	4	3	14
DVD Movies	2	2	3	1	3
Rings	4	1	6	2	7
Blu-Ray Movies	2	2	3	2	5
Musical Instruments	6	1	3	1	5
Ski and Snowboards	1	1	3	1	7
Necklaces	8	2	6	3	11

The difference between TLD and state-of-the-art metrics is even more evident if we consider the number of detected clusters for each gold standard category g (Table 2). WP and LC_q fail in properly partitioning the overall set V_k^g of facet values, thus failing in detecting groups (i.e. they detect only one or two clusters). They are too inclusive and thus they group facet values at a granularity level that is too high to be suitable for effectively supporting domain experts in bootstrapping a faceted classification system within the dataspace. From the other side, LC_n discards too much values to be effective.

In addition to standard evaluation metrics, we provide a more intuitive insight of results of the facet extraction process, using TLD for facet value clustering compare to state-of-the-art metrics. Table 3 depicts an example of facets discovered for the global category "Wines" by TLD, WP, LC_q, and LC_n compared to manually defined ones. Validating and refining groups discovered by TLD requires much less domain experts' effort than LC_q, LC_n and WP, thus sensibly reducing the cost of bootstrapping faceted classification.

Table 3 highlights a difficulty of TLD in grouping together different lexicalizations of same values (e.g., "Red Wine" and "Red"). One naive approach to overcome this difficulty is to normalize source category names by removing terms belonging to the global category for which the facets are extracted (e.g., the term "Wine" when extracting facets for global category "Wines"). However, this naive solution cannot be generalized to every global category. For example, if we remove from the source category "Dog Food" all the terms belonging to the gold standard global category "Dogs and Cats Food" we end up with an empty, inconsistent facet value. Moreover, also the more conservative approach of removing global category terms only if they *all* occur in the source category cannot be generalized. For example, if we consider the gold standard category "Musical Instruments", using the more conservative approach we will not normalize source categories "Wind Instruments" and "Winds".

We implemented and evaluated both the previously described naive solutions (we omit them due to space limitation), and found that they both decrease the effectiveness of our approach. We believe that effectively solving the problem of

Table 3. Discovered facets for TLD, WP and LC compared to manually discovered facets. Numbers after groups indicate group cardinality.

LC_q	F_1^g = {Wine, Red Wine, White Wine, ..., Piedmont, Lombardy, ..., Sicily, Donnafugata, Cusumano, ..., Alessandro di Camporeale, ..., France} (98)
LC_n	F_1^g = {Wine, Red Wine, White Wine, ..., France, ..., Chianti} (36)
WP	F_1^g = {Wine, Red Wine, White Wine, ..., Piedmont, Lombardy, ..., Sicily, Donnafugata, Cusumano, ..., France} (100)
TLD	F_1^g = { Piedmont, Tuscany, Sicily, , ..., France } (14) F_2^g = { Red, White, Rosé } (3) F_3^g = { Red Wine, White Wine, Rosé Wine } (3) F_4^g = { Moscato, Chardonnay, ..., Merlot } (13) F_5^g = { Tuscany Wine, Sicily Wine} (2) F_6^g = { Donnafugata, Cusumano, ..., Principi di Butera } (27)
Gold Standard	F_1^g = { Piedmont, Lombardy, ..., Sicily } (21) F_2^g = { Red Wine, White Wine, ..., Rosé Wine } (14) F_3^g = { Donnafugata, Cusumano, ..., Alessandro di Camporeale} (12)

different lexicalizations requires Natural Language Processing language specific techniques. NLP techniques can be used to discriminate between global category terms that refer to nouns, verbs, etc. and thus can be safely removed from source categories without creating inconsistencies or change category names' semantics. Introducing this kind of NLP language specific techniques comes at the cost of sacrificing the language independence of our approach. However, this represents an interesting extension of our approach.

5   Related Work

Many different approaches to the problem of extracting facets from structured and unstructured Web resources have been proposed (see [21] for a recent survey). Facets are usually extracted from a *document collection* (e.g., [2,18,13,20]), from search engine *query results* (e.g., [23,8,3,7]) or from the combination of documents and search engine *query logs* (e.g., [15,14,10]).

Document collection based approaches tackle the problem of extracting faceted taxonomies across a document collection. Faceted taxonomies represent a hierarchy topics to which document refer to. External structured resources such as WordNet [2,18], Wikipedia [2,20] or its Linked Data version DBPedia [13] are exploited to enrich the extracted set of facets. Our approach is different from document collection based ones because: (1) we extract facets and facet values in stead of a hierarchy of topics and (2) we analyze taxonomy structure in order to provide sets of mutually exclusive facet values.

The focus of query result based approaches is on classification of documents returned by a keyword query search. Facets for browsing results of a query are extracted from Wikipedia documents [23] analyzing, among other things, Wikipedia categories and reciprocal links between documents. In more general approaches facets are extracted by analyzing raw HTML pages in order to identify potential faceted classifications within them using unsupervised [3] or supervised [8] machine learning techniques. Facets are also extracted by images annotated with a folksonomy [7] and external resources are exploited for value disambiguation and hyponym detection. State of art query result based approaches deal with the specific problem of integrating and ranking heterogeneous facets that are already present in documents. Our approach takes in input source taxonomies and mappings between them and the global taxonomy.

The focus of query logs approaches is on the usage of user query statistics to identify facet values that are useful/relevant. Query logs are analyzed in order to select relevant facet values with respect to closed, fixed [15] or open, not defined a-priori [14,10] set of facets. Query log based approaches are strictly dependent on end-user queries: they do not consider currently available dataspace instances. Our approach analyzes classifications at the sources, and thus provide a more comprehensive fine-grained dataspace instances classification.

All the previously described approaches are complementary to ours. We extract facets from a different source than previous approaches: taxonomies used to categorize instances within a dataspace. We expect the facet extraction process to benefit from the integration of state-of-the-art facet extraction techniques.

Taxonomy structure analysis has been employed in the field of Ontology Matching [17]. In this field, several similarity metrics between ontology (and also taxonomy) concepts have been proposed and/or adapted from other domains [1,9,22,12]. However, experimental results provided in this paper prove that our proposed distance metric (i.e. TLD) is more effective in capturing the mutual exclusiveness of concepts across multiple heterogeneous taxonomies.

6 Conclusions

In this paper we proposed a semi-automatic, language independent approach to the problem of facets extraction from heterogeneous taxonomies within dataspaces. We proposed a novel metric designed ad-hoc to capture source categories mutual exclusivity across taxonomies. We used the proposed metric as a clustering distance metric for grouping together mutual exclusive facet values. Experimental results show that our approach outperforms state-of-the-art taxonomy concepts similarity metrics in capturing category mutual exclusiveness. Our approach provides valuable aid and reduces domain experts' effort in bootstrapping dataspace fine-grained classifications.

We plan to extend our approach along different directions. Advanced NLP techniques can be used to improve the facet labelling phase and to normalize source categories considering different lexicalizations. Finally, the effective integration of the proposed approach with evidence coming from the consideration of different additional input (e.g., user queries) as proposed in related work is currently under investigation.

References

1. Cheatham, M., Hitzler, P.: String similarity metrics for ontology alignment. In: Alani, H., Kagal, L., Fokoue, A., Groth, P., Biemann, C., Parreira, J.X., Aroyo, L., Noy, N., Welty, C., Janowicz, K. (eds.) ISWC 2013, Part II. LNCS, vol. 8219, pp. 294–309. Springer, Heidelberg (2013)

2. Dakka, W., Ipeirotis, P.G.: Automatic extraction of useful facet hierarchies from text databases. In: ICDE, pp. 466–475 (2008)
3. Dou, Z., Hu, S., Luo, Y., Song, R., Wen, J.R.: Finding dimensions for queries. In: CIKM, pp. 1311–1320 (2011)
4. Ester, M., Kriegel, H.P., S, J., Xu, X.: A density-based algorithm for discovering clusters in large spatial databases with noise. In: KDD, pp. 226–231 (1996)
5. Halevy, A.Y.: Why your data won't mix. ACM Queue 3(8), 50–58 (2005)
6. Halevy, A.Y., Franklin, M.J., Maier, D.: Principles of dataspace systems. In: PODS (2006)
7. Kawano, Y., Ohshima, H., Tanaka, K.: On-the-fly generation of facets as navigation signs for web objects. In: Lee, S.-G., Peng, Z., Zhou, X., Moon, Y.-S., Unland, R., Yoo, J. (eds.) DASFAA 2012, Part I. LNCS, vol. 7238, pp. 382–396. Springer, Heidelberg (2012)
8. Kong, W., Allan, J.: Extracting query facets from search results. In: SIGIR, pp. 93–102 (2013)
9. Leacock, C., Chodorow, M.: Combining local context and wordnet similarity for word sense identification, pp. 265–283. MIT Press (1998)
10. Li, X., Wang, Y.Y., Acero, A.: Extracting structured information from user queries with semi-supervised conditional random fields. In: SIGIR, pp. 572–579 (2009)
11. Madhavan, J., Cohen, S., Dong, X.L., Halevy, A.Y., Jeffery, S.R., Ko, D., Yu, C.: Web-scale data integration: You can afford to pay as you go. In: CIDR, pp. 342–350 (2007)
12. Mazuel, L., Sabouret, N.: Semantic relatedness measure using object properties in an ontology. In: Sheth, A.P., Staab, S., Dean, M., Paolucci, M., Maynard, D., Finin, T., Thirunarayan, K. (eds.) ISWC 2008. LNCS, vol. 5318, pp. 681–694. Springer, Heidelberg (2008)
13. Medelyan, O., Manion, S., Broekstra, J., Divoli, A., Huang, A.-L., Witten, I.H.: Constructing a focused taxonomy from a document collection. In: Cimiano, P., Corcho, O., Presutti, V., Hollink, L., Rudolph, S. (eds.) ESWC 2013. LNCS, vol. 7882, pp. 367–381. Springer, Heidelberg (2013)
14. Pasca, M., Alfonseca, E.: Web-derived resources for web information retrieval: from conceptual hierarchies to attribute hierarchies. In: SIGIR, pp. 596–603 (2009)
15. Pound, J., Paparizos, S., Tsaparas, P.: Facet discovery for structured web search: a query-log mining approach. In: SIGMOD, pp. 169–180 (2011)
16. Schwartz, H.A., Gomez, F.: Evaluating semantic metrics on tasks of concept similarity. In: FLAIRS (2011)
17. Shvaiko, P., Euzenat, J.: Ontology matching: State of the art and future challenges. IEEE Trans. Knowl. Data Eng. 25(1), 158–176 (2013)
18. Stoica, E., Hearst, M.A., Richardson, M.: Automating creation of hierarchical faceted metadata structures. In: HLT-NAACL, pp. 244–251 (2007)
19. Taylor, A.G., Wynar, B.S.: Wynar's introduction to cataloging and classification. Libraries Unlimited (2004)
20. Wei, B., Liu, J., Ma, J., Zheng, Q., Zhang, W., Feng, B.: Dft-extractor: a system to extract domain-specific faceted taxonomies from wikipedia. In: WWW (Companion Volume), pp. 277–280 (2013)
21. Wei, B., Liu, J., Zheng, Q., Zhang, W., Fu, X., Feng, B.: A survey of faceted search. J. Web Eng. 12(1-2), 41–64 (2013)
22. Wu, Z., Palmer, M.S.: Verb semantics and lexical selection. In: ACL, pp. 133–138 (1994)
23. Yan, N., Li, C., Roy, S.B., Ramegowda, R., Das, G.: Facetedpedia: enabling query-dependent faceted search for wikipedia. In: CIKM, pp. 1927–1928 (2010)

Towards a Form Based Dynamic Database Schema Creation and Modification System

Kunal Malhotra[1], Shibani Medhekar[1], Shamkant B. Navathe[1],
and M.D. David Laborde[2]

[1] College of Computing, Georgia Institute of Technology, Atlanta, Georgia, USA
{kmalhotra7,smedhekar3}@gatech.edu, sham@cc.gatech.edu
[2] Iconic Data Inc, Atlanta, Georgia, USA
dlaborde@aya.yale.edu

Abstract. The traditional approach to relational database design starts with the conceptual design of an application based schema in a model like the Entity-relationship model, then mapping that to a logical design and eventually representing it as a set of related normalized tables. The project we present has been motivated by needs of healthcare-IT where small group practices are currently in need of systems that will cater to their dynamic requirements without depending on EMR (Electronic Medical Record) systems. It is also relevant for researchers for mining huge repositories of data such as social networks, etc. and create extracts of data on the fly for data analytics. Based on user characteristics and needs, the data is likely to vary and hence, a dynamic back-end database must be created. This paper addresses a form-based approach to schema creation and modification.

Keywords: Dynamic user interface, Schema modification, Dynamic form generator, Schema evolution.

1 Introduction

It has been observed that a database schema frequently experiences a lot of changes with time [13]. In most of the domains, there is a lack of a set of common data elements, that users would like to store in the database thus requiring different database schemas. In such cases, a static database schema would pose a problem. One approach to modifying the schema would be to have a database administrator track the data elements and periodically modify the schema. This would require a lot of manual labor and periodic updates would eventually delay data entry. In most large organizations, the DBA staff has been entrusted with dealing with schema management however the costs associated with database management systems and other large-scale application systems such as EMR (Electronic Medical Record) systems tend to be prohibitive for most "small-business", or start-up operations. For most small outfits dealing with a specialty practice with a handful of physicians, adopting large generic systems is prohibitive in adoption, training and maintenance costs. We propose an approach in this paper to:

M. Jarke et al. (Eds.): CAiSE 2014, LNCS 8484, pp. 595–609, 2014.
© Springer International Publishing Switzerland 2014

1. Create schemas based on predefined forms
2. Update and customize schemas as per changing user needs
3. Align the back-end storage of data as the schemas evolve

Our primary goal is to reduce user intervention and to let the database "evolve" consistently as time progresses. For developing a generically applicable system, we base it on the relational model. Our approach to dynamic schema creation and management has been described here in the context of healthcare just for illustrative purposes. This project was motivated by our interaction with a local neurosurgery practice through Dr.Laborde, a neurosurgeon, who convinced us that there is merit to developing approached to "ad-hoc" database creation and management for applications where elaborate and costly solutions like EMR and EHR (Electronic Health Record) systems are an overkill.

We made some assumptions while developing the prototype. Our current implementation has been designed to cater to clinical researchers and physicians who want to use existing data for clinical trials and studies and want to add some parameters of their own. Very little knowledge about database modeling and query languages is assumed. The forms could then be made available to the end users such as patients. The users (physicians, nurses, etc. but not patients) are provided with predefined forms developed based on the underlying database schema. These forms are automatically generated based on the metadata, which is stored in a separate database. This process is discussed later in the paper.

The users can customize these existing forms by adding and deleting data elements of their choice. As a result of this the tables in underlying database will undergo appropriate schema modifications as discussed later in the paper. In our test implementation, we have used a neurosurgery application database from a local clinic called the ALIF (Anterior Lumbar Inter-body fusion) database [10]. We dealt with the ALIF data with Dr.Laborde's expertise as a domain expert in the specific specialty which deals with surgical procedures of the spine. The term "user" will apply to physicians , nurses, researchers etc. who are knowledgeable about the application domain, who can evaluate the suitability of existing forms and who can be guided in their choices when they undertake to modify the forms. Totally naive end users will not be a target audience for our approach.

2   Technical Challenges and Claims

One of the major challenges we faced while developing this system was to avoid anomalies or inconsistencies at the back-end when the user makes changes to the forms provided for entering the data. The traditional approach to constructing a relational database application involves building a conceptual schema of the relational database using a model like the extended entity-relationship model and then constructing a relational database schema [12]. For most advanced applications the schema of the relational database changes during development. We are interested in providing a solution to environments where the database schema needs to be adjusted in real time keeping all constraints and rules of a relational database intact while the user makes changes to the existing forms or creates new forms. This involves maintaining a metadata database to store metadata about the forms (FORMS DATABASE) and a domain specific database (DSD) to store the actual data entered by the user. The system also provides an easy to use Form Field Selection feature, which can be used by novice users to build their own forms.

A dialog based UI is designed to create a new database from scratch or modify an existing one. It would gather information about the nature of the form field (label in the form) being added which would in turn lead to appropriate changes in the schema of the DSD. Addition of a form field leads to formation of a new attribute in the appropriate table in the DSD. For the data which already exists in the database before adding a new field, the system populates default values for that particular field. Deletion of the form field does not lead to deletion of the corresponding attribute from the schema. These deletions are tracked and recorded in a metadatabase, and a customized form is presented to the user. Modification of a form field does not modify the field name at the back-end. Mappings are created between the field at the back-end and the ones in the UI. A new user may choose from any of the existing customized versions of a form and select the most appropriate one or he (henceforth we will use the pronoun "he" for the user without any intended bias) may customize them further based on his requirements. In order to ensure a smooth working of the system after plugging in any DSD which stores the data entered via the forms, the FORMS DATABASE stores the metadata of all forms and also the information about what tables a form is connected to.

A user is typically shown all available forms, which guide the user to use one that comes close to their requirements and to modify it. They are also given the option to create a form from scratch. Our algorithms for storing metadata, for defining the schema for the back-end, for storing actual data as well as displaying user defined forms are generic. We propose the mechanism by which a metadata layer called the FORMS meta-database is created to accommodate the current form definitions and subsequent changes to it. In this approach, a user can choose to display data elements that he would like to view together without providing an SQL query. At the back-end the algorithm performs joins between tables based on primary key-foreign key relationships and displays data elements requested by the user. The user can also request the system to perform aggregation operations on data elements, add conditions as well as sort the results. This is particularly geared for researchers who would want to do studies or clinical trials using patient treatment data related to a specific drug as the DSD. They would then create a new database after appropriate aggregation to define a cohort of patients.

3   Approach to Dynamic User Interface Management

The user interface of the system is a form-based UI since its functionality is guided by a set of forms. The user is provided with two modes; one of them deals with 'Data Entry' and the other with 'Data Retrieval'. Data entry can be done by either using the existing template forms provided by default based on the current state of the DSD, or the existing forms may be customized to suit new requirements before being used to insert data. The users can also create new forms if the requirements for the data they want to enter are not met. These changes are automatically translated into appropriate modifications at the schema level.

A large set of options is provided to the user as to what type of form field he wants to create for his form. The options are Radio buttons, Checkboxes, textboxes, dropdowns and buttons. Any of these options apply while modifying existing forms or creating new forms. On creating a new form field, the user is required to provide details about its data type, default value, ability to have multiple values, etc. helping the system to make appropriate modifications in the database. Similarly, creation of a new form requires some information from the user which helps in creating a new table at the back-end. E.g. information regarding its relationship with the existing forms, cardinality of the relationship, etc. The UI has help buttons to describe the semantics of these questions in simple language with examples.There may be a class of users such as researchers that may use an existing large database, create a form using our tool and then modify the form slightly to add some fields/attributes of their own using the data entry function.

The other important feature of this system is 'Data Retrieval' which is used for retrieving data by generating queries based on user input. The operations currently handled by the system are 'Select', 'Aggregation', 'Group By', and 'Having'. Appropriate selections may be made by the user and on doing so the system builds the query and displays the results after validation. This feature would be explained later in section 5. Figure 1 illustrates the process flow adopted by the system.

3.1 Data Entry

The user is presented with template forms based on the underlying DSD. He has a choice of either using the available forms to enter data or customize the forms appropriately. In the latter case he uses the Form Field Panel which displays the potential types of form fields available. A dialog is initiated with the user, which requires him to provide details about the form field chosen. For example, if a radio button is selected for a field 'Gender', then he is required to enter the number of options he wants to keep for this field and their corresponding labels. The new form field added to a form would become a new attribute in the corresponding table having the rest of the form fields of that form after the user provides information about this new attribute using an 'Add New Form Field' screen. This information consists of the label of the form field, it's data type, e.g Integer, String, etc. The user would also need to specify a default value of the field which would be stored if the field is left blank while entering data. This new field may have multiple values e.g If the new field which is getting added is 'Symptoms' then it may contain multiple values since a patient may have multiple symptoms. This can be specified in the 'Add New Form Field' screen.

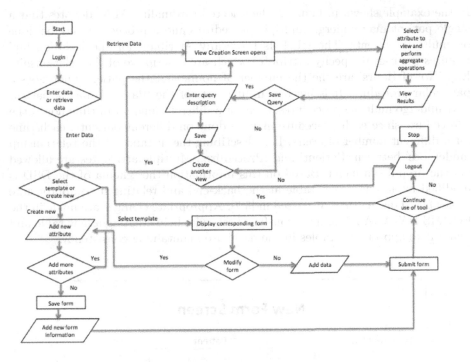

Fig. 1. Process flow of the system

Each modified template form would be stored as a new version of the existing template and will be annotated with the username of the user modifying it. E.g 'Form_A_User1' is 'Form_A' modified by 'User1' and 'Form_A_User2' is 'Form_A' modified by User2. All the versions of a template are shown to every user from which he can select one for data entry.

The user may create a new form from scratch for which he would be required to provide some information about the new type of data he would like to store (See Figure 2). As mentioned before the '?' marks alongside each label would assist the user in filling this form. The 'Form Name' is the name of the new form the user wants to create. The 'Unique Form Field' would be the field which uniquely identifies an observation. This is equivalent to the key for that form. Initially this field would be empty since it is a new form and no fields have been added. The user would use the 'Add New Form Field' screen to add fields to this form. The system allows selection of multiple fields for the cases when a combination of more than one fields uniquely identifies an observation. The 'Related to Form' field would require the user to choose from a list of existing forms to which this form is related to. As shown in the figure 'Patient' form has a relationship with 'Visits' form in the context of patients having visits in a hospital. The 'Cardinality' can have values 1:1, 1:N and M:N according to the standard cardinality ratio concept in database modeling [3]. Based on the nature of the relationship between the forms the user needs to select the cardinality.

In the example shown in figure 2, the selected cardinality 'M:N' denotes that a single patient may undergo multiple procedures and a procedure may be done on multiple patients. The label 'Is there any Attribute for the Relationship' requires the user to specify attributes which are descriptive of the relationship. E.g. 'No. of Hours' are the the number of hours that the patient undergoes a particular procedure. It is neither an attribute of the 'Patient' since a patient may undergo multiple procedures, each for a different amount of time nor of the 'Procedure' since each procedure may be done on different patients, each time for a different number of hours. It is describing the instance of the relationship 'undergoes' between 'Patient' and 'Procedure'. Multiple attributes are allowed via the drop-down menu. Based on this information the schema of the DSD is modified by adding a new table at the back-end and relating it to appropriate tables based on the rules discussed in [3,7]. Appropriate changes are made in the FORMS DATABASE simultaneously. These rules help creating a new table and relate it to appropriate tables in the database maintaining consistency.

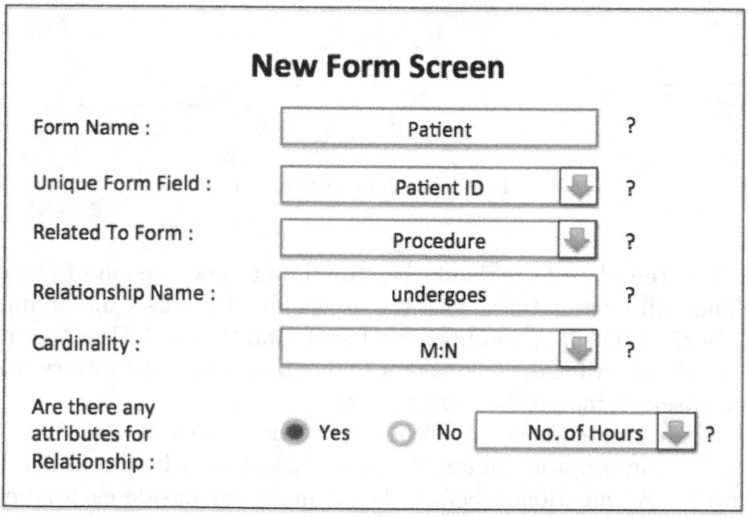

Fig. 2. New Form Screen

4   Approach to Dynamic Schema Management and Maintenance

Our system has two databases, one is the DSD, which primarily stores the actual data, that is entered by a user using the forms provided, and the other one is the FORMS DATABASE that stores the metadata about the forms. The FORMS DATABASE is the one primarily responsible for the dynamics of the system and is explained in more detail in the following section.

4.1   Meta-Database Schema

This database (see Figure 3) consists of all the information about the form structure such as the form name, the fields it consists of, the label of each form field, the type of form fields, etc. needed to build a form. The arrows in the figure stand for foreign-key to primary-key referential integrity constraints. In our present implementation the users are provided with already existing form templates pertaining to the data for a local neurosurgery practice. The database we used for our test was the already pre-populated ALIF database with information about the template forms.

The table 'Form' records a list of all forms provided by the system by default in a well-annotated format. Any new form created by the user gets added to the list. The modified form gets stored as a new form and there is a record of which form it originated from. This table is used to pull out all the forms existing in the current state of the database for the user to choose from to fill data or to select data elements to aggregate data as explained before. The table 'Form Field' stores information about the different fields present in the form along with the forms that they are a part of. It also stores the label of the form fields and a detailed explanation of the field which would translate into a tool tip description in the UI to assist the user in filling the data. The table 'Form Field Type' is created where values such as textbox, radio-button, check-box, drop-down,etc are stored. The table 'Form Modifications' is needed to keep a record of modifications made to the existing form. If a form field is added or deleted by a user to create his customized form then this table will keep track of the changes and pull out the customized form fields for users. The 'Form Field Option' table stores the enumerations of values for the aforementioned types of form fields. For instance, the form field 'Gender' has options 'Male' and 'Female' which are stored in the 'Form Field Option' table.

The table 'Table Information' stores the tables, which are present in the actual database holding the data, which in our case is the ALIF DATABASE. This table is required for the purpose of aggregating data using the view creation mode where users have an option of aggregating data elements, which they want to view together. The table 'Attribute Information' stores all the attributes present along with their data-types and default values in the actual database holding the data. We also keep track of attributes which are primary keys or foreign keys in a particular table. This enables the system to decide the table joins when user selects data elements to be aggregated in the view creation mode explained in the following sections. If a user selects some data elements from a set of tables, which cannot be joined due to the absence of Primary Key-Foreign Key relationship then the user is prompted against the action

This FORMS DATABASE is populated by acquiring the definition of the underlying DSD, say as an SQL file, with CREATE TABLE statements. The level of automation is being improved by providing this functionality. The system currently has the ability to filter out attributes which need not be displayed on the forms. Our strategy for dealing with schema evolution as the database creation progresses is explained below. The algorithm can be used to modify an

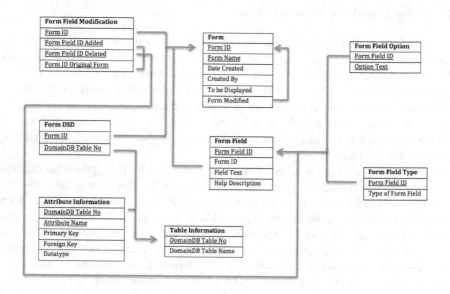

Fig. 3. Schema of the metadata database. The arrows show referential integrity constraints.

existing database at the back-end with the help of a dialog based UI or create a new database from scratch. When modifying an existing database by adding additional forms we already have the metadata database and the DSD at the back-end contrary to the case when a new database is created. In the latter case, an unpopulated metadata database exists at the back-end. As and when the user creates forms at the front-end, the DSD gets developed. We explain our approach for the 2 cases below:

Case 1: Database Schema Modification of the DSD

This is the case when a user chooses to modify existing forms to customize based on his requirements in turn leading to modification of the DSD schema. The modified form would be treated as a new form with a new 'Form ID'. The creation of this new form is recorded in the 'Form' table. In this table the 'Form ID' of the original form is stored, which was modified to create the new form. The modifications would be stored separately in another table 'Form Field Modification' where we store the form fields that were added or deleted from a particular form to create a new form. Any form field which gets added to a form first needs to be added to the 'Form Field' table, 'Form Field Type' table and the 'Form Field Option' table appropriately. For every new form field which gets added to a form, a corresponding attribute gets added to the existing table which has other attributes corresponding to the other form fields of the form. This requires population of the 'Attribute Information' table with all the information about the new attributes. The 'data entry' feature is used to populate the table with data. If there is data already existing in the table corresponding to the form being modified then default values of the newly added attributes would be inserted for these existing observations.

Case 2: Database Schema Creation

This is the case when a user does not want to use any of the existing templates and instead creates a new set of forms. This may occur if the data that the user wants to store pertains to a different domain. He would be required to create new forms from scratch which would guide the creation of a new domain specific database. At the metadata level this involves populating the 'Form' table with information about the new forms. The 'form modified' field would be 'NULL' since we are not modifying any existing forms to create the new forms. In this case we would also populate the 'Table Information' table with information about the new tables that would be formed in the new DSD corresponding to the new forms created. Subsequently the 'Form DSD' table and the 'Attribute Information' table would also be populated as and when new form fields are added in the forms. The process of creation of new form fields has been explained in CASE 1.

In both cases, when adding a form field to a form if the form field is supposed to have atomic values then the corresponding table in the DSD is updated but if the form field is expected to have multiple values then a new table is created in the DSD which references the original table corresponding to that form.

4.2   Guranteeing Consistencies during Schema Evolution

In our approach a lot of flexibility has been provided to the user in terms of freedom of choice of creating new forms when the existing form templates do not seem to be suitable. This can lead to a lot of redundancy at the back-end since a user may choose to build a new form instead of modifying existing templates even though his requirements differ from the existing forms by a small amount. For example, a user needs only 8 out of 10 form fields of a particular form and wants to add more fields of his own choice. We would assume that the user would use our feature of modifying this form by deleting the two irrelevant fields and adding the new extra fields. But instead it is possible that he creates a new form and adds all the form fields he needs to this new form. At the back-end this would result in an extra table in the DSD which would store data being entered via this new form. Periodic reorganization of the DSD and the metadata database is required. This would involve manually identifying such redundant tables and integrating them into one table by performing a full outer join between them. This would be done when the primary keys of the two tables which are getting integrated are the same. The two keys may have different labels but if they have the same semantics, we would go ahead with the join. Such merging would be done only with human approval. If the keys are different then we would keep the tables as they are. A full outer join may result in a lot of null values in the integrated tables. Due to the increase in the volume of data and creation of multiple redundant tables, the decision to go ahead with the integration would depend on the relative advantage of querying a single table with a lot of null values over querying multiple tables to get the data.

5   Data Retrieval: Query Creation and Validation

The system also supports data retrieval by giving the user a choice of either selecting existing result sets previously created by users or creating his own. The user is presented with four types of operations namely 'Select', 'Aggregation', 'Group By' and 'Having' to build a query.

1. **Select Operation**
   The user can select fields, which need to be displayed together in the result set. This may be done by selecting a table from a drop down list and on doing so the corresponding attributes of the selected table would be shown.
2. **Aggregation Operation**
   The operation may be used by user to perform aggregate functions like COUNT, MIN, MAX, AVG, etc on the fields.
3. **Group By and Having Operation**
   If the user decides to use the Aggregation operation then the 'Group By' and 'Having' operations would be enabled. Using them the aggregated results may be grouped with respect to certain fields which may or may not be based on some condition.

The system maintains consistency of the user request as well as of the back-end operations as follows. If the selected attributes belong to multiple tables then the system would perform a join between those tables using the Primary Key and Foreign Key constraints. A 'Where' clause is appended to the query being created, to reflect the join. If there are any attributes that the user has selected to group his result by then those attributes would be added to the attribute selection list already created by the 'Select' Operation in the first step. If the attributes that the user has selected require a join of tables, which cannot be joined due to absence of a primary key-foreign key relationship, then the user would be prompted to change the selection. If the user has selected some attributes and is also performing aggregation then the system would remove the selected attributes other than the ones he is grouping by from the SELECT clause. The user would be prompted of this action. The system would also check for validity of attributes selected for aggregation. E.g. Calculating 'Average' of a non numeric attribute is prevented. After validation the query is executed and the result is displayed. The user has the choice of saving the result set with a description of the same. At the back-end the query is stored in the DSD along with the description provided and can be executed again when selected by its query label.

6   Related Work

Some research has been done in the area of dynamic schema modification with respect to a clinical dental relational database [12]. Their approach primarily focuses on handling One-to-Many and Many-to-Many relationships between tables via concepts of 'detail' and 'link' tables. The user interface developed by the authors is limited to the dental domain. In our approach the metadata database remains unchanged and there exists a provision for plugging in any DSD which in turn can be modified by users. Our application can also be used to create a new database from scratch and store data while it is created in real time. In addition to this, in [12] the interface to manage the addition of datasets requires the user to be familiar with the dataset being loaded after which it is the responsibility of the user to map it to an existing domain or create a new domain. In our approach the user is oblivious about the back-end structure. While he creates new form fields or a whole new form, our application automatically begins to modify the existing schema by creating new attributes or relations respectively to accommodate the new data elements. In addition to the dynamic schema modification approach, a feature of aggregating data and presenting the results to the user, which he can store for future use is also supported by our system. Palisser et al [1] discuss drawbacks of the systems called Orion [5] and Encore [11]. The former constructs a version of the database state every time any transformation in the schema takes place. This leads to the problem of managing multiple versions. The latter focuses on versioning of object types when design environment object types change in an object oriented database. In our approach on the other hand the original schema is modified based on the changes requested by the user but the user is kept unaware of these changes. For instance, a user might modify an existing form to create a new customized version but at the back-end the original schema accommodates the new data elements in an appropriate manner to avoid resorting to versioning. Kim et al. [6] have handled versioning of object types as well as schemas for single as well as multi-user design environment in Orion and also provided semantics of versioning the schema. Ferran et al. [4] discuss an approach to handle schema and database evolution in O2 object database system. The algorithm proposed by the authors automatically makes the database consistent on any update operation performed on the schema. However, depending on what the updates are, either immediate or deferred transformations are made. Deferred transformations cause problems while implementing complex conversion functions,that the user needs to specify if the default functions do not suit their needs. Our approach on the other hand does real time modification of the original schema based on the changes requested by the user and avoids user intervention to a large extent.

7   Use Case

Let us describe the current interface for this prototype used by ALIF practitioners at a local neurosurgery practice.

1. **Basic menu for user [Figure 4]:** This figure shows the menu which will be presented to the user after logging in. It consists of all the template forms consisting of data elements currently in the back-end database. The last bullet is "Create New Form" which would be explained ahead. It has a

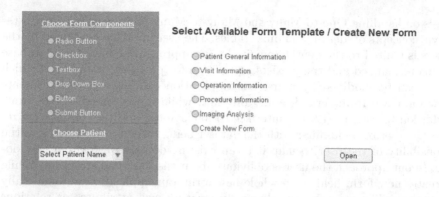

Fig. 4. Basic Menu

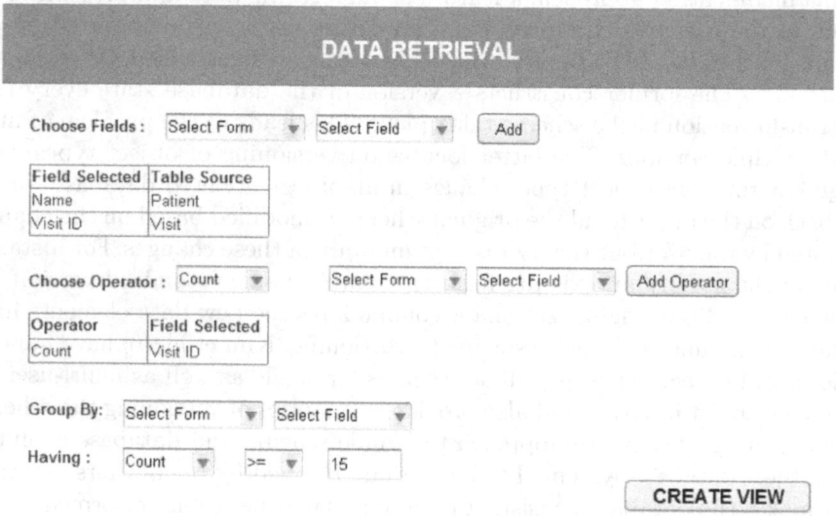

Fig. 5. View Creation Screen

'Form Field Selection' panel which the user can use when creating new form fields when needed. The main menu also consists of a 'Choose Patient' option which will help pulling up existing patients in the database when additional data needs to be entered about them.

2. **Ability to use existing forms :** On choosing a particular template the corresponding form is displayed for the user to fill in data. This data gets saved in the appropriate tables at the back-end.

3. **Creating / Updating forms :** If the user feels the need to update existing templates to accommodate data elements, which are not in the form, he can modify the form using the 'Add New Form Field' feature. This creates a new version of the existing form incorporating the changes requested by

the user. The new form fields added get saved in the back-end database at appropriate places. The "Create New Form" feature can be selected from the screen shown in Fig. 4 to create a new form from scratch and add new form fields.

4. **View Creation [Figure 6]:** The data retrieval feature allows users to select the fields they wish to integrate together, perform aggregation operations on them and also group the result set fields of their choice. The result set can be saved for future use. All screens could not be shown for space reasons.

8 Discussion and Conclusion

8.1 Why not NoSQL?

A lot of organizations which collect vast amounts of customer, scientific, sales data have traditionally stored data in a relational structure, but recently some of these organizations are tending to use various types of non-relational databases called NoSQL databases since they have been found to be efficient in handling unstructured data where there is no fixed schema [8]. In our case we also have a schema that is flexible since the user can modify it based on his requirement, but we chose not to go for NoSQL due to the following reasons.

1. Consistency, availability, and partition tolerance are the three properties taken into consideration when designing a database system. According to the CAP theorem [2] it is only possible to have two out of these three properties together in a database system at once. Traditional relational databases maintain consistency and availability but have trouble with partitions whereas NoSQL databases are able to maintain either consistency or availability along with partition tolerance. In our case the main goal of the system is providing the user with all the data in a consistent state and available in user's expected form.

2. The primary goal of our system is to add flexibility to existing schemas and dynamically modify them. Since most of the healthcare databases have a relational structure at the back-end, we formulated our approach using relational databases.

8.2 Metadatabase Flexibility

The metadata database in our system plays an important role in driving the dynamic nature of the DSD which stores tha actual content entered using the forms. The schema of the metadata database is designed in such a way that the DSD can be modified without any manual interference. It guides the UI formation and the selection process of the different UI components other than providing the forms with a particular structure under different circumstances. The metadata also has the capability to form queries based on information entered by the users along with verifying the correctness of those queries.

8.3   Summary and Future Work

In this paper we proposed a UI and metadata based approach to dynamically modify and create a database schema which would address the problem of dynamic data entry in data-rich environments where the schema can be "built" incrementally as new data becomes available. It is intended for users with needs for managing data for operational and research purposes but who have no access to DBAs or database design experts. Template forms are provided to the user but since there may be difference in requirements between users, the system facilitates modification of existing forms or create new forms from scratch resulting in appropriate real time modifications in the database schema keeping the user oblivious to the back-end The changes at the back-end involve adding new attributes to existing tables, adding new tables, creating relationships between these new tables and existing tables by assigning appropriate cardinality, etc. Unlike other systems such as Encore and Orion, our approach does not create versions of the schema whenever there is a change; instead it creates different versions of a single form if needed after modifying the schema appropriately. Our system also has a data retrieval feature which helps users to aggregate and extract data from the database, perform aggregate operations on them and storing the result sets for future use. This feature does not require the user to write queries instead it automatically generates and validates queries based on the data elements selected.

There is still a lot of scope for improvement in this system like making the system usable for novice users who do not have any knowledge of database modeling concepts. Given a good domain ontology about synonyms such as WordNet [9] we would like to automate the process of removing redundant tables. There is a possibility that a user modifies a form to add a form field, which has semantic equivalence with one of the existing fields in the form. This would result in redundancy. To avoid such cases we would like to incorporate semantic validation in the future. The paper represents preliminary work awaiting field experimentation with small group practices of physicians. It addresses the problems related to relational schema evolution in real-time which opens up a lot of room for improvement. We have been motivated for the need of such system in data-rich environments with relatively limited volume such as medical practices. We are addressing a large user population where the typical user is not very knowledgeable about database concepts but would like to be able to create robust databases on the fly. We would like to like to address the aforementioned ideas of improvement before making it available to the medical community.

References

1. Andany, J., Leonard, M., Palisser, C.: Management of Schema Evolution. In: VLDB, Barcelona, Spain (1991)
2. Brewer.E.A: Towards robust distributed systems (Invited Talk) Principles of Distributed Computing, Portland, Oregon (July 2000)
3. Elmasri, R., Navathe, S.: Fundamentals of Database Systems, 6th edn. Addison Wesley (2011)

4. Ferrandina, F., Ferran, G.: Schema and Database Evolution in the O2 Object Database System. In: VLDB, Zurich, Switzerland (1995)
5. Kim, W., Ballou, N., Chou, H.T., Garza, J.F., Woelk, D.: Features of the ORION Object-Oriented Database System. In: Kim, W., Lochovsky, F.M. (eds.) Object-Oriented Concepts, Databases and Applications. ACM Press Frontier Series, New York (1989)
6. Kim, W., Chou, H.: Versions of schema for object oriented databases. In: VLDB, Los Angeles (1988)
7. Kolp, M., Zimanyi, E.: Enhanced ER to relational mapping and interrelational normalization. Informaton and Software Technology 42, 1057–1073 (2000)
8. Leavitt, N.: Will NoSQL Databases Live Up to Their Promise? Technology News (February 2010), http://www.leavcom.com/pdf/NoSQL.pdf (retrieved)
9. Miller, G.A.: WordNet: A Lexical Database for English. Communications of the ACM 38(11), 39–41 (1995)
10. Sasso, R.C., Reilly, T.M.: Anterior Lumbar Interbody Fusion: Threded Bone Dowels Versus Titanium Cages. In: Resnick, D.K., Haid Jr., R.W., Wang, J.C. (eds.) Surgical Management of Low Back Pain, 2nd edn. American Association of Neurosurgeons, Rolling Meadows (2008)
11. Skarra, A., Zdonik, S.B.: The Management of Changing Types in an Object-Oriented Database? In: OOPSLA, pp. 483–495 (1986)
12. Taylor, D.,Naguib, R. N. G., Boulton, S.: A Dynamic Clinical Dental Relational Database. IEEE Transactions on Information Technology in Biomedicine 8(3) (September 2004)
13. Zhou, L., Rundensteiner, E.A.,Shin, K.G: Schema Evolution for Real-Time Object-Oriented Databases IEEE TKDE 9(6) (November 1997)

CubeLoad: A Parametric Generator
of Realistic OLAP Workloads

Stefano Rizzi and Enrico Gallinucci

DISI – University of Bologna,
V.le Risorgimento 2, 40136 Bologna, Italy
{stefano.rizzi,enrico.gallinucci2}@unibo.it

Abstract. Differently from OLTP workloads, OLAP workloads are hardly predictable due to their inherently extemporary nature. Besides, obtaining real OLAP workloads by monitoring the queries actually issued in companies and organizations is quite hard. On the other hand, hardware and software benchmarking in the industrial world, as well as comparative evaluation of novel approaches in the research community, both need reference databases and workloads. In this paper we present CubeLoad, a parametric generator of workloads in the form of OLAP sessions, based on a realistic profile-based model. After describing the main features of CubeLoad, we discuss the results of some tests that show how workloads with very different features can be generated.

Keywords: OLAP, Data Warehouse, Business intelligence, Benchmarks.

1   Introduction

The term *OLAP* (On-Line Analytical Processing) is now widely used to refer to multidimensional databases and to data warehouse systems. However, originally, it was meant to denote a specific class of queries characterized by high interactivity and flexibility, small formulation effort, read-only access, and data aggregation, run by decision makers to analyze their business trend and effectively explore key figures and indicators. While OLTP (On-Line Transactional Processing) queries are normally grouped into transactions that support the everyday operational processes in a company, OLAP queries are typically sequenced into *sessions*. Users create sessions by applying a sequence of OLAP operations (such as drill-down and slice-and-dice) that transform one multidimensional query into another, starting from an initial query that is usually predefined [15]. During an OLAP session the user analyzes the results of a query and, depending on the specific data she sees, applies one operation to determine a new query that will give her a better understanding of information. The resulting sequences of queries are strongly related to the issuing user, to the analyzed phenomenon, and to the current data.

Differently from OLTP workloads, that are 90% frozen within operational applications, OLAP workloads are hardly predictable due to their inherently extemporary nature. Besides, obtaining real OLAP workloads by monitoring

M. Jarke et al. (Eds.): CAiSE 2014, LNCS 8484, pp. 610–624, 2014.

the queries actually issued in companies and organizations is quite hard because
(i) OLAP queries are at the core of the decision-making process, hence they are
jealously guarded by managers and administrators, and (ii) reconstructing OLAP
sessions by interpreting the query log of a multidimensional engine operating in
a multi-user context is very complex.

On the other hand, hardware and software benchmarking in the industrial
world, as well as comparative evaluation of novel approaches in the research
community, both need reference databases and workloads. To this end, some efforts have been done over the years to provide standard benchmarks. Specifically,
in the OLAP context, the TPC-DS benchmark [14] has been recently developed;
it is based on a fixed set of star schemata including 7 fact tables and 17 dimension tables, and it provides a workload featuring queries that address complex
business problems and use a variety of access patterns.

The TPC-DS benchmark is carefully designed and offers a solid reference.
However, especially in research papers, there is often a need for using benchmarks based on schemata with varying characteristic and on multiple alternative workloads with different features. For instance, it could be interesting to
understand how the performance of a proposed approach varies with the number of dimensions in a cube, with the average branching factor of hierarchies,
with the maximum length of sessions, or with the average selectivity of queries.
In particular, generating parametric OLAP workloads is crucial to the experiments made in the context of OLAP prediction and recommendation, where the
features of sessions and queries may have a strong impact on the approach effectiveness and efficiency. So, the papers in this context often rely on synthetically
generated OLAP workloads, where queries and session are built in a completely
random way based on a set of structural and statistical parameters [1–4]. Unfortunately, while these synthetic workloads serve well for efficiency tests, they
cannot provide significant results for effectiveness tests because they do not lean
on a realistic user model.

To fill this gap, in this paper we present *CubeLoad*, a parametric generator of
OLAP workloads. The main features of CubeLoad are:

- No predefined multidimensional schema is used. The benchmarker[1] can create a workload for any multidimensional schema provided it has been exported in XML compliant with the Mondrian format.
- The workload is generated in the form of sessions, each including a variable
  number of aggregate queries. The main parameters used are related to a
  realistic profile-based workload model.
- Sessions are generated according to a set of four templates, that model recurrent types of user analyses.
- If an instance of the multidimensional schema is available (in particular,
  in the form of a set of dimension tables), its data are used for generating
  instance-dependent (hence, more realistic) workloads.
- The generated workload is exported in XML to ensure maximum usability.

---

[1] To distinguish users of OLAP front-ends from the users of CubeLoad, we will call
benchmarkers the latter.

CubeLoad is written in Java and can be downloaded at http://big.csr.unibo.it/downloads/CubeLoad.zip. It can be freely used by researchers, practitioners, and vendors whenever they need to create parametric bulk OLAP workloads for benchmarking and testing.

The paper outline is as follows. After discussing some related literature in Section 2, in Section 3 we describe the overall functional architecture of CubeLoad. Then we present our workload model and the session templates we defined so far in Sections 4 and 5, respectively. Finally, in Section 6 we discuss the results of some tests we made to profile the generated workloads and in Section 7 we draw the conclusions.

2 Related Works

A milestone in OLAP benchmarking is the TPC-DS [14], that models the decision support functions of a retail product supplier relying on multiple snowflake schemata with shared dimensions. The TPC-DS provides four classes of queries; in particular, the class of *iterative OLAP queries* is distinguished by the tendency of one query to be related to the previous query so as to create sequence of queries —essentially, OLAP sessions. Queries are randomly generated starting from four templates; however, there is no way of parameterizing the generation of sessions.

In [7] the authors introduce the concept of *workload profile* as a way for summarizing the features of an OLAP workload to support designers during logical and physical design. However, the profile used there has a merely statistical nature, and has no relationship with classes of users. Besides, only stand-alone queries are generated.

A workload for evolutionary analytics is proposed in [10] together with several test metrics and with a methodology for running the workload. The emphasis there is not on standard OLAP sessions but rather on queries that evolve over time (which may imply much more drastic changes than those obtained through OLAP operations) and are formulated over changing data and schemata.

A *Data Warehouse Engineering Benchmark* (DWEB) that allows to generate various ad-hoc synthetic data warehouses and workloads is presented in [6]. Though the DWEB workload is parameterized to fulfill data warehouse design needs, it does not create queries in sessions and is ruled by statistical parameters rather than by realistic assumptions.

The author of [13] starts from the query generator of the TCP-DS to define a set of rules that transform a SQL query into another SQL query similar to the original. However, this transformation works at a merely syntactical level (e.g., a new query can be created by changing the comparison operator in the selection predicate) and does not consider OLAP operations such as slicing and drilling.

In [18] the authors introduce a query generator to evaluate the quality of a query optimizer. Similarly to ours, the generator presented is schema-independent and is able to produce valid queries on any database. However, only OLTP queries are generated and, therefore, there is no mention of query sessions.

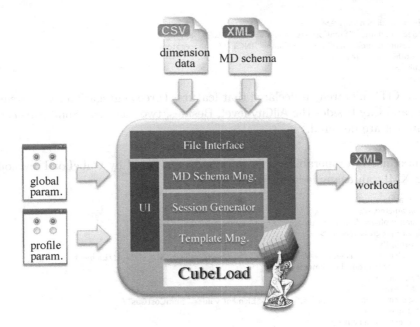

Fig. 1. Functional overview of CubeLoad

Finally, a benchmark on star schemata that extends the TPC-H is presented in [12]; the emphasis here is more on data schemata than on queries, so only 4 non-parameterized OLAP sessions (called query flights here) are provided.

3   Overview

A functional overview of the CubeLoad architecture is sketched in Figure 1. The main input is the multidimensional schema on which the workload is to be generated. To provide this input we adopt the XML specification used by Mondrian for its metadata [9].

Example 1. IPUMS is a public database storing census microdata for social and economic research [11]. An excerpt of the XML specification for its CENSUS multidimensional schema is given below.

```
<?xml version="1.0"?>
<Schema name="Ipums">
  <Cube name="CENSUS">
    <Table name="FACT500K"/>
    <Dimension name="CITY" foreignKey="CITY">
      <Hierarchy hasAll="true" primaryKey="IDCITY" allLevelName="AllCity" allMemberName="All">
        <Table name="CITY"/>
        <Level name="Region" column="REGION" type="String" uniqueMembers="true"/>
        <Level name="State" column="STATE" type="String" uniqueMembers="true"/>
        <Level name="City" column="CITY" type="String" uniqueMembers="false"/>
      </Hierarchy>
    </Dimension>
```

```
<!- other dimensions ->
<Measure name="SumCostGas" column="COSTGAS" aggregator="sum"/>
<Measure name="SumIncTot" column="INCTOT" aggregator="sum"/>
<!- other measures ->
</Cube>
</Schema>
```

Here, a CITY hierarchy is declared that features three aggregation levels, Region, State, and City besides the AllCity level. Besides, two measures SumCostGas and SumIncTot are declared.   □

To maximize interoperability, the workloads generated by CubeLoad are coded using XML; an example is shown below:

```
<Benchmark>
  <!- parameters ->
  <Session profile="Manager" progressive="1" template="Goal Oriented">
    <Query progressive="1">
      <GroupBy>
        <Element> <Hierarchy Value="CITY"/> <Level value="State"/> </Element>
        <!- other group-by elements ->
      </GroupBy>
      <Measures>
        <Element value="MaxCostGas"/> <Element value="SumCostGas"/>
      </Measures>
      <SelectionPredicates>
        <Element>
          <Hierarchy value="OCCUPATION"/> <Level value="Category"/>
          <Predicate value="Dentists"/>
          <YearPrompt value="false"/> <SegregationPredicate value="false"/>
        </Element>
      </SelectionPredicates>
    </Query>
    <!- other queries ->
  </Session>
  <!- other sessions ->
</Benchmark>
```

(an explanation of the parameters and of the other workload elements mentioned in this XML will be given in Section 4).

To generate realistic selection predicates and enable report sizes to be estimated, dimension data are needed. These data can be fed into CubeLoad using the CSV (comma-separated values) format, which can be easily obtained by benchmarkers by exporting dimension tables.

Internally, CubeLoad includes five components:

1. The **user interface**, that allows benchmarkers to select the XML multidimensional schema to be used and choose values for global and profile parameters.
2. The **file interface**, in charge of reading and parsing XML and CSV input files and of writing XML output files.
3. The **multidimensional schema manager**, that builds an internal representation of cubes and dimension data.
4. The **session generator**, that runs the basic procedures for creating sessions respecting the constraints posed by global and profile parameters.
5. The **template manager**, that gives the session generator additional rules for creating sessions based on each template.

4 The Workload Model

The output of CubeLoad is an OLAP workload, defined as a set of *sessions*. A session is a sequence of queries. In the current implementation, we support a basic form of multidimensional query consisting of (i) a *group-by* (i.e., a set of hierarchy levels on which measure values are grouped); (ii) one or more measures whose values are returned (the aggregation operator used for each measure is defined by the multidimensional schema); and (iii) zero or more *selection predicates*, each operating on a hierarchy level. We call *report* the result of a query; its size is the number of facts returned. Roughly, the size of a report can be estimated as the product of the domain cardinalities for all levels in the query group-by, reduced by considering the selectivity factors of the selection predicates; more accurate estimates can be computed if the sparsity of the cube is known [5]. Two consecutive queries within a session are normally separated by the application of one OLAP operation, that changes either the group-by, or the selection predicate, or the set of measures returned, as shown in the following example.

Example 2. An example of a session starting from seed query q_1 is $s = \langle q_1, q_2, q_3, q_4 \rangle$; the group-by's, selection predicates, and returned measures for the queries involved are shown in Table 1. Query q_2 is obtained from q_1 by drilling-down the cube along the CITY dimension; q_3 is obtained from q_2 by slicing-and-dicing the cube; q_4 is obtained from q_3 by changing the measure returned. □

Table 1. Queries for the sample session in Example 2

Query	Group-by	Selection predicate	Measures
q_1	State, Year	Region='South Atlantic'	SumCostGas
q_2	City, Year	Region='South Atlantic'	SumCostGas
q_3	City, Year	Occupation='Dentists'	SumCostGas
q_1	City, Year	Occupation='Dentists'	SumIncTot

In company settings, users of OLAP front-ends are normally grouped into profiles with different skills (e.g., CEO, marketing analyst, department manager) and involved in business analyses with different features (e.g., more or less repetitive, more or less complex). Importantly, different profiles generally have quite different permissions for accessing data; often, a profile has one or more *segregation predicates*, i.e., it can only view a specific slice of the cube data (e.g., a department manager can only access the sales for her department).

When a user logs to the OLAP front-end, she is typically shown a page where some predefined queries (which we call *seed queries*) are linked. Sometimes seed queries include a *prompt*, meaning that the front-end asks the user to select one value out of the domain of a level (often, the year). After choosing and executing one of these queries, the user starts applying a sequence of OLAP operations that progressively transform a query into another so as to build an analysis session.

Features such as the number of seed queries available, the maximum size and complexity of reports returned by seed queries, and the average length of sessions may significantly depend on the typical ICT skills and business understanding for the users of each profile —besides on the quality of the OLAP fron-end.

To simulate the above setting, CubeLoad uses a set of parameters that rule workload generation and are distinguished into *global parameters* and *profile parameters*. The global parameters rule:

- the **number of distinct user profiles** to be simulated. Each profile simulates a specific class of OLAP users and is characterized by different values of the profile parameters. Each session is generated for one profile, so the sessions in the resulting workload can be naturally grouped into clusters; the more different the parameters for the profiles, the sharper the clusters.
- the **maximum number of measures** that can be returned by a single query. A report including several measures is hardly readable by anyone, so the value for this parameter mainly depends on how sophisticated the visualization modes supported by the OLAP front-end are.
- the **minimum and maximum size of seed query reports**. The size (i.e., number of cells) of a query result depends on the query group-by and on the presence of selection predicates. While during an unconstrained OLAP sessions users can (either consciously or unconsciously) formulate a query that returns a report with either negligible or huge size, seed queries are typically created by front-end programmers in such a way that their report size is reasonable. This is reason the reason why in our model the size of seed query reports ranges within a parametric interval.
- the **number of surprising queries**, whose meaning will be explained in Section 5 in relationship to the explorative template.

Each profile is then associated to a further set of parameters, that rule:

- the **number of seed queries**. Specialists' profiles have a large number of seed queries; managers' profiles may have a low number of seed queries.
- the **minimum and maximum length of sessions**. The values for these parameters depend on the ICT skills of the users of each profile and on the complexity of the analyses they usually carry out.
- the **number of sessions** to be created. The more intensive the use of the OLAP front-end for the users of a profile, the higher the value of this parameter.
- the **fraction of seed queries that include a year prompt**. This fraction depends on the time scope of decision-making tasks for each profile (operative profiles typically analyze daily to monthly trends, while managerial profiles are often interested in yearly trends).
- the **presence of a segregation predicate**. A segregation predicate is typically present in departmental or geographically-distributed profiles (e.g., production manager and sales manager for Italy).

The workload model is summarized in Figure 2 in the form of a UML class diagram.

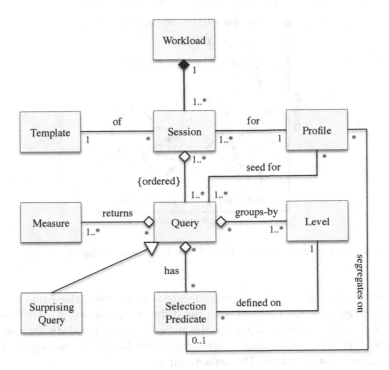

Fig. 2. UML workload model

5   Session Templates

Each session generated by CubeLoad for a given profile starts from one of the seed queries for that profile and evolves, consistently with global and profile parameters, according to a *template*. In its current implementation, CubeLoad uses four different templates for generating sessions:

1. **Slice-and-Drill.** In several OLAP front-ends, the default behavior when a user clicks on a row/column of a pivot table is to disaggregate the values for that row/column into its components, which in OLAP terms means slicing and drilling down. For instance, starting from a report showing sales per state and year, clicking on 2013 would trigger a query showing sales per state and month of 2013, while clicking on Florida would trigger a query showing sales per Florida cities and year. In sessions based on this template, (non-segregated) hierarchies are progressively navigated by choosing a hierarchy h, a member v of the current group-by level $l \in h$ and creating a new query with selection predicate $l = v$ and group-by on the level l that precedes l within h.

2. **Slice-All.** Users are sometimes interested in navigating a cube by slices, i.e., in repeatedly running the same query but with different selection predicates. In sessions based on this template, a level l of the group-by of the seed query

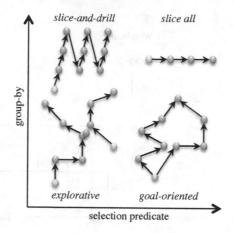

Fig. 3. Session templates (seed queries in green, surprising queries in red)

is chosen, and new queries are generated by keeping the same group-by and adding selection predicates on the different members of l. For instance, starting from a query asking for the monthly sales by state for the video department, the subsequent queries could ask for the same report for the audio, the photo, and the PC departments.

3. **Explorative.** Some queries may return reports that are particularly interesting for most users, for instance because they show unexpected results (e.g., they show that the impact of a social policy is not the one that had been predicted) or have a strong impact on business (e.g., they show that the level of qualified employment in a given area is extremely low, which requires a corrective action to be taken). Following [16], we call them *surprising queries*. The motivation for this template is the assumption that several users, while exploring the cube in search of significant correlations, will be "attracted" by one surprising query. So, sessions based on this template tend to converge "near" to one of the surprising queries, then they evolve casually. Note that the overall number of surprising queries is fixed by a global parameter, while each surprising query is randomly generated.

4. **Goal-Oriented.** Sessions of this type are run by users who have a specific analysis goal, but whose OLAP skills are limited so they may follow a complex path to reach their destination. All the goal-oriented sessions starting from the same seed query q end in the same (randomly-generated) query p, but the sequence of OLAP operations to be applied to reach p from q is generated randomly.

Figure 3 shows an intuition of sessions based on the four templates in a qualitative group-by/selection predicate space.

6 Experiments

To verify that the CubeLoad parameters and templates actually allow a wide spectrum of workloads to be generated, and to help benchmarkers better understand the relationships between those parameters/templates and the workload features, we use a similarity function that was specifically proposed in [2] for comparing OLAP queries and sessions. The query similarity function, σ_{que}, is a combination of three components: one related to group-by's, one to selection predicates, and one to measure sets.

Definition 6.1 (Similarity of OLAP queries). *Let q and q' be two queries on the same n-dimensional schema. The* similarity *between q and q' is*

$$\sigma_{que}(q,q') = 0.35\sigma_{gbs}(q,q') + 0.50 \cdot \sigma_{sel}(q,q') + 0.15 \cdot \sigma_{meas}(q,q') \in [0..1]$$

where:

- *The similarity between the group-by's of q and q', $\{l_1,\ldots,l_n\}$ and $\{l'_1,\ldots,l'_n\}$ respectively, is*

$$\sigma_{gbs}(q,q') = 1 - \frac{\sum_{i=1}^{n} \frac{Dist_{lev}(l_i,l'_i)}{L_i - 1}}{n}$$

  where L_i is the total number of levels in the i-th hierarchy, h_i, and $Dist_{lev}(l_i,l'_i) \in [0..L_i - 1]$ is the distance between its two levels l_i and l'_i.
- *The similarity between the selection predicates of q and q', $\{p_1,\ldots,p_n\}$ and $\{p'_1,\ldots,p'_n\}$ respectively, is*

$$\sigma_{sel}(q,q') = 1 - \frac{\sum_{i=1}^{n} \frac{Dist_{pred}(p_i,p'_i)}{L_i}}{n}$$

  where the distance $Dist_{pred}(p_i,p'_i)$ between predicates p_i and p'_i, both formulated on levels of hierarchy h_i, is 0 if they are expressed on the same level and using the same constant, 1 if they are defined on the same level but not on the same constant, greater than 1 if they are defined on different levels.
- *The similarity between the measure sets returned by q and q', M and M' respectively, is*

$$\sigma_{meas}(q,q') = \frac{|Meas \cap Meas'|}{|Meas \cup Meas'|}$$

The session similarity function, $\sigma_{ali}(s,s') \in [0..1]$, is based on the best alignment between the queries belonging to sessions s and s'. The best alignment is computed by means of the Smith-Waterman algorithm, which efficiently matches subsequences of two given sequences by ignoring the non-matching parts [17]. It is a dynamic programming algorithm based on a matrix whose value in position (i,j) expresses the score for aligning subsequences of s and s' that end in queries s_i and s'_j, respectively. This score is computed starting from the similarity between the queries included in the aligned subsequences [2].

Table 2. CubeLoad parameters used for generating the three sample workloads

Sample workload	$W1$	$W2$	$W3$
Number of profiles	1	1	1
Max number of measures	2	2	2
Size of seed query reports	$10 \div 100$	$10 \div 100$	$10 \div 100$
Number of surprising queries	5	2	1
Number of seed queries	50	5	1
Length of sessions	$7 \div 12$	$7 \div 12$	$7 \div 12$
Number of sessions per seed query	4	40	200
Year prompt fraction	0.25	0.50	1.00
Segregation predicate	No	Yes	Yes

To explore the range of possibilities of CubeLoad we generated three sample workloads with the following "extreme" features:

1. Workload $W1$ is a sparse one, i.e., the sessions generated are quite different one from another. This result is mainly obtained by using a high number of seed queries and generating a few sessions per seed.
2. Workload $W2$ is a clustered one, i.e., the sessions generated are similar to each other in five groups. This is mainly obtained by defining five seed queries.
3. Workload $W3$ is a dense one, i.e., the sessions generated are all quite similar to each other. This is mainly obtained by defining a single surprising query and by generating all sessions starting from the same seed query.

For a fair comparison, all three workloads include the same numbers of sessions (200); the values for the other parameters are summarized in Table 2.

A qualitative analysis of these three workloads can be made by observing Figure 4, that shows for each of them the session-to-session similarity. Each row and column corresponds to one of the 200 sessions of the workload, so each cell shows the similarity between two different sessions of the same workload: white means $\sigma_{ali} = 0$, black $\sigma_{ali} = 1$, gray shades mean $0 < \sigma_{ali} < 1$. As expected, in Figure 4.a we find a very low average similarity between sessions, while in Figure 4.c the average similarity is much higher. In Figure 4.b we can easily find the five cluster as areas with higher-than-average similarity. A quantitative confirmation of this fact can be found in Figure 5, that shows for each workload the average session-to-session similarity and its standard deviation: they are both lower for the sparse workload $W1$ (where all sessions are different), while they increasingly grow higher for the clustered workload $W2$ (where sessions in the same cluster are very similar to each other and very different from those in the other clusters) and the dense workload $W3$ (in the latter case, the standard deviation is high because the four templates adopted inevitably introduce a scattering in the sessions generated).

Figure 5 also shows the propensity of each workload to being clustered. The indicator we adopted to this end is the *Hopkins statistics* [8]. Given a workload W, i.e., a set of N sessions, we first generate a set S of m fake sessions ($m \ll N$)

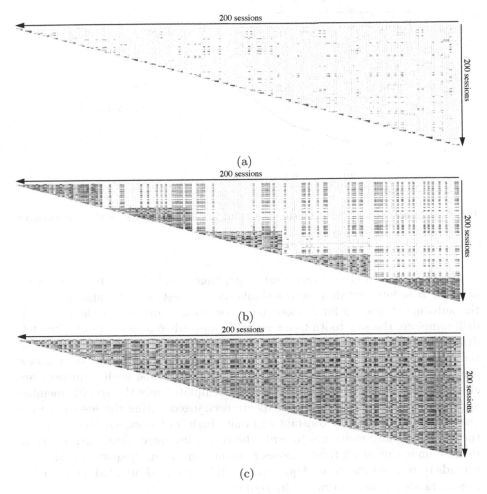

Fig. 4. Session-to-session similarities for the three sample workloads

that are randomly and uniformly distributed in the space of possible sessions. For each fake session $s_i \in S$, let u_i be its distance from the nearest-neighbor session in W (where $Distance(s, s') = 1 - \sigma_{ali}(s, s')$). Then, m sessions are randomly chosen from W; let w_i be the distance of the i-th of these sessions from its nearest-neighbor in W. The Hopkins statistics is then defined as

$$H = \frac{\sum_{i=1}^{m} w_i}{\sum_{i=1}^{m} u_i + \sum_{i=1}^{m} w_i}$$

For workload $W1$, H is near to 0.5; this means that the distance of each session in $W1$ from its nearest-neighbor is very similar to the distance of each fake session, i.e., that $W1$ has a random distribution. For $W2$ is quite small; this is because the w_i's are small, which means that sessions are well clustered. For $W3$ H is even smaller, because all sessions are part of a single, dense cluster.

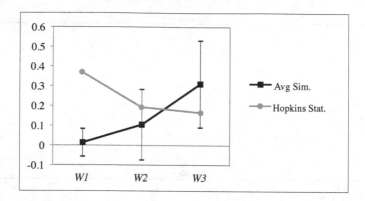

Fig. 5. Average session-to-session similarity and Hopkins statistics for the three sample workloads

Finally, Figure 6 gives a quantitative explanation of the differences between our four templates by showing the similarity σ_{que} between the first query and the subsequent queries for sessions based on each template. In the slice-and-drill template, the saw-tooth trend arises because when a sequence of slice-and-drill clicks along hierarchy h leads to a query grouped by the finest level of h, the simulated user behavior is to go back to the seed query and start a new slice-and-drill sequence along a different hierarchy (three such sequences are clearly visible in the figure). In the slice-all template, only the specific member appearing in the query selection predicate is changed during the session, so the query similarity is mostly constant and quite high. In the explorative template, the session rapidly converges towards the surprising query (the sixth query in the session in this case), then it moves randomly in the query space (in this case, it tends to reapproach the seed query). Finally, in the goal-oriented template the session randomly moves towards its goal query.

7   Final Remarks

In this paper we have described the features of CubeLoad, a generator of OLAP sessions aimed at simulating realistic workloads. The sessions generated are currently based on four templates and ruled by a set of parameters. The template features and the impact of parameters on the resulting workload have been discussed with the support of some tests using a similarity function specifically devised for OLAP sessions.

Some comparison between CubeLoad and TPC-DS is useful at this point. Overall, the focus in the TPC-DS is more on the complexity of single queries rather than on query sessions. Indeed, while the query model is more expressive than in CubeLoad because nesting is supported, three of the four classes of queries provided in the TPC-DS (namely, *ad hoc queries*, *reporting queries*, and *data mining queries*) only include stand-alone queries; as such, they could be

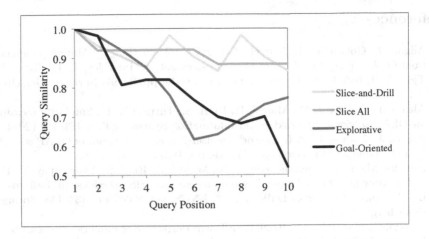

Fig. 6. Intra-session query similarity for the four templates

generated with CubeLoad by setting the maximum length of sessions to 1 and properly tuning the maximum size of seed query reports (differently from the first two classes, data mining queries are characterized by high cardinality of the results). Conversely, the class of *iterative OLAP queries* comprises four base sessions each including exactly 2 queries; more sessions can be generated from each base session by randomly changing a selection predicate. In two of the base sessions, the subsequent queries are not related by the application of a single OLAP operator like in CubeLoad, so they can be quite "distant" from each other, but still they are finalized to the same analysis goal. In the other two base sessions, the two subsequent queries differ from their selection predicate. Thus, an effective way to generate sessions like these ones with CubeLoad is to use the goal-oriented and the slice-all templates and fix the number of seed queries to 4, with a session length equal to 2.

Our future work on this topic will be mainly aimed at enhancing the capabilities of CubeLoad in three directions: (i) by allowing benchmarkers to distinguish *skilled* and *non-skilled* profiles, so as to enable a finer tuning of the workload features; (ii) by defining other templates, so as to make CubeLoad more flexible and usable for a wider array of benchmarks; and (iii) by adopting a more complex query model, so as to make the generated workloads more realistic still. From the engineering point of view, we plan to refactor the CubeLoad code according to an open architecture where each benchmarker can write her own templates in the form of a plugin.

Acknowledgements. We would like to thank Luca Spadazzi for his support in implementing and testing CubeLoad, and Patrick Marcel (Université François Rabelais, Tours, France) for the fruitful discussions about the features of a realistic OLAP workload.

References

1. Aligon, J., Golfarelli, M., Marcel, P., Rizzi, S., Turricchia, E.: Mining preferences from OLAP query logs for proactive personalization. In: Eder, J., Bielikova, M., Tjoa, A.M. (eds.) ADBIS 2011. LNCS, vol. 6909, pp. 84–97. Springer, Heidelberg (2011)
2. Aligon, J., Golfarelli, M., Marcel, P., Rizzi, S., Turricchia, E.: Similarity measures for OLAP sessions. Knowledge and Information Systems 39(2), 463–489 (2014)
3. Aligon, J., Marcel, P.: A framework for user-centric summaries of OLAP sessions. In: Proceedings EDA, Bordeaux, France, pp. 103–117 (2012)
4. Aufaure, M.-A., Kuchmann-Beauger, N., Marcel, P., Rizzi, S., Vanrompay, Y.: Predicting your next OLAP query based on recent analytical sessions. In: Bellatreche, L., Mohania, M.K. (eds.) DaWaK 2013. LNCS, vol. 8057, pp. 134–145. Springer, Heidelberg (2013)
5. Ciaccia, P., Golfarelli, M., Rizzi, S.: Efficient derivation of numerical dependencies. Inf. Syst. 38(3), 410–429 (2013)
6. Darmont, J., Bentayeb, F., Boussaid, O.: DWEB: A data warehouse engineering benchmark. CoRR abs/0705.1453 (2007)
7. Golfarelli, M., Saltarelli, E.: The workload you have, the workload you would like. In: Proceedings DOLAP, New Orleans, Louisiana, pp. 79–85 (2003)
8. Hopkins, B., Skellam, J.G.: A new method for determining the type of distribution of plant individuals. Annals of Botany 18, 213–227 (1954)
9. Hyde, J.: Mondrian documentation (2011), http://mondrian.pentaho.com/documentation/schema.php
10. LeFevre, J., Sankaranarayanan, J., Hacigümüs, H., Tatemura, J., Polyzotis, N.: Towards a workload for evolutionary analytics. CoRR abs/1304.1838 (2013)
11. Minnesota Population Center: Integrated public use microdata series (2008), http://www.ipums.org
12. O'Neil, P., O'Neil, E., Chen, X., Revilak, S.: The star schema benchmark and augmented fact table indexing. In: Nambiar, R., Poess, M. (eds.) TPCTC 2009. LNCS, vol. 5895, pp. 237–252. Springer, Heidelberg (2009)
13. Poess, M.: Controlled SQL query evolution for decision support benchmarks. In: Proceedings WOSP, Buenes Aires, Argentina, pp. 38–41 (2007)
14. Pöss, M., Smith, B., Kollár, L., Larson, P.Å.: TPC-DS, taking decision support benchmarking to the next level. In: Proceedings SIGMOD Conference, Madison, Wisconsin, pp. 582–587 (2002)
15. Sapia, C.: PROMISE: Predicting query behavior to enable predictive caching strategies for OLAP systems. In: Kambayashi, Y., Mohania, M., Tjoa, A.M. (eds.) DaWaK 2000. LNCS, vol. 1874, pp. 224–233. Springer, Heidelberg (2000)
16. Sarawagi, S.: User-adaptive exploration of multidimensional data. In: Proceedings VLDB, Cairo, Egypt, pp. 307–316 (2000)
17. Smith, T., Waterman, M.: Identification of common molecular subsequences. Journal of Molecular Biology 147, 195–197 (1981)
18. Stillger, M., Freytag, J.C.: Testing the quality of a query optimizer. IEEE Data Eng. Bull. 18(3), 41–48 (1995)

Task Specification and Reasoning in Dynamically Altered Contexts

George Chatzikonstantinou, Michael Athanasopoulos, and Kostas Kontogiannis

National Technical University of Athens, Greece
{athanm,kkontog}@softlab.ntua.gr, gchatzik@cslab.ece.ntua.gr

Abstract. Software systems are prone to evolution in order to be kept operational and meet new requirements. However, for large systems such evolution activities cannot occur in a vacuum. Instead, specific action plans must be devised so that evolution goals can be achieved within an acceptable level of deviation or, risk. In this paper we present an approach that allows for the identification of plans in the form of actions that satisfy a goal model when the environment is constantly changing. The approach is based on sequences of mutations of an initial solution, using a local search algorithm. Experimental results indicate that even for medium size models, the approach outperforms in execution time the weighted Max-Sat algorithms, while it is able to achieve an almost optimal solution. The approach is demonstrated on an example scenario of re-configuring a dynamically provisioned system.

Keywords: local search, weighted partial max-sat, task specification.

1 Introduction

Complex software systems are prone to continuous change and re-configuration. Software maintenance, hardware upgrades, and dynamic provision of resources in elastic or autonomic systems, are just a few of the factors that drive the need for designing systems that assist administrators to compile action plans. In this context, the focus is to devise *a*) models that represent system goals; *b*) models that associate such goals with tasks and actions ; and *c*) reasoning methodologies that allow for the selection of tasks and actions in order to form coherent plans. The software engineering community has responded with models to represent system-wide functional and non-functional properties as well as, formalisms to associate such functional properties with design decisions, tasks, actions, and stakeholder views. These models include i* [1], KAOS [2,3], the Goal-oriented Requirements Language (GRL) [4], the Extended Enterprise Modeling Language (EEML), and the Unified Modeling Language, to name a few. Similarly, reasoning on these models has emerged as a key problem in order for useful logical and sound conclusions to be reached. Such reasoning approaches are based on logic deductions (rules), propagation of labels, domain specific heuristics or, SAT solvers. SAT solvers in particular have been a focal point of the research conducted in this area. However, there are still open issues to be investigated when

M. Jarke et al. (Eds.): CAiSE 2014, LNCS 8484, pp. 625–639, 2014.
© Springer International Publishing Switzerland 2014

the goal models themselves are modified as a result of changes in the operating environment or, as a result of the actions incurred so far.

In this paper, we investigate the use of local search algorithms and boolean expression evaluators to reason with Decision Task Models introduced in Section 3, when labels related to cost and benefit values, for actions and tasks, are altered as a result of context changes. Experimental results indicate that the approach allows for obtaining a solution that is within 90% range of the optimal value at a fraction of time that is required by a Weighted Partial MAX-SAT algorithm to compute the optimal solution for the problem at hand. Applications of such reasoning include the formation of plans to re-configure autonomic systems, plan for software and hardware upgrades in a large scale where the administrators must conform to specific guidelines (e.g. ITIL), or devise alternative plans to meet specific goals and requirements. We illustrate the approach by a running example depicted in Fig. 2, that focuses on a goal model that denotes how high quality of service can be maintained in an elastic cloud based system. The approach has been evaluated on a large number of sizeable goal models that have been compiled by an automated construction process with positive results.

The paper is organized as follows: Section 2 provides an outline of the proposed approach. Section 3 introduces the elements of Decision Task Models (DTMs) and discusses their semantics. In Section 4 a formalization for DTMs is provided along with a process for the transformations of DTMs to CNF formulas. Subsequently, in Section 5 two reasoning approaches are discussed based on operating environment for the task model and in Section 6 experiment results are discussed to provide an evaluation for the proposed framework and algorithms. Finally, related work is discussed in Section 7 and Section 8 concludes the paper.

2   Process Outline

The outline of the proposed framework process is depicted in Fig. 1. Initially, certain tasks and actions, along with the relationships that exist between them are modeled in a Decision Task Model (DTM) like the one presented in Fig. 2, which describes what tasks and actions can be performed in order to maintain the QoS to a required level. Given such a model, we are interested in determining the optimal (or at least, suboptimal) plan to accomplish the root task while the weights assigned to each node change dynamically as a consequence of contextual changes. For example, for the model of Fig. 2, the weights of A5 and T11 change from $C1$ and $B1$ to $C2$ and $B2$ respectively, leading to different optimal solutions as this is summarized in Tables 3 and 4. An impossible low negative weight value (i.e. high cost) deems an action unachievable, while a high positive weight value (i.e. high benefit) deems a task achievable.

The first step towards plan determination is to extract a CNF formula that fully captures the logical dependencies modeled by the DTM. This enables the reduction of plan determination to the SAT problem, and as a consequence allow the use of a SAT solver. Moreover, as nodes in DTMs are annotated with weights which may change as a consequence of certain context changes, we are interested

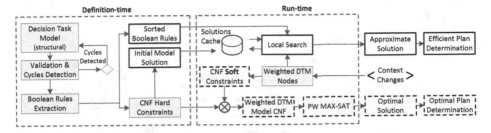

Fig. 1. The proposed framework for optimal and efficient plan determination

in finding an assignment that not only satisfies the CNF formula but also has the best score, in terms of node weights. This optimization problem, referred to as *optimal plan determination*, can be reduced to an instance of Weighted Partial Max-SAT problem, hence a Max-SAT solver can be utilized to solve it. The steps required for the determination of the optimal plan are depicted as dashed rectangles in Fig. 1.

However, as the context (and thus node weights) may change dynamically, computing an approximate solution may be a preferable alternative to optimal plan determination, as Max-SAT is a known NP-hard problem. In this paper, we propose the use of a local search algorithm as an effective technique for efficient plan determination. The steps required for the determination of an effective plan are depicted as bold rectangles in Fig. 1.

3   Decision Task Modeling

In order to model the actions that realize certain tasks, and to express semantic and temporal relationships that exist between tasks and actions, we propose a metamodel which borrows notions from the goal model theory. The proposed DTM metamodel, an instance of which is illustrated in Fig. 2, retains the AND/OR-decomposition schema used in goal models. However, additional modeling elements are used to capture logical and temporal relationships, increasing thus the expressiveness of the proposed notation. In the rest of this section we briefly describe the semantics of the various modeling artifacts.

Nodes: DTM nodes may be either *Tasks* or *Actions*. The former may be AND/OR decomposed and represent a collection of actions or subordinate tasks, where either more than one subtasks or actions should be combined together, or one or more subtasks or actions may be alternatively selected to accomplish the task. In contrast, action nodes represent atomic activities. In the example DTM of Fig. 2, tasks are depicted as ellipses and Actions as hexagons.

Links: The DTM metamodel contains three types of links between nodes namely, *Logical Preconditions* ($\xrightarrow{lp}$), *Temporal Preconditions* ($\xrightarrow{tp}$), and *Contributions*. The former two links interconnect task and action nodes and express temporal dependencies. More specifically, $\xrightarrow{lp}$ links resemble precedence links originally

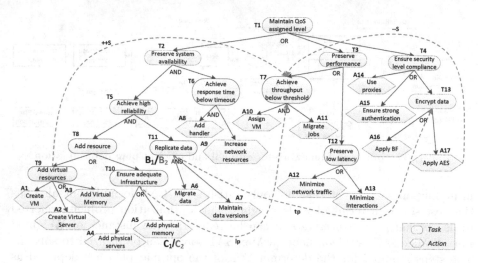

Fig. 2. An Example Decision Task Model

introduced in [5], and indicate the fact that the target node can only be performed as long as the source node has already been performed. In contrast, $\xrightarrow{tp}$
links denote a weaker notion of precondition, which implies that in case both
the target and the source node participate in a plan (i.e. a sequence of actions),
then the target task/action must performed after the source task/action.

Finally, in a similar manner as in [6], we consider four types of contributions
namely, $++S/--S$ meaning that the target node is satisfied/denied when the
source node is satisfied, and; $++D/--D$ meaning that the denial of the source
node leads to the denial/achievement of the target node. However, in the context
of this paper, contribution links can terminate only to task nodes as an action is
only satisfied when the corresponding atomic activity is performed and it cannot
be fulfilled otherwise.

4   DTM Formal Definition and CNF Generation

In this section we are going to introduce a process that transforms DTMs into
CNF formulas that fully capture the constraints modeled by the DTM. This
reduces the problem of plan determination to an instance of the SAT problem,
and allows for the use of SAT solvers. However, before going into the details of
CNF formula generation, we are going to formally define DTMs.

4.1   DTM Formal Definition

A DTM contains a set of task or action nodes which are connected with each
other through decomposition rules or rules that describe binary relations on the
set of nodes i.e. *binary rules* such as *Precondition*, and *Contribution* links. Hence,
we formulate the following definition for DTMs:

Definition 1. *A Decision Task Model is a tuple of the form* $\langle N, R_d, R \rangle$, *where* $N = N_t \cup N_a$ *with* N_t *and* N_a *denoting the sets of task and action nodes respectively,* R_d *is the set of decomposition rules, and* R *the set of binary rules.*

In the above definition, a decomposition rule $r_d \in R_d$ describes the way a *parent* task node p is AND/OR decomposed to a set $\{c_1, c_2, \cdots c_n\}$ of *child* task or action nodes. There must be one decomposition rule for each task node p, which is formally written as:

$$ r_d = \langle T, p, \{c_1, c_2, \cdots, c_n\} \rangle \quad \text{where} \quad T \in \{\text{AND}, \text{OR}\}. $$

For example, task node $T7$ ("Achieve throughput below threshold") in Fig. 2 is AND-decomposed to action nodes $A10$ ("Assign VM") and $A11$ ("Migrate Jobs"), so the corresponding decomposition rule is $\langle \text{AND}, T7, \{A10, A11\} \rangle$.

A binary rule $r \in R$ between source node s and target node t is denoted as:

$$ r = \langle T, s, t \rangle \quad \text{where} \quad T \in \{\text{lp}, ++S/D, --S/D\}. $$

where as discussed above, for contribution rules the target node $t \in N_t$. In the example DTM in Fig. 2, task node $T7$ participates as the target node of three binary rules, namely $\langle ++S, T9, T7 \rangle$, $\langle --S, A17, T7 \rangle$ and $\langle \text{lp}, T10, T7 \rangle$.

Finally, given a DTM $\langle N, R_d, R \rangle$ and a node $b \in N$, we can define for each type T of binary rule the following set of nodes:

$$ N^{[T]}(b) = \{s \in N | \exists r = \langle T, s, b \rangle \in R\} \quad \text{where} \quad T \in \{\text{lp}, ++S/D, --S/D\}, $$

which includes the source nodes of all rules of type T for which node b is the target node. Given the DTM of Fig. 2, the following sets can be defined for node $T7 : N^{++S}(T7) = \{T9\}$, $N^{--S}(T7) = \{A17\}$, and $N^{\text{lp}}(T7) = \{T10\}$.

4.2   Boolean Rules and CNF Formula Extraction

Given a DTM, a corresponding set of Boolean rules that capture all the constraints in the model can be generated. The semantics of those rules as well as their mappings to CNF clauses are originally presented in [7], and for the sake of presentation completeness summarized in Table 2. The required CNF formula can then be easily extracted by taking the conjunction of the CNF clauses corresponding to each individual Boolean rule.

The generation of Boolean rules starts by extracting set $N^{\text{lp}}(p)$, and also the following two sets for each task node $p \in N_t$ of the DTM :

$$ N^{\text{pos}}(p) = N^{++S}(p) \cup N^{--D}(p) = \{e_1, \cdots, e_k\} \cup \{f_1, \cdots, f_l\} \tag{1} $$

$$ N^{\text{neg}}(p) = N^{--S}(p) \cup N^{++D}(p) = \{g_1, \cdots, g_m\} \cup \{h_1, \cdots, h_o\} \tag{2} $$

which, along with the decomposition rule $r_d = \langle T, p, \{c_1, c_2, \cdots, c_n\} \rangle$ for node p, determine the set of Boolean rules that must be generated for this node. According to whether some or all of those sets are empty, a different set of rules

Table 1. AND/OR rules generation for task and action nodes. There is always a decomposition rule $r_d = \langle T, p, \{c_1, c_2, \cdots, c_n\}\rangle$ for each task node $p \in N_t$.

| $N^{pos}(p)$ | $N^{neg}(p)$ | $N^{lp}(p)$ | Generated AND/OR Rules | |
			$p \in N_t$	$p \in N_a$
$=\emptyset$	$=\emptyset$	$=\emptyset$	$p \leftarrow T(c_1, c_2, \cdots, c_n)$	-
$=\emptyset$	$=\emptyset$	$\{b_1 \cdots b_q\}$	$p \leftarrow AND(b_1 \cdots b_q, p\_d)$	$p \leftarrow AND(b_1 \cdots b_q, p\_leaf)$
$=\emptyset$	$\neq\emptyset$	$=\emptyset$	$p \leftarrow AND(p\_d, \neg p\_c\_neg)$	-
$=\emptyset$	$\neq\emptyset$	$\{b_1 \cdots b_q\}$	$p \leftarrow AND(p\_\ell, \neg p\_c\_neg)$ $p\_\ell \leftarrow AND(b_1 \cdots b_q, p\_d)$	-
$\neq\emptyset$	$=\emptyset$	$=\emptyset$	$p \leftarrow OR(p\_d, p\_c\_pos)$	-
$\neq\emptyset$	$=\emptyset$	$\{b_1 \cdots b_q\}$	$p \leftarrow OR(p\_\ell, p\_c\_pos)$ $p\_\ell \leftarrow AND(b_1 \cdots b_q, p\_d)$	-
$\neq\emptyset$	$\neq\emptyset$	$=\emptyset$	$p \leftarrow OR(p\_d, p\_c)$ $p \leftarrow AND(p\_c\_pos, \neg p\_c\_neg)$	-
$\neq\emptyset$	$\neq\emptyset$	$\{b_1 \cdots b_q\}$	$p \leftarrow OR(p\_\ell, p\_c)$ $p\_c \leftarrow AND(p\_c\_pos, \neg p\_c\_neg)$ $p\_\ell \leftarrow AND(b_1 \cdots b_q, p\_d)$	-

is generated as this is illustrated in Table 1. Additionally, the following apply for the pseudo-variables p_c_pos (contributions that positively affect the target node p), p_c_neg (contributions that negatively affect the target node p), and p_d (decomposition rule for node p) that appear in Table 1:

$$p\_c\_pos \leftarrow OR(e_1, \cdots, e_k, \neg f_1, \cdots, \neg f_l)$$
$$p\_c\_neg \leftarrow OR(g_1, \cdots, g_m, \neg h_1, \cdots, \neg h_o)$$
$$p\_d \leftarrow T(c_1, c_2, \cdots, c_n)$$

where T is the type of the decomposition rule and nodes e_i, f_i, g_i and h_i correspond to the ones in equations (1) and (2). It is important to note that p_c_pos (p_c_neg) is substituted by e_1 or $\neg f_1$ (g_1 or $\neg h_1$) in case $k = 0$ or $l = 0$ ($m = 0$ or $o = 0$) respectively, while if both of k and l (m and o) are equal to zero, set N^{pos} (N^{neg}) is empty, and the pseudo-variable p_c_pos (p_c_neg) does not appear in the rules. For example, given task node $T7$ of Fig. 2 for which $N^{lp}(T7) = \{T10\}$, $N^{pos}(T7) = N^{++S}(T7) = \{T9\}$, and $N^{neg}(T7) = N^{--S}(T7) = \{A17\}$, the following Boolean rules are generated based on the last case of Table 1:

$$T7 \leftarrow OR(T7\_\ell, T7\_c) \qquad (3) \qquad\qquad T7\_c \leftarrow AND(T9, \neg A17) \qquad (5)$$
$$T7\_\ell \leftarrow AND(T10, T7\_d) \qquad (4) \qquad\qquad T7\_d \leftarrow AND(A10, A11) \qquad (6)$$

Table 2. Mapping of Boolean rules to CNF Clauses

Boolean Rule	Equivalent Constraints	CNF Clauses
$o \leftarrow AND(i_1, i_2, \cdots, i_n)$	$\neg i_1 \Rightarrow \neg o, \cdots, \neg i_n \Rightarrow \neg o,$ $i_1 \wedge i_2 \wedge \cdots \wedge i_n \Rightarrow o$	$(i_1 \vee \neg o) \wedge \cdots \wedge (i_n \vee \neg o) \wedge$ $(\neg i_1 \vee \neg i_2 \vee \cdots \vee \neg i_n \vee o)$
$o \leftarrow OR(i_1, i_2, \cdots, i_n)$	$i_1 \Rightarrow o, \cdots, i_n \Rightarrow o,$ $i_1 \wedge i_2 \wedge \cdots \wedge i_n \Rightarrow o$	$(\neg i_1 \vee o) \wedge \cdots \wedge (\neg i_n \vee o) \wedge$ $(i_1 \vee i_2 \vee \cdots \vee i_n \vee \neg o)$

which can be directly mapped to CNF clauses as this is illustrated in Table 2. For example the following CNF formula corresponds to rule (5):

$$(T9 \vee \neg T7\_c) \wedge (\neg A17 \vee \neg T7\_c) \wedge (\neg T9 \vee A17 \vee T7\_c)$$

Finally, Boolean rules are also generated for action nodes when they are the target of $\xrightarrow{lp}$ links. This case is also presented in Table 1 (second row).

5 Reasoning

The extracted CNF formula for the DTM provides a formal model of logical relationships between the DTM nodes. Such a model can be used to apply reasoning techniques in order to identify possible DTM model resolutions as combinations of actions, that if performed in coordination, can realize the root task of the DTM model. In this respect, finding such a task resolution equals to solving the SAT problem for the extracted CNF which would assign truth values to both tasks and actions, and then executing all actions assigned as *true*. However, as discussed above, DTM nodes may be annotated with weights indicating either benefit (for task nodes) or cost (for action nodes). So we are not only interested in finding an assignment that satisfies the CNF formula, but also an assignment that has the best score taking into account the cost/benefit of each *true* node.

Given the nature of the problem, different strategies can be utilized based on whether the model resides in static or dynamic environments. The former are characterized by absent or extremely rare changes of assigned benefits and costs to DTM nodes, while the latter by frequent context changes that lead to changes for the weights associated to all or to a subset of the model's nodes.

5.1 Reasoning in Static Environment

Optimal plan determination is an optimization problem that can be reduced to an instance of Max-SAT problem called *Weighted Partial Max-SAT* (WP-MAXSAT). In WP-MAXSAT we have two sets of clauses namely, hard and soft clauses. The former are the clauses that a solution assignment must satisfy, while the latter are clauses that have weights and the solution must satisfy only those that ensure the maximum total weight.

In our case, the generated CNF corresponds to the hard constraints of the WP-MAXSAT, while the weight-node pairs are used to build the soft constraints of the problem. For example, given the weights illustrated in Table 3 two single literal soft clauses namely, $(T2)$ and $(A8)$ with weights 97 and -412 respectively are generated for nodes $T2$ and $A8$.

5.2   Reasoning in Dynamic Environment

An exhaustive WP-MAXSAT algorithm can be applied to get an optimal plan determination; however, having to apply such an algorithm for each context change can limit significantly the applicability of the approach, especially when working with task models of significant size and complexity in dynamically altering environments. In such cases, computing an approximate to optimal solution may be a preferable alternative instead of attempting to compute the optimal solution, for two primary reasons. First, the average time between any two context changes may be less than the average time required to compute the optimal solution, making the application of typical WP-MAXSAT algorithms impractical. Secondly, even when the time between any two context changes is adequate for WP-MAXSAT, the extra time required to compute the optimal solution may ultimately impose higher aggregate costs than utilizing a good-enough, approximate solution to perform the task right after the context change occurs. Before examining a search process to approximate optimal solutions for task models, we introduce certain concepts required for the definition and application of a local search algorithm that can efficiently explore the solutions space.

Boolean Rules Evaluation. Boolean rules, which have been introduced in the previous section, consist of a set of input variables (i.e. variables denoted as i_1 to i_n in Table 2) and a single output parameter (i.e. variable o in Table 2). Given a Boolean rule B_r, we are going to use the notations $In[B_r]$ and $Out[B_r]$ to signify the input variables and the output parameter of rule B_r respectively.

Definition 2. *We say that a Boolean rule B_{r_a} directly requires rule B_{r_b}, denoted as $B_{r_a} \xrightarrow{req} B_{r_b}$ iff $Out[B_{r_b}] \in In[B_{r_a}]$.*

For example, for the rules presented in the previous section, rule (4) *directly requires* rule (6) as variable $T7\_d$ appears in the input variables of the former and is also the output parameter of the latter rule.

Definition 3. *We say that a Boolean rule B_{r_a} requires rule B_{r_b}, denoted as $B_{r_a} \xrightarrow{req*} B_{r_b}$ iff $B_{r_a} \xrightarrow{req} B_{r_b}$ or there exist a Boolean rule B_{r_k} such that $B_{r_a} \xrightarrow{req} B_{r_k}$ and $B_{r_k} \xrightarrow{req*} B_{r_b}$.*

Rule (3) $\xrightarrow{req*}$ (6) as (3) $\xrightarrow{req}$ (4) because of $T7\_\ell$, and (4) $\xrightarrow{req}$ (6) as we have previously mentioned.

Furthermore, the $\xrightarrow{req*}$ operator provides a mechanism that allows us to create sequences of Boolean rules in which every rule depends *only* on rules that appear earlier in the sequence. More precisely:

Definition 4. *We say that a sequence of Boolean rules* $B_{r_1}, B_{r_2}, \cdots, B_{r_n}$ *is a proper one if for every pair* B_{r_i}, B_{r_j} *of Boolean rules in the sequence,* B_{r_i} *appears earlier than* B_{r_j} *in case* $B_{r_j} \xrightarrow{req*} B_{r_i}$.

Hence, sequence (6)(5)(4)(3) is a *proper* sequence of Boolean rules, while sequence (3)(6)(5)(4) is not, as (3) $\xrightarrow{req*}$ (6) and the latter appears after the former in the sequence. If circular dependencies exist in a set of Boolean rules, no proper sequence of those rules exists. However, as the DTMs used have no cycles because of the validation phase illustrated in Fig. 1, we ensure that no circular dependencies exist in the Boolean rules sets generated from DTMs, and so there is always a proper sequence for them. Proper sequences of Boolean rules can be computed at definition-time through typical topological sorting algorithms.

Additionally, given a set $B = \{B_{r_1}, B_{r_2}, \cdots, B_{r_n}\}$ of Boolean rules we define the following two sets of variables:

$$L[B] = \bigcup_{i=1}^{n} In[B_{r_i}] - \bigcup_{i=1}^{n} Out[B_{r_i}] \qquad I[B] = \bigcup_{i=1}^{n} Out[B_{r_i}] \qquad (7)$$

where the former contains the variables that appear only as input while the latter those that appear as output parameters in the Boolean rules of set B. We call variables in $L[B]$ and $I[B]$ *leaves* and *inner* respectively and we assign weights to them as follows: those that correspond to nodes of the initial model have the same weight as the node, while those that correspond to pseudonodes (i.e. nodes added during CNF generation) have a zero weight. Finally, using a proper sequence of Boolean rules and an assignment on $L[B]$ elements we can propagate the truth assignment to $I[B]$ elements, and by adding the weights of all true variables we can calculate the total weight of the given sequence.

Local Search on DTM Leaves. Motivated by the above scenarios, we propose a parameterized local search algorithm that can be applied as soon as context changes occur and provide solutions whose quality generally converge to the optimal after a number of iterations. The iterations of the search algorithm can be configured through input parameters so that the search process can be tunned to run within acceptable execution times. The defined search algorithm operates on $L[B]$ and attempts to rapidly reach solutions of improving quality. It should be noted that while a WP-MAXSAT algorithm has to be applied to the whole weighted model (that is, variables corresponding to both inner and leaf nodes) to compute the optimal solution, the proposed search algorithm constructs truth assignments for leaves only by mutating previous ones. In this way, the search space is considerably smaller, particularly for task models of significant depth and complexity (i.e. high inner to leaf nodes ratio). The search process begins by examining a fixed size pool of cached solutions that fulfill the model's hard constraints, and selects the best-performing one. For the process to start even one cached solution suffices, and this solution can be obtained with low computation cost by utilizing a simple SAT solver applied once and offline. The solutions pool is enriched with new solutions as these are discovered at execution-time. By keeping the solution pool with a fixed size we allow for better computation

---

Algorithm 1. Leaves Local Search

Input: X: Initial solution, B: Boolean rules, $L[B]$: Leaves of B, FF: flips-factor, NF: neighborhood-factor

1: $S \leftarrow X$
2: $x \leftarrow \{x_n\}$, where $x_n = \langle n, v \rangle$, $x_n \in X \wedge n \in L \wedge v \in \{TRUE, FALSE\}$
3: **for** $i = 1$ **to** $FF * |L[B]|$ **do**
4:    $y \leftarrow x$
5:    $d \leftarrow$ random integer $\in [1, NF * |L[B]|]$
6:    **for** $j = 1$ **to** d **do**
7:       $y_m \leftarrow \neg x_n$, where n random leaf
8:    **end for**
9:    **if** $evaluate(y, R)$ **then**
10:       $Y = propagate(y, R)$
11:       **if** $weight(Y) \geq weight(X)$ **then**
12:          $S \leftarrow Y$
13:          $x \leftarrow y$
14:       **end if**
15:    **end if**
16: **end for**
17: **return** S

---

complexity for seed selection when a context change occurs. Once such a solution is selected, the local search algorithm is applied on $L[B]$ in order to gradually reach better solutions.

The proposed Leaves Local Search (LLS) algorithm begins with setting as current solution the one provided and proceeds by computing an initial leaves truth assignment based on the provided solution (lines 1-2). Then, the algorithm applies a set of assignment mutating steps for a fixed number of times which is equal to a specified flips factor parameter (FF) times the number of leaves. During the mutating steps, the assignment's values are flipped in random pairs, for up to a different number of pairs in each iteration which is equal to a specified neighborhood factor (NF) parameter times the number of leaves (lines 5-8). The new leaves truth assignment is evaluated against a precomputed proper sequence of Boolean rules to examine whether it leads to a solution of the model, i.e. root R is satisfied (line 9). If the new leaves assignment leads to a solution for the model, then the respective DTM solution's weight is compared to the currently selected solution and provided that the former is better, it becomes the selected solution, while the next iteration of the mutating process will be applied to the leaves assignment that led to the new solution (lines 10-15). Finally, the algorithm returns the best solution met throughout the search.

5.3 Reasoning Example

To illustrate the application of the WP-MAXSAT algorithm and the execution of the LLS algorithm for different contexts (i.e. different weights t_1, t_2) and for different FF values, we use the DTM presented in Fig. 2. In this respect, Table 3 contains two weight assignments (t_1 and t_2) in the DTM example, where the second assignment (t_2) reflects changes in the initial weights (t_1) of nodes $A5$ and $T11$ as a result of a context change. As discussed before, task nodes are annotated with positive weight values indicating the benefit included in fulfilling the task while action nodes are annotated with negative values reflecting the associated

Table 3. Weights assignment for two context changes (DTM in Fig. 2)

	A11	A17	A4	**A5**	A6	A8	A9	**T11**	T2	T4	T5	T6	T7
Weight (t_1)	-709	-359	-26	**-957**	-841	-412	-79	**0**	97	608	643	664	976
Weight (t_2)	-709	-359	-26	**-593**	-841	-412	-79	**599**	97	608	643	664	976

Table 4. Results on Running Example

	Leaves Local Search							WP-MAXSAT
FF	0	1	2	3	4	5	≥ 6	-
Weight (t_1)	-395	1022	1172	1757	1731	1584	1757	1757
Weight (t_2)	568	1546	1520	2255	2255	2255	2255	2255

cost for executing the activity. The model's nodes that are not included in Table 3 have weights that are equal to zero. Based on the above weight annotations, we apply WP-MAXSAT and compute an optimal solution for the problem with total weights equal to 1757 for context t_1 and 2255 for context t_2.

In order to apply the LLS algorithm we utilize a solution computed by a SAT solver which will be used as a seed. Table 4 presents the results of the LLS algorithm with different FF values for both the initial weight assignment as well as the one after the context change. As the number of iterations increases the acquired solution converges to the optimal one. Also, the LLS algorithm required less iterations ($FF \geq 3$ for context t_2 vs. $FF \geq 6$ for context t_1) in order to reach the optimal solution during the second run. This relationship between the rate of context changes and the solution quality performance of LLS is examined in the next section. In this respect, in order to evaluate and assess the performance of the algorithm with regard to solution quality, as well as the computational requirements we discuss a series of experiments in the following section.

6   Case Studies and Experiments

In order to evaluate the applicability and the performance of the proposed framework we conducted a series of experiments with randomly generated task models of varying size and complexity. Using these models we evaluated the application of a WP-MAXSAT algorithm with regards to execution time required for models of different size. Additionally, using the same models, we evaluated and compared the performance of the search process presented in the previous section with regard to the execution time required as well as the quality of acquired solution for different FF values.

In order to evaluate the proposed framework we implemented a random task model generation mechanism which, given certain parameters, such as model size, task vs. actions ratio, AND vs. OR decompositions ratio and maximum binary rules coverage returned a randomly generated task model. Due to space limitations, the results presented and discussed in this paper were acquired with the following task model generation configuration: *a*) model size ($|N|$): 20 - 300, with an interval of 20 nodes *b*) task vs. actions ratio: 1 *c*) AND vs. OR decomposition ratio: 1 *d*) Maximum binary rules coverage: 30% (percentage of nodes participating in on or more binary rules) We used the above configuration and acquired 10 randomly generated models per model size, for 15 model sizes. For each model, we simulated five context changes each of which assigned different weight values to 10 percent of the nodes and for each context change we ran the WP-MAXSAT algorithm to get the optimal solution, as well as the WP-MINSAT algorithm to get the worst solution for the model with regard to total weight. In order to evaluate and compare the search process performance vs. the WP-MAXSAT results, we used the following measures:

- $t_{wp-maxsat}$: WP-MAXSAT algorithm execution time,

- t_{lls}^{FF}: LLS algorithm execution time with flips factor FF, and

- $Q_S = \frac{W_S - W_{worst}}{W_{optimal} - W_{worst}}$: solution quality,

where W_S is the total weight of the solution, and $W_{optimal}$ and W_{worst} being the total weights of the solutions computed by WP-MAXSAT and WP-MINSAT algorithms respectively. For each generated model the search process was executed for the following parameter values: $FF \in \{5, 10, 15, 20, 25, 30, 35, 40\}$, $NF = 0.2$ and average values were computed for the above measures.

6.1 Results

The presentation of the results is split into: (a) evaluation of *time performance* through considering $t_{wp-maxsat}$ and t_{lls}^{FF}, and (b) evaluation of *solution quality* through computing Q_S for different model sizes and flips factor values.

Time Performance. Fig. 3 depicts the average $t_{wp-maxsat}$ versus model size. The execution time required by the WP-MAXSAT algorithm scales exponentially with regard to model size, which is expected due to the nature of the problem. Additionally, Fig. 3 depicts the average t_{lls}^5 as well as the average t_{lls}^{40} for all examined model sizes ($FF = 5$ and $FF = 40$ are the minimum and maximum flips factor values considered in our experiments) while results for all intermediate FF values lie between the results for the two extreme values depicted. t_{lls}^5 is generally proportionate to FF; however, independent of the FF value, the average t_{lls} scales almost linearly to the number of nodes. For large models, LLS is significantly faster compared to applying WP-MAXSAT. For instance, for model size equal to 300 nodes and flips factor value equal to 40, LLS required on average $\frac{1}{1000}$ of the time that WP-MAXSAT required and compute solutions of high quality ($Q_S = 0.938$) as will be discussed in the next section.

Solution Quality. Fig. 4 presents how Q_S varies versus FF values for model sizes of 100 and 300 nodes. The quality of the initial solution is depicted for $FF = 0$ and it is around 0.5 for both model sizes. From that point on, as FF increases, the quality converges asymptotically to the optimal solution getting its maximum value for $FF = 40$ (0.961 for size = 100 and 0.938 for size = 300).

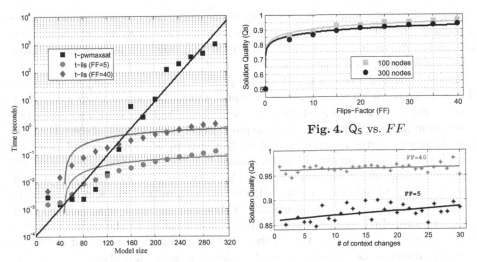

Fig. 4. Q_S vs. FF

Fig. 3. Execution time   **Fig. 5.** Q_S vs. number of context changes

Finally, Fig. 5 depicts the average solution quality for the proposed search process, with regard to the number of consecutive context changes using average values from 3 models of 200 nodes and 30 context changes. As the number of consecutive context changes in a dynamic environment increases and the LLS algorithm is applied more times, the solution quality provided by the algorithm is improved for each run. Also, the lower the FF, the more evident the improvement effect is. This effect can be explained by the fact that context changes are gradual, allowing for the algorithm's seed solutions that originate from the solutions' cache to be of higher quality. In this respect, as the starting point for each application of the algorithm gets better, the outcome with regard to solution quality is improved, indicating thus in environments with high rates of gradual context changes, using the proposed search technique can provide further benefit.

7   Related Work

Decision support and action selection for a given context and a given set of goals is a key problem that still motivates researchers and practitioners to devise solutions for. There are two main facets to this problem, namely decision support for static environments, and dynamic decision support for dynamic environments. In the first category, [8] discusses a qualitative approach as well as a numerical approach for reasoning with goal models. In [9] an approach of evaluating qualitative or quantitative satisfaction levels of goals and tasks through the propagation of appropriate values via the goal model links, is presented.

A variation to these approaches are utility based decision support approaches that aim also to maximize or minimize a utility function such as benefit or cost for each task and action, or the number of constraints that are satisfied for each possible plan. Assuming that a goal or other type of model can be represented as logic formulas a number of reasoning approaches based on SAT reasoners are applicable. In [10] an algorithm that implements Weighted Partial MAX-SAT by successively invoking a SAT solver and by attempting to minimize the penalty for not satisfying soft-constraints, is presented.

In [11], GRASP a search algorithm for propositional satisfiability is proposed. The search algorithm is based on the concept of identification of assignments that cause conflicts at a given level, and then non-chronologically backtrack to earlier levels to improve pruning of the search space. In [12] an extension of the GRAPSP algorithm augmented with path re-linking that attempts to intensify and focus the search around good-quality isolated solutions that have been originally computed by the GRASP algorithm is presented. The basic difference of the GRASP and also the path re-linking augmented GRASP algorithms from the approach here is that, in our approach we do not utilize backtracking or a and we are solely based on mutations of the possible assignments of truth values to the variables in the given set of clauses. The quality of the produced solution is based on the number of mutations (i.e. iterations) and the size of possible mutations in each flip. The augmented GRASP algorithm guarantees a better approximate solution to the Weighted MAX-SAT than ours, as it already starts from known good (elite) solutions, but on the other hand requires the use of GRASP as its initial input.

In the second category, the environment is considered dynamic in the sense that actions of a plan may become impossible once the plan is devised and started being enacted because the environment is dynamically altered. Work in this category relates to approaches proposed in autonomous agents and autonomic software systems. In [13] an approach that allows for reasoning about partial satisfaction of soft-goals is discussed. The approach is based on the annotation of softgoals with reward (e.g. benefit), and penalty (e.g. cost) functions. The approach utilizes Dynamic Decision Networks (DDN) in order to identify a selection of softgoals that provide an optimal decision with respect to softgoal satisfaction and the utility functions used. The difference from our approach is that we do not require the compilation of intermediate models such as a DDN, and we allow for utility functions (rewards, and penalties) to vary dynamically as the system operates. In [14] a framework that implements an adaptation manager for autonomic systems is proposed. The framework is based on the Goal-Attribute-Action model and allows for a decision to be reached regarding the selection of actions in order to adapt or re-configure an autonomic system according to specified goals that need be reached.

8   Conclusion

In this paper, we investigated the use of local search algorithms and boolean expression evaluators to reason with DTMs when labels related to cost and benefit values for actions and tasks are altered as a result of context changes. The approach allows for obtaining a solution that is within 90% of the optimal value at a fraction of time that is required by a Weighted Partial MAX-SAT algorithm to compute the optimal solution for the problem at hand. The applicability and the performance of the proposed framework was evaluated with promising results by conducting a series of experiments with randomly generated task models of varying size and complexity.

Acknowledgment. The research of G. Chatzikonstantinou is co-funded by the European Union (European Social Fund ESF) and Greek National funds through the Operational Program "Education and Lifelong Learning" of the National Strategic Reference Framework (NSRF) - Research Funding Program: Heracleitus II. Investing in knowledge society through the European Social Fund. The research of M. Athanasopoulos is supported by IBM Canada CAS Research under the Research Fellowship Project No. 754.

References

1. Yu, E.: Modelling strategic relationships for process reengineering. PhD thesis, University of Toronto Toronto (1996)
2. van Lamsweerde, A., Letier, E.: Handling obstacles in goal-oriented requirements engineering. IEEE Trans. Software Eng. 26(10), 978–1005 (2000)
3. Dardenne, A., van Lamsweerde, A., Fickas, S.: Goal-directed requirements acquisition. Sci. Comput. Program. 20(1-2), 3–50 (1993)
4. Amyot, D.: Introduction to the user requirements notation: Learning by example. Comput. Netw. 42(3), 285–301 (2003)
5. Liaskos, S., Khan, S.M., Litoiu, M., Jungblut, M.D., Rogozhkin, V., Mylopoulos, J.: Behavioral adaptation of information systems through goal models. Inf. Syst. 37(8), 767–783 (2012)
6. Chopra, A.K., Dalpiaz, F., Giorgini, P., Mylopoulos, J.: Reasoning about agents and protocols via goals and commitments. In: AAMAS, pp. 457–464 (2010)
7. Velev, M.N.: Efficient translation of boolean formulas to cnf in formal verification of microprocessors. In: Proceedings of the 2004 Asia and South Pacific Design Automation Conference, ASP-DAC 2004 (2004)
8. Giorgini, P., Mylopoulos, J., Nicchiarelli, E., Sebastiani, R.: Reasoning with goal models. In: Spaccapietra, S., March, S.T., Kambayashi, Y. (eds.) ER 2002. LNCS, vol. 2503, pp. 167–181. Springer, Heidelberg (2002)
9. Amyot, D., Ghanavati, S., Horkoff, J., Mussbacher, G., Peyton, L., Yu, E.S.K.: Evaluating goal models within the goal-oriented requirement language. Int. J. Intell. Syst. 25(8), 841–877 (2010)
10. Ansótegui, C., Bonet, M.L., Levy, J.: A new algorithm for weighted partial maxsat. In: AAAI (2010)
11. Silva, J.P.M., Sakallah, K.A.: Grasp: A search algorithm for propositional satisfiability. IEEE Trans. Computers 48(5), 506–521 (1999)
12. Festa, P., Pardalos, P.M., Pitsoulis, L.S., Resende, M.G.C.: GRASP with path-relinking for the weighted maximum satisfiability problem. In: Nikoletseas, S.E. (ed.) WEA 2005. LNCS, vol. 3503, pp. 367–379. Springer, Heidelberg (2005)
13. Bencomo, N., Belaggoun, A.: Supporting decision-making for self-adaptive systems: From goal models to dynamic decision networks. In: Doerr, J., Opdahl, A.L. (eds.) REFSQ 2013. LNCS, vol. 7830, pp. 221–236. Springer, Heidelberg (2013)
14. Salehie, M., Tahvildari, L.: A weighted voting mechanism for action selection problem in self-adaptive software. In: SASO, pp. 328–331 (2007)
15. Ernst, N.A., Mylopoulos, J., Borgida, A., Jureta, I.J.: Reasoning with optional and preferred requirements. In: Parsons, J., Saeki, M., Shoval, P., Woo, C., Wand, Y. (eds.) ER 2010. LNCS, vol. 6412, pp. 118–131. Springer, Heidelberg (2010)

Finding Optimal Plans
for Incremental Method Engineering

Kevin Vlaanderen, Fabiano Dalpiaz, and Sjaak Brinkkemper

Utrecht University,
Department of Information and Computing Sciences,
{k.vlaanderen,f.dalpiaz,s.brinkkemper}@uu.nl

Abstract. Incremental method engineering proposes to evolve the information systems development methods of a software company through a step-wise improvement process. In practice, this approach proved to be effective for reducing the risks of failure while introducing method changes. However, little attention has been paid to the important problem of identifying an adequate plan for implementing the changes in the company's context. To overcome this deficiency, we propose an approach that assists analysts by suggesting—via automated reasoning—optimal and quasi-optimal plans for implementing method changes. After formalizing the Process-Deliverable Diagrams language for describing the method changes to implement, we present a planning framework for generating plans that comply with different types of constraints. We also describe an implementation of the modeling and planning components of our approach.

Keywords: method engineering, evolution, planning, logic programming.

1 Introduction

Incremental method engineering [18,24] is a paradigm that proposes to change information systems development methods through a continuous improvement process. This strategy adheres to the common understanding that spreading changes over a time period is less risky and more efficient than introducing them all at once.

Empirical studies have provided significant evidence in favor of incremental method engineering [24,16,7], including cases on the introduction of Scrum [21], showing that it helps to cope with the major obstacles to change, including resistance to change, fear of ineffectiveness by the involved personnel, and resource constraints [2].

However, existing research has largely ignored the relevant problem of identifying a plan that specifies *when* to implement the changes. This requires defining which are the most (and least) urgent changes, how many changes can be implemented given time and budget constraints, and when a plan is better than another. See the following example.

Example 1. A software organization wants to improve customer satisfaction by introducing the Kano analysis [13]. However, introducing and learning the Kano analysis requires a significant effort, due to its complexity (Fig. 4). The management team is concerned with upfront costs and risks of resistance to change. A product manager suggests introducing it incrementally, but she cannot devise a proper plan. How can Kano analysis be embedded within the current process? Are there any variations possible? □

M. Jarke et al. (Eds.): CAiSE 2014, LNCS 8484, pp. 640–655, 2014.

In this paper, we address the problem of devising a plan for the incremental implementation of a set of method changes in an organization (as elaborated in Sec. 2). We use automated reasoning techniques for generating *optimal* and *quasi-optimal* plans. We propose a formalization of the Process-Deliverable Diagram (PDD) modeling language [23], that we use to describe the changes to be implemented.

We combine these elements into a method that, based on a description of the changes to be enacted, assists the analysts by suggesting possible plans, and helps to refine these plans to improve fitness with the organizational context. These plans have to satisfy mandatory constraints, and should *satisfice* [19] weak (nice-to-have) constraints.

While we are inspired by automated planning techniques, we develop a novel solution that copes with the specificities of method engineering. This includes defining sequencing based on deliverables rather than activities, and using weak constraints to derive a plan leading to an incremental maturity growth in the organization.

After stating our problem in Sec. 2, and discussing our research baseline in Sec. 3, we propose the following contributions:

- We formalize the PDD modeling language, adding clear semantics, so as to make it usable for automated reasoning. This formalization is described in Sec. 4.
- We define a formal framework that defines optimal and quasi-optimal plans with respect to an input PDD, an organizational context, and a set of time and budget constraints. The framework in Sec. 5.1 forms the basis for plan generation.
- We propose a process that guides the analysts in applying the framework to generate plans and to refine them by strengthening and relaxing constraints (Sec. 5.2).
- We develop tool support for our method: PDD models can be created via a graphical modeling environment, and automatically converted into input for a logic program in disjunctive Datalog [15] that generates (quasi-)optimal plans (see Sec. 6).

Sec. 7 illustrates our approach using the scenario in Example 1. Sec. 8 discusses related work, presents conclusions, and outlines future directions.

2   Problem Statement

Our research context is method evolution, i.e, the process through which an organization's methods change over time. We focus on incremental method engineering, a well-defined process for managing and incrementally introducing method changes.

This approach is illustrated in Fig. 1. Whenever the process is triggered (either by an occurred event, or every N months/years), the maturity of the current processes is assessed. If any process shows low maturity, the stakeholders' needs are considered to identify *what* to change, and, subsequently, by defining a plan that specifies *how* and *when* to deploy these changes in the organization. Finally, the changes are enacted as per the plan. This process is highly iterative, for organizations are in constant evolution.

In this paper, we focus on the important yet under-explored activity of *change planning*. The problem is that of determining a (quasi-)optimal scheduling for implementing the changes, based on all the constraints (hard and soft ones) of the stakeholders. To address this non-trivial problem, several sub-questions have to be answered:

- Which factors determine the optimality of a plan?
- Which elements describe the hard constraints that cannot be violated?

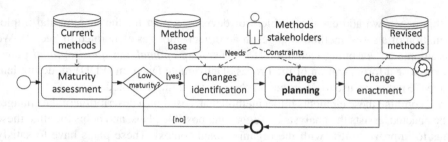

Fig. 1. Research context: systematic method evolution illustrated

- Which factors determine the priority of changes?
- How can one ensure that, even when partially deployed, the introduced changes can be effectively used in the organization?

In this paper, we consider the gradual introduction of new methods. In reality, it is more common to deal with changes to existing methods, which also requires to consider the removal and replacement of fragments. We leave dealing with the more complex case of decrements (as opposed to increments) for future research.

3   Baseline

We approach the challenges in Sec. 2 as part of the Online Method Engine (OME) [22], a knowledge management system for incremental method engineering. The OME consists of a method base that contains method fragments (generic descriptions of common approaches to software development tasks), rules for combining fragments, and organizational experience related to the fragments. These elements feed the four main functions of the OME: (a) disseminating method knowledge; (b) assessing the maturity of an organization's processes; (c) suggesting improvements based on method fragments and experience from similar organizations; and (d) enacting improvement proposals.

Process-deliverable Diagrams (PDDs) are a fundamental component of the method base: method fragments are modeled using a combination of UML activity diagrams—to describe the procedural aspects—and UML class diagrams—to express the data

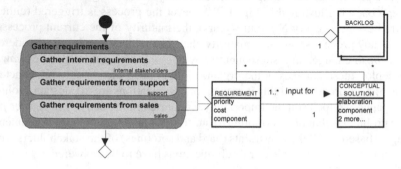

Fig. 2. Example of a Process-Deliverable Diagram (excerpt)

aspects (using classes called "deliverables"). These models are connected through a "results in" relationships from the activities to the deliverables. PDDs also distinguish between simple, closed, and open activities and deliverables [23]. Fig. 2 illustrates the core components of a PDD through an example. More details can be found in [23].

We also adopt the notion of focus area maturity matrix from the Situational Assessment Method (SAM) [4] (see Tab. 1). This matrix is filled in based on questions concerning situational factors as well as organizational capabilities. Each of these capabilities (with level A-F) contributes to the maturity of the organization in a specific focus/process area. For example, capability A in the focus area (row) "Requirements gathering" corresponds to a basic registration of the requirements, which contributes to maturity level 1, while capability F in the same area corresponds to the involvement of partners in the product management process, which contributes to maturity level 8.

By using a focus area maturity matrix instead of a fixed level maturity matrix, we are able to suggest more detailed improvement suggestions [4]. SAM enables assessing the maturity level of an organization and identifying the desired (target) maturity level.

Table 1. Example Capability Maturity Matrix (excerpt)

Focus Area Title	Code	Maturity Levels										
		0	1	2	3	4	5	6	7	8	9	10
Requirements Management												
Requirements Gathering	RG			A		B	C		D	E	F	
Requirements Identification	RI				A			B	C			D
Requirements Organizing	RO					A		B	C			

4   PDDs for Planning Method Changes

We formalize the relevant parts of the PDD language [23] so as to make it usable for automated reasoning. We state the requirements for our refinement in Sec. 4.1, and we present a revised metamodel and its semantics in Sec. 4.2.

4.1   Requirements

We want to leverage previous work: PDDs are a simple yet expressive means to model a method fragment's activities, deliverables, and their relationships. This choice is made to reuse the method base of fragments (modeled as PDDs) within the OME system.

PDDs were designed as a means to intuitively communicate methods and fragments to users. The price of this choice is that some constructs have ambiguous semantics that cannot be readily used for automated reasoning. Thus, we need to provide a clear semantics of the PDD metamodel, by fulfilling the three requirements (R_1 to R_3) below.

R_1: **Avoid Generic Associations.** Consider a directed association between two deliverables: "customer wish" and "theme". The original PDD metamodel does not specify a detailed semantics for associations, which inhibits determining the nature and the strength of the link. Thus, we require our language to avoid generic associations.

R_2: **Include Input and Output Relationships.** PDDs do not express input relationships, i.e., that an activity needs to use a deliverable. This choice eases readability, but does not express when a deliverable is needed. This obstacles planning for change: an activity that requires a deliverable cannot be introduced until that deliverable is produced. Our language needs to unambiguously express input and output relationships.

R_3: **Distinguish Deliverable Dependency Types.** Consider the following dependency between deliverables: the priority of a requirement is based on the input from customers and partners, but one of them suffices. This can be represented as an association between a requirement and an aggregated *input* deliverable in PDDs, but the semantics are not sufficiently detailed to indicate the choice. We thus require our language to support more specialized deliverable relationships.

4.2   PDD Metamodel

In Fig. 3, we present a refinement of the part of the PDD metamodel [23] that relates with describing method change. The semantics of the language should enable describing *what* changes have to be introduced, and expressing the dependencies between deliverables that pose constraints on *when* the different activities are introduced.

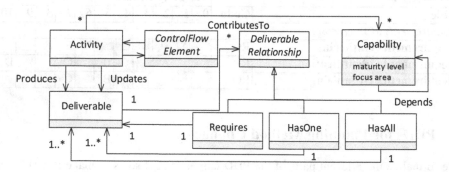

Fig. 3. Partial metamodel of the PDD language for describing method changes

Since we are interested in the implementation order of a set of activities, rather than in their execution order, our metamodel does not restrict the process side of the PDD: *ControlFlowElement* in Fig. 3 is a generic placeholder for all the control flow constructs of PDDs (sequence, decision point, fork and merge, etc.).

ContributesTo: this relationship indicates that an *Activity* contributes to a certain *Capability*, thus helping the organization to reach that capability's maturity level. An activity can contribute any number of capabilities, and a capability can be contributed by any number of activities. Graphically, contributions are textual annotations "FocusArea-Code:Capability" on the left of activities. In Fig. 1, e.g., activity "Analyze Product Environment" contributes to capability D of focus area "Requirements Gathering".

We implement several changes to fulfill $\mathbf{R_1}$–$\mathbf{R_3}$. We remove the distinction between simple, complex, and closed deliverables, as these concepts are not useful for our purposes. Also, we replace generic associations ($\mathbf{R_1}$) with the following relationships.

Requires: a transitive and asymmetric binary relationship between deliverables D_1 and D_2, indicating that the D_1 can be produced only when D_2 already exists. In Fig. 4, deliverable "Functional Questions" requires "Requirements".

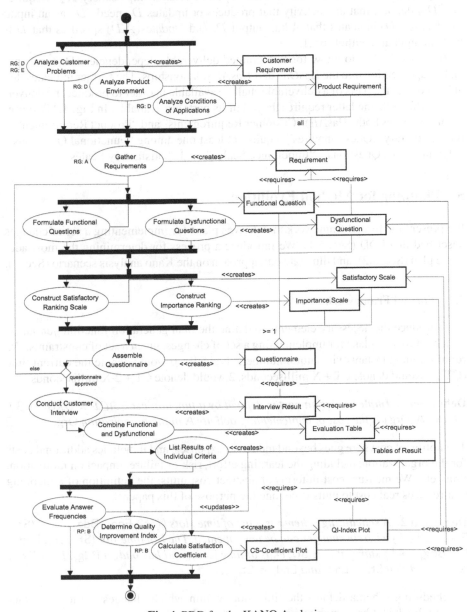

Fig. 4. PDD for the KANO Analysis

Produces/Updates: in a PDD, activities can be linked to deliverables only through the "results in" relationship between activity A and deliverable D. Here, we specialize this relationship into *Produces*, to denote that A creates a previously non-existent deliverable, and *Updates*, to indicate the modification of a previously available deliverable. In Fig. 4, activity "List Results of Individual Criteria" produces deliverable "Table of Results", while activity "Evaluate Answer Frequencies" updates it.

Together, the *Requires*, *Produces*, and *Updates* relationships satisfy $\mathbf{R_2}$: *Requires* (D_1, D_2) denotes that any activity that produces or updates D_1 needs D_2 as an input; *Produces*(A,D) indicates that A has output D; and *Updates*(A,D) specifies that D is both an input and output for A.

HasOne/HasAll: to allow for fine-grained deliverable dependencies ($\mathbf{R_3}$), we specialize aggregation into the *HasOne* and *HasAll* relationships. The former indicates that at least one of the parts of a deliverable shall be available in order to produce the deliverable itself, while the latter requires that all of its parts are available. In Fig. 4, "Requirements" requires both (*HasAll*) "Customer Requirements" and "Product Requirements"; on the contrary, "Questionnaires" requires at least one among "Functional Questions", "Dysfunctional Questions", "Importance Scales", and "Satisfactory Scales".

5   Planning for Method Evolution

We present the formal framework that derives plans for implementing a set of changes described in a PDD (Sec. 5.1). We introduce a process for determining the most adequate plan (Sec. 5.2), and illustrate our approach on the Kano analysis scenario (Sec. 7).

5.1   Formal Framework

We introduce the necessary elements to define the plan generation function *genplans*, which returns all plans for implementing a set of changes, given a set of constraints. We represent time instants via natural numbers: typically, 0 would denote the current time (CT), 1 would denote CT + X milliseconds, 2 would denote CT + 2·X milliseconds, etc.

Definition 1. *Implementation cost is defined by a function* $cst : \mathcal{ACT} \times \mathcal{ORG} \rightarrow \mathbb{R}^+$ *s.t.* $cst(\mathsf{A}, \mathsf{Org})$ *is the cost of implementing activity* A *in the organization* Org. □

The notion of cost here goes beyond monetary expenses, and it includes additional costs for the organization, including the learning effort, risk of failure, impact on motivation, time, etc. We measure cost in terms of abstract cost units; the definition of a mapping that reduces real cost to units is beyond the purpose of this paper.

Definition 2. *A* **scheduling schema** *is a list of time slots* $(\langle \mathsf{St}_1, \mathsf{End}_1, \mathsf{Bdg}_1 \rangle, \ldots, \langle \mathsf{St}_n, \mathsf{End}_n, \mathsf{Bdg}_n \rangle)$ *wherein changes can be implemented. The i-th time slot* $\langle \mathsf{St}_i : \mathbb{N}_0, \mathsf{End}_i : \mathbb{N}_0, \mathsf{Bdg}_i : \mathbb{R}^+ \rangle$ *starts at time* St_i, *ends at time* End_i, *and has budget* Bdg_i. *For all* i, *it is required that* $\mathsf{St}_i \leq \mathsf{End}_i$ *and* $\mathsf{End}_i < \mathsf{St}_{i+1}$. □

A scheduling schema defines the time slots within which changes are to be implemented. Each slot has a budget, i.e., an upper bound on the implementation cost in that

slot's time frame. The specification of a scheduling schema depends on the characteristics and strategy of the organization, and on the changes to implement. For example,
an organization may define a linear schema where all slots have the same duration and
budget, while another may start with low effort, and increase it in later slots.

Definition 3. *Given a PDD model* Mdl *and a scheduling schema* $(\langle St_1, End_1, Bdg_1 \rangle,$
$\ldots, \langle St_n, End_n, Bdg_n \rangle)$, *a set of* **scheduling constraints** Cstr *defines temporal restrictions on the allocation of the activities and the production of the deliverables of* Mdl
with respect to a time $T : \mathbb{N}_0$:

- actBefore(A, T): *activity* A *shall be scheduled in a slot* i, *s.t.* $End_i < T$;
- delBefore(D, T): *deliverable* D *shall be produced in a slot* i, *s.t.* $End_i < T$;
- actAfter(A, T): *like* actBefore, *but* $St_i > T$;
- delAfter(D, T): *like* delBefore, *but* $St_i > T$;
- actAt(A, T): *activity* A *shall be scheduled in a slot* i, *s.t.* $St_i \leq T \leq End_i$;
- delAt(D, T): *deliverable* D *shall be produced in a slot* i, *s.t.* $St_i \leq T \leq End_i$. $\square$

Scheduling constraints enable imposing fine-grained temporal restrictions on the allocation of activities and on the production of deliverables. In Sec. 7, we will show how
these constraints are a useful tool in our method to identify the most suitable plan.

Definition 4. *Given a PDD model* Mdl *and a scheduling schema* Schema, *a* **plan** *is a
set* $Pln = \{\langle A_1, T_1 \rangle, \ldots, \langle A_n, T_n \rangle\}$ *such that:*

- $A_1, \ldots, A_n$ *are all and only activities in* Mdl, *and*
- *for each* i, $1 \leq i \leq n$, *there exists exactly one slot* $\langle St_j, End_j, Bdg_j \rangle$ *in* Schema
  such that $St_j \leq T_i \leq End_j$. $\square$

A plan is an allocation of all and only the activities of a PDD model into a scheduling
schema. The activities shall be allocated within exactly one slot.

   We say that a plan is *feasible* if it respects budget constraints, i.e., if for each slot, the
sum of the implementation costs of the activities in that slot does not exceed the budget.
We say that a plan is *contiguous* when all slots have at least one allocated activity. In
this paper, we are concerned with the generation of feasible and contiguous plans.

   The function *genplans* brings together the concepts defined above and generates
the feasible and contiguous plans for implementing a set of changes described by a
PDD model in an organization, according to a specified scheduling schema, additional
temporal constraints, and considering a cost function for implementing the changes.

Definition 5. **Plan generation** *is a function that returns all feasible and contiguous
plans for implementing a set of changes in an organization. Formally,* genplans : $\mathcal{PDD}$
$\times \mathcal{ORG} \times \mathcal{CSTF} \times \mathcal{SS} \times \mathcal{CSTR} \times \rightarrow 2^{\mathcal{PLN}}$, *and* genplans(Mdl, Org, cst, Schema, Cstr) =
$\{Pln_1, \ldots, Pln_n\}$ *is such that:*

- Mdl *is a description of the changes to implement in PDD;*
- Org *is the organization where the changes are implemented;*
- cst *defines the cost of implementing the activities of* Mdl *in* Org *(Def. 1);*
- Schema *is a scheduling schema (Def. 2);*

- Cstr *is a set of constraints on scheduling (Def. 3);*
- *for each i,* $1 \leq i \leq n$, Pln_i *is a feasible and contiguous plan (Def. 4) for* Mdl *and* Schema *such that (i)* Pln *respects all constraints in* Cstr*; and (ii)* Pln *complies with the deliverable and capability dependencies in* Mdl.   □

While *genplans* deals with hard scheduling constraints that cannot be violated, it does not consider the optimality of a plan. In this paper, we conceive plan optimality in terms of *incremental maturity improvement*: the changes should be introduced in accordance with a growing maturity level of the organization. The activities that contribute to capabilities with lower maturity levels shall be introduced first, followed by the activities contributing to higher maturity levels, up to the highest maturity. Def. 6 introduces the notion of penalty for a plan, i.e., its distance from an optimal plan where activities are introduced with a monotonic increasing level of maturity.

Definition 6. *Plan penalty is a function that returns the distance between a given plan and an optimal plan that would introduce all activities in increasing order of maturity. Let the predicate* preceeds(A, A', Pln) *indicate that activity* A *is scheduled before activity* A' *in* Pln. *The maturity of an activity* mat(A) *is the lowest maturity level among the capabilities that the activity contributes to. Formally, penalty :* $\mathcal{PLN} \times \mathcal{PDD} \rightarrow \mathbb{N}_0$, *s.t.* penalty(Pln, Mdl) $= \sum_{A,A':preceeds(A,A',Pln)} \max(mat(A) - mat(A'), 0)$.   □

When an activity contributes to multiple capabilities, we consider the capability having the lowest maturity level, for that activity is important for the organization to achieve that level. The penalty is the number of "steps" that have been skipped in the plan: for instance, consider only activities "Gather Requirements" and "Analyze Customer Problems" in Fig. 4. The former activity has lowest maturity level 1 (it contributes to capability A in area requirements gathering), while the latter has lowest maturity level 6 (the contributed capability with lowest maturity is D in requirements gathering). If the former activity is introduced before the latter, the plan penalty would be 5.

We call a plan *optimal* when its penalty is zero, and *quasi-optimal* when its penalty is greater than zero but lower than Δ. This number Δ is domain-specific, and it depends on the number of activities in the plan, the organization, the cost of activities, etc.

In this paper, we limit ourselves to a special kind of scheduling schema, where for each slots i ($1 \leq i \leq n$), $St_i = End_i$, and the slots are such that $St_1 = 1, \ldots, St_n = n$.

We do not consider constraints related to organizational resources (other than the abstract unit Cost) and human factors (such as worker resistance), as such factors are harder to attribute to single activities and deliverables. The method we propose is a support tool for analysts, and does not replace their role as decision makers.

5.2   A Method for Identifying and Refining Plans

We present an elaboration of the **Change planning** step in Sec. 2 that uses *genplans* (Def. 5) for identifying plans and for refining them to fit well with the organization at hand. This method, illustrated in Fig. 5, helps to restrict or widen the space of alternative plans, depending on the plans that the function *genplans* returns.

The process begins with two preparatory steps that provide the inputs to the *genplans* function: the planning context is defined (the changes to implement, the organization,

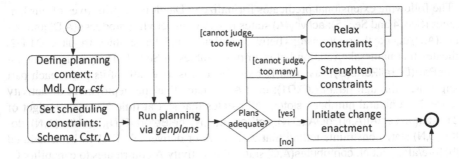

Fig. 5. A method for identifying and refining (quasi-)optimal plans

and the cost function), and an initial version of the scheduling constraints is created (the scheduling schema and constraints, and the quasi-optimality upper bound Δ). This input feeds the *genplans* function, which returns all optimal and quasi-optimal plans. The analyst then judges the adequacy of the returned plans:

- *Adequate*: a plan is identified and *change enactment* starts (see also Fig. 1);
- *Uncertain*: a final decision cannot be made at the moment, due to scarcity or excess of results. In order to identify a better plan, the analyst can modify the constraints:
  - *Relaxation*: when too few plans are returned, the scheduling constraints can be relaxed/weakened. Time slots can be merged to spread changes over a longer period with higher budget. Temporal scheduling constraints can be relaxed, or the quasi-optimality upper bound Δ increased. More intrusive options (from the organization's perspective) are to increase the number of slots or the budget.
  - *Strengthening*: if too many plans are returned, the analyst cannot make an informed choice, and the constraints can be tightened: the slots in the schema and their budget can be reduced, and temporal constraints can be added.
- *Inadequate*: no satisfactory plan can be devised in the current planning context, irrespective of the scheduling constraints. This terminates the process, which can be re-executed in a different context.

6   Realization

We have developed a graphical modeling tool for PDD within MetaEdit+ [20]. This tool is built around the Graph, Object, Property, Relationships, Role (GOPRR) metamodel, which we used to describe the PDD metamodel; instances of the latter metamodel are PDDs. The editor enforces syntactical rules, thereby ensuring the well formedness of the model. In addition, we have developed a set of code generators that transform any PDD model into a set of Datalog statements, which are needed to generate plans.

We have realized the mechanisms for identifying optimal and quasi-optimal plans via logic programming (specifically, via the disjunctive Datalog engine DLV [15]). The program consists of a set of inference rules (Tab. 2) that returns feasible and contiguous plans for a given input. The input consists of the Datalog statements that are generated from the PDD model, the temporal constraints, and the Δ quasi-optimality upper bound.

The following extensional predicates formalize in Datalog the primitives of our languages (Sec. 4 and Sec. 5): activity(A) states that A is an activity; produces(A,D) and updates(A,D) denote the relationships between activities and deliverables; requires(D1,D2) indicates that namesake relation between deliverables in Sec. 4. The predicate atLeastOnePart(D) (allParts(D)) says that D requires at least one (all) of its parts, each part being stated through hasPart(D,D1); cost(A,N) states that the deployment of activity A costs N (a natural number); slot(N1,N2) states that slot at time N1 has a budget of N2 cost units; actAt(A,N), delAt(D,N), actBefore(A,N), delBefore(D,N), actAfter(A,N), delAfter(D,N) state constraints telling that activity A or deliverable D shall be scheduled at/before/after slot N; contributes(A,C) states that activity A contributes to capability C; depends(C1,C2) says that capability C1 shall be implemented strictly after capability C2; maturity(C,N) states that capability C has maturity level N.

Tab. 2 presents the inference rules (syntax head :- tail.) to generate plans. By default, the program returns all possible plans that satisfy the constraints. A plan is defined as a set of predicates chosen(A,N), each stating that the deployment of activity A will be scheduled in slot N. Rules without a head (those starting with ":-") are integrity constraints: the condition expressed in the tail shall not become true in any model.

Table 2. Core disjunctive Datalog inference rules for deriving plans

Id	Rule definition
1	chosen(A,T) :- activity(A), slot(T,_), not chosenNotT(A,T), not missingReq(A,T).
2	chosenNotT(A,T) :- activity(A), chosen(A,T2), slot(T,_), slot(T2,_), T2!=T.
3	:- activity(A), 0=#count{T: chosen(A,T)}.
4	:- slot(T,_), 0=#count{A : chosen(A,T)}.
5	chosen(A,T) :- actAt(A,T).
6	:- delAt(D,T), T1=T-1, producedAt(D,T1).
7	:- delAt(D,T), not producedAt(D,T).
8	:- actBefore(A,T), chosen(A,T1), T1>=T.
9	:- delBefore(D,T), 0=#count{T1 : producedAt(D,T1), T1<T}.
10	:- actAfter(A,T), chosen(A,T1), T1<=T.
11	:- delAfter(D,T), 0=#count{T1 : producedAt(D,T1), T1>=T, not producedAt(D,T)}.
12	:- slot(T,B), #int(C), C=#sum{Cs,Act : cost(Act,Cs), chosen(Act,T)}, C>B.
13	missingReq(A,T) :- uses(A,D), #int(T), not producedAt(D,T), T2=#max{T1 : slot(T1,_)}, T2<=Z.
14	producedAt(D,T) :- chosen(A,T1), #int(T1), #int(T), T1<=T, produces(A,D), T3=#max{T2 : slot(T2,_)}, T3<=Z.
15	uses(A,D1) :- produces(A,D), requires(D,D1).
16	uses(A,D) :- updates(A,D).
17	requires(D1,D3) :- requires(D1,D2), requires(D2,D3).
18	hasOnePart(D) :- atLeastOnePart(D), produces(A,D), chosen(A,T), hasPart(D,D1), producedAt(D1,T).
19	:- atLeastOnePart(D), not hasOnePart(D).
20	:- allParts(D), produces(A,D), chosen(A,T), hasPart(D,D1), not producedAt(D1,T).
21	:- contributes(A1,C1), contributes(A2,C2), A1!=A2, depends(C1,C2), chosen(A1,T1), chosen(A2,T2), T1<=T2.
22	minmaturity(A,M) :- activity(A), M=#min{L : contributes(A,C), maturity(C,L)}.
23	penalty(Cs) :- #int(Cs), Cs=#sum{C,A1,A2 : chosen(A1,T1), chosen(A2,T2), T1<T2, minmaturity(A1,M1), minmaturity(A2,M2), M1>M2, C=M1-M2}.

Rules 1–3 ensure that all activities are assigned to exactly one slot. Rule 4 guarantees that all slots have at least one assigned activity. Rules 5–7 deal with actAt and delAt constraints: the activity (the deliverable) shall be scheduled (produced) in the specified slot. Rules 8–9 and rules 10–11 guarantee the fulfillment of the similar constraints in the before/after variant. Rule 12 ensures that the sum of the costs for implementing the activities in a slot does not exceed the slot budget. Rules 13–14 ensure that deliverables are produced before their use. Rule 15 states that an activity A uses a deliverable D1 if X produces D, and D requires D1. Rule 16 says that updating a deliverable implies using it. Rule 17 says that the requires relationship is transitive. Rules 18–20 take care of atLeastOnePart(D) (allParts(D)): at least one part of D (all parts) shall be available when D is produced. Rule 21 handles the depends(C1,C2) relationship between capabilities: all activities that contribute to C1 are scheduled strictly before any activity that contributes to C2. Rules 22–23 compute the penalty of the plan as in Def. 6.

The program can be run with different parameters to return only optimal and quasi-optimal plans. By adding the rule :∼ penalty(Cs). [Cs:1], only the plans with minimum penalty are listed (":∼" is a weak constraint that DLV optimizes by returning the models that minimize it). In order to return all quasi-optimal plans, the parameter "-costbound=Δ" can be specified when executing DLV.

7 Illustration

We apply our planning method to the scenario of Example 1 and Fig. 4. Kano analysis uses a two-dimensional quality model used for the analysis of customer requirements, which is useful to elicit customer needs about a service or product under design. It uses two types of questionnaires and an evaluation table for classifying the requirements into different categories [13]. We show how the company can use our method to identify an incremental plan to introduce the 15 activities and 13 deliverables of Kano analysis.

Step 1: Define the Planning Context. We begin with the creation of a PDD model that describes the changes to introduce (Kano analysis, as in Fig. 4), the organizational context (our example organization), and the cost function that returns the costs for each activity. In this example, we use a simple cost scheme, where we use natural numbers in the range [1,5] to describe the complexity of implementing and learning each activity. For each activity, we add a fact as input to our datalog program: cost(analyze_customer_problems, 4). cost(analyze_product_environment, 2)., etc.

Step 2: Set Scheduling Constraints. This activity involves the specification of the number of slots for implementing the plan, and the budget for each of them. Here, we define four slots, each with a budget of nine cost units (adopting the same unit as for activities cost). We do not define any temporal constraint, and we set $\Delta = 25$.

Step 3: Run Planning. When we run our planner with the settings above, we obtain 1,442 plans, with penalties between 8 and 22. Making a choice at this point would obviously be difficult; moreover, no optimal plan exists (no plan has penalty 0). Some constraints have to be introduced.

Step 4: Strengthen Constraints. The company wants to have a running implementation of Kano analysis in slot 0. This requires to have at least a table of results based on requirements from the customer and the product environment. More advanced tools, such as the QI-index plots and the CS-coefficient plots, can be introduced later. To such extent, the following temporal constraints are added:

delAt(tables_of_results, 0). delAfter(cs_coefficient_plots, 0). delAfter(qi_index_plots, 0). actAt(analyze_product_environment, 0). actAt(evaluate_answer_frequencies, 1).

When we re-run the planner, we obtain no results. By forcing the planner to schedule the activity that produces the table of results at slot 0, the require relationships between the deliverables imply that several other activities have to be schedules in slot 0 as well. Their total cost exceeds the budget of slot 0. This forces us to relax some constraints.

Step 5: Relax Constraints. To cope with the required effort for implementing the table of results in slot 0, the organization can either combine the effort of multiple slots, thereby lengthening the implementation time, or allocate more resources to slot 0. We assume the analyst opts for the latter: the budget of slot 0 is raised to 20, but a slight reduction in the overall budget is required (-4 units); the remaining units are allocated in two slots with budget 6, and the last slot is removed.

Table 3. Slot allocation for the activities of Kano analysis: the (quasi-)optimal plans in Step 5

Activity	Plan A	Plan B	Plan C	Plan D	Plan E
analyze_customer_problems	0	0	0	0	0
analyze_product_environment	0	0	0	0	0
analyze_conditions_of_applications	2	2	2	1	1
gather_requirements	0	0	0	0	0
formulate_functional_questions	0	0	0	0	0
formulate_dysfunctional_questions	0	0	0	0	0
assemble_questionnaire	0	0	0	0	0
conduct_customer_interview	0	0	0	0	0
combine_func._and_dysfunc._answers	0	0	0	0	0
list_results_of_individual_criteria	0	0	0	0	0
evaluate_answer_frequencies	1	1	1	1	1
construct_satisfactory_ranking_scale	1	1	2	2	1
construct_importance_ranking_scale	1	2	1	1	2
determine_quality_improvement_index	2	2	1	2	2
calculate_satisfaction_coefficient	2	1	2	2	2
penalty	8	8	8	12	12

When we re-run our planner, we obtain 5 plans. Tab. 3 shows them and outlines their differences via a gray background color. Two of them have a penalty of 12, the other three have a penalty of 8. The analyst is free to consider a restricted set of plans. The choice is between introducing both plots in slot 2, implementing QI index plots first and then CS coefficient plots, or vice versa.

8   Discussion and Future Directions

We have presented a method that assists analysts in the planning phase of method evolution, i.e., to identify plans for implementing a set of changes in an organization. Our method enables representing changes via PDD models, and is supported by our graphical modeling tool. The method includes the automated generation of plans that comply with scheduling constraints, and that maximize incremental growth in maturity, by trying to introduce changes according to an increasing maturity level. We also propose a process that guides analysts in refining plans by strengthening and relaxing constraints.

This work is performed within the context of the Online Method Engine, and it touches upon several related fields. We discuss our approach in the light of these fields.

Software Process Improvement. Research in the area of software process improvement has produced effective frameworks to determine what to change, including CMMI [6] and SPICE [8]. We complement these works by proposing a method for planning the implementation order of these changes.

Situational Method Engineering. This discipline deals with describing, constructing and adapting software development methods for a specific situational context, thus promoting reuse of standardized approaches while maintaining flexibility [11,12,3]. In this research, we employ the method fragment concept [5] for compatibility with the OME system; however, other notations can be used, as long as they satisfy the requirements of Sec. 4.1. There has been some work related to the notion of method evolution [18,17]. Most approaches in method evolution consist of manual activities, although some approaches support (semi-)automatic method construction [1].

Automated Planning. The problem of identifying a plan to reach a given goal is well-known in Artificial Intelligence [10]. Recent planners are able to deal with sophisticated planning constraints on state trajectory, preferences, soft constraints, and plan quality [9]. Our approach differentiates from existing solutions in that it employs a capability-driven planning policy that takes in to account deliverable-based constraints, as opposed the activity-based constraints that are typical of AI planning. We do not preclude that an extended version of our framework could employ PDDL.

Project Management. The implementation of a set of changes in the methods of an organization is usually executed in the form of a project. Project management is a very mature field, which offers effective mechanisms and tools to deal with change by planning, scheduling, and controlling it [14]. Our approach is inspired by this field, but focuses on a very specific type of scheduling that relates to method change.

We have focused only on introducing new fragments; the next step is to consider the removal and replacement of fragments. We will also explore the preceding step of *method construction*. Furthermore, we plan to convert our prototype into a comprehensive tool that supports the analysts in the plan refinement process by recommending possible refinements. We will evaluate the efficacy of our approach with case studies in the industry, and based on the feedback from practitioners, we will extend the supported constraints. Finally, we aim to assess the scalability of our reasoning techniques.

References

1. Aharoni, A., Reinhartz-Berger, I.: Semi-automatic composition of situational methods. Journal of Database Management 22(4) (2011)
2. Baddoo, N.: De-motivators for software process improvement: an analysis of practitioners' views. Journal of Systems and Software 66, 23–33 (2003)
3. Becker, J., Knackstedt, R.: Configurative method engineering – on the applicability of reference modeling mechanisms in method engineering. In: Proc. of AMCIS, pp. 1–12 (2007)
4. Bekkers, W., Spruit, M., van de Weerd, I., van Vliet, R., Mahieu, A.: A situational assessment method for software product management. In: Proc. of ECIS, pp. 22–34 (2010)
5. Brinkkemper, S.: Method engineering: engineering of information systems development methods and tools. Information and Software Technology 38(4), 275–280 (1996)
6. CMMI Product Team: Capability Maturity Model Integration (CMMI). Tech. Rep. December 2001, Carnegie Mellon Software Engineering Institute, Pittsburgh (2002)
7. Diaz, M., Sligo, J.: How software process improvement helped Motorola. IEEE Software 14(5), 75–81 (1997)
8. Dorling, A.: SPICE: Software Process Improvement and Capability Determination. Software Quality Journal 2(4), 209–224 (1993)
9. Gerevini, A., Long, D.: Plan constraints and preferences in PDDL3 – the language of the fifth international planning competition. Tech. rep., University of Brescia (2005)
10. Ghallab, M., Nau, D., Traverso, P.: Automated planning: theory & practice. Elsevier (2004)
11. Harmsen, F., Brinkkemper, S., Oei, J.L.H.: Situational method engineering for informational system project approaches. In: Proc. of the IFIP WG8.1 Working Conference on Methods and Associated Tools for the Information Systems Life Cycle, pp. 169–194 (1994)
12. Henderson-Sellers, B., Gonzalez-Perez, C.: Granularity in conceptual modelling: Application to metamodels. In: Parsons, J., Saeki, M., Shoval, P., Woo, C., Wand, Y. (eds.) ER 2010. LNCS, vol. 6412, pp. 219–232. Springer, Heidelberg (2010)
13. Kano, N., Seraku, N., Takahashi, F., Tsuji, S.: Attractive quality and must-be quality. The Journal of the Japanese Society for Quality Control 14(2), 39–48 (1984)
14. Kerzner, H.R.: Project management: a systems approach to planning, scheduling, and controlling. Wiley (2013)
15. Leone, N., Pfeifer, G., Faber, W., Eiter, T., Gottlob, G., Perri, S., Scarcello, F.: The DLV system for knowledge representation and reasoning. ACM Transactions on Computational Logic 7(3), 499–562 (2006)
16. Pino, F.J., Pedreira, O., García, F., Luaces, M.R., Piattini, M.: Using Scrum to guide the execution of software process improvement in small organizations. Journal of Systems and Software 83(10), 1662–1677 (2010)
17. Ralyté, J., Rolland, C., Ayed, M.B.: An approach for evolution-driven method engineering. In: Information Modeling Methods and Methodologies, pp. 80–202 (2005)
18. Rossi, M., Ramesh, B., Lyytinen, K., Tolvanen, J.P.: Managing evolutionary method engineering by method rationale. Journal of the Association for Information Systems 5(9), 356–391 (2004)
19. Simon, H.A.: Rational choice and the structure of the environment. Psychological Review 63(2), 129–138 (1956)
20. Tolvanen, J.P., Rossi, M.: MetaEdit+: Defining and using domain-specific modeling languages and code generators. In: Crocker, R., Steele Jr., G.L. (eds.) Proc. of OOPSLA (2003)

21. Vlaanderen, K., van Stijn, P., Brinkkemper, S., van de Weerd, I.: Growing into Agility: Process Implementation Paths for Scrum. In: Dieste, O., Jedlitschka, A., Juristo, N. (eds.) PROFES 2012. LNCS, vol. 7343, pp. 116–130. Springer, Heidelberg (2012)
22. Vlaanderen, K., van de Weerd, I., Brinkkemper, S.: On the design of a knowledge management system for incremental process improvement for software product management. International Journal of Information System Modelling and Design 3(4), 46–66 (2012)
23. van de Weerd, I., Brinkkemper, S.: Meta-modeling for situational analysis and design methods. In: Handbook of Research on Modern Systems Analysis and Design Technologies and Applications, ch. III, pp. 35–54 (2008)
24. van de Weerd, I., Brinkkemper, S., Versendaal, J.: Concepts for incremental method evolution: Empirical exploration and validation in requirements management. In: Krogstie, J., Opdahl, A.L., Sindre, G. (eds.) CAiSE 2007 and WES 2007. LNCS, vol. 4495, pp. 469–484. Springer, Heidelberg (2007)

On the Effectiveness of Concern Metrics to Detect Code Smells: An Empirical Study

Juliana Padilha[1], Juliana Pereira[1], Eduardo Figueiredo[1], Jussara Almeida[1],
Alessandro Garcia[2], and Cláudio Sant'Anna[3]

[1] Computer Science Department, Federal University of Minas Gerais, Belo Horizonte, Brazil
{juliana.padilha,juliana.pereira,figueiredo,jussara}@dcc.ufmg.br
[2] Informatics Department, Pontifical Catholic University of Rio de Janeiro (PUC-RIO), Brazil
afgarcia@inf.puc-rio.br
[3] Computer Science Department, Federal University of Bahia (UFBA), Brazil
santanna@dcc.ufba.br

Abstract. Traditional software metrics have been used to evaluate the maintainability of software programs by supporting the identification of code smells. Recently, concern metrics have also been proposed with this purpose. While traditional metrics quantify properties of software modules, concern metrics quantify concern properties, such as scattering and tangling. Despite being increasingly used in empirical studies, there is a lack of empirical knowledge about the effectiveness of concern metrics to detect code smells. This paper reports the results of an empirical study to investigate whether concern metrics can be useful indicators of three code smells, namely Divergent Change, Shotgun Surgery, and God Class. In this study, 54 subjects from two different institutions have analyzed traditional and concern metrics aiming to detect instances of these code smells in two information systems. The study results indicate that, in general, concern metrics support developers detecting code smells. In particular, we observed that (i) the time spent in code smell detection is more relevant than the developers' expertise; (ii) concern metrics are clearly useful to detect Divergent Change and God Class; and (iii) the concern metric Number of Concerns per Component is a reliable indicator of Divergent Change.

Keywords: Empirical evaluation, Metrics, Code Smells, Concerns.

1   Introduction

The modularization of the driving design concerns is a key factor to achieve maintainable information systems [16, 21]. A concern is any important property or area of interest of a system that we want to treat in a modular way [23]. Business rules, distribution, persistence, and security are examples of typical concerns found in many information systems and that are important, albeit hard, to achieve full modularization. The inadequate separation of concerns degrades design modularity and may lead to maintainability-related design flaws [6, 11]. Detection of these design flaws by programmers is far from trivial and requires effective support.

Software metrics are the key means for assessing the maintainability of information systems [3, 7]. The community of software metrics has traditionally explored quantifiable module properties, such as class coupling, cohesion, and interface size, in order to identify maintainability problems in a software project [3, 8, 19, 20].

M. Jarke et al. (Eds.): CAiSE 2014, LNCS 8484, pp. 656–671, 2014.
© Springer International Publishing Switzerland 2014

More specifically, software measurement is also seen as a pragmatic solution to find symptoms of particular design flaws, such as code smells [17, 19]. Code smells are symptoms that something may be wrong in the system code [12].

Marinescu [19], for instance, relies on traditional metrics to compose strategies aiming to detect code smells. However, some code smells are often a direct result of poor separation of concerns, and traditional module-driven measurement cannot be tailored to quantify properties of concern modularity. Whereas traditional metrics quantify the properties of modules, the concern metrics quantify properties of concerns, such as scattering and tangling [10]. A growing number of concern metrics have been proposed [5, 6] aiming to quantify key characteristics of concerns' implementation. Indeed, concern metrics have been applied with different purposes and used in several empirical studies. They are used, for instance, to compare aspect-oriented and object-oriented programming techniques [4, 11, 13, 14] and to identify crosscutting concerns that should be refactored [6]. However, we still lack empirical knowledge on the effectiveness of concern metrics to support code smell detection in information systems.

To fill this gap, this paper presents an empirical investigation of the effectiveness of concern metrics compared with traditional metrics on the identification of code smells. We report the results of a series of experiments relying on two benchmark information systems, named Health Watcher [14] and MobileMedia [11]. This study focuses on a two-dimension analysis comparing the trade-offs on the recall and time efficiency of code smell detection. To analyze the recall, we compare classes identified as suspects of exhibiting a code smell with the reference list of code smells provided by the actual developers in each information system. We also assess time efficiency based on the recorded time spent by each subject in the experimental tasks.

This empirical study involved 54 subjects, which were divided into three groups. Subjects of each group participated on the analysis of one of three different sets of metrics: (i) *only traditional metrics*, (ii) *only concern metrics*, and (iii) both traditional and concern metrics, called *hybrid metrics* from now on. These metrics were previously applied to the source code of both target information systems. Subjects then analyzed the values of metrics aiming to detect three specific code smells, namely Divergent Change [12], Shotgun Surgery [12], and God Class [22]. Our overall results confirmed that concern metrics, in fact, contribute to improve the detection of these code smells. More specifically, this study shows that (i) concern metrics are clearly useful to detect Divergent Change and God Class; (ii) the subject's level of experience does not have significant impact on detection rates; (iii) time explains most of the variations observed in detection rates; and (iv) recall of each metric suite is largely dependent on the adequacy of each metric to quantify a property explicitly mentioned in the smell definition.

The rest of this paper is organized as follows. Section 2 summarizes the concepts of software metrics and code smells. Section 3 describes the study procedures. Sections 4 and 5 discuss the main results of this empirical study. Section 6 discusses the study limitations and related work. Section 7 concludes this paper and points out directions for future work.

2   Software Metrics and Code Smells

Software metrics have played an important role in understanding and analyzing information systems [3, 7, 17]. For the purpose of this study, software metrics can be divided into three sets: traditional metrics (Section 2.1), concern metrics (Section 2.2), and hybrid metrics; i.e., a combination of both traditional and concern metrics. Section 2.3 describes the three code smells that we investigate in this study.

2.1   Traditional Metrics

We selected a set of the most widely used metrics to be a baseline in this study. The selected set includes object-oriented (OO) metrics proposed by Chidamber and Kemerer [3] and well-documented metrics in the software engineering literature [7]. Table 1 summarizes the metrics used in this study, while detailed definitions can be found elsewhere [3, 7].

Table 1. Definitions of Traditional Metrics

Metric	Definition
Coupling between Objects (CBO)	Number of classes from which a class calls methods or accesses attributes.
Lack of Cohesion in Methods (LCOM)	Divides pairs of methods that do not access common attributes by pairs that do access.
Lines of Code (LOC)	Total number of lines of code.
Number of Attributes (NOA)	Number of attributes defined in a class.
Number of Methods (NOM)	Number of methods defined in a class.
Weighted Methods per Class (WMC)	Number of methods and their parameters in a class

We selected the most common and widely used traditional metrics for several reasons. First, it is still not well known whether some particular combinations of these metrics can precisely detect specific code smells. Hence, finding combinations involving either concern or traditional metrics might be a relevant result of this paper. Second, we aim to select a reduced number of metrics since many metrics could make the analysis harder and with redundant measurements. Finally, the selected metrics have been used in previous work [8, 11, 19] and they seem to assist developers in software maintenance tasks.

2.2   Concern Metrics

Concern metrics have been defined aiming to capture modularity properties associated with the realization of concerns in software artifacts [10]. Their goal is the identification of specific design flaws [6] or design degeneration caused by poor modularization of concerns [9]. Some recent studies [6, 8] have also shown that concern metrics can be useful indicators of defect-prone modules. Concern is something that you may want to treat as a modular unit, including non-functional requirements and programming language idioms [23]. Concern metrics rely on a mapping between concerns and design elements [9, 10]. The mapping consists of assigning a concern to the corresponding design elements that realize it. Table 2 presents a brief definition of the concern metrics evaluated in this paper.

Table 2. Definitions of Concern-based Metrics

Metric	Definition
Concern Diffusion over Components (CDC)	Number of classes whose main purpose is to contribute to the implementation of a concern and the number of other classes that access them.
Concern Diffusion over Operations (CDO)	Number of methods whose main function is to implement a concern.
Concern Diffusions over LOC (CDLOC)	Number of transition points for each concern through the lines of code. Transition points are points in the code where there is a "concern switch".
Number Concerns per Component (NCC)	Number of concern in each class.

A more detailed description and discussion of these metrics can be found elsewhere [4, 6, 10, 13]. These metrics were selected for evaluation in this paper because they have been successfully used in a number of studies related to software maintainability [11, 13, 14]. However, no systematic study has been performed to evaluate whether these concern metrics support code smell detection.

2.3   Code Smells

Code smells were proposed by Kent Beck in Fowler's book [12] as a mean to diagnose symptoms that may be indicative of something wrong in the system code. This paper investigates the use of concern metrics to detect three code smells, namely Divergent Change [12], Shotgun Surgery [12] and God Class [22], which are described below. These code smells were chosen because they recurrently appear in information systems and are related to poor modularization of concerns [2, 19].

Divergent Change. This smell occurs when one class is often changed in different ways for different reasons [12]. For example, we have to change three methods of a class every time we get a new database or we have to change other four methods every time there is a new financial instrument. Depending on the number of assignments of a given class, it may undergo unrelated changes. The fact that a class undergoes various kinds of changes can be associated with a symptom of concern tangling [2].

Shotgun Surgery. This code smell is somehow the opposite of Divergent Change. We identify a Shotgun Surgery instance every time we make a kind of change that leads to a lot of small changes in many different classes [12]. In other words, this code smell can lead to small changes in classes that have a common concern [2].

God Class. This code smell describes an object that knows too much or does too much [22]. It represents a class that has grown beyond all logic to become the class that does almost everything in the system [22]. In a different view, we can say that God Class implements too many concerns and, so, it has too many responsibilities [2].

3   Study Settings

This study aims at evaluating the effectiveness of concern metrics in detecting code smells. Our study relies on traditional metrics as baseline. Therefore, we perform a comparative analysis between traditional and concern metrics in order to identify whether the latter supports the former in detecting three specific code smells. Section 3.1 introduces the two target information systems. Sections 3.2 and 3.3 present, respectively, the reference list of code smells and background information for the subjects that took part in this study. Finally, Section 3.4 explains the tasks assigned to each subject.

3.1   Target Systems

Our study involved two information systems: Health Watcher [14] and MobileMedia [11]. These systems were selected because they have been previously used in other maintainability-related studies [4, 8, 11, 18], and we have access to their developers and experts. Therefore, we were able to recover a reference list of actual code smells for each analyzed information system (see Section 3.2). A brief description of the Health Watcher and MobileMedia functionalities and their key concerns are described below. Most of these concerns recurrently appear in typical information systems.

Health Watcher. It is a Web-based information system that supports the registration and management of complaints to the public health system [14]. This system has about 6 KLOC. Some concerns implemented in Health Watcher that we used are: *Business*, *Concurrency*, *Distribution*, *Exception Handling*, *Persistence*, and *View*.

MobileMedia. Our study also involved the 7th version of the MobileMedia system [11]. This system is a software product line (SPL) with about 4 KLOC for applications that manipulate photo, music, and video on mobile devices. The concerns of our interest in MobileMedia are: *Sorting*, *Favorites*, *Exception Handling*, *Security*, and *Persistence*.

3.2 Code Smells Reference List

Before conducting the study, we performed a systematic code analysis of Health Watcher and MobileMedia aiming to determine which classes were affected by the relevant code smells. We also relied on two experts in each information system to help us building the reference lists. These experts participated of the development, maintenance, or assessment of the systems. Our goal was to detect actual instances of each code smell in both systems. Table 3 presents classes in the final reference list of each code smell per system.

Reference List Protocol. Each expert was instructed to individually use their own strategy for detecting code smells in the system classes. As a result, different strategies were used. One expert focused on code inspection following more traditional code analysis. Following a different path, another expert used a complementary set of automated detection strategies [18] to identify candidate instances of the three code smells. For each code smell, the sets of potential instances – one set from each expert – were not exactly the same, although they have many classes in common (approximately 80% and 75% for Health Watcher and MobileMedia, respectively). In order to achieve a consensus, we promoted discussions among experts of the same system. The result of their discussion was recorded as a joint decision and double-checked by ourselves.

Table 3. Code Smell Reference List for Health Watcher and MobileMedia

System	Smell	Classes in the Reference List
Health Watcher	Divergent Change	EmployeeRecord, HealthWatcherFacade, HealthUnitRecord, PersistenceMechanism, IFacade, HealthWatcherFacadeInit, IPersistenceMechanism, ServletInsertEmployee, ComplaintRecord, ServletSearchComplaintData, ServletUpdateComplaintData, ServletUpdateHealthUnitData
	Shotgun Surgery	PersistenceMechanism, ComplaintRecordRDB, EmployeeRepositoryRDB, IComplaintRepository, HealthUnitRepositoryRDB, IPersistenceMechanism, IHealthUnitRepository, IEmployeeRepository
	God Class	HealthWatcherFacade, HealthWatcherFacadeInit, PersistenceMechanism
Mobile Media	Divergent Change	ImageMediaAccessor, MediaController, MediaAcessor, MediaListController
	Shotgun Surgery	ControllerInterface, MediaAccessor, ScreenSingleton

3.3 Background of Subjects

This study involved a set of 54 subjects, named S1 to S54, from two different institutions (UFMG/Brazil and Lancaster/UK). Subjects from the 1st institution were 11 young IT professional taking an advanced SE course, 4 PhD candidates, and 12 undergraduate students. Subjects from the 2nd institution were 14 PhD candidates and 13 undergraduate students. We organized subjects in such a way that each group worked with only one set of metrics: traditional metrics, concern metrics, or hybrid metrics. The study was performed using the OO designs of both information systems. We conducted 13 rounds of the experiment in different dates. Subjects were organized as follows: (i) 24 subjects detected Divergent Change in 6 rounds, (ii) 20 subjects detected Shotgun Surgery in 5 rounds, and (iii) 10 subjects detected God Class in 2 rounds. Health Watcher was used by subjects of Lancaster to detect all three code smells, while MobileMedia was used by subjects of UFMG to detect Divergent Change and Shotgun Surgery. Further details about the distribution of subjects are available at the project website [1].

Before running the experiment, we used a background questionnaire (also available at [1]) to balance previous knowledge of each subject. Table 4 summarizes knowledge that subjects claimed to have in the background questionnaire. Although the subjects were asked to answer the questionnaire, it was not compulsory. Therefore, some subjects annotated in the last column (No Answer) in Table 4 have not answered the questionnaire. In fact, we asked subject to indicate their level of knowledge by choosing one of the following options: none, few, moderate, and high experience. The other columns list subjects who claimed to have moderate or high knowledge in a particular skill.

Subjects answered questions about their level of knowledge with respect to Class Diagrams, Java Programming, and Software Metrics. Furthermore, they indicated their previous academic and work experience. Some subjects do not appear in a row because they have few or none experience in that particular topic. For instance, with respect to work experience in detecting Divergent Change, subjects S1 to S3 (and others) have not answered the questionnaire, while subjects S4, S27, S39-S44, and S47 claimed to have none or little knowledge in Java Programming. In general, excluding 13 subjects who have not answered the background questionnaire, we have observed that (i) about 60% of the subjects have moderate to high knowledge in Class Diagram and Java Programming; and (ii) 70% of the subjects have moderate to high

Table 4. Background Data of Subjects

Divergent Change		Traditional	Concern	Hybrid	No Answer
Knowledge	Class Diagram	S5 - S6	S9 - S11	S14 - S24	S1, S2, S3, S7, S8, S12, S13, S18
	Java Programming	S5 - S6	S9 - S11	S14 - S24	
	Measurement	-	S9	S16, S20, S22, S24	
	Academic Experience	S4, S6	S9	S19, S21-S24	
	Work Experience	S5	S10,S11	S14 - S17, S20	
Shotgun Surgery					
Knowledge	Class Diagram	S28, S29	S31, S32	S34 - S37	S25, S26, S30, S33, S38
	Java Programming	S28, S29	S31, S32	S34 - S37	
	Measurement	-	S31	S35, S36	
	Academic Experience	S27, S29	S31	S39, S41-S44	
	Work Experience	S28	S32	S33 - S37, S40	
God Class					
Knowledge	Class Diagram	S46	S48 - S50	S51- S54	
	Java Programming	S45, S46	S48 - S50	S51- S54	-
	Measurement	-	S49 - S50	S52 -S54	
	Academic Experience	S46, S47	S49, S50	S52-S54	
	Work Experience	S45	S48	S51	

knowledge in at least one topic. Therefore, in general, all subjects have at least basic knowledge required to perform the experimental tasks, and subjects are fairly distributed among the groups of metrics.

3.4   Experimental Tasks

The study was preceded by a 30-minute training session to allow subjects to familiarize themselves with the evaluated metrics and the target code smells. After the training session, each subject received a document containing: (i) a brief explanation and a partial view of the system design as a Class Diagram, and (ii) a description of the concerns involved in the respective information systems. The document also described steps and guidelines that subjects should follow, the questions they should answer, and information they should register. In addition, we provided subjects with the results of the metrics in the respective information system under analysis. In order to identify the classes with code smells, we asked subjects to reason about the metrics and identify which of them (alone or combined with other metrics) provide relevant indicators based on the code smell description. We also asked subjects to register the time taken to conclude the experimental tasks and to explain which metrics they used or not to detect each code smell. Each group of subjects (traditional, concern or hybrid) only had access to the results of metrics to which they were assigned. Subjects had no access to source code of the information systems.

4   Results

This section presents the results of our experiments. Section 4.1 introduces the recall and precision metrics, while Sections 4.2 to 4.4 report the results per code smell.

4.1   Evaluation Metrics: Recall and Precision

We rely on three metrics, namely True Positive (TP), False Positive (FP), and False Negative (FN), collected based on the reference lists (Section 3.2). True Positive and False Positive quantify the number of correctly and wrongly identified code smells by a subject. False Negative, on the other hand, quantifies the number of code smells a subject missed out. Based on these metrics, we quantify recall and precision, presented below, to support our analysis. Recall measures the fraction of relevant classes listed by a subject. Relevant classes are classes that appear in the reference list (TP + FN). Precision measures the ratio of correctly detected smells by the total classes a subject listed (TP + FP).

$$\text{Recall (R)} = \frac{TP}{TP + FN} \qquad \text{Precision (P)} = \frac{TP}{TP + FP}$$

We focus our discussion mainly on recall because it is a measure of completeness. That is, high recall means that the subject was able to identify most code smells in the system. High precision, on the other hand, means that a subject indicated more relevant (TP) than irrelevant (FP) code smells. For code smell detection, a large number of false positives are preferred over a large number of false negatives, because manual inspection, which is inevitable, tends to uncover false positives.

4.2   Concern Metrics Support Divergent Change Detection

Table 5 presents the results for the identification of Divergent Change. Rows in this table present three pieces of data: Recall (R), Precision (P), and the Time (T) in minutes used by subjects to complete their tasks. In total, 24 subjects had to identify Divergent Change in the target systems. Table 5 shows that subjects in the concern and hybrid groups achieved better results than those in the traditional group. The average recall of the concern group was 62%. Two out of five subjects in this group identified all code smells (100% of recall). On the other hand, the best achievement by a subject using only traditional metric was 33% of recall. Results of subjects in the hybrid group vary from 0% to 100% of recall (S19 and S16) being on average 41%. These results reveal that, even when analyzed in isolation, concern metrics are an effective means for Divergent Change detection.

Table 5. Results for Divergent Change

Group	Traditional						Concern						
Subject	S1	S2	S3	S4	S5	S6	S7	S8	S9	S10	S11		
R(%)	17	17	17	33	25	25	100	100	33	25	50		
P(%)	67	50	40	50	17	25	63	100	100	25	29		
T(min)	15	15	40	38	41	36	26	29	29	15	33		
Group	Hybrid												
Subject	S12	S13	S14	S15	S16	S17	S18	S19	S20	S21	S22	S23	S24
R(%)	75	8	25	50	100	25	50	0	50	25	50	25	50
P(%)	100	50	75	25	67	33	40	0	67	17	40	17	50
T(min)	40	31	23	36	27	39	24	11	18	19	13	13	12

4.3   Hard to Detect Shotgun Surgery with Metrics

Table 6, which follows the same structure of Table 5, presents the results for Shotgun Surgery. Note that no group of subjects stands out with good results in this scenario. In fact, only one subject in each group achieved more than 60% of recall: S28 scored 67% analyzing traditional metrics, S30 scored 75% in the concern group, and S35 scored 67% of recall analyzing hybrid metrics. The concern group performed a little better: all subjects scored more than 25% of recall and the average recall was 44%. However, the poor detection rates for almost all subjects suggest that the used metrics cannot properly indicate Shotgun Surgery instances.

Table 6. Results for Shotgun Surgery

Group	Traditional					Concern							
Subject	S25	S26	S27	S28	S29	S30	S31	S32					
R(%)	13	13	0	67	33	75	25	33					
P(%)	25	33	0	25	25	35	40	25					
T(min)	6	10	27	12	14	13	28	14					
Group	Hybrid												
Subject	S33	S34	S35	S36	S37	S38	S39	S40	S41	S42	S43	S44	
R(%)	13	50	67	33	33	33	0	0	33	0	0	0	
P(%)	25	80	6	33	25	33	0	0	20	0	0	0	
T(min)	35	14	19	15	4	10	14	9	21	3	7	5	

In addition to a poor recall, almost all subjects (except S34) also had low precision rates. In fact, more than half of the Shotgun Surgery instances detected by the subjects were incorrect, regardless of the metrics used. Interestingly, the subjects detecting Shotgun Surgery in general spent less time (on average) in their tasks than the subjects assigned to detect other code smells. That is, although subjects could not succeed detecting Shotgun Surgery, they did not take much longer to conclude their tasks. This result might indicate that, if developers do not have appropriate means to detect a code smell, they give up with their duties soon.

4.4   Joint Data Analysis Favor God Class Detection

Table 7 presents the results of God Class. Data in this table suggests that traditional metrics when used in isolation do not offer appropriate means to detect God Class. Two subjects (S45 and S46) in the traditional group scored only 33% of both recall and precision. This low performance is much worse than the one achieved by the concern and hybrid groups. For example, two out of three subjects in the concern group and three out of four subjects in the hybrid group scored 100% of recall. Subjects S49 and S51 are exceptions. In addition, S52 in the hybrid group achieved full precision and recall. Therefore, joint analysis of concern and traditional metrics seems to succeed in detecting this particular code smell.

Table 7. Results for God Class

Group	Traditional			Concern			Hybrid			
Subject	S45	S46	S47	S48	S49	S50	S51	S52	S53	S54
R(%)	33	33	67	100	67	100	33	100	100	100
P(%)	33	33	67	75	100	75	50	100	60	75
T(min)	18	25	27	37	66	43	22	53	51	35

5   Statistical Analysis and Discussions

This section aims to answer three research questions. We focus on the most interesting results, but the complete raw data can be found on the project website [1]. Section 5.1 analyzes the recall of concern metrics compared to the traditional metrics. Section 5.2 discusses to which extent the background of subjects and the time spent impact the recall of code smell detection. Section 5.3 analyzes possible combinations of metrics that increases the recall of identifying each code smell.

5.1   Comparing Concern Metrics and Traditional Metrics

The main goal of this paper is to evaluate the effectiveness of concern metrics to detect code smells. Towards that goal, this section aims to answer the following specific research question: **RQ1.** *How accurate do concern metrics perform in comparison with traditional metrics to detect code smells?*

We start by investigating whether the type of system (Health Watcher and MobileMedia) influences the detection of code smells. Table 8 shows average recall results for traditional, concern and hybrid metrics, along with corresponding values of variance, sample size (i.e., number of subjects who participated in the experiment) and 90% confidence intervals. Results are presented separately for each system - Health Watcher and MobileMedia - and for each type of code smell. We also show results for all code smells combined (row *All*). In order to check for statistically significant differences across systems, metrics and/or types of code smell, we perform an unpaired t-test[1] with 90% confidence level [15].

---

[1] We perform an analysis of unpaired observation since we got independent samples from two populations.

Focusing first on the use of concern metrics to detect code smells in general (i.e., row *All*); we note that the confidence intervals computed for subjects who used concern metrics for the two systems do not overlap. Therefore, we can state that the results for the two systems are significantly different at the 90% confidence. As shown in Table 8, the results for the system analyzed – Health Watcher – are significantly better (75% higher recall, on average). In other words, detection of code smells using the concern metrics leads to higher recall while using the Health Watcher system. On the other hand, the two confidence intervals computed for the group of subjects who used traditional metrics do overlap. This fact indicated that the results for both systems are *not* statistically different, with 90% confidence. The same behavior is observed for the group of subjects who used hybrid metrics. In other words, whereas the system used does impact the detection of code smells using concern metrics, the detection using traditional and hybrids metrics is not significantly influenced by it.

Table 8. Confidence Intervals (CI) for the average recall in Health Watcher and MobileMedia

Systems	Health Watcher (HW)			Mobile Media (MM)		
Groups	*Traditional (T)*	*Concern (C)*	*Hybrid (H)*	*Traditional (T)*	*Concern (C)*	*Hybrid (H)*
All	(13.26, 35.34)	(54.59, 95.40)	(20.98, 91.02)	(18.70, 46.49)	(22.94, 49.32)	(19.08, 43.32)
DC	(11.6, 30.4)	(12.5, 142.9)	(-22.7, 94.8)	(23.9, 26.5)	(-41.4, 116.4)	(27.2, 57.9)
SS	(-4.0, 21.3)	(-107.9, 207.9)	(-85.3, 148.3)	(-57.3, 157.3)	(28.9, 37.9)	(6.4, 33.4)
GC	(11.2, 77.4)	(56.9, 121.1)	(43.8, 123)	-	-	-

Next, we applied the unpaired t-test (90% confidence level) to evaluate whether the concern metrics lead to significantly different results compared to the other groups of metrics for a fixed system, considering all code smells combined (row *All*). We found that the concern metrics produce significantly higher recall, compared to traditional metrics for the Health Watcher system. For the MobileMedia system, there is a statistical tie, at 90% confidence, though average results are better for the concern metrics. Moreover, we also found that the concern metrics outperform the hybrid metrics in both systems. Thus, we can state that, in general, concern metrics are the best ones, among those analyzed, for the detection of three types of code smells studied. Our intuition is that when the subjects use a greater set of metrics, such as hybrid metrics, they are not likely to obtain better accuracy compared to the concern metrics, since the quantity of metrics could hinder the detection of the code smell. We may argue that concern metrics would be more time efficient because (i) the set only includes four metrics, and (ii) their definitions capture concerns properties that might be related to the code smells.

We also examine whether the type of code smell detected influences the recall of concern metrics in comparison with traditional ones. We restrict our analysis to two code smells, Divergent Change and Shotgun Surgery, because God Class was not analyzed on MobileMedia. Our results indicate that there is no significant difference between the two systems in terms of recall, for any code smell. In other words, subjects were able to recover around the same rates of code smells, regardless of the analyzed system. This is an interesting result because it supports the claims that metrics abstract most of the system complexity [7]. Therefore, metric-based detection of code smells is expected to scale up to larger systems.

After ascertaining that the difference between the systems in terms of recall is not significant, we applied t-tests (90% confidence level) to compare concern metrics against traditional and hybrid metrics for each of three code smells separately, considering the results for both systems together (Table 8). Our results show that the superiority of the concern metrics varied according to the type of code smell. We observed that the use of concern metrics was consistently better in comparison with traditional metrics in the Divergent Change and God Class detection cases. However, the difference between both types of metrics for Shotgun Surgery is not statistically significant (with 90% confidence). Additionally, we observed that the difference between concern and hybrid metrics is not significant, independently of the type of code smell to be identified. These results indicate that the accuracy of the metric suite is largely dependent on the adequacy of each metric to quantify a property explicitly mentioned in the smell definition. For instance, God Class is characterized by the "high amount of class members with the realization of multiple responsibilities" [12].

This property is better captured by concern metrics. This probably explains why the concern metrics outperformed the traditional ones for God Class detection. Data also suggests that detecting Divergent Change with only traditional metrics seems harder when compared to the support of concern metrics. The explanation could be that this code smell is closely related to poor separation of concerns. Divergent Change often occurs when several concerns are tangled into a module [2]. Therefore, this module is likely to be changed by different reasons. Focusing on subjects that used concern metrics (concern and hybrid groups), it is interesting to note that 10 out of 18 subjects in either groups achieved 68% of recall on average.

5.2   Background of Subjects

Our goal in this section is to analyze whether the background of subjects can impact the results. In other words, we aim to answer the following research question: *RQ2. Does background of subjects impact the efficiency of the detected code smell?*

To answer RQ2, we evaluate the impact of both the background of subjects and the time spent by them on the effectiveness of the detection when using concern metrics. To that end, we apply a 2^k full factorial design with k=2 factors, namely the developers' work experience and the time spent in detected code smells [15]. As discussed in Section 3.3, all subjects have at least basic knowledge in the relevant topics of software development, namely UML Class Diagram, Java Programming, and Measurement. Therefore, we decided to draw this analysis with respect to work experience of subjects which varied a lot among subjects [1]. In this analysis, we excluded subjects that did not answer the background questionnaire (Section 3.3).

We focus on the recall of the detected code smells using the concern metrics as the response variable. For this analysis, we consider the results for all code smells and both systems together. Since we did not observe statistical difference in the recall of detection across systems when using concern metrics (Section 5.1), we grouped the results for both systems together for this analysis. Moreover, we also consider all three code smells indistinctly.

We divided subjects into two categories according to their work experience: (i) no experience indicates those subjects who never worked, or worked for fewer than 6 months, and (ii) some experience identifies those subjects who worked for at least 6 months in software development industry. Additionally, we also divided subjects into two categories according to the time spent in detected code smells: (i) short time indicates those subjects who took less than 33 minutes (overall average) to detect the code smells, and (ii) long time indicates those subjects who took at least 33 minutes.

In general, results show that the recall tends to increase with the work experience and the time spent in the detection, as one might expect. In order to quantify the relative impact of each of these factors on the subjects' recall, we compute the percentage of the variation in the measured recall that can be credited to each factor in isolation, as well as to the interaction of both factors. The higher the percentage of variation explained by a factor/interaction, the more important it is to the response variable [15].

Out of the total variation observed in our measurements, 96% can be attributed to the time spent in the detection, whereas only 4% is due to variations in the subjects' work experience and 1% can be attributed to the interaction of these two factors. Thus, both the work experience factor and the interaction seem of little importance to the final recall, compared to the time subjects spent in detecting the code smells. The latter has a major impact on the final recall. Indeed, the results clearly show that the subjects who spent more time to analyze the concern metrics achieved the better results in terms of recall. One possible explanation is the complexity of concern metrics, which require more time from subjects to successfully perform the detection. Additionally, even the subjects who have no experience tend to obtain a higher recall when they spend a longer time to detect the smell.

5.3   Metrics Flocking Together

In this section, we analyze possible metrics that might be useful to detect specific code smells and answer the following research question. *RQ3. Is there a combination of metrics that increases recall of code smell detection?*

As explained in Section 3.4, subjects reported the metrics they considered useful for each code smell. Based on their answers, we analyzed in this section the metrics that were considered useful by at least three subjects. In order to determine which metrics were used together to detect code smells, we performed analysis of subjects who used the same metrics and scored high in terms of recall. Table 9 shows the metrics that at least three subjects claimed to have used for Divergent Change. In this case, we also restricted our analyzes to metrics with average of recall higher than 30%. Both the Number Concern per Component (NCC) and Lack of Cohesion in Methods (LCOM) metrics were considered useful to detect Divergent Change by eleven subjects. Subjects that considered these metrics useful achieved 60% and 34% of recall in average, respectively. Additionally, the concern metric Concern Diffusion over Components (CDC) was considered useful by 3 subjects. It is interesting to observe that subjects that considered concern metrics NCC and CDC useful achieved better results in terms of recall.

Table 9. Metrics Considered Useful for Divergent Change

Metrics	NCC	LCOM	CDC	LOC
Subjects who used this metric	S7, S8, S9, S11, S12, S14, S15, S16, S20, S23, S24	S1, S2, S4, S6, S12, S13, S14, S15, S17, S22, S24	S8, S10, S23	S2, S17, S20
Average of recall	60%	34%	50%	31%

In particular, NCC seems the most effective metric (among the analyzed ones) to detect Divergent Change. For instance, S7, S8, S12 and S16 used NCC - solo or in combination with other metrics - and achieved 94% of recall. We also observed that subjects who indicated NCC as not being useful achieved less than 11% of recall; as it is the case of S10, S13 and S19. Additionally, subjects who indicated NCC and LCOM as being useful achieved 50% of recall in average. For instance, we observed that the metrics were used together by subjects S12 and S15. These subjects achieved 75% and 50% of recall respectively. Interestingly, while S12 had 100% of precision, S15 had only 25%. We also observed that subjects who indicated NCC and LCOM as not being useful achieved 0% of recall; as it is the case of S19.

Since most subjects had poor performance for detecting Shotgun Surgery, Table 10 presents metrics considered useful by at least three subjects when detecting this code smell. Coupling between Object (CBO) was considered useful by eleven subjects. However, these subjects achieved only 15% of recall in average. On the other hand, five subjects indicated Concern Diffusion over Components (CDC) as being useful and achieved 23% of recall in average. In addition, Number Concern per Component (NCC) was considered useful by four subjects who achieved 42% of recall in average. Hence, the concern metrics NCC achieved better results in terms of recall. A combination of these metrics, i.e.., NCC and CBO, was used together by subject S37 who achieved 33% of recall. In fact, all subjects that used NCC, solo or in combination with other metrics, scored higher than 30% of recall. This is the case of subjects S32 (33%), S35 (67%), S36 (33%), and S37 (33%). However, a combined analysis of Tables 6 and 10 does not allow us to conclude that these metrics (and any other) are good to detect Shotgun Surgery due to the global symptoms associated with this code smell.

Table 10. Metrics Considered Useful for Shotgun Surgery

Metrics	CBO	CDC	NCC
Subjects who used this metric	S25-S29, S37, S39, S40, S42-S44	S30, S31, S33, S40, S43	S32, S35, S36, S37
Average of Recall	15%	23%	42%

Table 11 shows for God Class the metrics (i) considered useful by at least three subjects and (ii) with average of recall for these subjects higher than 60%. Coupling between Object (CBO) and Lack of Cohesion in Methods (LCOM) were considered useful to detect God Class by at least four subjects. Subjects using these metrics achieved about 67% of recall in average. On the other hand, three metrics also considered useful achieved recall rates above 85%, namely Weighted Methods per Class (WMC), Lines of Code (LOC), and Concern Diffusions over LOC (CDLOC). This result suggests that size metrics, such as LOC and WMC, and the concern metric CDLOC are good indicators of God Class. Additionally, we observed some cases of metrics that were used together. WMC with LOC seems the best combination of metrics. It was used by S52 and S53 and worked well since both subjects achieved 100% of recall. In addition, the combination of WMC and CBO, was used by S47 and S53 and worked well since subjects achieved 67% and 100% of recall respectively. Another case was the combination of CBO with LCOM used by the subjects S51, S53 and S54. These Subjects achieved 78% of recall in average.

Table 11. Metrics Considered Useful for God Class

Metrics	CBO	LCOM	WMC	LOC	CDLOC
Subjects who used	S46, S47, S51, S54	S45, S51, S53, S54	S47, S52, S53	S52, S53, S54	S48, S49, S53
Average of recall	67%	67%	89%	100%	89%

6   Threats to Validity and Related Work

The conclusions obtained here are restricted to the involved metrics, code smells, and target information systems. These limitations are typical of studies like ours. Although we acknowledge these limitations, we note that our study fills a gap in the literature by reporting original analyses on the benefits of using concern metrics for detecting code smells. Additionally, this paper describes an experimental framework that can be used in further rounds of this study.

Ultimately, the recall of concern metrics depends on how accurate the mapping (assignment) of each concern to code elements was. Fortunately, we observed in a previous study [9] that, apart from Concern Diffusion over Lines of Code (CDLOC), the mapping process does not significantly impact the concern metrics assessed in this paper. Additionally, in order to mitigate this threat, we relied on concern mappings produced by the original developers. Whether the concern mapping was fully correct or not, it just reflects how concern metrics would be used in practice.

Detection strategies of code smells have been the subject of recent studies reported in the literature. They are usually based on exploiting information that is extracted from the source code [6, 8, 9, 11, 14, 17, 19] and rely on the combination of metrics. Metrics has been historically used to detect code smells [17, 19]. Marinescu [19] proposed the use of strategies composed of traditional metrics for detecting code smells. He observed that multiple metrics are required to capture all factors in the code smell definition. He relied on several traditional metrics also used in their study, but have not used concern metrics.

Several studies have used traditional and concern metrics to assess diverse maintainability attributes of information systems, such as instability [11, 14] and error-proneness [6, 8]. Some of these studies [11, 14] rely on concern metrics to support the comparison of aspect-oriented and object-oriented decompositions. Unlike our work, these studies implicitly assume that concern metrics are reliable indicators of the respective quality attribute assessed. This paper, on the other hand, aims to verify whether concern metrics can provide appropriate means to detect code smells.

Eaddy and his colleagues [6] have carried out three experiments to evaluate the usefulness of concern metrics to identify error-prone modules. Their experiments evaluated six concern metrics; two of them are also used in our experiment, namely CDC and CDO. They found a moderate to strong correlation between the concern metrics and defects in modules for all three experiments. The purpose of our study is different, due the fact that we are not focused on error-proneness analysis. Our work complements and extends Eaddy's findings since we observed that concern metrics could also serve as reliable indicators of code smells.

7   Conclusions and Future Work

The evaluation of software maintainability is largely dependent on the availability of metrics that accurately detect code smells. Concern metrics are increasingly being used in empirical studies [4, 11, 13, 14]. Our study aims at examining the effectiveness of concern metrics to detect code smells. Our results revealed that concern metrics are clearly useful to detect Divergent Change and God Class and that experience of developers does not have influence on the effectiveness of code smell detection. Additionally, we observed that the effectiveness of each metric suite is largely dependent on the adequacy of each metric to quantify a property explicitly mentioned in the smell definition. For instance, we observed that the concern metric Number of Concerns per Component (NCC) was efficient to detect Divergent Change even when used alone because it seems to quantify a dimension of module cohesion that is not captured by other metrics.

This study represents a first stepping-stone towards the evaluation of concern metrics to detect code smells. We are currently working on strategies to detect code smells based on the concern metrics we found useful. We also plan to perform further empirical studies to analyze the role of concern metrics at different levels of abstraction, such as architectural and detailed design.

Acknowledgments. This work was partially supported by FAPEMIG, grants APQ-02376-11 and APQ-02532-12, and CNPq grant 485907/2013-5.

References

1. Data of the Experiment with Metrics, http://www.dcc.ufmg.br/~juliana.padilha/caise2014
2. Carneiro, G.F., et al.: Identifying Code Smells with Multiple Concern Views. In: Proc. of the Brazilian Symposium on Software Engineering (SBES), pp. 128–137 (2010)
3. Chidamber, S.R., Kemerer, C.F.: A Metrics Suite for Object Oriented Design. Trans. on Software Engineering (1994)
4. Conejero, J. M. et al.: On the Relationship of Concern Metrics and Requirements Maintainability. Inf. and Sof. Technology (IST) (2011)
5. Ducasse, S., Girba, T., Kuhn, A.: Distribution Map. In: Proc. of ICSM, pp. 203–212 (2006)
6. Eaddy, M., et al.: Do Crosscuting Concerns Cause Defects? IEEE Trans. on Software Engineering, 497–515 (2008)
7. Fenton, N.E., Pfleeger, S.L.: Software Metrics: A Rigorous and Practical Approach. Thomson (1996)
8. Ferrari, F., et al.: An Exploratory Study of Fault-Proneness in Evolving Aspect-Oriented Programs. In: Proc. of the Int'l Conf. on Software Engineering (ICSE), pp. 65–74 (2010)
9. Figueiredo, E., et al.: On the Impact of Crosscutting Concern Projection on Code Measurement. Proc. of the Int'l Conf. on Aspect-Oriented Soft. Develop, AOSD (2011)
10. Figueiredo, E., et al.: On the Maintainability of Aspect-Oriented Software: A Concern-Oriented Measurement Framework. In: Proc. of CSMR (2008)
11. Figueiredo, E., et al.: Evolving Software Product Lines with Aspects: an Empirical Study on Design Stability. In: Proc. of the Int. Conf. on Soft. Engineering (ICSE), pp. 261–270 (2008)
12. Fowler, M.: Refactoring: Improving the Design of Existing Code. Addison Wesley (1999)
13. Garcia, A.: Modularizing Design Patterns with Aspects: A Quantitative Study. In: Proc. of the Int. Conf. Aspect Oriented Software Development (AOSD), March 14-18 (2005)
14. Greenwood, P., et al.: On the impact of aspectual decompositions on design stability: An empirical study. In: Ernst, E., et al. (eds.) ECOOP 2007. LNCS, vol. 4609, pp. 176–200. Springer, Heidelberg (2007)

15. Jain, R.: The Art of Computer System Performance Analysis: Techniques for Experimental Design, Measurement, Simulation and Modeling, pp. 1–702. John Wiley & Sons (1991)
16. Kiczales, G., et al.: Aspect-oriented programming. In: Akşit, M., Matsuoka, S. (eds.) ECOOP 1997. LNCS, vol. 1241, pp. 220–242. Springer, Heidelberg (1997)
17. Lanza, M., Marinescu, R.: Object-Oriented Metrics in Practice. Springer (2006)
18. Macia, I. et al.: Are Automatically-Detected Code Anomalies Relevant to Architectural Modularity? In: Proc. of Int'l Conf. on Aspect-oriented Soft. Dev. (AOSD), pp. 167–178 (2012)
19. Marinescu, R.: Detection Strategies: Metrics-Based Rules for Detecting Design Flaws. In: Proc. of Int'l Conf. on Software Maintenance (ICSM), pp. 350–359 (2004)
20. Nguyen, T., Nguyen, H., Nguyen, H., Nguyen, T.: Aspect recommendation for evolving software. In: Proc. of the Int'l Conf. on Soft. Eng (ICSE), pp. 361–370 (2011)
21. Parnas, D.L.: On The Criteria to Be Used in Decomposing Systems into Modules. Comm. of the ACM 15(12), 1053–1058 (1972)
22. Riel, A.J.: Object-Oriented Design Heuristics. Addison-Wesley Professional (1996)
23. Robillard, M. and Murphy, G. Representing Concerns in Source Code. Trans. on Soft. Eng. and Meth. (2007)

Author Index